The Upper Paleolithic of the Central Russian Plain

STUDIES IN ARCHAEOLOGY

Consulting Editor: Stuart Struever

Department of Anthropology
Northwestern University
Evanston, Illinois

A complete list of titles in this series is available from the publisher.

The Upper Paleolithic of the Central Russian Plain

Olga Soffer

Department of Anthropology
University of Illinois
Urbana, Illinois

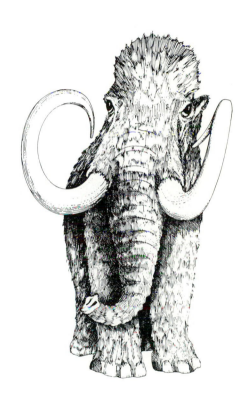

1985

ACADEMIC PRESS, INC.
Harcourt Brace Jovanovich, Publishers
Orlando   San Diego   New York   Austin
London   Montreal   Sydney   Tokyo   Toronto

ACADEMIC PRESS, INC.
Orlando, Florida 32887

United Kingdom Edition published by
ACADEMIC PRESS INC. (LONDON) LTD.
24–28 Oval Road, London NW1 7DX

LIBRARY OF CONGRESS CATALOGING-IN-PUBLICATION DATA

Soffer, Olga.
  The Upper Paleolithic of the Central Russian Plain.

  Bibliography: p.
  Includes index.
  1. Paleolithic period—Russian S.F.S.R.   2. Russian
S.F.S.R.—Antiquities.   I. Title.
GN824.R8S64   1985   947′.01   84-24391
ISBN 0-12-654270-8 (alk. paper)
ISBN 0-12-654271-6 (paperback)

To

Eric Delson
Mikhail Ivanovich Gladkih
Gregory A. Johnson
Andrei Alekseevich Velichko

and especially
Ninel' Leonidovna Kornietz

Contents

1
Introduction

2
Upper Paleolithic Sites on the Central Russian Plain

3
The Environmental Given

8
Conclusions and Implications

List of Figures

List of Tables

Preface

In this work I examine hunter–gatherer adaptations on the Upper Paleolithic central Russian Plain, offering both a culture history for the area and an explanation for the changes in human adaptation. This is an exercise in what Marquardt (1985) terms "synthetic processual anthropology"; I view human adaptations as multicomponent systems, and use insights from evolutionary cultural ecology and historical materialism to examine and model the various components of Upper Paleolithic cultures.

The volume is addressed to archaeologists, paleoecologists, and anthropologists interested in hunter–gatherers and late Pleistocene adaptations. It is of interest to archaeologists because it presents a culture history for a large portion of Upper Paleolithic Europe—one which is poorly known to Anglophones. Biological, geographic, geological, and archaeological data are presented on 29 major archaeological sites in the study area—a region of 180,000 km². This record spans some 14,000 years of occupation, from 26,000 to 12,000 B.P. Sections of this work, especially Chapters 3 and 4, which deal with environments and issues of chronology, will be of interest to paleoecologists concerned with questions of resource abundance and distribution in low-latitude periglacial steppes during the last glacial. Finally, and most important, the volume is also addressed to anthropologists interested in hunter–gather subsistence practices and settlement systems; it extends the known range of variability in these adaptations to include an example of logistically organized affluent inland groups who employed extensive storage. The diachronic perspective employed in this volume also offers relevant insights on patterns of behavior. A comparison of sociopolitical relationships in the study area through time demonstrates fluctuational rather than unidirectional changes in culture.

The organization of this volume closely follows its multiple purposes. In the first four chapters the pertinent data are presented. Details of the archaeological inventories and assemblages found at the 29 sites are given in Chapter 2, along with a discussion of the geography and geology of the study area. Environmental data, presented in Chapter 3, are used to model environmental conditions and resource distribution during the various periods of human occupation, as well as to predict optimal strategies for exploiting the available resources. Relative and chronometric dating schemes are offered in Chapter 4.

After formulating and testing various hypotheses about late Pleistocene human behavior, I reconstruct the subsistence pratices, settlement systems, and sociopolitical integration in the area through time. Man–land relationships and ensuing subsistence strategies are examined in Chapter 5. In Chapter 6, I define and classify the settlement types present in the archaeological record and outline the settlement systems. Analyses of sociopolitical behavior are offered in Chapter 7. I examine the differences observed in this behavior through time for their evolutionary significance and suggest models for the different systems in existence during each of the two periods of Upper Paleolithic occupation—the first before 20,000 B.P. and the second after 18,000 B.P.

In the final chapter, I summarize the general conclusions reached in the course of this work and examine the implications these conclusions have both for the archaeological record of Upper Paleolithic Europe and for theoretical issues in archaeology and anthropology.

Finally, a few words about the genesis of this monograph. It is a revised version of my doctoral dissertation, which resulted from some five years of transatlantic research. I came to this region and period through an extremely convoluted path, from Picasso to primitive art to prehistoric art to prehistoric lifeways to the Paleolithic. Early in graduate school, I realized that my fluency in Russian gave me an entrée into what I considered and still consider the most fascinating region of the Paleolithic Old World— Eastern Europe and the USSR. The rest was just time and excess baggage charges.

Acknowledgments

Any research project requires the cooperation, assistance, advice, and criticism of a great many people. This is especially true when data collecting is conducted on foreign soil. Work abroad also calls for appropriate official permissions and institutional support. My research visits to the USSR in 1977–1978, 1979, and 1983, on which this work is based, occurred under exchange agreements between the International Research and Exchange Board and the National Academy of Sciences in the United States and the Ministry of Higher Education and the Academy of Sciences of the Union of Soviet Socialist Republics. In this day and age when many places are becoming off limits to foreign scholars, Soviet colleagues deserve special credit for their generosity with data, archives, and collections.

I was fortunate to work with and benefit from the help and advice of scholars on both sides of the Atlantic. Andrei Alekseevich Velichko and Mikhail Ivanovich Gladkin served as my advisers in the Soviet Union—their interest, assistance, and insightful comments are greatly appreciated. Although not in an official capacity of adviser, Ninel' Leonidovna Kornietz always fulfilled the role of mentor and friend. She taught me a great deal about the central Russian Plain, encouraged me to work with her and Mikhail Ivanovich Gladkin at Mezhirich, shared her data and insights, and was always there when help was needed either with academic or everyday problems. To all these scholars I owe a great deal and hope that this work will be partial compensation for their efforts on my behalf.

In Moscow, my research exposed me to many scientists whose wealth of knowledge, constructive criticism, and help willingly volunteered in an atmosphere of friendship and cooperation was most valuable. For this I thank Andrei Leonidovich Chepalyga, Lyudmila Vadimovna Grekhova, Vadim Polikarpovich Grichuk, Marianna Davidovna Gvozdover, Elena Ivanovna Kurenkova, Nataliya Borisovna Leonova, Irina Il'inishna Spasskaya, Marina Ivanovna Sotnikova, Viktor Pavlovich Udartsev, Eleonora Alekseevna Vangengeim, and Rima Petrovna Zimina. I am especially grateful to the late Academician Innokentii Petrovich Gerasimov for his support and help with this project.

In Leningrad, Pavel Iosifovich Boriskovskii, Pavel Markovich Dolukhanov, Anatolii Kuz'mich Filippov, the late Emil Evseevich Fradkin, Gennadi Pavlovich Grigor'ev,

Rudolf Ferdinandovich Its, Vasilii Prokofievich Liubin, and Nikolai Kuzmich Vereschagin facilitated and greatly enriched my work.

Colleagues in Minsk who deserve many thanks are Vladimir Dimitrievich Budko,
Elena Gennadievna Kalechitz, and Leonid Davidovich Pobol'.

My frequent stays in Kiev were always enjoyable and productive and permitted me
access to the wealth of knowledge of Sergei Nikolaevich Bibikov, Valentina Ivanovna
Bibikova, Natalia Grigor'evna Belan, and Ivan Gavrilovich Shovkoplyas. I thank them
for their consultations, comments, and interest.

My familiarity with the archaeology of the central Russian Plain came as a result of
working in the field both at Avdeevo and Mezhirich. I learned a great deal at both sites
and thank the principal investigators for those field seasons. I also owe a debt of
gratitude to the following Soviet archaeologists, who generously showed me their
ongoing excavations: Zoya Aleksandrovna Abramova, Valentina Ivanovna Belyaeva,
Nikolai Dmitrievich Praslov, the late Aleksandr Nikolaevich Rogachev, and Viktor
Yakovlevich Sergin.

I am equally in debt to teachers, colleagues, and friends on the other side of the
Atlantic. Eric Delson, Greg Johnson, Tom McGovern, and Martin Wobst provided sound
critical advice and encouragement while displaying superhuman endurance during the
many months this manuscript was in preparation. Gary Feinman and especially John
Speth served stoically as kindly editors. Rich Davis, Jim Moore, Art Keene, Bob Paynter,
and Alex Marshack never tired of discussing various aspects of my research. Pat Gray
and Lynne Goldstein were dutifully on hand for consultation on methodological issues.
My thanks also go to Michele Patin, who is responsible for all the drawings in this
volume.

Finally, and most important, I wish to thank my family for unfailing encouragement,
self-sacrifice, and support moral and otherwise during my years of work on this project.

This research was also generously supported by the Fulbright Doctoral Dissertation
Fellowship, the Wenner–Gren Foundation for Anthropological Research, the Foundation for Research into the Origins of Man, the National Geographic Committee for
Research and Exploration, and The Explorers Club. Their financial support is gratefully
acknowledged.

1

Introduction

By studying the external configurations of the existing land and its inhabitants, we may restore in imagination the appearance of the ancient continents which have passed away. . . . the human mind is not only enabled to number worlds beyond the unassisted ken of mortal eye, but to trace the events of indefinite ages.

Lyell 1889: 319–320, orig. 1830–1833

There are more things in heaven and earth, Horatio, than are dreamt of in your philosophy.

Shakespeare, Hamlet

OBJECTIVES AND SIGNIFICANCE

Future generations of archaeologists will wonder why we, their predecessors, viewed the Upper Paleolithic prehistory of Europe, a continent over 10,000,000 km² in area, primarily as an extension of the prehistory of the Périgord region of France, an area that measures under 10,000 km² (White 1980: 37). Yet as any introductory textbook clearly shows, that is precisely what we have done and continue to do. Even when we enlarge this Upper Paleolithic core area, one that is overtly or covertly treated as the center of the Upper Paleolithic world in our literature, to include all of southwestern France (an area under 100,000 km²; Wobst 1976) and acknowledge the richness of the archaeological record there, the lack of congruence between the French microcosmos and the European macrocosmos is startling. This Francophile perspective, however, one with us since the beginning of prehistoric archaeology, is a direct result of historical and linguistic factors rather than a reflection of prehistoric realities. As Wobst and Keene (1983) point out, this distorted view of the European Upper Paleolithic came into existence because Paleolithic archaeology had the longest history in southwestern France. Since Paleolithic researchers in both Western Europe and North America were always fairly well versed in the essential Romance and Germanic, but not in Slavic, languages, linguistic barriers further enhanced this Francophile orientation.

While I do not intend to debate that southwestern France, most notably in its Périgord region, does have a very rich late Pleistocene archaeological record, I empha-

1

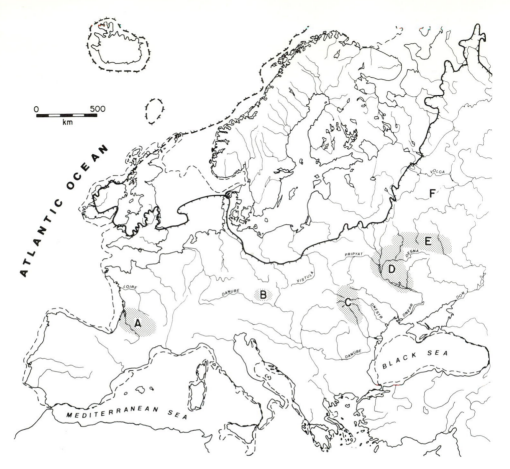

Figure 1.1 Upper Paleolithic Europe: (⊢⊢) extent of Scandinavian Ice Sheet at glacial maximum; (−−) Europe after the retreat of glaciers; A, sites in Southwestern France; B, Pavlov culture in Czechoslovakia; C, sites of the Molodova culture; D, sites on the central Russian Plain; E, sites of the Kostenki–Avdeevo and Kostenki–Borschevo cultures; F, Sungir (after Praslov 1982:113).

size that an equally rich record exists on the Russian Plain, well to the east of France (Figure 1.1). As Gvozdover and Rogachev (1969) note, by 1969 over 1000 Paleolithic sites and localities had been discovered in the European portion of the USSR. In this work I concentrate on one of the sections of the Russian Plain, dealing with the Upper Paleolithic archaeological record of the central Russian Plain, an area some 180,000 km² in size. Today this area is administratively divided between the Byelorussian, Russian, and Ukranian Soviet Socialist Republics (Figure 1.2). It is a region with a rich archaeological record and a long history of research.

The purpose of this work is multifold; the following three objectives can be singled out as the most significant: (1) to present as completely as possible all of the data available on the sites in the study area, including geographic, geological, biological, and

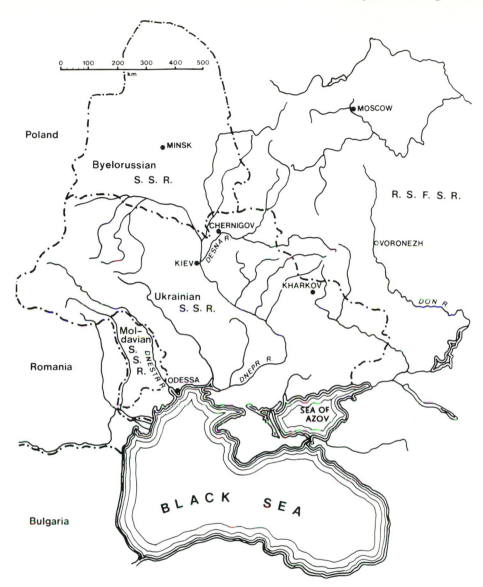

Figure 1.2 Administrative map of the Russian Plain.

archaeological information, (2) to examine both man–land and man–man relationships during the Upper Paleolithic period in the study area and to offer models for late Pleistocene hunter–gatherer adaptations, and (3) to examine evidence for change in human adaptation strategies during the 14,000 years of Upper Paleolithic occupation, as well as to delimit the ecological and social variables responsible for these changes. This volume is intended as an exhaustive treatment of what has been found at 29 major

Upper Paleolithic sites occupied over a period of some 14,000 years (see Figure 2.1). As such, covering as it does almost all one ever wanted to know about this or that site and then some, the volume is hardly "a good read." The story line is multistranded, and the cast of characters huge and confusing. The reader is therefore well within his or her rights to know answers to a series of questions before embarking on this reading venture.

Why These Sites?

This question is indirectly answered in the introduction: because the sites are there and because their features and assemblages are spectacular. The central Russian Plain is the area where Upper Paleolithic groups built their dwellings out of mammoth bone. Eleven of the sites considered in this work have such dwellings—some, such as Mezhirich, Mezin, and Yudinovo, very elaborate and complex structures. Rich inventories of portable art and jewelry come from these sites—some made of materials obtained from regions 600–800 km away. Lithic remains are varied and rich, numbering in tens of thousands at many of the sites. Faunal assemblages include impressive numbers of mammoth: 93 individuals at Dobranichevka, 116 at Mezin, and 149 found to date at Mezhirich. This wealth of archaeological data, however, is poorly known to Western specialists and only schematically considered in our literature. This data base is indispensible for our understanding of human adaptations in the late Pleistocene in the Old World and can be used henceforth by other researchers to answer a number of different questions of both archaeological and anthropological interest.

Why This Region?

My second objective—to examine both man–land and man–man relationships during the Upper Paleolithic period and to offer models for late Pleistocene hunter–gatherer adaptations—could be met only by treating the region rather than specific sites as the analytic universe. I work with a region rather than a particular site or sites because human adaptations, both in their ecological and sociopolitical components, can only be comprehended from a regional perspective (Johnson 1977; Moore 1983; Wobst 1976,1977). For some questions requiring different spatial scales, I modify this analytic universe to include, in some cases, intrasite variability, and in others to encompass the whole Russian Plain.

This specific region has been chosen for a number of reasons, including its ambiguous status as an Upper Paleolithic culture area. As Figure 1.3 shows, the central Russian Plain is bracketed on both the eastern and western sides by equally rich archaeological regions. To the east along the Don lie the famed Kostenki–Borschevo sites assigned to various well-defined archaeological cultures (see Praslov and Rogachev 1982). To the west along the Dnestr lie numerous Upper Paleolithic sites assigned to the Molodova culture (see Dolukhanov 1982; Grigor'ev 1970; Gvozdover and Rogachev 1969). While Soviet researchers are far from agreement about the specific cultural assignment of some of the Don and Dnestr sites, all agree that both the Dnestr and Don Upper Paleolithic regions represent distinct cultural areas (Grigor'ev 1983; Lazukov et al. 1981; Praslov and Rogachev 1982). The archaeological record from the central Russian

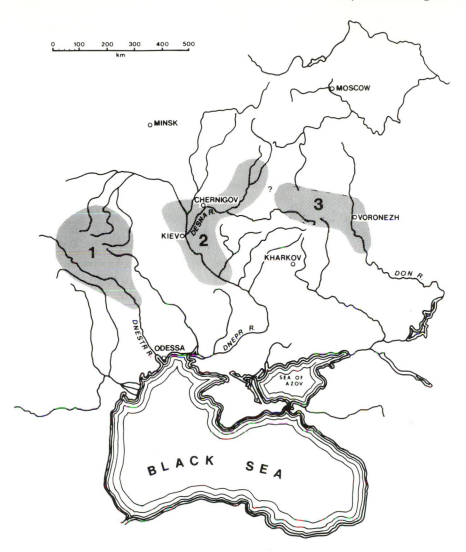

Figure 1.3   Upper Paleolithic sites on the Russian Plain: 1, sites assigned to the Molodova culture; 2, sites on the central Russian Plain; 3, sites assigned to the Kostenki–Avdeevo and Kostenki–Borschevo cultures; ?, boundaries unclear (after Gerasimov and Velichko 1982:Map 15).

Plain, on the other hand, has been far more enigmatic and difficult to assign to specific archaeological cultures. Most Soviet researchers are in agreement that the sites in this region exhibit some sort of unity, but they have not been able to agree on just what this unity represents. Some, like Shovkoplyas (1965a), see all the sites as belonging to a diachronically evolving Mezin culture. Others, like Grekhova (1970), delimit numerous synchronic archaeological cultures, some of which have genealogical ties to one another. Gladkih (1973, 1977a,b) assigns all of the sites to one technoeconomic complex. Grigor'ev (1983) claims that whatever similarities exist between the assemblages found at some of the sites, they are not sufficient to assign any of them to either synchronic or diachronic archaeological cultures. In brief, judging by assemblages found at the sites, the Upper Paleolithic archaeological record of the central Russian Plain is a classic example of a "cultural muddle in the middle." This situation is clearly interesting and is one that merits a closer examination.

Why This Period?

Two answers can be offered to this question. First, this work offers a culture history of a major portion of the Upper Paleolithic world and does so from the vantage point of human behavior. The models I offer for the adaptation strategies of late Pleistocene hunters–gatherers in this region expand our knowledge about the prehistory of both the specific study region and Upper Paleolithic Europe in general. Second, and perhaps more important, past hunter–gatherer adaptations are also of general anthropological interest. Our knowledge about these adaptations can come only from archaeological research. This work specifically approaches two major anthropological concerns: our theoretical constructs about hunter–gatherer adaptations in general, and our evolutionary theories of culture change

Extant theories about hunter–gatherer adaptations, be they based on economic behavior (Sahlins 1972), social relationships (Service 1962), or political integration (Fried 1967), all rely on behavior known from ethnographies. Yet, as numerous authors have pointed out, the ethnographic record does not reflect the full range of variability in human adaptation that existed in the past (e.g., Wobst 1978, on "the tyranny of the ethnographic record"). Thus, archaeology offers us our only chance of documenting this range of variability. This work amply attests to the fact that adaptations extant on the Upper Paleolithic central Russian Plain have no known ethnographic analogues and that important aspects of late Pleistocene subsistence behavior and sociopolitical integration were unique to that time. This uniqueness is not absolute: It is only evident when we compare the archaeological record to our ethnographic sample of hunter–gatherers. Human adaptations in the study area, like those of other late Pleistocene groups in Europe, differ from those we know ethnographically. An understanding of these differences, available only through archaeology, is therefore important for our theoretical constructs in anthropology (see Chapter 8 for a more extensive discussion of this issue).

Archaeological research in general, and this work on Upper Paleolithic groups on the central Russian Plain in particular, are also significant for theories about culture change. Our theoretical constructs view change in culture through time as unidirectional, accretional increases in complexity, where cultural complexity (after Flannery 1972), is defined as an increase in the number of structural components of a cultural system. Our archaeological record, on the other hand, operating on smaller time scales, is filled with evidence to the contrary. We have, for example, numerous cases of collapses of early states in the Near East before this complex entity became fully established (Redman 1978). In Europe, we have evidence that greater cultural complexity in the

Upper Paleolithic was followed by simpler patterns during the early Mesolithic. In the New World we have the enigmatic Hopewell phenomenon, which did not develop into a more complex cultural entity but simply fell apart in time (Bender 1982, but also see Braun 1977 for a different interpretation). Thus it appears that our theoretical trajectories for general cultural evolution are not congruent with the archaeological record of culture change. This incongruence can in part be explained by invoking the classic distinction between "general" and "specific" evolution (see Sahlins and Service 1960). This explanation, however, does not integrate the two phenomena: We are left with a general anthropological question of how changes on smaller time scales are related to large-scale general trajectories. This question, again, can only be answered through archaeological research.

In the course of this work, using time scales of thousands of years, I document fluctuations in cultural complexity through time. These fluctuations, however, disappear from view if the temporal scale is increased to hundreds of thousands of years. They would probably appear even more pronounced on time scales smaller than those employed in this work. I argue, therefore, that while on one time scale cultural change can indeed be seen as accretional and unidirectional, on another this smooth ascending line in fact consists of a conglomeration of fluctuations. The existence of these fluctuations in cultural complexity during the Upper Paleolithic, like those documented for other parts of the world throughout the Holocene, suggests that much "trial and error" took place before more complex forms of economic and sociopolitical integration became fully established.

PAST RESEARCH IN THE STUDY AREA

Western specialists not versed in Russian know the Upper Paleolithic record of the central Russian Plain only from summarized and descriptive accounts. The sole English-language volume on the area is Klein's (1973) brief *Ice-Age Hunters of the Ukraine*. Some information on the study area is offered in two long articles, by McBurney (1975) and Shimkin (1978); both, unfortunately, contain some errors (see Chapter 2 on Timonovka I). Bhattacharya's (1977) volume on Paleolithic Europe has some basic, although at times erroneous, information on some of the sites. Earlier work by Golomshtok (1938) includes mention of some of the sites. These, along with abstracts of papers presented by Soviet researchers at various International Union for Quaternary Research (INQUA) congresses, represent the total information available in English on the region. All these sources offer summary information, are neither inclusive nor exhaustive, and, most important, offer little or no quantitative data on the assemblages and features found at the sites.

A vast amount of information on the sites is available in Russian—too often, however, published in difficult to obtain serial publications. In spite of the very site-specific focus prevalent in Soviet Paleolithic archaeology, very few of the sites have been published in monograph form. Detailed monographic treatment exists only for Mezin, Mezhirich, and Timonovka II. Large segments of Polikarpovich's (1968) volume are devoted to Eliseevichi and Yudinovo. Other sites, even those excavated relatively recently (e.g. Dobranichevka), are known from a few short articles published in the USSR. Readers interested in a full listing of publications available for each site are referred to Chapter 2.

No single volume exists on this archaeological region in Russian. The most complete work, Boriskovskii's (1953) *Paleolit Ukraini,* includes only those sites located within the borders of the Ukranian SSR. Polikarpovich's (1968) posthumous monograph discusses only those sites along the Desna, Pripyat', Sozh, and Sudost' that he excavated. Pidoplichko's (1969) book on Upper Paleolithic mammoth-bone dwellings discusses these features at sites within the Ukraine only.

Prior to the relatively recent work by Pidoplichko and Velichko and his associates, the focus in Soviet Paleolithic research has been on describing the archaeological features and assemblages found at particular sites. The sum of these works concentrates on describing the behavior of objects either through time or across space. In more recent years, joint research by paleogeographers and archaeologists, most notably seen in the Velichko *et al.* (1977a) monograph on Timonovka II, has finally begun focusing on human adaptation—albeit on the scale of a specific site.

In general, Russian-language literature on the study area can be characterized as (1) site specific publications, (2) publications dealing exclusively with either specific features or objects, or (3) regional compilations of site-specific information on discoveries within specific confines of present-day administrative regions. In brief, no work in either Russian or any other language systematically examines human adaptations on the central Russian Plain during the Upper Paleolithic period.

HISTORY OF PALEOLITHIC ARCHAEOLOGY IN THE USSR

In a recent paper I argued that archaeology is not an acultural phenomenon and that what we see as archaeological problems, as well as how we attempt to solve them, is profoundly affected by the culture that surrounds us (Soffer 1983; see also Wobst and Keene 1983). The views of Soviet archaeologists, like those elsewhere, reflect cultural and historic realities. It is, therefore, germane to briefly examine the history of prehistoric research in the USSR.

It is not my objective here to undertake an all-inclusive review of the history of Soviet archaeology. In the subsequent discussion I focus only on those issues that I see as most relevant to archaeological research in the study area. Readers interested in a fuller treatment of the subject are referred to Bulkin *et al.* (1982), Davis (1983), Gellner (1975), Howe (1976, 1980), Klejn (1977), Miller (1956), and Thomson's translator foreword in Mongait (1961).

Soviet archaeologists are exceedingly prolific. The literature that their work generates is, however, molded and directed by a specific historical and theoretical context. Gellner (1975) wrote that the first culture shock that Western researchers receive when entering the world of Soviet anthropology—be it physical anthropology, cultural anthropology, or archaeology—is the fact that it is all heavily historical. This historicism, however, is a relatively recent phenomenon, dating to the late 1920s. The history of prehistoric archaeology in the USSR can be divided into three periods, which I delimit as the Formative period, the Developmental period, and the Period of Crisis.

FORMATIVE PERIOD: 1873–1928

As both Howe (1976, 1980) and Mongait (1961) show, interest in Russia in general archaeology blossomed in the nineteenth century in response to imperial expansion and focused on the excavation of gold-laden Scythian barrows and object-rich Greek settlements around the Black Sea. The organization of this research, unlike that elsewhere in Europe, was controlled by the state from the very beginning. The supervising agency was the Imperial Archaeological Commission, a department of state and a part of the ministry of the court.

Paleolithic archaeology began in Russia with the discovery of Gontsy on the central Russian Plain in 1873–1874 (Boriskovskii 1953). From its very inception it was associated with the radical elements of Russian society—the Narodniks. Volkov, the founder of Russian Paleolithic archaeology, was a mathematician, physicist, and ethnologist by training and an ardent evolutionist and Darwinist by persuasion. He emphasized the differences between Paleolithic archaeology, which he called "paleoethnology," and the established historical grounding of traditional or institutionalized archaeology of the Imperial Archaeological Commission (Howe 1976, 1980). Briefly exiled for his political activities in the 1890s, he spent his banishment in France at Broca's school of anthropology, where he became both a student and a follower of de Mortillet.

Volkov's background in natural science was similar to that of other prehistoric researchers at the time: Feofilaktov was a geologist, Hvoika a natural scientist, Kaminsky a geographer and teacher of natural sciences (Boriskovskii 1953). Like Volkov, all were evolutionists.

The salient point of the history of Russian Paleolithic archaeology for this discussion is that both its origin and early development were profoundly affected by the work of the French, most notably de Mortillet and Abbe Breuil. After an initial period of disagreement on the dating of some sites (e.g., between Hvoika and Volkov on Kirillovskaya; see Efimenko 1928), Breuil's revision of de Mortillet's classic French scheme for subdividing the Paleolithic was accepted and used widely, as was the French methodology of excavation and the use of *indexes fossil* as chronological markers. A few researchers acknowledged local differences and attempted to subdivide the unilineal and uniform French stages. Most notable among these was Gorodtsov (1923), who used stylistic differences in art as criteria for dividing the Magdalenian into three provinces: the Western (Atlantic), the Middle and Eastern European, and the Mezin–Eastern European variants. His scheme, however, was not accepted, and lithics dominated all attempts at classification.

This Formative period lasted until 1928. Throughout this period, Paleolithic archaeology was tied to the natural sciences and separated from classical historical archaeology. The 1917 revolution brought with it some organizational changes in the archaeological superstructure. But as Thompson notes (in Mongait 1961), until 1928 these changes had no serious ideological consequences for archaeological research.

DEVELOPMENTAL PERIOD: 1928–1950s

Soviet prehistoric archaeology took a different turn when the first Five-Year Plan was instituted in 1928. After a large-scale removal from institutes, museums, and universities of all non-Marxists and of pre-revolutionary elements, by 1935 Soviet archaeology became fully and dogmatically Marxist (Thompson in Mongait 1961; Miller 1956; Howe 1976, 1980). Paleolithic archaeology became separated from the natural sciences, fully and vocally accepting Marx's periodizations of history as Marxist philosophy of history was applied wholesale and became scientific dogma in all disciplines.

This presented particular problems for Paleolithic archaeologists, because Marx himself did not focus at length on the period of "primitive society." As he wrote in the *Grundrisse,* people engaged exclusively in hunting and fishing predated the time when real social and economic development began (Marx and Engels 1939, vol. 46, pt. 1, p. 44, orig. 1857–1858). While Marx's texts offered a plethora of theoretical constructs for archaeologists researching later periods, there was relatively little original material for Paleolithic archaeologists. Such typological constructs as the "feudal period" or the "slave-owning period" were, as Gellner (1975) notes, quite concrete, while the first one, "primitive society," was not. It was, and to some extent still remains, a sort of grab bag catch-all category held together by the absence of certain features: classes, states, and so on. In a sense, people engaged only in the collection of food produced and reproduced only themselves and not the means of their subsistence—hence production during this stage remained outside economic and historical criteria.

Theoretical guidelines for prehistoric archaeology were sought in Engels' *The Origin of the Family, Private Property, and the State* (1884). The answers, a sequence of set stages and periods, were based on the unilineal evolutionary schemes of Morgan and Tylor. Based on this text, firm periodizations and stadiality was worked out for human prehistory by the mid-1930s (e.g., Efimenko 1938; Ravdonikas 1939). The scheme saw the primitive and promiscuous herd of the Ancient (Lower) Paleolithic transformed into the matrilineal primitive community in the Late (Upper) Paleolithic. These socioeconomic stages or formations of primitive society were both value-laden and theory-laden constructs. All groups at this level of historical development were expected to share certain traits as well as a certain historical role—to be transformed into the next and higher stage. Biology and tools became linked in a cause-and-effect relationship and biological evolution was tied to social evolution. No need was felt to discover social laws underlying sociocultural transformations—economic means were equated with a particular social structure. In brief, it was speculative evolutionism in which quantitative changes brought about qualitative changes.

Because what happened in the past was known, what was needed, in effect, were just illustrations. Inferential machinery was, therefore, left underdeveloped. Typology and classification were, as before, mainly adopted from the French, slightly modified, and generally ignored. In fact, interest in any classificatory ordering of archaeological data was derogatorily labeled "thingization" and considered ideologically deviant (see Boriskovskii and Okladnikov 1953 for attitudes; Howe 1976 for history). The focus was on "paleoethnology"—on illustrating the various known stages through this approach.

Since no typological or classificatory work was conducted, different typological concepts led different researchers to classify materials found at the sites differently, as can be seen in the comparison of Voevodskii's chronology to that of Efimenko, for example, in Figure 4.1. The lack of uniformity in typology likewise resulted in the different classification of sites, as is illustrated in Table 4.1.

While such a focus had these and other flaws, it is also important to note that it was responsible for the institution of large-scale horizontal excavations in Paleolithic research. This new methodology, originally developed by Pitt-Rivers, was used by Efimenko in his work at the Kostenki sites. He concentrated on opening Upper Paleolithic living floors and on recognizing features (Boriskovskii 1953). This change from excavating via trenching resulted in the recognition of mammoth-bone dwellings and storage pits—features that were previously interpreted as kitchen debris.

Efimenko, who came to dominate Soviet Paleolithic research during this period, had been a student of Volkov. He in turn trained most of the senior Paleolithic archaeologists working in the USSR through the late 1970s. Given Efimenko's firm and vocal commitment to evolutionary stages, it is not surprising that he unearthed a "longhouse" at Kostenki I-1 or that Boriskovskii, his student, found one at Pushkari I in the 1930s. They were, after all, exactly the sort of dwellings that matrilineal clans of the Upper Paleolithic stage would be expected to live in. Small round dwellings, which dominate our literature today and represent the majority of Upper Paleolithic constructions in the study area, did not fit as well into this model—either they were not discovered or, when found, as in Gagarino on the Don and Malta and Buret in Siberia, their implications were not examined (see Boriskovskii 1953 for his reconstruction of Mezin and compare with Shovkoplyas 1965a). The discovery of female figurines was taken ipso facto as confirmation of the existence of matrilineal clans, and so on.

Natural sciences continued to play an important role in Paleolithic archaeology during this period in the Ukraine only, where such paleontologists as V. Gromov and Pidoplichko were actively involved in Paleolithic research.

During this period, little if any attention was paid to any synchronic variability in the archaeological record. This variability, however, refused to abate, and under its onslaught Paleolithic archaeology in the early 1950s entered its third period.

THE PERIOD OF CRISIS: 1950–1980s

By the early 1950s, firm periodization and stadiality, known in the USSR as the "Theory of Stages," began crumbling under an avalanche of irrefutable, synchronic variability in the data base. Rogachev's (1957) work at the Kostenki–Borschevo sites showed the inadequacies and errors in the previously held unilineal evolutionary schemes based on megacultural stages. At Kostenki I-1, Rogachev discovered that the Aurignacian layer was sandwiched between two Solutrean layers. At Telmanskaya, he found the Magdalenian layer below the Mousterian layer. With these discrepancies at hand, Rogachev called for the recognition of local synchronic archaeological cultures. He saw these cultures as material reflections of distinct and bounded ethnographic groupings. This concept, one very similar to the constructs of Bordes (1961) and Sonneville-Bordes (1960), was accepted and widely adopted by Paleolithic archaeologists in the USSR. Archaeological research on the central Russian Plain began increasingly to focus on delineating the different archaeological cultures reflected in the archaeological record.

This adoption of archaeological culture as an analytic unit and research objective undermined the validity of previously held megatheory (i.e., the Theory of Stages) and indirectly raised a theoretical disagreement not unlike that present in American anthropology at about the same time. This was the debate between the unilineal evolutionary schemes of White (1949) and multilineal evolutionism of Steward (1955), which was rephrased and reconciled into "specific" and "general" evolution approaches by Sahlins and Service (1960). In Soviet archaeology, which was considered a historical science, this disagreement surfaced in debates on classification and chronological ordering. It is not surprising that the classic problem of data versus theory and universality versus exception that plagued and continue to plague Western archaeologists committed to evolutionary paradigms disturbed their Soviet colleagues as well.

The need for revamping megatheory was acutely felt and responded to by Soviet cultural anthropologists, who in the 1960s began dealing with large-scale theoretical issues on the level of socioeconomic formations. While undoubtedly more debate was generated for the socioeconomic formations of more advanced stages, "primitive society" also received its share of attention. Averkieva (1971, with references) tried to reconcile slave and property ownership as well as class differences among the groups of the Pacific Northwest Coast with the classic constructs of "primitive society." Y. Semenov (1979, 1980) attempted to modernize the evolutionary stages in the light of archaeological data—particularly the "primitive horde" and "primitive community" stages. Ter-Akopian (1979) sought to reconcile the diachronic focus of classic Marxist constructs with the synchronic basis of the ethnographic method. Fainberg (1975) focused on reconstructing the origins of clan societies and descent ideologies.

Paleolithic archaeologists, by and large, did not involve themselves with issues of megatheory. The one exception was Grigor'ev, who in *Hunters, Gatherers, Fishermen* (1972), an admitted response to *Man The Hunter* (1968), used archaeological data to argue for both the existence and importance of the nuclear family in the Upper Paleolithic as a minimal social unit. He argued that the herd stage never existed historically and questioned the validity of the long-held assumptions that the appearance and presence of female figurines indicated high female status and proved the existence of matrilineal clans in the Upper Paleolithic.

In summary, the legacy from this period was one that saw a switch in prehistoric research from illustration of "prehistoric lifeways" during a particular stage of human prehistory to focus on synchronic as well as diachronic archaeological cultures. These cultures, as elsewhere in Europe, were defined by lithic assemblages and, like elsewhere, in time presented archaeologists with a new set of problems.

The effects of cracking megatheory were also felt in the excavations done after 1950.

It is not accidental that the discovery of a plethora of sites with small round or oval dwellings, definitely not like Iroquois longhouses envisioned by Efimenko, occurred after 1950.

PALEOLITHIC RESEARCH TODAY

The effects of this complex and mixed legacy still influence Paleolithic archaeology in the USSR. Although research interests are clearly centered on a level of middle-range issues (i.e., on archaeological cultures and not on stages of culturo-historic evolution), the ghost of the Theory of Stages can still be felt on the level of unstated assumptions. Davis characterizes this traditional view today as one that "focuses specifically on transitions from one stage to another, and highlights the points of transition. At the moment, however, available theory provides no universally accepted transition points to look for within the Paleolithic" (1983:414).

The theoretical turmoil of the 1950s and 1960s, which led some archaeologists to questions of isolating archaeological cultures and interpreting them in ethnic terms, also brought problems of selecting attributes for defining archaeological cultures, finding their ethnographic correlates, and of tracing their existence through time (e.g., Kabo 1979; Zaharuk 1978).

Since the mid-1960s, another major analytic cultural concept has been introduced as an explanation for the observed synchronic variability in the archaeological record: the idea of *techno-economic,* or as Davis (1983) terms them, *economico-cultural,* groupings. Some researchers, including Shovkoplyas (1965a) and Gladkih (1977a,b), see archaeological cultures reflecting past similarities in techno-economic behavior. This interpretation is in marked contrast to Rogachev's idea that archaeological cultures represent historico-cultural groups. As Davis (1983) points out, the basic task for Soviet archaeologists is to denote how archaeological assemblages and features reflect these two potential axes of variability. This ambiguity in how to interpret recognized archaeological cultures has become even more vexing for the study area, where, as noted, no unanimity exists on the demarcation of archaeological cultures.

Perhaps the most significant recent development in Soviet Paleolithic archaeology, however, one of greater significance for this work, is the tenuous but growing cooperation between archaeology and other natural sciences. While paleoenvironmental questions were always prominent in the work of Ukranian researchers, such as Pidoplichko (1976), today, mostly through the efforts of Academician I. P. Gerasimov, Velichko, and Dolukhanov, paleogeography and paleoecology have become important features of research in the study area. This focus, however, has been either very site specific, as in the work of Velichko and colleagues (e.g., Velichko *et al.* 1977a and the discussion in Chapter 3), or on spatial and temporal scales too gross for concrete questions about human adaptations (e.g., Dolukhanov 1979, 1982; Dolukhanov *et al.* 1980).

In summary, Soviet Paleolithic archaeology today lacks overt and concrete mega-theoretical constructs. The use of archaeological culture as an organizing principle for research has inadvertently led to focusing research on the behavior of objects and features. As elsewhere in Europe, this research focus is necessarily site specific, with the objects as the units of analysis and a particular site the analytic universe. While growing paleoenvironmental interests, centered as they are on man–land relationships, can potentially change this focus to one of regional perspective, they have to date not done so. Interests in paleoecology, by and large, are seen as secondary in importance by many Soviet archaeologists. Because of this, questions about human adaptation have to be asked within the analytic universe delimited by the primary interests of archaeologists—the site and its cultural identity.

Thus, in spite of a rather different history of prehistoric archaeology in the USSR, the state of research there today is not too dissimilar from that in other parts of Europe. I find great similarities between the current state of research in France and in the USSR. The Francophile orientation, present in Russian archaeology since the very beginning of Paleolithic research in the 1870s, still prevails today and presents Soviet researchers with problems similar to those faced by their colleagues elsewhere on the European continent.

INTERPRETATIONS OF THE DATA FROM THE STUDY AREA

As I noted previously, while today no unanimity exists in opinions about the cultural affinity of the sites in the study area, all researchers do distinguish the central Russian Plain from Upper Paleolithic regions lying to the east and west. This regional delimitation did not always exist; it is a by-product of the recognition of archaeological cultures elsewhere. In those areas of the Russian Plain (e.g., Dnestr and Don basins) where research was conducted or directed by a small number of researchers, unified typological concepts and classificatory criteria were employed and regional classificatory typologies and chronologies were constructed that permitted a delineation of synchronic and diachronic cultures.

The central Russian Plain, on the other hand, was investigated by a greater number of researchers who were not institutionally or academically allied with one another. As a result, no firm or widely accepted regional typologies or chronologies emerged. Researchers working there from the 1870s to the early 1950s treated the sites as illustrations of this or that period or stage of culturo-historical development (Boriskovskii 1953; Efimenko 1938; Polikarpovich 1968). During the earlier part of this period, heated debates were heard about the assignment of this or that site either to the Solutrean, or to the Magdalenian, or to some other evolutionary chronological period. With the introduction of archaeological culture as a research focus, archaeologists began trying both to isolate these cultures on the central Russian Plain and to connect them to cultures delimited elsewhere (e.g., Budko 1966,1967b,1969a). Their successors attempted to delimit localized archaeological cultures within the study area itself (Grekhova 1970; Grigor'ev 1970,1983). With the advent of the techno-economic explanation for observed synchronic variability in the archaeological record, some researchers advocated seeing regional similarities as reflecting similar techno-economic behavior in the past (see Gladkih 1977a,b). Thus no consensus exists on the interpretation of the data from the study area. The area is delimited as a distinct region of Upper

Paleolithic occupation, but no agreement exists on what specifically distinguishes it from other areas—historical ethnic differences, different economic pursuits, or both.

METHODOLOGY AND ASSUMPTIONS

ASSUMPTIONS

While my theoretical assumptions can easily be deduced from the objectives guiding this work, it is useful to state them explicitly. First, following White (1949), I understand culture as people's extrasomatic means of adaptation. Second, after Binford (1962), I view the archaeological record as material remains of past human behavior and, therefore, as an entrée into past cultural systems. The second assumption necessarily presupposes a certain degree of uniformitarianism in human behavior through time. In brief, it suggests that past behavior, as revealed through its material correlates in the archaeological record, can be understood through analogy with the behavior known from the ethnographic record. I am well aware of the inherent dangers in using analogies of this sort in archaeology, but I would argue that they are appropriate when used with due caution (see Chapter 8 for a fuller discussion of this issue). In this work I use analogy as a heuristic or exploratory device to outline possible contours of past behavior but in no way to delimit it.

Last, after Flannery (1972), I view culture as a system composed of numerous interrelated subsystems. I see past human adaptations, therefore, as products of the interaction of two major components of culture: the ecological (man–land) relationships and the sociopolitical (man–man relationships). In my analyses and interpretations of the data from the study area I give no preference to either one of these two components and argue that both were crucial in shaping Upper Paleolithic adaptations on the central Russian Plain.

METHODOLOGY

To some extent this work can be seen as an exercise in remedial archaeology. The data were collected through (1) archival and library research and (2), when possible, an examination of archaeological and paleontological collections in the pertinent libraries, museums, and institutes in the USSR. Information was also gathered during three field seasons of excavation at the Upper Paleolithic sites of Mezhirich and Avdeevo, as well as from research visits to Dobranichevka, Gontsy, Novgorod–Severskii, the Pushkari group of sites, Yudinovo, and the Kostenki–Borschevo sites. In selecting to work with the archaeological record of this region, one with over a 100-year history of excavation which generated an abundance of data, I was also interested in seeing how information already on hand can be used to answer questions of interest to archaeology today. Since many of the collections, especially organic remains, were excavated prior to the 1950s and are no longer available for restudy, much of the data this work is based on are problematic. This situation is clearly less than ideal, but it is an archaeological reality not only for the sites on the central Russian Plain but for many major Upper Paleolithic sites in the Old World in general. Working with "kitchen" or "laundry" lists instead of collections is all that we can do for many sites; the challenge lies in using them both to explain the archaeological record better than has been done heretofore, to raise new questions, and to suggest new directions for research.

The approach used in this work for reconstructing past adaptations can best be characterized as "descriptive modeling." I selected this approach rather than the more sophisticated and rigorous one of predictive modeling for a number of reasons that are related to both the nature of the data base and epistemological problems. As numerous researchers have indicated, predictive modeling is beset by problems of justification for specific behavioral assumptions, methodological difficulties in reconstructing past environments, and scalar problems (Bettinger 1980; Jochim 1983; Keene 1983; Yessner 1981). Predictive modeling is, first and foremost, predicated on accurate environmental reconstruction, which at present is not possible for the late Pleistocene central Russian Plain. Furthermore, as I argue in Chapter 5, modeling constructs erected on ethnographic analogies fail to consider a potential uniqueness of past adaptations. Thus, by limiting ourselves to what we already know from ethnographies as a starting point for our predictive models, we stand in danger of interpreting the archaeological record of the past as just carbon copies of ethnographically known groups.

Because of these operational and theoretical considerations, I elected instead to investigate and model past adaptations using the excavated archaeological, geological, and biological evidence. This approach, likewise, is beset with problems. These difficulties have been widely discussed in the literature and are considered in the ensuing chapters (Binford 1983). I chose to work directly with the record itself in spite of all the biases distorting it, because the record does, in the case of the study area at least, come closer to past behavioral realities than do modeling constructs erected on recent ethnographic analogies. Thus, the data from the study sites were used in formulating a series of hypotheses about past human behavior. These hypotheses, when possible, were then tested by a set of simple parametric and nonparametric procedures commonly employed in archaeological research. Particular statistical calculations used are described in detail in pertinent sections of this work.

PROBLEMS WITH THE DATA

The nature of available data, as I have already noted and as can be clearly seen in discussions in ensuing chapters, is both problematic and leaves much to be desired. My analytic universe, 29 Upper Paleolithic sites that span some 14,000 years of occupation, is clearly very small. Many problems exist with the accuracy and representativeness of the data from each site. Only a handful of the sites have been completely excavated and the majority are known from very small excavations and limited test trenches. Chronological controls are another major source of difficulties with the data. These complex problems, discussed in detail in Chapter 4, show that much work remains to be done before we can state with certainty either that different parts of any one site or different sites were occupied at the same time. Finally, chronometric dating is available for only some of the sites considered in this work.

Given these problems, some will argue that no research objectives beyond a purely descriptive presentation of the data are warranted. I suggest, however, that available data are not too weak to use for hypothesis formulation. This is precisely how they have been used traditionally—in this work it is only the nature of the questions that has changed. Instead of formulating hypotheses about the relationship of objects, I focus on the behavior of the makers and users of the objects. The models offered in the following pages are meant not as firm and unequivocal reconstructions of the past, but rather as tentative approximations that can be evaluated in future research using the same traditional media of archaeological research—objects and features. They account for the archaeological record better than has been done heretofore, and they indicate the kinds of new data needed for future work. I argue, furthermore, that our only hope for obtaining better data—data more suitable to questions about human adaptations, lies in asking new questions—questions that call for something other than the kinds of information we have on hand.

In conclusion, I agree that the data are of poor quality, that numerous problems exist with our assumptions and methodologies, and that, as Leach (1973:768) notes, our modeled constructs will never be able to go beyond "well-informed guesses." But without a focus on human behavior we will not have better data, nor will we ever realize the problems with our assumptions or generate work to overcome them. And finally, at least our guesses will be more interesting and better informed than those of our predecessors.

2

Upper Paleolithic Sites on the Central Russian Plain

GEOGRAPHY AND GEOMORPHOLOGY OF THE STUDY AREA ———

The Russian Plain, a vast area occupying the southern half of the European USSR, is the easternmost extension of the East European Plain. It is bordered on the west by the uplands and foothills of the Carpathian Mountains and on the east by the increasing elevations that terminate in the Ural Mountains. The plain is drained by a number of major river systems flowing from north to south either into the Black Sea or the Sea of Azov. The majority of the known Upper Paleolithic sites are located in the river valleys and form distinct site-cluster regions. These are the Dnestr sites of Molodova and Korman, the Don Kostenki–Borshevo sites, and the Dnepr–Desna sites discussed in this work and illustrated in Figure 2.1 (Gvozdover and Rogachev 1969; Ivanova 1969).

The study area of sites discussed in this work covers approximately 180,000 km.[2] This region is drained by the river Dnepr and its main tributaries: Desna, Pripyat', Sozh, and Sudost' (Figure 2.2). As Figure 1.2 shows, the central portion of the Russian Plain is predominantly located in the Ukranian Soviet Socialist Republic, although its northern segments lie within the territories of the Byelorussian Soviet Socialist Republic and the Russian Soviet Federated Socialist Republic.

The midsection of the Russian Plain, called the "central Russian Plain" in this work, consists of three contrasting geomorphological units, illustrated in Figure 2.3. They are the Polissya Lowlands in the north (located to the west of the Dnepr River), the Dnepr Uplands, lying south of the Polissya and west of the Dnepr, and the Dnepr–Donetsk Lowlands to the east of the Dnepr. All three units are part of the Russian Platform, which is made of crystalline bedrock formed at the beginning of the Devonian period and covered through the subsequent Paleozoic, Mesozoic, and early Cenozoic with sedimentary deposits of clay, sand, marl, and chalk. In the Polissya these sedimentary layers are in turn covered by Dneprovskiye (Riss) terminal moraines. The crystalline bedrock, sedimentary layers, and moraines are overlaid by Pleistocene loess deposits (sandy loam, loam, loess–loam) which range in thickness from 30–50 m in the south to under 10 m in the north (*Geografiya Byelorussi* 1977; *Soviet Ukraine* 1965; Velichko 1961; Voznyachuk and Budko 1969).

The altitudinal differences between the uplands and the lowlands are due to the

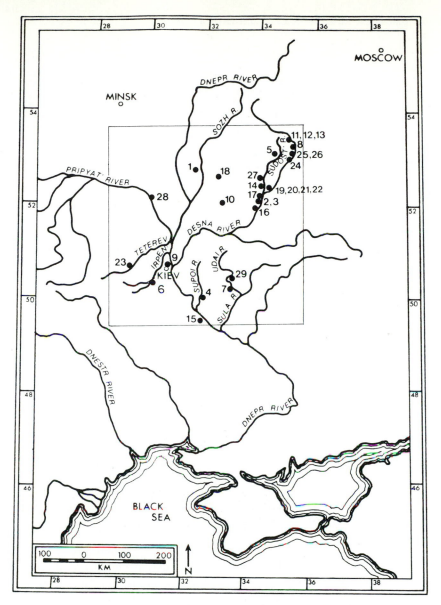

Figure 2.1   Upper Paleolithic sites on the central Russian Plain.

1. Berdyzh	11. Korshevo I	21. Pushkari I
2. Chulatovo I	12. Korshevo II	22. Pushkari II
3. Chulatovo II	13. Kositsa	23. Radomyshl'
4. Dobranichevka	14. Kurovo	24. Suponevo
5. Eliseevichi	15. Mezhirich	25. Timonovka I
6. Fastov	16. Mezin	26. Timonovka II
7. Gontsy	17. Novgorod-Severskii	27. Yudinovo
8. Khotylevo II	18. Novo-Bobovichi	28. Yurovichi
9. Kirillovskaya	19. Bugorok	29. Zhuravka
10. Klyusy	20. Pogon	

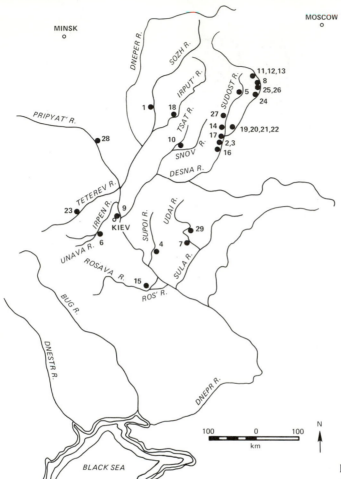

Figure 2.2 Tributary system of the study area.

irregularities in the crystalline foundation of the Russian Platform and are minor in nature. The Dnepr–Donetsk and Polissya Lowlands lie on the undisturbed portion of the platform, while the Dnepr Uplands are on the uplifted southwestern part of the platform known as the Ukrainian Shield. The Dnepr–Donetsk Lowlands average 100–130 m above sea level in the south and 140–160 m in the north, the Polissya Lowlands are from 100–150 m above sea level, and the average elevation of the Dnepr Uplands is about 175 m with a maximum of 220 m above the sea level (*Geografiya Byelorussii* 1977; *Ukraina—Obschii Obzor* 1969).

RIVER TERRACES

The main relief-forming factor on the central Russian Plain is erosion as seen in river valleys and ravines. The Dnepr and its major tributaries are all mature rivers with broad

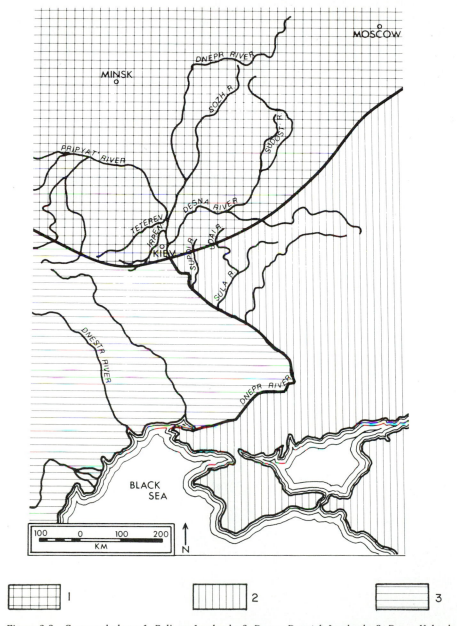

Figure 2.3   Geomorphology: 1, Polissya Lowlands; 2, Dnepr–Donetsk Lowlands; 3, Dnepr Uplands.

flat valleys, which show up to four terraces representing different erosional episodes during the late Pleistocene. Each was cut during a warm interglacial or interstadial period. An important feature of the river valleys here is their asymmetry. They all have one steep and terraced erosional bank (the right, western or northern) and one low-lying depositional (the left, eastern or southern) bank (*Ukraina—Obschii Obzor* 1969). As Velichko (1961) points out, this asymmetry is due to the Coriolis force and is more pronounced on the rivers that flow diagonally or horizontally across the plain (e.g., parts of the Desna, Pripyat', and Sudost'). The valleys of the Desna and Sudost' extensively investigated by Velichko (1961) over a 20-year period, show this feature of asymmetry most clearly. The Desna and its numerous tributaries all form a large valley-lowlands system up to 40 km wide. The right or nothern banks are steep and terraced while the left or southern banks are expansive and low-lying valleys filled with alluvium (Figure 2.4). The present-day floodplains are wide as well, stretching up to 5 km. The low-lying left banks of both the Desna and Sudost' are heavily forested and swampy.

The Pripyat' is a more meandering river and shows similar asymmetry in its valley. The Polissya Lowlands through which the Pripyat' flows were partially covered by ice during the last glaciation, and the retreat of the Scandinavian Ice Sheet from this region activated thermocarstic processes and resulted in the formation of hundreds of lakes and extensive swampy areas (Voznyachuk *et al.* 1969).

The Dnepr valley has the same asymmetrical construction—especially pronounced in its northeastern section, where the river meanders a great deal, as well as in its middle section, where it flows along the Ukrainian Shield (from just south of Kiev to Dnepropetrovsk).

Table 2.1 shows the heights of the river terraces along the Dnepr and its main tributaries. The higher and older fourth and third terraces were formed prior to and during the Mikulino (Riss–Würm) Interglacial (Figure 2.5). These terraces, because of differential erosion, are not seen along all of the rivers. The second terrace, lying approximately 10–25 m above the present river levels, was formed during an in-

Figure 2.4 Desna floodplain from the Novgorod-Severskii site.

Table 2.1   HEIGHTS OF THE RIVER TERRACES ALONG THE DNEPR AND ITS TRIBUTARIES

River	Terraces (m)			References
	First	Second	Third	
Dnepr	6–8	10–12	15–20	Voznyachuk and Budko 1969
				Kornietz *et al.* 1981
Desna	10–12	20–25	30–40	Velichko 1961:
				Velichko, Grekhova *et al.* 1981
				Velichko, Zavernyaev *et al.* 1981
				Gromov 1948
Sozh	6–8	10–12	14–17	Voznyachuk and Budko 1969
Sudost'	6–7	10–12	—	Gromov 1948
	8–12	15–18	—	Velichko 1961
Pripyat'	4–6	25–40	—	Voznyachuk, Budko, and Kalechitz 1969
				Geografiya Byelorussii 1977
Udai	20	25	60	Gromov 1948

Figure 2.5   Environs of Gontsy viewed from the third terrace of the Udai River.

terstadial of the last Valdai glaciation, possibly during or just prior to the Bryansk Interstadial, and it dates, according to Velichko (1961), to some 25,000–30,000 B.P. Voznyachuk *et al.* (1969; Voznyachuk and Budko 1969) date the formation of this second terrace somewhat earlier. Their ^{14}C dates for the alluvial deposits on this terrace taken at the locality of Krasnaya Gorka span a period from 30,000 to 45,000 B.P. The second terrace is important for archaeology, as most Upper Paleolithic sites are found either on it or in nearby plauteau and slope deposits associated with it.

The first terrace lies up to 12 m above the present river and was formed at the end of the Valdai glacial period, well past the cold maximum. Voznyachuk *et al.* state that the alluvium of the first terrace of the Dnepr and Sozh was deposited between the start of the recession of the Scandinavian Ice Sheet from its terminal moraines and the Alleröd or Late Dryas. This would date the alluvium to a period between 15,000 and 12,000 B.P.

It is important to note here that only the terraces of the Desna and Sudost' have been adequately investigated. As a result, because of extensive work by Velichko, our best and firmest terrace chronology comes from these river valleys. The history of the terrace formation of other rivers is far less clear. Klein (1973) notes that because of the different erosional, depositional, and tectonic histories of the different regions of the Russian Plain, terraces along the different rivers are neither in phase with each other nor, in some cases, are the terraces of the different segments of the same river in phase with each other. This last observation is especially true for the longer rivers such as the Dnepr, which flows through areas with very different tectonic and glacial histories. In the upper reaches of the Dnepr, eustatic uplift occurred during the late Pleistocene as the Scandinavian Ice Sheet receded, while in the lower reaches, the fluctuations of sea level created different erosional and depositional sequences.

RAVINES

The other relief-generating feature found in the central Russian Plain is the ravine. These are erosional features which occur on loess plateaus adjacent to the river valleys

Figure 2.6   Pogon promontory viewed from the Desna floodplain.

as well as on terraces. Ravine formation appears to have gone on throughout the late Pleistocene along the Dnepr and its tributaries, facilitated by the presence of soft loess matrix. The ravine-indented topography of the river valleys is most clearly seen along the Desna, where today some of the older ravines run 5–10 km in length with 20–40-m wide bottoms and 10–12-m depths (Figure 2.6). In places these ravines resemble small river valleys. Their importance for archaeology is twofold. First, at many Upper Paleolithic sites, post-depositional ravine formations have either totally eroded parts of the living floor or eroded and relocated them down the ravine slopes (e.g., Berdyzh, Chulatovo II, Kurovo, Mezin). Second, late Pleistocene ravines created plateau and terrace promontories over the rivers, and these promontories were preferred locales for Upper Paleolithic sites. Finally, the ravines may have played an important role in mammoth-procurement strategies during the Upper Paleolithic. Figures 2.6 and 2.7 depict the topography of the area of the Pushkari group of sites, clearly illustrating the character of the Desna ravines.

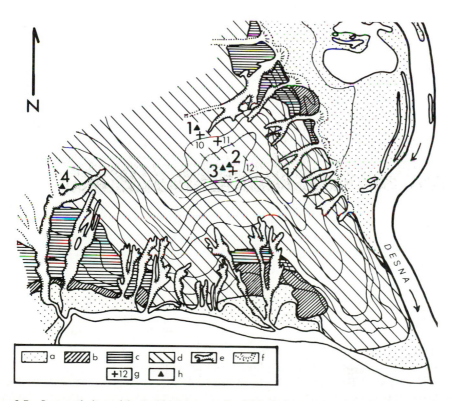

Figure 2.7 Geomorphology of the Pushkari group: a, floodplain; b, first terrace; c, second terrace; d, plateau; e, growing ravines; f, old ravines; g, bore holes; h, sites: 1, Pushkari I; 2, Pogon; 3, Bugorok; 4, Pushkari II (after Velichko 1961: Fig. 38).

PLEISTOCENE STRATIGRAPHY AND CHRONOLOGY ─────────

INTRODUCTION

The geological dating of the Upper Paleolithic sites of the Russian Plain has undergone a major revision since 1960. Inasmuch as many of the sites discussed in this work were investigated and published in the 1920s and 1930s, before Soviet geologists and archaeologists accepted the glacial chronology used in the West, it is germane to briefly discuss the state of Pleistocene chronology in the USSR both today and in the recent past. At the onset of this discussion it is important to note that Soviet Paleolithic research has a long history of collaboration between archaeologists and geologists. As the previous chapter showed, Soviet Paleolithic archaeology was modeled after and grew out of the classical French school of prehistory of de Mortillet—a school heavily committed to geology. This collaboration, however, while firmly grounding archaeological sites in a geological and stratigraphic context, also produced a number of major difficulties with the chronology of the sites. At the end of the nineteenth century and during the first 30 years of the twentieth century, Russian and Soviet geologists working at such sites as Gontsy, Kirillovskaya, Mezin, and Suponevo accepted and used the classic European Penck and Brückner scheme of Pleistocene glaciations, as can be seen in the works of Mirchink (1934, 1937).

This generation of geologists, however, was succeeded by a new breed of "monoglacialists" led by Gromov (1933a,b, 1936). Gromov's major thesis on the Pleistocene chronology and geology of the Paleolithic sites, published only after the war in 1948, was based on a theory that saw the one-stadial penultimate Dneprovskoye glaciation as the only Pleistocene glaciation. Gromov saw the following Mikulino interglacial and Valdai periods as a post-glacial time devoid of any advances of the ice sheet or climate deterioration. This view was widely accepted and Gromov's stratigraphies were used by archaeologists as well (e.g., Efimenko 1939). This resulted in the assignment of the Upper Paleolithic period to the end of the Mikulino and the beginning of the Valdai period. Gromov, for example, accepted the French subdivision of the Upper Paleolithic cultural sequence and equated the Aurignacian with the second half of the Riss–Dneprovskoye and the first half of the Eem–Mikulino, the Solutrean with the Eem–Mikulino, and the Magdelenian with the Würm–Valdai.

The existence of a glaciation after the Riss–Dneprovskoye was again advocated in the work of Gerasimov and Markov (1939). Their monograph not only showed evidence for this glaciation on the Russian Plain but also firmly placed Upper Paleolithic sites of the Russian Plain within the Valdai deposits. It is only with this reacceptance of the European glacial sequence that the Russian Upper Paleolithic sites once again became consistant with Western European sites. The 1961 monograph by A. Velichko, *Geologicheskii Vozrast Verhnego Paleolita Tsentral'nih Raionov Russkoi Ravnini,* firmly established the late Valdai age of the sites and proposed a uniform stratigraphic scheme and chronology for the major river valleys and adjacent plateaus of the Russian Plain. This scheme is currently widely used by Soviet archaeologists and serves as a basis for the following discussion.

Valdai Glaciation

Chronology

The late Pleistocene chronology and climatic oscillations based on the data from the Russian Plain and widely accepted by Soviet scholars are as follows (Gerasimov and Velichko 1982; Velichko 1973; Vigdorchik *et al.* 1974): Holocene from about 10,000 B.P., Valdai glacial period from about 70,000 B.P., and Mikulino interglacial from about 130,000 B.P.

However, this scheme does not take into account the most recent revisions suggested for the late Pleistocene chronology based on the work of Woillard (1978, 1979; Woillard and Mook 1982) and Mörner (1974). Briefly, these data indicate that the Eem–Mikulino interglacial period was a brief episode lasting some 10,000–20,000 years at maximum and that the last glacial period, the Weichsel–Valdai, began much earlier than hitherto accepted—some 105,000–115,000 B.P.

Soviet researchers divide the Valdai period itself into three stages: late Valdai (~24,000–10,000 B.P.), middle Valdai (24,000–50/55,000 B.P.), early Valdai (50/55,000–70,000 B.P.) (Dolukhanov 1982; Velichko 1973; Vigdorchik *et al.* 1974). This subdivision of the last glacial is somewhat at odds with the current views of such Western European researchers as Woillard and Mook (1982). The disagreements, however, pertain to the subdivision of the first half of the period as well as to the location of the last interglacial—last glacial boundary. Woillard and Mook (1982), for example, writes that the early Weichsel can be dated from approximately 105,000–115,000 B.P. to about 70,000 B.P. and the middle Weichsel from 70,000–25,000 B.P.

In Soviet literature, the early and middle Valdai was until recently seen as a non-glacial part of the last glaciation with a long expanse of time that saw no ice on the Russian Plain (Chebotareva and Makaricheva 1974, Velichko 1973, Vigdorchik *et al.* 1974, Voznyachuk 1973). It was, however, a period of some warm–cold oscillations. This long period was not fully recognized or segmented but was seen as a long "megainterstadial" (Klein 1973). Work by Zarrina *et al.* (1980) and Dolukhanov (1982) has analyzed this period of oscillations into the sequence illustrated in Figure 2.8. In general, it can be concluded that while this long period was one of fluctuating climate, these fluctuations are not major in nature when compared to those of the late Valdai (Figure 2.9).

The end of this middle Valdai period is of particular relevance to this work, as three of the Upper Paleolithic sites may date to this time: Berdyzh, Khotylevo II, and Yurovichi. The period between the onset of cooling at 30,000–35,000 B.P. and the Valdai maximum is not that finely delineated on the Russian Plain into clear sequences of fluctuations (Dolukhanov and Pashkevich 1977; Gerasimov 1973) (see Figure 2.9). The presence of several relic soils in the Dnestr–Molodova stratigraphy suggests that some minor fluctuations did occur (Ivanova 1977; Polevoi 1974: Fig. 4). The overall trend for this 10,000-year period between 35,000 and 25,000 B.P. was toward decreasing temperature, increasing aridity, and increasing continentality in the area, with just minor fluctuations of the ice sheet.

Damper, but still cold interstadial conditions existed at the close of the middle Valdai

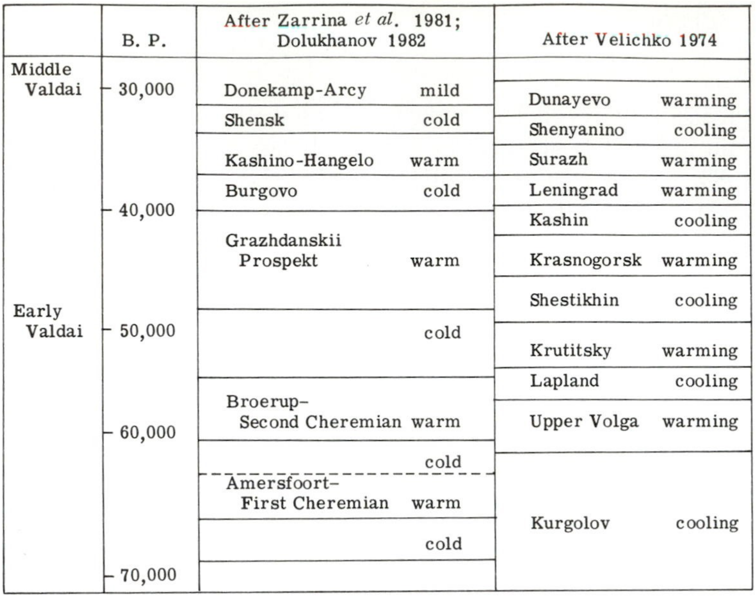

	B. P.	After Zarrina et al. 1981; Dolukhanov 1982		After Velichko 1974	
Middle Valdai	30,000	Donekamp-Arcy	mild		
				Dunayevo	warming
		Shensk	cold		
				Shenyanino	cooling
		Kashino-Hangelo	warm	Surazh	warming
		Burgovo	cold	Leningrad	warming
	40,000			Kashin	cooling
		Grazhdanskii Prospekt	warm	Krasnogorsk	warming
Early Valdai				Shestikhin	cooling
	50,000		cold		
				Krutitsky	warming
				Lapland	cooling
		Broerup– Second Cheremian	warm	Upper Volga	warming
	60,000				
			cold		
		Amersfoort– First Cheremian	warm	Kurgolov	cooling
			cold		
	70,000				

Figure 2.8   Early and middle Valdai chronology.

(27,000–24,000 B.P.), called the Bryansk Interstadial by Velichko (1973). Chebotareva and Makaricheva (1974) place the Bryansk interval in a period between 30,000 and 24,000 B.P. Dates for the humus of the soils formed at this time are 24,000 ± 300 (IGAN) at Arapovich; 24,200 ± 1680 (Mo 342), 24,300 ± 370 (IGAN 88), and 24,210 ± 270 (IGAN 80) at Mezin; 24,920 ± 1800 (Mo 337) at Bryansk (Grichuk 1982a; Velichko, Morozava et al. 1969). This interstadial period of soil formation has been correlated with the Paudorf or Stillfried B period of Western Europe (Dolukhanov and Pashkervich 1977; Gerasimov 1973; Velichko 1973, 1982a). Fink (1969), however, warns that it is preferable to use the term "Stillfried B" for the correlate, as the Paudorf soil is not synchronized all over Europe, and this presents a confusing picture for correlation. Austrian Stillfried B is firmly dated to 28,120 ± 200 (Gro. 2533) and 27,990 ± 300 B.P. (Gro. 2523). This same soil layer appears in many stratigraphic sequences of Eastern and Western Europe, and it is thus classified under different terms, ranging from the PKI soil of Czechoslovakia to Paudorf to Mende F in Hungary.

A number of problems exist, however, in correlating soil profiles not only between sequences separated from each other by long distances but also from those within smaller geographic regions. As Voznyachuk (1978, personal communication) notes, even the Bryansk soil of the Russian Plain is discontinuous, is found at different heights in different localities, varies in thickness, and presents too wide a range of dates to be an unquestionable chronological or stratigraphic marker. Veklich (1974) correlates the formation of the Bryansk soil (in his terminology, Vitachevskaya; see Table 2.2) not with the 25,000–30,000-year period but with an earlier interstadial episode dating to 48,000–

B. P.	After Dolukhanov and Pashkevich 1977		After Gerasimov 1969		After Grichuk, Mangushina, and Monoszon 1969		After Frenzel 1973		After Leroi-Gourhan 1965	
	Dryas III	S	Younger Dryas	S	Younger Dryas	S	Youngest Tundra	S		
	Alleröd	I	Alleröd	I	Alleröd	I	Alleröd	I		
12,000	Dryas II	S	Middle Dryas	S	Middle Dryas	S	Middle Tundra	S		
	Bölling	I	Bölling	I	Bölling	I	Bölling	I		
	Dryas I	S	New Estonian	I	Older Dryas	I	Older Tundra	S		
14,000	Raunis	I	Luga	S						
			Plyussa-Raunis	I					stadial	
	Lascaux	I	Vepsovo	S	Pomeranian	S				
16,000			Somino-Ula	I	Blankendorf	I	Lascaux-Ula	I	Lascaux	I
	Laugerie	I								
18,000									Laugerie	I
			Edrovo	S	Frankfurt	S				
20,000			Berezaika	I						
			Bologoye	S	Brandenburg	S			Maximal cold	
22,000										
									Tursac	I
24,000	Tursac	I								
			Bryansk	I						
26,000										
					Paudorf	I				
28,000							Stillfried B-Arcy	I		
	Salpetriere	I								
30,000										

Figure 2.9   Late Würm–Valdai chronology and tentative Western correlations: I, interstadial; S, stadial.

52,000 B.P. Great difficulties exist when correlations are attempted between more distant locales. Frenzel (1973) rejects the correlation of Stillfried B with the soil level dating from 23,000–24,000 B.P. He suggests that this soil level, found in Arcy-Sur-Cure, Dolni Vestonice, Molodova, and, by extension, at the central Russian Plain sites, lies above the Stillfried B soil, is younger, and in fact reflects a different warming period than the Stillfried B interstade. He suggests that it may possibly correlate with the Tursac interstade.

As Fink (1969) notes, the correlation of Stillfrield B and Bryansk soils is also problematic because the Stillfried B horizon is pale brown-gray steppe soil and the Bryansk soil is a chernozem. The correlations offered in this work, therefore, should be taken only as approximate and tentative and should be used only for establishing relative chronologies. The discontinuity of strata formation as well as the fact that erosional and depositional sequences are out of step over large areas all combine to create both spatial and chronological discontinuities in stratigraphy and therefore to limit the usefulness of specific deposits as time markers.

It was during the late Valdai, a period that Velichko (1973; 1982a) calls Glacial Valdai that the Scandinavian Ice Sheet reached its maximal size and covered over 828,000 km² of northern Europe, including approximately 300,000 km² of the USSR (Chebotareva

1969a; Chebotareva and Makaricheva 1982; Voznyachuk 1973). As Figure 2.10 shows, during the Belogoye stage of its maximal spread (18,000–20,000 B.P.) the ice sheet extended down to about 53°. The massive Scandinavian Ice Sheet was 3000 m thick. On the Russian Plain the ice sheet was separated into three lobes: the southwestern, southern, and southeastern. The southwestern and southern lobes penetrated furthest onto the plain (Grichuk *et al.* 1975). During this Belogoye glacial maximum the ice front was located some 150–200 km north of the northernmost Upper Paleolithic sites.

The occurrence of the Valdai glacial maximum at 20,000–18,000 B.P. can be dated worldwide. Chebotareva (1969a) and Makaricheva (Chebotareva and Makaricheva 1982) correlate it with the Brandenburg deposits in Germany. It finds correlates in the Würm in France, in Mörner's (1972) data from Sweden, and Mania's (1969) German data. Global sea-level- and marine-isotope curves place the Würm–Valdai–Wisconsin ice volume maximum at 18,000 B.P. (CLIMAP Project Members 1976). The history of the Wisconsin glaciation of North America also shows that the maximal spread of the Laurentian Ice Sheet occurred between 20,000 and 17,000 B.P. (Andrews and Barry 1978; Dreimanis and Goldthwail 1973; Mörner and Dreimanis 1973).

Two important features of the Russian Plain during the Valdai maximum should be noted here. First, on the southern border of the plain the two bodies of water, the Black Sea and the Sea of Azov, were very different than at present. Chebotareva and Makaricheva (1974, 1982) state that there was no Sea of Azov and that the Black Sea was from 87 to 90 m lower than today. This drop in the sea level decreased the area of the Black Sea by some 320,000 km^2 and turned it into the New Euxine Basin—a body of fresh water that was fed glacial meltwater by the enlarged Dnepr and its tributaries (Vigdorchik *et al.* 1974). The second important feature found on the Russian Plain at the Valdai maximum is the presence of glacial lakes at the edges of the ice sheet. During the Valdai glaciation, glacial meltwater in this area drained into large glacial lakes, which at peak stadial periods overflowed and drained along the interfluves into the rivers of the Russian Plain (Aseev *et al.* 1973). This suggests, as Dolukhanov (1982) points out, that the nature of both the drainage system and load carried by the rivers of the Russian Plain were indeed vastly different during the late Würm–Valdai period. According to Dolukhanov, in late Würm–Valdai "the ice-dammed lakes obtained access to the rivers flowing in the southerly direction, towards the Black and Caspian Seas. These rivers became channels which drained the ice-dammed basins, and in many cases turned themselves into chains of lakes" (1982:10). As he notes, the great majority of Upper Paleolithic sites of the Russian Plain were situated either on the shores of these channels or on the shores of the ice-dammed lakes. The presence of these bodies of water profoundly affected the distribution of vegetation on the Russian Plain, as well as the distribution of fauna, which is discussed in Chapter 3.

The second important phase of the late Würm–Valdai glaciation occurred in the late glacial period of 18,000–10,000 B.P.—the period of ice retreat. As elsewhere, the ice retreat did not occur unidirectionally but rather was spasmodic, with a series of readvances followed by greater retreats. The recessional intervals of the Würm–Valdai glaciation on the Russian Plain are illustrated in Figure 2.11. This figure shows a series of sequential advances and retreats which resulted in extremely fluctuating climatic

Figure 2.10 Maximal extent of Valdai glaciation: 1, ice sheet; 2, lakes; 3, mountains (after Gerasimov and Velichko 1982: Map 1; Grosswald 1980: Fig. 7).

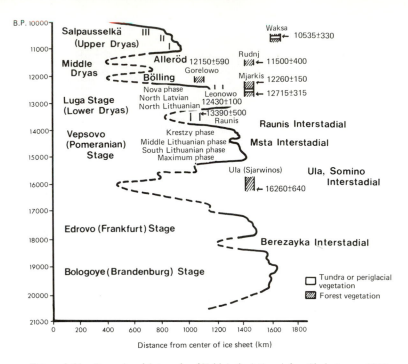

Figure 2.11   Recessional intervals of Valdai glaciation (after Chebotareva 1969a: Figure 3).

conditions. The Edrovo–Frankfurt and Vepsovo–Pomeranian stages were major, for then the ice sheet readvanced almost to its previous moraines. The ice sheet was present in Byelorussia until approximately 14,000 B.P. (Voznychuk 1973).

The rate of the ice retreat varied greatly, from approximately 190–200 m/year during the early stages of retreat (ca. 15,000 B.P.) to over 400 m/year in later stages. It is important to note that the drainage pattern described here prevailed until approximately 14,000–15,000 B.P., when the ice sheet retreated sufficiently for meltwater to begin draining north into the Baltic Sea (Chebotareva 1969b).

The spasmodic fluctuations in the Scandinavian Ice Sheet during this time created a series of alternating stadial–interstadial climatic conditions, the major interstadials being Ula–Somino–Lascaux(?) (16,260 ± 640), Raunis (13,390 ± 500), Bölling (12,430 ± 100 and 12,260 ± 150), and Alleröd (11,500 ± 400) (Chebotareva 1969a; Gerasimov 1969). These are discussed in Chapter 3.

The evidence for the readvances and retreats of the ice sheet on the Russian Plain correlates well with the data collected elsewhere in Europe. Similar patterns are shown by the Frenzel (1973), Leroi-Gourhan (1965), and White (1980) data. Mörner (1969) and Mörner and Dreimanis (1973) report that the Scandinavian, Belgian, German, and British data show the existence of at least two glacial maxima, with the second, the Zurich phase, dating to 14,470 ± 385 B.P. As Mörner and Dreimanis (1973) show, the presence of three glacial maxima, the major at 20,000 to 17,000 B.P. and the others at 16,500 to 15,000 B.P. and at 14,850 B.P., is reflected both in the ^{18}O curves of the Greenland ice cores and in ocean levels. The universality of this pattern and the degree of synchronization of the different readvances and retreats of the different ice lobes of the major ice sheets and mountain glaciers is very difficult to assess. Dreimanis and Goldthwail (1973), for example, argue for their worldwide occurrence, presenting the Erie interstade (15,500 ± 500) and the Cary–Pt. Huron interstade (13,300 ± 400) in North America as evidence. Mörner and Dreimanis (1973) write that the New World glacial record shows that the Laurentian Ice Sheet retreated during the Erie interstade from its Wisconsin maximum position in central Ohio all the way to the eastern portion of Lake Erie and then returned back to Ohio during the subsequent stadial phase. Wright (1976) also reports three or more ice lobe fluctuations in the Wolf Creek area between 20,000 and 12,000 B.P. This evidence clearly suggests that the late glacial period was one of extreme fluctuation, with some of the oscillations of major magnitude and continental, if not worldwide, in extent.

Stratigraphy

Velichko (1961, 1973, 1979, 1982a) and his paleogeographic team from the Institute of Geography of the Academy of Sciences of the USSR have since 1960 been developing a late Pleistocene stratigraphy of the Dnepr and Desna. This stratigraphic scheme serves as a basis for the following discussion. This section focuses on the delineation of the middle and late Valdai deposits that contain Upper Paleolithic sites. We must briefly, however, mention the glaciofluvial deposits that date to the penultimate glacial, as well as the soils formed during the last Mikulino interglacial. These pre-Valdai deposits often find surface exposure along the river banks in the Dnepr and Desna basins.

The penultimate glaciation covered much of the Russian Plain with ice, which left in its wake the terminal moraines. These moraines are present in the northern parts of the study area. As the section on geomorphology shows, these glaciofluvial deposits overlie Tertiary marls and chalks. The moraines are in turn overlaid by the Mikulino cher-nozem soil that Velichko (1961) calls Mezin soil. Velichko's general Valdai stratigraphy is illustrated in Figure 2.12.

Velichko's scheme shows that climatic conditions during interglacials and in-terstadials favored chemical erosion and soil formation, while those during glacial and stadial periods favored the action of wind as the main agent of erosion. These glacial and stadial periods witnessed the deposition of windblown sands, sandy loams, and loams collectively called *loess* (Velichko *et al.* 1969). He describes loess as a dust deposit with characteristic diffractional and chemical properties and includes size-graded deposits from loam to silt to sand, all of which were transported by wind as well as water. The origin of loess is still a moot point for geologists. Kukla writes that while it was once widely held that European loess originated in glacial outwash, "it is now believed that the bulk of the sediment was picked up by wind from seasonally dried floodplains of the intermittent Pleistocene rivers and from the mechanically weathered hard rock out-crops in the neighboring highlands" (1975:105). The northernmost limit of loess depos-its lies some 50 km south of the margin of Valdai ice. These deposits range in thickness

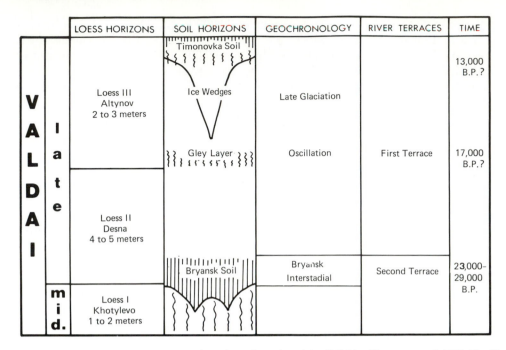

LOESS HORIZONS	SOIL HORIZONS	GEOCHRONOLOGY	RIVER TERRACES	TIME
	Timonovka Soil			
		Late Glaciation		13,000 B.P.?
Loess III Altynov 2 to 3 meters	Ice Wedges			
	Gley Layer	Oscillation	First Terrace	17,000 B.P.?
Loess II Desna 4 to 5 meters				
	Bryansk Soil	Bryansk Interstadial	Second Terrace	23,000– 29,000 B.P.
Loess I Khotylevo 1 to 2 meters				

Figure 2.12   Late Pleistocene stratigraphy and geochronology (after Velichko, Morozova *et al.* 1969: Fig. 8)

from 1–2 m in Byelorussia, to some 30–50 m in the southern Ukraine (*Ukraina— Obschii Obzor* 1969; Voznyachuk *et al.* 1969). Pleistocene loess deposits are found all along the East European Plain (Kukla 1975). On the Russian Plain they stretch from the Carpathians to the Don and beyond and can be seen best in undisturbed conditions along the plains and plateaus of the area. On sloped terraines such as old ravines, as well as along the river valleys, alluvial and colluvial processes predominate. As a result, the Valdai deposits in the valleys and ravines include glaciofluvial moraine sands and loess, as well as reworked loess–colluvium, alluvial sands, and clays (Velichko *et al.* 1969). In the study area, loess deposits are the thinnest and most patchily distributed in the northern part of the Russian Plain in Byelorussia and the Polissya, where they appear in patches on morainic hillocks (Velichko *et al.* 1969; Voznyachuk 1973).

As Figure 2.12 shows, the Valdai loess contains relic soil within it as well as embryonic humic gley layers. These gley layers are evidence for the early stages of soil formation. The presence of these relic soils and gley layers permit Velichko (1961) to divide the Valdai loess deposits into Loess I, Loess II, and Loess III. Loess I (Kohtylevo loess) was formed during early Valdai. It is 5–6 m thick in the Desna region and it is separated from Loess II (Desna loess) by the fossil Bryansk soil. This Bryansk soil is humus poor and is divided into two horizons. For ^{14}C dates on the humic content of this soil see p. 28.)

As Morozova (1969) and Velichko *et al.* (1969; Velichko and Morozova 1982) show, the Bryansk soil demonstrates many permafrost deformation features. These include funnel-shaped wedges filled with humus, which suggest that periglacial polygon-like nets with 2–3-m polygons and medallions were present in the soil during the Bryansk interstadial. Morozova (1969) describes this soil as quite unique, having been formed under permafrost conditions and having no analogues today. She sees it as somewhat similar in microstructure to the soils found in central Yakutia, USSR, where cryogenic processes cause similar periglacial deformations. Velichko *et al.* (1969) suggest that Bryansk soil was formed on permafrost that had a seasonal thaw layer ranging from less than 0.4–0.5 m around Bryansk, 0.8–1.0 m in the center of the Russian Plain, and as much as 1.0–1.5 m in the Ukraine. The presence of these periglacial deformations is extremely important for paleoclimatic and paleoenvironmental reconstruction and is discussed in Chapter 3.

The Bryansk soil is topped by the Loess II deposit. This loess layer does not contain permafrost deformations, although its structure suggests that the bottom of the layer, that part overlying the Bryansk soil, was formed in a warmer and wetter period than the top of the layer (Morozova 1969; Velichko and Morozova 1982). Both Loess II and the overlying Loess III show much swifter rates of deposition than does Loess I. Grichuk 1969b) postulates that Loess I accumulated at the rate of approximately 0.07 mm/year (or less), while Loess II and Loess III were deposited at 0.6–0.7 mm/year. This observation reinforces Pashkevich and Dubnyak's (1978) and Gerasimov's (1969) views that the late-middle and late Valdai periods were characterized by greatly increased aridity, decreased temperatures, and increased continentality—culminating in the Valdai maximum at 20,000 to 18,000 B.P. Loess II was deposited during the interval between the Bryansk interstadial and the Valdai maximum, that is, between 24,000 and 18,000 B.P.

Velichko reports that a relatively thin, single gley layer separates Loess II from Loess III (Altynov loess). It is a layer that ranges in thickness from 0.2 to 0.3 m. Velichko *et al.* (1969) correlate the deposition of this layer with the occurrence of an interstadial period, possibly the Ula-Somino-Lascaux interstade at approximately 16,000 B.P.

Loess III is present in the Desna region in 2–3 m thick deposits that contain 4–5 m deep ice wedge casts that extend into Loess II. In addition to these casts, other localities, such as the village of Timonovka, show the presence of ice wedge polygons along both the river valleys and on the plateaus during the time that Loess III was deposited, indicating frost conditions during that time. Grichuk (1969b) as well as Chebotareva (1969b) indicate that Loess III continued to be deposited all through the Dryas I and Dryas II periods, terminating only at the onset of the Alleröd some 11,500 years ago.

The permafrost phenomena found in Loess III are far more extensive and severe than in the Bryansk soil layer, suggesting much more severe cryogenic processes and seasonal thaw layers from 1.5 to 2 m deep in the northern part of the Russian Plain and from 2 to 3 m deep in the southern part (Velichko 1969b). Velichko and Morozova (1982) believe that extensive polygonal nets extended as far down as the 46th–48th Parallel during this period.

The Valdai stratigraphic column terminates with a layer of relic Timonovka soil formed during the Bölling and pre-Boreal periods. This soil is in turn covered by the contemporary soil, which began forming at the onset of the Holocene (Velichko and Morozova 1969, 1982).

Stratigraphic Problems

As noted before, the working scheme for the periodization of the late Valdai used here is modeled closely on that offered by Velichko and is based on the loess stratigraphy of the Desna region. However, there are a number of problems with this sequence evident in both the Desna stratigraphy itself and in other river valleys. First, both the Bryansk soil layer and the single gley layer found below Loess III are not equally well represented in all localities or at equal depths. This makes the use of either one as a chronological marker quite difficult. For example, Velichko (1961) reported that the cultural layer of Pushkari I was found directly above the Bryansk soil and postulated that Pushkari inhabitants walked on this soil surface. Later reexcavations at Pushkari I now indicate that the cultural layer overlies the gley layer and not the Bryansk soil, as this soil is to be found farther down in the deposit (Grigor'ev 1981, personal communication).

The Ukrainian geologist Veklich (1974), working in the Dnepr region on loess stratigraphy, as outlined a rather different and more complex scheme which often appears in the Ukrainian literature (Pashkevich and Dubnyak 1978). Veklich's late Valdai chronology can, however, be loosely correlated with Velichko's; these correlations are presented in Table 2.2.

A different stratigraphic scheme for this same period is offered by the Byelorussian geologist Voznyachuk (Voznyachuk *et al.* 1969). His work, based on the alluvial, colluvial, and morainic deposits of Byelorussia (a region north of the extensive late Pleistocene loess deposition), also suggests a more complex stratigraphic history than that outlined by Velichko. For example, Voznyachuk's scheme suggests the existence of an interstade between the Bryansk Interstadial (27,000–24,000 B.P.) and the interstadial Velichko associates with the gley layer (16,000–17,000 B.P.). Voznyachuk's scheme suggests an interstade prior to the Valdai maximum (18,000–20,000 B.P.)—a period of climatic amelioration occurring around 21,000 B.P.

This amelioration does not find corroboration at present in the Desna or Dnepr loess

Table 2.2 LATE PLEISTOCENE STRATIGRAPHIC TERM EQUIVALENCES FOR CENTRAL RUSSIAN PLAIN DEPOSITS

	Sequences	
	Velichko 1962	Veklich 1974
HOLOCENE ↑ 12,000 B.P. ↓	Present-day soil	Present-day soil
LATE PLEISTOCENE	Relic soil—Timonovka soil	Relic soil
	Loess III	Prichernomorskii loess
	Gley layer	Dofinov soil—Embryonic layer
	Loess II	Bug loess
	Bryansk soil	Vitachevskaya soil
	Loess I	Udai loess

sequences, where the Loess II deposits (laid between 24,000 and 18,000 years ago) appear uninterrupted by any soil formation processes. Kozłowski and Kozłowski (1979) report that German scholars also find evidence that the Valdai maximum (termed Last Pleniglacial) was divided into two segments: They recognize the existence of an earlier phase of the Pleniglacial taking place between 24,000 and approximately 21,000 B.P., then a warmer interphase or interstade dated at approximately 21,000 B.P., and finally the Valdai (Pleniglacial) maximum itself at 20,000–18,000 B.P. In brief, this suggests that the period 24,000–18,000 B.P., which Velichko sees as a period of slow and uniform growth of the Scandinavian glacier to its maximal size, may indeed have been interrupted by a warm fluctuation or interstade at about 21,000 B.P.

Similar problems exist in correlating the Desna Loess III stratigraphy. This deposit is dated by Velichko from about 16,000–17,000 B.P. to approximately 12,000 B.P. It terminated with the layer of Timonovka relic soil, the only soil associated with Loess III. Pashkevich and Dubnyak (1978) report a gley layer (or relic soil layer) at the site of Dobranichevka that seems to lie higher than Velichko's Desna gley layer and below the Timonovka soil layer; this layer is not reflected at present in the Desna sequence. Ivanova's (1977) late Valdai stratigraphy from the Dnestr terraces shows the presence of a layer of humic loam above the Bryansk soil (a correlate of the gley layer in the Desna sequence?) as well as the presence of two gley layers above that in Loess III. All of these observations again point to the difficulties in correlating the observed Desna sequence with those of other river valleys in the study area. They suggest that the scheme offered by Velichko may indeed be too simplistic and should be used only tentatively and only for a first approximation when dating cultural layers of the Upper Paleolithic sites on the Russian Plain. It is used in this work not because of its strict accuracy and comparability with all of the other sequences—but because it is the most extensive and uniform scheme for the study region at the present time and the only one that incorporates a number of the Upper Paleolithic sites considered in this work.

It should also be noted that the stratigraphic scheme for the Desna late Pleistocene deposits offered by Velichko, problematic though it may be, does find broad agreement in the stratigraphies of Central and Eastern Europe. For example, the Mende exposure in Hungary similarily shows the broad loess subdivisions outlined by Velichko (Pécsi, Pevzner, and Szébenyi 1979). The difficulties in using this scheme for stratigraphic dating of the sites is discussed in Chapter 4.

PROFILES OF THE SITES

Introduction

Disparate amounts of information exist on the 29 sites considered in this work. Some, like Kirillovskaya, were excavated at the end of the last century when field methods were considerably less rigorous than they are today. Others, such as Fastov, were investigated over very short periods. Materials recovered from many excavations prior to the Second World War were inadvertantly lost during the political turmoil of the time. All this adds up to a sad reality that data from many of the sites are most incomplete, often available only in archival form and not as original materials—a fact that makes this work to somewhat an exercise in remedial archaeology replete with all the advantages and disadvantages of such an exercise.

In this section I briefly describe the location and stratigraphy of each site, as well as the nature of its cultural layer or layers. Additional names by which the sites have appeared in the literature, as well as their approximate latitude and longitude, raion, and oblast', are indicated in parentheses following the name used in this work. The sites will be considered in alphabetical order with the exception of the Pushkari group (Puskhari I, Pushkari II, Bugorok, and Pogon), which are discussed as a unit. Site numbers here and in the following tables are those of Figure 2.1. See Figure 2.2 for location of tributaries. I offer my own analysis and interpretation of these central Russian Plain sites in Chapters 5 and 6.

Data on the geographic particulars of each site, the nature of archaeological remains, the nature and quantity of features unearthed, and the composition of organic remains per site all appear in Tables 2.3–2.12 at the end of this chapter. Table 2.3 presents summarized locational and geological data on the sites, as well as data on their cultural layers. Their location and orientation on plateaus or river terraces, their present-day altitudes above the rivers, stratigraphic information on the cultural layers, areas excavated, and postulated total site areas are given in Table 2.3 as well. Data on the exact geographic location of the sites (longitudinal and latitudinal measurements) are never given in Soviet archaeological publications and, therefore, I derived them from the locations of the nearest villages listed in the *Official Standard Names Gazeteer* No. 42 (2nd edition). In some cases where the villages were not listed, I estimated locational measurements from maps. Because the locational measurements had to be extrapolated in this manner, they should be taken as close estimates of the true site locations and not their absolute coordinates. Similarily, some of the measurements listed in Table 2.3 (distances of the sites from the river) were estimated from sketch maps provided in the literature. They, likewise, should be taken as approximate and not absolute measures. The most approximate measures are those listed for distances of the sites to their nearest neighbor sites. They represent the shortest linear measurements between the two sites across a flat and undifferentiated landscape and were taken from contemporary maps of the region. The problems and errors involved in using raw linear distance measurements in settlement system studies have been discussed in the literature (Johnson 1977). I present them in this work because no alternatives are presently available. To date Soviet researchers have focused solely on the sites themselves and not on the distribution of the sites across the late Pleistocene landscape. In the case of the late Pleistocene central Russian Plain, the most obvious problem with raw linear distance measures is that in many cases they involve crossing large bodies of water (e.g., Dobranichevka and Mezhirich are located across the Dnepr from each other). As I mentioned earlier and further discuss in Chapter 3, late Valdai rivers of the central Russian Plain were much larger and more powerful than their present-day counterparts. Today, for example, the widest river, the Dnepr, is less than 2 km in width at its widest point in the study area. In the past, however, the rivers of the central Russian Plain carried glacial runoff and meltwater and were greatly enlarged. Boriskovskii (1953) postulates that the Dnepr at the latitude of Kiev may have been quite a bit wider than 10 km. Aseev *et al.* (1973), Dolukhanov (1982), and Voznyachuk *et al.* (1969) postulate great widths for the other rivers in the study area as well. Late Pleistocene hunter–gatherers, therefore, could have crossed the rivers in two ways: in warm months using boats, and in cold months by walking across the frozen surface of the rivers. At present there is no evidence for the use of boats on the central Russian Plain during this period. Therefore, I assume in this discussion that rivers could have been crossed only in cold months after freezing and before the spring breakup of ice.

PROBLEMS WITH THE DATA

Features uncovered at the sites are presented in Table 2.4 and lithic remains in Tables 2.5 and 2.6. As my discussion of various sites shows, these lists are far from complete and represent in some cases a basal minimum. Data offered in these tables come from both the extant literature and archival notes; the exact sources for the data can be found in the pertinent tables.

Tables 2.7–2.10 lists faunal remains at the sites. These tables are possibly the most problematic of all the data tables and are bound to elicit the greatest objections (see Grayson 1984 on optimal methods of quantifying organic remains). The nature of the available data, discussed briefly below, precludes me from using the optimal methods, and the remains are presented as MNB (minimum number of bones) and MNI (minimum number of individuals) values. Values listed in the table are taken from the literature and archival sources and in some cases are modified after my own examination. The MNI and MNB statistics are most problematic. Optimal methods for calculating these values are still widely discussed in the literature (Binford 1981; Clason 1975; Daly 1969; Gilbert 1980; Grayson 1973, 1974, 1978, 1984; Lyman 1982). Binford (1982), among others, has pointed out some basic problems with the use of these statistic as representative of live weight of animals. As I have already noted and reiterate below, optimal methods of quantifying faunal remains are simply not possible when the assemblages are no longer available. Under such conditions, two options are open to archaeologists: either dismiss available information (archival notations, "faunal laundry lists," etc.) altogether because it does not meet current standards and collect and record new data properly, or, when the first solution is not feasible, work with what is available to salvage as much information, problematic though it may be, as is possible. I follow the second course and see the faunal treatment in this work as an exercise in *salvage archaeozoology.*

Soviet researchers very rarely state the methods they use in reaching MNI figures. Vereschagin (1977) is the only author who mentions that his figures are based on the calculation of the greatest number of specific skeletal elements (e.g., right or left mandibles). Since no discussion exists in the Soviet literature on the methodologies used to calculate the MNI, I have assumed that all figures were derived by the method used by Vereschagin. This constrains me to use the same method when augmenting and amending the MNI estimates in the extant lists. I add to the MNI statistic only when extant collections contain more of a particular skeletal element than is accounted for in the MNI statistic of the faunal list. I elect to use this problematic and highly inaccurate method to assure some comparability between the lists.

The faunal lists are most often taken from the literature, and in indicated cases they are amended to reflect my own reexamination of both available collections and archival information not previously considered. In other cases I add to extant lists information on fauna unearthed after the published faunal lists were compiled. This is done for Dobranichevka, Eliseevichi, Gontsy, Khotylevo II, Timonovka II, and Yudinovo. In other cases, two or more faunal lists published at different times and reflecting different years of collection for the same site are combined and presented summarily. This is the case for Berdyzh, Eliseevichi, Novgorod-Severskii, Timonovka I, and Yudinovo. In some cases, such as Suponevo, where no collections have been preserved, amendments to the published information are made on the basis of field notes of the excavator.

The treatment of faunal remains varies greatly in the USSR. In general, the excavations conducted either by paleontologists or where paleontologists were present contain the most accurate account of faunal remains. These biases, unfortunately cannot be rectified. Many of the sites were excavated in the 1920s, 1930s, and 1940s, and their faunal collections no longer exist. In most cases, both in the past and even today, it was and is not the habit of Soviet excavators to bring back complete faunal assemblages from the field. Faunas from the sites currently under excavation—Gontsy, Khotylevo II, Mezhirich, Pushkari I, and Yudinovo—vary in their inclusiveness. The Mezhirich fauna has been analyzed and tabulated through the 1980 field season. The Gontsy, Pushkari I, and Yudinovo faunal lists do not reflect remains found in recent excavations, as these remains were not available for my examination. The Khotylevo II faunal list is quite incomplete. The assemblages found in different years of excavation are located at different institutes in different cities of the European USSR. Some of these I was unable to examine. The faunal list for Khotylevo II published by Velichko, Zavernyaev *et al.* (1981) records only those remains housed at the Paleolithic Sector of the Institute of Geography of the Academy of Sciences of the USSR in Moscow. I have added to this list the material excavated at the site during the 1970 field season—a collection I was able to examine at the Zoological Institute of the Ukrainian Academy of Sciences in Kiev. The faunal lists presented in this work should be used only for tentative comparisons; they are by no means firm enough for any but the simplest statistical manipulations.

Taxa presented in Tables 2.7–2.10 are grouped according to the role they played in the economies of the Upper Paleolithic hunter–gatherers. The category of "economically important species" (Table 2.7) includes species the remains of which show cultural modification in the form of dismembering, butchering, burning, or use in tool or artifact manufacturing. Species the remains of which bear no cultural-use markings are listed as "economically unimportant" (Tables 2.8 and 2.9). It is presumed they represent either food debris from nonhuman predators or, in some cases, remains of animals that lived and died at the sites after they were abandoned by man.

There are two problematic taxa in the assemblages: equids and leporids. I have identified all horses excavated at the central Russian Plain sites as *Equus* sp. even though some researchers have classified them as distinct species. For example, the faunal list presented by Shovkoplyas (1965a) for Mezin lists *Equus equus*. Pidoplichko (1976) identifies the equids of Mezhirich also as *Equus equus*. Vereschagin (1977) lists the Yudinovo equid as *Equus caballus*, and Gromov (1948) classifies all equid remains from the central Russian Plain as *Equus* sp. Kornietz *et al.* (1981) assign the Mezhirich equid remains to the species of *Equus latipes Gromova*. They thus follow Kuzmina (1978), who has examined the remains of the late Valdai horses from Novgorod-Sever-skii, Mezin, and Kostenki sites hitherto variously classified as *Equus equus, Equus caballus latipes,* or *Equus* sp. Kuzmina concludes that they all belong to the same extinct late Pleistocene species and names it *Equus latipes*. Azzaroli (1982, personal communication) states, however, that late Pleistocene horses should be classified as subspecies of *Equus caballus*. Since Kuzmina has not examined all of the equid remains from the central Russian Plain, and since other classifications exist for them in the literature, I have decided to place all equid remains into the undifferentiated category of *Equus* sp., which must await further delineation.

A similar classificatory difficulty exists with the leporids. The literature abounds with different species identifications, ranging from *Lepus europaeus* for Mezhirich (Kornietz *et al.* 1981) to *Lepus* sp. for Mezin, Mezhirich, and Dobranichevka (Pidoplichko 1969) to *Lepus timidus* (Velichko, Grekhova *et al.* 1981). Gureev (1964) has proposed a new species for late Pleistocene leporids of the Russian Plain—the large extinct form of *Lepus tenaiticus*. My own examination of the leporids from Mezhirich, Gontsy, Khotylevo II, Mezin, and Novgorod—Severskii indicates close metric and morphological similarities. I have therefore decided to combine all the fossils into one taxon, *Lepus* sp., until further examination leads to an evaluation of Gureev's proposal.

Organic inventories found at the sites (bone, antler, and shell) are quantified in Table 2.11; these values, like values found in the preceding tables, represent minimum counts. Radiocarbon dates for the sites are given in Table 2.12; the reliability of these dates is discussed in Chapter 4.

Finally, there are a few sites or localities mentioned in the Soviet literature that are not considered in this work (e.g., Karachizh, Kladbischenskaya Balka, Podluzhye III, and Dovginichi). I do not include them because their status is most unclear. In some cases, such as Karachizh and Kladbischenskaya Blaka, it is unclear if they were sites or just locales where some worked flint was found. In other cases, such as Podluzhye III, the existence of the site is in question (Kaletchitz 1978, personal communication).

THE SITES

1. **Berdyzh** (52°50′ N, 30°58′ E; Chechevskii, Gomel).   The site is located on the right or eastern banks of the river Sozh, some 500 m south of the village of Podluzhye and 3 km south of the village of Berdyzh. The site was discovered by Polikarpovich in 1926. Polikarpovich and Zamyatnin excavated small and often discontinuous sections of Ber-dyzh from 1927 through 1954 (Polikarpovich 1968). Budko continued excavating Ber-dyzh from 1965 to 1970. Berdyzh is one of the oldest sites on the central Russian Plain, although the precise date of occupation remains problematic (see discussion of chro-nology in Chapter 4).

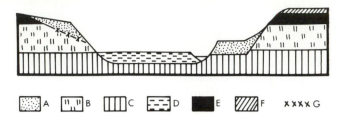

Figure 2.13 Berdyzh stratigraphy: A, sands; B, deposits under the moraine; C, bedrock; D, floodplain deposits; E, moraine; F, loam; G, cultural materials (after Gromov 1948: Fig. 79).

The geography and geology of the site are described by Budko *et al.* (1971), Budko and Voznyachuk (1969), Gromov (1948), and Voznyachuk and Budko (1969) (see Figure 2.13). The site was found on the promontory of an 8–10-m-deep ravine that cut through the high, steep plateau and terrace deposits. The ravine in which the site was located was in turn cut through by a younger ravine that partially disturbed and dislocated the cultural layer. Voznyachuk and Budko (1969) suggest that the location of the site is associated with the second terrace of the Sozh. Isaenko (1968) reports that the site was in a ravine that cut through the first Sozh terrace.

In total some 350 m² of the site have been investigated to date. The cultural layer was found 1.5 to 10 m below the present soil surface in green-gray colluvial loam and loess–loam. Both Polikarpovich (1968) and Gromov (1948) interpret the different depths of the cultural remains as well as the presence of associated periglacial deformations to imply that the cultural remains have been redeposited down the slope of a ravine. Budko (1966), Budko and Voznyachuk (1969), and Voznyachuk and Budko (1969), on the other hand, state that parts of the site are in situ. They also postulate that two cultural layers are present at Berdyzh and that at present it is impossible to determine if (1) two different sites are represented; (2) the cultural layers at different depths and locations represent two locales of the same site, or (3) one of the two observed layers is a redeposited section of the other layer. To date the site is known from a handful of very brief articles and has

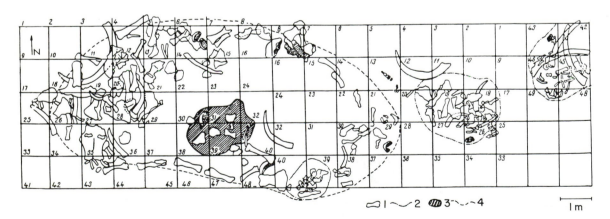

Figure 2.14   Berdyzh excavation, 1938–1939: 1, mammoth bones; 2, outline of storage pits; 3, hearth and ash spots; 4, outline of dwelling (after Polikarpovich 1968: Fig. 10).

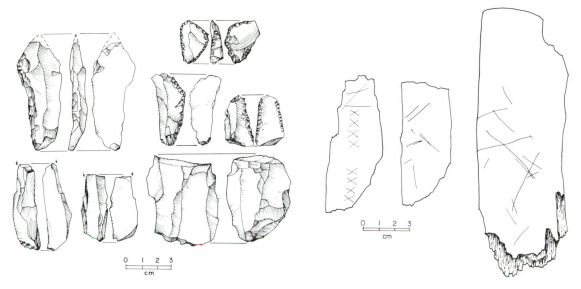

Figure 2.15   Berdyzh lithics (after Polikarpovich 1968: Figs. 5,6,7).

Figure 2.16   Berdyzh: engraved bone.

not been adequately studied either archaeologically or geologically. This precludes firm conclusions about either its precise stratigraphy or the possible areal extent of the site. At least parts of the cultural layer have been disturbed by erosion and solifluction, as well as by periglacial deformations such as ice wedge casts, tundra hillocks, involutions (Kalechitz 1972, 1984).

Although the original excavator of the site, Polikarpovich, does not recognize the presence of any features at Berdyzh, subsequent excavations and reconstructions reveal that the site contained at least two mammoth-bone dwellings, interior hearths, and both interior and exterior storage pits (Figure 2.14).

Lithic and organic inventories from Berdyzh have not been fully published; a sampling is offered in Figures 2.15 and 2.16.

2. **Chulatovo I** (Kreidyanoi Maidan) (51°50′ N, 33°07′ E; Novgorod–Severskii, Chernigov).   The site is located on the right or northern bank of the Desna some 500 m from the site of Chulatovo II. It was discovered in 1935 by Zaharchenko and excavated by Pidoplicho in 1935 and Voevodskii in 1937 (Boriskovskii 1953). Cultural remains were discovered in a chalk quarry in the process of quarrying, and the site was subsequently destroyed by quarrying operations. The geology of the site is illustrated in Figure 2.17.

The geomorphology of this part of the Desna is such that the right or northern bank consists of a 40-m-high interfluve plateau that comes right to the river and is cut by deep ravines. Velichko (1961) suggests that man settled close to the Desna floodplain here, possibly at the foot of a ravine. The cultural remains, according to Velichko, are not in situ but have been redeposited by erosion and possibly solifluction from a location higher

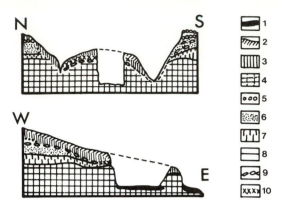

Figure 2.17   Chulatovo I stratigraphy: 1, top-soil; 2, soil; 3, loess; 4, chalk; 5, boulder loam; 6, yellow Tertiary sand; 7, yellow-grey sand; 8, buried soil; 9, sandstone lenses; 10, cultural layer (after Pidoplichko 1947a: Figs. 1,2).

in the ravine, or possibly from the edge of the plateau itself. Boriskovskii (1953) and Pidoplichko (1947a), however, report that some 20 m² of the site held an in situ cultural layer. In light of this it is impossible to state with any certainty where the exact location of the original site was, but it appears to have been both in the ravine and close to the floodplain. A major part of the cultural remains was destroyed prior to investigation, and only some 390 m² have been excavated. Faint remain of from one to three hearths are the only features found (see Figures 2.18 and 2.19).

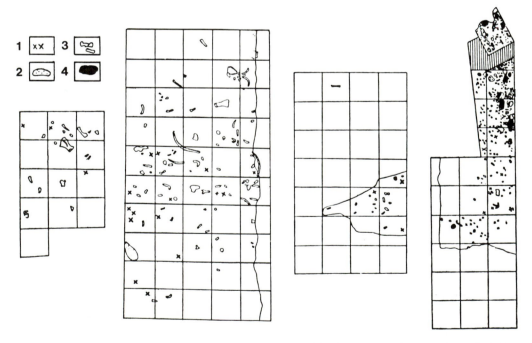

Figure 2.18   Chulatovo I excavations: 1, flint; 2, sandstone slabs; 3, bones; 4, ash spots (after Pidoplichko 1947a: Fig. 3).

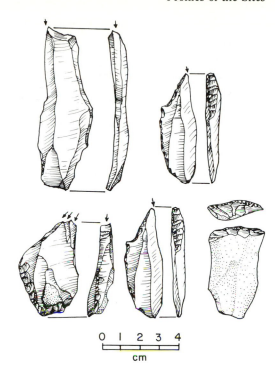

Figure 2.19 Chulatovo I flint tools (after
Voevodskii 1947b: Figs. 3,4).

0 1 2 3 4

cm

3. **Chulatovo II** (Rabochij Rov).   The site is located on the right banks of the Desna
some 500 m downstream of Chulatovo I. It was discovered in 1935 by Pidoplichko and
Galich and was excavated by them in 1936 (Boriskovskii 1953). In 1937 and 1938 more
extensive excavations at Chulatovo II were conducted by Voevodskii (1952a). The geography and geology of the site have been described by Gromov (1948) and Velichko
(1961) and are illustrated in Figures 2.20 and 2.21.

The cultural layer was found on a back part of an old ravine which cut through the
37–40 m-high interfluve plateau that abutted the river. The formation of the ravine
took place after the site was occupied and the subsequent ravine erosion destroyed
approximately half of the site. Cultural remains were found some 35–37 m above the
river and some 100–125 m from the steep shore. Velichko, Grekhova, and Gubonina
(1977) postulate that the height of the Desna in the late Valdai was 15–20 m higher than
it is today, which would suggest that the site was then located at the edge of the plateau
15–25 m over the river and its floodplain. The cultural layer was found in the upper part
of a loess–loam layer 2.0–2.5 m below present-day surface. Below the cultural layer, at a
depth of approximately 2.5 m, Velichko (1961) reports finding traces of the humic layer
which he identified as remnants of a badly eroded Bryansk soil.

Voevodskii (1952a) excavated approximately 1000 m² of the site, which he considers
to be one-half of the area originally occupied, by opening up large contiguous areas of
50 to 200 m². One very thin cultural layer was found at the site. It was spread discon-

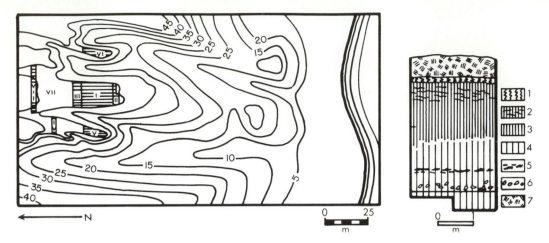

Figure 2.20   Chulatovo II geomorphology: I–VI, excavations (after Voevodskii 1952a: Fig. 1)

Figure 2.21   Chulatovo II stratigraphy: 1, humic layer; 2, loess–loam with sand; 3, loess–loam dark tan; 4, loess–loam, light tan; 5, humic loess–loam; 6, cultural layer; 7, plow zone (after Velichko 1961: Fig. 36).

tinuously over the excavated area and found concentrated in three locations. Seven hearths and a number of small pits were excavated at Chulatovo II, and Leonova (1977) delineates the presence of at least three work areas on the living floor (Figures 2.22 and 2.23). Leonova is also the first Soviet archaeologist to investigate the spatial aspects of site use, and she did so using Chulatovo II lithic data. Her conjoining of flint pieces is illustrated in Figure 2.24. Although the majority of conjoinables are located in close proximity, some, found in disparate work areas, suggest a contemporaneity of occupa-

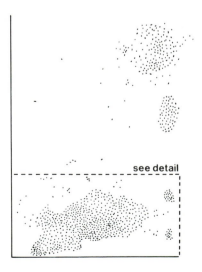

Figure 2.22   Chulatovo II: distribution of cultural remains; see detail, Figure 2.23 (after Leonova 1977: Tab. 19).

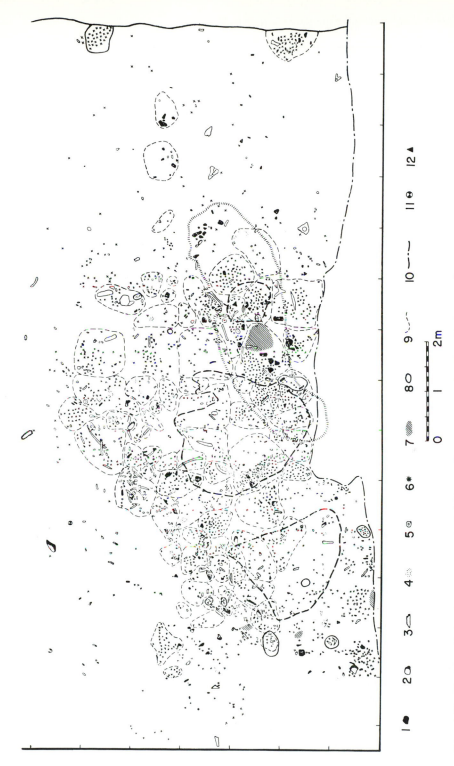

Figure 2.23 Chulatovo II: details of excavation: 1, flint; 2, quartzite; 3, bones; 4, ocher; 5, shell; 6, charcoal; 7, chalk slab; 8, pit; 9, border of complex; 10, extent of erosion; 11, flint nuclei; 12, amber (after Leonova 1977: Tab. 20).

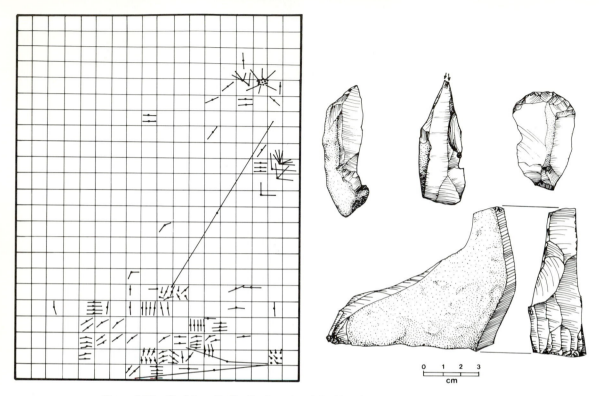

Figure 2.24   Chulatovo II: distribution of conjoinables. Squares are 1 × 1-m sections (after Leonova 1977: Table 3).

Figure 2.25   Chulatovo II flint tools (after Voevodskii 1952a: Figs. 4,5).

tion for the different areas. The lithic and bone inventory of the site is listed in Tables 2.5, 2.6, and 2.11, and a sample of worked flint is illustrated in Figure 2.25.

   4. Dobranichevka (50°02′ N, 32°40′ E; Yagodinskii, Kiev).   Dobranichevka was dis-covered in 1952 in the course of road construction and was excavated through 1975 by Shovkoplyas. Data on the site has been only partially published by Shovkoplyas (1971, 1972, 1974, 1976) and Shovkoplyas *et al.* (1981). Four dwellings, hearth, work areas, and pit complexes have been found at the site, two of which have been partially de-scribed; a third was transported in blocks and reconstructed at the Periyaslov–Khmelnitsky open-air museum (see Figure 6.4), and a fourth was left open but unexca-vated and is now a part of the local site museum at Dobranichevka.

   The geography and geology of the site have been studied by Pidoplichko (1969), Pashkevich and Dubnyak (1978), and Shovkoplyas *et al.* (1981) and are illustrated in Figure 2.26. The site is located on a left-bank promontory formed by the second terrace of the river Tashanka as the river enters the valley of the river Supoi. The site today is

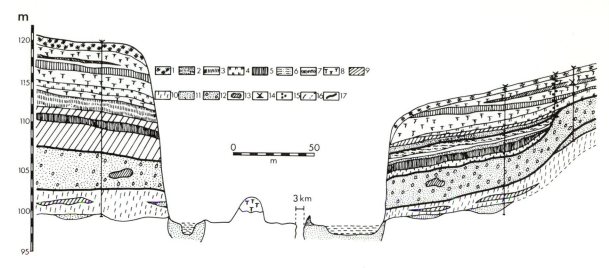

Figure 2.26 Dobranichevka: geomorphology and stratigraphy of the Supoi valley: 1, chernozem; 2, dark grey forest soil; 3, grey forest soil; 4, dark brown-grey forest soil; 5, grey-brown soil; 6, meadow soil; 7, embryonic soil; 8, loess; 9, loam; 10. sandy loam; 11, sand; 12, boulder loam (moraine); 13, boulders; 14, cultural layer; 15, pollen cores; 16, stratigraphic boundaries; 17, erosional boundaries (after Paskevich and Dubnyak 1978: Fig. 1).

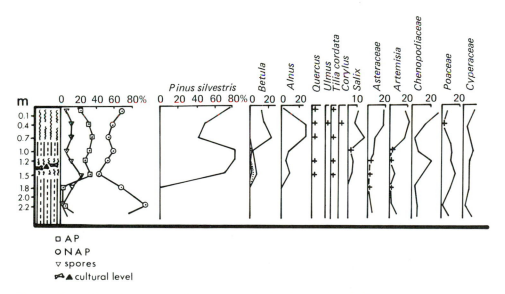

Figure 2.27 Dobranichevka pollen diagram (after Shovkopylas *et al.* 1981: Fig. 28).

less than 100 from Tashanka. The promontory on which man settled is 16–17 m above the river today. At the time of occupation, the promontory had a gentle northeast–southwest slope; the site was therefore open to the south and protected from the north.

The cultural layer was found in the Loess III deposits and overlay a thin layer of embryonic soil. The stratigraphy of the Dnepr and its tributaries has been studied far less extensively than that of the Desna, and it is therefore difficult to say at present if this layer of fossil soil is contemporaneous with the gley layer of the Desna sequence. It is also possible, as Dolukhanov and Pashkevich (1977) and Pashkevich and Dubnyak (1978) suggest, that this layer accumulated during a younger warm episode than that which resulted in the formation of the gley layer in the Desna sequence. Such a conclusion seems warranted, given the pollen data from Dobranichevka (Figure 2.27, and see Pashkevich and Dubnyak 1978; Tab. I). I return to this question, as well as to pollen data from the sites in general, in Chapter 3, where I consider the environment of the central Russian Plain in the late Valdai.

Dobranichevka is one of the two sites in the study area that has been totally exca-

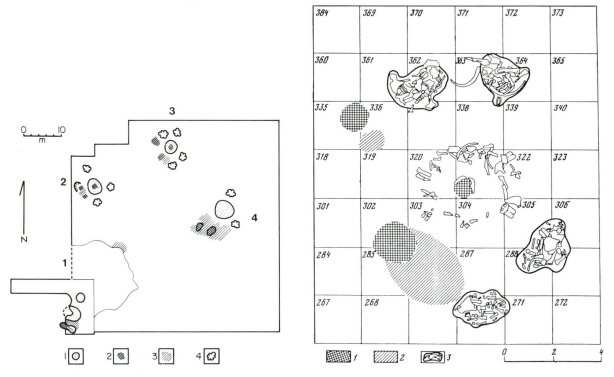

Figure 2.28. Dobranichevka excavations: 1, dwellings; 2, hearths; 3, work area—lithic and bone concentrations; 4, storage pits (after Leonova 1977: Fig. 44).

Figure 2.29 Dobranichevka Complex 3: 1, hearths; 2, bone and lithic work areas; 3, storage pits (after Shovkoplyas et al. 1981: Fig. 29).

vated. Shovkoplyas (1972) and Shovkopylas *et al.* (1981) report that the site was 5500 m² in area, but only about 2000 m² have been carefully investigated. A single, in situ cultural layer was found, but parts of the site were destroyed by road building prior to archaeological excavations. In spite of some problems with Dobranichevka, it remains one of most "classic" sites on the central Russian Plain. The features found there, as the plan (see Figures 2.28 and 2.29) of the excavation shows, consist of mammoth-bone dwellings, hearths, storage pits, and work areas grouped into four distinct complexes. While Leonova (1977), because of provenience problems, was unable to conjoin lithics at this site, Gladkih, using a comparability index for lithics, argues that the four complexes were occupied at the same time (see a discussion of contemporaneity of occupation at the sites in Chapter 6).

Dobranichevka lithics, made of both local cobble flint and exotic mountain crystal, feature much microlithization, a trait once considered diagnostic for chronology but now recognized as dependent on geography (Figure 2.30). Gladkih (1973) persuasively argues that microlitization occurred earlier at more southerly sites on the central Russian Plain than at their northern equivalents (see Chapter 4). It is interesting to note that both locally available and exotic lithic materials were used without discrimination at Dobranichevka, an issue I return to in Chapter 7 in considering the points of origin and distribution of nonlocal materials found at the sites. Dobranichevka has also yielded an impressive array of bone tools, as well as amber and sandstone pieces which Shov-koplyas (1972) interprets as female figurines (Figure 2.31).

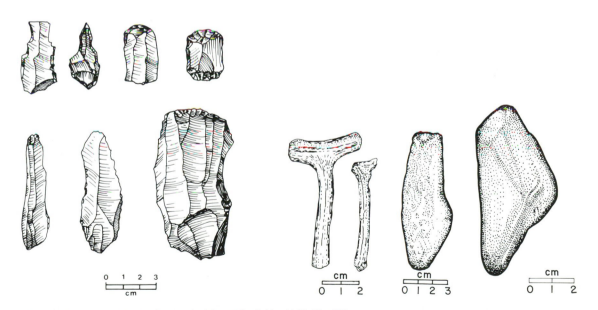

Figure 2.30 Dobranichevka flint tools (after Pidoplichko 1969: Fig. 22).

Figure 2.31 Dobranichevka: antler tool and amber and sandstone figurines (after Shovkoplyas *et al.* 1981: Fig. 30).

5. **Eliseevichi** (Yeliseevichi, Eliseyevichi) (53°08′N, 33°37′E; Zhiryatinskii, Bryansk). The site was discovered in 1930 by Polikarpovich. It was subsequently excavated by Polikarpovich, Voevodskii, and Zavernyaev in 1935, 1936, 1946, and 1948. Budko excavated parts of the site from 1963 to 1967. From 1970 to 1978 Grekhova excavated the site, since 1972 with Velichko and his staff. While a monograph on Eliseevichi is being prepared by Grekhova and Velichko, no unified plan of all Eliseevichi excavations is available that coordinates all the work done there since 1930. Figure 2.32 represents my compilation of all available information on past work at Eliseevichi. The geography and geology of the site have been reported by Gromov

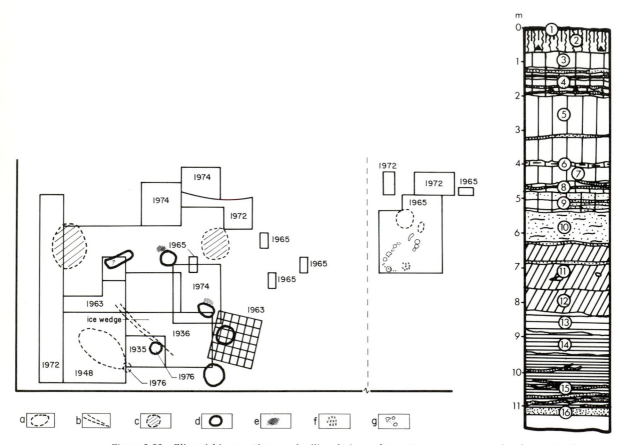

Figure 2.32 Eliseevichi excavations: a, dwelling; b, ice wedge cast; c, contemporary pits; d, storage pits; e, hearths; f, flint; g, bones.

Figure 2.33 Eliseevichi stratigraphy: 1, humic loam; 2, sandy loam, light grey; 3, sandy loam, light brown; 4, layering of 2 and 3 with cultural layer at depth of 1.90 to 1.95 m; 5, loess-like sandy loam; 6, sandy loam, grey-brown; 7, sandy loam, loess-like; 8, sand; 9, sandy loam, light grey; 10, sandy loam, brown-grey; 11, loam, brown-grey; 12, loam, greyish; 13, clay, marly and compact; 14, clay, marly, light; 15, clay, marly, light, sith sand lenses; 16, sand, dark grey (after Velichko 1961: Fig. 56).

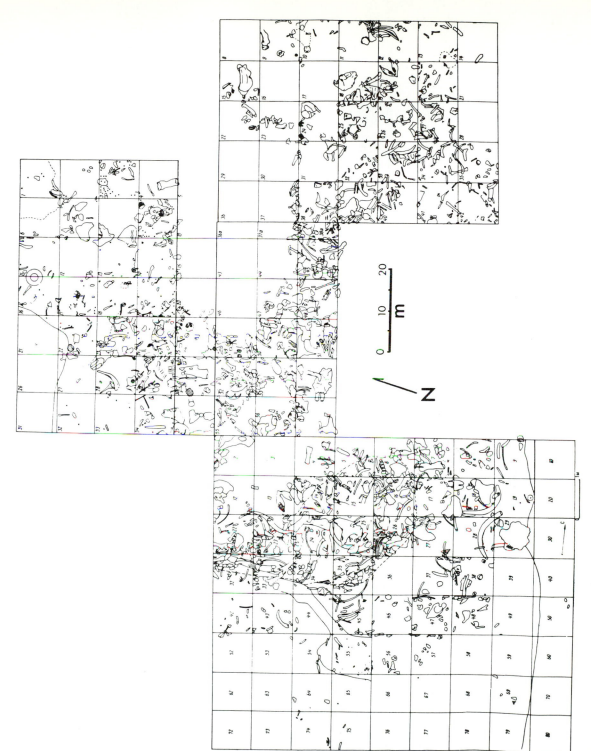

Figure 2.34 Eliseevichi (1935–1948) distribution of large mammoth bones (after Polikarpovich 1968: foldout map).

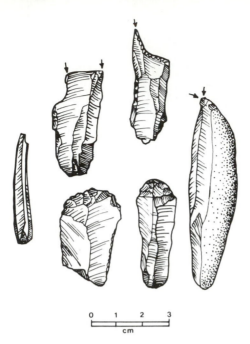

0   1   2   3
cm

Figure 2.35   Eliseevichi flint tools (after Polikarpovich 1968: Fig. 18).

(1948), Polikarpovich (1968), Velichko (1961), and Velichko, Grekhova, and Udarsev (1977) (see Figure 2.33.)

The site is located on the (northern right-bank promontory of the second terrace formed by the terrace and two ravines that delimit the promontory in the north and south. The promontory is bounded on the north by a steep river bank and on the west it rises gradually into the interfluve plateau. Velichko (1961) postulates that at the time of occupation the site was located on the floodplain. Today the river is no more than 10–15 meters away from the site.

Velichko, Grekhova, and Udartsev (1977) report that the cultural remains are associated with a faint fossil soil layer that was formed during a warm, late Valdai episode. It is not clear if this layer is to be equated with the gley layer of the Desna sequence or if it represents another warming episode.

Approximately 620 m² of the area have been excavated. Polikarpovich (1968) supposes the original site may have been as large as 5000 m². Parts of the site have been eroded by the river and the cultural layer itself has been severely disturbed in parts by such periglacial phenomena as ice wedge casts and possibly solifluction. In 1965, Budko (1978, personal communication) excavated a section of the site located 20–50 m to the northeast of the main excavations, behind the northern ravine next to the river. He suggests that this locale, which he calls Eliseevichi II, is a different complex and perhaps a different site from Eliseevichi. Grekhova (1981) reports excavating an area 200 m northeast of the previous excavations (in the area of Budko's 1965 excavation?) and finding a very disturbed cultural layer. She suggests that this is another site and calls it Eliseevichi II. The justification for claiming that either of these two finds represents yet another site is unclear. Budko seems to assume that the location of the remains behind the ravine justify this, and Grekhova offers as evidence the observation that cultural remains at her Eliseevichi II are found at an elevation of 6.7 m above those of Eliseevichi. The question of whether one or two (or more) sites are represented in this locality cannot be answered until extensive geological investigations are done to determine, among other things, the stratigraphies involved and the age of the north ravine.

In addition, the presence of severe periglacial disturbances at Eliseevichi has only recently been recognized (see Velichko *et al.* 1977 for discussion). Because of this, I discuss only the materials found at the main Eliseevichi location and assume that both the 1965 excavation and the 1980 excavation unearthed other portions of the same site. If this is so, then it seems quite possible that the maximal areal extent for Eliseevichi suggested by Polikarpovich (5000 m^2) is much too small. I trust that the forthcoming monograph on Eliseevichi by Velichko and Grekhova will clarify many of these questions.

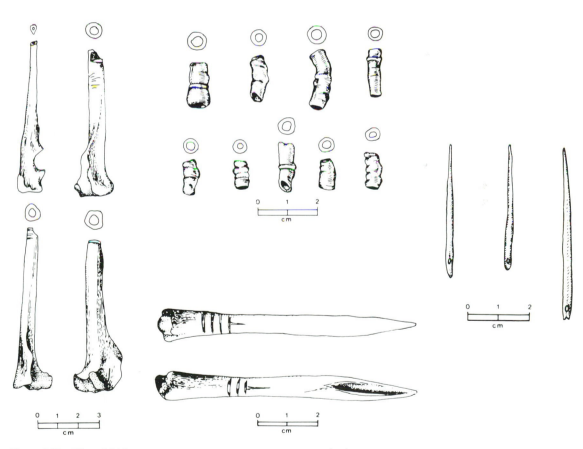

Figure 2.36   Eliseevichi bone tools and shell beads (after Polikarpovich 1968: Figs. 31,32,53,54).

Figure 2.37 Eliseevichi: ivory plaque 8 (from Marshack, 1979, "Upper Paleolithic Symbol Systems of the Russian Plain," *Current Anthropology*, 20(2), © 1979 University of Chicago Press).

Polikarpovich and Budko after him mistook some of the periglacial deformations of the cultural layer for man-made features. This gave rise to reports of a "mammoth-bone corridor" at Eliseevichi which found their way into both the Russian-language and Western literature (see Figure 2.34). While there is no agreement on the exact number and nature of the features found at the site, at least two mammoth-bone dwellings, numerous storage pits (exterior and possibly interior), and stone- and bone-working areas existed at the site. Storage pits at Eliseevichi, like those at Timonovka II, were

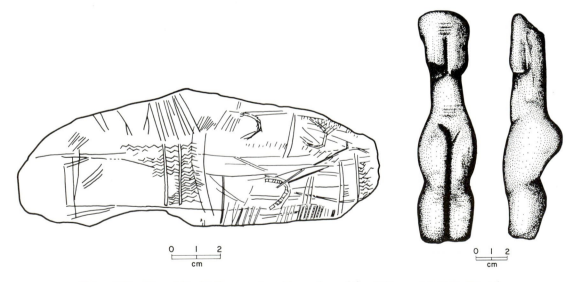

Figure 2.38 Eliseevichi: details on engraved ivory plaque (after Polikarpovich 1968: Fig. 44).

Figure 2.39 Eliseevichi: ivory female figurine (Soffer 1985).

probably "fenced" by mammoth crania (Velichko, Grekhova, and Gubonina 1977; Grekhova 1979, personal communication). While I report no hearths for Eliseevichi in Table 2.4, their absence is not surprising given the severe periglacial deformations.

Archaeological inventories from Eliseevichi are numerous, varied, and impressive. A sampling of flint tools from the site is illustrated in Figure 2.35. Worked bone found at the site includes a large assortment of bone awls, needles, piercers, hoes, digging implements, pendents, and beads (Figure 2.36). Numerous engraved ivory plaques (Figures 2.37 and 2.38), termed "churingas" by Polikarpovich (1968) and an ivory female figurine (Figure 2.39) quite different from the classic Venus figurines of Upper Paleolithic Europe have also come from this extremely rich and complex site.

6. Fastov (50°05' N, 29°55' E; Fastovskii, Kiev).   Fastov was found by Shovkoplyas in 1954 on the second terrace of the river Unava. The site is known from just one 6-page article by Shovkoplyas (1956) and is summarized in the Boriskovskii and Praslov volume (1964). To the best of my knowledge no geological investigation was done here and no stratigraphic schemes are available.

Shovkoplyas (1956) and Gladkih (1973) report that the site is located on the right (southern) slope of a ravine somehow associated with the second terrace of Unava. Shovkoplyas postulates that man settled here on a ravine promontory above a stream or brook that flowed at the bottom of the ravine. The cultural layer is in loess-like loam 12 m above the river at depth of 3.2 m below the present surface. The site is currently less than 10 m from the river. It seems reasonable to assume that both Unava and Irpen' flowed at much higher elevations during the late Valdai and were, like the Desna, found at elevations of at least 10 m above their present levels. This in turn suggests that man settled at Fastov in a ravine on or very near the floodplain.

Shovkoplyas excavated 220 m² at Fastov and found one thin but apparently in situ central layer. He considers Fastov to have been occupied very briefly—only six flint working areas and two hearths were found. Unfortunately Shovkoplyas did not illustrate any of his discoveries at Fastov. As I argue in Chapter 6, Fastov appears to have been a very interesting special-purpose hunting camp—a type of site poorly represented in the archaeological record of the central Russian Plain.

7. Gontsy (Hontsy) (50°10' N, 32°49' E; Lubenskii, Poltava).   Gontsy was the first Upper Paleolithic site to be found on the central Russian Plain. It was discovered in 1871 when a landowner, in the process of some construction on his property, found mammoth bone and reported it to the local schoolteacher, Kaminskii. Both Boriskovskii (1953) and Pidoplichko (1968) report that the site underwent sporadic and unsystematic excavations from 1873 to 1914. The first planned excavations were conducted in 1914–1915 be Schervakivskii and Gorodtsov. The site was subsequently investigated in 1935 by Levitskii (1947). The results of these excavations were published in a handful of articles—no monograph was ever done on this important Upper Paleolithic site (Boriskovskii 1953; Levitskii 1947; Pidoplichko 1969). Sergin began working again at the site in 1976, conducting small-scale salvage-type excavations in an attempt to recover new evidence from parts of the site excavated earlier (Sergin 1978, 1979a, 1981a,) (Figure 2.40).

Gontsy is located on the right (southern) promontory formed by the second terrace of

Figure 2.40 Gontsy excavations (1979 season).

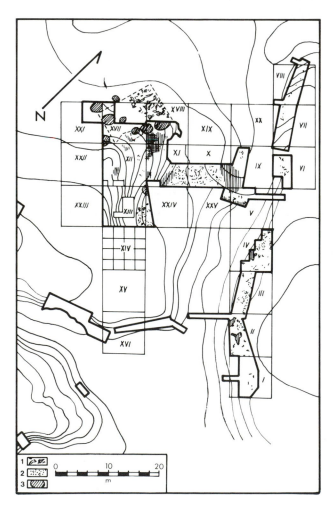

Figure 2.41 Gontsy: plan of past excavations: 1, bones; 2, flint; 3, storage pits; I–XXIII, excavations (after Levitskii 1947: Fig. 9).

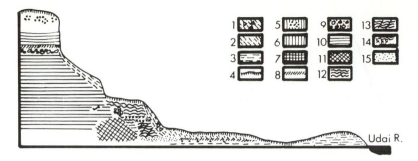

Figure 2.42   Gontsy: stratigraphy of the right bank of the Udai River: 1, soil creep; 2, colluvial ravine deposits; 3, alluvial deposits; 4, present-day soil; 5, loess with burrows; 6, pale yellow loess; 7, brown loam; 8, fossil soil; 9, boulder clay; 10, stratified pale loam; 11, Pliocene clay; 12, bandy loam; 13, dislocations; 14, cultural layer; 15, stratified sand (after Pidoplichko 1969: Fig. 13).

the Udai. The promontory faces south and is bordered today, as it was at the time of occupation, by ravines and the floodplain. Today the site lies 1.2 km from the river. The site's stratigraphy led both Gromov (1948) and Pidoplichko (1969) to conclude that people here settled on the floodplain itself and that the site was periodically flooded during the time Upper Paleolithic groups inhabited it (Figures 2.41 and 2.42). As best I can surmise, some 820 m^2 have been excavated to date.

Figure 2.43   Gontsy excavations (1979).

Soviet archaeological literature is divided on the question of how many cultural layers were found at Gontsy. Levitskii (1947) reports five layers. Boriskovskii (1953) reviews the geology and archaeology of Gontsy and concludes that only two layers were present. Pidoplichko (1969), in his reconstruction of past excavations at Gontsy, concludes that only one layer existed. These discrepancies arose in part because insufficient geological work was done at the site in the past, and we lack a clear understanding of taphonomic processes that operated at Gontsy. Periodic flooding, noted by Gromov and Pidoplichko, undoubtedly disturbed sections of the site and possibly redeposited some cultural material. Since the site was originally discovered because mammoth bones were eroding out of the deposits, it is probable that erosion took its toll as well.

While the early discovery of Gontsy initiated Upper Paleolithic archaeology on the central Russian Plain, the status of "first site found" was a costly one. Excavators working at Gontsy through the 1930s consistently mistook remains of mammoth-bone dwellings for remains of kitchen middens. This leaves us unable to determine how many dwellings and storage pits originally existed at the site. Sergin, working with ambiguous archival materials, reports at least two dwellings and at least five or six exterior storage pits. These pits purportedly surrounded one of the dwellings. (Figures 2.43–2.45). Sergin's reconstructions are in agreement with those undertaken by Pidoplichko

Figure 2.44   Gontsy Storage Pit 5 (1979).

(1969). Two of these exterior pits, left in situ by previous excavators, were reexcavated by Sergin (Figures 2.43 and 2.44). Both researchers have also determined the existence of numerous hearths, both interior and exterior.

Gontsy lithics, like those from Dobranichevka and Mezhirich, feature much micro-lithization (Figure 2.46; for discussion of the significance, see Chapter 4). Examples of worked bone are illustrated in Figure 2.47. Because of the history of archaeological work at Gontsy, lithic and organic inventories and faunal remains reported in Table 2.5–2.11 are minimal at best.

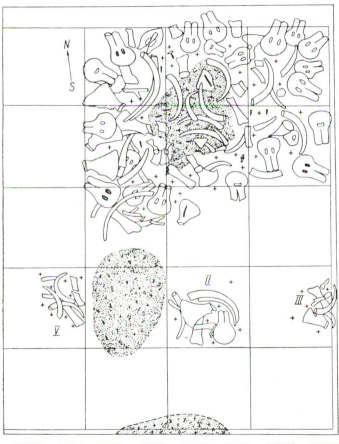

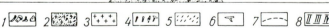

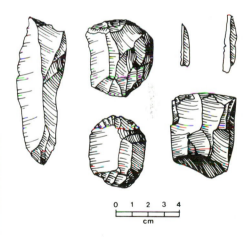

Figure 2.46   Gontsy lithics (after Pidoplichko 1969: Fig. 15).

Figure 2.45   Gontsy mammoth-bone dwelling reconstruction: 1, mammoth bones; 2, ash lenses; 3, flint; 4, worked bone; 5, bone charcoal; 6, reindeer antler; 7, eroded ash lens; 8, storage pits; excavation grids = 2 × 2 m (after Pidoplichko 1969: Fig. 14).

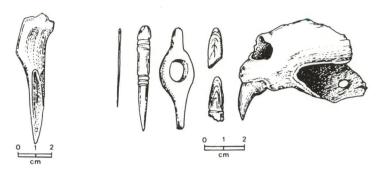

Figure 2.47   Gontsy worked bone (after Boriskovskii 1953: Fig. 167).

8. **Khotylevo II**   (53°20′ N, 34°07′ E: Bryanskii, Bryansk).   Khotylevo was dis-covered by Zavernyaev in 1967 and has been continuously excavated by Zavernyaev and Velichko and his staff since then. The site is located on the right (northern) bank of the Desna on a promontory formed on two sides by the interfluve plateau and the river. This promontory, 300 m wide, sits 15–16 m above the floodplain. Velichko, Gribchenko *et al.* (1977) postulate that both the ravines and river were situated much as today at the time Khotylevo II was occupied, but that the promontory itself was only from 5 to 7 m above the Desna.

As Figures 2.48 and 2.49 illustrate, cultural remains were found from 4.0 to 4.5 m below the present surface in a layer of laminated sandy loam. Below this layer is a humic layer that Velichko, Gribchenko *et al.* 1977 argue is similar to Bryansk soil. The cultural

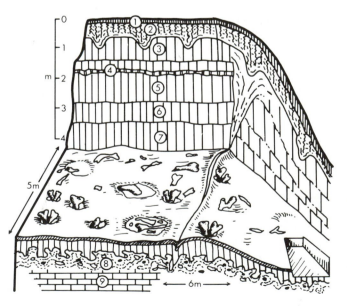

Figure 2.48   Khotylevo II: 1, humic layer; 2, Horizon B; 3, loess–sandy loam; 4, faint humic layer; 5, loess–sandy loam; 6, loess–sandy loam, faintly banded; 7, heavy loess–sandy loam with sand lenses; 8, loam; 9, marl (after Velichko, Zavernyaev *et al.* 1981: Fig. 17).

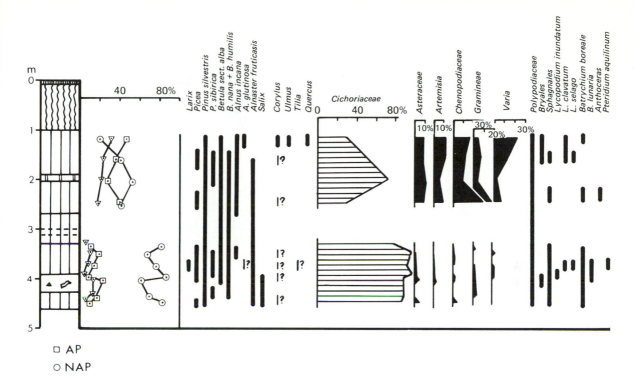

□ AP
○ NAP
▽ spores
◞▴ cultural level

Figure 2.49   Khotylevo II pollen diagram (after Velichko, Zavernyaev *et al.* 1981; Fig. 19).

layer is in situ but has been disturbed by ice wedge casts as well as other periglacial phenomena.

Over 500 m² have been excavated at Khotylevo II (Zavernyaev 1978). The extent of the site is still unknown. Velichko, Zavernyaev *et al.* (1981) report finding a cultural layer in test trenches 200 m up the plateau, farther away from the river. All reports indicate that only one Upper Paleolithic cultural layer has been found.

Little information about this site has appeared in print, but it is startling just how unlike Khotylevo II is to other sites on the central Russian PLain and how like those Upper Paleolithic sites farther east along the Sejm and Don. Unlike most other sites in the study area, it lacks mammoth-bone dwellings. Its living floor, replete with numerous small and large pits, resembles those at Avdeevo and Kostenki I. Its lithic inventory (Figure 2.50) is more akin to those from the Don sites (Lazukov *et al.* 1981; Zavernyaev 1981). Worked bone and ivory found at Khotylevo II (Figure 2.51) are stylistically similar to organic inventories at both Avdeevo and Kostenki I. Finally, the only examples of classic or almost classic Venus figurines found on the central Russian Plain come from Khotylevo II. I return to these observations in ensuing chapters of this work (see especially Chapters 6–8).

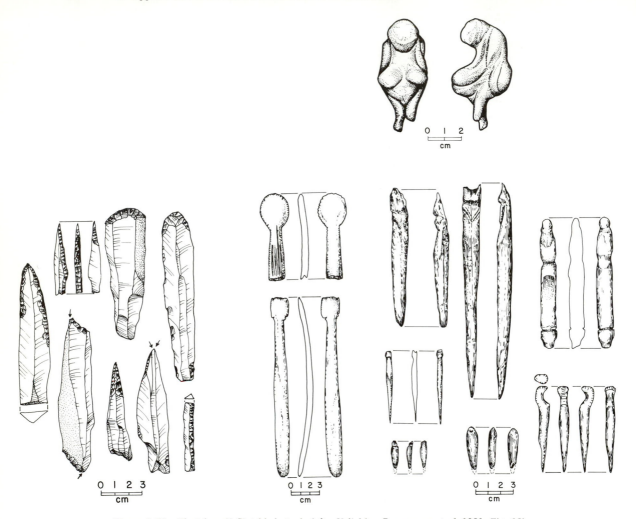

Figure 2.50   Khotylevo II flint blade tools (after Velichko, Zavernyaev *et al*. 1981: Fig. 18).

Figure 2.51   Khotylevo II mammoth-ivory portable art and worked pieces (after Zavernyaev 1978: Figs. 5,6).

9. Kirillovskaya (Kievo–Kirillovskaya) (50°26′ N, 30°31′ E; Kievskii, Kiev).   The site was discovered and excavated fully from 1893 to 1902 by Hvoiko (Boriskovskii 1953; Pidoplichko 1969). It is located in the city of Kiev itself on a promontory formed by the Dnepr shore and two ravines. The site is less than 100 m from the river. The geology and geography have been reconstructed by both Gromov (1948) and Pidoplichko (1969), primarily from unpublished archival holdings (see Figure 2.52).

Gromov and Pidoplichko agree that the west–east ravines that delimited the site at the time of excavation formed after the site was occupied and abandoned. Both state that, at the time of occupation, man settled on a gently sloping Dnepr floodplain, but

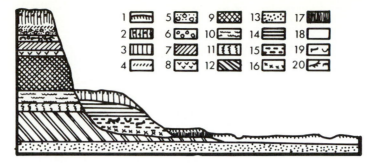

Figure 2.52   Kirillovskaya stratigraphy: 1, present-day soil; 2, loess with burrow; 3, loess; 4, fossil soil on boulder clay; 5, boulder clay; 6, banded boulder loam and sand; 7, brown clay; 8, mottled clay; 9, Poltava sand; 10, Kharkov sand; 11, sandy clay; 12, Kiev marl; 13, Buchaksky sand; 14, loess, sandy, banded loam; 15, clayey stratified sand; 16, cultural layer; 17, alluvial–colluvial deposits; 18, alluvium; 19, bones of megafauna; 20, separate bones of reindeer and musk-ox (no musk-ox reported in faunal assemblage at the site) (after Pidoplichko 1969: Fig. 4).

they interpret the stratigraphy of the site somewhat differently. Pidoplichko (1969) believes that man settled on the second terrace of the Dnepr when that terrace was a floodplain, and that the cultural remains were found in alluvium. Gromov (1948) writes that in the 1940s it was impossible to reconstruct the exact stratigraphy of the site. He entertains the geological interpretation presented by Pidoplichko but also thinks that the cultural remains could have been in colluvial ravine deposits. Gromov tends to favor the first interpretation but warns that the second should not be totally discounted. Both agree that man settled on the floodplain itself, and that the site was oriented toward the east.

Cultural remains at Kirillovskaya were found at depths ranging from 13 to 22 m. No information exists about the thickness of the cultural layer. The different depths at which different sections of the site were found led some investigators to speculate that a number of cultural layers were present. As Gromov (1948) and Boriskovskii (1953) report, Hvoiko saw two layers, Gorodtsov believed that three layers were present, and Gromov himself felt that as many as eight layers were excavated. More recent reconstructions of the site by Boriskovskii (1953) and Pidoplichko (1969) have narrowed this range: Boriskovskii suggests two layers, and Pidoplichko covincingly argues that Kirillovskaya, like most other Upper Paleolithic sites on the central Russian Plain, contained only one cultural layer. Pidoplichko's arguments are based on a model of the surface relief of the site at the time of occupation. The large size of the site (7840–10,000 m²) appears to support Pidoplichko's argument that man settled here on a large sloping surface which dipped toward the river, and that the differences of elevation between different cultural remains just reflects the surface relief.

All accounts report that the cultural layer was in situ. That conclusion, however, should be only tentatively accepted, since both the projected slope of the site and possible seasonal flooding would have favored some modification of at least parts of the site. Some confusion exists in the literature about the exact size of the area excavated at

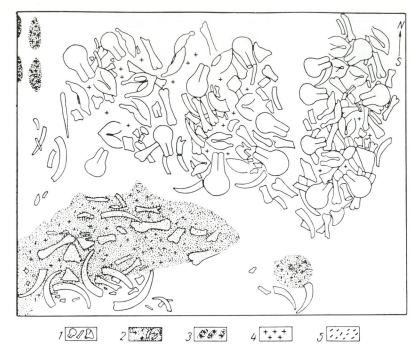

Figure 2.53   Kirilloskaya: partial reconstruction of the cultural layer: 1, mammoth bones; 2, ash lenses; 3, ash spots (former "upper layer"); 4, flint; 5, bone charcoal (after Pidoplichko 1969: Fig. 8).

Kirillovskaya as well. Pidoplichko (1969) discusses the discrepancies found in the original accounts. In this work I use 7840 m², the figure offered by Pidoplichko as the excavated area that he could document securely through archival sources.

    The contents of Kirillovskaya's living floor is known very patchily because apparently no inventories were kept at the time of excavation. Therefore both the faunal remains and the archaeological assemblage listed for this site represent just a fraction of what

Figure 2.54   Kirillovskaya: engraved mammoth tusk (photograph by Alexander Marshack).

was probably unearthed. Similarly, the mammoth-bone dwellings and hearths reported by Pidoplichko (1969) are based on his reconstruction of what existed at Kirillovskaya when Hvoiko excavated it (Figures 2.53 and 2.54).

10. **Klyusy** (52°05′ N, 36°56′ E; Shorskii, Chernigov).   The site was discovered in 1964 and excavated in 1966 by Shovkoplyas (1967). No work has been done at the site since then, and, to the best of my knowledge, no additional analyses were performed on the cultural remains found. The brief three-page notices by Shovkoplyas offer only sketchy details about the geography and geology of the site. It is located on a south-facing left (north) promontory of a large old ravine which entered into the valley of the river Tsat.

Shovkoplyas excavated about 1300 m² of the site but suggests that it may have been originally much larger—over 2 ha. He does not indicate the thickness of the cultural layer at Klyusy, but he writes that it varied depending on the state of preservation of the different areas of the site and the depth at which it was found. He reports that at least parts of the site were in situ and undisturbed. The predominance of lithics among the cultural remains, the absence of any features, and the exclusive presence of highly fragmented mammoth bone has led other researchers to see the Klyusy cultural layer as totally redeposited (Grigor'ev 1982, personal communication). This issue cannot be resolved without additional research at the site.

As best as I can surmise, no features of any kind have been found at Klyusy. The presence of a sizable lithic assemblage (approximately 10,500 pieces) together with the absence of any features and faunal remains strongly suggests that the cultural layer may have indeed been redeposited, and that the site was used primarily for lithic production.

11 and 12. **Korshevo I and II**   (~53°21′ N, 34°09′ E; Bryanskii, Bryansk). The discovery of Korshevo I and Korshevo II has only recently been reported in the literature, and the sites are known from less than page-long articles (Tarasov 1976, 1977, 1981). The two sites, along with Kositsa were discovered in the mid-1970s in the process of an investigation of the environs of a Mousterian site—Betovo. No maps or stratigraphic diagrams have appeared, and neither have the exact geographic locations of the sites. According to Tarasov (1976), Korshevo I and II are located on the southern outskirts of the village of Betovo, not far from the town of Bryansk. Cultural remains were found on a promontory facing a small river, the Betovka, a left (eastern) tributary of the Desna.

Both Korshevo I and Korshevo II are multilayer sites in which the Upper Paleolithic layer is found between deeper lying Mousterian and overlying Neolithic layers. At Korshevo I, 25 m² have been excavated, and at Korshevo II, approximately 60 m². No information exists on the thicknesses of these layers; from Tarasov's accounts it would appear that they are quite thin <10 cm). No information exists on either features or assemblages.

13. **Kositsa** (~53°21′ N, 34°09′ E; Bryanskii, Bryansk).   Kositsa was discovered in 1972 by Tarasov (1981), who excavated it from 1976 on. The site is known presently from two brief notices and one 6-page article (Tarasov 1976, 1977, 1981). It is located in the vicinity of Korshevo I and II. The cultural layer was found on a left-bank slope of a

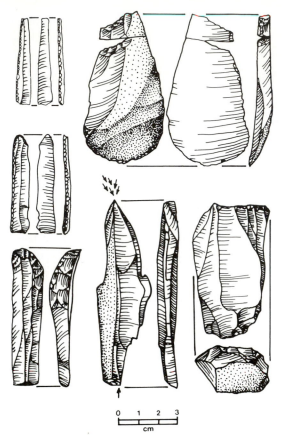

Figure 2.55 Kositsa flint tools (after Tarasov 1981: Fig. 2).

promontory bordered on two sides by brooks that flow into a small river, the Betovka, a left tributary of the Desna.

No geological profiles have been published for Kositsa. Remains were found in a loam stratum which overlies loess (Loess III?). Tarasov (1981) noted that the central section of the cultural layer (~20 m²) was undisturbed, whereas the remaining 105 m² showed varying degrees of erosion. The Upper Paleolithic layer at Kositsa, like those at Korshevo I and II, was found interstratified between Mousterian and Neolithic layers. Tarasov has not found any clear features at Kositsa. Lithics (Figure 2.55) show no unique tool types and conform to a general pattern of Upper Paleolithic inventories of the central Russian Plain.

14. **Kurovo**   (52°32′ N, 33°17′ E; Pogarskii, Bryansk).   The site was discovered in 1930 and excavated in 1930, 1936, and 1947 by Polikarpovich (1968). Cultural remains were found at the outskirts of the village of Kurovo on the right (northwest) bank of the Sudost'.

The stratigraphy of the area was never studied directly. Gromov (1948) notes that the data provided by Polikarpovich are insufficient to reconstruct the geography of the area

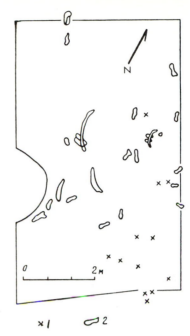

Figure 2.56 Kurovo cultural layer: 1, flint; 2, bones (after Polikar-povich 1968: Fig. 77).

for the time the site was occupied. Polikarpovich mentions a possibility that the prom-ontory on which man settled was located next to a ravine—it is uncertain from his writing if the promontory with the cultural remains was in the ravine or just adjacent to it. What can be concluded at this point is that man probably settled here either on a floodplain itself or on a ravine promontory very close to the floodplain.

Two hundred forty-eight square meters were excavated at Kurovo in discontinuous blocks. No estimates exist on the total area of the site. According to Polikarpovich, the cultural layer was found at depths from 1.1 to 1.4 m from the present soil surface. Gromov, however, indicates that cultural remains come from greater depths (see Figure 2.59 for Gromov's estimates). No information exists on the thickness of the cultural deposit. Both Gromov and Polikarpovich indicate that the remains were probably not in situ.

Polikarpovich does not report finding any features at Kurovo (Figure 2.56), and Kurovo's lithic collection contains approximately 25 pieces of flint, only two of which have been classified as tools.

15. Mezhirich (49° 38′ N, 31° 24′ E; Kanevskii, Cherkassy).   The Upper Paleolithic site was discovered in Mezhirich in 1965 when a local farmer, Zakhar Novitsky, began excavating for a cellar a few feet from the front door of his house. From 1966 through 1974 the site was excavated by I. G. Pidoplichko, and after 1976 by N. L. Kornietz and M. I. Gladkih. I participated in the excavations in 1978, 1979, and 1983 and was responsible for the faunal analyses. The geography and geology of the site were studied by Pidopli-chko (1969, 1976) and by Velichko and his staff (Kornietz *et al.* 1981) (Figures 2.57 and

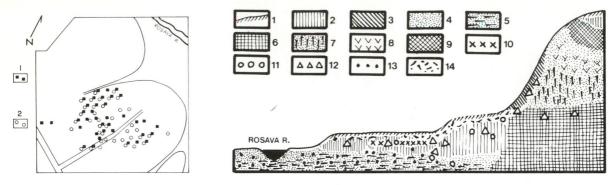

Figure 2.57   Mezhirich location: 1, contemporary structures; 2, bore holes (after Pidoplichko 1976: Fig. 3).

Figure 2.58   Mezhirich stratigraphy: 1, soil; 2, loess, loess-like loam; 3, colluvium; 4, alluvium; 5, relic stratified alluvium; 6, Paleogene deposits; 7, Kharkov sand; 8, Poltava sand; 9, clay; 10, cultural remains; 11, isolated small granite boulders; 13, isolated pieces of silica pebble and siliceous chips; 13, shells, fresh water molluscs; 14, burrows (after Pidoplichko 1976: Fig. 5).

2.58). The site is located on a north-facing promontory overlooking the valleys of the Ros' and Rosava Rivers at the point where the two merge (Figure 2.59).

This area of the Ukraine is located on the Cenozoic Kanev dislocation, which makes the right or western banks of the rivers high and fairly steep and cut by a number of ravines. The promontory on which Mezhirich is located (southern in Pidoplichko's description) today lies 9–10m above the level of the Rosava. Pidoplichko (1976) writes that at the time man settled here, it was no more than 1 or 2 m above the river. Today the site is found approximately 200 m from the river (Figure 2.60).

Some disagreement exists in the literature about the exact geological history of the site. Pidoplichko (1976) writes that the cultural layer was located in colluvial laminated loess–loam on a promontory between two ravines. Kornietz et al. (1981) state that cultural remains were found in a colluvial fan deposit of an ancient ravine. They date the

Figure 2.59   Mezhirich: view toward the site and Ros' and Rosava floodplain. Arrow indicates site location.

Figure 2.60 Mezhirich site: view from the floodplain. Arrow indicates site location.

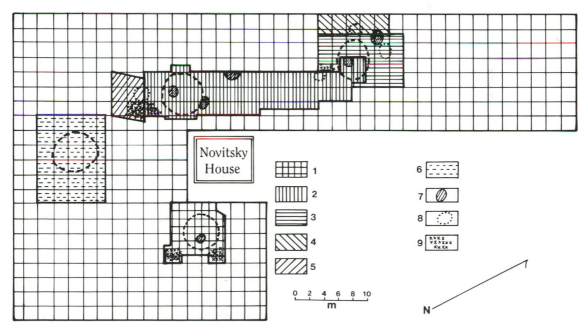

Figure 2.61 Mezhirich excavation plan: 1, 1966 excavation—Dwelling 1; 2, 1969–1970 excavation—Dwelling 2; 3, 1972 excavation—Dwelling 3; 4, 1974 excavation; 5, 1976 excavation; 6, 1978–1983 excavation—Dwelling 4; 7, hearths; 8, dwellings; 9, storage pits.

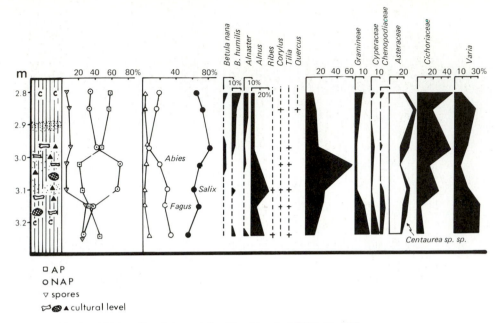

Figure 2.62   Mezhirich pollen diagram (after Kornietz *et al.* 1981: Fig. 33).

deposition of the cone to about the same time that alluvium was being deposited on the second terraces of the Dnepr and its tributaries.

The promontory itself is around 10,000 m² in area; 508 m² have been excavated. While there are no estimates of the total size of the site, Pidoplichko (1976) reports finding cultural remains in cores bored on the adjacent northern promontory, 200–300 m away. Kornietz (1979, personal communication) reports finding cultural material in cores from the southern promontory as much as 100 m from the excavated area of the site. Both these observations suggest that the site is much larger than the segment excavated to date.

Cultural remains were found at depths ranging from about 2.7 to 3.1 m below the present surface (Figures 2.61 and 2.62). Pidoplichko writes that only one cultural layer up was present at the site. Kornietz and Gladkih, however, suggest that two cultural layers are present at some parts of the site (Kornietz *et al.* 1981). The bottom layer (10–15 cm thick) is associated with the foundation of mammoth-bone Dwelling 4, and a much thinner upper layer is associated with the middle and upper level of the construction. The two layers are separated by a sterile layer up to 12 cm in thickness. The significance of these two layers will be difficult to interpret until a clear taphonomic history of the site is reconstructed. Such a reconstruction may well indicate that at least parts of the site underwent two separate periods of utilization, or that the two layers resulted from erosional episodes. The different depths at which mammoth-like dwellings have been found at Mezhirich (see Table 2.4) suggest that the surface of the

Figure 2.63 Mezhirich Dwelling 1: 1, mammoth bones; 2, hearths and ash lenses; 3, bone charcoal; 4, worked bone; 5, marine shells; 6, reindeer antlers; excavation grid = 2 × 2 m (after Pidoplichko 1976: Fig. 18).

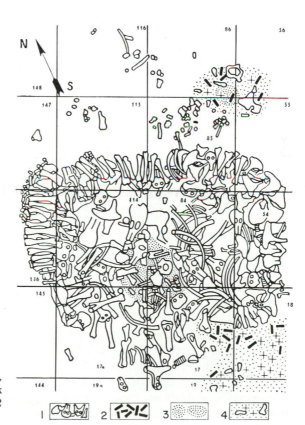

Figure 2.64 Mezhirich Dwelling 2: 1, bones; 2, bone charcoal; 3, hearths; 4, work areas near hearths; excavation grid = 2 × 2 m (after Pidoplichko 1976: Fig. 19).

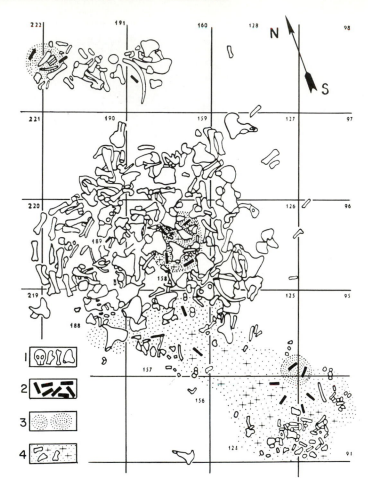

Figure 2.65 Mezhirich Dwelling 3: 1, mammoth bones; 2, bone charcoal; 3, hearths; 4, work areas near hearths and storage pit; excavation grid= 2 × 2 m (after Pidoplichko 1976: Fig. 20).

promontory at the time of occupation was not flat but sloped toward the floodplain. Because of this, pending future research, it is possible to speculate that the thiner upper layer found during the 1979 excavation may have been redeposited from higher upslope. Kornietz *et al.* (1981) and Pidoplichko (1976) agree that cultural remains were in situ. The loess matrix above the layer, however, shows extensive burrowing.

Mezhirich is the latest spectacular Upper Paleolithic site to be discovered on the central Russian Plain. It has yielded the most complete archaeological record we have for late Pleistocene settlements in the area. The thickness of loess deposit above the cultural remains assured perfect preservation for organic materials at the site. Four mammoth-bone dwellings have been unearthed at Mezhirich (Figures 2.63–2.67). Although we at Mezhirich have not been able to locate postholes in these dwellings and

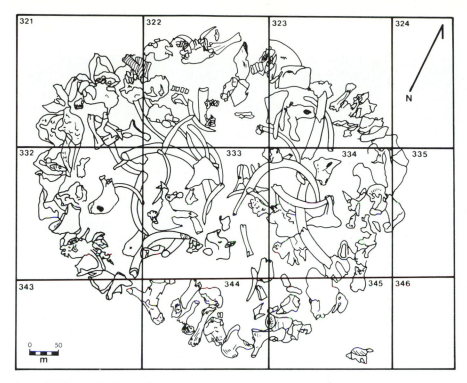

Figure 2.66   Mezhirich Dwelling 4.

thus be confident in reconstructing the contours of the dwellings, Pidoplichko (1976) argues that they were dome shaped. His reconstruction of Dwelling 1 is on display at the Museum of Paleontology in Kiev (see Figures 6.5 and 6.6). Although lacking postholes, dwellings in Mezhirich as well as inventories in Berdyzh, Gontsy, and Yudinovo contained a number of large mammoth bones with man-made holes in them, which may have been used as post supports (Pidoplichko 1976; Kornietz 1979, personal communication) (Figure 2.68).

In addition to the dwellings, large exterior storage pits, exterior and interior hearths, exterior piles of mammoth bones, and flint- and bone-working areas have been excavated at Mezhirich (Figure 2.69). Archaeological inventories are equally impressive. To date 149 mammoths have been found, mandibles of 95 of them went into the construction of base walls of Dwelling 1. Flint tools, made of locally available cobble flint, show a fair degree of microlithization typical for inventories from southern sites (Figure 2.70). Organic assemblages (see Figure 2.71), are extensive, as well, and contain awls, needles, piercers, shaft straighteners, toggles, and items of personal adornment such as beads of nonlocal amber (see a discussion of Mezhirich amber in Chapter 7.

Art objects found at Mezhirich fall into three categories: anthropomorphic representations (Figure 2.72), mammoth bones painted in red ocher (Figure 2.73) in geometric

Figure 2.67.   Mezhirich: excavation of Dwelling 4 (1979 season).

Figure 2.68   Mezhirich Dwelling 4: mammoth scapula with artificially cut hole.

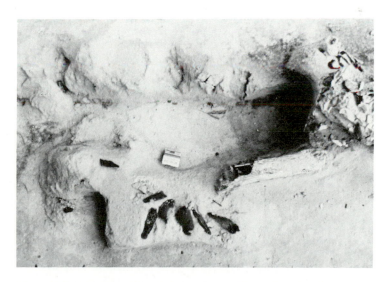

Figure 2.69   Mezhirich: flint blades in Square 345 near Dwelling 4.

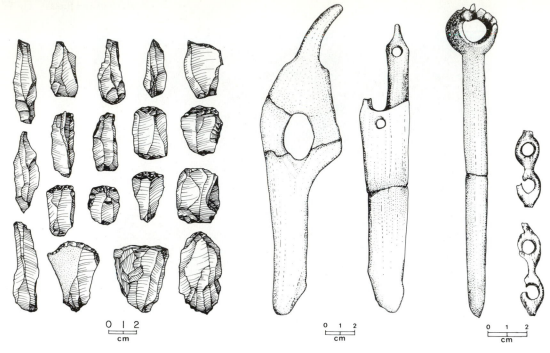

Figure 2.70 Mezhirich lithics (after Pidoplichko 1969: Fig. 52).

Figure 2.71 Mezhirich mammoth-ivory objects (after Pidoplichko 1976: Figs. 58,66).

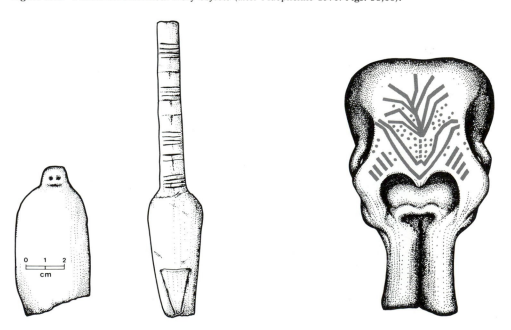

Figure 2.72 Mezhirich mammoth-ivory portable art (Soffer 1985).

Figure 2.73 Mezhirich: mammoth skull painted with red ocher (reconstructed drawing after Pidoplichko 1969: Fig. 57).

Figure 2.74 Mezhirich ivory plaque (from Marshack, 1979, "Upper Paleolithic Symbol Systems of the Russian Plain," *Current Anthropology,* 20(2), © 1979 University of Chicago Press).

Figure 2.75 Mezhirich plaque: detail of engraving.

patterns similar to those found at Mezin, and engraved pieces of ivory (Figures 2.74 and 2.75).

Soviet researchers classify this site, as they do other elaborate Upper Paleolithic sites with dwellings, storage pits, and rich inventories, as a permanently occupied base camp or settlement. I address this at length in Chapter 6 when I consider questions of duration of occupation at the sites.

16. Mezin (51°45′ N, 33°05′ E; Koropskii, Chernigov). Mezin, like many other sites on the central Russian Plain, was discovered during excavation for a cellar. It was under excavation in 1908–1909, 1912–1916, 1930, 1932, and 1940. Such prominent researchers as Efimenko, Rudenko, Voevodskii, and Volkov worked at Mezin. Shovkoplyas returned to the site in 1954 and both reexcavated parts of the site previously opened and investigated new areas. He completed his research at the site in 1961 (Boriskovskii 1953; Shovkoplyas 1965a). The geography and geology of the site has been described by numerous authors, including Boriskovskii (1953), Gromov (1948), Pidoplichko (1969), and Shovkoplyas (1965a) (Figure 2.76).

Cultural remains were located on the left-bank promontory of an old ravine that cut through the interfluve deposits. The ravine is located on the north (right) bank of the river in an area where the interfluve plateau first gently descends to the river and then abuts the river in steep 40–70 m cliffs. The promontory on which the cultural layers were deposited is today 10–12-meters above the river, approximately 300 m up the ravine from its entrance into the Desna. A difference of opinion exists on the height of the site above the river at the time of occupation. Gromov (1948) assumes a similar height as today for the promontory during the late Valdai. Velichko, Grekhova, and Gubonina (1977), on the other hand, postulate that the Desna in the late Valdai was from 15 to 20 m above its present level, which would place the late Valdai settlement fairly close to the floodplain. The site was open to the south and protected by the plateau to the north.

Cultural material was found in colluvial loess deposits laminated with sandy and clayey layers (Pidoplichko 1969). The surface on which man settled, as can be judged from the cultural layer, sloped in two directions: a 40–45° northwest–southwest decline

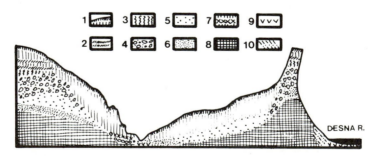

Figure 2.76 Mezin stratigraphy: 1, loess and present-day soil; 2, fossil soil; 3, stratified loam; 4, boulder clay; 5, redeposited Paleogene sand; 6, sand; 7, cultural remains; 8, chalk; 9, alluvium; 10, colluvium (after Pidoplichko 1969: Fig. 25).

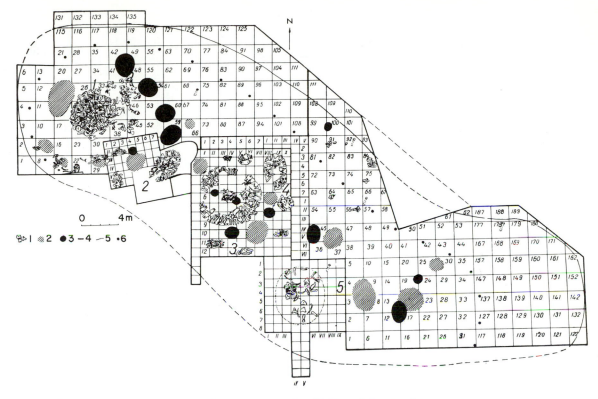

Figure 2.77 Mezin excavations: 1, bones; 2, concentration of small objects; 3, hearths; 4, border of excavation; 5, limits of the site; 6, border of the core and periphery areas of the site (after Shovkoplyas 1965a: Fig. 15).

toward the river and a 20–25° north–south slope toward the ravine itself. Because of this dual slope, cultural deposits were found lying 1–1.5 m below the present-day surface in the southern part of the site and to depths of 7 to 8 m below present-day surface in the northern part of the site. Maximal slope of 15 to 20° for some parts of the living floor is reported both by Boriskovskii (1953) and Shovkoplyas (1965a).

Shovkoplyas (1965a) reports excavating, sampling, and reconstructing 1200 m² of the site and considers this area the total size of the site (Figure 2.77); the cultural layer was mostly in situ, with some minor downslope redeposition. One cultural layer, averaging 10 cm in thickness, is reported for the site. Shovkoplyas also reports finding five storage pits with large bones up to 0.6 m below hearths outside Dwelling 1. The hearths were a part of the cultural layer, they overlie the storage pits, and they are separated from them by a sterile layer of colluvial loess. Shovkoplyas (1965a) explains the absence of a second cultural layer on the level of the storage pits by rapid downslope erosion that purportedly occurred when man first occupied the promontory—possibly during a spring thaw. He argues that sheets of running water not only drove late Pleistocene

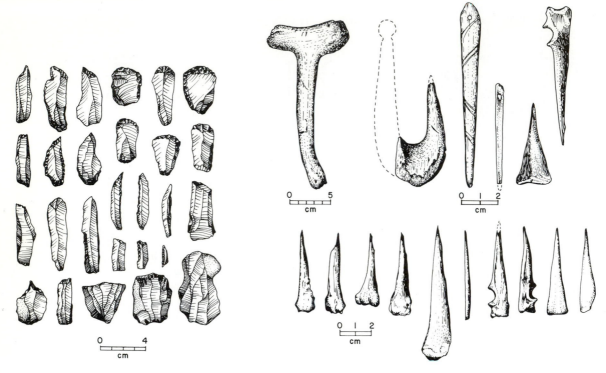

Figure 2.78 Mezin flint tools (after Pidoplichko 1969: Fig. 38).

Figure 2.79 Mezin worked bone (after Pidoplichko 1947a: Figs. 5,8,9; Shovkoplyas 1965a: Figures XLII,XLIII).

settlers off the promontory that spring, but also eroded away cultural remains either into the pits themselves or downslope into the ravine. People returned and settled on the promontory, according to Shovkoplyas, later in the season, possibly fall.

Shovkoplyas sees the thickness of the deposits separating the storage pits from the hearths (0.6 m) as resulting from accumulation over a few years. Kukla (1975) reports that during a single particularily rainy spring day in Czechoslovakia in May of 1960 up to 25 cm of loess was deposited. This suggests that a thickness of up to 0.6 m, as observed by Shovkoplyas, may have accumulated quickly, possibly during just one particularily rainy spring–summer period.

The archaeology of Mezin is complex at best. Since Shovkoplyas actually excavated only one of the complexes there (Complex 1—which included a mammoth-bone dwelling plus surrounding hearths atop storage pits) and reconstructed the other features from archival data of previous excavations, numerous serious questions still exist about the nature and quantity of various features found. Whereas Shovkoplyas (1965a) claims that five mammoth-bone dwellings were found, Boriskovskii (1953) offers a radically different reconstruction of the Mezin living floor, with the absence of bone dwellings

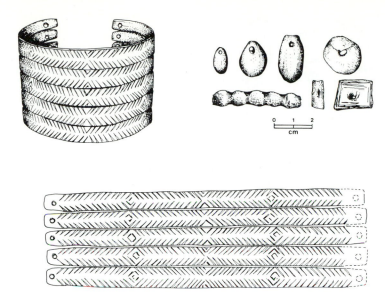

Figure 2.80   Mezin mammoth-ivory jewelry (after Shovkoplyas 1965a: Figs. XLVI,LI,LII).

and the presence of numerous storage and dwelling pits as in Kostenki I–1. Although, as I indicated in the introductory chapter, investigators working prior to the 1950s tended not to find small-sized round or oval dwellings and favored seeing the presence of "long houses," it is unclear that differences in theoretical outlook are a sufficient explanation for the sizable differences between Shovkoplyas' and Boriskovskii's reconstructions of the Mezin living floor. Since the site is no longer in existence, future work cannot resolve these discrepancies. Because of the differing interpretations, I list features reported for the site as a range in Table 2.4. The site contained from two to five

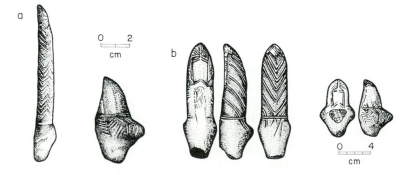

Figure 2.81   Mezin portable art: mammoth-ivory "phallic figurines" and "birds" (a, after Shovkoplyas 1965a: Figs. 58,59; b, after Filippov 1983: Fig. 2).

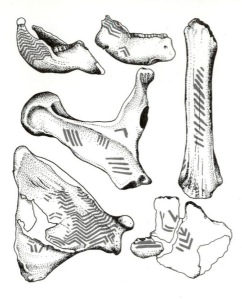

Figure 2.82   Mezin: mammoth bones painted in red ocher (after Pidoplichko 1969: Fig. 31).

mammoth-bone dwellings (116 mammoths were found there), numerous storage pits filled with large bones, some interior and exterior hearths, and about four exterior work areas.

Assemblages at Mezin are exceedingly rich—the numerous pieces of portable art are nothing short of spectacular. Numerous stone tools, all made of locally available flint, include a sizable number of microliths (Gladkih 1973) (Figure 2.78). Bone tools are numerous and, as elsewhere in the study area, include eyed needles (Figure 2.79). Numerous items of personal adornment from Mezin include pendants, two incised bracelets of mammoth ivory, and over 600 perforated fossil marine shells used as beads (Figure 2.80) (see Chapter 7 for a discussion of the nonlocal shells). Portable art from Mezin (Figure 2.81) has excited much comment ever since a few pieces were shown at the Paris World's Fair in the beginning of the century. They have been variously interpreted in the past as "birds" and "phallic figurines," while today most Soviet researchers see them as abstracted representations of the female form (see Abramova 1966; Bibikov 1981; Filippov 1983). Finally, mammoth bones painted in geometric designs in ocher (Figure 2.82) have also been found at Mezin.

17. Novgorod-Severskii (Novgorod-Severskaya; Novgorod-Severskij) (52°00′ N, 33°16′ E; Novgorod-Severskii, Chernigov).   The site was discovered in 1933 as a result of sandstone and quartzite quarrying on the outskirts of the town of Novgorod-Severskii on the northwest (right) banks of the Desna. It was excavated by Pidoplichko (1947b) from 1936 through 1939. The geography and geology of the site were studied and described by Boriskovskii (1953), Gromov (1948), Pidoplichko (1947b), and Velichko (1961) (Figures 2.83 and 2.84).

Cultural remains, consisting of redeposited flint and bones, were found on a promontory on the left slope of a northern ravine which runs into the Desna. The ravine cuts

Figure 2.83   Novgorod-Severskii: Desna valley from the site's promontory.

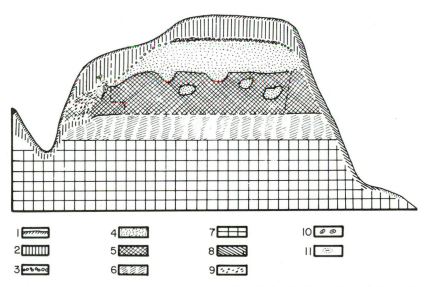

Figure 2.84   Novgorod-Severskii stratigraphy: 1, soil; 2, loess; 3, boulder loam; 4, sand; 5, sandstone; 6, chalky sand; 7, chalk; 8, colluvial soil; 9, bones; 10, flint "gigantoliths"; 11, worked tusk (after Pidoplichko 1947b: Fig. 6).

into a steep interfluve plateau. Archaeological remains lay some 30 m above the present level of the river, at depths from 6 to 7 m from the soil surface. Both Gromov (1948) and Velichko (1961) indicate that the geology and geomorphology of this locality is poorly understood. Figure 2.84 illustrates Pidoplichko's stratigraphic reconstructions and shows that cultural materials were found in boulder gravels mixed with sand and loam. Velichko (1961) associates cultural remains with the base of the loess-like loam.

Pidoplichko and Gromov speculate that man settled here in a sandstone rockshelter, and such shelters are found in the area today. If their speculation is correct, then Novgorod-Severskii is unique for the study area; it is the only rockshelter (albeit collasped) on the central Russian Plain that was occupied during the Upper Paleolithic. Such an interpretation also suggests that much of the material at the site was found in situ (Figure 2.85). Velichko, on the other hand, rejects such a reconstruction and argues that cultural remains were clearly redeposited. While it is impossible today to reconstruct the paleogeography of the area and determine the locale where man settled with full certainty, both the presence of rockshelters in the area and the context in which cultural material was found favor views held by Pidoplichko and Gromov. Although the materials may have been in places in situ, the site probably was severely disturbed.

Pidoplichko excavated 238 m² and notes that the remains were not evenly spread but found in clusters both under and between the sandstone and quartzite slabs. He does not indicate the average thickness of these clusters. The small numbers of both lithic and faunal remains suggest that the clusters were no thicker than 10 cm at most.

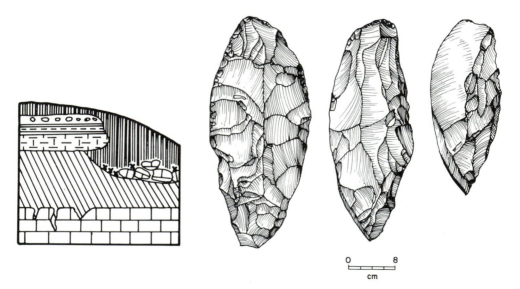

Figure 2.85   Novgorod-Severskii: location of cultural remains; X = flint (after Boriskovskii 1953: Fig. 148).

Figure 2.86   Novgorod-Severskii "gigantoliths": Pieces are 45.4 × 19.3 × 9.9 cm, 44.0 × 17.5 × 12.1 cm, and 33.9 × 13.9 × 9.2 cm (after Pidoplichko 1947b: Fig. 13).

Being a redeposited or at least severely disturbed site, Novgorod-Severskii contained no features. Fauna recovered consists of a ubiquitous mix of species found at most of the Upper Paleolithic sites, but it also contains a large number of fish remains. The lithic assemblage found is small, but it does contain three large flint pieces which are termed "gigantoliths" in the Soviet literature (Figure 2.86). Boriskovskii (1953:203) gives their weights as 8050, 8250, and 4550 g.

18. Novo-Bobovichi (52°38′ N, 31°45′ E; Novo-Zybkovskii, Bryansk). Novo-Bobovichi was discovered in 1927 when mammoth-bone accumulations were found in local earthworks. It was excavated from 1951 through 1953 and is known from a handful of brief notices, the most extensive of which is a five-page article by Polikarpovich (1968). The geology and geography of the site were described by Gromov (1948) and Polikarpovich (1968) and are presented in Figure 2.87.

The site was located at the outskirts of a village of the same name, on the right (western) banks of the river Irput'. Remains consisted mostly of mammoth bones. No features were found, and Polikarpovich (1968) reports finding a single flint tool with the mammoth bones. Both he and Gromov (1948) indicate that the cultural material was redeposited. Gromov lists a number of possible erosional episodes that could have placed the remains at the bottom of a ravine, and he favored massive soil creep or mud flow as the most likely of them. Polikarpovich, on the other hand, thought that down-slope erosion associated with ravine formation may have redeposited the remains from a terrace promontory some 10 m above the river. Both of these views are clearly spec-

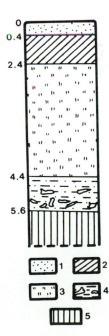

Figure 2.87   Novo-Bobovichi stratigraphy: 1, present-day soil; 2, brownish loam; 3, yellow-brown loam; 4, cultural layer; 5, loess-like loam (after Gromov 1948: Fig. 82).

ulative and cannot be accepted or rejected until additional studies are conducted at the site.

There is no indication in the literature on the total area excavated. What I surmise from Polikarpovich's descriptions is that less than 100 m² were excavated via discontinuous trenches. No information exists on the thickness of the cultural remains. Polikarpovich does note, however, that remains were found at varying depths and that one excavation trench showed a 1.75–2.0-m dip in the cultural layer over a distance of approximately 6 m.

19–22. The Pushkari Group (52°51′ N, 33°14′ E; Novgorod–Severskii, Chernigov).   The existence of a number of Upper Paleolithic sites in the vicinity of the village of Pushkari was first reported by Rudinsky in 1932 (Boriskovskii 1953). Throughout the 1930s additional sites or localities were discovered in the area. Today at least 10 Upper Paleolithic sites are known—all found within an area of approximately 1 km². They are known collectively as the Pushkari group. All are located on the right (western) banks of the Desna on a promontory formed by the interfluve plateau, ravines, and the river (Figure 2.6 and 2.88). The plateau is some 40 m above the river. The geomorphology of the right (western) bank of the Desna is such that the interfluve plateau directly abuts the river itself, river terraces are absent due to river erosion, and the plateau hangs above the river, separated from it by steep cliffs at angles of 40–50°. The geography and geology of the sites is illustrated in Figures 2.89 and 2.90.

Four sites found on the promontory have been described in the literature in some detail and are considered in this work: Bugarok, Pogon, Pushkari I, and Pushkari II. The others, as Boriskovskii (1953) pointed out, are known either from very small test trenches or from surface collections only. It should be emphasized that (1) the geology of the promontory is imperfectly known, (2) the sites themselves are known from very small excavations (e.g., the largest excavation, at Pushkari I, is 400 m²), and (3) the sites are in very close proximity. This precludes definite conclusions as to whether the sites are

Figure 2.88   The Pogon promontory from upstream.

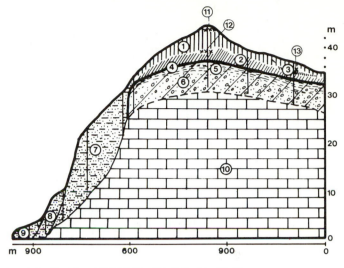

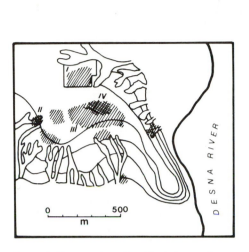

Figure 2.89   Location of Pushkari sites on the promontory (after Boriskovskii 1953: Fig. 87): I, Pushkari I; II, Pushkari II; III, Pogon; IV, Bugorok.

Figure 2.90   Pushkari group stratigraphy: 1, loess-like sandy loam; 2, loess-like loam; 3, humic layer (gley?); 4, buried soil; 5, stratified sandy loam; 6, moraine loam; 7, second ravine terrace (stratified sandy loam); 8, first ravine terrace (stratified sandy loam); 9, ravine bottom (loam and sandy loam); 10, chalk, 11, Bugorok; 12, Pogon; 13, Pushkari I (after Velichko 1961: Fig. 39).

independent sites occupied at different periods, and not just redeposited sections of other sites, or even simply remnants of the daily surface of a late Valdai promontory. Soviet researchers assigned different locales the status of independent sites based on stylistic differences observed in the lithic assemblages. It may well be that this promontory contains both remnants of in situ sites and redeposited layers, as well as a highly utilized late Valdai surface covered with lithic and faunal scatters that have been subsequently interpreted as sites.

In many ways this region is reminiscent of the Kostenki–Borschevo region on the Don, where a number of Upper Paleolithic sites are found within a short distance of each other. Our understanding of the Pushkari sites is much poorer, however, because much less work has been done there to date.

19. Bugorok.   Bugorok was discovered by Voevodskii in 1940, who excavated it with Gvozdover (Gvozdover 1947; Voevodskii 1952b). As Figures 2.89 and 2.90 show, it is located at the highest elevation on the Pogon promontory, near the center, 50 m above the Desna. If we assume that the Desna in Late Valdai was 15–20 m higher than today, this would place Bugorok 30–35 m above the river at time of occupation.

Although Gvozdover and Voevodskii excavated only 13 m² of Bugorok, they test-trenched the area extensively and conclude that the site may have been as large as 13,000 m². The cultural layer was found at depths from 0.3 to 0.5 m from the present soil surface. It was in loess that Velichko (1961) characterized as Loess III. Some of the material, according to the excavators, was in situ, whereas other sections showed signs of both redeposition and disturbance by periglacial processes.

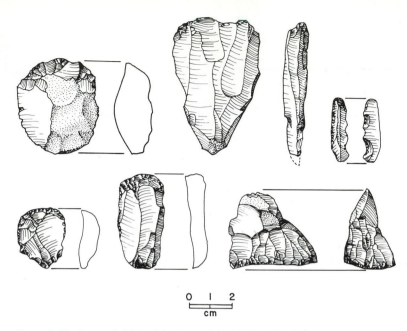

Figure 2.91   Bugorok lithics (after Voevodskii 1952b: Tabs. 2,3).

No features were found at Bugorok, and the archaeological assemblage consists of flint and bone (Figure 2.91). The site, as all Upper Paleolithic sites in the study area without elaborate mammoth-bone dwellings or bone accumulations, has received very little attention in the Soviet literature; it is impossible to even discern what sort of site Soviet researchers consider Bugorok to be.

20. **Pogon** (Pyatii Metr).   Voevodskii (1949) discovered cultural remains at Pogon in 1940 and investigated the site in 1940 and 1946. He excavated 63.3 m² and estimated that the site may have been as large as 40,000 m². The layer was found in the center of the Pogon promontory in the lower layer of Loess III (Velichko 1961). Material was in situ, and in the center of the promontory it was 5 m below the Bugorok cultural layer; some 200 m to the northwest (in the vicinity of Pushkari I) it lay on the surface. At Pushkari I, the Pogon cultural material was found above the Pushkari I layer. Both Voevodskii and Velichko explain the different depths of the Pogon layer as resulting from differential erosional episodes on different sections of the promontory. Thus, we can conclude that a part of the Pogon cultural material, that found in the center under the Bugorok layer, was in situ, whereas other remains assigned to Bugorok were subjected to erosion and possibly redeposition.

Pogon, like Bugorok, has yielded an unquantified number of highly fragmented bones, no features, and a small (671-piece) lithic assemblage.

21. **Pushkari I** (Paseka).   Puskhari I was the first site discovered on the Pogon promontory. It was found in 1932 by Rudinsky, who excavated it in 1932 and 1933. Boriskovskii (1953) excavated the site in 1937 and 1939. Excavations as Figure 2.92

Figure 2.92 Pushkari I excavations (1932–1937): Dotted area is possible extent of the site; I–IV are trenches (after Boriskovskii 1953: Fig. 88).

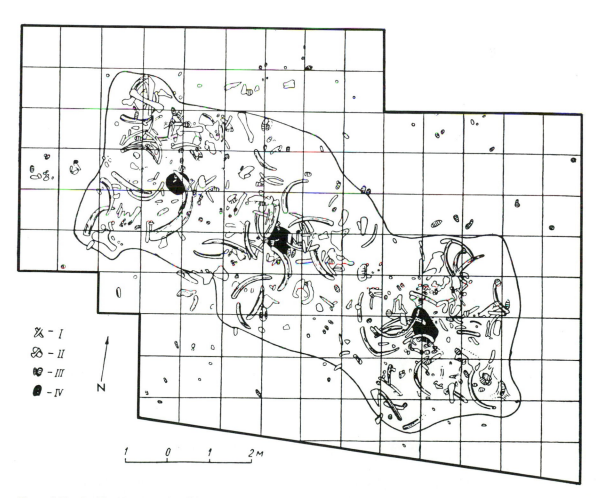

Figure 2.93 Pushkari I: Excavation II (1937–1939): I, tusks; II, mammoth bones; III, mammoth teeth; IV, hearths (after Boriskovskii 1953: Fig. 89).

shows, were conducted in three discontinuous localities. Pushkari I is located on the northern part of the promontory, 32–35 m above the current level of Desna. During the late Valdai the site would have been 12–20 m above the river (Velichko 1961).

Cultural material was found in loess at depths ranging from 0.5 to 1.1 m below the soil surface. Velichko identifies the faintly humic layer below this loess stratum as Bryansk soil and concludes that the remains were in Loess II. Belyaeva began new excavations at Pushkari I in 1981 and reports that the layer is in loess above the gley layer and not Bryansk soil (Belyaeva 1981, personal communication). This suggests that the Pushkari I layer is in Loess III and not loess II. This new geological information puts into question the stratigraphic location of the Pushkari material shown in Figure 2.90, as well as the

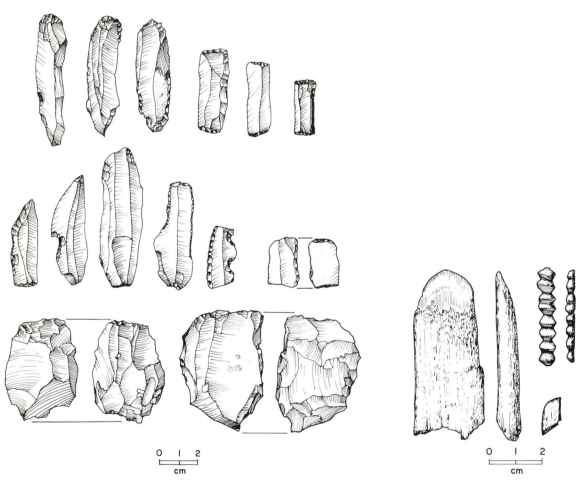

Figure 2.94   Pushkari I flint nuclei and blade tools (after Boriskovskii 1953: Figs. 100,102,107).

Figure 2.95   Pushkari I: worked bone found inside dwelling (after Boriskovskii 1953: Fig. 111).

stratigraphic dating of the site. It is also in better accord with the one ^{14}C date for
Pushkari—16,775 ± 605 (QC 899) (see Table 2.12 and Chapter 4).

Approximately 400 m[2] had been excavated at Pushkari I by 1981 (Boriskovskii *et al.*
1981). Test-trenching led Boriskovskii (1953) to suggest that at the time of occupation
the site was as large as 30,000 m[2].

Boriskovskii sees the site as a long-term base camp and interprets the distribution of
lithic and faunal remains as representing the remnants of one three-hearth longhouse
that measured 4 × 12 m (Figure 2.93). More recently, Shovkoplyas (1965a) questions
this reconstruction and argues that it is just as likely that three small round dwellings,
each containing a single hearth, were present at Pushkari I. I have listed the site in
Table 2.7 as containing either one or three mammoth-bone dwellings. In addition to
both interior and exterior hearths, Pushkari I also contains about 50 small pits ranging
in diameter from 0.1 to 0.2 m (up to 0.1 m in depth), some of which Boriskovskii thinks
may have been postholes.

Faunal remains recovered Pushkari I include 69 mammoths (MNI). It is significant to
note that a large number of the mammoth bones found were tusks. While no complete
list of all elements per taxon recovered at Pushkari I have been published, anecdotal
descriptions of the remains in Boriskovskii's (1953) monograph clearly suggest that a
much smaller number of mammoths than the 69 estimated by tusks is represented by
other body parts. Pushkari I has yielded a huge (160,000-piece) lithic inventory (Figure
2.94) and a negligible number of artifacts of worked bone (Figure 2.95).

22. **Pushkari II** (Anikeev Rov I).   This site was discovered in 1933 by Pidoplichko
and excavated by him and Voevodskii in 1933, 1937, and 1939 (Voevodskii 1952c). The
geology of the site have been described by Gromov (1948) and Voevodskii (1952c)

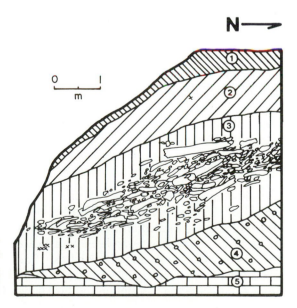

Figure 2.96   Pushkari II stratigraphy: 1, present-day soil; 2, colluvial loam; 3, loam with
traces of colluvium and ravine alluvium; 4,
moraine; 5, chalk; x, flints (after Voevodskii
1952c: Fig. 3).

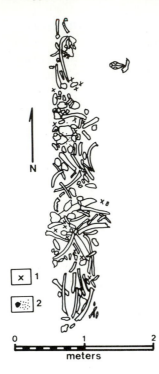

Figure 2.97 Pushkari II excavation: 1, flint; 2, charcoal. (after Voevodskii 1952c: Fig. 2).

(Figure 2.96). Cultural remains were found 400 m southwest of Pushkari I in the upper part of an old ravine where it had been cut through by a younger post–late Valdai ravine. Geological work in the area conducted by Gromov in 1939 and 1940 shows that man settled at Pushkari II on the banks of a small lake at the point where a small river entered it.

The cultural layer was found on the northeast–southwest sloping surface and lay from 1.7 to 4.4 m below the present soil. Voevodskii excavated 58 m² and suggested that cultural remains here were partially redeposited by soil creep or solifluction (Figure 2.97).

No features were found at the site, but Voevodskii notes that some of the large mammoth bones found may have been deliberately placed in a small river or brook that ran by the site at the time of occupation. He unfortunately did not offer any ideas as to the function of such a bone accumulation. Lithics recovered consisted of 85 pieces.

23. Radomyshl' (50°33′ N, 29°14′ E; Radomyshl'skii, Zhitomir).   The site was discovered in 1956 and excavated by Shovkoplyas in 1957, 1959, and 1963 (Shovkoplyas 1964, 1965b). It is located on the right (western) banks of the Teterev. The geography and geology of the site have been investigated only perfunctorily by Shovkoplyas (1965b) and Pidoplichko and Shovkoplyas (1961). The stratigraphic column in Figure 2.98 is taken from a description in Pidoplichko and Shovkoplyas (1961), which differs in minor detail from the description in Shovkoplyas (1964).

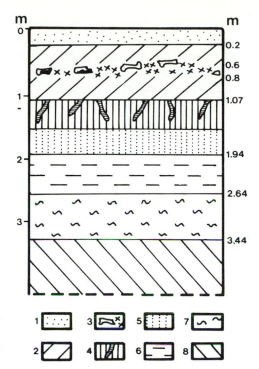

Figure 2.98 Radomyshl' stratigraphy: 1, present-day soil; 2, loam; 3, cultural remains; 4, loam with burrows and concretions; 5, loam with limestone veins; 6, buried soil; 7, sand; 8, boulder clay.

The location of Radomyshl' differs somewhat from that of other sites in the study area. The site is located in flat and swampy Polissya lowlands where, because of past erosion, loess accumulations are absent. The area today contains a myriad of swamps, small lakes, and rivers. Cultural remains were found on four small hillocks that measured from 20 to 40 m in diameter and no more than 2–3 m in height. Shovkoplyas (1965b) suggests that these hillocks were somewhat higher in elevation until recent times, when intensive plowing and erosion removed a substantial part of their soil cover. At the time of occupation the area was located on the upper parts of a ravine on its right or northern side; today the ravine is totally buried. The site was located some 3 km from the river, and, judging by Shovkoplyas' description of the topography of the area, it was elevated just a few meters above the present level of the river.

Cultural remains were found in loam, 60–80 cm below the soil surface. Lazukov et al. (1981) note that the cultural materials were in terminal moraine deposits of the penultimate glaciation. While Shovkoplyas does not specify the thickness of the cultural layer, his and Pidoplichko's descriptions suggest that it was no thicker than 20 cm.

Shovkoplyas investigated the site by means of three discontinuous excavations that opened a total of about 1500 m². Excavation I, totaling some 600 m², is the best studied and the only one documented in the literature (sometimes referred to as Radomyshl' I). Shovkoplyas (1964, 1965b) reports a single cultural layer in all excavations and suggests that all of the hillocks were occupied at the same time, which implies that the site was far larger than either the 600 m² excavated at Radomyshl' I or the total 1500 m² excavated to date. Since he only reported on his discovered at Radomyshl' I, we simply do not know if the cultural remains at the three sampled hillocks do indeed represent parts of one site or different occupational events in the area. In this work I restrict myself to a discussion of Radomyshl' I.

Shovkoplyas saw Radomyshl' I as a permanently occupied settlement with mammoth-bone dwellings and a single centrally located storage pit (Figure 2.99). A number of serious, as yet unresolved, problems exist with Radomyshl' data, including questions of just how many dwellings and pits were found, and how many hearths were excavated. The relatively small number of mammoths (47 individuals) for a site with numerous dwellings is problematic. Kornietz (1962) argues that taphonomic factors were responsible for the paucity of mammoths, and indeed faunal remains at the site were in a very bad state of preservation. I suspect, however, that taphonomy is not the sole explanation and that some bone accumulations interpreted as dwellings may have served other purposes.

Using stylistic criteria, Shovkoplyas (1965b) argues that the mixture of Mousterian and Upper Paleolithic elements in the lithic assemblage indicates a very early age for

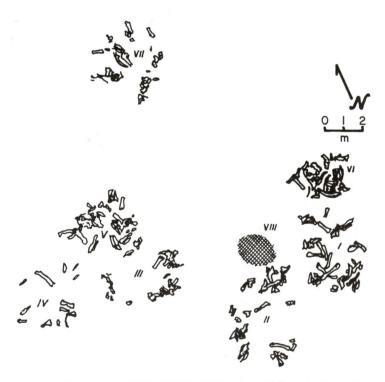

Figure 2.99 Radomyshl' excavations (1957–1959): I–IV,VII: mammoth-bone dwellings; VI, storage pit; VIII, flint working area (after Shovkoplyas 1964: Fig. 3).

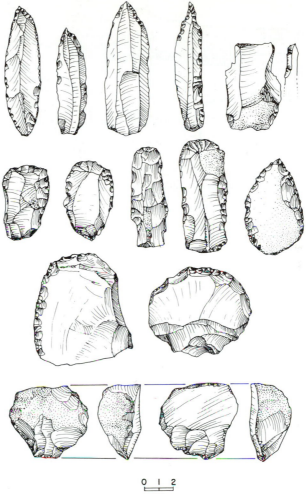

Figure 2.100 Radomyshl' lithics
(after Shovkoplyas 1964: Plates I–IV).

0 1 2
cm

Radomyshl' and that the site represents the oldest Upper Paleolithic site on the central Russian Plain (Figure 2.100). I address the question of Radomyshl's age in considering the dating of the sites in detail in Chapter 4. In all subsequent discussions I refer to the site simply as Radomyshl'.

24. Suponevo (53°19′ N, 34°20′ E; Bryanskii, Bryansk).   Suponevo was excavated by Efimenko and Zhukov from 1925 to 1927. This, unfortunately, was before bone accumulations were recognized as remains of mammoth-bone dwellings. The materials found at the site were not analyzed or published. Shovkoplyas (1950, 1951) worked with archival notes made by Efimenko and Zhukov and published brief summaries on their excavations as well as his reinterpretations and reconstructions of the features they

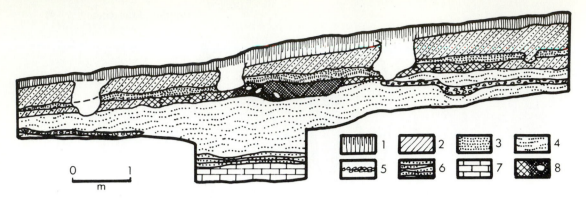

Figure 2.101 Suponevo stratigraphy: 1, present-day soil; 2, loamy sand; 3, light grey sand; 4, laminated sand; 5, chalk fragments; 6, green-grey loamy sand; 7, chalk; 8, cultural remains (after Velichko 1961: Fig. 52).

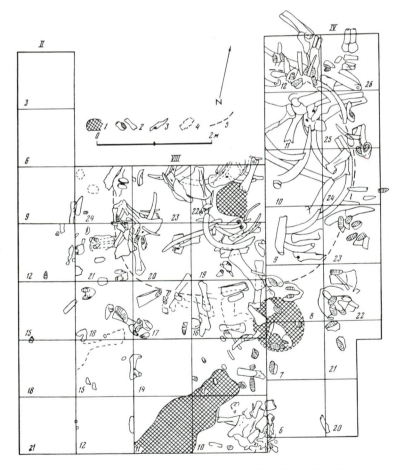

Figure 2.102 Suponevo excavation reconstructed from archival data: 1, hearths and charcoal lenses; 2, mammoth bones; 3, mammoth bones with artificial holes; 4, disintegrated bones; 5, contour of dwelling (after Sergin 1979b: 17).

excavated. The geology and geography of Suponevo were described by Gromov (1948) and Velichko (1961) (Figure 2.101).

The site is located on the right (western) bank of Desna on a 70–80-m wide promontory 20–25 m above the river. Opinion on the geomorphology of the promontory is divided. Earlier investigators, Gromov and Mirchink in particular, feel that the site lay on the second terrace of Desna. Gromov (1948) suggests that man settled here after the soil-forming processes occurred on top of the second-terrace alluvium. Velichko (1961), however, convincingly argues that the promontory was an old hanging bottom of a ravine which cut through the interfluve plateau. Man, in Velichko's scheme, settled on the bottom of this ravine when the ravine was on the floodplain. This ravine was subsequently filled in and cut through by a much younger one. From the literature on Suponevo, it can at best be surmised that the site was oriented toward the river. Velichko equates the position of the promontory with the second terrace of the Desna and assigns its time of occupation to a period immediately after the formation of the second terrace and deposition of Loess III.

Shovkoplyas (1950) reports that some 200 m² of the site were excavated. No estimates exist on the possible size of the site. A single, apparently undisturbed cultural layer was found at depths from 0.7 to 0.9 m. According to Velichko, the cultural remains lay in colluvial laminated loam and sandy loam.

Suponevo was excavated by trenching, and accumulations of mammoth bone found were interpreted as kitchen debris. Various researchers subsequently recognized that at least some of these "bone heaps" probably represented mammoth-bone dwellings, as well as storage pits. These attempts at posthumous reconstruction led researchers to

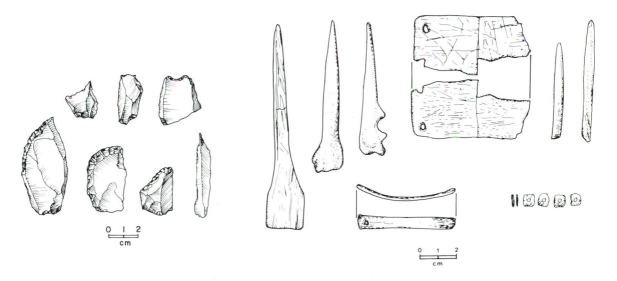

Figure 2.103 Suponevo flint tools (after Shovkoplyas 1952: Fig. iii).

Figure 2.104 Suponevo worked bone (after Shovkoplyas 1952: Fig. IV).

very divergent conclusions. Shovkoplyas (1964, 1965a), for example, discerns the presence of both short-term tent-like structures and long-term mammoth-bone dwellings, whereas Sergin (1979b) states that only one mammoth-bone dwelling was unearthed at the site (Figure 2.102). Similarly, it is impossible to accurately quantify the number and sizes of hearths and storage pits. Thus the tables of features and assemblages from Suponevo list only a fraction of what existed (Tables 2.4–2.8, 2.11).

25. **Timonovka I** (53°20′ N, 34°20′ E; Bryanskii, Bryansk).   The site was discovered in 1927 by Voevodskii and excavated by Gorodtsov from 1928 through 1933 (Gorodtsov 1935a,b). In 1955 it was excavated by Rogachev, Krainov, and Velichko. Both Timonovka I and Timonovka II are located on the same high promontory on the right (western) bank of Desna. The geography and geology of the site has been thoroughly presented in the literature by Velichko (1961; Velichko, Grekhova, and Gubonina 1977; Velichko, Grekhova *et al.* 1981) and are illustrated in Figures 2.105 and 2.106. The narrow (80–100-m-wide), long plateau promontory was formed by the erosional action of the Desna and by a southwest–northeast large ravine.

As was the case with Suponevo, geologists working in the 1920s and 1930s interpret

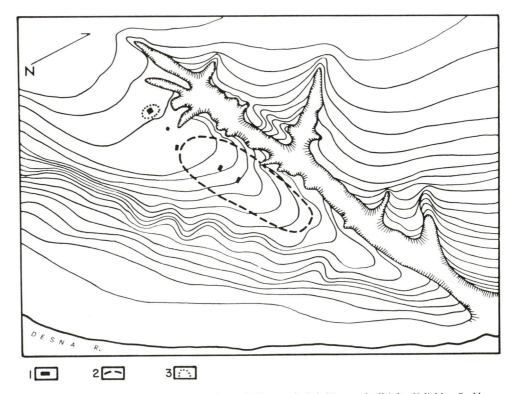

Figure 2.105   Timonovka sites: 1, excavated area; 2, Timonovka I; 3, Timonovka II (after Velichko, Grekhova, and Gubonina 1977: Fig. 7).

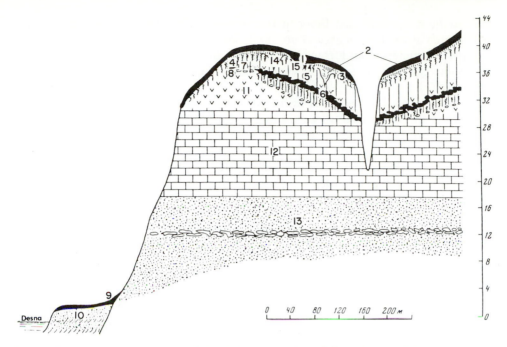

Figure 2.106   Timonovka stratigraphy: 1, humic layer, present-day; 2, humic layer, relic Timonovka soil; 3, 4, colluvium; 5, loess; 6, Mezin soil complex; 7, sand; 8, rock detritus; 9, colluvial deposits; 10, present-day alluvium; 11, diatomaceous clay; 12, chalk; 13, Senomanian sand; 14, ice wedge casts; 15, cultural remains (after Velichko, Grekhova *et al*. 1981: Fig. 20).

the geography of Timonovka somewhat differently. Gromov (1948) after Mirchink, states that Timonovka I, like Suponevo, was located on the second terrace of the Desna. This work follows the fuller and more exhaustive geological study of the sites done by Velichko. Timonovka I lies 240 m northeast of Timonovka II, slightly downslope and closer to the Desna. At the time of excavation it was located approximately 200 m from the river. Gorodtsov (cited in Gromov 1948) test-trenched 18,378 m² (an oval measuring 90 × 260 m) and believes that this represented the maximal area of the site. He excavated 1178 m² of this area. Velichko, Grekhova, and Gubonina (1977), in reviewing Gorodtov's excavations, felt that his areal estimates for the site were greatly exaggerated and that the site probably was about 3200 m² in size.

A single cultural layer was found 0.25–0.5 m below the soil surface. According to Velichko and his associates, cultural material was found in humified loam associated with both Profile B of the relic Timonovka soil and the very top of Loess III.

Both Gorodtsov (1935a,b) and Krainov (1956) consider the cultural layer to be in situ. But extensive work at the site by Velichko clearly shows that the layer was serverely disturbed by various periglacial phenomena including numerous ice wedges and solifluction. Apparently man settled on the Timonovka promontory on top of an extensive ice wedge polygon system which melted after man abandoned the site and severely disturbed the cultural remains. Unfortunately, these periglacial features were not recognized as such at the time of excavation. Both Gorodtsov and Krainov (1956) interpret them as semi-subterranean rectangular dwellings or earth lodges. This erroneous interpretation can still be found in contemporary English-language literature (e.g., Shimkin 1978).

Since Timonovka I was severely disturbed, it is impossible today to state with any certainty whether any dwellings were found or to ennumerate features. Grekhova (in Velichko, Grekhova, and Gubonina 1977) hypothesizes that there may have been two or three mammoth-bone constructions. Since, however, Eliseevichi, Timonovka II, and possibly Yudinovo contained storage pits with some above-ground structural elements of mammoth bone, the constructions Grekhova thinks were possibly mammoth-bone dwellings could have as likely been storage pits. Storage pits were indeed found at Timonovka I. In this work I treat this site as one with storage pits but no mammoth-bone dwellings: No direct evidence exists for the presence of mammoth-bone dwellings

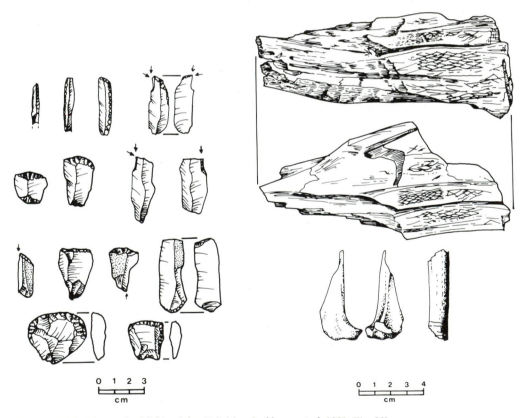

Figure 2.107   Timonovka I lithics (after Velichko, Grekhova, *et al.* 1981: Fig. 22).

Figure 2.108   Timonovka I: engraved mammoth ivory and worked bone (after Velichko, Grekhova, and Gubonina 1977: Fig. 46).

and the site's fauna contains a small number of mammoths for a site with mammoth-bone dwellings. The extensive lithic assemblage was made primarily of locally available material but also contained some exotic lithics (Figure 2.107). Worked bone was sparce but contained some engraving (Figure 2.108).

26. **Timonovka II** (53°20′ N, 34°20′ E).   Timonovka II was discovered in 1965 and excavated by Grekhova from 1965 to 1968. The geology and geography here are the same as at Timonovka I. Grekhova excavated 163 m² (Velichko, Grekhovo, and Gubonina 1977). Test-trenching indicated that the site may have been as large as 500 m². A single cultural layer was found lying in humic loam at depths of 0.6 to 0.8 m below the contemporary soil. Cultural material was unevenly distributed over the excavated area (Figure 2.109 and 2.110). The layer was in situ but had been fairly severely disturbed by various periglacial phenomena. Test-trenching between Timonovka I and II showed no

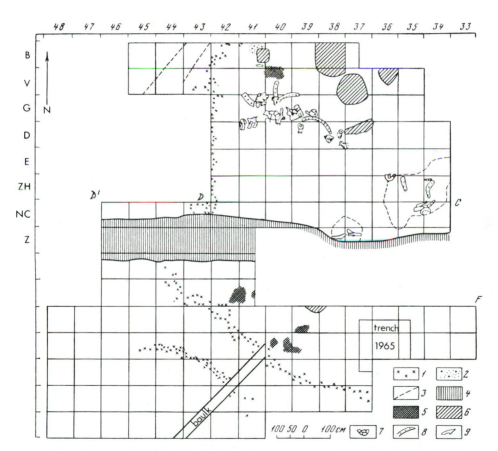

Figure 2.109   Timonovka II excavations: 1, extent of cultural layer around casts; 2, colored spot; 3, storage pits; 4, construction trench—contemporary; 5, ash spots; 6, present-day disturbed areas; 7, mammoth skulls; 8, mammoth tusks; 9, bones (after Velichko, Grekhova, and Gubonina 1977: Fig. 32).

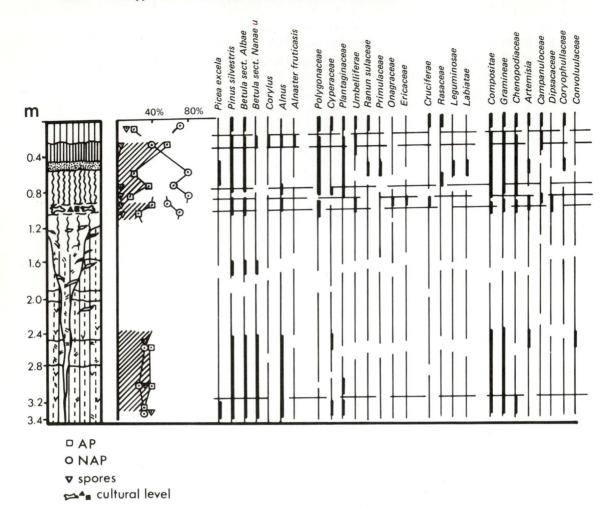

Figure 2.110   Timonovka II pollen diagram (after Velichko, Grekhova *et al.* 1981: Fig. 21).

cultural remains and Velichko *et al.* consider Timonovka I and II to be separate sites reflecting two slightly different periods of occupation.

The site contained three large storage pits filled with mammoth bone, as well as remnants of some hearths, work areas, and surface accumulations of mammoth bone. Using stylistic criteria, Grekhova assigned both Timonovka sites to the same culture and worked out an occupational sequence for the Timonovka promontory that sees first the occupation of a part of Timonovka I together with all of Timonovka II and then a second occupation (or a continuation of occupation at a slightly later time) of other sections of Timonovka I.

27. **Yudinovo** (52°40′ N, 33°17′ E; Pogarskii, Yudinovo).   The site was first investigated and test-trenched in 1934 by Polikarpovich, who returned in 1947 to conduct excavations and do additional test-trenching in the area. Today Yudinovo remains the least-known major Upper Paleolithic site in the study area—one known in print from a handful of short articles and one-page notices. The most extensive description of the site is in Polikarpovich (1968), which only describes his 1947 excavation. Since 1947 the site has been investigated by Budko (1966, 1967a, 1969b) from 1961 to 1966 and by Sergin (1977, 1981c) in 1976 and 1980. In 1980 Abramova and Grekhova began new excavations at Yudinovo that have continued every field season but have not been published in detail.

The site is located on the right (northern) bank of the Sudost' on a promontory formed by the river terrace and a buried ravine (Figure 2.111). The geology and geography of the area have been reported by Kalechitz (1972), Polikarpovich (1968), and Velichko (1961) (Figure 2.112). The promontory itself lies 9–11 m above the summer level of the Sudost' and is horizontal for the most part, with a slight dip toward the river to the east. Today three small, seasonal lakes are present in the vicinity of the site; similar lakes are thought to have existed in the area during the late Valdai as well.

A major disagreement exists in the literature about the river terrace on which the site was found. Velichko (1961) and Budko (1969a) after him write that the site is on the first terrace and that man settled here on the floodplain itself. Kalechitz (1972), Polikarpovich (1968), and Vereschagin and Kuzmina (1977) write that the promontory is part of the second Sudost' terrace. These differences of opinion, which put into question the stratigraphic dating of the site, are discussed in Chapter 4.

Cultural materials lie in a single layer in alluvial loess-like sandy loam at depths ranging from 2.35 to 2.75 m from the present surface. From all accounts, the layer appears in situ, although Polikarpovich (1968) notes that mammoth bone had been

Figure 2.111   Yudinovo excavations (1983 season).

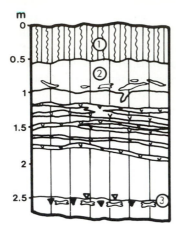

Figure 2.112   Yudinovo stratigraphy: 1, humic layer; 2, sandy loam; 3, cultural layer (after Velichko 1961: Fig. 55).

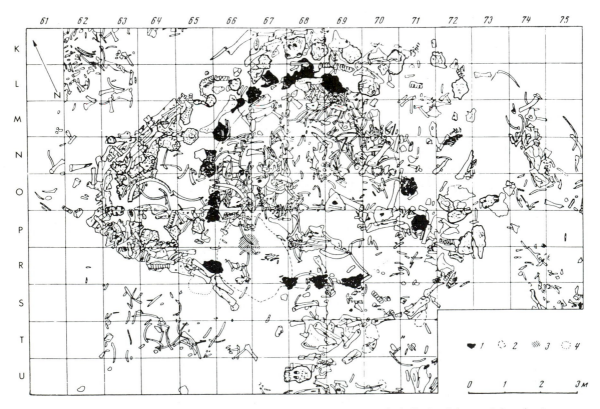

Figure 2.113   Yudinovo excavations (1947, 1961): 1, mammoth skulls; 2, ash lenses; 3, hearths; 4, contemporary pit (after Sergin 1974a: 237).

eroding into the nearby Sudost' for a long time. This suggests that parts of the site may have been destroyed in the past.

Today it is still unclear if all the cultural remains found at Yudinovo come from a single site or a number of nearby sites. Polikarpovich in 1947 confined his excavations to the southeastern section of the promontory and called this area the Yudinovo site. His test trenches, up to 500 m to the north and west of the excavated area, revealed the presence of thick cultural layers. The similarity of the cultural remains and their analogous stratigraphic positions led Polikarpovich to conclude that these discoveries were all of a single, very large site which may have occupied 13,500–18,000 m². In 1975 and again in 1979, Sergin test-trenched an area of the promontory 150 m away from Polikarpovich's 1947 excavation and called the two spots where he found cultural remains Yudinovo II and III. Sergin considers these remains, especially at Yudinovo III, to be a part of a different and independent site. Unfortunately Sergin (1977, 1981c) published his observations in two half-page articles in *Arheologicheskiye Otkritiya 1976*

Figure 2.114 Yudinovo excavations (1983).

Goda and *Arheologicheskiye Otkritiya 1980 Goda* with neither maps to show where he conducted his excavations nor justification for considering them separate sites. As best as I can estimate, approximately 500 m² have been excavated at Yudinovo from 1934 up to and including the current work by Abramova and Grekhova.

Materials excavated at Yudinovo from 1947 through 1979 have been neither studied nor described, and in fact many of them are still to be found in their original field crates scattered between the Institute of History of the Byelorussian SSR and the Byelorussian Historical Museum in Minsk. Much confusion exists in the literature on both sides of the Atlantic about the nature and number of features found at Yudinovo. Judging from the Soviet literature and archival materials I examined, three mammoth-bone dwellings were uncovered at the site prior to Abramova and Grekhova's excavation. Two of these were small, round-to-oval constructions, whereas the third may have been a much larger oval construction measuring as much as 10 × 17 m along the outside perimeters (Figure 2.113). This construction is a most complex one, and the dimensions cited above reflect the accumulations of bone concentrated in one part of the site. It appears that this bone concentration includes both remains of a smaller dwelling and a surrounding bone wall or fence that went around at least half of the dwelling and was located approximately 1 m from its outside walls. I interpret this large bone accumulation, after both Rogachev (1970) and Sergin (1979b), not as remnants of a single large dwelling but as an architectural complex of dwelling and surrounding wall. Abramova

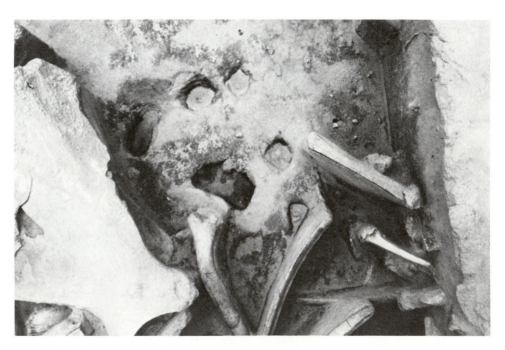

Figure 2.115   Yudinovo living floor inside dwelling.

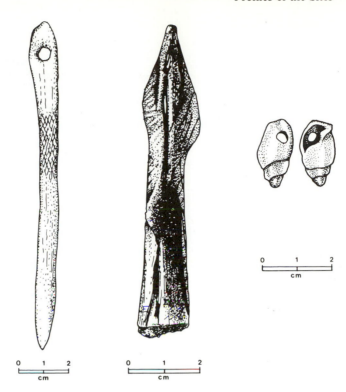

Figure 2.116 Yudinovo: engraved bone, ivory, and perforated shells (after Budko 1967a: Fig. 2).

and Grekhova's recent work at Yudinovo has produced another mammoth-bone dwelling which is small and either round or oval in contour (Figure 2.114). In addition to dwellings, the site also contained an unspecified number of large storage pits filled with bone as well as about 11 small interior pits in one of the dwellings excavated before 1965 (which Budko, 1966, 1967a, interpreted as postholes). Similar pits have also been found in the recently uncovered dwelling (Figure 2.115). Both exterior and interior hearths were also found, but again their exact number and dimensions remain uncertain.

Faunal remains listed in Tables 2.7 and 2.8 reflect just a part of fauna found at the site—those bones excavated prior to 1980 that were taken back from excavations conducted by Polikarpovich and Budko. Values given in Tables 2.5, 2.6, and 2.11 are the best estimates I could derive from the literature and archival sources. Since, however, all Yudinovo researchers have commented on the paucity of lithics at the site, the estimated figure of some 12,500 pieces may not be too inaccurate. The lithic inventory, as in Eliseevichi, appears to consist of nonlocal flint. Abramova (1983, personal communication) speculates that it may have come from Desna deposits. Yudinovo, like Mezin and Eliseevichi, has yielded a sizable collection of worked bone, decorative objects in the form of bone beads, and numerous perforated exotic marine shells used as beads or pendants (Figure 2.116).

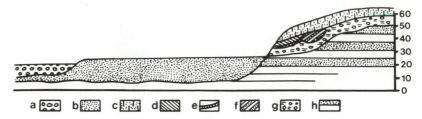

Figure 2.117 Yurovichi stratigraphy: a, present-day alluvium; b, loess-like sands; c, laminated sands; d, cultural material; e, rubble and gravel layer; f, glaciofluvial laminated sands; g, moraine; h, glaciofluvial sands (after Gromov 1948: Fig. 83).

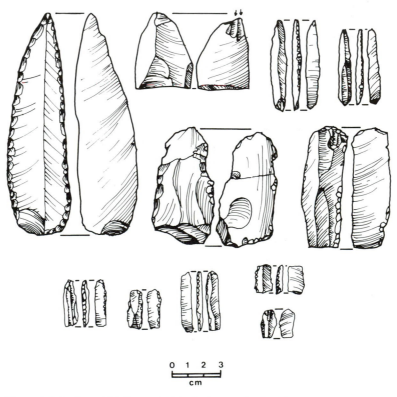

Figure 2.118 Yurovichi flint tools (aftr Budko 1967b: Fig. 7).

28. **Yurovichi** (Yurevichi) (53°47′ N, 28°41′ E; Kalinkovicheskii, Gomel'). This site was excavated from 1929 to 1931 by Polikarpovich (1968) and by Budko (1967b) in 1959 and 1960. Ksenzov (Ksenzov *et al.* 1977) conducted two small excavations there in 1976. The site is located on the high (30–40 m) left (northeastern) bank of the Pripyat' on the southern slope of a northeast–southwest ravine. The geology and geography of the site are reported in the literature by Budko (1967b), Gromov (1948), Kalechitz (1972, 1984), Mirchink (1934), and Polikarpovich (1968) (Figure 2.117).

According to most of these sources, the site was found on the second (middle) terrace of the Pripyat' at heights ranging from 15 to 30 m over the present summer level of the river. Gromov (1948), however, indicates that the geomorphology of the area is insufficiently clear to justify this conclusion. It is possible that the site was located either on a promontory or on the side of a ravine that cut into the interfluve plateau.

A little less than 300 m² have been excavated at Yurovichi since 1929. Cultural remains were found in alluvial and colluvial laminated sand and sandy loam at depths ranging from 1.6 to about 10 m below the surface. Opinions vary about the condition of the cultural material, as well as on how many layers were opened. Both Gromov and Polikarpovich suggest that only one, redeposited layer was found, one which had been moved down the slope of the ravine. Budko, on the other hand, claims that remains were in situ and represented at least two separate cultural layers. Work by Ksensov and the geologist Voznyachuk demonstrate that Gromov and Polikarpovich were correct (Ksenzov *et al.* 1977). Only one redeposited layer is present at Yurovichi; the different depths at which remains were found just reflect post-depositional processes that eroded and redeposited the materials.

Budko (1967b) reports finding one hearth at Yurovichi, but its existence, after Ksensov and Voznyachuk's restudy, is highly suspect. Lithic and organic remains from the site have never been fully published (Figure 2.118). The sole ^{14}C date obtained for Yurovichi—26,470 ± 420 (LU 125)—is problematic but suggests that this site is one of the oldest in the study area.

29. **Zhuravka** (50°39′ N, 32°36′ E; Varvaskii, Zhuravka). Zhuravka was excavated by Rudinskii and Voronov from 1927 to 1930. It is located on the left (eastern) bank of a very meandering river, the Udai. The geology and geography of the site have been amply described in the literature by Rudinskii (1928, 1929, 1930) and subsequently summarized in Boriskovskii (1953), Boriskovskii and Praslov (1964), and Gromov (1948) (Figures 2.119 and 2.120).

Cultural remains were found on a river terrace promontory 12 m above the summer level of the Udai. This terrace is 2–3 km wide in the area, and cultural remains were found on the edge of the terrace closest to the river. Strong disagreement exists in the literature on the geomorphology of the area and on whether the site was found on the first or second terrace. Gromov (1948) discussed these differences of opinion in detail. They can be summarized by saying that earlier geologists and archaeologists (e.g., Pidoplichko, Reznichenko, Rudinskii, and Voronov) believed it was located on the second terrace, whereas later researchers, working with both published and archival

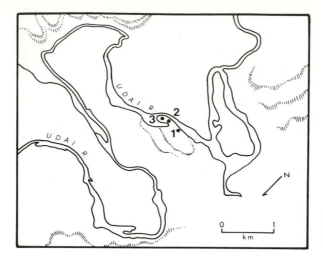

Figure 2.119   Zhuravka: location; 1–3 = excavations (after Gromov 1948: Fig. 34).

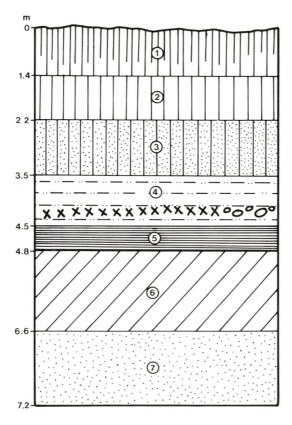

Figure 2.120   Zhuravka stratigraphy: 1, present-day soil; 2, porous loess with burrows; 3, sandy loess; 4, laminated loess-like loam; 5, laminated and gley loam; 6, laminated sandy and loess-like loam; 7, sand; x, cultural remains.

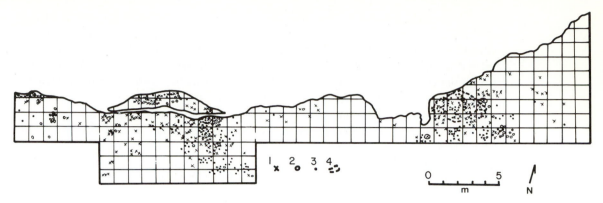

Figure 2.121 Zhuravka excavations: 1, flint; 2, bones; 3, bone fragments; 4, boundary of the concentration of cultural remains (after Boriskovskii and Praslov 1964: Table XXXI).

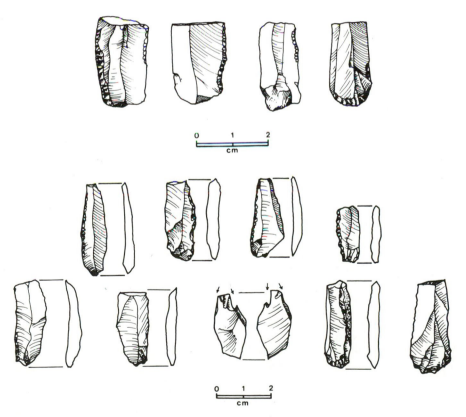

Figure 2.122 Zhuravka lithics (after Boriskovskii 1953: Figs. 198,201).

materials, place the site on the first terrace of the Udai (Boriskovskii 1953; Gladkih 1973). This disagreement stems in part from archaeological data. Lithics found at the site show a large percentage of microliths. This led those researchers who saw micro-lithization as a chronological marker par excellence to assign Zhuravka to the very end of the Upper Paleolithic or even to the Mesolithic. Together with Gromov, I favor the older view that the site was located on the second Udai terrace.

Gromov suggests that man settled here after the floodplain began steady erosion. The presence of laminated layers of sand in the strata suggest that the site was periodically (seasonally?) flooded. This flooding eliminated parts of the cultural layer and subjected the rest to some erosion and redeposition. A single cultural layer was found from 3.5 to 4.3 m below the soil surface. The differences of depth at which remains were found reflect the late Valdai surface of the promontory—it sloped toward the southwest, in the direction of the river. Rudinskii excavated a total of 330 m² at Zhuravka. No estimates exist on the total size of the site. Zhuravka's thin cultural layer contains the remains of three work areas, each of which had a small hearth (Figure 2.121). Its small lithic inventory consists of both locally available cobble flint and a superior nonlocal block flint (Figure 2.122). Soviet researchers, following Rudinskii's early interpretation, see Zhuravka as a temporary camp occupied by a small group for a short time.

RAW DATA TABLES

SITE NUMBER KEY

1. Berdyzh	11. Korshevo I	21. Pushkari I
2. Chulatovo I	12. Korshevo II	22. Pushkari II
3. Chulatovo II	13. Kositsa	23. Radomyshl'
4. Dobranichevka	14. Kurovo	24. Suponevo
5. Eliseevichi	15. Mezhirich	25. Timonovka I
6. Fastov	16. Mezin	26. Timonovka II
7. Gontsy	17. Novgorod–Severskii	27. Yudinovo
8. Khotylevo II	18. Novo-Bobovichi	28. Yurovichi
9. Kirillovskaya	19. Bugorok	29. Zhuravka
10. Klyusy	20. Pogon	

Reference Key for Tables 2.3–2.12

1. Abramova and Grekhova 1981
2. Abramova: personal communication 1983
3. Boriskovskii 1953
4. Boriskovskii and Praslov 1964
5. Boriskovskii *et al.* 1981
6. Budko 1966
7. Budko 1967a
8. Budko 1967b
9. Budko 1969a
10. Budko 1969b
11. Budko and Voznyachuk 1969
12. Budko *et al.* 1971
13. Budko, archive
14. Gladkih 1973
15. Gladkih 1977a
16. Golomshtok 1938
17. Gorodtsov 1935a
18. Grekhova 1970
19. Grekhova: personal communication 1977
20. Grekhova: personal communication 1978
21. Gromov 1948
22. Gvozdover 1947
23. Ivanova *et al.* 1963
24. Klein 1973
25. Kornietz 1962
26. Kornietz *et al.* 1981
27. Kornietz, archive and field notes
28. Kornietz: personal communication 1983
29. Ksenzov *et al.* 1977
30. Kurenkova 1978
31. Kurenkova 1980
32. Kurenkova 1985
33. Lazukov *et al.* 1981
34. Leonova 1977
35. Levitskii 1947
36. Pidoplichko 1947a
37. Pidoplichko 1947b
38. Pidoplichko 1969
39. Pidoplichko 1976
40. Pidoplichko and Shovkoplyas 1961
41. Pidoplichko, archive
42. Polikarpovich 1968
43. Rogachev 1970
44. Rudinskii 1928
45. Rudinskii 1929
46. Sergin 1974a
47. Sergin 1979b
48. Sergin 1979b
49. Sergin 1981a
50. Sergin 1983
51. Shovkoplyas 1950
52. Shovkoplyas 1951
53. Shovkoplyas 1956
54. Shovkoplyas 1964
55. Shovkoplyas 1965a
56. Shovkoplyas 1965b
57. Shovkoplyas 1965c
58. Shovkoplyas 1967
59. Shovkoplyas 1972
60. Shovkoplyas *et al.* 1981
61. Sklenar 1976
62. Soffer-Bobyshev 1984
63. Tarasov 1976
64. Tarasov 1977
65. Tarasov 1981
66. Umanskaya 1975
67. Velichko, Grekhova *et al.* 1981
68. Velichko, Grekhova, and Gubonina 1977
69. Velichko, Grekhova, and Udartsev 1977
70. Velichko, Gribchenko *et al.* 1977
71. Velichko, Zavernyaev *et al.* 1981
72. Vereschagin and Kuzmina 1977
73. Voevodskii 1947b
74. Voevodskii 1949
75. Voevodskii 1950
76. Voevodskii 1952a
77. Voevodskii 1952b
78. Voevodskii 1952c
79. Voznyachuk and Budko 1969
80. Zavernyaev 1978
81. Zavernyaev 1981
82. Collections at History Museum, BSSR, Minsk
83. Collections at Institute of Geography, AN SSSR, Moscow
84. Collections at Institute of History, BSSR, Minsk
85. Collections at State Historical Museum (GIM), AN SSSR, Moscow
86. Collections at Zoology Institute, AN Uk.SSR, Kiev
87. Collections at Zoology Institute, Leningrad
88. Mezhirich field notes, 1978–1983

Table 2.3 GEOGRAPHY, GEOMORPHOLOGY, AND STRATIGRAPHY OF THE SITES

Site	River	Location[a]	From modern river (m)	Above river (m) modern	Above river (m) B.P.[b]	Orientation	Area excavated (m²)
1. Berdyzh	Sozh	P?, R, T-1?	60–70	6–12	nd	NE	~350
2. Chulatovo I	Desna	P, R	50–70	19–25	0–5	SE	390
3. Chulatovo II	Desna	P, R	100–125	35–40	15–20	S	~1000
4. Dobranichevka	Toshanka	T-2, M	<50	16–17	nd	S	2000
5. Eliseevichi	Sudost'	T-2, M	5–10	11–12	0	E	623
6. Fastov	Unava	T-2, R	<10	12	nd	nd	220
7. Gontsy	Udai	T-2	1300	7–8	0	S	820
8. Khotylevo II	Desna	P, M	<100?	17	5–7	SE	500?
9. Kirillovskaya	Dnepr	T-2?, R?, M	<100?	nd	0	E	7840
10. Klyusy	Tsat	R	<100?	8–10	nd	S	1300
11. Korshevo I	Korshevka	R, M	nd	nd	nd	nd	25
12. Korshevo II	Korshevka	R, M	nd	nd	nd	nd	60
13. Kositsa	Betovka	R, M	nd	nd	nd	nd	125
14. Kurovo	Sudost'	T-2, R?	200	nd	nd	nd	248
15. Mezhirich	Ros' and Rosava	T-2, R, M	~200	9–10	1–2	SE	508
16. Mezin	Desna	T-2, R, M	100	6–16	0?	S–SW	1200
17. Novgorod-Severskii	Desna	P?, R, M	<1000	30	10–15	NW	238
18. Novo-Bobovichi	Irput'	T?, R?	~70	under water	10?	nd	nd
19. Bugorok	Desna	P, M	200	50	35–40	S	13.6
20. Pogon	Desna	P, M	200	35–40	15–20?	S	63.3
21. Pushkari I	Desna	P, M	300	35–40	15–20?	NW–SE	400
22. Pushkari II	Desna	P, M	200	35–40	15–20?	SW	58
23. Radomyshl'	Teterev	R?	~3000	2–3	4–5?	N	600
24. Suponevo	Desna	T-2?, P, R	80–100	20–25	0	E	200
25. Timonovka I	Desna	P, M	~200	38	18–23	SE	1178
26. Timonovka II	Desna	P, M	500	40	15–20	SE	163
27. Yudinovo	Sudost'	T-2?, M	40–50	11	0	S–SE	~500
28. Yurovichi	Pripyat'	T-2?, P?, R?, M?	<2000	30	nd	NW	<300
29. Zhuravka	Udai	T-2, M	~250	8–12	0	SW	330

[a]M, promontory; P, plateau; R, ravine; T, terrace.
[b]At time of occupation.
[c]IS, in situ; D, disturbed; P, partially, R, redeposited.
[d]E, erosion; P, periglacial deformation; S, solifluction.
[e]Presence (+) or absence (−) of mammoth-bone dwellings.
[f]Disagreement exists in literature.

Est. total area (m²)	Cultural layer					Dwelling[e]	Number of mammoth	Nearest neighbor	
	No.	Condition[c]	Disturbance[d]	Depth (m)	Thickness (cm)			Site	Distance (km)
nd	1?	IS?, D	S	1.5–10	30–40	+	45	18	55
nd	1	R, PR?	E, S	4.2–4.5	to 25	−	11	3	.20–.25
2000	1	IS, PD	E	2–2.5	2–5	−	13	2	.20–.25
5500	1	IS, PD	E	1.5–2.5	10–12	+	91	7, 15	70
5000	1	IS, PD	P, E	1.2–1.9	10–12	+	60	13	30
nd	1	IS	—	3.2	10	−	11	9	60
nd	1?	IS, PD	P?, E	2–3.8	5–7	+	93	29	40
nd	1	IS, D	P	4–4.5	20–40	−	nd	11–13	12
9000–10,000?	1?	IS, PD, PR?	E, S	13.5–22.5	nd	+	70	6	60
>20,000?	1	R?, IS?	nd	nd	nd	−	nd	18, 19–22	55
nd	1	IS, PD	E	nd	nd	−	nd	12, 13	1
nd	1	IS, PD	E	nd	nd	−	nd	11, 13	1
nd	1	IS, PD	E	0.5	10–15	−	nd	11, 12	1
nd	1?	R?	E, S?	1.1	nd	−	1	19–22	25
>10,000?	1	IS	—	2.7–3.1	10–15	+	149	4	70
nd	1?	IS, PD	E, S	1–8	to 10	+	116	2, 3	18
nd	1	D, R	E	6–7	nd	−	15	2, 3	7
nd	1?	R	S, E	5–6	nd	−	11	10	55
~13,000?	1	IS, PD, R	E, P	0.3–0.5	20–30	−	nd	20–22	.20
~40,000?	1?	D, R	E	0–5	nd	−	nd	19, 21, 22	.20
~30,000?	1?	IS	—	0.5–1.1	to 10	+	69	19, 20, 22	.20
nd	1	IS?, PD?	S, E	1.7–4.4	to 10	−	17	19–21	.20
nd	1	IS	—	0.6–0.8	to 20	+	47	6	65
nd	1?	IS	—	0.7–0.9	to 30	+	7	25, 26	2–3
2400–18,000	1	IS, PD	P	0.2–0.5	7–15	−	15	26	.24
500	1	IS, PD	E	0.6–0.8	5–15	−	12	25	.24
13,500–18,000	1	IS	—	2.3–2.7	to 20–40	+	56	14	40
nd	1?	R	E, P	1.6–10	nd	?	15–20	1, 9	140
nd	1	IS, D	E	3.5–4.3	5–6	−	—	7	40

Table 2.4 FEATURES AT THE SITES

	Mammoth-bone dwellings				Hearths						Storage pits		
					In dwelling			Outside			In dwelling		
	No.	Shape[a]	Dim. (m)	Area (m²)	No.	Dim. (m)	Vol. (m³)	No.	Dim. (m)	Vol. (m³)	No.	Dim. (m)	Vol. (m³)	Contents
1. Berdyzh	2	1) R?	d = 4	~12.5	2?	nd	nd	—	—	—	1?	0.5 × 0.4 × 0.5	0.2	bone
		2) O?	11 × 5.2	~45.0	1?	d = 2.0 depth = 0.7	1.8							
2. Chulatovo I	—							1–3?	0.75 m² × 0.01	0.008	—			—
3. Chulatovo II	—							7?	1–5 m², depth to 0.02	0.02–0.1	—			—
4. Dobranichevka	4	1) R	d = ~4	~12.5	—			1	d = 2.0, depth = nd	nd	—			—
		2) R	d = ~4	~12.5	1	d = 1.0 depth = 0.2	0.2	2	1) 1.8 × 1.4 × 0.1	0.2	—			—
									2) d = 0.5, depth = 0.1	0.02				
		3) R	d = ~4	~12.5	1	d = 0.7 depth = 0.17	0.07	2	1) d = 1.7, depth = 0.12	0.3	—			—
									2) d = 1.2, depth = 0.1	0.1				
		4) R	d = ~4	~12.5	—			2	1) 1.0 × 2.0 × nd	nd	—			—
									2) 1.0 × 1.5 × nd	nd				
5. Eliseevichi	2?	1) R?	nd	~20.0?	—			—		—	1?[d]		nd	worked bone
6. Fastov	—				—			2	nd	nd	—			—
7. Gontsy	2?	both R? or O?	d = 5	both ~20.0	1	d = to 1.0?	nd	2?	nd	nd	3	1) d = 0.4 depth = 0.4	0.05	bone charcoal
												2) d = 0.4 depth = 0.1 to 0.2	0.01	bone charcoal
												3) d = 0.4 depth = 0.1 to 0.2	0.01	bone charcoal
8. Khotylevo II	—				—			some	nd	nd	—			—
9. Kirillovskaya	3?4?	R?O?	d = 5	~20.0?	same?	nd	nd	>20	depth 0.1–0.2	nd	nd	nd	nd	nd
10. Klyusy	—				—			—			—			

| | Storage pits | | | Pits with bone constructions | | Work areas | | | | | |
| | Outside | | | | | In dwelling | | Outside | | Outdoor large bone heaps | References |
No.	Dim. (m)	Vol. (m³)	Contents	No.	Material	No.	Size	No.	Size		
3	1) 1.1 × 1.6 × 0.6 2) 2.4 × 2.7 × 0.4 3) nd	0.8	large bone	1?	mammoth tusks	—		—			11, 12, 61
— few	d = 0.15–0.25 depth = 0.1–0.2	0.004–0.005	bone and burned bone	—		— 3	5.0 × 0.1	— 3?			3, 36 34, 76
2	1) d = 2.0, depth = 1.2 2) d = 2.0, depth = 0.9	3.8 2.8	large bone burned bone	—		1	d = 3.0	—		Some	38, 59, 60
4[b]	1) 2.8 × 2.0 × 0.8 2) 2.5 × 2.0 × 0.8 3) 1.6 × 1.2 × 0.8 4) 2.2 × 1.8 × 0.8	3.5 3.1 1.2 2.5	large bone large bone large bone large bone			1	d = ~3.0	—			
4[c]	1) 2.5 × 1.7 × 0.8 2) 2.1 × 1.5 × 0.8 3) 2.3 × 1.6 × 0.8 4) 2.3 × 1.25 × 0.8	2.7 2.0 2.8 1.8	large bone large bone large bone large bone			2	1) d = 1.0 2) 4.0 × 2.0	—			
2	1) d = 2.0, depth = 0.8? 2) d = 2.0, depth = 0.8?	~2.5 ~2.5	large bone large bone			1	8.0 × 4.0	—			
5	1) 2.6 × 2.7 × 0.7 2) 2.05 × 1.05 × 0.5 3) 2.0 × 1.3 × 0.5 4) nd 5) 1.53 × 1.0 × nd[d]	3.9 0.8 1.02 nd nd	large bone large bone large bone large bone worked bone	2–3?	mammoth skulls?	2?	nd	1?			6, 18, 19, 42
— 5–6	1) d = 1.5, depth = 0.75 2) d = 1.2, depth nd 3) nd 4) d = 2.0, depth = 0.6 5) d = 2.0, depth = 0.6	1.3 1.0 nd 1.9 1.9	large bone large bone large bone large bone large bone	— —		6 1?	all to d = 1.0 nd	>1 nd			4, 53 35, 38, 49, 50
— nd —		nd	nd	some? — —	nd	>2 —	nd	some nd —	nd		71, 80 3, 38 57, 58

(*continued*)

Table 2.4   FEATURES AT THE SITES (*Continued*)

	Mammoth-bone dwellings				Hearths						Storage pits			
					In dwelling			Outside			In dwelling			
	No.	Shape[a]	Dim. (m)	Area (m²)	No.	Dim. (m)	Vol. (m³)	No.	Dim. (m)	Vol. (m³)	No.	Dim. (m)	Vol. (m³)	Contents
11. Korshevo I	—				—			—			—			—
12. Korshevo II	—				—			—			—			—
13. Kositsa	—				—			—			—			—
14. Kurovo	—				—			—			—			—
15. Mezhirich	4	1 R)	d = ~5.5	24.0	1	d = 0.5–0.7 depth = 0.1–0.2	0.04	1	d = 0.9 depth = 0.15	0.1	—			—
		2) R	d = ~5	20.0	1	d = 0.6 depth = 0.2	0.06	2	1) d = 0.8 depth = 0.2	0.01	—			—
									2) d = 0.8 depth = 0.4	0.02				
		3) R	d = ~2	12.0	1	nd	nd	1	d = 0.9 depth = 0.8	0.05	—			—
		4) O	5.8 × 4.6	~20.0	nd	nd	nd	2	nd	nd	nd			
16. Mezin	2–5	1) R	d = ~5.5	24.0	3? ash spots	d = 0.5–0.7 depth[f]	0.003	4	1) 2.5 × 2.0 × 0.1	0.04	4	small	nd	postholes?
		2) O	4.0 × 2.0	8.0	—			1	d = 1.0	nd	—			—
		3) R	d = 6	28.0	2 ash spots	d = 0.5–0.7 depth[f]	0.003	—			—			—
		4) O	4.0 × 2.0	8.0	—			1	d = 1.0 depth = 0.3	0.2	same	small	nd	caches
		5) R	d = 6	28.0	1 ash spot	d = 1.0 depth[f]	0.008	3	1) 2.5 × 1.5 × 0.1	0.3	—			
									2) d = 1.0 depth = 0.02	0.02				
									3) 2.0 × 1.5 × 0.1	0.2				
17. Novgorod-Severskii	—				some charcoal			—			—			—
18. Novo-Bobovichi	—				—			—			—			—
19. Bugorok	—				—			—			—			—
20. Pogon	—				—			—			—			—
21. Pushkari I	1?	O?	12.0 × 4.0	~48.0	3	1) 1.2 × 0.8 × 0.1	0.2	2	1) d = 1.5, depth = 0.1	0.2	~50	d = 0.1–0.2 depth to 0.1	~ 0.007	postholes? some flint, charcoal, ocher, worked bone
	3?	R?	d = 4.0	~12.6 each		2) 2.5 × 1.2 × 0.2	0.2		2) d = 1.0 depth = 0.1	0.1				
						3) 2.2 × 2.5 × 0.1	0.1							

| | Storage pits | | | Pits with bone constructions | | Work areas | | | | | |
| | Outside | | | | | In dwelling | | Outside | | | |
No.	Dim. (m)	Vol. (m³)	Contents	No.	Material	No.	Size	No.	Size	Outdoor large bone heaps	References
—				—		—		2	nd		63, 64, 65
—				—		—		—			63, 64, 65
—				—		—		—			63, 64, 65
—				—		—		—			21, 42
—				—		2	nd	—		some	15, 26, 38, 39
1	d = 1.5, depth = 1.4	2.5	large bone and cultural layer	—		1	nd	—			
1e	d = 1.0, depth = 0.8	0.6	large bone and cultural layer	—		1	nd	1	nd		
								2	nd		
6	1) d = 0.5, depth = 1.0	0.2	large bone	—		4	1) ~8.0	1–3		3?	38, 55
	2) 2.0 × 1.5 × 1.0	2.4	large bone				2) ~3.0				
	3) d = 2.0, depth = 1.0	3.1	large bone				3) ~3.0				
	4) 2.3 × 1.9 × 1.0	3.4	large bone				4) ~2.0				
	5) 2.5 × 1.5 × 1.0	2.9	large bone								
	6) d = 0.9, depth = 1.0	0.6	large bone								
	1.0 × 0.7 × 0.65g	~0.5		—		1	~4.0	2?		2?	
—				—		2	1) ~6.0	5?		4?	
							2) ~4.0				
—				—		1	~2.0	2?		2?	
—				—		4	1) ~7.0	—		—	
							2) ~5.0				
							3) ~4.0				
							4) ~1.0				
—				—		—		—			3, 21, 37
—				—		—		—			21, 42
—				—		—		—			3, 22, 77
—				—		—		—			3, 75
				—			nd	—			3, 5
3	d = 0.25, depth = 0.15	~0.007	burned bone and flint			many					

(continued)

Table 2.4   FEATURES AT THE SITES (*Continued*)

| | Mammoth-bone dwellings | | | Hearths | | | | | | Storage pits | | | |
| | | | | In dwelling | | | Outside | | | In dwelling | | | |
	No.	Shape[a]	Dim. (m)	Area (m²)	No.	Dim. (m)	Vol. (m³)	No.	Dim. (m)	Vol. (m³)	No.	Dim. (m)	Vol. (m³)	Contents
22. Pushkari II	—				—			some ash spots	nd	nd	—			—
23. Radomyshl'	5–6	1) O	3.0 × 5.0	~12.5	some	nd	nd	some	nd	nd	—			—
		2) O	3.0 × 5.0	~12.5										
		3) O	4.0 × 3.0	~10.0										
		4) O	4.0 × 3.0	~10.0										
		5) O	4.0 × 3.0	~10.0										
		6) R	d = 4.0	~12.5										
24. Suponevo	1–3	1) R	d = 5.5?	~23.76	1–2?	1) d = 1.0, depth = 0.2–0.3	0.2	2?	1) d = 2.1, depth = 0.2–0.3	0.2	—			—
		2) O	5.0 × 7.0?	~27.50					2) d = 3.0, depth = 0.2	1.4?				
25. Timonovka I	?				some?			some	1) d = 1.0, depth to 0.6	0.5	—			—
26. Timonovka II	—				—			1–3 wash outs	depth to 0.1	nd	—	—		—
27. Yudinovo	3? 4?	1) O	10.0 × 17.0[h] d = 5.0–7.5	44.0? ~20.0	2?	1) d = 0.6 depth = 0.1	0.04	5?	1) 2.0 × 2.0	nd	—			—
						2) nd			2) 4.2 × 2.4					
									3) 5.4 × 3.0					
									4) and 5) nd					
		2) O?	5.0 × 6.0	~24.0	1	d = 2.1	nd	—?			—			—
		3) R?	d = 5.0–6.0	20–28	—			—			11	d = 0.05–0.2 depth = 0.1–0.2	0.003	postholes?
		4) R?	nd	20–30[i]	nd			1?	nd		nd			—
28. Yurovichi	—				—			1?	nd	nd	—			—
29. Zhuravka	—				—			3? washed out	nd	nd	—			—

[a] R, round; O, oval.
[b] Depths of pits around Dwelling 2, 0.5–1.0 m (Shovkoplyas 1972).
[c] Depths of pits around Dwelling 3, up to 1.0 m (Shovkoplyas et al. 1981).
[d] Location inside or outside dwelling questionable; possibly the same pit.
[e] Not fully excavated.
[f] All depths assumed to be .001 m.
[g] Association with any complex uncertain.
[h] Dwelling 1 with outer walls.
[i] Currently under excavation.

| Storage pits | | | | Pits with bone constructions | | Work areas | | | | Outdoor large bone heaps | References |
| | Outside | | | | | In dwelling | | Outside | | | |
No.	Dim. (m)	Vol. (m³)	Contents	No.	Material	No.	Size	No.	Size		
—				—		—		—			3, 78
1	d = 2.0 depth = 1.0	~3.14	large bone	nd		1	~2.0 × 1.7	—			33, 54, 56
1–2?	1) d = 1.0 depth = 0.95 2) nd	0.8 nd	nd nd	nd		3? 4?	1) 3.0 × 2.0 2) r = ~6.0 3) 8 m² 4) 5.0 × 3.0	some			3, 47, 51, 52
2?	nd	nd	large bone	?				1	2.7 × 1.3		17, 67, 68
3	1) 0.1 × 0.1 × 0.1 2) d = 2.0 depth = 0.7 3) 0.6 × 1.0 × 0.6	0.0007 2.2 0.3	posthole? large bone large bone	2?	mammoth skulls			2	nd	some	67, 68
some?	association? nd		nd	nd		nd		some	nd	bone wall of 20 mammoth skulls around dwelling	1, 8, 9, 42, 43, 46, 48
— —											
— —				—				— 3?	d = 4.0	—	8, 29, 42 4, 44, 45

Table 2.5 LITHIC INVENTORIES

Site	Area excavated (m²)	Lithics found	Density of lithics (m²)	Tools found	Density of tools (m²)	% of all lithics	Flint	Sandstone	Other	Ocher	References
							Lithic materials and sources[a]				
1. Berdyzh	~350	~1500	4.9	nd	nd	nd	nd	nd	—	—	42, 79
2. Chulatovo I	390	1200	3.0	42	0.10	3.5	L	L	—	+ L	3, 36, 73
3. Chulatovo II	~1000	13387	13.4	535	0.50	4.0	L	L	quartzite-L	+ L	34, 76
4. Dobranichevka[b]	2000	13688	6.8	1153	0.60	8.4	L	L	granite-L; gneiss-L; mountain crystal-E[c]	+ nd	14, 34, 60
5. Eliseevichi	623	80,000[d]	128.4	~4000	6.40	5.0	E?	E?	quartzite-L; granite-L; marl-nd	—	20, 42
6. Fastov	220	1888	8.6	170	0.80	9.0	L	—	—	+ nd	14
7. Gontsy	820	~3000	3.7	~300	0.40	~10.0	L	—	hematite-nd, mountain crystal-E; opaline-nd	+ nd	3, 35
8. Khotylevo II	500	20,714	41.4	5029	10.00	24.3	nd	nd	nd	+ nd	71
9. Kirillovskaya	7840	>4000[e]	0.5[e]	~75	0.01	9.4	L	—	nd	—	3, 38
10. Klyusy	1300	10,500	8.1	~400	0.30	3.8	L	—	granite-L	—	58
11. Korshevo I	25	nd	nd	nd	nd	nd	nd	nd	nd	—	63, 64
12. Korshevo II	60	nd	nd	nd	nd	nd	nd	nd	nd	—	63, 64
13. Kositsa	125	2500	20.0	250	2.00	~10.0	L	L?	quartzite-L?	+ nd	65
14. Kurovo	248	~25	0.1	2	<0.01	8.0	nd	nd	nd	—	42
15. Mezhirich	508	14,870	29.3	1290	2.50	8.7	L	L	granite-L?, gneiss-L?, mountain crystal-E	+ L	26, 39
16. Mezin	1200	113,238	94.4	4429	3.70	3.9	L	—	slate-L?, granite-L, gneiss-L	+ L	55
17. Novgorod-Severskii	238	570	2.4	12	0.05	2.1	L	—	—	+ nd	3, 37
18. Novo-Bobovichi	nd	1	nd	1	nd	100.0	L?	—	—	—	42
19. Bugorok	13.6	4197	308.6	268	19.70	6.4	L, E	—	—	+ nd	3, 22, 77
20. Pogon	63.3	671	10.6	67	1.10	10.0	L, E	—	—	+ E	3
21. Pushkari I	~400	160,000	400.0	~3200	8.0	2.0	L	—	quartzite-L, slate-L?	+ nd	3
22. Pushkari II	~58	85	1.5	2	0.03	2.4	L	—	—	+ nd	3, 77
23. Radomyshl'	1500[f]	10,000	16.7	1145	1.90	11.5	L, E	—	—	+ nd	54, 56
24. Suponevo	~200	~30,000	150.0	nd	nd	nd	L, E	nd	quartzite-nd, slate-nd	+ nd	3, 51, 52
25. Timonovka I	1178[g]	110,095	85.0	10,447	8.90	10.4	L	nd	slate-E?, iron ore-nd, phosphorite-nd	+ nd	17, 68
26. Timonovka II	163	13,932	85.5	632	3.90	4.5	L	L	—	+ nd	68
27. Yudinovo	~500	~12,500?	25.0[h]	nd	nd	nd	E?	—	limestone-nd	+ nd	2, 7, 10, 42, 84
28. Yurovichi	<300	nd	nd	~211	~0.70	nd	L	L?	—	+ nd	8, 29, 42
29. Zhuravka	330	3700	11.2	77	0.20	23.3	L, E	L?	—	—	4, 44, 45

[a] E, exotic; L, local; +, present; —, absent.
[b] Shovkoplyas opened up about 5500 m², but information available on only ~2000 m²; data comes only from Complexes 1 and 3.
[c] For potential sources see Chapter 7.
[d] Grehova (1978), personal communication states that about 80,000 lithics were found in toto.
[e] Boriskowskii (1953) reported that >4000 lithics were found, but only 800 could be found after the Second World War; all calculations are based on the 800.
[f] Shovkoplyas opened up ~1500 m² but described only 600 m²; all calculations based on 600 m².
[g] Excavated area after Velichko, Grekhova, and Gubonina (1977).
[h] Density estimate after Sergin (1977, 1981c).

Table 2.6 COMPOSITION OF LITHIC TOOL ASSEMBLAGE

	Axes	Blades and fragments (unretouched)	Blades and fragments (retouched)	Burins	Burin spalls	Combination tools (end scrapers and burins)	End scrapers	Grinding stones and slabs	Knives	Nuclei and fragments	Piercers and points	Push plane (rabot)	Waste flakes and debitage	Reference
1. Berdyzh	—	nd	nd	nd	nd	nd	nd	nd	nd	nd	nd	nd	nd	3, 36, 73
2. Chulatovo I	—	60	4	—	28	—	—	22	—	15	—	3	1080	34, 76
3. Chulatovo II	—	1473	53	374	150	—	86	>1	—	160	some[a]	—	11, 178	14, 34, 60
4. Dobranichevka[b]	—	2107	49	~182	—	—	~160	—	—	~305	33	40	4060	20, 42
5. Eliseevichi	—	6908	149	436	314	—	28	—	—	321	—	—	749?	14
6. Fastov	—	216	1	3	—	1	5	—	—	92	—	1	1393	14
7. Gontsy	—	>200	some	105	—	3	>150	some	—	13	some	—	nd	3, 14, 35
8. Khotylevo II	—	many	many	many	nd	some	many	—	—	nd	some	—	many	71
9. Kirillovskaya[c]	—	>180	~50	13	—	2	21	—	—	5	some	—	>210	3, 38
10. Klyusy	—	some	some	some	some	some	some	—	—	nd	some	some	nd	58
11. Korshevo I	—	nd	nd	nd	nd	nd	nd	—	nd	nd	nd	nd	nd	63, 64
12. Korshevo II	—	nd	nd	nd	nd	nd	nd	—	nd	nd	nd	nd	nd	63, 64
13. Kositsa	—	>1000	>90	>100	50	—	some	some	—	>30	some	—	>500	65
14. Kurovo	—	3	1	1	—	—	—	—	—	1	—	—	nd	42
15. Mezhirich	17	5461	123	575	297	29	84	~8	—	337	73	38	7475	26, 39, 88
16. Mezin	—	14,828	317	2659	3021	143	714	~13	—	576	574	—	83,058	55
17. Novgorod-Severskii	—	>20	5	2	—	—	2	—	—	9[d]	2	1	—	3, 37
18. Novo-Bobovichi	—	—	—	—	—	—	—	—	—	—	—	—	—	42
19. Bugorok	3	250	26	112	15	—	66	—	—	130	14	—	nd	3, 22, 77
20. Pogon	—	~100	8	18	5	—	6	—	—	24	13	—	nd	3
21. Pushkari I	~20	~15,000	~1000	~160	~30	—	~250	some	~10	~3200	~550	~30	nd	3
22. Pushkari II	—	11	1	1	—	—	—	1	—	17	—	—	26	77
23. Radomyshl'	few	nd	many	many	—	some	some	—	—	many	many	1	10,000	54, 56
24. Suponevo	nd	some	some	many	nd	nd	some	—	nd	some	>20	nd	nd	51, 52
25. Timonovka I	—	6895	109	4714	>1615	140	1098	84	—	~3000	304	—	nd	17, 68
26. Timonovka II	—	nd	78	328	nd	10	180	some	—	215	41	—	nd	68
27. Yudinovo	nd	nd	nd	nd	nd	nd	nd	nd	nd	nd	nd	nd	nd	7, 10, 42
28. Yurovichi	—	>70	>40	61	nd	—	91	some	nd	58	18	nd	nd	8, 29, 42
29. Zhuravka	—	200	34	18	20	—	1?	—	—	3	5	1?	3400	4, 44, 45

[a] Assume ~20.

[b] Shovkoplyas opened up about 5500 m², but information available on only ~2000 m²; data comes only from Complexes 1 and 3.

[c] Boriskovskii (1953) reported that >4000 lithics were found, but only 800 could be found after the Second World War; all calculations based on 600 m².

[d] Three "gigantoliths" counted as nuclei.

Table 2.7 ECONOMICALLY IMPORTANT FAUNA[a]

							Sites							
		1	2	3	4	5	6	7	8	9	10	11	12	13
OSTEICHTYIES															
Salmo sp. (salmon family)															
MNB	number	—	—	—	—	—	—	—	—	—	—	—	—	—
	% of MNB													
MNI	number													
	% of MNI													
Esox lucius (pike)															
MNB	number	—	—	—	—	—	—	—	—	—	—	—	—	—
	% of MNB													
MNI	number													
	% of MNI													
Cyprinidae sp. (carp family)															
MNB	number	—	—	—	—	27 (14)[b]	—	—	—	—	—	—	—	—
	% of MNB					ins								
MNI	number					14 (7)[b]								
	% of MNI					1.7								
Rutilus rutilus (roach)															
MNB	number	—	—	—	—	—	—	—	—	—	—	—	—	—
	% of MNB													
MNI	number													
	% of MNI													
Leuciscus sp. (chub or dace)															
MNB	number	—	—	—	—	—	—	—	—	—	—	—	—	—
	% of MNB													
MNI	number													
	% of MNI													
Abramis brama (bream)															
MNB	number	—	—	—	—	—	—	—	—	—	—	—	—	—
	% of MNB													
MNI	number													
	% of MNI													
Silurius glanis (cat fish)															
MNB	number	—	—	—	—	—	—	—	—	—	—	—	—	—
	% of MNB													
MNI	number													
	% of MNI													
Lota lota (burbot)															
MNB	number	—	—	—	—	—	—	—	—	—	—	—	—	—
	% of MNB													
MNI	number													
	% of MNI													
Lucioperca lucioperca (pike-perch)															
MNB	number	—	—	—	—	—	—	—	—	—	—	—	—	—
	% of MNB													
MNI	number													
	% of MNI													
Perca fluviatilis (perch)															
MNB	number	—	—	—	—	—	—	—	—	—	—	—	—	—
	% of MNB													
MNI	number													
	% of MNI													
Pisces sp. (fish)															
MNB	number	—	50	—	—	—	—	—	—	—	—	—	—	—
	% of MNB		4.2											
MNI	number		1											
	% of MNI		2.6											

						Sites									
14	15	16	17	18	19	20	21	22	23	24	25	26	27	28	29
—	—	—	6	—	—	—	—	—	—	—	—	—	—	—	—
			0.4												
			1												
			0.5												
—	1	—	10	—	—	—	—	—	—	—	—	—	—	—	—
	ins		0.7												
	1		2												
	0.3		0.9												
—	—	—	3	—	—	—	—	—	—	—	—	—	—	—	—
			0.2												
			1												
			0.5												
—	—	—	2	—	—	—	—	—	—	—	—	—	—	—	—
			0.1												
			1												
			0.5												
—	—	—	3	—	—	—	—	—	—	—	—	—	—	—	—
			0.2												
			1												
			0.5												
—	—	—	1	—	—	—	—	—	—	—	—	—	—	—	—
			ins												
			1												
			0.5												
—	—	—	1	—	—	—	—	—	—	—	—	—	—	—	—
			ins												
			1												
			0.5												
—	—	—	2	—	—	—	—	—	—	—	—	—	—	—	—
			0.1												
			1												
			0.5												
—	—	—	1	—	—	—	—	—	—	—	—	—	—	—	—
			ins												
			1												
			0.5												
—	—	—	1	—	—	—	—	—	—	—	—	—	—	—	—
			ins												
			1												
			0.5												
—	—	—	290	—	—	—	—	—	—	2	—	—	—	—	—
			19.9							0.5					
			25							1					
			11.2							5.9					

(continued)

Table 2.7   ECONOMICALLY IMPORTANT FAUNA[a] (Continued)

		Sites												
		1	2	3	4	5	6	7	8	9	10	11	12	13
AVES														
Lagopus lagopus (willow ptarmigan)														
MNB	number	—	—		1	1	—	—	80	—				
	% of MNB				ins	ins			5.8					
MNI	number				1	1			10					
	% of MNI				0.9	0.2			21.3					
Lyrurus tetrix (black grouse)														
MNB	number	—	—	—	—	—	—	—	—	—	—	—	—	—
	% of MNB													
MNI	number													
	% of MNI													
Larus argentatus (silver gull)														
MNB	number	—	—	—	—	—	—	34	—	—	—	—	—	—
	% of MNB							2.4						
MNI	number							14						
	% of MNI							30.0						
Larus rudibundus (black-headed gull)														
MNB	number	—	—	—	—	—	—	—	—	—	—	—	—	—
	% of MNB													
MNI	number													
	% of MNI													
Gavia arctica (Arctic loon)														
MNB	number	—	—	—	—	—	—	3	—	—	—	—	—	—
	% of MNB							0.2						
MNI	number							2						
	% of MNI							4.2						
Anas sp. (duck)														
MNB	number	—	—	—	—	—	—	2	—	—	—	—	—	—
	% of MNB							0.1						
MNI	number							2						
	% of MNI							4.2						
Anser sp. (field geese)														
MNB	number	—	—	—	—	—	—	—	—	—	—	—	—	—
	% of MNB													
MNI	number													
	% of MNI													
Bucephala clangula (golden eye)														
MNB	number	—	—	—	—	—	—	—	1	—	—	—	—	—
	% of MNB								ins					
MNI	number								1					
	% of MNI								2.1					
Cygnus sp. (swan)														
MNB	number	—	—	—	—	—	—	—	—	—	—	—	—	—
	% of MNB													
MNI	number													
	% of MNI													
MAMMALIA														
Hyaena sp. (hyena)														
MNB	number	—	—	—	—	—	—	—	—	1	—	—	—	—
	% of MNB									0.2				
MNI	number									1				
	% of MNI									1.3				
Felis spelaea[c] (cave lion)														
MNB	number	—	—	—	—	—	—	—	—	2	—	—	—	—
	% of MNB									0.4				
MNI	number									1				
	% of MNI									1.3				

								Sites							
14	15	16	17	18	19	20	21	22	23	24	25	26	27	28	29
—	66	14	21	—	—	—	—	—	—	—	—	—	—	—	—
	1.0	0.2	1.4												
	21	7	5												
	6.7	1.4	2.3												
—	5	—	1	—	—	—	—	—	—	—	—	—	—	—	—
	ins		ins												
	1		1												
	0.3		0.5												
—	—	—	—	—	—	—	—	—	—	—	—	—	—	—	—
—	—	—	1	—	—	—	—	—	—	—	—	—	—	—	—
			ins												
			1												
			0.5												
—	—	—	—	—	—	—	—	—	—	—	—	—	—	—	—
—	1	—	31	—	—	—	—	—	—	—	—	—	—	—	—
	ins		2.1												
	1		13												
	0.3		5.8												
—	3	—	2	—	—	—	—	—	—	—	—	—	—	—	—
	ins		0.1												
	3		2												
	1.0		0.9												
—	—	—	—	—	—	—	—	—	—	—	—	—	—	—	—
—	1	—	—	—	—	—	—	—	—	—	—	—	—	—	—
	ins														
	1														
	0.3														
—	—	—	—	—	—	—	—	—	—	—	—	—	—	—	—
—	3	—	—	—	—	—	—	—	—	—	—	—	—	—	—
	ins														
	2														
	0.6														

(continued)

Table 2.7   ECONOMICALLY IMPORTANT FAUNA[a] (Continued)

		1	2	3	4	5	6	7	8	9	10	11	12	13
Lynx lynx (lynx)														
MNB	number	—	—	nd	—	—	—	2	—	—	—	—	—	—
	% of MNB			nd				ins						
MNI	number			2				2						
	% of MNI			1.6				1.3						
Gulo gulo (wolverine)														
MNB	number	—	1	—	7	5	—	5	159	1	—	—	—	—
	% of MNB		0.1		0.2	ins		0.09	11.5	0.2				
MNI	number		1		1	1		2	6	1				
	% of MNI		2.6		0.9	0.2		1.3	12.8	1.3				
Mustela erminea (ermine)														
MNB	number	—	—	—	—	—	—	—	—	—	—	—	—	—
	% of MNB													
MNI	number													
	% of MNI													
Mustela eversmanni (polecat)														
MNB	number	—	—	—	—	6	—	—	—	—	—	—	—	—
	% of MNB					ins								
MNI	number					2								
	% of MNI					0.5								
Mustela nivalis (weasel)														
MNB	number	—	—	—	—	—	—	—	—	—	—	—	—	—
	% of MNB													
MNI	number													
	% of MNI													
Putorius sp. (fitch)														
MNB	number	—	—	—	—	—	—	—	—	—	—	—	—	—
	% of MNB													
MNI	number													
	% of MNI													
Alopex lagopus (Arctic fox)														
MNB	number	nd	42	nd	64	15,374	—	68	191	—	—	—	—	—
	% of MNB	nd	3.2	nd	2.3	53.5		1.2	13.7					
MNI	number	1	6	17	7	278		12	2					
	% of MNI	1.9	15.9	13.7	6.0	68.5		7.6	4.2					
Canis lupus (wolf)														
MNB	number	nd	13	nd	53	1045	—	44	276	2	—	—	—	—
	% of MNB	nd	1.0	nd	1.8	3.6		0.7	19.8	0.4				
MNI	number	1	3	3	3	36		5	6	1				
	% of MNI	1.9	7.9	2.4	2.6	8.9		3.2	12.8	1.3				
Vulpes corsac (corsac)														
MNB	number	—	—	—	—	16	—	—	—	—	—	—	—	—
	% of MNB					ins								
MNI	number					4								
	% of MNI					1.0								
Vulpes vulpes (red fox)														
MNB	number	—	—	—	2	2	—	—	—	—	—	—	—	—
	% of MNB				ins	ins								
MNI	number				1	2								
	% of MNI				0.9	0.5								
Ursus arctos (brown bear)														
MNB	number	nd	2	nd	13	96	—	5	6	4	—	—	—	—
	% of MNB	nd	0.2	nd	0.4	0.3		0.09	0.4	0.9				
MNI	number	2	1	1	1	10		2	1	2				
	% of MNI	3.9	2.6	0.8	0.9	2.5		1.3	2.1	2.5				

						Sites									
14	15	16	17	18	19	20	21	22	23	24	25	26	27	28	29
—	—	—	5	—	—	—	—	—	—	—	—	—	—	—	—
			0.3												
			3												
			1.4												
—	61	28	—	—	—	—	—	—	—	—	—	4	—	—	—
	0.9	0.4										3.2			
	8	5										1			
	2.5	1.0										4.3			
—	—	—	4	—	—	—	—	—	—	—	—	—	—	—	—
			0.3												
			2												
			0.9												
—	—	—	—	—	—	—	—	—	—	—	—	—	—	—	—
—	—	—	14	—	—	—	—	—	—	—	—	—	—	—	—
			0.9												
			5												
			2.2												
—	—	—	2	—	—	—	—	—	—	—	—	—	—	—	—
			0.1												
			1												
			0.5												
—	146	1842	169	—	—	—	93	—	—	27	nd	78	147	2	—
	2.2	22.4	11.7				18.0			6.5	nd	62.9	29.1	0.5	
	11	112	23				4			1	2	6	25	1	
	3.5	22.7	10.3				4.7			5.9	8.3	26.2	25.0	4.3–5.5	
1	89	1004	9	—	—	—	159	10	—	38	nd	5	32	—	nd
2.0	1.3	12.3	0.6				30.7	0.8		9.1	nd	4.0	6.3		nd
1	12	59	4				6	4		2	1	1	3		1
20.0	3.8	11.9	1.8				7.0	14.8		11.7	4.2	4.3	3.0		4.3
—	2	—	—	—	—	—	—	—	—	—	—	—	1	—	—
	ins												0.2		
	2												1		
	0.6												1.0		
—	2	1	3	—	—	—	—	—	—	—	—	—	1	—	nd
	ins	ins	0.2										0.2		nd
	2	1	1										1		1
	0.6	0.2	0.5										1.0		4.3
—	12	35	4	—	—	—	1	3	—	1	nd	1	13	—	—
	0.2	0.4	0.3				0.2	0.2		0.2	nd	0.8	2.6		
	3	7	2				1	1		1	2	1	1		
	1.0	1.1	0.9				1.2	3.7		5.9	8.3	4.3	1.0		

(continued)

Table 2.7   ECONOMICALLY IMPORTANT FAUNA[a] (*Continued*)

		1	2	3	4	5	6	7	8	9	10	11	12	13
							Sites							
Mammuthus primigenius (woolly mammoth)														
MNB	number	nd	1045	nd	2766	>12,187	256	~4000	>616	~440	some	some	some	some
	% of MNB	nd	88.0	nd	93.9	42.4	80.3	70.4	44.3	96.8	nd	nd	nd	nd
MNI	number	45	11	13	91	60	11	93	nd	70	nd	nd	nd	nd
	% of MNI	86.6	29.1	10.4	78.3	14.9	68.8	58.8	nd	88.5	nd	nd	nd	nd
Equus sp.[d] (wild horse)														
MNB	number	nd	6	nd	—	1	63	—	—	—	—	—	—	some
	% of MNB	nd	0.5	nd		ins	19.7							nd
MNI	number	1	2	7		1	5							nd
	% of MNI	1.9	5.2	5.6		0.2	31.2							nd
Coelodonta antiquitatis (woolly rhinoceros)														
MNB	number	nd	2	nd	2	—	—	—	2	4	—	—	—	—
	% of MNB	nd	0.2	nd	ins				0.1	0.9				
MNI	number	1	2	12	1				1	2				
	% of MNI	1.9	5.2	9.6	0.9				2.1	2.5				
Sus scrofa (boar)														
MNB	number	—	—	—	—	—	—	4	—	—	—	—	—	—
	% of MNB							ins						
MNI	number							1						
	% of MNI							0.6						
Cervus elaphus (red deer)														
MNB	number	—	—	—	—	1	—	—						
	% of MNB					ins								
MNI	number					1								
	% of MNI					0.2								
Cervus sp. (deer)														
MNB	number	—	—	—	—	—	—	—	—	—	—	—	—	—
	% of MNB													
MNI	number													
	% of MNI													
Megaceros euryceros (giant deer)														
MNB	number	—	—	—	—									
	% of MNB													
MNI	number													
	% of MNI													
Rangifer tarandus (reindeer)														
MNB	number	—	21	nd	30	2	—	991	—	—	—	—	—	—
	% of MNB		1.7	nd	1.0	ins		17.5						
MNI	number		6	20	5	1		14						
	% of MNI		15.9	16.2	4.2	0.2		8.8						
Bison priscus (steppe bison)														
MNB	number	—	3	nd	2	—	—	5	15	—	—	—	—	—
	% of MNB		0.3	nd	ins			0.09	1.1					
MNI	number		2	4	1			2	1					
	% of MNI		5.2	3.2	0.9			1.3	2.1					
Bos sp. (wild cattle)														
MNB	number	nd	—	—	—	—	—	—	—	—	—	—	—	—
	% of MNB	nd												
MNI	number	1												
	% of MNI	1.9												
Ovibos moschatus (musk-ox)														
MNB	number	—	—	—	2	—	—	—	—	—	—	—	—	—
	% of MNB				ins									
MNI	number				1									
	% of MNI				0.9									

								Sites							
14	15	16	17	18	19	20	21	22	23	24	25	26	27	28	29
44	3677	3979	373	nd	some	some	198	1170	1138	287	nd	>21	246	383	—
88.0	54.4	48.3	25.5	nd	nd	nd	38.3	97.1	99.1	69.0	nd	16.9	48.6	99.1	
1	149	116	15	11	nd	nd	69	17	47	7?	15	12	56	15–20	
20.0	47.3	23.6	6.7	100	nd	nd	81.2	63.0	92.4	44.1	62.5	52.3	56.0	83.5–87.0	
3	2	659	53	—	—	—	64	1	6	53	—	—	—	1	—
6.0	ins	8.0	3.6				12.4	ins	0.5	12.8				0.2	
1	2	61	8				3	1	1	1				1	
20.0	0.6	12.4	3.5				3.5	3.7	1.9	5.9				4.4–5.5	
2	—	17	95	—	—	—	—	14	—	2	—	—	13	—	—
4.0		0.2	6.5					1.3		0.5			2.6			
2		3	13					2		1			7			
40.0		0.6	5.8					7.4		5.9			7.0			
—	2	1	—	—	—	—	—	—	—	—	—	—	—	—	nd
	ins	ins													nd
	1	1													1
	0.3	0.2													4.3
—	—	—	—	—	—	—	1	—	—	—	—	—	—	—	nd
							0.2								nd
							1								1
							1.2								4.3
—	—	—	—	—	—	—	—	—	—	—	—	—	1	—	—
													0.2		
													1		
													1.0		
—	—	1	—	—	—	—	—	—	—	—	—	—	1	—	—
		ins											0.2		
		1											1		
		0.2											1.0		
—	41	444	117	—	—	—	1	6	2	2	nd	10	15	—	—
	0.6	5.4	8.1				0.2	0.5	0.2	0.5	nd	8.2	2.9		
	10	83	25				1	1	1	1	3	1	nd		
	3.2	6.9	11.2				1.2	3.7	1.9	5.9	12.5	4.3	nd		
—	17	19	13	—	—	—	—	—	1	1	—	—	26	—	—
	0.3	0.2	0.9						0.09	0.2			5.1		
	6	5	5						1	1			2		
	1.9	1.0	2.2						1.9	5.9			2.0		
—	—	—	—	—	some	—	—	—	—	—	—	—	—	1	nd
					nd									0.2	nd
					nd									1	1
					nd									4.3–5.5	4.3
—	—	118	—	—	some	—	—	—	—	—	—	—	—	—	—
		1.4			nd										
		17			some										
		3.5			nd										

(continued)

Table 2.7   ECONOMICALLY IMPORTANT FAUNA[a]   (Continued)

		1	2	3	4	5	6	7	8	9	10	11	12	13
Marmota bobac (steppe marmot)														
MNB	number	—	2	nd	4	—	—	37	—	—	—	—	—	—
	% of MNB		0.2	nd	0.1			0.6						
MNI	number		2	25	1			6						
	% of MNI		5.2	20.3	0.9			3.8						
Castor fiber (beaver)														
MNB	number	—	—	—	—	—	—	—	—	—	—	—	—	—
	% of MNB													
MNI	number													
	% of MNI													
Lepus sp. (hare)														
MNB	number	—	—	nd	3	4	—	514	8	1	—	—	—	—
	% of MNB			nd	0.1	ins		9.1	0.6	0.2				
MNI	number			20	2	2		16	1	1				
	% of MNI			16.2	1.7	0.5		10.1	2.1	1.3				
Total count of MNB		nd	1188	nd	2949	>28,754	319	5678	1393[e]	455	nd	nd	nd	nd
Total cost of MNI		52	38	124	116	406	16	158	47[e]	79	nd	nd	nd	nd
References		21, 42	3, 21, 25	25	25, 38, 60, 86	21, 42, 69, 72, 84	40	21, 25, 27, 38	66, 68, 71, 83, 86	38, 40	58	63, 64	63, 64	65

[a]MNI and MNB for economically important and unimportant taxa counted separately. All MNI and MNB are *minimal* and vary in reliability.

[b]Polikarpovich 1968 reported 28 MNB and 14 MNI of Cyprinids; spectral analysis (1978 Geology Institute, AN USSR, Moscow indicate that only half were organic. Calculations here use 14 MNB and 7 MNI.

[c]Genus assigned by excavator or identifier; current taxon category is *Panthera*.

[d]Various Soviet researchers identify this taxon as either *Equus* sp. or *Equus latipes*.

[e]Does not include mammoth.

								Sites								
14	15	16	17	18	19	20	21	22	23	24	25	26	27	28	29
—	—	5	140	—	—	—	—	—	1	—	—	—	3	—	nd
		0.1	9.7						0.09				0.6		nd
		4	31						1				1		18
		0.8	13.9						1.9				1.0		78.5
—	—	—	—	—	—	—	—	—	—	—	—	—	3	—	—
													0.6		
													1		
													1.0		
—	2633	37	86	—	—	—	—	—	—	3	nd	5	4	—	—
	38.9	0.5	5.9							0.7	nd	4.0	0.8		
	79	11	26							1	1	1	nd		
	25.2	2.2	11.6							5.9	4.2	4.3	nd		
50	6764	8273	1463	nd	nd	nd	517	1205	1148	416	nd	124	506	387	nd
5	315	492	222	11	nd	nd	85	27	51	17	24	23	100	18–23	23
21, 42	26, 39, 86	55	37, 66	21, 42	22, 77	3, 74	3, 25	21, 25	25, 40, 86	21, 83, 86	21	70,83, 85	10, 13, 42, 72, 84	8, 21, 42	4, 21

Table 2.8 ECONOMICALLY UNIMPORTANT FAUNA[a]

	Sites						
	1	2	3	4	5	7	8
AVES							
Bubo bubo							
MNB (% of MNB)	nd	—	—	—	1 (2.3)	—	—
MNI (% of MNI)	1 (20.0)				1 (7.7)		
Nyctea scandiaca							
MNB (% of MNB)	—	—	—	—	—	—	—
MNI (% of MNI)							
Alanda arvensis							
MNB (% of MNB)	—	—	—	—	—	—	1 (0.4)
MNI (% of MNI)							1 (nd)
Galerida cristata							
MNB (% of MNB)	—	—	—	—	—	—	1 (0.4)
MNI (% of MNI)							1 (nd)
Corvus corax							
MNB (% of MNB)	—	—	—	—	1 (2.3)	—	—
MNI (% of MNI)					1 (7.7)		
Oenanthe oenanthe							
MNB (% of MNB)	—	—	—	—	—	—	—
MNI (% of MNI)							
Emberiza citrinella							
MNB (% of MNB)	—	—	—	—	—	—	1 (0.4)
MNI (% of MNI)							1 (nd)
Aves sp.							
MNB (% of MNB)	—	—	—	1 (2.6)	—	1 (3.2)	—
MNI (% of MNI)				1 (12.5)		1 (8.3)	
Cricetus cricetus							
MNB (% of MNB)	—	—	nd	10 (26.3)	13 (30.2)	—	—
MNI (% of MNI)			9 (1.2)	3 (37.5)	3 (23.1)		
Cricetus sp.							
MNB (% of MNB)	—	—	—	—	—	—	—
MNI (% of MNI)							
Dicrostonyx ex. gr. *gulielmi-hanseli*							
MNB (% of MNB)	—	—	—	—	—	—	13 (5.9)
MNI (% of MNI)							nd
Dicrostonyx torquatus							
MNB (% of MNB)	—	4 (3.3)	nd	—	7 (16.3)	—	—
MNI (% of MNI)		1 (11.1)	105 (15.1)		1 (7.7)		
Ellobius talpinus							
MNB (% of MNB)	—	—	—	—	—	—	—
MNI (% of MNI)							
Lagurus lagurus							
MNB (% of MNB)	—	—	nd	—	—	—	—
MNI (% of MNI)			248 (35.5)				
Lagurus luteus							
MNB (% of MNB)	—	—	nd	—	—	2 (6.5)	—
MNI (% of MNI)			6 (0.8)			2 (16.8)	
Lemmus obensis							
MNB (% of MNB)	—	—	nd	—	17 (39.5)	—	49 (22.4)
MNI (% of MNI)			7 (1.0)		5 (38.4)		nd

				Sites					
15	16	17	21	22	24	25	26	27	29
3 (0.8)	—	—	—	—	—	—	—	—	—
3 (3.0)									
—	1 (0.3)	—	—	—	—	—	—	2 (4.5)	—
	1 (1.2)							nd	
—	—	9 (0.1)	—	—	—	—	—	—	—
		3 (0.2)							
—	—	4 (ins)	—	—	—	—	—	—	—
		3 (0.2)							
3 (0.8)	—	—	—	—	—	—	—	—	—
1 (1.0)									
3 (0.8)	1 (0.3)	—	—	—	—	—	—	—	—
1 (1.0)	1 (1.2)								
—	—	1 (ins)	—	—	—	—	—	—	—
		1 (ins)							
22 (6.3)	2 (0.6)	315 (6.6)	—	—	1 (100)	nd	1 (100)	1 (2.2)	—
11 (10.9)	2 (2.4)	30 (1.7)			1 (100)	1 (100)	1 (100)	nd	
3 (0.8)	—	—	—	—	—	—	—	—	nd
2 (2.0)									1 (10.0)
—	—	—	—	—	—	—	—	3 (6.8)	—
								nd	
—	—	—	—	—	—	—	—	—	—
—	291 (88.5)	510 (10.8)	—	—	—	—	—	35 (79.6)	—
	56 (69.3)	216 (12.5)						nd	
—	1 (0.3)	—	—	—	—	—	—	—	—
	1 (1.2)								
46 (13.4)	—	1232 (25.8)	—	—	—	—	—	—	—
11 (10.9)		576 (33.3)							
—	—	28 (0.6)	—	—	—	—	—	—	—
		10 (0.6)							
—	—	16 (0.3)	—	3 (60.0)	—	—	—	—	—
		10 (0.6)		1 (50.0)					

(continued)

Table 2.8   ECONOMICALLY UNIMPORTANT FAUNA[a]   (Continued)

	Sites						
	1	2	3	4	5	7	8
MAMMALIA[b]							
Desmana moschata							
MNB (% of MNB)	—	—	nd	—	—	—	—
MNI (% of MNI)			3 (0.4)				
Sorex araneus							
MNB (% of MNB)	—	—	nd	—	—	—	—
MNI (% of MNI)			3 (0.4)				
RODENTIA							
Citellus major							
MNB (% of MNB)	—	—	nd	—	—	15 (48.4)	—
MNI (% of MNI)			15 (2.1)			1 (8.3)	
Citellus rufensis							
MNB (% of MNB)	nd	—	—	—	—	—	—
MNI (% of MNI)	4 (80.0)						
Citellus suslicus							
MNB (% of MNB)	—	—	—	3 (7.9)	—	—	—
MNI (% of MNI)				1 (12.5)			
Citellus sp.							
MNB (% of MNB)	—	—	—	—	—	—	1 (0.4)
MNI (% of MNI)							nd
Arvicola sp.							
MNB (% of MNB)	—	—	nd	—	—	8 (25.8)	—
MNI (% of MNI)			3 (0.4)			4 (33.3)	
Microtus arvalis							
MNB (% of MNB)	—	—	—	—	—	—	—
MNI (% of MNI)							
Microtus gregalis[c]							
MNB (% of MNB)	—	100 (82.6)	nd	—	2 (4.7)	—	43 (19.5)
MNI (% of MNI)		7 (77.8)	247 (35.3)		1 (7.7)		nd
Microtus oeconomus							
MNB (% of MNB)	—	—	—	—	—	—	—
MNI (% of MNI)							
Microtus sp.							
MNB (% of MNB)	—	—	—	—	2 (4.7)	—	111 (50.6)
MNI (% of MNI)					1 (7.7)		nd
Silvimus sibvaticus							
MNB (% of MNB)	—	—	—	—	—	—	—
MNI (% of MNI)							
Allactaga jaculus							
MNB (% of MNB)	—	17 (14.1)	nd	20 (52.7)	—	—	—
MNI (% of MNI)		1 (11.1)	18 (2.5)	1 (12.5)			
Spalax microphthalmus							
MNB (% of MNB)	—	—	—	4 (10.5)	—	5 (16.1)	—
MNI (% of MNI)				2 (25.0)		4 (33.3)	
Spalax podolicus							
MNB (% of MNB)	—	—	—	—	—	—	—
MNI (% of MNI)							
Ochotona pusilla							
MNB (% of MNB)	—	—	nd	—	—	—	—
MNI (% of MNI)			37 (5.3)				
Total count of MNB	nd	121	nd	38	43	31	220
Total count of MNI	5	9	695	8	13	12	nd
References	21	21, 25	25	25, 38, 60	21, 42, 72, 84	21, 25, 38	66, 68, 71

[a]MNI and MNB for economically important and unimportant taxa counted separately. All MNI and MNB are *minimal* and vary in reliability.
[b]For *Homo sapiens*, see Table 2.10.
[c]Genus assigned by excavator or identifier; current taxon category is *Stenocranius*.

	Sites								
15	16	17	21	22	24	25	26	27	29
—	—	43 (0.9) 6 (0.3)	—	—	—	—	—	—	—
—	—	12 (0.2) 6 (0.3)	—	—	—	—	—	—	—
4 (1.2) 3 (3.0)	1 (0.3) 1 (1.2)	90 (1.9) 19 (1.1)	—	—	—	—	—	3 (6.8) nd	—
—	—	—	—	—	—	—	—	—	—
41 (11.8) 13 (12.8)	—	48 (1.0) 16 (0.9)	—	—	—	—	—	—	nd 2 (20.0)
41 (11.8) 13 (12.8)	1 (0.3) 1 (1.2)	—	—	—	—	—	—	—	—
—	1 (0.3) 1 (1.2)	27 (0.6) 17 (0.9)	8 (66.7) 2 (66.7)	—	—	—	—	—	—
19 (5.5) 8 (7.9)	—	—	—	—	—	—	—	—	—
6 (1.7) 3 (3.0)	29 (8.8) 16 (19.9)	1412 (29.5) 620 (35.8)	4 (33.3) 1 (33.3)	—	—	—	—	—	—
—	—	25 (0.5) 11 (0.6)	—	—	—	—	—	—	—
71 (20.6) 11 (10.8)	—	—	—	—	—	—	—	—	—
1 (0.3) 1 (1.0)	—	—	—	—	—	—	—	—	—
—	1 (0.3) 1 (1.2)	629 (13.1) 28 (1.6)	—	2 (40.0) 1 (50.0)	—	—	—	—	—
—	—	—	—	—	—	—	—	—	nd 5 (50.0)
20 (5.8) 7 (6.9)	—	—	—	—	—	—	—	—	—
56 (16.1) 7 (6.9)	—	329 (6.8) 118 (6.8)	—	—	—	—	—	—	—
see Table 2.9 26, 39, 66	329 81 55	see Table 2.9 37, 66	12 3 3, 25	5 2 21, 25	1 1 21	nd 1 21	1 1 21, 70	44 nd 13, 21, 42, 72	nd 9 4, 21

Table 2.9   ECONOMICALLY UNIMPORTANT FAUNA AT MEZHIRICH AND NOVGOROD-SEVERSKII

	MNB		MNI		
	Number	%	Number	%	References
15. MEZHIRICH	347		101		26, 39, 66
Amphibia					
Pelobates fuscus	4	1.1	4	3.0	
Aves					
Vultur vel Gyps	1	0.3	1	1.0	
Haliaetus albicilla	1	0.3	1	1.0	
Strix uralensis	2	0.6	1	1.0	
17. NOVGOROD-SEVERSKII	4783		1732		25, 37, 66
Aves					
Accipitres sp.	1	ins	1	ins	
Circus sp.	1	ins	1	ins	
Falco tinumculus	18	0.4	4	0.2	
Crex crex	1	ins	1	ins	
Porzana porzana	1	ins	1	ins	
Rallus aquaticus	1	ins	1	ins	
Charadrius morinellus	1	ins	1	ins	
Limicola falcinellus	1	ins	1	ins	
Tringa glareola	1	ins	1	ins	
Tringa orythropus	1	ins	1	ins	
Tringa tonatus	1	ins	1	ins	
Vanellus vanellus	1	ins	1	ins	
Chlidonias leucoptera	1	ins	1	ins	
Sterna albifrons	2	ins	2	0.1	
Dryobates medius	1	ins	1	ins	
Jynx torquilla	1	ins	1	ins	
Calandrella cinerea	1	ins	1	ins	
Delichon urbica	1	ins	1	ins	
Hirundo rustica	7	0.1	5	0.3	
Parus cristatus	1	ins	1	ins	
Parus major	1	ins	1	ins	
Anthus campestris	2	ins	2	0.1	
Motacilla alba	1	ins	1	ins	
Lanius collurio	1	ins	1	ins	
Sturnus vulgaris	1	ins	1	ins	
Carduelis carduelis	1	ins	1	ins	
Chloris chloris	1	ins	1	ins	
Passer domesticus	1	ins	1	ins	
Fringica coelebs	1	ins	1	ins	
Mammalia					
Cricetulus migratorius	16	0.3	11	0.6	
Microtus oeconomus	25	0.5	11	0.6	

Table 2.10   HOMINID REMAINS

	Chulatovo I	Khotylevo II	Mezin	Novgorod-Severskii	Pushkari I	Yudinovo
Number of pieces	6	2	1	4	1	1?
Nature of remains	cranial fragments: frontal, parietal	fragments of deciduous tooth and mandible	fragment of lower right molar	one fragment of humerus, three fragments of cranium	crown of deciduous molar	humerus fragment
Age	adult	juvenile	nd	adult	juvenile	nd
References	3	70	55	37	3	10

Table 2.11 ORGANIC ASSEMBLAGES

Site	MNB[a]	MNB/m²	MNI[a]	MNI/m²	Worked bone	Worked bone/m²	Amber	Art[b]	Jewelry[b]	Marine shells	MNB + lithics/m²	MNI + lithics/m²	References
1. Berdyzh	nd	nd	52	0.15	some	nd	—	—	—	—	nd	0.15	42, 79
2. Chulatovo I	1188	3.04	38	0.10	12	0.0300	—	—	—	—	6.10	3.20	3, 36, 73
3. Chulatovo II	nd	nd	124	0.10	6	0.0060	1	—	1 B?	4	nd	13.50	34, 76
4. Dobranichevka[c]	2949	1.50	116	0.06	9	0.0050	12	2 R,S	—	—	8.32	6.90	14, 34, 60
5. Eliseevichi	28,754	46.10	406	0.70	280	0.5000	—	1 M	8 A, 24 B	105	174.57	129.10	20, 42, 82, 84
6. Fastov	319	1.45	16	0.07	—		—	—	—	—	10.00	8.70	14
7. Gontsy	5678	6.90	158	0.20	16	0.0200	some	—	2 Pe	—	10.60	3.90	3, 35
8. Khotylevo II	1393	2.80	47[d]	0.09[d]	300	0.6000	—	16 M	—	—	44.20	41.50	71, 80, 81
9. Kirillovskaya	455	0.06	79	0.01	1?	0.0009	—	3 M	—	—	0.60	0.50	3, 38
10. Klyusy	nd	nd	nd	nd	—		—	—	—	—	nd	nd	58
11. Korshevo I	nd	nd	nd	nd	—		—	—	—	—	nd	nd	63, 64
12. Korshevo II	nd	nd	nd	nd	—		—	—	—	—	nd	nd	63, 64
13. Kositsa	2	0.02	2	0.02	—		—	—	—	—	20.00	20.00	65
14. Kurovo	50	0.20	5	0.02	—		—	—	—	—	0.30	0.10	42
15. Mezhirich	6764	13.30	315	0.60	271	0.5000	348	15 M,R	16 A, 2 P	3	42.60	29.90	26, 39
16. Mezin	8273	6.90	492	0.40	293	0.2000	1	40 M	44 B,A,Pe, 2 Br	800	101.30	94.80	55
17. Novgorod-Severskii	1463	6.10	222	0.90	3	0.0100	—	—	—	—	8.50	3.30	3, 37
18. Novo-Bobovichi	nd	nd	11	nd	—		—	—	—	—	nd	nd	42
19. Bugorok	nd	nd	nd	nd	—		—	—	—	—	nd	nd	3, 22, 77
20. Pogon	nd	nd	nd	nd	—		—	—	—	—	nd	nd	3
21. Pushkari I	517	1.30	85	0.20	5	0.0100	—	—	1 Pe	—	401.30	400.20	3
22. Pushkari II	205	3.50	27	0.50	—		—	—	—	—	5.00	1.50	78
23. Radomyshl'	1148	1.90	51	0.09	—		—	—	—	—	18.60	16.80	54, 56
24. Suponevo	416	2.08	17	0.09	200	1.0000	—	2 M	14 B, 1 Pe, 1 P?	—	151.00	150.00	51, 52
25. Timonovka I	nd	nd	24	0.02	147	0.1000	—	27 M	—	—	nd	85.00	17, 68
26. Timonovka II	124	0.80	23	0.10	2	0.0100	—	1 M	—	9	86.20	85.60	68
27. Yudinovo	506	1.01	100	0.20	some	nd	—	some M	some	150	nd	nd	7, 10, 42, 82, 84
28. Yurovichi	387	1.30	18–23	0.06–0.07	4?	0.0100?	—	1 M	—	—	nd	nd	8, 29, 42
29. Zhuravka	nd	nd	23	0.07	—		—	—	—	—	nd	11.30	4, 44, 45

[a] MNB and MNI from Tables 2.7–2.9.
[b] A, amulet; B, bead; Br, bracelet; E, engraving; M, mammoth ivory; P, pin; Pe, pendant; R, amber; S, sandstone.
[c] Complexes 1 and 3 only.
[d] Exclusive of mammoth.

Table 2.12 RADIOCARBON DATES FOR UPPER PALEOLITHIC SITES

Site and date	Lab No.[a]	Material dated	Provenience	Reference
1. Berdyzh				
23,430 ± 180[b]	LU 104	mammoth tooth	cultural layer	30
5. Eliseevichi				
33,000 ± 400[c]	GIN 80	wood? bone? loess–loam?	cultural layer	24
20,570 ± 430	LE 450	burned wood	unclear	30
17,340 ± 170	LU 360	mammoth tooth	cultural layer	30
15,600 ± 1350	QC 889	burned bone (gas count)	cultural layer	62
14,470 ± 100	LU 126	mammoth tooth	cultural layer	30
12,970 ± 140	LU 102	mammoth tooth	cultural layer	30
7. Gontsy				
13,400 ± 185	QC 898	burned bone	cultural layer, storage pit	62
8. Khotylevo II				
24,950 ± 400	IGAN 73	mammoth tooth	cultural layer	71
23,660 ± 270	LU 359	mammoth tooth	cultural layer	71
15. Mezhirich				
19,280 ± 600	KI 1058	mammoth bone	cultural layer, Dwelling 1	28
19,100 ± 500	KI 1057	burned bone	cultural layer, Dwelling 1	28
18,470 ± 550	KI 1056	burned bone	cultural layer, 1976 excav.	28
18,020 ± 600	KI 1055	burned tooth	cultural layer	28
17,855 ± 950	KI 1054	burned bone	cultural layer, Dwelling 4	26
15,245 ± 1080	QC 900	burned bone (gas count)	cultural layer	62
14,700 ± 500	GIN 2593	mammoth tooth	cultural layer, Dwelling 3	32
14,530 ± 300	GIN 2595	burned bone	cultural layer, Dwelling 2	32
14,320 ± 270	QC 897	burned bone	cultural layer, Dwelling 1	62
14,300 ± 300	GIN 2596	burned bone	cultural layer, Dwelling 4	32
16. Mezin				
29,700 ± 800	KI 1053	shell	cultural layer, 1953 excav.	28
29,100 ± 700	KI 1052	shell	cultural layer, 1953 excav.	28
27,500 ± 800	KI 1051	mammoth tooth	cultural layer, 1953 excav.	28
21,600 ± 2200[b]	GIN 4	mammoth tooth	nd	23
20. Pogon				
18,690 ± 770	LU 361	mammoth tooth	cultural layer	30
21. Pushkari I				
16,775 ± 605	QC 899	burned bone	cultural layer	62
25. Timonovka I				
15,300 ± 700	GIN 2003	burned bone	cultural layer	31
12,200 ± 300	IGAN 82	mammoth tooth	cultural layer	31
26. Timonovka II				
15,110 ± 530	LU 358	mammoth tooth	cultural layer	30
27. Yudinovo				
15,660 ± 180	LU 127	mammoth tooth	cultural layer	30
13,830 ± 850	LU 103	burned bone	cultural layer	30
13,650 ± 200	LU 153	nd	cultural layer	30
28. Yurovichi				
26,470 ± 420[b]	LU 125	mammoth tooth	cultural layer	30

[a]GIN, Institute of Geology, Academy of Sciences, USSR; IGAN, Institute of Geography, Academy of Sciences, USSR; KI, Institute of Geochemistry and Mineral Physics, Academy of Sciences, Uk. SSR; LE, Institute of Archaeology, Leningrad Division, Academy of Sciences, USSR; LU, Leningrad University, USSR; QC, Queens College, City University of New York, USA.

[b]Problematic dates: redeposition.

[c]Problematic date: provenience.

3

The Environmental Given

THE STUDY AREA TODAY

CLIMATE

The climate of the central part of the Russian Plain can be characterized as moderately warm with continentality from west to east (*Soviet Ukraine* 1965). Average annual temperatures, precipitation, and number of frost-free days are listed in Table 3.1. The most prominent climatic feature is an almost latitudinal north-northeast to south-southwest zonation in the distribution of temperature, precipitation, and humidity with maximal temperatures in the southeastern part of the plain. Precipitation and humidity grade from a maximal in the west to a minimal in the east.

The central Russian Plain is an area where two large atmospheric pressure systems meet: the moisture bearing Atlantic air and the southern, hot and dry air mass. The interaction of these air masses throughout the year results in the predominance of mostly southwesterly and westerly winds in the winter and northwesterly and westerly winds in the summer. Maximal precipitation in the form of rain falls in the warm months (July and August). The thickness of the snow cover varies greatly and exhibits a gradation from west to east, with the thickest snow cover in the vicinity of the Carpathians (20–30 cm/year) and the lightest in the steppe region (5–10 cm/year) (*Ukraina—Obschii Obzor* 1969).

FLORA

The area encompasses three distinct ecological zones: (1) the northern mixed forest belt of the Polissya region extending approximately as far south as the city of Kiev (50°26′N); (2) the broad forest–steppe zone from Kiev to approximately Kharkov (50°00′N); and (3) the steppe zone south of Kharkov (*Ukraina—Obschii Obzor* 1969). Upper Paleolithic sites discussed in this work are all found in today's mixed forest and forest–steppe zones.

The Polissya mixed forest belt is a subprovince of the East European deciduous forest, which in the past was far more heavily forested than today. This low-lying area was much affected by the degradation of the Scandinavian Ice Sheet and today is a forest and

Table 3.1   PRESENT-DAY TEMPERATURES AND PRECIPITATION ON THE RUSSIAN PLAIN

City/ locality	Annual temperature (°C)			Annual precipitation (mm/year)		Season of greatest precipitation	Frost-free days (average)
	Average	January	July	General	As snow		
Bryansk[a]	+6	−8.5	+18	560	150	summer	160
Gomel[b]	+6.5	−6.5	+18,5	600	200	summer	220
Kiev[c]	+7.0	−6.5	+19,5	622	190	summer	180

[a]From Markova (1975: Tab. III).
[b]From *Geografiya Byelorussii* (1977: 30, 253).
[c]From *Ukraina—Obschii-Obzor* (1969: 270–273).

swamp biotope. The forest mix is approximately 62% conifer (pine and spruce) and 38% deciduous (oak, birch, aspen, and alder) (*Geografiya Byelorussii* 1977). Nonarboreal meadow grasses primarily grow along the river valleys.

The forest–steppe zone lies south of the Polissya and today has only about 11% of its territory covered by forest. This is a broadleaf forest with a mixture of oak, hornbeam, maple, and linden and a thick undergrowth of hazel (*Ukraina-Obschii Obzor* 1969). Arboreal vegetation predominates on higher elevations and on the right banks of rivers. Grasslands are classified as meadow–steppe, increasing in territory to the south, where they grade off into the true steppe.

FAUNA

Much of the fauna as well as the flora indigenous to the Dnepr–Desna area in the past has disappeared as a result of man's agricultural activities in the last two centuries. Many of the species that played a role in the subsistence practices of Upper Paleolithic hunter–gatherers existed in the area until the recent past. Paleolithic mammals that still existed in the East European forest–steppe in the tenth to the sixteenth centuries are given in Table 3.2. Several species of fish and bird of the Upper Paleolithic exist on the plain today. The avifauna is rich and varied. A comparison of the bird remains found at the Upper Paleolithic sites listed by Umanskaya (1975, 1978) with those currently present in the area (Voitenko 1965) shows that several species of migratory water fowl exploited by Upper Paleolithic hunter–gatherers still exist in the region today (see Table 3.3). Fish present in the Dnepr, Desna, and their tributaries represent both local river varieties and a decreasing number of anadromous fish that come up to spawn from the Black Sea (*Soviet Ukraine* 1965). Lebedev's (1944, 1952) list of fish extant in the rivers today that were exploited by Upper Paleolithic groups is given in Table 3.3. In addition, the presence of anadromous fish such as *Salmo* sp. (salmon) in the Dnepr and Desna in historic times is reported both by Lebedev (1944) and Casteel (1976).

Table 3.2   EAST EUROPEAN FOREST–STEPPE FAUNA, 10–16TH CENTURIES A.D.[a]

Order	Family	Species/common name
Carnivora	Felidae	*Lynx lynx* lynx
	Mustelidae	*Gulo gulo* wolverine
		Lutra lutra otter
		Meles meles badger
	Canidae	*Canis lupus* wolf
		Vulpes corsac corsac fox
		Vulpes vulpes red fox
	Ursidae	*Ursus arctos* brown bear
Perissodactyla	Equidae	*Equus caballus* horse
Artiodactyla	Suidae	*Sus scrofa* wild boar
	Cerviadae	*Alces alces* moose
		Capreolus capreolus roe deer
		Cervus elaphus red deer
	Bovidae	*Bison priscus* bison
		Bos sp. cattle
		Saiga tatarica saiga antelope
Rodentia	Scuiridae	*Marmota bobac* steppe marmot
	Castoridae	*Castor fiber* beaver
Lagomorpha	Leporidae	*Lepus europaeus* European hare

[a]Adapted from Kirikov (1979).

Table 3.3   PLEISTOCENE BIRDS AND FISH STILL REPORTED IN THE AREA TODAY

Order	Family	Species/common name
Bird		
Anseriformes	Anatidae	*Anas* sp. duck
		Anser sp. geese
		Cygnus sp. swan
Charadriiformes	Laridae	*Larus* sp. gull
Fish		
Protacanthepterygii	Essocidae	*Esox lucious* pike
Cypriniformes	Cyprinidae	*Abramis* sp. bream
		Luciscus sp. ide fish
		Rutilus rutilus roach fish
Saluriformes	Saluridae	*Salurius glanis* cat fish
Perciformes	Percoidae	*Lucioperca lucioperca* pike-perch
		Perca fluviatilis perch

GENERAL FEATURES OF THE LATE VALDAI

SOME CAUTIONARY NOTES ON PALEOENVIRONMENTAL RECONSTRUCTION

The nature of the evidence used for paleoenvironmental reconstruction—geological, paleobotanical, and paleontological—involves a number of major problems. While our record to Pleistocene climate and environment is most complete for the late Pleistocene, and especially for the terminal period considered in this work, the evidence itself is problematic. Often, for example, information derived from one line of evidence is either not confirmed or even contradicted by that from another. It is important, therefore, to briefly consider some limitations of the data base as paleoenvironmental indicators.

Geological data in the study area come from strata that may be either discontinuous or absent at key localities. The nature of particular deposits is also innately connected with highly localized events. Granulometric, morphometric, and chemical analyses of sediments have produced some important though controversial paleoenvironmental information in France, information that appears to be fine enough for reconstruction of climate on the 10^3-year time scale (see Laville *et al.* 1980; Movius 1977). Such gross scales, however, while of general interest, are not fine enough for most questions about past human adaptations. Similar analyses of sediments in the study area have not yielded information fine enough to record climatic oscillations within the late Valdai (i.e., the period between 25,000 and 10,000 B.P.) (e.g. figures and tables in Velichko, Zavernyaev *et al.* 1981; Gerasimov and Velichko 1982).

Paleobotanical evidence has always been an important component in the reconstruction of past environments in the study area. But a number of problems exist with this data source as well. First, as Gubonina (1975) notes, pollen and spores preserve better in relic soils than in loess. This means that the amount of pollen and spores present in deposits on the central Russian Plain is inversely related to the thickness of loess cover—increasing from north to south. Another important factor that contributes to possible error is the differential preservation rates for various plants. Birks writes: "Studies of modern pollen deposition in arctic and subarctic areas have shown that several major components of the vegetation are poorly registered in the pollen rain. . . . for example, the abundant lichens, mosses, and low-growing herbs are absent or are barely represented in modern assemblages" (1981:338). Because the late Valdai central Russian Plain was covered by periglacial forest–steppe vegetation and was climatically similar to present-day high latitude regions, this factor is an important one to consider in the reconstruction of late Valdai environment.

A more serious problem is pointed out by Davis (1976). She notes that plant migration does not occur instantaneously after a climatic change, but that it occurs at varied rates for various species and, most important, is limited by the migration speed of different species. This means that the sudden arrival of a species, limited as it is by its migration speed, cannot be attributed to a change in climate. Nor, by analogy, can the absence of a species be taken as evidence of unfavorable conditions. Davis' work implies that pollen evidence should not be synchronic with the geological evidence—the two sets of data clearly must be out of step with each other. This factor is confirmed by Wright (1976), who reports that the three or more ice lobe fluctuations in the Wolf Creek area of the New World between 20,000 and 12,000 B.P. are not matched by systematic change in the pollen profile. He postulates that the reason for this discrepancy may be either that the glacial advances resulted from nonclimatic causes or, more likely, that pollen is not sensitive enough to show climatic changes of the magnitude involved in glacial fluctuations.

Paleontological data are also problematic. As the faunal tables in this chapter demonstrate, species that were exploited by man in late Valdai—presumably fairly sympatric— are today found in very different biogeographic zones. This necessarily points to the existence of unique environmental conditions that have no present-day analogues. Microfauna, avifauna, and molluscs, both economically important and unimportant species, also demonstrate unique environmental mixes. Furthermore, avifauna are not particularly direct environmental barometers, reflecting presence or absence of arboreal vegetation rather than climatic factors, and molluscs are at best indicators of fresh- or saltwater and crude water-temperature categories.

Finally, paleontological data, coming as they do from primary and secondary consumers, cannot be perfectly synchronized with paleobotanical data. Bones of consumers, by necessity, will appear later than the paleobotanical data that reflects the presence of primary producers. The presence of a particular species in the record cannot signal the onset of a climatic change but, rather, can only reflect events that have already occurred.

In summary, this enumeration of problems with paleoenvironmental data indicates that at present we cannot with any degree of accuracy document small-scale climatic fluctuations in the late Valdai, nor can we reconstruct an uninterrupted climatic sequence. All that can be done is to present more or less synchronized glimpses into paleoenvironments at different points in the late Valdai. Disparate amounts of information are available for this, however. In this section I describe general climatic, floral, and faunal features of late Valdai environments. In the following sections I focus on changes that can be monitored through time.

CLIMATE

The late Valdai was a period of climatic degradation that saw a progression of ever-increasing cold temperatures coupled with decreasing precipitation. Halcheva's (1975) granulometric and chemical analyses of Valdai loess and soils show that the period saw a progressive reduction of the role played by chemical agents in erosion and an increase in the importance of wind erosion. Chebotareva and Makaricheva (1974) document the correlation of warm episodes with increased presence of moisture and the co-occurance of cold and dry periods. Grichuk (1969a,b) has profiled Valdai stadials as beginning with cold and wet conditions that in time changed to cold and dry ones.

Extremely cold temperatures and the presence of permanently frozen ground in the study area is documented by two cryogenic horizons in the deposits. Velichko (1979) notes such periglacial features as ice wedge casts and polygons both in Loess II and Loess III. These features are associated with permanently frozen ground. The extent of the permafrost and the distribution of periglacial features is illustrated in Figure 3.1.

Low temperatures in the late Valdai resulted from the maximal advance of the Scandinavian Ice Sheet, which not only lowered the overall temperatures but also possibly created temperature inversions. Butzer (1971) suggests that the area affected by such an inversion would have extended 1000–1500 km beyond the major continental glaciers. Such an inversion would have affected the whole of the central Russian Plain. The presence of the ice sheet also profoundly affected the atmospheric circulation and resulted in precipitation sequences different from those of today. The progressively increasing aridity of this period is well documented in the literature (see Butzer 1976; Colinvaux 1981; Davis 1976; Peterson *et al.* 1979; Velichko 1961; Wright 1976). Wright (1976) attributes this increasing aridity to the secondary effects of the presence of the huge ice sheets to the north. Butzer (1976) adds the contributing role of cooler ocean surface water and greater atmospheric stability over the tropics.

Estimated precipitation figures for this period are presented in Table 3.4. They show a reduction in both annual precipitation averages and also a substantial decline in the amount of winter precipitation in the form of snow. Butzer (1971), citing Poser's work, reports that much of the Russian Plain was in a low-pressure zone in the summers, and Frenzel (1973) writes that the prevailing wind directions during the last glacial were similar to today's. Voznyachuk *et al.* (1969) suggest a difference in the wind patterns for this period. They believe that the presence and growth of the ice sheet to the north of the study area would have effectively blocked much of the moisture-bearing Atlantic and oceanic currents. Finally, Velichko (1982a) writes that multielement anticyclonic circulation during winter months with prevailing north and northeast air-mass direction would have resulted in both low temperatures and low humidity during the late Valdai and especially during the Valdai maximum. This indicates that the bulk of precipitation during the period fell in warm months and that the study area had a light winter snow cover.

FLORA

The uniqueness of the late Valdai vegetation has been amply attested to in the literature (Butzer 1971; Colinvaux 1967; Frenzel 1973; Grichuk 1969a, 1975; Lundelius 1976). The central Russian Plain, which today lies in the forest belt, was during the late Valdai covered by open, nonarboreal vegetation, which has been variously classified. Grichuk (1969a) writes that it was neither a tundra, a forest, nor a steppe, but a unique periglacial floral community, and he terms the tundra and steppe-like vegetation of the interfluves and loess plains "periglacial steppe." Numerous other terms have appeared in the literature to describe this environment, both in the Old and New Worlds, and numerous arguments still exist as to whether it was more steppe-like or tundra-like (Butzer 1971; Colvinaux 1967; Frenzel 1973; Grichuk 1969a,b, 1972; Grichuk *et al.* 1975). We can, however, generally characterize the central Russian Plain as covered by a

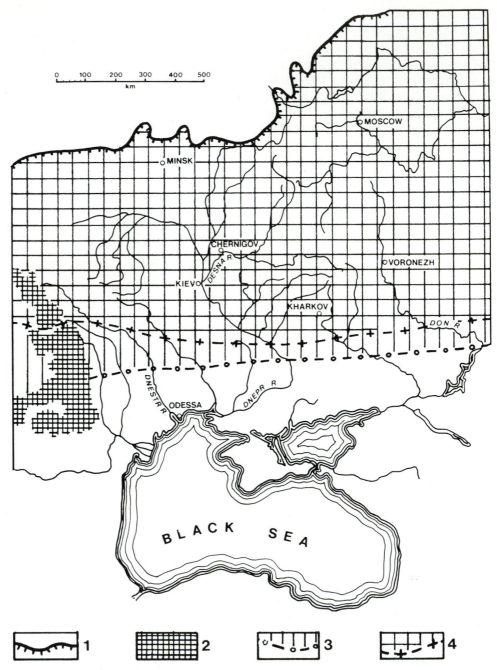

Figure 3.1 Extent of permafrost on the Russian Plain during the Valdai Glaciation: 1, ice sheet; 2, mountains; 3, after the glacial maximum; 4, after Bryansk Interstadial (after Velichko 1977: Maps 14,15).

Table 3.4   LATE VALDAI CLIMATE

	Temperature (°C)			Frost-free days per year	Precipitation (mm)	
	January	July	Annual averages		Average per year	As snow per year
Bryansk Interstadial 25,000 B.P.						
—[a]	−30−−40°	nd	nd	nd	600	200
microfauna[b]	−16−−18°	−18−+20°	nd	nd	150–400	20–120
Post-Bryansk time 24,000–20,000 B.P.						
Khotylevo II[c]	−17−−18°	+17.0°	+0.4	nd	300–400	60–120
flora[d]	−32.5°	+13.5°	nd	106.5	350	110
fauna[d]	−18.0°	+17.0°	nd	106.5	350	110
Valdai maximum 20,000–18,000 B.P.						
—[e]	nd	nd	−2−−4°	nd	nd	nd
—[f]	−32−−35°	+8−+12°	−9−−14°	90?	60–110	20–120
microfauna[b]	−30−−40°	+16−+18°	nd	nd	nd	nd
Post-maximum 18,000–12,000 B.P.						
Chulatovo II[b]	−12−−18°	+16−+20°	nd	nd	120–400	30–120
Mezin[b]	−20−−40°	+17−+21°	nd	nd	60–500	20–120
Novgorod-Severskii[b]	−13−−16°	+22−+23°	nd	nd	80–380	30–120
Timonovka II[d]	−30−−34°	+18−+20°	−3−−10°	80–100	200	50

[a]From Velichko (1973).
[b]From Markova (1975, 1982).
[c]From Zelikson and Monoszon (1974).
[d]From Velichko, Zavernyaev et al. (1981).
[e]From Frenzel (1973).
[f]From Butzer (1976).

unique tundra–grassland with sparce arboreal vegetation that was most densly distributed along the river valleys in the form of gallery forests. A comparison of pollen diagrams reflecting the vegetation of the area at various times during the late Valdai (see Figures 2.27, 2.49, 2.62, and 2.110) shows the predominance of nonarboreal vegetation at all times after the Bryansk Interstadial. The diagrams, however, also show that some tree growth was always present in the area in the form of *Pinus* sp., *Betula* sp., and *Larix* sp. stands; these at times included some deciduous elements, such as *Quercus* sp.

As was indicated in the introduction to this chapter, the central Russian Plain today includes three distinct ecological zones: the northern mixed forest, the broad forest–steppe, and the southern steppe. This zonation reflects the distribution of climatic belts in the area. Vastly different climatic conditions during the late Valdai created a different biogeography in the study area. Velichko (1973; Velichko and Morozova 1969, 1982) postulates the absence of these broad climatic and vegetational belts during the late

Valdai. Instead he suggests that the central Russian Plain was part of a vast "hyperzone" that existed south of the Scandinavian Ice Sheet. During this period of periglacial hyperzonality, which lasted until the retreat of the ice sheets, there was no vegetational differentiation by latitude as today—rather, the whole plain was thickly covered by very similar vegetation—herbaceous plants with components of semidesert or salt-tolerant species (Butzer 1976; Grichuk 1972).

Caution must be taken, however, with this reconstruction. Many of the arguments presented to support Velichko's thesis focus on the uniqueness of this environment, and various theories have been offered to explain the supposed high productivity of these "low-latitude tundras" (Butzer 1971; Vereschagin 1979). An important component of these arguments, however, is paleontological evidence showing that large numbers and a great variety of herbivores were supported by the environment. Using analogies to present-day grasslands and their carrying capacities, the arguments state that a region supporting such a mass of primary consumers must indeed have been very productive. A discordant note, however, has been sounded by the work of Cwynar and Ritchie (1980; Ritchie and Cwynar 1982) in the Yukon. Working with late Glacial environments in Alaska, a Pleistocene environment considered to be quite similar to that of periglacial Eurasia, they note that the pollen record does not support the "Arctic steppe" concept. Specifically, they suggest that the pollen diagrams from the late Pleistocene period are not that dissimilar from those of the area today—implying that the environment was not a rich-grazing, cold steppe capable of supporting teeming multitudes of herbivores, but rather a type of an arctic steppe–tundra. They caution researchers modeling the environment of the period to concentrate on models of a harsh environment supporting small populations of vertebrates and not to use the analogues of the species-rich contemporary African savanna (cf. Matthews 1982).

Extensive research in Alaska and Siberia suggests that these seeming incongruities can be resolved by considering not only the overall numbers of species present but also their distribution across the Pleistocene landscape (Schweger 1982; Yurtsev 1982). This important issue is considered in greater detail in the final section of this chapter.

Fauna

Some Additional Problems and Caveats.   In Chapter 2, I presented a listing of faunal remains found at the Upper Paleolithic sites in the study area (Tables 2.7–2.10). These lists constitute most of our late Valdai collection. There are no late Valdai paleontological collections from sites or localities away from river valleys. This precludes the possibility of considering possible differences in the spatial distribution of the different species across the central Russian Plain landscape.

As Guthrie (1968, 1982) has shown, differences existed in Pleistocene Alaska between the herbivore communities inhabiting the floodplains and those in the interfluves. Similar differences probably also existed on the central Russian Plain, but at present they have neither been recognized nor studied.

The presence of extinct species in the collections creates numerous difficulties for paleoenvironmental reconstruction as well. The ecological requirements for some of the extinct species are still a subject of debate among specialists. Mammoths, for example, are considered by some to have been grazers (Butzer 1971; Guthrie 1968; Kurten 1968; Vereschagin 1979), others see them as browsers (Pidoplichko 1969, 1976), and still others argue that they were mixed browser–grazers (Bliss and Richards 1982; Ermolova 1963; Velichko, Grekhova, and Gubonina 1977). Kornietz (1962) reported that stomach contents of frozen mammoths found in Siberia were ambiguous: The Indigirka mammoth of Yakutia had remains of *Pinus* and *Picea* shoots in its stomach, the Berezovka mammoth's stomach held steppe grasses, and the Novosibirskii Island and Taymyr mammoths showed a mixture of twigs, leaves, and grasses. Vereschagin and Baryshnikov (1982) have pointed out that at present we know only summer feeding habits of mammoths which were those of grazers. They postulate that in winter months browsing would have played a far more important role in the subsistence strategies of this taxon. Because of this, the mammoth should be considered a mixed browser–grazer whose presence in the assemblages need not reflect the exclusive presence of either grassland or forest environments. I have therefore placed this taxon in a category of species found widely distributed in different vegetational zones.

Even less is known of the ecological requirements of *Coelodonta antiquitatis*. Opinion in the literature tends to link the distribution of the woolly rhinoceros with that of the mammoth (Butzer 1971; Kurten 1968). Vereschagin and Baryshnikov (1982) postulate a mixed seasonal strategy of grazing in the summer and browsing in the winter for the woolly rhinoceros. I have placed this taxon, too, in a category of widely distributed species not suitable as environmental indicators.

Taxa Recovered.   Table 3.5 groups various species found in the study area into specific ecological zones. This table reflects a unique mix of species that today are either extinct or found in very different environments. The late Pleistocene central Russian Plain contained megafauna that are now present only in the tundra (e.g., *Ovibos moschatus*) or tundra and boreal forests (e.g., *Rangifer tarandus*), together with pure steppe forms such as *Equus* sp. and forest forms such as *Cervus elaphus*. Smaller herbivores, carnivores, and omnivores also reflect this unique mix. We find such species as *Sus scrofa,* found in deciduous forests today, with tundra dwellers such as *Alopex lagopus,* steppe dwellers like *Marmota bobac* and *Vulpes corsac,* and boreal forest dwellers such as *Lynx lynx.*

The microfauna (Tables 3.6–3.8) also shows this mix of steppe (e.g., *Citellus* sp.), tundra (e.g., *Dicrostonyx torquatus, Microtus gregalis*), forest–steppe (*Silvimus sybvaticus*) and forest (*Sorex araneus*) species.

Remains of birds (Tables 3.9–3.12) are mixed as well, and we find such tundra species as *Lagopus lagopus* and *Nyctea scandia* together with forest–steppe dwellers like *Crex crex, Corvus corax,* and *Bubo bubo.*

The mollusca (Tables 3.13–3.15), like the mammals, reflect both the economic pursuits of late Pleistocene hunter–gatherers and the late Valdai environment. Some marine shells found at the sites were collected as fossils from the Karangat and possibly Sarmat marine deposits around the Black Sea and Sea of Azov (Motuz 1969; Polikarpovich 1968; Rudenko 1959; Shovkoplyas 1965a). Their presence obviously reflects the

Table 3.5   ECOLOGICAL PROVENIENCE OF FAUNA[a]

	Tundra	Tundra–forest	Forest						Forest–steppe		Steppe		Wide range						
	Arctic fox	Musk-ox	Beaver	Boar	Brown bear	Giant deer	Lynx	Wolverine	Bison	Wild cattle	Corsac fox	Horse	Fox	Hare	Hyena	Red deer	Wolf	Mammoth	Woolly rhinoceros
Berdyzh	+				+					+		+					+	+	+
Chulatovo I	+				+			+	+			+					+	+	+
Chulatovo II	+				+	+			+			+		+	+		+	+	+
Dobranichevka	+	+			+			+	+				+[b]	+			+	+	+
Eliseevichi	+				+			+				+	+[b]	+		+	+	+	
Fastov													+						
Gontsy	+		+		+		+	+	+					+			+	+	
Khotylevo II	+				+			+	+					+			+	+	+
Kirillovskaya					+			+						+			+	+	+
Korshevo I																		+	
Korshevo II																		+	
Kositsa																		+	
Kurovo												+					+	+	+
Mezhirich	+		+		+			+	+		+[b]	+	+	+			+	+	+
Mezin	+	+	+		+	+		+	+			+	+	+			+	+	+
Novgorod-Severskii	+				+		+		+			+	+	+			+	+	+
Novo-Bobovichi																		+	
Bugorok		+								+								+	
Pogon																		+	
Pushkari I	+				+							+				+	+	+	
Pushkari II	+				+							+		+			+	+	+
Radomyshl'									+			+						+	
Suponevo	+				+				+			+		+			+	+	+
Timonovka I	+				+									+			+	+	+
Timonovka II	+				+			+						+		+	+	+	
Yudinovo	+		+	+	+				+		+[b]		+				+	+	+
Yurovichi	+									+	+							+	
Zhuravka			+							+			+			+	+		

[a] + = present.
[b] Questionable classification; may be arctic fox.

cultural practices of Upper Paleolithic groups in the region, and so they are omitted from this discussion. The remainder of the mollusca represent a mix of species that today also inhabit very different environments. Zhadin (1965) and Likhachev and Rammel'meier (1962) list the present-day distribution of both aquatic and terrestrial mollusca in the USSR. These lists show that such species as *Unio pietorium* and *Sphaerium solidum,* which were found in late Valdai deposits together with such cold-loving forms as *Anisus contorius* and *Pupilla muscorum,* today prefer warm waters.

The co-occurrence of species that today have widely different ecological requirements ostensibly supports Velichko's concept of environmental hyperzonality during the late Valdai. As I noted previously, however, the paleoenvironmental reconstructions available in the literature fail to consider the question of the distribution of these species across the landscape. The same criticism can be addressed to the faunal data presented in this section. It too gives the overall presence of a multitude of species but fails to consider their distribution. The co-occurrence of these disparate taxa at the sites was a result of the late Pleistocene environment and, more important, of the cultural practices of late Pleistocene hunter–gatherers.

Table 3.6   ECOLOGICAL PROVENIENCE OF MICROFAUNA: MNI

	Sites											
	1	2	3	4	5	7	15	16	17	21	22	29
Tundra												
Dicrostonyx torquatus	—	1	105	—	1	—	—	56	216	—	—	—
Lemmus obensis	—	—	7	—	5	—	—	—	10	—	1	—
Microtus gregalis	—	7	247	—	1	—	—	16	620	1	—	—
total	—	8	362	—	7	—	—	72	846	1	1	—
percent	—	88.9	51.3	—	63.6	—	—	93.5	50.6	25.0	50.0	—
Forest–tundra												
Sorex araneus	—	—	3	—	—	—	—	—	6	—	—	—
Microtus arvalis	—	—	—	—	—	—	8	—	—	—	—	1
Microtus oeconomus	—	—	—	—	—	—	—	—	11	—	—	—
total	—	—	3	—	—	—	8	—	17	—	—	1
percent	—	—	0.4	—	—	—	10.5	—	1.0	—	—	11.1
Forest												
Sorex araneus	—	—	3	—	—	—	—	—	6	—	—	—
total	—	—	3	—	—	—	—	—	6	—	—	—
percent	—	—	0.4	—	—	—	—	—	0.4	—	—	—
Forest–steppe												
Desmana mochata	—	—	3	—	—	—	—	—	6	—	—	—
Silvimus sibvaticus	—	—	—	—	—	—	1	—	—	—	—	—
total	—	—	3	—	—	—	1	—	6	—	—	—
percent	—	—	0.4	—	—	—	1.3	—	0.4	—	—	—
Steppe												
Citellus major	—	—	15	—	—	1	3	1	19	—	—	—
Citellus rufensis	4	—	—	—	—	—	—	—	—	—	—	—
Citellus suslicus	—	—	—	1	—	—	13	—	16	—	—	2
Citellus sp.	—	—	—	—	—	—	—	1	—	—	—	—
Cricetulus migratorius	—	—	—	—	—	—	—	—	11	—	—	—
Cricetus cricetus	—	—	9	3	3	—	2	—	—	—	—	1
Ellobius talpinus	—	—	—	—	—	—	—	—	1	—	—	—
Lagurus lagurus	—	—	248	—	—	—	11	—	576	—	—	—
Lagurus luteus	—	—	6	—	—	2	7	—	10	—	—	—
Allactaga jaculus	—	1	18	1	—	—	13	1	28	1	1	—
Spelax microtus	—	—	—	2	—	4	—	—	—	—	—	—
Spelax podolicus	—	—	—	—	—	—	7	—	—	—	—	5
Ochotona pusilla	—	—	37	—	—	—	—	—	118	—	—	—
total	4	1	333	7	3	7	56	4	778	1	1	8
percent	100	11.1	47.1	100	37.3	64.0	73.7	5.2	46.6	25.0	50.0	88.9
Wide-ranging												
Arvicola sp.	—	—	3	—	—	4	—	1	17	2	—	—
Microtus sp.	—	—	—	—	1	—	11	—	—	—	—	—
total	—	—	3	—	1	4	11	1	17	2	—	—
percent	—	—	0.4	—	9.1	36.0	14.5	1.3	1.0	50.0	—	—
	4	9	707	7	11	11	76	77	1670	4	2	9

Table 3.7   ECOLOGICAL PROVENIENCE OF MICROFAUNA: MNB

	Sites										
	2	4	5	7	8	15	16	17	21	22	27
Tundra											
Dicrostonyx ex. gr. *gulielmi-hanseli*	—	—	—	—	13	—	—	—	—	—	—
Dicrostonyx torquatus	4	—	7	—	—	—	291	510	—	—	35
Lemmus obensis	—	—	17	—	49	—	—	16	—	3	—
Microtus gregalis	100	—	2	—	43	6	29	1412	4	—	—
total	104	—	36	—	105	6	320	1938	4	3	35
percent	86.0	—	70.6	—	48.3	1.9	98.5	43.8	33.3	60.0	85.4
Forest-tundra											
Sorex araneus	—	—	—	—	—	—	—	12	—	—	—
Microtus arvalis	—	—	—	—	—	19	—	—	—	—	—
Microtus oeconomus	—	—	—	—	—	—	—	25	—	—	—
total	—	—	—	—	—	19	—	37	—	—	—
percent	—	—	—	—	—	6.2	—	0.8	—	—	—
Forest											
Sorex araneus	—	—	—	—	—	—	—	12	—	—	—
total	—	—	—	—	—	—	—	12	—	—	—
percent	—	—	—	—	—	—	—	0.2	—	—	—
Forest–steppe											
Desmana mochata	—	—	—	—	—	—	—	43	—	—	—
Silvimus sibvaticus	—	—	—	—	—	1	—	—	—	—	—
total	—	—	—	—	—	1	—	43	—	—	—
percent	—	—	—	—	—	0.3	—	1.0	—	—	—
Steppe											
Citellus major	—	—	—	15	—	4	1	90	—	—	3
Citellus suslicus	—	3	—	—	—	41	—	48	—	—	—
Citellus sp.	—	—	—	—	1	—	1	—	—	—	—
Cricetulus migratorius	—	—	—	—	—	—	—	16	—	—	—
Cricetus cricetus	—	—	13	—	—	3	—	—	—	—	—
Cricetus sp.	—	10	—	—	—	—	—	—	—	—	3
Ellobius talpinus	—	—	—	—	—	—	1	—	—	—	—
Lagurus lagurus	—	—	—	—	—	46	—	1232	—	—	—
Lagurus luteus	—	—	—	2	—	—	—	28	—	—	—
Allactaga jaculus	17	20	—	—	—	4	1	629	—	2	—
Spelax microtus	—	4	—	5	—	56	1	—	—	—	—
Spelax podolicus	—	—	—	—	—	20	—	—	—	—	—
Ochotona pusilla	—	—	—	—	—	—	—	329	—	—	—
total	17	37	13	22	1	211	5	2372	—	2	6
percent	14.0	100.0	25.5	73.4	0.5	68.6	1.5	53.6	—	40.0	14.6
Wide-ranging											
Arvicola sp.	—	—	—	8	—	—	—	27	8	—	—
Microtus sp.	—	—	2	—	111	71	—	—	—	—	—
total	—	—	2	8	111	71	—	27	8	—	—
percent	—	—	3.9	26.6	51.2	23.0	—	0.6	66.7	—	—
	121	37	51	30	217	308	325	4429	12	5	41

Table 3.8   ECOLOGICAL PROVENIENCE OF MICROFAUNA: NUMBER OF SPECIES

	Sites													
	1	2	3	4	5	7	8	15	16	17	21	22	27	29
Tundra														
number	—	2	3	—	3	—	3	1	2	3	1	1	1	1
percent	—	66.7	23.0	—	60.0	—	60.0	9.0	28.6	20.0	25.0	50.0	50.0	25.0
Forest–tundra														
number	—	—	1	—	—	—	—	1	—	2	—	—	—	—
percent	—	—	7.7	—	—	—	—	9.0	—	13.3	—	—	—	—
Forest														
number	—	—	1	—	—	—	—	—	—	1	—	—	—	—
percent	—	—	7.7	—	—	—	—	—	—	6.7	—	—	—	—
Forest–steppe														
number	—	—	1	—	—	—	—	1	—	1	—	—	—	—
percent	—	—	7.7	—	—	—	—	9.0	—	6.7	—	—	—	—
Steppe														
number	1	1	6	4	1	3	1	7	4	7	1	1	1	3
percent	100.0	33.3	42.6	100.0	20.0	75.0	20.0	64.0	57.1	46.6	25.0	50.0	50.0	75.0
Wide-ranging														
number	—	—	1	—	1	1	1	1	1	1	2	—	—	—
percent	—	—	7.7	—	20.0	25.0	20.0	9.0	14.3	6.7	50.0	—	—	—
Total number of taxa	1	3	13	4	5	4	5	11	7	15	4	2	2	4
Ecology of taxa[a]	S	Ts	Stf	S	Ts	S	Ts	Stf	ST	Stf	Ts?	TS	TS	St

[a] F, forest; S, steppe; T, tundra; capitals denote major ecology; lower-case letters denote minor ecology. Reference on ecology of microfauna after Markova (1975, 1982).

--------- **THE BRYANSK INTERSTADIAL: 27,000–24,000 B.P.**

CLIMATE

This relatively warm period of the late Valdai, according to Velichko and his associates, had a slightly warmer climate and an appreciably greater precipitation than existed later. Levkovskaya (1977) describes this period as one with climate warmer than in the subsequent glacial maximum but colder and wetter than found in the area today. During the Bryansk Interstadial the annual precipitation was greater than 600 mm/year, of which more than 200 mm fell as snow (Table 3.4).

Analysis of the Bryansk soil layer itself has led Morozova (1969) to conclude that it was formed under permafrost conditions. She notes that the soil horizon is similar in microstructure to the soils in central Yakutia, where cryogenic processes operate today. Translating these observations into climatic implications, Velichko, Gribchenko *et al.* (1977) suggest that the January temperatures may have been as low as those found in central Yakutia: −30° to −40°C. The nature of the periglacial deformations associated

Table 3.9 ECOLOGICAL PROVENIENCE OF AVIFAUNA[a]

	Berdyzh		Dobrani-chevka		Eliseevichi		Khotylevo II		Mezhirich		Mezin		Novgorod-Severskii		Yudinovo	
	MNB	MNI	MNB	MNI	MNB	MNI	MNB	MNI	MNB	MNI	MNB	MNI	MNB	MNI	MNB	MNI
TUNDRA																
All Terrestrial																
Lagopus lagopus[b]																
number	—	—	1	1	1	1	80	10	66	21	14	7	21	5	2	nd
percent			50.0	50.0	33.3	33.3	65.1	31.3	59.5	45.7	77.9	63.6	5.8	5.2	66.7	nd
Nyctea scandica																
number	—	—	—	—	—	—	—	—	—	—	1	1	—	—	—	—
percent											5.5	9.1				
FOREST																
Terrestrial																
Limicola falcinellus																
number	—	—	—	—	—	—	—	—	—	—	—	—	1	1	—	—
percent													0.2	1.0		
Tringa glareola																
number	—	—	—	—	—	—	—	—	—	—	—	—	1	1	—	—
percent													0.2	1.0		
Tringa orythropus																
number	—	—	—	—	—	—	—	—	—	—	—	—	1	1	—	—
percent													0.3	1.0		
Tringa tonatus																
number	—	—	—	—	—	—	—	—	—	—	—	—	1	1	—	—
percent													0.2	1.0		
Chlidonias leucoptera																
number	—	—	—	—	—	—	—	—	—	—	—	—	1	1	—	—
percent													0.2	1.0		
Sterna albifrons																
number	—	—	—	—	—	—	—	—	—	—	—	—	2	2	—	—
percent													0.4	2.0		
Strix uralensis																
number	—	—	—	—	—	—	—	—	2	1	—	—	—	—	—	—
percent									1.8	2.1						
Dryobates medius																
number	—	—	—	—	—	—	—	—	—	—	—	—	1	1	—	—
percent													0.2	1.0		
Jynx torquilla																
number	—	—	—	—	—	—	—	—	—	—	—	—	1	1	—	—
percent													0.2	1.0		
Alanda arvensis																
number	—	—	—	—	—	—	1	1	—	—	—	—	9	3	—	—
percent							0.8	3.1					2.1	3.0		
Galerida cristata																
number	—	—	—	—	—	—	1	1	—	—	—	—	4	3	—	—
percent							0.8	3.1					0.9	3.0		
Calandrella cinerea																
number	—	—	—	—	—	—	—	—	—	—	—	—	1	1	—	—
percent													0.2	1.0		

Table 3.9   (Continued)

	Berdyzh		Dobrani-chevka		Eliseevichi		Khotylevo II		Mezhirich		Mezin		Novgorod-Severskii		Yudinovo	
	MNB	MNI	MNB	MNI	MNB	MNI	MNB	MNI	MNB	MNI	MNB	MNI	MNB	MNI	MNB	MNI
Delichon urbica																
number	—	—	—	—	—	—	—	—	—	—	—	—	1	1	—	—
percent													0.2	1.0		
Hirundo rustica																
number	—	—	—	—	—	—	—	—	—	—	—	—	7	5	—	—
percent													1.7	5.1		
Parus cristatus																
number	—	—	—	—	—	—	—	—	—	—	—	—	1	1	—	—
percent													0.2	1.0		
Sturnus vulgaris																
number	—	—	—	—	—	—	—	—	—	—	—	—	1	1	—	—
percent													0.2	1.0		
Chloris chloris																
number	—	—	—	—	—	—	—	—	—	—	—	—	1	1	—	—
percent													0.2	1.0		
Passer domesticus																
number	—	—	—	—	—	—	—	—	—	—	—	—	1	1	—	—
percent													0.2	1.0		
Emberiza citrinella																
number	—	—	—	—	—	—	1	1	—	—	—	—	1	1	—	—
percent							0.8	3.1					0.2	1.0		
Aquatic																
Larus argentatus[b]																
number	—	—	—	—	—	—	34	14	—	—	—	—	—	—	—	—
percent							27.7	43.7								
Larus ridibundus[b]																
number	—	—	—	—	—	—	—	—	—	—	—	—	1	1	—	—
percent													0.2	1.0		
Gavia arctica[b]																
number	—	—	—	—	—	—	3	2	—	—	—	—	—	—	—	—
percent							2.4	6.3								
Porzana porzana																
number	—	—	—	—	—	—	—	—	—	—	—	—	1	1	—	—
percent													0.2	1.0		
Rallus aquaticus																
number	—	—	—	—	—	—	—	—	—	—	—	—	1	1	—	—
percent													0.2	1.0		
Charadrius morinellus																
number	—	—	—	—	—	—	—	—	—	—	—	—	1	1	—	—
percent													0.2	1.0		
Motacilla alba																
number	—	—	—	—	—	—	—	—	—	—	—	—	1	1	—	—
percent													0.2	1.0		

(continued)

Table 3.9   ECOLOGICAL PROVENIENCE OF AVIFAUNA[a]   (*Continued*)

	Berdyzh		Dobrani-chevka		Eliseevichi		Khotylevo II		Mezhirich		Mezin		Novgorod-Severskii		Yudinovo	
	MNB	MNI	MNB	MNI	MNB	MNI	MNB	MNI	MNB	MNI	MNB	MNI	MNB	MNI	MNB	MNI
FOREST/FOREST–STEPPE																
Terrestrial																
Lyrurus tetrix[b]																
number	—	—	—	—	—	—	—	—	5	1	—	—	1	1	—	—
percent									4.5	2.1			0.2	1.0		
Crex crex																
number	—	—	—	—	—	—	—	—	—	—	—	—	1	1	—	—
percent													0.2	1.0		
Parus major																
number	—	—	—	—	—	—	—	—	—	—	—	—	1	1	—	—
percent													0.2	1.0		
Oenanthe oenanthe																
number	—	—	—	—	—	—	—	—	3	1	1	1	—	—	—	—
percent									2.7	2.1	5.5	9.1				
Anthus campestris																
number	—	—	—	—	—	—	—	—	—	—	—	—	2	2	—	—
percent													0.5	2.0		
Aquatic																
Anas sp.[b]																
number	—	—	—	—	—	—	2	2	1	1	—	—	31	13	—	—
percent							1.6	6.3	0.9	2.1			7.2	13.3		
Anser sp.[b]																
number	—	—	—	—	—	—	—	—	3	3	—	—	2	2	—	—
percent									2.7	6.4			0.5	2.0		
Bucephala clangula[b]																
number	—	—	—	—	—	—	1	1	—	—	—	—	—	—	—	—
percent							0.8	3.1								
Cygnus sp.[b]																
number	—	—	—	—	—	—	—	—	1	1	—	—	—	—	—	—
percent									0.9	2.1						
Circus sp.																
number	—	—	—	—	—	—	—	—	—	—	—	—	1	1	—	—
percent													0.2	1.0		
Vanellus vanellus																
number	—	—	—	—	—	—	—	—	—	—	—	—	1	1	—	—
percent													0.2	1.0		
FOREST–STEPPE																
All Terrestrial																
Haliaetus albicilla																
number	—	—	—	—	—	—	—	—	1	1	—	—	—	—	—	—
percent									0.9	2.1						
Bubo bubo																
number	nd	1	—	—	1	1	—	—	3	3	—	—	—	—	—	—
percent	nd	100.0			33.3	33.3			2.7	6.4						

Table 3.9   (Continued)

	Berdyzh		Dobrani-chevka		Eliseevichi		Khotylevo II		Mezhirich		Mezin		Novgorod-Severskii		Yudinovo	
	MNB	MNI	MNB	MNI	MNB	MNI	MNB	MNI	MNB	MNI	MNB	MNI	MNB	MNI	MNB	MNI
Corvus corax																
number	—	—	—	—	1	1	—	—	3	1	—	—	—	—	—	—
percent					33.3	33.3			2.7	2.1						
Lanius colluria																
number	—	—	—	—	—	—	—	—	—	—	—	—	1	1	—	—
percent													0.2	1.0		
Fringica coelebs																
number	—	—	—	—	—	—	—	—	—	—	—	—	2	2	—	—
percent													0.5	2.0		
WIDE-RANGING																
Vultur vel Gyps																
number	—	—	—	—	—	—	—	—	1	1	—	—	—	—	—	—
percent									0.9	2.1						
Accipitres sp.																
number	—	—	—	—	—	—	—	—	—	—	—	—	1	1	—	—
percent													0.2	1.0		
Falco tinumculus																
number	—	—	—	—	—	—	—	—	—	—	—	—	18	4	—	—
percent													4.0	4.0		
Carduelis carduelis																
number	—	—	—	—	—	—	—	—	—	—	—	—	1	1	—	—
percent													0.2	1.0		
Aves																
number	—	—	1	1	—	—	—	—	22	11	2	2	315	30	1	nd
percent			50.0	50.0					19.8	24.1	11.2	18.2	71.8	30.7	33.3	nd
		1	2	2	3	3	123	32	111	46	18	11	440	98	3	

[a]From Landsborough-Thompson (1964); Umanskaya (1975, 1978).
[b]Economically important taxa.

with this layer led Velichko (1969b) to conclude that permafrost was present and had a seasonal thaw layer ranging from 0.4 m in the north to perhaps as much as 1 to 1.5 m in the south. The moderate nature of these deformations and the fact that only medallions and not full-scale polygon nets are present suggest that the climate was less severe than in subsequent periods.

No data exist about the location of atmospheric pressure belts over the region during this period. This information is lacking for all of the subdivisions of the late Valdai considered in this section.

FLORA

The vegetational cover during the Bryansk Interstadial is fairly well known from extensive pollen samplings (Table 3.16). Grichuk (1969a, 1969c), working with pollen

Table 3.10 COMPOSITION OF AVIFAUNA (NUMBER AND PERCENTAGE)[a]

	Berdyzh	Dobranichevka	Elisee-vichi	Khotylevo II	Mezhirich	Mezin	Novgorod-Severskii	Yudinovo
TOTAL								
taxa	1	2	3	8	12	4	37	2
MNB	nd	2 (100.0)	3 (100.0)	123 (100.0)	111 (100.0)	18 (100.0)	440 (100.0)	3 (100.0)
MNI	1 (100.0)	2 (100.0)	3 (100.0)	32 (100.0)	46 (100.0)	11 (100.0)	98 (100.0)	nd (100.0)
AQUATIC								
Economically important								
Forest								
taxa	—	—	—	1 (12.5)	—	—	1 (2.7)	—
MNB	—	—	—	34 (27.7)	—	—	1 (0.2)	—
MNI	—	—	—	14 (43.7)	—	—	1 (1.0)	—
Forest/forest–steppe								
taxa	—	—	—	2 (25.0)	3 (25.0)	—	2 (5.4)	—
MNB	—	—	—	3 (2.4)	5 (4.5)	—	33 (7.9)	—
MNI	—	—	—	3 (9.4)	5 (10.6)	—	15 (16.0)	—
Forest–steppe								
taxa	—	—	—	—	—	—	—	—
MNB	—	—	—	—	—	—	—	—
MNI	—	—	—	—	—	—	—	—
Total								
taxa	—	—	—	3 (37.5)	3 (25.0)	—	3 (8.1)	—
MNB	—	—	—	37 (30.1)	5 (4.5)	—	34 (8.1)	—
MNI	—	—	—	17 (53.1)	5 (10.6)	—	16 (17.0)	—
Economically unimportant								
Forest								
taxa	—	—	—	1 (12.5)	—	—	4 (10.8)	—
MNB	—	—	—	3 (2.4)	—	—	4 (0.8)	—
MNI	—	—	—	2 (6.3)	—	—	4 (4.0)	—
Forest/forest–steppe								
taxa	—	—	—	—	—	—	2 (5.4)	—
MNB	—	—	—	—	—	—	2 (0.4)	—
MNI	—	—	—	—	—	—	2 (2.0)	—
Forest–steppe								
taxa	—	—	—	—	—	—	—	—
MNB	—	—	—	—	—	—	—	—
MNI	—	—	—	—	—	—	—	—
Total								
taxa	—	—	—	1 (12.5)	—	—	6 (16.2)	—
MNB	—	—	—	3 (2.4)	—	—	6 (1.2)	—
MNI	—	—	—	2 (6.3)	—	—	6 (6.0)	—
Total aquatic								
taxa	—	—	—	4 (50.0)	3 (25.0)	—	9 (24.3)	—
MNB	—	—	—	40 (32.5)	5 (4.5)	—	40 (9.3)	—
MNI	—	—	—	19 (59.4)	5 (10.6)	—	22 (23.0)	—
TERRESTRIAL								
Economically important								
Tundra								
taxa	—	1 (50.0)	1 (33.3)	1 (12.5)	1 (8.3)	1 (25.0)	1 (2.7)	1 (50.0)
MNB	—	1 (50.0)	1 (33.3)	80 (65.1)	66 (59.5)	14 (77.9)	21 (5.1)	2 (66.7)
MNI	—	1 (50.0)	1 (33.3)	10 (31.3)	21 (45.7)	7 (63.6)	5 (5.4)	nd

(continued)

Table 3.10   (*Continued*)

	Berdyzh	Dobranichevka	Elisee-vichi	Khotylevo II	Mezhirich	Mezin	Novgorod-Severskii	Yudinovo
Forest								
taxa	—	—	—	1 (12.5)	—	—	1 (2.7)	—
MNB	—	—	—	1 (0.8)	—	—	4 (1.0)	—
MNI	—	—	—	1 (3.1)	—	—	3 (3.3)	—
Forest/forest–steppe								
taxa	—	—	—	—	1 (8.3)	—	1 (2.7)	—
MNB	—	—	—	—	5 (4.5)	—	1 (0.2)	—
MNI	—	—	—	—	1 (2.1)	—	1 (1.0)	—
Forest–steppe								
taxa	—	—	—	—	—	—	—	—
MNB	—	—	—	—	—	—	—	—
MNI	—	—	—	—	—	—	—	—
Total								
taxa	—	1 (50.0)	1 (33.3)	2 (25.0)	2 (16.7)	1 (25.0)	3 (8.1)	1 (50.0)
MNB	—	1 (50.0)	1 (33.3)	81 (65.9)	71 (64.0)	14 (77.9)	26 (6.3)	2 (66.7)
MNI	—	1 (50.0)	1 (33.3)	11 (34.4)	22 (47.8)	7 (63.6)	9 (9.7)	nd
Economically unimportant								
Tundra								
taxa	—	—	—	—	1 (25.0)	—	—	—
MNB	—	—	—	—	1 (5.5)	—	—	—
MNI	—	—	—	—	1 (9.1)	—	—	—
Forest								
taxa	—	—	—	2 (25.0)	1 (8.3)	—	16 (43.3)	—
MNB	—	—	—	2 (1.6)	2 (1.8)	—	32 (7.7)	—
MNI	—	—	—	2 (6.2)	1 (2.1)	—	24 (25.1)	—
Forest/forest–steppe								
taxa	—	—	—	—	1 (8.3)	1 (25.0)	3 (8.1)	—
MNB	—	—	—	—	3 (2.7)	1 (5.5)	4 (0.9)	—
MNI	—	—	—	—	1 (2.1)	1 (9.1)	4 (4.2)	—
Forest–steppe								
taxa	1 (100.0)	—	2 (66.7)	—	3 (25.0)	—	2 (5.4)	—
MNB	nd	—	2 (66.7)	—	7 (6.3)	—	3 (1.2)	—
MNI	1 (100.0)	—	2 (66.7)	—	5 (10.6)	—	3 (2.2)	—
Wide-ranging								
taxa	—	1 (50.0)	—	—	2 (16.7)	1 (25.0)	4 (10.8)	1 (50.0)
MNB	—	1 (50.0)	—	—	23 (20.8)	2 (11.2)	335 (75.1)	1 (33.3)
MNI	—	1 (50.0)	—	—	12 (26.2)	2 (18.2)	36 (34.8)	nd
Total								
taxa	1 (100.0)	2 (100.0)	2 (66.7)	2 (25.0)	7 (58.3)	3 (75.0)	25 (67.6)	1 (50.0)
MNB	nd	2 (100.0)	2 (66.7)	2 (1.6)	35 (31.6)	4 (22.1)	374 (84.9)	1 (33.3)
MNI	1 (100.0)	2 (100.0)	2 (66.7)	2 (6.2)	19 (41.0)	4 (36.4)	67 (66.3)	nd
Total terrestrial								
taxa	1 (100.0)	2 (100.0)	3 (100.0)	4 (50.0)	9 (75.0)	4 (100.0)	28 (75.7)	2 (100.0)
MNB	nd	2 (100.0)	3 (100.0)	83 (67.5)	106 (95.6)	18 (100.0)	390 (91.2)	2 (100.0)
MNI	1 (100.0)	2 (100.0)	3 (100.0)	13 (40.6)	41 (88.8)	11 (100.0)	76 (76.0)	nd
Ecology based on all economically unimportant terrestrial avifauna[b]	FS (100.0)	WR (100.0)	FS (100.0)	F (100.0)	T (12.5) F (12.5) FFS (12.5) FS (37.5) WR (2.5)	FFS (50.0) WR (50.0)	F (64.0) FFS (12.0) FS (8.0) WR (16.0)	WR (100.0)

[a] From Landsborough-Thompson (1964); Umanskaya (1975, 1978).
[b] F, forest; FFS, forest/forest–steppe; T, tundra; WR, wide-ranging.

Table 3.11   ECOLOGY BASED ON ECONOMICALLY UNIMPORTANT AVIFAUNA (NUMBER AND PERCENTAGE)[a]

	Berdyzh	Dobrani-chevka	Elisee-vichi	Khotylevo II	Mezhirich	Mezin	Novgorod-Severskii	Yudinovo
All taxa	1	2	3	8	12	4	37	2
Economically unimportant								
taxa	1 (50.0)	1 (50.0)	2 (66.7)	3 (37.5)	6 (50.0)	3 (75.0)	32 (86.5)	1 (50.0)
MNB	nd	1 (100.0)	2 (100.0)	5 (100.0)	34 (100.0)	4 (100.0)	384 (100.0)	1 (50.0)
MNI	1 (100.0)	1 (100.0)	2 (100.0)	4 (100.0)	18 (100.0)	4 (100.0)	77 (100.0)	nd
Tundra								
taxa	—	—	—	—	—	1 (33.3)	—	—
MNB	—	—	—	—	—	1 (25.0)	—	—
MNI	—	—	—	—	—	1 (25.0)	—	—
Forest								
taxa	—	—	—	3 (100.0)	1 (16.7)	—	20 (62.5)	—
MNB	—	—	—	5 (100.0)	2 (5.9)	—	39 (10.1)	—
MNI	—	—	—	4 (100.0)	1 (5.6)	—	31 (40.2)	—
Forest/forest–steppe								
taxa	—	—	—	—	1 (16.7)	1 (33.3)	5 (15.6)	—
MNB	—	—	—	—	3 (8.8)	1 (25.0)	6 (1.6)	—
MNI	—	—	—	—	1 (5.6)	1 (25.0)	6 (7.8)	—
Forest–steppe								
taxa	1 (100.0)	—	2 (100.0)	—	3 (50.0)	—	2 (6.3)	—
MNB	nd	—	2 (100.0)	—	7 (20.5)	—	3 (0.8)	—
MNI	1 (100.0)	—	2 (100.0)	—	5 (27.8)	—	3 (3.9)	—
Wide-ranging								
taxa	—	1 (100.0)	—	—	1 (16.6)	1 (33.3)	5 (15.6)	1 (100.0)
MNB	—	1 (100.0)	—	—	22 (64.8)	2 (50.0)	336 (87.6)	1 (100.0)
MNI	—	1 (100.0)	—	—	11 (61.0)	2 (50.0)	37 (48.0)	nd
Ecology based on[b]								
taxa	FS (100.0)	WR (100.0)	FS (100.0)	F (100.0)	F (16.7)	T (25.0)	F (62.5)	WR (100.0)
					FFS (16.7)	FFS (25.0)	FFS (15.6)	
					FS (50.0)	WR (50.0)	FS (6.3)	
					WR (16.6)		WR (15.6)	
MNB	nd	WR (100.0)	FS (100.0)	F (100.0)	F (5.9)	T (25.0)	F (10.0)	WR (100.0)
					FFS (8.8)	FFS (25.0)	FFS (1.7)	
					FS (20.5)	WR (50.0)	FS (6.8)	
					WR (64.8)		WR (87.6)	
MNI	FS (100.0)	WR (100.0)	FS (100.0)	F (100.0)	F (5.6)	T (33.3)	F (39.4)	nd
					FFS (5.6)	FFS (33.3)	FFS (8.4)	
					FS (27.8)	WR (33.3)	FS (4.2)	
					WR (61.0)		WR (48.0)	

[a]From Landsborough-Thompson (1964); Umanskaya (1975, 1978).
[b]F, forest; FFS, forest/forest–steppe; FS, forest–steppe; T, tundra; WR, wide-ranging.

data from nine geological localities, reconstructed the vegetational cover of the northern portion of the central Russian Plain as a mixed forest of at least 45% arboreal vegetation. The forests had a mix of coniferous and deciduous species such as *Quercus* sp. and *Tilia* sp. Such warmth-loving species as *Carpinus betulus* and *Tilia* sp. led Grichuk to conclude that the climate may have been milder than today—a suggestion clearly at odds with Levkovskaya's (1977). He further indicates, however, that per-

Table 3.12   ECOLOGY BASED ON ECONOMICALLY IMPORTANT AVIFAUNA (NUMBER AND PERCENTAGE)[a]

	Berdyzh	Dobrani-chevka	Elisee-vichi	Khotylevo II	Mezhirich	Mezin	Novgorod-Severskii	Yudinovo
All taxa	1	2	3	8	12	4	37	3
Economically important								
taxa	—	1 (50.0)	1 (33.3)	5 (62.5)	5 (41.7)	1 (25.0)	6 (16.2)	1 (50.0)
MNB	—	1 (100.0)	1 (100.0)	118 (100.0)	72 (100.0)	14 (100.0)	60 (100.0)	2 (100.0)
MNI	—	1 (100.0)	1 (100.0)	28 (100.0)	27 (100.0)	7 (100.0)	25 (100.0)	nd
Tundra								
taxa	—	1 (100.0)	1 (100.0)	1 (20.0)	1 (25.0)	1 (100.0)	1 (16.7)	1
MNB	—	1 (100.0)	1 (100.0)	80 (67.9)	66 (91.5)	14 (100.0)	21 (35.0)	2 (100.0)
MNI	—	1 (100.0)	1 (100.0)	10 (35.7)	21 (77.8)	7 (100.0)	5 (20.0)	nd
Forest								
taxa	—	—	—	2 (40.0)	—	—	2 (33.3)	—
MNB	—	—	—	35 (29.6)	—	—	5 (8.3)	—
MNI	—	—	—	15 (53.6)	—	—	4 (16.0)	—
Forest/forest–steppe								
taxa	—	—	—	2 (40.0)	3 (75.0)	—	3 (50.0)	—
MNB	—	—	—	3 (2.5)	6 (8.5)	—	35 (56.7)	—
MNI	—	—	—	3 (10.7)	6 (22.2)	—	16 (64.0)	—
Forest–steppe								
taxa	—	—	—	—	—	—	—	—
MNB	—	—	—	—	—	—	—	—
MNI	—	—	—	—	—	—	—	—
Wide-ranging								
taxa	—	—	—	—	—	—	—	—
MNB	—	—	—	—	—	—	—	—
MNI	—	—	—	—	—	—	—	—
Ecology based on[b]								
taxa	—	T (100.0)	T (100.0)	T (20.0) F (40.0) FFS (40.0)	T (25.0) FFS (75.0)	T (100.0)	T (16.7) F (33.3) FFS (50.0)	T (100.0)
MNB	—	T (100.0)	T (100.0)	T (67.9) F (29.6) FFS (2.5)	T (91.5) FFS (8.5)	T (100.0)	T (35.0) F (8.3) FFS (56.7)	T (100.0)
MNI	—	T (100.0)	T (100.0)	T (35.7) F (53.6) FFS (10.7)	T (77.8) FFS (22.2)	T (100.0)	T (20.0) F (16.0) FFS (64.0)	nd

[a]From Landsborough-Thompson (1964); Umanskaya (1975, 1978).
[b]F, forest; FFS, forest/forest–steppe; FS, forest–steppe; T, tundra.

Table 3.13   UTILIZED MOLLUSCS[a]

	Chulatovo II	Eliseevichi	Mezhirich	Mezin	Timonovka I	Yudinovo
	n	n	n	n	n	n
Gastropoda						
Gibbula mega	—	—	—	—	—	1
Nerita sp.	—	—	—	—	3	—
Theodoxus pullasi[b]	—	—	—	—	—	3
Cyclope neritea	—	—	—	—	—	2
Cerithium rubiginosum	—	—	—	1	—	—
Cerithium vulgatum	—	—	—	31	1?	—
Vermicularia sp.[c]	—	>101	—	—	—	—
Buccinum carbianum	—	—	—	91	—	—
Buccinum dublicatum	—	—	—	39	—	—
Buccinum opinabile	—	—	—	29	—	—
Buccinum subspinosum	—	—	—	1	—	—
Buccinum superabile	—	—	—	1	—	—
Buccinidae	—	—	—	45	—	—
Nassa reticulata[d]	—	—	2	40	1?	141
Bivalva						
Cardium edule	—	—	—	—	—	2
Cardium sp.	—	—	—	1	—	—
Ostrea sp.	>2	—	—	—	—	—
Didacna pullasi	—	—	—	—	—	1
Cephalopoda						
Balemnites sp.	—	—	—	10	—	—
Mollusca	—	4	1	—	6	—
References[e]	(1)	(2,3,10)	(4,11)	(4,5)	(2,10)	(2,9)

[a]Fossil shells used for personal decoration. All numbers represent minimal values; Shovkoplyas (1965a) reported over 800 at Mezin, but only those identified are listed here.

[b]Genus assigned by excavator or identifier; *Nerita* in current terminology.

[c]May also include *Serpula*.

[d]Genus assigned by excavator or identifier; *Nassarius* in current terminology.

[e]1, Chepalyga (1983) personal communication; 2, Polikarpovich (1968). 3, Museum of History, Minsk, and Institute of History, An BSSR, Minsk; 4, Pidoplichko (1969); 5, Rudenko (1959); 8, Pidoplichko (1947b); 9, Motuz (1969); 10, Museum of Anthropology and Ethnology, Leningrad; 11, Institute of Zoology, AN UK SSR, Kiev.

iglacial hyperzonality was already present, as no changes are detected in the soil zones over 1000-km stretches of the central Russian Plain.

The southern part of the central Russian Plain, around the middle reaches of the Dnepr, had more open vegetation. Paskevich and Dubnyak (1978) and Dolukhanov and Paskevich (1976) report that a number of pollen profiles from the Ukraine suggest a forest–steppe zone with a mix of 52% NAP and 44% AP in the profiles from Dobranich-evka. The forest was mixed, with *Pinus silvestris* predominating, but remains of *Betula* sp. and *Alnus* sp. are also represented, as is the pollen of such broadleaves as *Quercus* sp., *Ulmus* sp., *Tilia* sp., *Capriaus* sp., and *Corylus* sp. Grasses are represented by Gramineae, Chenopodiaceae, and Labiatae. These authors reconstruct the landscape of the mid-Dnepr valley as one where terraces were covered by pine forests, while river

Table 3.14   NONUTILIZED MOLLUSCS[a]

	Ecology of taxa[b]	Gontsy	Eliseevichi	Mezhirich	Mezin	Novgorod-Severskii	Yudinovo
Aquatic							
Gastropoda							
Valvata piscinalis	C	—	—	x	—	—	—
Valvata pulchella	T	—	—	x	—	—	—
Radix lagotis	C	—	—	x	—	—	—
Radix ovata	C	—	—	x	—	—	—
Galba truncatula	C	—	—	x	—	—	—
Physa fontinalis	C	—	—	x	—	—	—
Planorbis planorbis	C	—	—	x	—	—	—
Anisus contortus	C	—	—	x	—	—	—
Anisus spirorbis	C	—	—	x	—	—	—
Gyraulus grendleri	C	—	—	x	—	—	—
Segmentina nitida	T	—	—	x	—	—	—
Lithoglyphus natocoides	H	—	—	—	—	—	x
Bivalva							
Anodonta sp.	WR	—	—	—	—	x	—
Unio sp.	H	3	—	—	—	—	—
Sphaerium solidum	H	—	—	—	—	x	—
Pisidium amnicum	H	—	—	x	—	—	—
Terrestrial							
Gastropoda							
Carychium minimum	T	—	—	x	—	—	—
Succinea elegans	T	—	—	x	—	—	—
Succinea oblonga	C	—	—	x	xxx	—	—
Succinea putris	C–WR	—	—	x	—	—	—
Cochlicopa lubrica	WR	—	—	x	—	—	—
Vertigo antivertigo	T	—	—	x	—	—	—
Vertigo costata	nd	—	—	x	—	—	—
Columella edentula	WR	—	—	x	—	—	—
Pupilla muscorum	C	—	—	x	xxx	x	—
Vallonia costata	WR	—	—	—	x	—	—
Vallonia oblongata	WR	—	—	x	—	—	—
Vallonia pulchella	WR	—	—	x	—	—	—
Vallonia tenuilabris	C	—	—	x	xxx	—	—
Chondrula tridens	WR	—	—	x	—	—	—
Retinella hammonis	WR	—	—	x	—	—	—
Euconulus fulvus	T	—	—	x	—	—	—
Helicolomax pellucidus	C	—	—	—	x	—	—
Eulota fruticum	WR	—	—	x	—	—	—
Zenobiella rubiginosa[c]	C	—	—	x	x	x	—
Mollusca		—	4	—	—	—	—
References[d]		(4)	(2,3,10)	(4,11)	(4,5)	(8)	(2,9)

[a]Ordering of taxa per Morton 1979. x, some; xxx, many.
[b]Ecology of Mollusca from Likhachev and Rammel'meier (1962); Zhadin (1965). C, cold-loving; T, temperate-loving; H, warm-loving; WR, wide-ranging.
[c]Genus assigned by excavator or identifier; Monacha is current terminology.
[d]See references, Table 3.13.

Table 3.15 ECOLOGY OF NONUTILIZED MOLLUSCS

	Gontsy		Eliseevichi		Mezhirich		Mezin		Novgorod-Severskii		Yudinovo	
	n	%	n	%	n	%	n	%	n	%	n	%
Wide-ranging	—		—		8	29.0	1	16.6	1	25.0	—	
Cold-loving	—		—		12	43.0	4	66.8	2	50.0	—	
Temperate-loving	—		—		6	21.0	1	16.6	—		—	
Warm-loving	1	100	—		1	3.5	—		1	25.0	1	100
No data	—		some	100	1	3.5	—		—		—	
	1		1?		28		6		4		1	

valleys and other low-lying regions such as ravines held broadleaf growth, including *Alnus* sp. on especially moist terraines. The interfluves and plateaus were covered with meadow–steppe vegetation. Pashkevich notes that, as today, the regions on the right bank of the Dnepr probably had greater tree cover than those on the left bank, where a more open steppe vegetation prevailed.

It is important to note here a caveat offered by Grichuk (1969a) to the accuracy of this pollen-based climatic reconstruction for the period of Bryansk soil formation. The pollen profiles, because of the nonsynchronized nature of the relationship of climate

Table 3.16 POLLEN FROM BRYANSK SOIL DEPOSITS[a]

	Arapovichi	Mezin	Priluki	Vyazovok	Gun'ki	Kamenka	Molochnaya	Kostenki I	Kostenki XVII
Total AP (%)	45	70	44–70	58–74	8	18–43	10–22	12–35	15–50
Picea	+	−	+	+	−	−	−	+	+
Pinus (*P. silvestris*)	+	+	+	+	+	+	+	+	+
Betula (*B. pubescens* and *B. verucosa*)	+	+	+	+	+	+	+	+	+
Alnus	+	+	+	+	+	+	−	+	+
Carpinus (*C. betulus* L.)	+	+	−	−	−	+	−	+	+
Corylus (*C. avellana*)	+	+	+	−	+	−	+	+	+
Quercus (*Q. robur*)	+	+	+	+	+	+	+	+	+
Ulmus	−	+	−	+	+	−	+	+	+
U. campestris and *U. laevis*	−	−	−	−	+	−	−	−	+
Tilia (*T. cordata* Mill.)	−	+	+	+	−	+	+	+	+
Tilia platyrhylica	−	−	−	−	−	−	−	−	+
Acer	−	−	−	−	+	−	−	−	−
Fraxinus	−	−	−	−	−	−	−	−	−
Elaeagnus sp.	−	−	−	−	+	−	−	−	+

[a]After Grichuk (1969c: 455).

and vegetation, may well represent the climate of an earlier and warmer part of the Bryansk Interstadial and, therefore, reflect the vegetation that existed earlier than the formation of the dated soil layer. This nonsynchronic relationship also explains the divergent climatic evidence for this period presented by pollen and soil data. Since soil processes respond quicker to climatic conditions, the pedological evidence presented above probably reflects more accurately the climate of this time than does the pollen.

Fauna

Only one Upper Paleolithic site, Yurovichi, has yielded a ^{14}C date (26,470 ± 420 [LU 125]) that falls in the Bryansk Interstadial (Table 2.12). As noted in Chapter 2, the assemblage found at Yurovichi has been redeposited, the site has been only superficially examined, and the date itself is quite unfirm. Fauna collected at the site is very sparse and contains the ubiquitous late Pleistocene mix of large herbivores and a single carnivore. The mix can in no way contribute to paleoclimatic reconstruction. No microfauna, avifauna, ichthyofauna, or molluscs are known from the site.

According to Frenzel (1973), fauna dating to the warm periods of the last glacial tend to suggest a tundra environment and, as such, are out of step with the pollen data. This observation holds true for the microfauna found at key Bryansk soil horizon localities (e.g., Mezin, Arapovichi). Markova (1975) reports the presence of such steppe forms as *Citellus* sp., *Alactaga jaculis,* and *Lagurus lagurus* together with such tundra species as *Dicrostonyx torquatus*. She reconstructs the climate at this time as severe continental, colder than found in the region today.

Conclusion

Keeping in mind the contradictory evidence presented by the paleobotanical and paleontological data, we can reconstruct the environment of the Bryansk Interstadial as follows: (1) it was one with a continental climate possibly slightly colder than today; (2) annual precipitation was at least as great as today; and (3) the central Russian Plain was covered by a mixed forest in the north and a mosaic of mixed forest and meadow–steppe in the south.

ENVIRONMENT BETWEEN 24,000 AND 20,000 b.p.

Soviet researchers see the period between 24,000 and 20,000 b.p. as one with steadily deteriorating climatic conditions during which the Scandinavian Ice Sheet gradually reached its maximal size (e.g. Chebotareva and Makaricheva 1974). They do not delineate any oscillations during this time, although evidence from points further west in Europe suggest that there may have indeed been a halt in the growth of the ice and a warm episode at about 21,000 b.p. Two sites have been dated to this period: Khotylevo II (23,660 ± 270 [LU 359]) and the problematic site of Berdyzh (23,430 ± 180 [LU 104]).

CLIMATE

The lower section of Loess II dates from this period. Morozova (1969) indicates that this lower section was deposited in warmer and wetter periods than was the top of Loess II. While conditions were still relatively mild, cryogenic processes continued to operate during this period and permafrost conditions were present in the study area (Velichko 1973, 1979; Velichko, Grekhova, and Gubonina 1977). In general, we can conclude that moderately continental and moist conditions prevalent during the Bryansk Interstadial increased in severity and continentality and were accompanied by a decrease in precipitation. Estimated temperatures and precipitation rates show that summer temperatures decreased by as much as 5–7°C for July, while mean January temperatures did not differ that much from the preceding Bryansk period. January temperatures were perhaps as much as 10–25°C lower than today, with the mean year-round temperature as much as 4°C lower (Velichko, Grekhova, and Gubonina 1977; Velichko, Grekhova, and Udartsev 1977). Increasing aridity during this time appears to have been continent wide. Peterson *et al.* (1979) report a major precipitation decline occurring in continental climates at about 21,000 B.P.

FLORA

A number of pollen profiles exist for this period. Pollen diagrams from the Upper Paleolithic sites of Khotylevo II and Dobranichevka are presented in Figures 2.27 and 2.49. Layers dating to this time are indicated on the diagrams. In general, they show that the northern part of the central Russian Plain was covered by a periglacial forest–steppe. Grichuk (1972) notes some lateral differentiation in the distribution of the vegetation: The presence of forest–steppe in the western part of the plain, which gradually increased in steppe associations to the east.

Pollen from Khotylevo II shows that the surrounding countryside was covered by a periglacial, cold forest–steppe with NAP vegetation represented by 76–91% of the pollen. The 9–24% AP pollen present represents such species as *Picea abies, Pinus silvestris, Betula pubescens, B. verrucosa, B. nana,* and *B. humilis*—all cold-loving boreal and arctic forms. These were distributed in sparce stands and primarily concentrated in gallery forests along the low-lying river valleys. Somewhat greater presence of tree cover is suggested for this period by Serebryannaya (1972). She analyzed pollen from the geological site of Karachizh near the city of Bryansk and found Loess II profiles more boreal than steppe in nature. She suggests that the landscape was covered by *Pinus* and *Betula* forests with widespread green moss cover and scattered meadows with open vegetation.

Grichuk (1969a,b) noted a change in climate in Loess II at the Arapovichi type-site on the Desna. Pollen spectra here included such cold but moisture loving taxa as *Chenopodium vulgaria, Altiplacs tatarica,* and *Artemisia lat.*

No pollen sampling was done at Berdyzh, but Kalechitz (1972, 1973) suggests that the spectra collected at a nearby geological locality, Shapurovo, are contemporaneous with the Berdyzh strata. These indicate a periglacial tundra–steppe vegetation with presence of *Picea* and *Betula* riverine gallery forests. As noted before, great problems exist with both the stratigraphic context at this site and the nature of the cultural layer; the paleoenvironmental evidence offered by Kalechitz, therefore, can be considered only tentative.

Vegetation of the mid-Dnepr basin can be reconstructed from Dobranichevka pollen data. Pashkevich and Dubnyak (1978) date samples from the 3.5-m depth to this period: AP represents 32% of the sample and includes *Pinus, Betula,* and *Alnus,* as well as singular grains of *Salix;* 50% is of NAP vegetation and includes *Chenopodiaceae, Poaceae, Cyperaceae, Rosaceae, Plumaginaceae,* and *Convolvulaceae* families. Pashkevich reconstructs the landscape as one where higher elevations of plateaus and interfluves were covered by meadow–steppe, while low-lying regions held forest stands with *Alnus* and *Salix. Pinus* and *Betula* forests covered very small areas—probably sandy terraces and ravines at the edge of river valleys, and the presence of *Botrychium borealis,* a tundra form, is interpreted to mean that climatic conditions were colder than exist in the region today.

FAUNA

Species found at Berdyzh and Khotylevo II (Tables 2.7 and 2.8) show the usual late Pleistocene mix of forms that today have differing ecological requirements. At both sites tundra, forest, and forest–steppe megafauna co-occur. Forest dwellers predominate in both assemblages, suggesting, perhaps, a greater forest cover in the area than indicated by paleobotanical data. Berdyzh microfauna consists only of *Citellus rufensis,* which today inhabits steppes. Microfauna at Khotylevo II includes a mix of steppe (*Citellus* sp.), cold forest (probably some of the microtines assigned to the broad category *Microtus* sp.), and the predominance of tundra species (*Dicrostonyx gregalis, Lemmus obsnsis, Microtus stenocranius*). Today, 60% of rodents at Khotylevo II are tundra dwellers, 20% steppe forms, and 20% found in a wide range of environments. These figures support conclusions of both Markova (1975) and Velichko, Gribchenko *et al.* (1977), who interpret rodent data to suggest a cold, open vegetation of a periglacial tundra–steppe. A plot of open vegetation forms versus forest forms (Figure 3.2a) and a plot of steppe versus tundra forms (Figure 3.2b) indicate the predominance of open-landscape species at both Berdyzh and Khotylevo II. Khotylevo II rodents indicate a colder tundra environment, while Berdyzh fauna indicate warmer steppe conditions.

Markova (1975, 1982) used microfaunal data to construct climatograms for this period, and they show an increase in precipitation from the preceding Bryansk Interstadial (see Table 3.4). She also notes that strata laid down after the Bryansk Interstadial show permafrost deformation—another indicator of great precipitation. These conclusions are thus somewhat at odds with those offered by Grichuk of increasingly arid conditions between 24,000 and 20,000 B.P.

Avifauna from the sites (Tables 3.9–3.12) indicate substantial forest cover, another barometer of adequate and not diminished precipitation. At Berdyzh only one individual of a forest–steppe species (*Bubo bubo*) was found. At Khotylevo II seven of the eight species present represent forest or forest–steppe forms and only one, *Lagopus lagopus,*

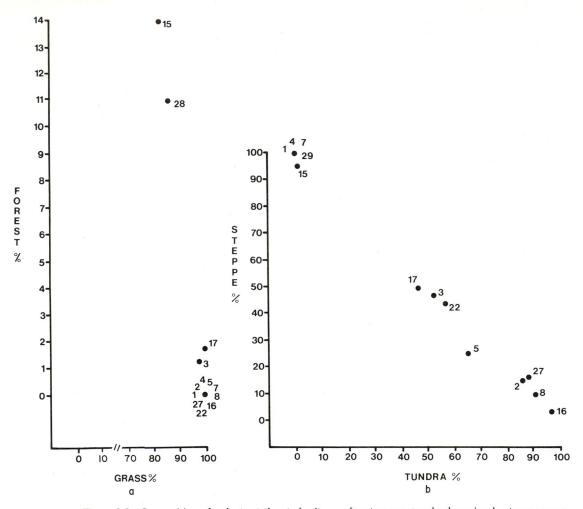

Figure 3.2 Composition of rodents at the study sites: a, forest versus grassland species; b, steppe versus tundra species. Numbers indicate sites as per Figure 2.1. Percentages of taxa calculated from data in Tables 3.6–3.8.

is found in tundras. If we divide Khotylevo II birds into the categories of economically important species and those not exploited by man (Tables 3.11 and 3.12), we see that those not exploited by man, in MNI, MNB, and number of species, could come from the forest zone. Species of economic importance show that a mix of both forest and tundra was exploited (40% of species, 53.6% MNI, and 29.3% MNB are of forest species; 20% of species, 35.7% MNI, and 67.9% MNB belong to tundra varieties). A combined list of all the avifauna similarly shows the presence of both open-space and forest species—but here the forest and forest–steppe types predominate, with only 12.5% of the species, 31.3% MNI, and 65.1% MNB belonging to tundra forms. The disproportionately large percentage of bones of tundra species reflects the fact that *Lagopus lagopus* was exploited as a food resource—a practice that led to greater fragmentation of bone than found among species not exploited. A further analysis of the categories of exploited and not exploited avifauna into water birds and land birds (Table 3.10) shows that all nonexploited species come from the forest, whereas exploited water birds come from the tundra, the forest, and forest–steppe, and exploited land birds from the forest and tundra. I conclude, therefore, that avifauna indicate a greater forest cover than is suggested by the microfauna. This indirectly supports Markova's claim for greater precipitation in the region than postulated by Grichuk. My figures also confirm conclusions reached by Serebryannaya (1972). These data also suggest that figures for mean January temperatures offered by Velichko, Grekhova, and Gubonina (1977) of $-32.5°$ may be too low and that Markova's (1975, 1982) and Zelikson and Monoszon's (1974) estimate of -17 to $-18°C$ are more accurate.

CONCLUSION

In general, we can characterize the environment of the central Russian Plain during the 24,000–20,000 B.P. interval as colder than the preceding period. Evolution of precipitation during this period is still unclear, but the general trend, certainly, was one of increasing aridity. This period may have begun with an increase in precipitation. The extent of forest cover is still an open question as well. The data in general suggest that colder periods saw deforestation. The study area was covered by a periglacial tundra–steppe in the north and a meadow–steppe in the south. Gallery forests as well as shrub vegetation existed all across the plain.

The effect of these trends on climate and landscapes at any particular time is unclear. Serebryannaya's (1972) pollen data, Markova's (1975, 1982) microfaunal data, and my own avifaunal information to some extent contradict this general picture and suggest greater precipitation, forest cover, and more moderate temperatures. It is impossible, at present, to resolve these contradictions. They may reflect the fact that Soviet researchers do not recognize any climatic oscillations during this 4000-year period. As noted previously, data from points farther west in Europe suggest a warmer oscillation some time around 21,000 B.P.

THE VALDAI MAXIMUM: 20,000–18,000 B.P.

A radiocarbon date from only one Upper Paleolithic site falls in this period: Pogon, at $18,690 \pm 770$ (LU 361). The date for Mezin of $21,600 \pm 2200$ is not reliable (see Chapter 4). The date for Pogon appears firmer, but there are no paleontological or paleobotanical remains to corroborate it.

Ivanova (1977) notes a break in human occupation at the Molodova sites on the Dnestr during the Valdai maximum. A similar break can be seen in data from the Kostenki–Borschevo sites on the Don (Klein 1969; Levkovskaya 1977). The sparcity of evidence for human occupation from the entire Russian Plain appears to indicate that it was either not occupied or only sparsely inhabited during the Valdai maximum.

CLIMATE

Broad consensus exists in the literature that this period saw the maximal spread of the Scandinavian Sheet accompanied by extremely dry, cold conditions. Compiled figures for annual averages, seasonal temperature maxima, and rates of precipitation show (1) a decrease of at least 2–4°C in annual temperature when compared to the previous period, and (2) substantial decreases in both July and January high temperatures and in annual precipitation.

Morozova's (1969) pedological data indicate that the upper part of Loess II was deposited under dryer conditions than the lower part. Frenzel (1973) notes that the predominance of steppe animals in the fauna all across Europe suggests low precipitation over wide areas. Some divergence exists in the estimated July temperature. Markova (1975, 1982) models July temperatures as fairly close to modern temperatures, at 16 to 18°C, and Butzer (1976) and Frenzel (1973) project a fall in mean July temperatures of 7 to 10°C from the previous period. No figures are offered for the length of the frost-free period (growing season), but we can project a reduction in that as well from the previous periods' average of 106.5 days to about 90 days.

Velichko (1982a) suggests that the position of the high-pressure belt insured long anticyclonic cold-weather months with low precipitation and light snow cover.

FLORA

Grichuk (1982a) indicates that the study area was covered by a mixture of periglacial steppe and forest–steppe (Figure 3.3). In the north the periglacial steppe contained sparce *Betula, Salix, Pinus,* and *Larix* stands. The periglacial forest–steppe in the south contained some sparce broadleaf species. Forest growth in both parts of the study area was primarily restricted to river valleys, with lower-lying valleys containing broadleaf species and sandy terraces showing *Pinus* forms. Both Grichuk (1969c) and Velichko and Morozova (1982) underscore the uniqueness of this vegetation and note that concentric floral distribution can only be modeled for the vegetation belt next to the ice sheet, whereas further south the main changes were not latitudinal but submeridial, going from northeast to southwest.

FAUNA

Since no site in the study area has been securely dated to the Valdai maximum, I omit a consideration of faunal evidence from this discussion.

CONCLUSION

We can summarize the environment of this period as one with colder and dryer conditions than found in the preceding period. As the following discussion shows, this was not necessarily the most severe interval. Chebotareva and Makaricheva (1974) suggest that the full glacial climatic peak was probably reached well after ice growth reached its maximal limits. This again underscores the lack of synchronization between

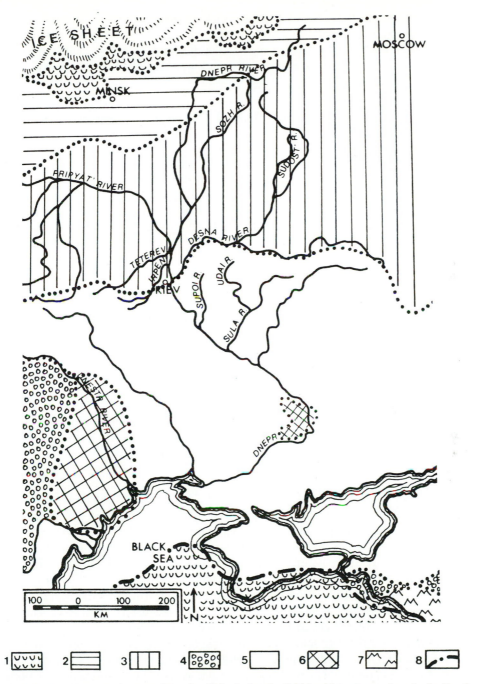

Figure 3.3   Vegetation on the central Russian Plain during the Valdai cold maximum: 1, water bodies; 2, shrub tundra–steppe; 3, periglacial forest–steppe; 4, mixed forest; 5, periglacial steppe; 6, southern periglacial forest–steppe; 7, mountainous areas; 8, limit of the New Euxine Sea (after Grichuk 1982b: Map 10).

pedological, paleobotanical, and paleontological evidence. And this, in turn, suggests that the sparseness or lack of human occupation cannot be directly attributed to unfavorable climatic conditions between 18,000 B.P. and 20,000 B.P. Other mitigating factors, such as possible changes in the distribution of exploited resources, will have to be considered as well.

CLIMATE AFTER THE GLACIAL MAXIMUM:
18,000–12,000 B.P.

The majority of Upper Paleolithic sites on the central Russian Plain date from after the Valdai maximum (see Table 2.15). Radiocarbon dates for Eliseevichi, Gontsy, Mezhirich, Pogon, Pushkari I, Timonovka I and II, and Yudinovo show these sites occupied after 18,000 B.P. I show in Chapter 4 that sites lacking chronometric dates, Bugorok, Chulatovo I and II, Dobranichevka, Novgorod-Severskii and others, were also probably occupied during this interval.

In Chapter 2 I noted that the retreat of the Scandinavian Ice Sheet from the study area was not a smooth and gradual process but rather one marked by spasmodic retreats and readvances. During such readvances as the Edrovo–Frankfurt or Vepsovo–Pomeranian stages, the ice sheet moved up almost to its previous moraines. The advances and retreats did not occur at uniform rates. Soviet researchers, although documenting these fluctuations, have not seriously considered the effect that they were bound to have on the environment in the study area. Velichko (1982a), for example, recognizes significant oscillations only after 12,000 B.P. and sees the preceding 18,000–12,000 B.P. interval as a climatically stable one. Both Chebotareva and Makaricheva (1982) and Khodakov (1982) suggest that the period between the maximal extent of the ice and its retreat from the Russian Plain was indeed one with great climatic fluctuations. But their observations have generally not impressed Soviet paleogeographers sufficiently to reexamine firmly held assumptions about climatic and environmental stability (e.g. environmental "hyperzonality") between 18,000 and 12,000 B.P. In this chapter I argue emphatically that fluctuating climatic conditions between 18,000 and 12,000 B.P. were real, significant, and had a profound effect on the environments and on human adaptation. Glacial advances and retreats after the Valdai maximum created a series of rapidly alternating stadial–interstadial climatic oscillations. A tentative sequence is illustrated in Figure 2.9. The table delimits four warm episodes: the Laugerie, Lascaux, Raunis, and Bölling. Lamb (1977) notes the presence of at least five climatic cycles in European Russia between 20,000 and 10,000 B.P.—each with an approximate 2000-year duration. Soviet authors are still debating the exact number of warm oscillations and whether these represent true interstadials or should be considered just interphases (Chebotareva and Makaricheva 1974; Veklich 1974; Vigdorchik et al. 1974).

The reasons for this periodic cyclicity are still being argued in the literature (Kukla 1972; Lamb 1977). As Lamb notes, the repetitiveness and regularity of the cycles clearly points to the importance of external causes such as solar fluctuations or variations in tidal forces. The evolution of each oscillation shows that they were also not gradual. Each oscillation, both warm and cold, began and reached its peak very quickly, and this peak was followed by a long period of transition (Kukla 1972). Warm peaks occurred at intervals of approximately 2000 years and were separated by cold peaks occurring at about the same intervals. Documentation exists from numerous data sources for these fluctuations on a worldwide scale.

No coherent global chronology exists for these fluctuations, and comparable episodes at times appear nonsynchronized. This is partially because there is a lack of synchronization between local perturbations and response. Also there are latitudinal differences in responses to perturbations. The last observation is especially pertinent for the study area. Lamb (1966, 1977) and Butzer (1971, 1976) concur that higher latitudes and those regions lying closer to the ice sheet cooled first and warmed last during these oscillations. These regions were also affected by greater climatic deviations than were lower latitudes. Frenzel (1973) writes that the beginning of postglacial warm periods in such regions as south Alaska may have lagged 1500–2000 years behind those in British Columbia and Washington state in the New World; or those in the Baltic 1500–2000 years behind those in south central Europe in the Old World. Principles of uniformitarianism suggest that similar regional differences existed because of the late Valdai oscillations as well. Because of this, climatic information collected from different points on the central Russian Plain will probably show a lack of synchronization between more southern and more northern regions. Watts (1980) reports precisely this sort of regional lag for late Glacial Europe.

EVIDENCE FOR CLIMATIC FLUCTUATION IN THE STUDY AREA

As noted previously, Soviet researchers have not focused on delimiting climatic fluctuation on the central Russian Plain. Yet the accumulated geological, paleobotanical, and paleontological evidence clearly indicates that these fluctuations were both real and significant. These data, however, are not sufficiently fine to allow either construction of a firm chronology for the oscillations or detailed paleoenvironmental reconstruction for each fluctuation.

Geological Evidence

In late Valdai stratigraphy, the period between 18,000 and 12,000 B.P. is represented by the gley layer, loess III, and relic soil layer in Velichko's (1961) scheme (see Figure 2.12). The presence of embryonic soil formation represented by the gley layer, as well as the relic soil horizon on top of the Loess III, indicate the presence of at least two warmer oscillations in the northern part of the central Russian Plain. Pashkevich and Dubnyak (1978) note the presence of an additional layer of embryonic soil in the Loess III deposits of the Ukraine and suggest the occurrence of an additional, third, warm oscillation. This oscillation is not documented in Desna Loess III deposits.

Grichuk (1969c) and Chebotareva (1969b) suggest that Loess III accumulated until the onset of the Alleröd some 11,500 years ago. This suggests that the relic soil layer (Timonovka soil) was deposited during the Alleröd. Velichko (Velichko, Grekhova, and Gubonina 1977), however, dates the formation of the contemporary soil to the Alleröd and indirectly implies that the relic soil layer under the contemporary soil must have been formed prior to the Alleröd. It is possible that the Timonovka relic soil can be correlated with the warmer Bölling period. This would tentatively date this layer to approximately 13,000 B.P. Unfortunately the Bölling oscillation is not correlated to any specific stratigraphic layer in the deposits of the central Russian Plain.

The top of the Loess III also contains a cryogenic horizon that shows the widespread presence of polygonal systems, ice wedge casts 4–5 m deep, and other periglacial phenomena (Velichko, Morozova *et al.* 1969; Velichko, Grekhova, and Gubonina 1977). A comparison of the extent of permafrost on the central Russian Plain during the 24,000–20,000 B.P. period and the 18,000–12,000 B.P. period shows that periglacial phenomena were more widespread during the latter. The ground was permanently frozen, with a summer thaw layer of 1.5–2 m in the north and as much as 2–3 m in the south. The presence of more extensive permafrost perturbations during this period agrees with the interpretation of Chebotareva and Makaricheva (1974, 1982) that the severest and coldest climate occurred after the Valdai maximum during subsequent stadials. Data for these disturbances come from Eliseevichi and Timonovka II and constitute evidence for the existence of cold oscillations during this period.

The modeled statistics for the temperatures and precipitation during this period (Table 3.4) reflect much disagreement. Velichko, Grekhova, and Gubonina (1977), using data from Timonovka II, suggest mean January figures of −30 to −35°C, mean July temperatures of 18 to 20°C, and annual precipitation of 200 mm/year with 50 mm in the form of snow. Markova (1975), on the other hand, using data from the sites of Chulatovo II, Mezin, and Novgorod-Severskii, has a range of January temperatures from −20 to −24°C, July temperatures from 16 to 23°C, and equally varying estimates for precipitation. These discrepancies again appear to reflect data collected from sites dated to different periods. Some of these sites were probably occupied during the warmer oscillations, others during the colder ones. The Velichko *et al.* statistic for 80 to 100 frost-free days should, likewise, be considered suitable for one of the colder oscillations.

Paleobotanical Evidence

I have previously discussed the difficulties in coordinating the fluctuations of the ice sheet, climatic oscillations, and evidence for these in pollen spectra. Paleobotanical evidence from the central Russian Plain is somewhat contradictory, as can be expected for a time interval with climatic oscillations. More agreement exists for the vegetational cover during the time the gley layer was deposited than for the subsequent period of Loess III deposition. I first outline the summarized data for this warm oscillation, which is tentatively dated to either the Lascaux warm period at 16,000 B.P. or the Laugerie oscillation at 18,000 B.P. I then discuss deposits found in the Loess III at the sites of Dobranichevka, Mezhirich, and Timonovka II.

Grichuk (1972) reconstructs the vegetational cover in the northern part of the study area as predominantly arboreal. These forests were boreal in nature with *Pteridium, Picea, Pinus, Betula,* and *Alnus* present. Deciduous trees represented less than 1% of pollen remains. The frequency of deciduous species increased farther south, where *Quercus* sp. formed an important component. While Grichuk classifies vegetation of the north as a form of boreal forest, he also points to the increase in steppe associations in the southern part of the plain. Serebryannaya (1972) reports that pollen profiles from Karachirzh show 65% AP, and she notes an increase of *Picea* and a decrease of *Pinus* in forests. Nonarboreal vegetation is represented by *Artemisia, Ephedra, Corispermum,* and *Chenopodium rabrium.* Serebryannaya suggests that the vegetation was similar to present-day south Ural taiga, with the boreal–deciduous forest border lying just south of the Desna.

Pashkevich's (Pashkevich and Dubnyak 1978) Dobranichevka pollen spectra taken from strata contemporary with the Desna gley layer indicate the increased role of arboreal vegetation in the south. *Pinus* represents the majority of remains (64–87% AP), with *Alnus* and *Betula,* as well as *Salix* and deciduous species, also present. The NAP (47–60% of pollen) contains *Poacea, Cypracea,* and *Asteracea.* Pashkevich reconstructs the landscape in the south as one covered by a mosaic of meadows and forests.

Unfortunately no ^{14}C dates exist for the gley layer and it is therefore impossible to date accurately the time span represented by the subsequent Loess III deposits. Loess III was probably deposited between about 17,000 and 13,000 B.P. The pollen spectra collected from the Loess III again show some contradiction. Serebryannaya (1972) reports a climatic amelioration, as seen in the spread of *Betula* forests with a presence of *Quercus, Tilia, Ulmus,* and *Fagus.* Grichuk (1972) sees a simplification and homogenization of the ecologicozonal structures and underscores the existence of hyperzonality during this period. He reconstructs the landscape of the north as covered by a periglacial forest–steppe, with NAP representing 87–88% and AP 7–8% of the species. The predominantly riverine forests consisted of *Pinus, Betula,* and *Larix.*

Pashkevich and Dubnyak (1978) recognized two distinct climatic episodes reflected in the Loess III deposits—a time during which the loess itself was deposited and a time during which the embryonic soil layer found within it was formed. During the former, the surrounding countryside was covered by steppe vegetation, with NAP representing 67–95% of the grains. The AP primarily belongs to *Pinus,* with *Betula, Salix,* and *Alnus* also present. In comparison to the preceding period (i.e., the gley layer), NAP shows an increase in the role of Chenopodiaceae and Artemisiae. The presence of spores of *Seliginella selaginoides,* a representative of tundra and boreal floras, suggests a deterioration of climate. Pashkevich and Dubnyak (1978) also recognized the existence of a climatic oscillation to warmer temperatures and increased humidity during the time the Loess III was deposited. This oscillation is indicated by a layer of embryonic soil found at depths of 1.0 to 1.1 m in Loess III. It may be that this embryonic layer, found in the middle of Loess III in the south, is a contemporary of the relic soil (Timonovka soil) layer that Velichko places at the top of Loess III in the Desna sequence (see Chapter 4 for discussion). Pollen spectra from Dobranichevka show that steppe associations of Loess III gave way to forest–steppe formations at this time. Arboreal species appeared in greater variety, including such deciduous species as *Quercus, Tilia,* and *Corylus.* The NAP vegetation consisted of Polygonaceae, Ranunculaceae, Caryophyllacea, Brassiaceae, Rosaceae, Fabaceae, and a considerable presence of Poaceae and Cyperaceae (see Figure 2.27). Pashkevich and Dubnyak (1978) argue that tree cover was still concentrated in river valleys, while open spaces of the interfluves and plateaus were covered by meadows or meadow–steppe.

Complete pollen diagrams exist from two sites chronometrically dated to this time: Mezhirich and Timonovka II. Paleobotanical data from Mezhirich show the predominance of NAP (45–70%) and suggest dominant presence of steppe associations, including Compositae, *Artemisia,* and *Plantago laceolata.* The AP (20–45%) is mostly represented by *Pinus,* with *Alnaster, Betula nana, B. humilis,* and *Ribes* found along the valley floor. In general, Kornietz *et al.* (1981) suggest that Mezhirich was occupied during one of the warm oscillations—possibly the Laugerie. A combination of paleobotanical evidence and chronometric dates from the site, however, do not preclude the possibility that it was occupied during the subsequent Lascaux oscillation.

Eliseevichi, possibly dating close in time to Mezhirich, is located some 400 km north of Mezhirich. While, as Velichko, Grekhova, and Udartsev (1977) indicate, the amount of pollen recovered there is insufficient for the construction of a pollen diagram, the data collected indicate the predominance of cold-loving grasses. This implies the presence of a periglacial steppe environment with some forest cover (probably gallery forests) of *Pinus, Picea,* and *Betula.* The stratigraphy at the site associated the cultural layer with the gley soil horizon tentatively dated at 17,000 B.P., which is associated with a warm oscillation. Like Mezhirich, then, Eliseevichi was probably occupied during a warm fluctuation—possibly either the Laugerie or Lascaux interstadial.

The pollen diagram from Timonovka II is presented in Figure 2.110. The cultural layer from which the samples were taken is associated with the very end of Loess III accumulation and the beginning of formation of the relic soil layer (Timonovka soil). Pollen sampling yielded a very small number of grains, among which NAP predominated slightly (about 55%). Grasses are represented by Cruciferae, Polygonaceae, Origraceae, Cyperaceae, Chenopodiaceae, Ericaceae, and Polypodiaceae. Dry-loving forms predominate the NAP spectra. Arboreal pollen, found to the maximum of 40%, show the presence of such species as *Pinus, Betula,* and *Alnus.* Velichko, Grekhova, *et al.* (1981) conclude that the surrounding countryside was covered by a periglacial forest–steppe. The fairly high percentage of AP in the cultural layer as well as the decrease of tree vegetation in strata overlying the cultural layer indicate that the site was also occupied during a warm climatic oscillation—possibly during the Lascaux or even perhaps as late as the Bölling. The chronometric date of 15,110 ± 530 favors the earlier of these two.

Cultural remains at Dobranichevka are associated with a layer of embryonic soil that may correlate with either the gley layer or the relic soil layer (Timonovka soil) of the Desna sequence. It may, however, also date to a warm fluctuation not recorded in the Desna sequence. As Figure 2.27 shows, AP represents up to 32% of the sample, with *Pinus* as the predominant species. The NAP (to 50%) indicates the preponderance of Cyperaceae and Graminaea families. Comparing these spectra to ones from underlying layers, Shovkoplyas *et al.* (1981) see an increase in both the extent and variety of forest cover in the area. The forests, however, while covering both river valleys and terraces, were found near river courses, while the rest of the area was covered by a cold meadow-steppe. Shovkoplyas *et al.* conclude that the site was occupied while climate was still severely continental but milder than in the preceding or subsequent times. This indicates that the site was also occupied during one of the warm oscillations.

Paleontological Evidence

There are no perceptible changes in the exploited fauna found at the sites dating to the period 18,000–12,000 B.P. The same wide mix of species discussed previously is found at such sites as Mezhirich, Dobranichevka, Gontsy, and Timonovka II (see Tables 2.7 and 2.8). Microfauna from Eliseevichi, Gontsy, Mezhirich, Pushkari I, and Yudinovo appear to indicate the presence of climatic oscillations and show that some sites were occupied at cold times and others at warmer times. Thus, for example, rodents from Dobranichevka and Gontsy belong exclusively to steppe species and indicate warmer climates. Rodents from Yudinovo and Eliseevichi reflect cold, tundra conditions. Mezhirich rodents indicate the presence of a cold but mixed forest and grassland environment. The high percentage of steppe species suggests milder climatic conditions than indicated by paleobotanical evidence, but it is in agreement with the conclusion that the site was occupied during a warmer climatic oscillation.

Similar variation can be seen in the microfaunal remains from sites that have no reliable chronometric dates. Rodents from Novgorod-Severskii and Mezin suggest colder climates and open tundra or tundra–steppe vegetation. Chulatovo I rodents suggest that the site was occupied in colder climates when the surrounding landscape was a tundra–steppe, while Chulatovo II data indicate that this site was occupied at warmer times. Samples from Pushkari I and Pushkari II indicate an open, cold landscape and little tree cover, which indirectly suggests occupation during a colder oscillation. Finally, Dobranichevka and Zhuravka microfauna point to open steppe-like landscapes and occupation during warmer times.

Avifaunal remains show that the sites were occupied during different climatic oscillations as well. For example, as Tables 3.9–3.12 show, no tundra species appears on the list of birds not exploited by man at Novgorod Severskii. Here forest and forest–steppe forms predominate in all figures, including number of species, MNI, and MNB calculations. This suggests that the environment was warmer and that greater tree cover existed than at such nearby sites as Mezin. Mezin avifauna data show the importance of tundra-dwelling species in all calculations and indicate a cold climate at the time of occupation. Birds found at Dobranichevka reflect primarily economic pursuits of man and are not very diagnostic for paleoenvironmental reconstruction. They do show the presence of tundra species (i.e., *Lagopus lagopus*) near the site. This taxon, however, is a typical late Pleistocene denizen and not diagnostic for any climatic oscillations. Avifaunal remains from Mezhirich agree with paleoenvironmental reconstruction suggested by pollen diagrams. A mix of forest and forest–steppe birds are represented in the assemblage of birds not exploited by man, while tundra species (*Lagopus lagopus*) predominate in the list of exploited forms. Avifaunal remains from Yudinovo show primarily the exploitation of tundra species as well.

Molluscan remains found at Gontsy, Chulatovo II, Eliseevichi, Mezin, Mezhirich, Novgorod-Severskii, Timonovka I, and Yudinovo are listed in Tables 3.13–3.15. These data also indicate the existence of climatic oscillations between 18,000 and 12,000 B.P. Here I consider only those molluscs that were not specifically exploited by man. Molluscs from Gontsy and Yudinovo, where 100% of the species represented are thermophilous, indicate occupation of the sites during warmer climatic oscillations. Molluscs from Mezin, on the other hand, where four species (66.8%) are cryophilous, suggest occupation during a cold oscillation. A comparison of molluscan remains from Mezhirich and Novgorod-Severskii shows that while only one taxon, representing less than 4% of the mollusca, is thermophilous at Mezhirich, the presence of one thermophilous species at Novgorod-Severskii reflects 25% of all the molluscan taxa there. The percentage of cryophiles at both sites is approximately equal (50% at Novgorod-Severskii and 43% at Mezhirich). These data, although sparce, do suggest that Novgorod-Severskii was occupied during a warmer climatic episode than Mezhirich.

The Magnitude and Effects of Climatic Oscillations

Climatic oscillations after the Valdai maximum contrast sharply with the gradual climatic changes documented for the preceding 25,000–18,000 B.P. interval. As I noted previously, climatic fluctuations after 18,000 B.P. occurred at intervals of approximately 1000 years and produced cyclicity on time scales of some 2000 years. Oscillations of such magnitude, while important for large-scale paleometeorological reconstructions, are too gross for questions of change in the environment and change in the environmental stress. Clearly, for questions of human adaptation we must focus on climatic and environmental changes that occur at intervals considerably shorter than 1000 years.

Sizable literature exists on Pleistocene climates, but as Butzer (1976) notes, there is undue neglect in paleometeorological literature of the short-range periodicities. I cannot offer a scheme that directly and succinctly translates the effect of long-term fluctuations into short-term cyclicity. Instead, I focus on two pertinent aspects of the late Valdai environment that permit me to offer tentative models of the effects of shorter-term fluctuations: (1) the nature of long-term fluctuations; and (2) the relationship of short- to long-term climatic cyclicity.

As already discussed, neither the warm nor the cold oscillations were gradual, smooth processes of climatic change; rather, they demonstrate an asymmetrical sawtooth-like pattern. This asymmetrical pattern Kukla (1972) attributes to the behavior of the snow line in response to changes in the solar index. The asymmetrical nature of the long-term late Valdai oscillations is illustrated in Figure 3.4. The time scale employed in this illustration is very tentative and is based on Kukla's (1972) model for the relationship of insolation and the snow line. It indicates that the actual climatic deterioration or amelioration, and the stress conditions presented by such changes in climate, were most severe for shorter periods than the length of the oscillation cycle itself, periods of stress perhaps lasting 100–200 years. This makes each oscillation's disturbance to environmental equilibrium brief and spasmodic enough for adaptation responses to be brought into play.

The general aridity in the study area was an additional factor contributing to the severity of these climatic jolts in the late Valdai. Wiens (1976) notes that arid environ-

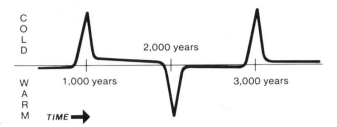

Figure 3.4 Profile of late Valdai climatic fluctuations after 18,000 B.P.

ments are more sensitive to climatic fluctuations and that the repair process following such disturbances is notoriously slow, perhaps persisting for decades and even centuries.

Paleobotanical data corroborate the rapidity of climatic and environmental changes within each long-term cycle. Woillard's (1979) pollen data from Grand Pile in northeastern France show a change from temperate forest to pine–spruce–birch taiga occurring within 150 ± 75 years during the last interglacial and projects that the "dramatic borealization of West European forests" may have taken less than 20 years.

The nature of the relationship between short- and long-term climatic cyclicity is the second factor to be considered in this discussion. Meteorological literature addressing questions of contemporary climatic oscillations indicates that long-term (10^3 or more years) oscillations that appear as smooth and gradual curves of climatic change in fact mask the existence of more rapid and violent short-term oscillations (Kukla 1972; Lamb 1966; Yoshino 1975). Flohn (1979), writing about climatic fluctuations of the late Würm, notes that much greater variability probably existed in climates within 100-year periods. Lamb (1977), in noting the existence of long-term climatic oscillations in European Russia between 20,000 and 10,000 B.P., also states that these long-term main fluctuations were superimposed on shorter-term fluctuations of about 25, 60, 100, and 400 years. His work with the paleoclimate of Great Britain leads him to conclude that short-term fluctuations (year to year and decade to decade) during the late Pleistocene were from two to three times as great as observed today. In another work, Lamb (1966) notes that the Holocene climatic fluctuations in Great Britain show slow and smooth changes of no more than 1–1.5°C/1000 years on the 10^3-year time scale. These long-term curves mask more extreme shorter-term fluctuations of both temperature and precipitation. Extensive climatic records from Greenland that span the last 1000 years also show these short-term fluctuations.

Kukla (1972) writes that the solar index is cyclical in nature as well, and he models the length of each cycle at approximately 200 years. This adds yet another short-term cycle to the inventory of meteorological cyclicity relevant to this study.

The presence of the Scandinavian Ice Sheet on the central Russian Plain was another factor contributing to the presence of short-term climatic cyclicity in the late Valdai. Spjeldnaes (1964) suggests that deviation-amplifying mechanisms exist in both northern latitudes and glaciated areas that tend to magnify even minor perturbations and lead to climatic oscillations. The existence and importance of these climatic oscillations (much shorter than 10^3 years in length) is confirmed by numerous researchers.

In conclusion, current meteorological research confirms both the existence and importance of short-term climatic oscillations today and their existence in the recent past. These oscillations are imperceptible on the scale of 10^3 years, because the very construction of long-term scales summarizes and averages all shorter-term deviations. We can, by analogy, presume that these short-term climatic oscillations also existed in the late Valdai, although the current state of paleometeorological and paleoenvironmental research does not permit us to delineate them.

The data presented here lead me to conclude that both the evolution of each major large-scale oscillation and the presence of undelineated short-term oscillations combined to create climatic and environmental instability on the central Russian Plain, probably in terms of year-to-year, decade-to-decade, and century-to-century deviations. These perturbations can be expected to have had profound effects on biotic communities of the central Russian Plain and to have influenced both the subsistence practices and settlement patterns of late Pleistocene hunter–gatherers.

THE STRUCTURE OF THE LANDSCAPE IN THE LATE VALDAI ———

INTRODUCTION

The preceding sections of this chapter present information on paleoenvironments in the study area through time and space on time scales significant for our understanding of the late Valdai in general but too gross for specific questions about human adaptations. The conclusions reached—namely that the region was a periglacial forest–steppe supporting numerous species of large mammals—offer very little additional insights to our understanding of specific subsistence strategies employed by groups who inhabited the region.

The literature on the subject until very recently, presented us with very static models for both late Pleistocene Eurasia and Alaska. Extant models tended to implicitly assume either a random or even distribution of biotic resources across an undifferentiated landscape (Butzer 1971, 1976; Frenzel 1973; Kurten 1968; Gerasimov and Velichko 1982; Velichko 1969a, 1973, 1974, 1977). Authors in the 1982 volume *Paleoecology of Beringia* have challenged these long-held assumptions (Ager 1982; Bliss and Richards 1982; Guthrie 1982).

Three environmental parameters—patchiness, temporal variability, and climatic instability—are of particular significance for our discussion. All three have been extensively discussed in the ecological literature. They profoundly affect the spatial and temporal variability in resource distribution and should be briefly considered before we turn to modeling the structure of the landscape in the study area.

Environmental Patchiness

Wiens notes that

> In the real world, environments are patchy. Factors influencing the proximate physiological or behavioral state or the ultimate fitness of individuals exhibit discontinuities on many scales in time

and space. The patterns of these discontinuities produce an environmental patchwork which exerts powerful influences on the distribution of organisms, their interactions, and their adaptations. (1976:81)

In terrestrial ecosystems, the most obvious framework of spatial patchiness is created by vegetational patterns (1976:85).

Wiens concludes that arid systems, in general, for a variety of factors including climatic effects, abiotic disturbances, soil effects, and consumer effects, are more sensitive to factors promoting vegetational patchiness and are temporally less predictable. Dunbar (1973) and Bunnell (1980) both characterize north-latitude environments as especially patchy due to the large spatial scale of the systems there. Patchiness is species defined, and my discussion focuses on patchiness as perceived by human populations in a specific environment—the late Valdai central Russian Plain—and as expressed in the archaeological record.

Guthrie (1968, 1982), working with large mammalian communities of late Pleistocene Alaska, clearly shows that differential distribution of both fauna and vegetation existed there. He notes a differential distribution of three large herbivore species (mammoth, horse, and bison) across the landscape, with mammoth and horse more prevalent on the floodplain. His underlying assumption is that there is a general correlation between the representation of animals in paleontological collections and their actual importance in contemporaneous faunal communities—an assumption that is also used in this work. The ecological requirements of these three species suggest that vegetation favored by each (short grass for bison, medium and tall grasses for mammoth and horse) was differentially distributed, too, with short grasses prevailing in the interior interfluves and medium and tall grasses predominating near the floodplain.

Ecological theory and Guthrie's Alaskan research indirectly imply that biotic resources of the central Russian Plain were discontinuous and patchily distributed in the late Valdai. Extant data do not permit me to specify this patchiness beyond the broad generalizations that cryophilous grassland vegetation predominated in the interfluves and arboreal vegetation predominated near river valleys and floodplains. Using Guthrie's Alaskan data, I argue that there was a proportional increase in medium and tall grasses toward the floodplain and an increase in more xerophytic short-grass associations away from water courses.

Temporal Variability

Temporal fluctuation in biotic resources is widely reported in the ecological literature (Budyko 1977; Odum 1971; Pianka 1974; Wiens 1976). These temporal population fluctuations occur on a number of scales, from seasonal to annual, as well as on longer time scales. They are especially significant in northern environments.

Shorter-term (seasonal, annual, decadal) population oscillations are well documented for several small animal species (e.g., lemming, arctic fox, hare, and lynx): (Butler 1953; Elton 1924, 1942; Finerty 1981; May 1980; Vibe 1967, 1970). As Amsden (1979) notes, with some important exceptions such as Burch's (1972) work on the caribou, there has been little in the way of systematic research to determine which other species of large mammals are subject to long-term population oscillations. Vibe's (1967, 1970) work in

Greenland has tentatively outlined long-term oscillations for such species as the musk-ox, polar bear, ptarmigan, caribou, and various species of whale. Similar observations are offered by White *et al.* (1980), Naumov (1972), Batzli (1981), and Peterson *et al.* (1984).

Temporal population oscillations result from a number of factors, most of which are still poorly understood. Climate, however, appears to be one of the prime factors. Dunbar (1973), for example, considers climatic cyclicity as an important variable. Formozov (1946, 1970) and Pruitt (1970) point to the changes in both the amount and nature of the snow cover as factors affecting population numbers of different species. The relationship between the faunal population oscillations and changes in floral communities is less than clear as well.

The documented existence of temporal population fluctuations in northern-latitude species, whatever their ultimate causes, offers us a plausible model for the late Valdai central Russian Plain as well. We can expect that similar population oscillations were an important feature of that environment and a variable that played a role in human adaptation strategies.

Climatic Instability

The effect that climatic fluctuations had on the temporal and spatial distribution of the biotic resources of the area is a third factor to be considered in this discussion. I have postulated the existence of both temporal and spatial patchiness or fluctuations in both animal and plant communities. I have also suggested that these are natural aspects of all environments—but of greater significance in northern latitudes. Greater fluctuations necessarily create greater instability, and northern-latitude environments are considered to be less stable than those to the south.

May (1973a, 1977) draws a distinction between reactions of stable and unstable ecological systems to perturbation. A central feature of a stable system is the presence of feedback that restores perturbed populations to equilibrium. In unstable systems, on the other hand, population disturbances tend to be amplified. May (1973a) notes that fluctuations both decrease average numbers and increase oscillations in population sizes. Budyko (1977) states that when population oscillations occur during periods of unstable climate, their parameters are amplified and place the populations involved under stress and at times in danger of extinction. The net result of perturbations, then, is both to decrease population numbers and to make the populations temporally less predictable as a stable resource.

Applying these observations to the central Russian Plain, we can postulate that climatic fluctuations documented for the 18,000–12,000 B.P. period resulted in both temporal and spatial fluctuations in the biotic resources. Specifically, the rapid fluctuations from warm to cold to warm conditions produced changes in vegetation, favoring grasslands over forests during cold periods and forests over open vegetation in warmer times. The rapidity of these changes was on a scale short enough to profoundly affect vegetation. The changes in distribution of different plant resources also affected the animal species that fed on them. Colder periods would have created particularly stressful conditions for animals inhabiting forests, while warmer conditions would have stressed those inhabiting grasslands.

The reaction of species to stress can be predicted to take the most energy-efficient form. As Slobodkin and Rappaport (1974) succinctly put it, the object is to stay alive with a minimum of change necessary to ensure survival. We can, therefore, expect that environmental stresses were met by adaptive behavioral changes. For mobile animal species, these involved changes in the geographic location and distribution as well as possible changes in seasonal aggregations and dispersals. It is also reasonable to assume that changes occurred in overall population numbers of specific species.

Patchily distributed resources, which also fluctuate in numbers and therefore in overall availability through time, constitute less reliable and less predictable food sources than evenly distributed and stable ones. Exploitation of these resources presents specific problems that have to be met through particular adaptation strategies if the dependent populations are to stay alive (Wiens 1976).

In the ensuing discussion I focus on the fine structure of the late Pleistocene land-scape in the study area. First I examine the ecological requirements and behavioral parameters of taxa exploited, and then, because past research does not address this issue and extant data are quite biased in favor of Upper Paleolithic cultural practices, I construct models using relevant information from other periods and regions as well.

The Faunal Record and its Implications

Seven species found at the sites contributed more than 95% by weight, MNI, and MNB of prey taken by Upper Paleolithic hunter–gatherers. Table 3.17 lists taxa used as food. A wide consensus exists in Russian language literature that carnivores were not used as food (Kornietz 1962; Kornietz et al. 1981; Pidoplichko 1969; Polikarpovich 1968; Shovkoplyas 1965a; Vereschagin 1971). Remains of these species show neither bone fragmentation nor charring associated with food processing and consumption. The seven species considered to have played a major role in Upper Paleolithic economies are (1) food resources—mammoth, reindeer, horse, steppe marmot, and hare, and (2) nonfood resources—artic fox and wolf. In this section I consider the distribution of these taxa across the landscape, delimit their ecological requirements, model their possible behavioral patterns, and project optimal locations and times for harvesting these species (Table 3.18).

Woolly Mammoth (*Mammuthus primigenius*).   The ecological requirements of this extinct species are subject to disagreement in the literature. Stomach contents of frozen carcasses found in Siberia yielded ambivalent data. Information on the closest living analogues, African and Indian elephants, suggests seasonal and even gender differences in the amount of browsing or grazing (Bliss and Richards 1982; Cornwall 1968; Guthrie 1968, 1982; Laws et al. 1975; Oliver 1982; Wilson 1975; Wing and Buss 1970). Guthrie (1982, 1982 personal communication), who considers mammoth to be primarily grazers, notes that this taxon would have satisfied most of its dietary needs with a large-volume, high-fiber, low-nutrient plant diet composed of medium and tall grasses with

Table 3.17 SPECIES USED AS FOOD: PERCENTAGE CONTRIBUTION[a]

		Sites												
		1	2	3	4	5	6	7	8	9	10	11	12	13
Number of food taxa		4	7	7	7	7	2	6	5	3	nd	nd	nd	nd
Fish	taxa	—	14.7	—	—	14.7	—	—	—	—	—	—	—	—
	MNB		4.6			0.1–0.2								
	MNI		7.4			9.8–17.7								
Bird	taxa	—	—	—	14.7	—	—	—	20.0	—	—	—	—	—
	MNB				ins				15.7					
	MNI				1.0				nd					
Mammoth	taxa	25.0	14.6	14.6	14.6	14.6	50.0	16.7	20.0	33.4	100?	100?	100?	50.0
	MNB	nd	92.1	nd	98.7	99.8	80.3	72.1	80.9	98.9	nd	nd	nd	nd
	MNI	93.7	40.8	12.8	89.2	75.9–83.5	68.8	70.5	nd	95.9	nd	nd	nd	nd
Horse	taxa	25.0	14.7	14.7	—	14.7	50.0	—	—	—	nd	nd	50.0
	MNB	nd	0.5	nd		ins	19.7				nd	nd	nd
	MNI	2.1	7.4	7.0		1.3–1.5	31.2				nd	nd	nd
Woolly rhinoceros	taxa	25.0	14.7	14.7	14.7	—		—	20.0	33.3	—	—	—	—
	MNB	nd	0.2	nd	ins				0.3	0.9				
	MNI	2.1	7.4	11.8	1.0				nd	2.7				
Boar	taxa	—	—	—	—	—	—	16.6	—	—	—	—	—	—
	MNB							ins						
	MNI							0.8						
Red deer	taxa	—	—	—	—	14.7	—	—	—	—	—	—	—	—
	MNB					ins								
	MNI					1.3–1.5								
Deer	taxa	—	—	—	—	—	—	—	—	—	—	—	—	—
	MNB													
	MNI													
Giant deer	taxa	—	—	—	—	—	—	—	—	—	—	—	—	—
	MNB													
	MNI													
Reindeer	taxa	—	14.7	14.7	14.7	14.7	—	16.7	—	—	—	—	—	—
	MNB		2.0	nd	1.2	ins		17.9						
	MNI		22.2	19.8	4.9	1.3–1.5		10.6						
Steppe bison	taxa	—	14.7	14.7	14.7	—	—	—	20.0	—	—	—	—	—
	MNB		0.3	nd	ins				0.3					
	MNI		7.4	4.0	1.0				nd					
Wild cattle	taxa	25.0	—	—	—	—								
	MNB	nd												
	MNI	2.1												
Musk-oxen	taxa	—	—	—	14.7	—	—	—	—	—	—	—	—	—
	MNB				ins									
	MNI				1.0									
Steppe marmot	taxa	—	14.7	14.7	—	—	—	16.7	—	—	—	—	—	—
	MNB		0.2	nd				0.7						
	MNI		7.4	24.8				4.5						
Beaver	taxa	—	—	—	—	—	—	—	—	—	—	—	—	—
	MNB													
	MNI													
Hare	taxa	—	—	14.7	14.7	14.7	—	16.7	20.0	33.3	—	—	—	—
	MNB			nd	0.1	ins		9.3	1.1	0.2				
	MNI			19.8	1.9	2.5–2.8		12.1	nd	1.4				

[a] Insignificant, ins ≤ 0.09%.
[b] All MNI percentages at Yudinovo calculated without reindeer or hare.

Sites															
14	15	16	17	18	19	20	21	22	23	24	25	26	27b	28	
3	8	11	9	1	3	1	4	4	5	7	3	3	9	3	
—	12.5 ins 0.4	—	11.1 25.6 19.9	—	—	—	—	—	—	14.7 0.6 7.7	—	—	—	—	
—	12.5 1.2 9.8	9.0 0.3 2.3	11.1 4.5 12.2	—	—	—	—	—	—	—	—	—	—	—	—
33.4 89.8 25.0	12.5 57.1 54.3	9.0 75.1 37.5	11.2 29.8 8.3	100 100 100	33.3 nd nd	100 100 100	25.0 75.0 93.2	25.0 98.3 81.1	20.0 99.2 92.0	14.6 82.0 53.8	33.4 nd 78.9	33.4 58.3 85.5	11.2 78.8 81.1	33.4 99.6 88.2–91.0	—
33.3 6.1 25.0	12.5 ins 0.4	9.0 12.5 19.7	11.1 4.2 4.4	—	—	—	25.0 24.2 4.0	25.0 ins 4.8	20.0 0.6 2.0	14.7 15.0 7.7	—	—	—	33.3 0.2 4.5–5.9	—
33.3 4.1 50.0	—	9.0 0.3 1.0	11.1 7.6 7.1	—	—	—	—	25.0 1.2 9.2	—	14.7 0.6 7.7	—	—	11.1 4.2 10.0	—	—
—	12.5 ins 0.4	9.0 ins 0.3	—	—	—	—	—	—	—	—	—	—	—	—	25.0 nd 4.7
—	—	—	—	—	—	—	25.0 0.4 1.4	—	—	—	—	—	—	—	25.0 nd 4.7
—	—	—	—	—	—	—	—	—	—	—	—	—	11.1 0.3 1.5	—	—
—	—	9.0 ins 0.3	—	—	—	—	—	—	—	—	—	—	11.1 0.3 1.5	—	—
—	12.5 0.6 3.6	9.0 8.4 26.9	11.1 9.4 13.8	—	—	—	25.0 0.4 1.4	25.0 0.5 4.8	20.0 0.2 2.0	14.7 0.6 7.7	33.3 nd 15.8	33.3 27.8 7.1	11.1 4.8 nd		
—	12.5 0.3 2.2	9.0 0.4 1.6	11.1 1.0 2.8	—	33.3 nd nd	—	—	—	20.0 ins 2.0	14.7 0.3 7.7	—	—	11.1 8.3 2.9	—	—
—	—	—	—	—	—	—	—	—	—	—	—	—	—	33.3 0.2 4.5–5.9	25.0 nd 4.7
—	—	9.1 2.2 5.5	—	—	—	—	—	—	—	—	—	—	—	—	—
—	—	9.0 0.1 1.3	11.1 11.2 17.1	—	—	—	—	—	20.0 ins 2.0	—	—	—	11.1 1.0 1.5	—	25.0 nd 85.9
—	—	—	—	—	—	—	—	—	—	—	—	—	11.1 1.0 1.5	—	—
—	12.5 40.8 28.2	9.0 0.7 3.6	11.1 6.7 14.4	—	—	—	—	—	—	14.7 0.9 7.7	33.3 nd 5.3	33.3 13.9 7.1	11.1 1.3 nd	—	—

Table 3.18 SPATIAL AND TEMPORAL DISTRIBUTION OF KEY LATE VALDAI RESOURCES

	Mammoth	Horse	Reindeer	Steppe marmot	Hare	Arctic fox	Wolf
Spatial Distribution							
warm season	Desna floodplain	local floodplain	?	interfluves	local gallery forest	gallery forest?	gallery forest
cold season	mid-Dnepr floodplain	local floodplain	gallery forest floodplain	interfluves, hibernation	local gallery forest	gallery forest?	gallery forest
Social Behavior							
aggregation	late summer	late summer	nd	permanent	late summer, to 700 indiv.	during migration	none
dispersal	local north & south	fall, winter, spring	nd	none	fall, winter, spring	nd	permanent
Temporal Distribution							
seasonal migration	north in warm weather, south in cold weather	local	nd	available warm months only	north in warm weather? south in cold weather?	migrate in winter into study area?	local
short-term fluctuation	nd	nd	warm-weather births	warm-weather births	warm-weather multiple litters	warm-weather births	warm-weather births
supraseasonal fluctuation	nd	nd	100-year population density oscillations	nd	9–10 year population oscillations	3–4 year population cycles; 10–20 year population cycles	9–10 year population cycles
Prime Pelt Condition	—	—	—	—	mid-October–mid-December	December–February	November–January
Optimal Hunting							
season	south: October–May north: July–August	late summer–August	October–April?	July–August	Late summer–August, also December	December–February	November–January
location	gallery forest	floodplain	floodplain	interfluves	gallery forest	gallery forest	floodplain, gallery forest

high stem content. Mammoths, like other nonruminants, would have also had to balance their amino acids and fatty acids by adjusting intake variety and compensate for nonsynthesis of vitamins by supplementing a grass diet with forbs, woody dicots, and other arboreal materials. Such a mixture of nutritional requirements would place the mammoth, like the present-day elephant, in a mixed grassland–forest biome that on the late Valdai central Russian Plain existed around riverine gallery forests.

Paleontological collections from late Pleistocene localities in Alaska and Siberia show that precisely this biome contained the greatest densities of mammoth (Table 3.19). Localities from which the Siberian data are summarized are all found in or near the floodplains (Kuzmina 1977). Statistics in Table 3.19 indicate that mammoth represent 56.5% of individuals and 82.7% of the biomass of mammalian remains in Siberia. Summarized Alaskan data show a smaller overall representation of mammoth—6.5% of individuals and 33.3% of the biomass. A comparison of the percentages of mammoth found at the different Alaskan localities reveals the increase of mammoth densities toward the floodplain. Mammoth represents 50.8% of the biomass and 10.9% of individuals at Cripple Creek, located 6 km from the floodplain, 36.0% of the biomass and 6.7% of individuals at Engineers Creek, 12 km from the floodplain, and 25.9% of the biomass and 4.7% of individuals at Fairbanks Creek, 30 km from the floodplain. Using these data, one could presume that late Valdai mammoth in the study area lived predominantly near the floodplains.

While it is relatively simple to postulate where the mammoth lived, it is more difficult to project just how many of them there were. Summarized Alaskan data suggest that mammoth accounted for about 33.3% of the mammalian biomass, while Siberian data indicate 82.7% for this species. These differences may reflect sampling biases. As noted, Siberian data come directly from the floodplains. It is not unreasonable to assume, given the percentage increases in both numbers of individuals and overall biomass toward the floodplains in Alaska, that faunal assemblages exclusively from floodplains would likewise indicate high mammoth densities. At present it is impossible to resolve the differences recorded in Alaskan and Siberian data. Further research in both Alaska and the USSR will have to empirically determine if real differences did exist in the mammoth ratios there. Problematic as these data are, they do permit some heuristic modeling. I use mammoth densities estimated by Guthrie (1968) nearest the floodplain (i.e., approximately 50% of the biomass) for some calculations of mammoth densities on the late Valdai central Russian Plain. In other cases, I work with Siberian data.

Temporal variability also played a role in the distribution of mammoths. While, to the best of my knowledge, no paleontological data exist that addresses this question, data on African elephants indicate the occurrence of various seasonal migration patterns. These migrations, like all migrations of ungulates, are related to the availability of food and are more prominent among elephants living in regions with fluctuating precipitation. In such regions, elephants congregate during the dry season around the few available bodies of water where vegetation is to be found (Bourliere 1963; Laws *et al.* 1975; Wing and Buss 1970). Seasonal migrations for the African elephant have been reported as short as 15 to 25 km in Uganda (Laws *et al.* 1975) and as long as seasonal journeys

Table 3.19   PERCENTAGES OF MAMMALS IN SIBERIAN AND ALASKAN LATE PLEISTOCENE ASSEMBLAGES[a,b]

	Live weight (kg)	Fairbanks Creek		Engineers Creek		Cripple Creek		Gold Hills		Summarized Alaska		Berelekh		Siberia		Summarized Siberia	
		Ind.	Bio.	Ind.	Bio.	Ind.	Bio.	Ind.	Bio.	Ind.	Bio.	Ind.	Bio.	Ind.	Bio.	Ind.	Bio.
Felis sp.	110	0.8	0.2	0.2	0.1	0.5	0.1	—	—	0.4	0.1	—	—	—	—	—	—
Panthera spelaea	240	—	—	—	—	—	ins	—	—	ins	ins	0.6	ins	0.9	ins	0.8	ins
Smilodon sp.	100	—	—	—	—	ins	ins	—	—	—	—	—	—	—	—	—	—
Gulo gulo	25	—	—	—	—	—	—	—	—	—	—	2.6	ins	1.5	ins	2.0	ins
Alopex lagopus	5	—	—	—	—	—	—	—	—	—	—	—	—	0.9	ins	0.5	ins
Canis latrans	15	—	—	—	ins	0.1	ins	0.7	ins	ins	ins	—	—	—	—	—	—
Canis lupus	30	0.9	0.1	0.5	ins	1.2	0.1	—	—	0.8	0.1	—	—	2.7	ins	1.4	ins
Thalarctos maritimus	500	—	—	—	—	—	—	—	—	—	—	—	—	0.2	ins	0.1	ins
Ursus arctos	150	ins	ins	ins	ins	0.2	0.1	0.2	0.1	0.1	ins	—	—	0.2	ins	0.1	ins
Mammuthus primigenius	3000	4.7	25.9	6.7	36.0	10.9	50.8	3.4	20.9	6.5	33.3	89.8	98.9	23.1	66.5	56.6	82.7
Mastodon americanus	2500	ins	ins	—	—	—	—	—	—	ins	ins	—	—	—	—	—	—
Equus caballus[c]	290	17.3	9.2	36.8	19.1	41.0	18.5	35.4	21.1	32.7	17.0	1.9	0.2	21.5	6.0	11.7	3.1
Coelodonta antiquitatis[d]	2800	—	—	—	—	—	—	—	—	—	—	0.6	0.5	5.9	15.9	3.3	8.2
Camelops sp.	180	ins	ins	ins	ins	0.1	0.1	0.3	0.2	0.1	0.1	—	—	—	—	—	—
Alces alces	370	4.7	3.3	0.3	0.2	0.7	0.4	0.3	0.2	1.5	1.0	—	—	2.2	0.8	1.1	0.4
Cervalces sp.	350	0.1	0.1	0.2	0.1	0.3	0.2	—	—	0.1	0.1	—	—	—	—	—	—
Cervus elaphus	220	0.3	0.1	0.7	0.3	0.7	0.2	0.4	0.2	0.5	0.2	—	—	0.5	ins	0.2	ins
Rangifer tarandus	100	4.7	0.9	2.9	0.5	6.6	1.0	3.0	0.1	4.3	0.6	2.6	<0.1	14.9	1.5	8.8	0.8
Bison priscus	500	64.6	59.4	44.9	40.2	35.9	27.9	54.9	56.4	50.1	45.9	1.3	0.2	16.6	8.2	9.0	4.2
Bos sp.	300	ins	ins	0.3	0.2	ins	ins	ins	ins	ins	0.2	—	—	—	—	—	—
Ovibos moschatus	180	0.9	0.5	6.4	3.4	1.7	0.8	1.2	0.7	2.6	1.4	—	—	6.4	1.1	3.2	0.6
Ovis nivicola	80	0.1	ins	ins	ins	ins	ins	ins	ins	ins	ins	—	—	—	—	—	—
Saiga tatarica	50	—	—	—	—	ins	ins	ins	ins	ins	ins	—	—	0.5	ins	0.2	ins
Symbos sp.	180	0.6	0.2	0.2	0.1	ins	ins	0.2	0.1	0.3	0.1	—	—	—	—	—	—
Lepus tenaiticus	6	—	—	—	—	ins	ins	ins	ins	—	—	—	—	2.0	ins	1.0	ins
Sample size		2073		595		2293		1004		5965		156		409		565	
Distance from floodplain (km)		30		12		6		nd		—		on it		nd		—	

[a] Alaskan data from Guthrie (1968). Berelekh data from Vereschagin (1977). Siberian data from Kuzmina (1977).
[b] By individuals (Ind.) and biomass (Bio.). Insignificant, ins ≤ 0.09%.
[c] Vereschagin (1977) identifies horses at Berelekh as Equus lenensis.
[d] Vereschagin (1977) identifies this taxon as Coelodonta tichorhinus.

between 250 and 550 km (1100 km round trip) in South Africa (Roberts cited in Churcher 1980).

Churcher (1980) has surveyed the literature on the rates of movement of migrating elephants and reports that African elephants spend from 2 to 3 hours daily asleep and the remainder of the day feeding and moving. He notes that elephants migrate in two ways: (1) by slowly feeding and moving at an effective rate of approximately 8 km/hour, and (2) with a rapid nonfeeding march of 10 to 15 km/hour. The rates for slow feeding and moving appear to be too rapid to be steadily sustained, and Churcher suggests that the effective rate of slowly feeding and moving in a particular direction is closer to 1 km/hour. This rate permits elephants to cover approximately 20 km/day.

The question of whether mammoths were seasonal migrants has received very little attention in the literature. Soviet researchers tend to assume, usually leaving the reasons for these assumptions unstated, that they were seasonal migrants (Kornietz 1962; Vereschagin 1971, 1977, 1979). The possible migration patterns of mammoths are treated equally vaguely. Kornietz (1962) suggests that mammoths on the central Russian Plain migrated laterally—spending the winter in river valleys and the summer on the interfluves. This suggestion is offered without any qualification and has been picked up in the English-language literature (e.g., Klein 1973). But the nutritional requirements of mammoths (see pp. 187–191) argues strongly against this model and suggests that mammoths were found fairly close to the river valleys year round.

In addressing the issue of North American mammoth migration, Churcher (1980) suggests that nutritional requirements would have favored a latitudinal migration— north in the summers and south in the winters. This model is supported by Vereschagin (1971, 1977, 1979), who theorizes that late Valdai mammoths on the central Russian Plain behaved similarly.

Guthrie (1980) and Shilo *et al.* (1983) indicate that the daily food intake of mammoths was probably of such magnitude that one area would be grazed over rather quickly, and therefore that the animals would have to be rather mobile with some seasonal fidelity in range use. More recently, Guthrie (1982) speculates that the mammoth may have been even more mobile than the modern elephant. Vereschagin (1979), using data on African and Indian elephants, postulates that mammoths were highly efficient feeders capable of depleting local vegetal resources quickly and consequently mobile. Given the nature of paleoenvironments in the study area in the late Valdai, it seems reasonable to suggest that no one region could have steadily produced sufficient fodder to maintain year-round stable mammoth populations. The co-occurance of maximal precipitation and warm weather would have made summer months the most favorable for the mammoth. I suggest that during these times mammoth groups were most sedentary. With the advent of cold weather and the disappearance of annual grasses, the mammoth diet would increasingly consist of perennials as well as the woody vegetation that remained available in and near gallery forests. During these cold-weather months, especially by the end of winter, mammoths faced their greatest dietary stress. I further suggest that due to linear constriction in their habitat in or near the floodplains, the mammoth's seasonal mobility was also linear and placed the herds in the north during summer months and in the south during the cold season.

Both Guthrie (1982) and Tieszen *et al.* (1980) note the high nutritional content and rapid growth in deciduous forbs and shrubs in northern latitudes in the beginning of the warm season. These resources become available some 2–4 weeks after melt-off, in contrast to meadow grasses, which grow more slowly and are not available until late spring or early summer. I suspect that it was the appearance of the deciduous plant materials that set the mammoths off on their migrations to the north. Their return southward may have been triggered by an earlier onset of cold weather in the north and quicker depletion of food resources there.

Figure 2.1 shows that longitudinal distances in the study area are sufficiently small to have been within annual migration ranges of the mammoth. Mezhirich, for example, is some 515 km south of the northernmost Khotylevo II. The greatest distance—between Gontsy and Korshevo I and II is approximately 540 km. These values are within the range of distances covered by African elephants in their seasonal migrations. If we postulate moving rates for mammoths suggested by Churcher (1980), mammoths covering about 20 km/day would have been able to reach the most northerly regions in approximately 26 days. Thus mammoths may have spent some 8 months in the south, 2 months in transit, and 2 months in the north of the study area.

My conclusions about the spatial and temporal distribution of mammoths in the study area, and particularly the optimal time and location for harvesting this species (Table 3.18), are based on some standard assumptions about hunting behavior in the past—that it had as its goal the maximization of some desirable value (e.g., energy) per unit of energy expanded. I assume that a particular taxon would be most profitably hunted during the period of its greatest local abundance. Given my modeled distribution of mammoth per season, they would have been procured in the north during warm months (July and August) and in the mid-Dnepr region during the October–May cold season.

Horse (*Equus* sp.).   Large-size late Pleistocene horses, possibly belonging to the subspecies *Equus caballus latipes,* were a second important food species for Upper Paleolithic hunter–gatherers. As Table 3.17 shows, remains of horses were found at most of the Upper Paleolithic sites in the area, and at some, equids represent a substantial percentage of the faunal remains of food species (e.g., at Fastov equids represent 31.2% MNI; at Mezin, 19.7% MNI).

Freeman (1973) notes that there is no general agreement on the requirements of *Equus caballus.* Both he and Vereschagin (1979) suggest that late Pleistocene horses were a fairly widely adapted form that could have inhabited both open and partially forested landscapes. Guthrie's (1968, 1982) work with late Pleistocene Alaskan fauna shows a co-occurrence of horse with mammoth. Overall, this taxon represented 32.7% of individuals and 17% of the biomass in Alaska and 11.7% of individuals and 3.15% of the biomass in Siberia (Table 3.19). Alaskan data indicate an increase in horses, both percentage of individuals and percentage of biomass, toward the floodplain. Horses make up 41.0% of individuals and 18.5% of the biomass at Cripple Creek (6 km from the floodplains); 36.8% of individuals and 19.1% of the biomass at Engineers Creek (12 km from the floodplain), and 17.3% of individuals and 9.2% of the biomass at Fairbanks

Creek (30 km from the floodplain). This distribution leads Guthrie (1968, 1980) to conclude that horses fed primarily on medium and tall grasses high in fiber content.

Horses of the central Russian Plain probably also co-occured with mammoths and exploited medium and tall grasses, as well as sedges and small amounts of brush. We can conjecture that they were found in stallion-led groups along the river valleys (Spiess 1979). The numerous sheltered ravines on the central Russian Plain would probably have been suitable horse locales, especially in winter months.

Discussions of the seasonal behavior of this species is very sparce in the literature. There are no reports of long-distance seasonal migrations for horses. Kornietz (1962) proposed that late Pleistocene horses, like their contemporary analogues, aggregated in warm-weather months. She suggests that these aggregations reached maximal sizes during the rutting season in late summer.

The local distribution of *Equus* sp. near the floodplains would have made the vicinity of the gallery forests the locale for their procurement. Their possible seasonal aggregations in late summer suggest that the optimal time for procuring this species would have been sometime in August.

Reindeer (*Rangifer tarandus*).   It is difficult to estimate the role that reindeer played in subsistence practices, because of the superficial treatment that archaeozoological remains have received in the literature. No information exists on what specific skeletal elements were found at the sites, and, as numerous researchers have noted, most of the reindeer appear to be represented by antlers only (Klein 1973; Pidoplichko 1969; Shovkoplyas 1965a). Since both male and female reindeer shed antlers, it is possible that many antlers were collected in shed form; their presence in assemblages is thus not indicative of active hunting of the species. At some sites, skeletal remains other than antlers have been found, as well as antlers still attached to crania—suggesting that at these sites (e.g., Mezin) some reindeer hunting did take place.

As both Burch (1972) and White *et al.* (1980) report, present-day reindeer belong to two behaviorally distinct forms—the woodland and barren-ground varieties. The latter undertake seasonal migrations of up to 2400 km between winter and summer pastures, whereas woodland reindeer migrate over shorter distances of up to 200 km. Spiess' (1979) study of both present-day and late Pleistocene reindeer of southwestern France indicates, however, that no fast and easy way exists to determine the ecology of reindeer of specific regions. Spiess writes:

> The typologizing of caribou behavior into tundra and forest forms is a falsehood by gross over-simplification. . . . We are reduced to considering each archaeological span of time and geographic area as an individual case, using osteoarchaeological techniques on several sites, before deciding what the caribou behavior and migration patterns were like. Much more work is needed before we can be precise about migration patterns beyond the certainty that they varied over geographic distances and time as conditions changed. (1979:137–138)

> Caribou tend to live in smaller population aggregations at a lower overall density in areas with a more diverse ungulate fauna. In such areas, usually of microenvironmental diversity . . . *Rangifer* does not form large herds or migrate long distances over highly predictable paths. (1979:247)

He uses these observations to state that late Pleistocene reindeer populations of south-western France in all probability were not analogous to tundra forms of today and did not undertake long-distance migrations. This does not, however, mean that they were locally available year round, as Bouchud (1966, 1975) thought, because shorter seasonal migrations were certainly both possible and feasible.

Table 3.19 shows that reindeer composed 8.8% of individuals and 0.8% of the bio-mass in late Pleistocene Siberian paleontological assemblages and 4.3% of individuals and 0.6% of the biomass in Alaskan assemblages. Alaskan data show no directional increase in this species either toward or away from the floodplain.

Siberian data, as well as faunal assemblages from the central Russian Plain, indicate that late Pleistocene environments in both regions contained diverse ungulate faunas, and by extension implies that reindeer of the central Russian Plain lived in small population aggregations at lower overall densities than found among tundra reindeer today. Spiess (1979) notes that during winter months most populations of most species, including reindeer, seek shelter in grassy river floodplains and deep-cut valleys. This suggests that the reindeer of the central Russian Plain would also have been located in and near the river valleys during the cold months.

Pidoplichko (1969) notes that no young reindeer were present in the faunal as-semblages of several major sites in the study area (Chulatovo I, Dobranichevka, Mezin, Mezhirich, and Novgorod-Severskii) and argues that this indicates that reindeer were harvested during cold months. He and Vereschagin (1971, 1977, 1979) after him argue that late Pleistocene reindeer undertook north–south seasonal migrations and may have been present on the central Russian Plain only during winter months. This hy-pothesis does not take into account the differential preservation rates for various ages—that the absence of immature reindeer may just reflect natural taphonomic processes and not cultural behavior (Grayson 1984).

Reindeer, like many other northern-latitude species, undergo long-term oscillations in population numbers (Amsden 1979; Vibe 1967, 1970; White *et al.* 1980). The length of these cycles for reindeer has been reported in the magnitude of approximately 100 years, and we can expect that late Pleistocene reindeer were also subject to such fluctuations.

In summary, then, all that can be concluded about reindeer of the late Pleistocene central Russian Plain is that they may have exhibited spatial patchiness in distribution during cold-weather months at least. During the 8–9-month winter season they may have tended toward the floodplains and may have undertaken seasonal north–south migrations of uncertain length or duration. Finally, we can postulate that long-term temporal fluctuations in the population of this species may have made them a more patchily distributed resource both temporally and spatially. Given these data, I suggest that optimal harvesting season would have been October–April and the optimal location riverine gallery forests.

Steppe Marmot (*Marmota bobac*).   Marmot remains have been found in great abun-dance at some Upper Paleolithic sites. As Table 3.17 shows, this species represents 24.8% MNI of food taxa at Chulatovo II, 17.1% at Mezin, and a high percentage of 85.9%

at Zhuravka. The ecology of this species is fairly well understood and has been reported on extensively by Zimina (1953) and Zimina and Gerasimov (1970, 1971). As a species, it is a relatively recent form that made its appearance in the Pleistocene from ancestral Asian stock. *Marmota bobac* formed an important component of late Pleistocene rodent communities, becoming especially widespread during the second half of the Valdai glaciation. These typical grassland dwellers, found today in areas with continental climate, were extremely well adapted to the cold climates of the past. Present-day steppe marmots feed on herbaceous vegetation (*Artemisia* and *Stipa* predominantly), augmenting it occasionally with insects. Marmots are highly social, living in family units of 10 to 15 individuals in burrows. These coresidential groups are further aggregated into colonies that sometimes number in the hundreds of animals. Zimina and Gerasimov report that, while today they dig deep and complex multiple burrows, during the Valdai glaciation steppe marmots probably lived in shallower burrows extending no deeper than 1–1.5 m (the permafrost thaw layer at the time).

Steppe marmots are highly seasonal and hibernate in the winter. Freeman (1973) reports that marmots hibernate when ambient temperatures drop below 3 or 4°C. Present-day marmots in northern parts of Siberia spend as many as 9 months in hibernation, and Zimina and Gerasimov (1970) postulate a 9-month hibernation period during the late Valdai.

As all hibernating species, marmots have a highly seasonal accumulation of fat, weighing 800–1200 g at the onset of hibernation. This weight is drastically reduced during the cold months, and marmots emerge from their burrows in the spring weighing 100–200 g (Zimina and Gerasimov 1971).

These observations suggest the following for late Pleistocene steppe marmots of the central Russian Plain: (1) They were a temporally variable species available for exploitation during 2 or 3 warm months only. (2) Their seasonal accumulation of fat would have made late summer the optimal time for exploiting this species. (3) They inhabited open grassland environments and thus would have been more numerous away from the riverine gallery forests and more concentrated in the interfluves. And though they were most likely procured in these locales, their small size would have allowed transportation of harvested individuals to habitation sites, and we can expect to find all skeletal elements represented in the archaeozoological assemblages.

It is interesting to note that both Kirikov (1979) and Zimina (1953) report that exploitation of this species as a food resource still persists in the southern part of European USSR, and marmots historically formed an important food source during periods of nutrition shortage. Marmot pelts are still in use as well.

Hare (*Lepus* sp.).   Hare remains figure prominently in faunal remains at some sites. At Mezhirich they represent 28.8% MNI of food taxa and at Chulatovo II 19.8%. As I noted in Chapter 2, classification of leporid remains found at the sites is still unclear. Gureev (1964) argues that these late Pleistocene denizens belong to the extinct form *Lepus tenaiticus*. He suggests that they were considerably larger than any modern species and at least 50% larger than their closest modern relatives, *Lepus timidus* (Gureev 1978, personal communication). Present-day arctic hares inhabit boreal forest and tundra biomes, feed on grasses in summer months, but switch to forbs, shrubs, and more arboreal vegetation during the winter (Naumov 1948). They are predominantly found in protected river valleys where a mix of grassland and arboreal vegetation is found year round. When local food supplies fail, hares undertake migrations, although both the direction and extent of these remain unclear (Gureev 1964). Arctic hares undergo two molts a year—to lighter summer pelage sometime from mid-March to the end of May and to winter pelage from mid-October to mid-December (Gaiduk 1970).

Hare populations are not stable year round but are largest by late summer after two litters are born (Gaiduk 1970; Gureev 1964). These large populations aggregate in summer months into local groupings of up to 700 individuals (Bliss *et al.* 1973; Naumov 1972). In addition, hare populations undergo regular oscillations in population and sharp declines occur on the average of every 9–10 years (Bliss *et al.* 1973; May 1980; Vibe 1970).

We can deduce the following for hares exploited by Upper Paleolithic hunter–gatherers in the study area: (1) The species was patchily distributed, predominantly in the gallery forest ecotone. (2) During the warm months they were more abundant—more patchily distributed but in larger patches. (3) The species may have exhibited some limited latitudinal seasonal migration, possibly moving short distances to the north in summers and south in winters. (4) Population numbers of leporids probably underwent periodic declines at intervals of about 10 years. Given this reconstruction, I suggest that late summer was the best time for harvesting the hare if their food value was being optimized (see Table 3.18). Since this taxon probably reached optimal pelt conditions sometime later, in late fall–early winter, a December–January harvest would have selected for pelt condition.

Arctic Fox (*Alopex lagopus*).   Although the arctic fox was not used for food, its remains are extremely abundant at some sites. This species is represented by 68.5% MNI and 53.3% MNB at Eliseevichi, 26.2% MNI and 62.9% MNB at Timonovka II, 22.7% MNI and 22.4% MNB at Mezin, and 11.7% MNB and 10.3% MNI at Novgorod–Severskii. Since this species represents only 0.5% of MNI in the summarized Siberian late Pleistocene assemblages (Table 3.19), the high numbers from the sites clearly indicate that arctic foxes were selectively exploited by Upper Paleolithic hunter–gatherers.

Benesz (1975) indicates that present-day arctic foxes, although somewhat larger, are very similar to their late Pleistocene relatives. Today this taxon is a characteristic representative of tundra–boreal forest fauna, found in the tundra in the summer months and the forest zone in winter (Adlerberg *et al.* 1935; Formozov 1970; Shilyaeva 1970; Vibe 1967). As Benesz (1975) points out, this specialization to an extremely cold climate appeared fairly recently, as late as the middle Würm.

There is no clear indication in the literature of spatial patchiness in the distribution of this species other than the prevalence of pupping dens near water. We must therefore assume that late Valdai foxes were also fairly evenly distributed, possibly favoring proximity to water (i.e., gallery forests) in warm months. Great temporal variability, however, does exist in the distribution of this species. The arctic fox regularly undertakes extensive fall and late winter–early spring migrations, covering over 1000 km one way in their seasonal treks. These migrations are especially important in lean years—

when prey rodents are scarce. As mentioned, the arctic fox spends winter months in the forest zone in the south and returns north to the tundra in spring and summer. Their migration routes follow the river valleys.

As this discussion indicates, a number of demographic changes occur in arctic fox populations throughout the year. First, population sizes and densities fluctuate, with greater numbers present after the birth of litters by mid-May. Marakov (1970) reports that average densities of 3.25–3.4 individuals/km^2 in Siberia increase to 5.25–5.5/km^2 after pupping. This suggests an approximately 62% increase in arctic fox numbers after the birth of new litters. Second, presence of immature individuals is felt only during summer and fall months (by winter all are adult), although the yearlings are still recognizable in skeletal morphology. Noting that remains of *Alopex lagopus* found at the Upper Paleolithic sites show sites show the presence of only adult individuals, Pidoplichko (1969) concludes that the arctic fox probably did not reproduce in the area but rather migrated there during winter months. Vereschagin (1977) reports the following demographic composition of *Alopex lagopus* at Eliseevichi: yearlings, 44.3%; adults, 47.7%; old, 8.4% ($n = 287$). He concludes that such a demographic profile could have resulted only from winter hunts. While taphonomic factors alone would select for an underrepresentation of juvenile individuals in faunal assemblages, the much higher numbers of arctic fox found in northern sites (Table 2.7) suggest that the species may have been far more abundant in the north. This greater availability may well have been a seasonal phenomenon.

Additional temporal variability is reported for this species as well. Numbers and densities of arctic fox are tied to densities of the lemming, and like the lemming, the fox undergoes regular population oscillations every 3–4 years (Braestrup 1941; Butler 1953; Formozov 1970; Marakov 1970; Shilyaeva 1970; Vibe 1967). Data from both fur trade and ecological studies suggest the existence of another long-term cycle in population of arctic foxes—one occurring on the average every 10–20 years (Butler 1953; Vibe 1967).

We can conclude the following for the distribution of arctic foxes in the study area in the late Valdai: (1) They were patchily distributed, favoring areas near the river valleys both in warm months while pupping and in the cold months while migrating north to south. (2) Their population densities varied seasonally, being significantly greater after pupping and during periods of migration along the migration routes. (3) Their numbers fluctuated at regular intervals of approximately every 3–4 years as well as every 10–20 years. Some circumstantial and conjectural evidence suggests that the species was present in the study area during cold months and reproduced elsewhere. This evidence is still tenuous and must await further research. Since optimal pelt conditions for this taxon would have co-occured with their maximal abundance in the study area (December–February), I suggest that early winter would have been optimal for harvesting arctic foxes.

Wolf (*Canis lupus*).   The wolf occurs in sizable numbers at three sites: Khotylevo II (12.8% MNI and 19.8% MNB), Mezin (11.9% MNI and 12.3% MNB), and Pushkari I (7.0% of MNI and 30.7% of MNB). Siberian paleontological collections show only 1.4% MNI belonging to this species. Alaskan data indicate that wolves account for 0.8% MNI.

A comparison of the statistics from the central Russian Plain with those from Alaska and Siberia indicates that wolves were selectively exploited at some sites during the Upper Paleolithic, as remains are found in much higher percentages than could be expected from nonselective random catches.

Some interesting differences appear between the Alaskan and Siberian data. Guthrie (1968) notes that the ratio of *Canis lupus* to ungulates in Pleistocene Alaska was 1:130 and that this is fairly similar to present-day proportions. Siberian late Pleistocene data show a much greater number of wolves and suggest a ratio of approximately 1:35. These differences may imply that a greater density of both predators and prey existed in late Pleistocene Eurasia than in Alaska. Highest present-day wolf densities in Siberia are reported to range from 1 to 3 wolves/100 km^2 in unpopulated regions (Kirikov 1979). I assume that these densities are fairly close to that during the late Valdai.

Canis lupus is a widely distributed Holarctic species with highly plastic ecological requirements that permit habitation of a wide variety of environments ranging from tundra to deciduous forest to steppe (Mech 1970; Naumov and Gentner 1967; Pimlott 1975; Stroganov 1969). Stroganov reports greater patchiness in the distribution of this predator in forested regions, where snow conditions make wolves favor river valleys with harder and more compact snow. In general, distribution of this species is associated with distribution of the medium- and large-size ungulates on which it preys. The species is fairly sedentary, living in monogamous familial packs in specific territories. Gurskii (1978) reports a lifetime range of wolves in European Russia as averaging between 120 and 160 km^2. Pimlott (1975) states that the long-held assumption that the social organization and territoriality of wolves breaks down in summer with increased mobility has been proven incorrect, and that packs persist throughout the year. It still remains unclear, according to Pimlott, whether wolves in areas without geographic barriers are locally restricted in their movements. These reports all suggest that wolf distribution is controlled by the distribution of ungulates. Where suitable densities of ungulates are present, wolf packs occupy specific and distinct territories year round. I have previously postulated greater ungulate densities for the gallery forest–steppe ecotone on the central Russian Plain. If this is correct, it would suggest that greater wolf densities existed along the riverine gallery forest–floodplains than in the interfluves. The noted increase in wolf densities along river valleys reported for Siberia also supports this conclusion.

Temporal variability in wolf population is also reported in the literature. Stroganov (1969) writes that population numbers of this species vary greatly from year to year. Little work exists on the long-term population fluctuations of the wolf. Pulliainen (1975) shows that a clear predator–prey relationship exists between the population density of the lynx (*Lynx lynx*) and *Canis lupus*. Lynx are reported to undergo regular long-term population oscillations on the scale of every 9–10 years (Butler 1953; Vibe 1967, 1970; White *et al.* 1980). Both wolves and lynx are probably also tied into the predator–prey oscillation cycles of their prey, such as hares. The predator–prey relationship between wolf, lynx, and other small animals implies that wolf populations also undergo regular long–term population oscillations.

We can conclude the following for the late Valdai population of *Canis lupus* on the central Russian Plain: (1) They were patchily distributed across the landscape, with greater densities found in and near the gallery forests. (2) They were a fairly localized species that did not undertake seasonal migrations. (3) Some temporal variability existed in the population numbers of the species, with greater numbers found in a region following spring pupping. (4) The population of wolves may have undergone regular long-term oscillations of as yet undetermined magnitude. (5) Optimal pelt conditions occurred in the late fall–early winter months.

Domesticated Dogs?   Soviet researchers have suggested from time to time that some of the *Canis lupus* remains found at the central Russian Plain Upper Paleolithic sites are of domesticated dogs. Pidoplichko (1969) postulates that some of the canid remains at Mezin represent dogs. Polikarpovich (1968) likewise suggests that dogs were present at Eliseevichi. He did not undertake a specific study of the canid remains to determine the morphological characteristics but rather extrapolated from literature on canid remains from other sites (particularly from Afontova Gora in Siberia). Gromov (1925) examined canid remains excavated at the Afontova Gora and concluded that the small size and forshortened muzzles of some of the crania indicates that domestication had taken place. In general, Soviet paleontologists in the 1920s and 1930s assumed that small sizes in canid remains reflected domestication, and thus the presence of domestic dogs was ascribed to canid remains from many Upper Paleolithic sites (Bonch-Osmolovskii 1931; Gerasimov 1931; Gromov 1925).

Pidoplichko (1969) based his conclusions about the presence of domestic dogs at Mezin on the measurement of a single cranium (specimen #5-490) and reported both a small size and foreshortening of the muzzle as evidence for the domestication of the animal. He estimated the age of the animal as about 1 year. My own examination of the specimen, housed in the Museum of Zoology of the Academy of Sciences of the Ukranian USSR in Kiev, resulted in a somewhat younger age for the cranium than that postulated by Pidoplichko. The aging criteria I used were derived from work by Allan (1920), Dolgov and Rossolimo (1966), Gilbert (1973), Mech (1970), and Silver (1969) for the sequence of suture fusings on the crania, and Dolgov and Rossolimo (1966), Mech (1970), Silver (1969), and Taber (1971) for the tooth-eruption sequence. My examination showed that adult canines were fully erupted, unworn, and about three-fourths of the way in—suggesting that the specimen was approximately 8 or 9 months old at the time of death. Some of the cranial sutures were still open (the vomer as well as the basioccipital–basisphenoid suture), confirming that the animal was less than 1 year old. Ample zoological literature exists to show that only adult, full-grown individuals should be used for morphological evaluations. The Mezin specimen, therefore, cannot be used to prove the existence of domestic dogs.

Lawrence (1966) and Lawrence and Bossert (1967, 1975) have done an exhaustive review of the suitable criteria for determining the domestication of *Canis lupus* and conclude that only a battery of measurements (42 cranial measurements) subjected to multiple character analysis can reveal whether a particular individual is a wild or domestic form. As both Lawrence and Bossert and Rossolimo and Dolgov (1965) amply indicate, populations of *Canis lupus* show a great deal of skeletal variability of size, both within particular populations and between different populations inhabiting different regions. Rossolimo and Dolgov report that divisions of variation for certain characteristics differ by as much as 32.8% from the mean value.

I could not take the cranial measurements suggested by Lawrence and Bossert because the Mezin specimen is damaged and many of the necessary cranial parts are missing (e.g., zygomatic arches). However, the previous discussion does indicate that small size of the specimen from Mezin is more likely due to immaturity and falls within the normal range of variability in wolf populations. Pidoplichko's measurements of specimen #5-490, of a wild *Canis lupus* from Mezin, and of present-day dog and wolf from the Ukraine are offered in Table 3.20.

The foreshortening of the muzzle observed by Pidoplichko in specimen #5-490, the second criterion offered by for domestication, is also problematic due to the age of the specimen. The length of the muzzle is 226 mm and is just 22% shorter than the length he reported for the wild form of *Canis lupus* from Mezin (specimen #5-488)—a size variation well within the normal range of variation for *Canis lupus*. In conclusion then, there is no evidence that specimen #5-490 from Mezin represents a domestic dog.

Skeletal remains of *Canis lupus* from Eliseevichi were likewise not complete anough for measurement using Lawrence and Bossert's criteria. In fact, all the crania were

Table 3.20   CRANIAL MEASUREMENTS OF LATE PLEISTOCENE AND PRESENT-DAY CANIDS[a]

Measurements (mm)	Specimen[b]			
	Mezin "dog"	Present-day dog	Mezin wolf	Present-day wolf
Maximal length	226	237	257	283
Candylo-basal length	210	215	233	248
Zygomatic width	$120\pm$[c]	123	$148\pm$[c]	147
Width across postorbital processes	57.5	67	61.5	64
Minimal interorbital width	39	44	39	40
Width between orbits	48	47	55	53
Maximal width of rostrum at canines	45	48	51	51.5
Length of rostrum from alveolus of I^1 to orbit	110	121	127	143
Length of nasal bones	80	93	92	106
Maximal width of nasal bones	23	25	26	25.5
Maximal width at of brain case at parieto-temporal suture	44.5	45	48.5	52
Maximal width between outside bulla walls	70	71.5	78	80
Alveolar length of tooth row	121	117	132	136
Maximal length and width of P^4	25×15	22×12	25×13	28×12
Maximal length and width of M^1	16×22	15×19	17×22	17×22
Maximal palate width between P^4	63	62	75	71

[a]From Pidoplichko (1969: 103).
[b]Provenience of specimens: (1) "dog" from Mezin cultural layer; (2) present-day Ukranian sheepdog from Dnepropetrovskaya Oblast'; (3) wolf from Mezin cultural layer; (4) present-day wolf from the village of Semivokli in Kiev Oblast'.
[c]Archaeological specimen incomplete; measurements estimated.

highly fragmented and the vast majority of skeletal remains in the faunal collection belong to post-cranial elements. To date, no paleontological examination of the remains has been conducted to determine if the size variation present in the assemblage is beyond the range of normal size variation for wild canids. Vereschagin (1978, personal communication) believes that all of the remains, in fact, represent *Canis lupus* and that no evidence exists for the presence of domestic dogs anywhere on the central Russian Plain during the late Valdai.

Olsen and Olsen (1977) have recently proposed that the presence of a "turned-back" apex of the coronoid process of the ascending ramus is a good criteria for establishing the domestic status of a canid. They report this feature present in domestic dogs and absent in all wild canids with the exception of the Chinese wolf. S. Olsen (1981, personal communication) reports that this feature is absent in all of the canid mandibles he has examined from the central Russian Plain and, like Vereschagin, concludes that no evidence exists that some of the canids were domesticated in the late Valdai.

In summary then, both my own examination and those of Olsen and Olsen and of Vereschagin reveal no solid justification for the claim that some of the *Canis lupus* remains from the area belong to domestic dogs. The remains found to date all belong to the wild species *Canis lupus*.

FAUNAL DISTRIBUTION AND CLIMATIC FLUCTUATION

Faunal assemblages found at Eurasian Upper Paleolithic sites, as well as at the late Pleistocene paleontological localities of Alaska and Siberia, have led many scholars to postulate that the periglacial forest–steppe environments provided conditions as favorable for ungulates as the temperate grasslands today (Butzer 1971, 1976; Frenzel 1973; Guthrie 1968; Martin 1973). These authors suggest that the carrying capacity of present-day tundras (ca. 800 kg of ungulates/km^2) is considerably lower than that of late Pleistocene grasslands. Butzer (1971) reports that the temperate Eurasian steppe-grasslands today have an ungulate carrying capacity of 350–3000 kg/km^2. Guthrie's work with Alaskan faunas suggests that late Pleistocene grassland supported a crop close to or above the maximum estimates for present-day temperate grasslands. Martin (1973) assumes even greater ungulate biomass for late Pleistocene North America and, basing his estimates on the ungulate crop of African grasslands today, offers a figure of 9000 kg/km^2. The most conservative estimates for the ungulate biomass are to be found in the work of Budyko (1977), who uses 800 kg/km^2.

These estimates, however, must be modified if they are to be used for estimating man–land relationships. The potential carrying capacity of an area is meaningless for such calculations, and as numerous authors have pointed out, we must take into consideration human perceptions since carrying capacities are culturally defined (e.g., Jochim 1976, 1981). The following discussion, therefore, focuses on the abundance and distribution of only those species significantly represented in the archaeological record of the study area.

I have noted previously that patchiness of distribution is a natural spatial feature of all environments; so, too, is carrying capacity. Extensive research in Africa, Beringia, and

North America indicates that ungulate biomass rises when proceeding from grassland to riverine gallery forests (Andreev and Aleksandrova 1981; Bourliere and Hadley 1970; Guthrie 1968; Martin 1973). My previous discussion on the ecological requirements of taxa exploited by Upper Paleolithic hunter–gatherers likewise suggests that this biome contained most ungulates. I conclude that late Pleistocene gallery forest–periglacial steppe ecotones in the study area also had higher carrying capacities than periglacial steppes of the interfluves.

Temporal variability can be postulated as well for the carrying capacity of the study area. I have postulated migratory behavior for the mammoth as well as the arctic fox. Other researchers have suggested that both reindeer and woolly rhinoceros may have migrated into the area only in winter months (Chernysh 1959; Pidoplichko 1969).

Ecological literature also suggests that gallery forests and their vicinities present important refuge for animal species during critical periods (Bourliere 1963; Bourliere and Hadley 1970; Laws *et al.* 1975). Both Jochim (1976) and Spiess (1979) argue that in northern latitudes winter months are such a critical period, and that during cold-weather months the distribution of large game tends to overlap that of plants, fish, and small game—that is, in and near floodplains. As Table 3.18 indicates, greater numbers of reindeer, wolf, and hare would have been found near floodplains in cold months.

These variables as well as specific seasonal aggregations for some taxa all demand qualifications to estimates of carrying capacity. Lack of fine-scale paleoenvironmental reconstructions forbid consideration of five-scale taxa densities; what data are available suggest that much higher carrying capacities existed near the river valleys than further inland on the interfluves, and that these differences were especially notable during the cold months in the late Valdai.

Density of Mammoth

Mammoth is the most abundant species found in faunal assemblages at Upper Paleolithic sites in the study area both in MNI and MNB calculations. The sheer abundance of mammoth (e.g., 149 at Mezhirich, 116 at Mezin) has led researchers to assume that the central Russian Plain was inhabited by large populations of mammoth and that mammoth was the most important resource in Upper Paleolithic subsistence practices (e.g., Klein 1973; Pidoplichko 1969, 1976; Shovkoplyas 1965a). But actual discussion of mammoth population in the literature has been cursory and indirect (e.g., Bibikov 1969). Some will argue that, given the coarse nature of our paleoenvironmental reconstructions, any estimate of mammoth density is an exercise in futility. I suggest, however, that reasonable estimates, offered as heuristic devices and not iron-clad reflections of past realities, can offer us new understanding and delimit important parameters relevant to past human cultural practices.

Table 3.21 offers various population estimates based on different carrying capacities. The assumptions I employed in all calculations are (1) an average live weight of mammoths for all age classes of 3000 kg (after Guthrie 1968), and (2) an estimate that mammoths represent 50% of the ungulate biomass in the area. (See previous discussion on mammoth ecology; the various published carrying capacity estimates express the carrying capacity of ungulate biomass only.) Populations are estimated for three areas.

Table 3.21   ESTIMATED MAMMOTH POPULATION IN THE STUDY AREA

	Ungulate carrying capacity[a]				Siberian wolf–ungulate ratio[b]
	Budyko 1967 800 kg/km²	Butzer 1971 3,000 kg/km²	Martin 1973 9,000 kg/km²	Bourliere 1963 (African grassland) 18,000 kg/km²	
Kilograms of mammoth per square kilometer	400	1,500	4,500	9,000	
Square kilometers per mammoth	7.5	2.0	0.67	0.33	
(A) total number of mammoth in study area	24,000	90,000	270,000	540,000	28,000–84,000
(B) total number of mammoth in river valleys	12,000	45,000	135,000	270,000	14,000–42,000
(C) total number of mammoth if species migrated seasonally	6,000	22,500	67,500	135,000	7,000–21,000

[a]Assumes mammoth live weight of 3000 kg and mammoth represents 50% of ungulate biomass.
[b]Assumes wolf density of 1–3 individuals per 100 km² (Kirikov 1970), late Pleistocene wolf–wolf ungulate ratio of 1:35 (see Table 3.19), and mammoth represents 44.7% of ungulate individuals (see Table 3.19).

The first (A) applies carrying capacities to the whole study area of 180,000 km²; (B) presumes the linearized distribution of mammoths close to the river valleys, with an estimated 1500 km of rivers and 60-km river valley widths for an area of 90,000 km²; (C) estimates a 50% reduction in overall numbers of linearly distributed mammoths. This last calculation is based on the assumption of seasonal north–south migration. African elephant data suggest much lower overall densities in regions where long-distance seasonal migrations are important (Bourliere 1963; Laws *et al.* 1975; Sikes 1971). To the best of my knowledge, no precise figures exist that express these density differences, and I have therefore adopted a 50% reduction in the population estimates. Paleontological data from Siberian late Pleistocene faunal assemblages allow an independent estimate of mammoth populations, also shown in Table 3.21. Here I take present-day wolf densities reported for Siberia (1–3 individuals/100 km²) and apply them to the wolf–ungulate ratios found in the Siberian paleontological assemblages (reported in Table 3.19). This permits an estimate of possible numbers of ungulates in the study area. I arrive at the estimates for mammoth population by employing the ratio of the number of mammoths to other ungulates found in the Siberian paleontological assemblages; this ratio shows that mammoths represent 44.7% of all ungulate individuals in the collection. The figures derived from these calculations (28,000–84,000 mammoths in an area of 180,000 km²; 14,000–42,000 mammoths if linearized in distribution along the river valleys; 7000–21,000 mammoths if linearized and seasonal migrations assumed) suggest that the carrying capacities suggested by Budyko (1967) and Butzer (1971) come closer to the possible late Valdai carrying capacity of the area than figures derived after either Martin (1973) or contemporary African grassland data.

It should be noted that these calculations are based on carrying capacities of ungulate biomass in open landscapes—either tundra or northern grasslands. I have shown, however, that climatic fluctuations during the period 18,000–12,000 B.P. varied the vegetational cover of the study area from open landscapes during cold periods to various degrees of forestation during the warm periods. These vegetational changes profoundly affected the ungulate carrying capacities of the area. Under conditions of greater fore-station, mammoth population would be considerably less. Butzer (1971) suggests a carrying capacity of 500 kg/km^2 for ungulates for mixed forest zones in northern latitudes—representing an 83% reduction from mammoth population estimates based on his cold-period carrying capacity figure, or a 37% reduction from populations based on Budyko's (1967) figure.

The populations presented in Table 3.21 are only rough estimates. Lack of chronolog-ical controls, absence of fine environmental reconstructions, as well as a lack of present-day mammoth populations all combine to preclude precision. I offer these estimates purely as heuristic devises—to be used in constructing adequate models for man–land relationships during the late Valdai. Varying environmental conditions throughout the period would cause fluctuations in mammoth densities. The relatively more stable period of 25,000–20,000 B.P. should have had a more stable population, whereas the more fluctuating period of 18,000–12,000 B.P. would have seen much greater popula-tion oscillations (see also Ukraintseva 1979). The magnitude of such oscillations is impossible to determine precisely—my estimates just offer some possible parameters.

Research on population oscillations has focused on the fluctuations on the wave-length of years or, at most, decades. No work exists that examines the relationship of such fluctuations to longer term (i.e., wavelength of centuries) oscillations. Haber (1980) has shown that population fluctuations combined with predation pressures create three population equilibria for moose. Under natural circumstances, subarctic moose populations are expected to fluctuate about the equilibrium point for a relatively long time (to 10 years), but the population reacts differently at the three equilibrium thresholds. Moose increment rates decrease at threshold levels of both high and low population densities, but increments to populations are positive at the medium density equilibrium levels. This leads Haber to conclude that oscillating moose populations have two recovery thresholds—from both medium and high density equilibria. Moose, however, are most vulnerable at the third, low, equilibrium. The natural predator–prey relationships between moose and their main predators are such that additional preda-tion pressure added to the low population threshold, even at small percentages, could be catastrophic for the moose population.

Haber's model for the wolf–moose relationship uses catastrophe theory to explain the predator–prey relationship and ensuing prey population densities. May (1977), while rejecting the specific use of the catastrophe theory as an explanatory devise in ecology, likewise reports the presence of several different equilibria in both plant and animal species. This implies the existence of different population thresholds and breakpoints for different species. Using fishery data for example, May shows that the presence of different equilibrium levels is responsible for the differential reaction to steady predation. In some cases, as when the particular population is at an equilibrium of low population, continuous harvesting rates can cause discontinuous collapse in fisheries.

Haber (1980) suggests that such a model may be quite applicable to population fluctuations recorded in many north-latitude species, including reindeer and musk-ox. A decrease in populations of north-latitude ungulates has been reported and related to climatic oscillations and especially climatic deterioration (Spiess 1979; White *et al.* 1980). These decreases occur as a result of decreased fertility and greater mortality among the juveniles of the species. Lack of long-term studies of northern ungulates precludes me from either assessing the universal applicability of such a model to ungulate populations in general or applying it to the late Valdai central Russian Plain. The model does suggest, however, that additional stress—either predator-generated or climatic, may be more detrimental to some species than to others, as well as at some times and not others. Specifically, the longevity and low reproduction rates of large ungulates would make them more vulnerable to stress and catastrophy. If late Valdai populations of large ungulates, especially mammoth, were in as complex predator–prey relationships as Haber reports for moose, then either additional climatic stress (such as induced by climatic fluctuations between 18,000 and 12,000 B.P.) or increased predation may have been catastrophic for the population.

Firm data on African elephants is available only for the period since about 1960. This time span is insufficient for establishing long-term population changes for the species with the longevity (approximately 50–60 years) and slow reproduction rates (gestation period of 22 months, at 3- to 7-year intervals) of elephants. We simply do not know whether African elephant populations are at equilibrium or have more than one equilibrium point.

Laws *et al.* (1975) report population growth rates as averaging 4.6%/year for African elephants and mortality rates as 28.5% for the 0–5-year age set and 6.4% for the 5–50-year age set. They note that mortality rates are uniformly spread within the latter set. These statistics suggest that the studied populations are not at equilibrium. Saunders (1980) reports average increment rates for African elephants of about 6%, with a range from 0 to 20%. Saunders' figure approaches the mortality rate more closely and indicates that at least some of the elephant populations are close to equilibrium. Populations at some equilibrium levels, as Haber's work has shown, can sustain only the most limited stress.

The effects of inclement climate on the recruitment (i.e., the numbers of newborn) of African elephants has been studied by Laws *et al.* (1975), who report a cyclical fluctuation with a wavelength of 6 to 8 years, which correlates with rainfall cycles. Laws' findings of decreased recruitment rates associated with climatic stress have been confirmed by Douglas-Hamilton (1972). Laws *et al.* (1975) reports that changes in habitat result in decreased reproduction, lower pregnancy rates, and increased calf mortality. In short, elephants react to climatic stress in a way that is detrimental to population numbers.

All of these data suggest that habitat changes during the climatic fluctuations in the late Valdai may have created similar effects on mammoth populations. As noted, populations under climatic stress may react catastrophically to added stress—such as presented by additional predation, for example. It can be postulated that even the same levels of predation could catastrophically effect populations that are under climatic stress. These observations suggest that mammoth populations during the 18,000–12,000 B.P. period may have been under stress brought about by the oscillating climate. Mammoth on the central Russian Plain were prey to Upper Paleolithic hunter–gatherers. The additional stress may have ultimately brought about decreases in the population beyond recovery thresholds.

Budyko (1967, 1977, 1980) has attempted to model the effects of just such stress on mammoth populations during the late Valdai. His model assumes that this species was at or near equilibrium and that the added stress was generated by increasing human predation. This assumption employs an increase in population of hunter–gatherers as a necessary and sufficient variable and postulates that this increase in stress brought about the ultimate crash in mammoth numbers and was responsible for the subsequent extinction of the species. Budyko's model is, in this aspect, quite similar to that offered by Martin (1973) for the extinction of the mammoth in North America. The problems with the assumptions underlying these models (i.e., increases in population of hunter–gatherers as well as single equilibrium levels for the species) have been widely discussed in the literature (e.g., Hassan 1981; Zubrow 1976). What is interesting about Budyko's work, however, is his modeling of the temporal effects of stress on mammoth populations. As I have shown, added stress can be caused by a number of factors. I have also documented the increased climatic stress during the late Valdai. We can consider Budyko's model, therefore, either by substituting climatic stress for predation stress or by combining the two.

Budyko postulates that added stress to mammoth populations would have resulted in little population change over a long period of time. This is because of both the low birthrate and the longevity of the species. Mammoth populations would have faced a slow decline in numbers imperceptible in the archaeological or paleontological record. At some point, though, the population would have reached and crossed a low threshold and then proceeded to decrease rapidly. Archaeologically and paleontologically this would appear in the record as a population crash or extinction. While Budyko's assumptions about the carrying capacity of the area and increased predation resulting from population increases of hunter–gatherers are quite problematic, the scenario he offers is a most interesting one worth further investigation. Precise modeling is needed to study mammoth populations through time to see if different density thresholds with differing responses existed for this species. Likewise, much finer chronological controls are needed to determine if human predation rates were stable or varied in the late Valdai. Data on hand suggest a general increase in mammoth hunting from the Middle to the Upper Paleolithic all across the Russian Plain (Vereschagin 1971). I consider the question of changing predation rates for the mammoth in Chapter 5. For the purposes of this discussion I assume a stable rate during the late Valdai.

I have postulated that mammoth densities varied during late Valdai—they were higher during the colder periods and lower during the warmer ones. It is interesting to consider the effects that such differences in population numbers would have had on the recruitment group sizes of mammoths. Table 3.22 uses the carrying capacity for the area postulated after Budyko (1977) and Butzer (1971), as applied to the river valleys, and calculates the recruitment age population with and without an assumption of seasonal migration (see Table 3.21). The estimated recruitment rate of 4.7%/year is taken from elephant data reported by Laws *et al.* (1975). The calculations show a population of recruitment age mammoths (0–2 years) ranging between a low of 280 and a high of 2100 individuals during cold times. During warm times, recruitment age mammoths number from 180 to 350. The small, warm-weather recruitment age set could have been critically susceptible to human predation. (I am assuming that the population of mammoths was at any one time at an equilibrium—an assumption that may not be warranted.) The MNI estimates for mammoths at some Upper Paleolithic sites in the area (Table 3.22) show that the numbers of mammoth found at each site represent a very large proportion of the annual recruitment rate, particularly when warm-weather carrying capacities are assumed. Since we do not know what time span is represented in each of these assemblages, we cannot estimate the rate of human predation. The figures are offered here as heuristic devices to show that human predation may have been especially significant during the period of climatic oscillations between 18,000–12,000 B.P.

Another assumption underlying these calculations is a steady natural mortality rate for mammoths. This assumption may be unwarranted; mortality rates probably varied greatly and increased during periods of climatic stress. During periods of equilibria, if

Table 3.22   ESTIMATES OF MAMMOTH POPULATIONS BY RECRUITMENT RATES[a]

| | Ungulate carrying capacity | | |
Condition	Budyko 1967 800 kg/km^2	Butzer 1971 3,000 kg/km^2	Butzer 1971 mixed forest—500 kg/km2
Total number in area	12,000	45,000	7,500
if mammoth migrated seasonally	6,000	22,500	3,750
Annual recruitment number			
in area of 90,000 km^2	564	2,100	350
if mammoths migrated seasonally	280	1,050	180
Mezhirich: MNI = 149			
MNI as percentage of recruitment			
in area of 90,000 km^2	26.40	7.04	42.30
if mammoth migrated seasonally	52.80	14.10	84.60
Mezin: MNI = 116			
MNI as percentage of recruitment			
in area of 90,000 km^2	20.60	5.50	33.00
if mammoth migrated seasonally	41.20	11.00	66.00
Dobranichevka: MNI = 93			
MNI as percentage of recruitment			
in area of 90,000 km^2	16.50	4.40	26.4
if mammoth migrated seasonally	33.00	8.80	52.80

[a]Mammoth recruitment rate = 4.7% per year after Laws *et al.* (1975) for elephants.

such were present, we can estimate that natural mortality of mammoths would have been at or near the recruitment rate. During periods of climatic stress it may have increased appreciably. Vereschagin (1979), for example, postulates a mortality rate of 15% for late Valdai mammoths—occurring during times of oscillating climate, especially periods of increased precipitation and snowfall. Spiess (1979) reports an increase of from 5 to 10% of the mortality of such north-latitude ungulates as reindeer during periods of climatic deterioration. Laws *et al.* (1975) report an increase in the mortality of elephant calves from an average of 28.5% to a high figure of 42.9%/year during periods of habitat change. These observations suggest that mammoth calf mortality probably also increased greatly during periods of climatic oscillations.

Future work on mammoth populations in the late Valdai will also have to consider the probable lack of synchronization between climatic stress and the population response of mammoths. The slow recruitment rates and longevity of the species indicate that at least one mammoth generation (50–60 years) would have to pass before the population would feel the effects of reduced recruitment. This initial decrease in mammoth numbers would be felt in the recruitment age set only, while the effect on the whole population would be felt even later than one mammoth generation—after a few age sets born under climatic stress had entered the population—some 100–150 years later. This lack of synchronization between climatic stress and population response would create apparently stable mammoth numbers beyond the period of climatic stress and make the stress of predation doubly detrimental. Archaeologically and paleontologically it could create a picture of steady predation on steady populations, whereas in fact the situation would have been very different.

My postulation of the 200-year duration of acute climatic perturbation followed by a slow, long period of climatic recovery for the profile of climatic oscillations between 18,000 and 12,000 B.P. implies that mammoth populations may have showed decreasing population numbers long after the stress period, all the way through at least half of the recovery period of climatic stabilization. It also implies that particular dangers to mammoth populations existed during these long periods of climatic recovery and suggests that the length of time for build-up of population numbers came close to coinciding with the periods of climatic stress. The shortness of the period of acute climatic stress (i.e., 100–200 years) may have been insufficient to restore populations to previous sizes. Admittedly these postulations are highly speculative. I offer them here as an indication of the direction that future research must take before we can consider the late Valdai man–land relationships on the central Russian Plain on anything beyond a speculative or anecdotal level.

This discussion can be summarized as follows: (1) Mammoth populations probably fluctuated greatly during the late Valdai and decreased appreciably during the warmer periods. (2) Recruitment rates in mammoth populations probably also fluctuated— decreasing during times of climatic stress. (3) Mortality rates of the population also varied, increasing during periods of unfavorable climate. (4) Overall population of mammoths were fairly low on the central Russian Plain—during favorable times mammoth densities may have ranged from 0.5 to 0.13 mammoth/km² to a low of 0.08 mammoth/km² during warm periods. (5) Steady human predation on mammoths would have been especially detrimental to the population during the warm climatic episodes. (6) Predation and climatically induced stresses to mammoth populations may have resulted in rare but periodic crashes of populations that would be the only population phenomenon visible in the record.

I have also suggested the possibility of multiple equilibrium points for mammoth populations. If these did exist, then predation pressure or climatic stress may have affected the population differently depending on the particular density equilibrium that the population was near. Lack of research on multiple equilibria precludes consideration of changing reactions to stress that the mammoth may have undergone. I have had to treat the mammoth populations statically, suggesting some variables that may have affected them through time. This static modeling is most inaccurate and fails to consider crucial variables involved. But the current state of research permits no other options.

Density of Other Species

The ecological requirements of other species which played a major role in the economies of the hunter–gatherers in the study area also indicate that these species, like the mammoth, probably underwent changes in population during the period of climatic oscillations. In general, we can expect that increased forestation during warmer episodes would have seen an overall reduction in the populations of equids and wolves. Equids would have decreased because increased forestation would have reduced their medium to tall grass pastures and wolves because of the projected general decrease in ungulate numbers.

The reservations about reconstructing behavioral patterns of late Pleistocene reindeer, discussed previously, do not allow for any speculations about the effect of climatic fluctuations on this species. Reindeer densities, however, as Spiess (1979) reports, appear greater overall in open landscapes and less in forests. Therefore, warmer times with greater forest cover may have seen an overall reduction in the size of *Rangifer* populations in the study area. Greater forestation would have also favored a reduction in the population of steppe marmots. It is unclear what effect fluctuations may have had on the population numbers of hares and arctic foxes.

In addition to changing the overall numbers of the different species, climatic fluctuations also affected their behavior. We can expect that changes occurred in spatial distribution as well as in migration patterns. Specifically, the pattern of linearization of many food species near the river valleys postulated for the cold periods may have changed to greater dispersal in warmer periods. It is also possible that during some of the warmer periods such migrants as the arctic fox may not have wintered in the study area at all, or been present in greatly reduced numbers.

4

Chronology and Land Use

RELATIVE DATING OF THE SITES

Upper Paleolithic sites of the central Russian Plain have been dated by a variety of relative methods that can be divided into two distinct categories: (1) archaeological chronological ordering based on the stylistic criteria of lithic assemblages, and (2) biostratigraphic methods, which utilize geological data as well as on the more recent, and as yet undeveloped, schemes that incorporate biological information. As elsewhere, relative dating has been used the longest in the area and is the most prevalent in the literature.

STYLISTIC DATING

Today, while problematic but fairly inclusive stylistic chronologies exist for some regions of the Russian Plain, such as the Molodova sites on the Dnestr (Chernysh 1959, 1973; Ivanova 1969; Klein 1973) and the Kostenki–Borschevo sites on the Don (Klein 1969; Lazukov *et al.* 1981; Rogachev 1957), no agreement exists on the chronological ordering of the sites in the Dnepr–Desna region. As I mentioned in the introductory chapter, there is uniform agreement among Soviet and Western researchers that the central Russian Plain constituted a uniform cultural unit (whether single or with multiple subdivisions) during the Upper Paleolithic. At the same time, strong disagreements exist on how to segment the region either synchronically or diachronically. The range of opinions and schemes offered by researchers extends from the unified mono-cultural scheme of Shovkoplyas (Figure 4.1), who sees all of the sites of the study area belonging to a single Mezin culture and explains the observed differences between the sites by chronology alone, to the other extreme as expressed by Grigor'ev (1970), who thinks there is insufficient information to either clearly separate the sites into different archaeological cultures, or to order these cultures chronologically. Table 4.1 shows some of the variety of dating established by various researchers. Mezin, for example, has been assigned from the Aurignacian to the Azilian cultures, and Kirillovskaya from the Mousterian all the way to the late Magdalenian.

These differences of opinion in part reflect changes in classification criteria through time. Archaeologists working in the area at the end of the nineteenth and the beginning of the twentieth century generally based their chronological ordering on lithic classifi-

	Boriskovskii 1953	Efimenko 1938	Shovkoplyas 1965a, 1967	Voevodskii 1952
MESO-LITHIC — EARLY	II Zhuravka I Chulatovo II, Kirillovskaya (ul), Gontsy (ul)			
UPPER PALEOLITHIC (LATE MAGDALENIAN)	VII Bugorok, Gontsy (ll) VI Chulatovo I, Suponevo, Timonovka I	*AZILIAN* Yurovichi *MAGDALENIAN* LATE Kirillovskaya (ul), Zhuravka MIDDLE Gontsy, Timonovka I(?) EARLY Suponevo, Eliseevichi, Timonovka I, Kirillovskaya Mezin→	*MAGDALENIAN* LATE Fastov MIDDLE Bugorok, Chulatovo II, Dobranichevka, Gontsy EARLY Chulatovo I, Eliseevichi, Kirillovskaya, Suponevo, Timonovka I, Yudinovo, Mezin	*MAGDALENIAN* LATE Bugorok, Chulatovo II, Gontsy, Kirillovskaya, Timonovka I MIDDLE EARLY Chulatovo I, Mezin, Suponevo
(MIDDLE MAGDALENIAN)	V Eliseevichi, Kirillovskaya (ll), Pogon		*AURIGNACO-SOLUTREAN* Novgorod-Severskii, Pogon Berdyzh Yurovichi	*SOLUTREAN* LATE MIDDLE EARLY Pogon, Pushkari I
(DDL AURIGNACO-SOLUTREAN)	IV Novgorod-Severskii, Pushkari I	*SOLUTREAN* LATE MIDDLE Berdyzh EARLY	Klyusy Pushkari	
EARLY (SOLUTREAN)	III II	*AURIGNACIAN*	*AURIGNACIAN* Radomyshl'	*AURIGNACIAN*

Figure 4.1 Stylistic chronologies. (ll) lower layer; (ul) upper layer.

cation and adopted the classic French scheme of de Mortillet for subdividing the Paleolithic. Efimenko's scheme (Figure 4.1 and Table 4.1) is a good case in point. Like its French progenitor, it was based on the use of *indexes fossil* as chronological markers, but to some extent it did take into account local data at odds with the classic scheme.

In the 1940s and early 1950s Rogachev's (1957) work at the Kostenki–Borschevo sites challenged previously held unilineal evolutionary schemes. At Kostenki I-l he discovered the Aurignacian middle layer sandwiched between two Solutrean layers. At Kostenki IV he observed that the Solutrean layer was found overlying the Magdalenian. At Telmanskaya the Magdalenian layer was found below the Mouseterian. With these upsetting observations in hand, Rogachev called for (1) the abandonment of unilineal evolutionary stages, (2) the recognition of local cultural units and sequences, and (3) the construction of local chronological sequences based on changes in the local cultures

Table 4.1   STYLISTIC DATING OF THE SITES BY VARIOUS RESEARCHERS[a]

	Mousterian	Upper Paleolithic	Early Upper Paleolithic	Late Upper Paleolithic	Aurignacian	Solutrean	Gravettian	Magdalenian	Azilian
Berdyzh					15,17,28——7—8M			26E	
Chulatovo I								27E,20L,27L	
Chulatovo II								1L,20L,27L	
Dobranichevka				23L				9L	
Eliseevichi							4	8E,17,20	
Fastov								L2,19L,20L	
Gontsy	14							2M,19M,8M,20L	
Khotylevo II								1E,20E,27L	
Kirillovskaya	12								
Klyusy			21L						
Korshevo I					24				
Korshevo II					24				
Kositsa					25				
Kurovo		17							
Mezhirich					15	7L,8L	1E,9L,20E		
Mezin								9L,23L	
Novgorod-Severskii						20L		20E,26E,16	
Novo-Bobovichi		2							
Bugorok								Il,19L,27L	
Pogon						-22—27E,1L,20L		1E,20E	
Pushkari I			3		L1,27L-22—	27E			
Pushkari II				27E					
Radomyshl'					13,21				
Suponevo					28	11,8L		20E,27E,17,7L	
Timonovka I					11L			20E,1,8,27L	
Timonovka II				10					
Yudinovo							5L	17L,20E	
Yurovichi				6	——20——		5L	20E,17	8
Zhuravka					18			9,8L	2

[a]E, early; M, middle; L, late; follows author where specified in text. References: 1, Boriskovskii 1953; 2, Boriskovskii and Praslov 1964; 3, Boriskovskii *et al.* 1981; 4, Budko 1962; 5, Budko 1966; 6, Budko and Mitrofanov 1967; 7, Efimenko 1938; 8, Efimenko 1953; 9, Gladkih 1973; 10, Grekhova 1970; 11, Gorodtsov 1923; 12, Hvoika 1901; 13, Ivanova 1969; 14, Kaminskii 1873; 15, Mirchink 1934; 16, Pidoplichko 1947b; 17, Polikarpovich 1968; 18, Rudinskii 1929; 19, Shovkoplyas 1956; 20, Shovkoplyas 1965a; 21, Shovkoplyas 1967; 22, Shovkoplyas 1971; 23, Shovkoplyas 1976; 24, Tarasov 1977; 25, Tarasov 1981; 26, Voevodskii 1940; 27, Voevodskii 1952b; 28, Zamyatnin 1951.

through time. During this period, some archaeologists, like Zamyatnin (1951), undertook the general classification of Upper Paleolithic cultures using a mixture of lithic and nonlithic criteria. For the Old World, Zamyatnin introduced three distinct cultural zones: the Siberian (Asian), the Atlantic (European periglacial), and the circum–Mediterranean-African. This was still within the old French classificatory tradition—it just segmented the Upper Paleolithic world somewhat more than had been allowed under the classic scheme. Others, like Boriskovskii (1953), refined the classic scheme and tailored it to the data from the Russian Plain. Boriskovskii chose to segment the Upper Paleolithic into seven stages and to classify the sites in the study area along this continuum (see Figure 4.1). His scheme, while ostensibly not tied to the French version, still offered the local equivalents of classic stadiality. In this chronology, however, we already see a collapse of a clear distinction between the Aurignacian and the Solutrean periods and the emergence of an Aurignaco–Solutrean period. This collapse finds its somewhat later expression in the chronological scheme of Shovkoplyas, also illustrated in Figure 4.1. Here we see the elimination of an independent Solutrean stage or period and the follow-up of the Aurignacian by an Aurignaco–Solutrean period. Both of these schemes, unlike their predecessors, are unilineal but regional. In this they are an update of the classic scheme, reflecting the growing recognition of the importance of regional differences.

A second and perhaps more serious problem responsible for differences in classification stemmed from a lack of uniformity in typology. Efimenko and his immediate successors in general had limited interest in typology and classification—these interests, at the time, were derogatorily labeled "thingization" and research focus was on "paleoethnology" (see Boriskovskii and Okladnikov 1953 for attitude; Howe 1976 for history). Since no typological work was conducted, different typological concepts led different researchers to classify materials found at the sites differently—as can be seen in the comparison of Voevodskii's chronology with Efimenko's, for example (Figure 4.1). This lack of uniformity in either taxonomy or classificatory criteria can be also seen by comparing Boriskovskii's and Shovkoplyas's schemes. For example, Shovkoplyas saw material from Pogon as Aurignaco–Solutrean, whereas Boriskovskii assigned it to his Stage V (early Magdalenian); parts of the Gontsy material were seen by Boriskovskii as belonging to Stage I of the early Mesolithic and by Shovkoplyas as middle Magdalenian. Still other archaeologists augmented both the classic French and Efimenko's schemes by introducing new regional cultural classifications. Budko (1966, 1969), for example, classified assemblages from some sites as Gravettian (see Table 4.1; see also Valoch 1968).

Reacting to the severe problems of noncomparability of the different typologies in use, Klein wrote that

> Because not all Soviet authors use the same typological concepts or are equally rigorous in applying their concepts, it is currently impossible to obtain a detailed notion of the typological variability among Ukranian Upper Paleolithic assemblages. (1973:76)

> Comparison of Ukranian Upper Paleolithic artifact assemblages with contemporaneous assemblages from elsewhere in Europe suggests that the cultures which are represented were more or less restricted to the Ukraine and its immediate neighbors. (1973:89)

Klein noted that Soviet investigators in the past tended to underestimate the originality of their lithic assemblages and to describe them in cultural terms adopted from points well west of the Russian Plain (e.g., Magdalenian, Solutrean, Eastern Gravettian). This tendency, unfortunately, still prevails today.

Recently some researchers in the Soviet Union have begun focusing on uniform typologies. Isaenko (1978) and Gladkih (1973) have worked to establish explicit standards for classification for some of the Byelorussian and Dnepr valley sites, respectively. These attempts, however, are of a most preliminary kind and no firm typologies have been offered for the study area as a whole. This problem with typological criteria has also been compounded by debates on the meaning of the observed (though unsystematized) differences in lithic assemblages from site to site. Some argue that these differences, seen primarily in lithics, reflect "archaeological cultures" that have ethnographic significance (e.g., Grigor'ev 1970). This position is quite akin to Bordes' in the now famous Binford–Bordes debate on the significance of variability in Mousterian industries of southwestern France (Binford and Binford 1966; Bordes 1968). Others, such as Shovkoplyas (1965a) and Gladkih (1973, 1977a), using a wider data base that includes stone tool typologies as well as features, argue for the recognition of techno-complexes that reflect a broader scale of differences than ethnographic identities and have both temporal and spatial unity. Gladkih (1977, personal communication), for example, has argued for the recognition of an overall cultural unity of the area through time. His chronological scheme (Figure 4.2a) has the earlier Upper Paleolithic assemblages, such as found at Radomyshl', Pushkari I, and Klyusy, evolved into three coeval cultural subgroups during the Magdalenian period: one that includes Gontsy, Mezhirich, and, somewhat later in time, Dobranichevka; another represented by Zhuravka; and a third by Mezin. Gladkih's scheme again suffers the fate of other such attempts. No clear justification is made for the selection of specific variables or attributes and no distinction is made about the significance and meaning of the observed

a.

b.

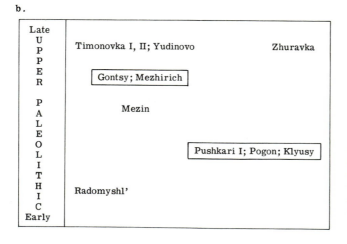

Figure 4.2 Stylistic chronologies after (a) Gladkih (1973; personal communication 1977) and (b) Gvozdover in Lazukov *et al.* (1981) and personal communication (1978). Enclosures indicate roughly contemporaneous sites.

variability—whether they reflect functional, structural, or cultural differences. Gladkih constructed his scheme on a study of nuclei and pieces with secondary retouch. Using the Brainerd–Robinson technique of coefficient correlation, he compared materials found within the four complexes at Dobranichevka, both among themselves and with those from Gontsy, Mezhirich, and Mezin. His results show a close similarity between Dobranichevka, Gontsy, and Mezhirich and a lesser degree of similarity between this group of sites and Mezin. These observations, while interesting and suggestive, still fail to be totally convincing because of the problems of attribute selection.

Grekhova (1970), working with intuitive typologies, has postulated a great similarity in the lithic inventories of Bugarok, Chulatovo I, Chulatovo II, Suponevo, Timonovka I and II, and Yudinovo. She interprets this similarity as showing both cultural unity and the synchronic occupation of the sites.

Gvozdover (Lazukov et al. 1981) recognizes the presence of the Pushkari culture (which includes Klyusy, Pogon, and Pushkari I), the Dobranichevka culture outlined originally by Gladkih (which includes Dobranichevka, Gontsy, and Mezhirich), the Mezin culture represented by just that site, and the Timonovka culture as delimited by Grekhova (Figure 4.2b). In this scheme, while chronological relationship between the cultures is not specified, the Pushkarian is considered earlier than the others.

Finally, increasing cooperation between paleogeographers and archaeologists has led to a new synthesis of observed variability in lithic assemblages with documented climatic fluctuations and to the creation of stylistic geochronologies, as those offered by Dolukhanov (1979), Kozłowski and Kozłowski (1979), and Dolukhanov, Kozłowski, and Kozłowski (1981) (Figure 4.3). This scheme fits into the category of a general evolutionary scheme for the Upper Paleolithic of all of Europe. Here again, however, attribute selection is neither explained nor justified, the correlation between environmental conditions and specific industries is moot, and so the significance of the scheme is open to debate.

As the above discussion shows, no unequivocable classificatory or typological schemes exist for the assemblages found at the sites in the study area to either (1) assign particular collections to specific archaeological cultures, or (2) clearly differentiate assemblages or cultures in time. While today Upper Paleolithic regional typologies for other parts of the Old World are coming under increasing scrutiny (e.g., White 1980, 1982; Wobst and Keene 1983), they still offer some scale for chronological ordering. The absence of such schemes for the study area make this method of relative dating nearly impossible here. The problems caused by this lack of chronological ordering can best be exemplified in the dating of two sites: Radomyshl' and Zhuravka. Shovkoplyas (1964, 1965a,b) argues that the presence of crude Mousterian tool types together with Aurignacian elements in the assemblage at Radomyshl' indicates a very early Upper Paleolithic date for the site. The criterion he used is an evolution and refinement of tool types through time. The fallacy of this uniformitarian assumption is pointed up by Rogachev's work at Telmanskaya, where, as noted before, upper layers contain Mousterian tools and lower layers Magdalenian. In the case of Zhuravka, early assignment of the site's assemblage to the Aurignacian (Rudinskii 1929) was later amended by Boriskovskii (1953) to the Mesolithic and still later to the Azilian (Boriskovskii and Praslov 1964). This change in typological dating of the

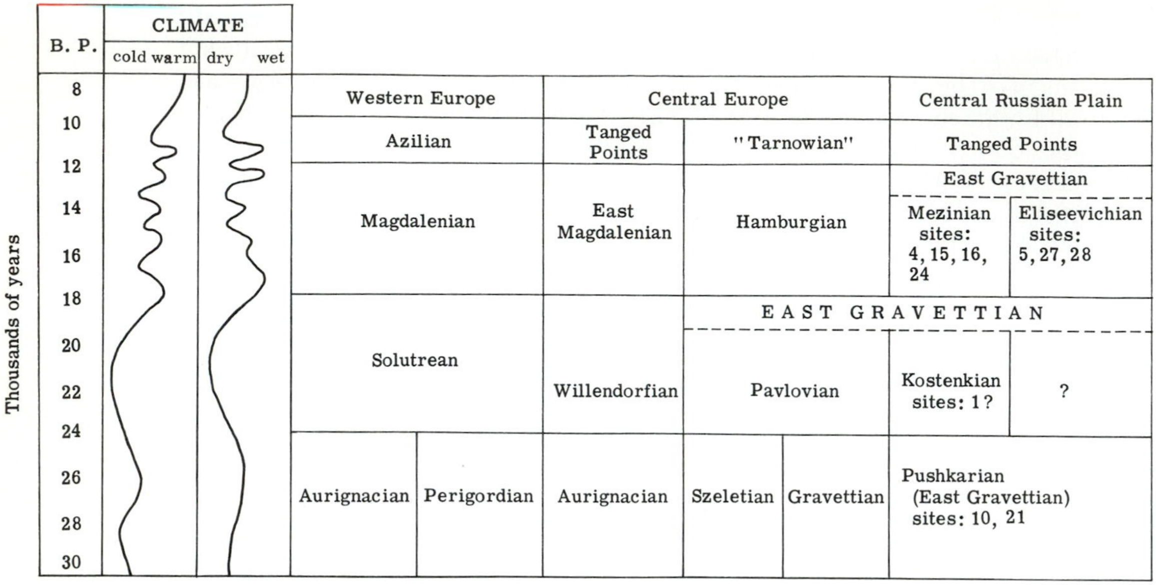

Figure 4.3 Stylistic geochronology of the Upper Paleolithic. Site numbers as in Figure 2.1 (climate curve after Dolukhanov 1979: Fig. 18; Chebotareva and Makaricheva 1982: Fig. 2; stylistic geochronology after Dolukhanov 1979: Fig. 18; Dolukhanov, Kozlowski, and Kozlowski 1980).

site occurred because microlithization of tools in general came to be considered a development of the very late Upper Paleolithic (primarily of the Mesolithic) and one that happened more or less synchronically everywhere. The implicit argument was that since the inventory at Zhuravka shows a good deal of microlithization, the site must necessarily date either to the very end of the Upper Paleolithic or, more probably, to the Mesolithic. Gladkih (1973) and Smirnov (1973) point out, however, that other sites in the southern part of the study region also show fairly high percentages of microlithization (7% at Dobranichevka, 11% at Mezhirich, and 6% at Mezin). They suggest that this feature should not be taken as a chronological marker, and that microlithization of tools and the concomitant use of composite or insert tools may have arisen at different times in different areas. By implication then, Gladkih argues that the presence of microlithization reflects a possible spectrum of variables, including functional and stylistic as well as chronological ones.

In conclusion then, while undoubtedly chronological differences do exist between the sites in the study area, unequivocable archaeological methods for specifying these differences do not exist at present.

Biostratigraphic Chronologies

Geological Dating

The history of stratigraphic dating of sites in the study area is a turbulent one that can be roughly divided into two periods. Geological work done before the middle of this century (e.g., Mirchink 1934, 1937, and, most notably, Gromov 1948) was primarily based on correlation of sites with specific river terraces and on construction of chronologies for these terraces. As I note in Chapter 2, Gromov's chronological scheme won wide acceptance and predominated in geological literature until the middle of the 1960s. The crux of Gromov's position was that Upper Paleolithic sites dated as far back as the last interglacial (see Table 4.2 and Figure 4.4).

Late in the 1950s, Velichko undertook a major revision of Gromov's scheme, one that

Table 4.2   STRATIGRAPHIC DATING OF THE SITES BY VARIOUS RESEARCHERS[a]

	General stratigraphy			Velichko's scheme				Terraces	
	Valdai	Early Valdai	Late Valdai	Bryansk soil	Loess II	Gley layer	Loess III	First	Second
Berdyzh					6				23,8,10
Chulatovo I	19								8
Chulatovo II					19		22		
Dobranichevka							17		
Eliseevichi			~8	6,23		19,20			7,16
Fastov					UNDATED				
Gontsy									8
Khotylevo II				21					
Kirillovskaya									8,13
Klyusy					UNDATED				
Korshevo I					UNDATED				
Korshevo II					UNDATED				
Kositsa							18?		
Kurovo									8
Mezin			15,19						~15
Mezhirich									~12
Novgorod-Severskii					UNDATED				
Novo-Bobovichi									14
Bugorok							19		
Pogon					19				
Pushkari I					19		1?		
Pushkari II			8						
Radomyshl'					UNDATED				
Suponevo							19		8,19
Timonovka I				6			19,21L		
Timonovka II							21L		10,8,25
Yudinovo							19L	19	10,14,25
Yurovichi									10,8,14,5
Zhuravka								2,3,7	8

[a]L, late; ~, equivalent to assigned terrace. References: 1, Belyaeva, pers. comm. 1982; 2, Boriskovskii 1953; 3, Boriskovskii *et al.* 1981; 4, Boriskovskii and Praslov 1964; 5, Budko 1967b; 6, Budko and Voznyachuk 1969a; 7, Gladkih 1973; 8, Gromov 1948 (present-day equivalents); 9, Ivanova 1969; 10, Kalechitz 1972; 11, Klein 1973; 12, Kornietz *et al.* 1981; 13, Pidoplichko 1969; 14, Polikarpovich 1968; 15, Shovkoplyas 1965a; 16, Shovkoplyas 1967; 17, Shovkoplyas 1981; 18, Tarasov 1981; 19, Velichko 1961; 20, Velichko, Grekhova, and Udartsev 1977; 21, Velichko, Zavernyaev *et al.* 1981; 22, Voevodskii 1952a; 23, Voznyachuk 1973; 24, Voznyachuk and Budko 1969; 25, Voznyachuk *et al.* 1969.

Gromov 1948	Klein 1973	Velichko 1961
LATE	LATE	TIMONOVKA SOIL
Gontsy, Yurovichi		Timonovka I, II, Yudinovo
		LOESS III
Bugorok, Chulatovo I, II, Eliseevichi, Mezin, Suponevo, Pushkari II	Berdyzh, Bugorok, Chulatovo I, Dobranichevka, Eliseevichi, Fastov(?), Gontsy(?), Kirillovskaya (?), Klyusy(?), Mezhirich(?), Mezin, Novgorod-Severskii(?), Novo-Bobovichi(?), Radomyshl'(?), Suponevo, Timonovka I, II, Yudinovo, Yurovichi, Zhuravka(?)	Bugorok, Suponevo Mezin—⌉ ? GLEY LAYER Eliseevichi
Novgorod-Severskii, Pogon Pushkari I		LOESS II
	WÜRM	Chulatovo II Pogon, Pushkari I
EARLY	MIDDLE	
Novo-Bobovichi(?)	Chulatovo II, Pogon, Pushkari I	
Berdyzh(?)		BRYANSK SOIL
		Khotylevo II

Figure 4.4   Geological chronologies for the central Russian Plain.

took into account the rest of the Old World and that placed Desna and Sudost' sites into a new geochronological framework. Velichko's (1961) basic stratigraphy and geochronology have already been discussed in detail in Chapter 2 (see pp. 33–35). This scheme incorporates erosional as well as depositional episodes of plateau and terrace building (see Tables 4.2 and Figure 4.4). His stratigraphic reconstructions for Desna and Sudost' sites are illustrated in Figure 4.5. As that figure shows, this stratigraphic sequence was established only for the Desna and Sudost' region of the study area and incorporates only 10 of the sites considered in this work.

Isaenko (1968), working with geological data from the Sozh and Pripyat', has offered a comparable scheme for dating Berdyzh and Yurovichi (Figure 4.6). This scheme is based on geological work of Voznyachuk (1973) and Kalechitz (1972, 1973, 1984). Their scheme for Sozh and Pripyat' valley stratigraphy and terrace-forming processes is in general agreement with Velichko's, but it differs on a number of important issues. Data from the southern part of the study region has led Ukranian geologists to construct a stratigraphic scheme also somewhat at odds with that of Velichko. These various schemes indicate a number of problems for extending Velichko's sequence to the central Russian Plain as a whole. Some of these problems have already been mentioned in Chapter 2; those most germane to the dating of the sites are examined in the following.

Other sites in the study area have either not been included in any of the schemes and have been tentatively dated by analogy to the Desna sequence, or, especially for the sites excavated and studied prior to the 1960s, by their association with specific river terraces. This information is presented in Table 4.2.

Finally, a number of the sites remain beyond the scope of geological dating. In some cases, such as the newly discovered sites of Korshevo I, II, and Kositsa, their geology has

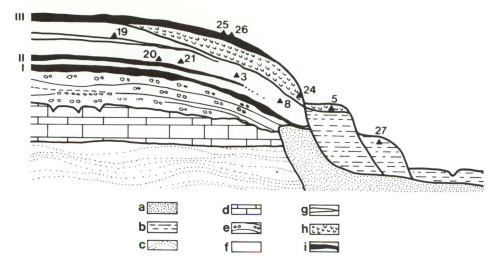

Figure 4.5 Geological age of Desna and Sudost' Upper Paleolithic sites: a, buried alluvium; b, alluvium; c, Upper Cretaceous sand; d, Upper Cretaceous limestone; e, early and middle Pleistocene deposits; f, loess; g, gley layer; h, reworked loess; i, relic soils—(I) Mikulino; (II) Bryansk; (III) Timonovka. Sites: 3, Chulatovo II, 5, Eliseevichi; 8, Khotylevo II; 19, Bugorok; 20, Pogon; 21, Pushkari I; 24, Suponevo; 25, Timonovka I; 26, Timonovka II; 27, Yudinovo (after Velichko 1961; Klein 1973; Kurenkova 1978).

not been studied. In others, such as Radomyshl', sites remain undated because erosional episodes played a far greater role in the stratigraphy of the region than did deposition. For yet a third group of sites, such as Novgorod-Severskii and Fastov, local stratigraphy remains poorly understood.

A comparison of geochronologic dating schemes offered by Gromov and Velichko (Figure 4.4) shows numerous divergences. These in part reflect different paradigms used by the two geologists. They also exist because insufficient research does not permit an extension of local stratigraphic schemes over large sections of the central Russian

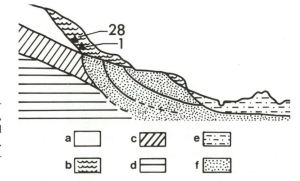

Figure 4.6 Geological age of Sozh and Pripyat' Upper Paleolithic sites: a, loess; b, slope deposits in ravine; c, moraine; d, basal strata; e, alluvium; f, buried alluvium. Sites: 1, Berdyzh; 28, Yurovichi (after Isaenko 1968: Fig. 1).

Plain. Velichko's 1961 monograph was the last attempt in the Soviet literature to construct a large-scale regional geochronology for the Russian Plain.

In the English-language literature, Klein (1973) presents a synthesis of extant Soviet views and attempts to resolve the divergences by (1) broadly following Velichko's scheme, (2) tentatively extending this scheme to the whole of the study region, and (3) collapsing possible geochronological distinctions. He divides the occupation of the sites into two distinct periods—one during the middle Valdai and one during the late Valdai (see Table 4.2 and Figure 4.4). This attempt is likewise unsatisfactory, because it obscures significant chronological differences. It does, however, clearly point out a number of difficult issues that existed and still exist in geochronological dating of the sites: (1) dating and synchronization of the river terraces, (2) synchronic and diachronic uniformity of plateau and terrace deposition, both intra and interregionally, and (3) precise dating and synchronization of ravine formation.

River Terrace Dating.   Only the Desna and Sudost' terraces have been adequately studied (Chapter 2). Major disagreements exist on the dating of individual terraces. Velichko (1961), for example, considers the second terrace of the Desna and Sudost' to have formed during or just prior to the Bryansk Interstadial (25,000–30,000 B.P.), whereas Voznyachuk and Budko (1969) and Voznyachuk *et al.* (1969) date the formation of the second terraces of the Dnepr, Sozh, and Pripyat' much earlier—between 30,000 and 45,000 B.P. This disagreement brings into question not only the synchronization of terrace formation but also the dating of the sites found on second terraces, as well as the overall antiquity of the Upper Paleolithic period in the area. As a result, it is not at all clear that the second terrace of the Sozh, for example, necessarily formed at the same time as did the second terrace of the Sudost' or Sula.

Other more concrete problems add to the difficulties in dating of the sites. In the case of Yudinovo, for example, Velichko (1961) associates the cultural remains with the first terrace, whereas Kalechitz (1972, 1973, 1984), Polikarpovich (1968), and Gromov (1948) place the site on the second Sudost' terrace. Zhuravka has been similarly assigned to either the first or the second terrace of Sula (see Table 4.2).

In summary then, much more stratigraphic work on both local erosional sequences and areal applicability of terrace formations as concrete time markers is needed before river terrace dating can offer chronological information fine enough for archaeological questions.

Local Stratigraphies and Their Synchronic and Diachronic Significance.   Velichko's late Valdai stratigraphy for the study area distinguishes two depositional sequences: (1) loess deposits during cold stadial periods and (2) formation of the soil and gley layer during warmer periods. Velichko divides the late Valdai loess deposits into Loess I, II, and III. This division is in broad agreement with the loess sequences observed elsewhere in Central and Eastern Europe. Recent radiometric dating of sites found in comparable loess strata, however, shows some major difficulties. For example, Velichko notes that such central Russian Plain sites as Eliseevichi, Suponevo, and Yudinovo were found in Loess III, as were such sites as Dolni Vestonice and Pavlov in Czechoslovakia. Radiometric dating, however, shows that Dolni Vestonice dates to 25,600 ± 170 (Gro. 1286), and Pavlov to 26,400 ± 230 (Gro. 1272), and 24,800 ± 150 (Gro. 1325) (Klima 1963). Kukla (1975) reports that the corrected dates for these sites are 25,020 ± 150 for Dolni Vestonice and 26,730 ± 250 for Pavlov. But such sites as Yudinovo and Timonovka II, found in Loess III, date between 13,650 ± 200 and 15,110 ± 530, respectively (see Table 2.15). These chronological discrepancies are of large magnitude. They can reflect either errors in the processing of the sample for dating or, more likely, the noncomparability of the strata.

Similar difficulties exist also with the use of the Bryansk soil layer, the gley layer, and the layer of Timonovka relic soil as chronological markers. I have already discussed the difficulties with the Bryansk soil layer itself—namely, its dating and its correlation with Stillfried B (see pp. 27–29). In addition, work at Pushkari I indicates a possible error there in the identification of the strata underlying the cultural remains. Velichko (1961) wrote that cultural remains at both Pushkari I and Pogon were found immediately above the Bryansk soil and dated the whole Pushkari group accordingly, Belyaeva (1982, personal communication) reports finding the cultural layer at Pushkari I right above the *gley layer,* not the *Bryansk soil*—the latter is present farther down in the stratigraphic column.

Velichko's stratigraphic column for the Desna shows the presence of a single gley layer that separates Loess II from Loess III (see Figure 4.5). As I have noted previously, stratigraphic sequences from other parts of the Russian Plain show the presence of additional gley or humic layers that date to the same period. Pashkevich and Dubnyak (1978) report that the cultural materials at Dobranichevka were found over a humic or gley layer in Loess III itself, above the gley layer that separates Loess II from Loess III. Ivanova likewise reports at least two gley layers above Loess II in the Dnestr sequence (see p. 37). Thus, data from both the Dnestr area and Dobranichevka strongly imply that Velichko's scheme may be too simplistic to reflect the complexity of climatic events and local responses over the entire study area.

Radiometric dating of Timonovka II creates additional problems for Velichko's stratigraphic scheme. As Figure 4.5 shows, he dates the occupation of this site to the very end of Loess III deposition and the beginning of the Timonovka relic soil formation. This relic soil is found directly beneath present-day Holocene soil. The ^{14}C date for Timonovka II (15,110 ± 530) is thus too old. Loess deposition continued until the onset of the Alleröd some 11,500 years ago (see Chapter 2). This incongruity may in part stem from the operation of unrecognized erosional episodes in the Desna and Sudost' regions—erosion that interrupted or obliterated subsequent loess depositions in the Timonovka area.

The rapid climatic fluctuations between 18,000 and 12,000 B.P. (Figure 4.1) suggest the formation of more than one gley layer (or relic soil layer) during this period. It may well be that these additional layers are better preserved in regions to the south of the Desna and Sudost', at the more southerly Dnestr and Dnepr sites. If this is so, the gley layer of Dobranichevka (found in Loess III) may well be a chronological equivalent to the Timonovka relic soil layer.

In summary, while the geochronological scheme developed by Velichko remains the only one available for the area, recent data strongly suggest that it be used only tentatively—as a first approximation that requires a great deal of additional geological research and refinement before it can be extended over the entire study region.

Ravines and Geochronological Dating.   As Table 2.6 shows, nine of the sites are found in ravines. Erosional and depositional processes responsible for ravine formations are the most localized of geological events and cannot be broadly correlated over large regions. The correlation of specific ravine deposits with either nearby terraces or plateau strata is, hence, an even more complex procedure than is the identification of the terrace on which particular cultural deposits are found. It is, therefore, not surprising that disagreements exist on the association of ravine deposits with terraces. For example, Klein (1973), using some Soviet geological interpretations, associates such ravine sites as Berdyzh and Yurovichi with the first terraces of the rivers, whereas Kalechitz (1972, 1973, 1984) states that both Berdyzh and Yurovichi ravines were associated with second terraces.

At some of the sites (e.g., Berdyzh, Mezin), Upper Paleolithic hunter–gatherers apparently settled in the ravines themselves. In such cases, the dating of cultural remains geologically is somewhat easier than in cases where the location of the remains in the ravines is a result of post-depositional taphonomic processes. This means that, while we can tentatively accept the association of some ravine sites with particular strata (e.g., the association of Mezin with the second terrace of the Desna), in cases where cultural remains in ravines were not in situ, no such chronological reconstruction can be made (e.g., at Novo-Bobovichi and Yurovichi, and possibly Klyusy and Kurovo).

Biological Data and Chronologies

Climatic information derived from floral and faunal data provides an additional source of chronological information (see Chapter 3). This data base, however, is not independent of the stratigraphy and geomorphology of an area. Since pollen and faunal remains are found in particular strata, their significance is relevant to these strata, and the diachronic information they carry necessarily also depends on stratigraphic reconstruction. Information provided by flora and fauna, however, can be used as a control to check the accuracy of stratigraphic schemes and indicate their deficiencies or inconsistencies.

The use of biological information on a time scale relevant for archaeological questions addressed in this work is beset by a number of problems. First and foremost these is a lack of synchronization between geological and biological data, and within the biological framework between floral and faunal data. Second, floral and faunal data cannot be taken as absolute indicators of climate, because neither their past nor their present-day proveniences need reflect the boundaries of their ecological tolerance. Additional difficulties arise because of the gross nature of information collected. For example, a discovery of warm-climate flora or fauna at a site on a scale of 10^3 years may equally well reflect the general climate or the season of occupation. Because of this, "noise" is created in the record which precludes us from using biological information as an unequivocable indicator of climate alone. To compensate for this problem, I use only ichthyofauna, microfauna, and avifauna in this discussion. Last, as noted previously, biological data from the study area necessarily reflect geographic (i.e., latitudinal) differences. These must be taken into account when using biological data for biostratigraphic reconstructions and modeling.

I have discussed in detail in Chapter 3 climatic inferences made on the basis of biological data from the sites in the study area. This information is presented in Table 4.3, where reconstructions based on avifauna, microfauna, molluscan fauna, and pollen data are given. As can be readily seen from this table, the use of different taxa leads to divergent interpretations. For example, at Berdyzh cold climate is suggested by both avifauna and pollen, whereas microfauna indicate a warmer climate at the time of occupation. At Yudinovo as well, microfaunal and malacofaunal data are in conflict.

Table 4.3 also offers a tentative ranking of the sites along a cold–warm axis. Since four sources of biological information are used, each is assigned a weight of 25%; absence of information from any one source is treated as contributing no information, and the remaining sources are weighed accordingly for the estimates. The ranking is then done along the following gradient:

Climate	Rank	Weight of score
Warm	1	<25% of biological data indicate cold conditions
	2	25–50% of biological data indicate cold conditions
	3	50–75% of biological data indicate cold conditions
Cold	4	>75% of biological data indicate cold conditions

Table 4.3 also presents ranked geological estimates on climate at the time of occupation. The ranking here is achieved in a similar manner. Paleoclimatic information (Table 3.4) is used to rank the various geological strata with which the sites are associated. To make the biological and geological rankings comparable, I collapse some of the paleoclimatic information in the following manner:

Climate	Rank	Stratigraphic layer
Warm	1	Bryansk soil
	2	Gley layer
	3	Timonovka soil
Cold	4	Loess II and Loess III

A comparison of rankings again shows numerous contradictions. In order to control for latitudinal differences, I divide the sites into northern and southern regions. Sites found in the north appear to reflect a much wider range of climatic conditions than do the sites in the south: Occupation is shown in the north during both very cold climate at such sites as Mezin and Chulatovo I and warmer conditions such as at Chulatovo II and Timonovka II; only relatively warm times can be reconstructed for the southern sites.

Table 4.3 BIOSTRATIGRAPHIC DATA ON THE TIME OF OCCUPATION OF THE SITES[a]

	Avifauna	Microfauna	Molluscs	Pollen	Climatic oscillation rank		Geological
Northern Sites							
1. Berdyzh	C	W	nd	C	C?	3	4
2. Chulatovo I	nd	C	nd	nd	C	4	nd
3. Chulatovo II	nd	W	nd	nd	W	1	4
5. Eliseevichi	nd	C	nd	C?	C?	3	2
8. Khotylevo II	W	C	nd	C	C	3	1
16. Mezin	C	C	C	nd	C	1	nd
17. Novgorod-Severskii	W	C	W	nd	W	2	nd
21. Pushkari I	nd	C	nd	nd	C	4	4
22. Pushkari II	nd	C	nd	nd	C	4	4
26. Timonovkka II	nd	nd	nd	W	W?	1	4?
27. Yudinovo	nd	C	W	nd	C/W?	2/3	4
Southern Sites							
4. Dobranichevka	nd	W	nd	W	W	1	2/4
7. Gontsy	nd	W	W	nd	W	1	nd
15. Mezhirich	W	W	C/W	W	W	2	nd
29. Zhuravka	nd	W	nd	nd	W	1	nd

[a]C, cold predominance; W, warm predominance; C/W, no predominance.

Within this warmer climate, however, some differences can also be observed in the southern sites: Mezhirich, for example, appears to have been occupied during colder times than were Dobranichevka, Gontsy, and Zhuravka.

Conclusions

All methods of relative dating, stylistic, geological, and biological, show significant chronological differences between the sites of the study area. However, there are also many contradictions and inconsistencies between and within these approaches. These can be related to a number of factors, some of which were discussed in Chapter 3: (1) insufficient information, (2) biased sampling, (3) non-synchronization of the different data bases, and (4) the fallacy of using biological analogies for paleoclimatic reconstructions when insufficient information exists on the ecological limits or tolerances of the species. In addition to this, it is my contention that these discrepancies also demonstrate the inadequacy of extant stylistic, stratigraphic, and geochronological models. This contention can be put more specifically as follows:

1. Stylistic (Table 4.1, Figure 4.1) and stratigraphic (Table 4.2, Figure 4.4) chronologies show extensive contradiction. Various authors have dealt with this differently. Soviet archaeologists, by and large, have favored chronological schemes based on unspecified stylistic criteria. Non-Soviet archaeologists have either glossed over the differences and tacitly used modified versions of stylistic schemes (see Kozłowski and

Kozłowski 1979; Bhattacharya 1977) or, as Klein (1973), abandoned stylistic criteria totally in favor of stratigraphy. Still others, like Shimkin (1978), have abandoned all efforts at any chronological ordering and opted for a descriptive presentation of the data instead. Clearly, none of these approaches can be considered satisfactory.

2. Disagreement and contradictory data within the literature of geological dating, as well as problematic and ambiguous measures, indicate that Velichko's late Valdai depositional sequence cannot be relied on throughout the central Russian Plain.

3. Biological data, particularly when limited to small regions, show some regularity as a chronological indicator. They also contradict generalized geological depositional sequences. This and (2) above suggest that Velichko's scheme for the study area has oversimplified earlier climatic occurrences and sectional and microgeographic variations; consequently, it may offer valid indicators for specific localities only, not the whole study area.

4. Particular care should be taken with biostratigraphic data from the post-maximum period of 18,000 to 12,000 B.P., when the Desna stratigraphic sequence appears most in conflict with data from the Dnepr and its more southerly tributaries.

The most salient point of the discussion of extant relative chronologies for the study area is that *biostratigraphic dating methods have not been applied with sufficient rigor in the study area to offer firm and acceptable chronologies.* Much additional work remains to be done before this important dating technique can produce a working scheme for the occupation of the study area during Late Valdai.

CHRONOMETRIC DATING OF THE SITES

Radiometric dating of materials from Upper Paleolithic sites of the Russian Plain has had a brief and turbulent history. First attempts at dating materials by the ^{14}C method resulted from the work of Ivanova and Chernysh at Molodova in the 1960s (Ivanova *et al.* 1963). Since then, radiometric dating has had a problematic history in the USSR and has received a mixed reception from Soviet archaeologists. This reception, as elsewhere, has been based primarily on how well the obtained dates upheld or rejected the chronological models developed on stylistic criteria. In those parts of the Russian Plain where archaeological research coincided with geological research and the use of chronometric dating (such as at the Molodova sites on the Dnestr), the chronological information provided by ^{14}C did not have to contest extant schemes and the dates were more readily accepted. In other parts of the plain, such as at the Kostenki–Borschevo sites on the Don, where archaeological research and stylistic periodizations preceded radiocarbon dating by a good 80 years or so, radiometric dates found more limited acceptance (e.g., Grigor'ev 1979).

The history of research on the central Russian Plain saw a progression of numerous researchers neither administratively connected to one institution (as in the case of Kostenki–Borschevo sites) nor engaged in long-term research in the area (as in the case of the Molodova sites). This produced a plethora of stylistic chronologies and geological schemes which were, as often as not, in conflict with one another. The advent of

Table 4.4   RADIOCARBON DATES FOR SUNGIR[a]

Lab & no.[b]	Date	Provenience	Material dated
Gro. 5425	25,500 ± 200	cultural layer at 3.2 m	wood charcoal
Gro. 5446	24,430 ± 400	cultural layer	collagen from reindeer bone
GIN 326b	22,500 ± 600	cultural layer	wood charcoal
GIN 326a	21,800 ± 1000	hearth, cultural layer	wood charcoal
GIN 16	20,540 ± 120	soil, 1 m below cultural layer	soil
LE 1058	19,780 ± 80	cultural layer, Excavation II, Horizon V	mixture of charcoal and soil
GIN 15	16,200 ± 400	soil under cultural layer	soil
GIN 14	14,600 ± 600	cultural layer	bone

[a]Reported by Bader (1978).
[b]Gro., Gronigen; GIN, Geology Institute, AN SSSR; LU, Leningrad University; LE, Leningrad Division, Institute of Archaeology AN SSSR.

radiometric dating methods had, therefore, minimal impact on the study of the Upper Paleolithic sites in the area. Overcoming initial problems with suspect proveniences and lack of acceptance by a number of major researchers in the area (e.g., Grigor'ev 1979; Pidoplichko 1976; Shovkoplyas 1978, personal communication), this dating technique is now used routinely by Velichko and his staff, who have been providing a steady stream of dates for the sites since the 1970s (see Kurenkova 1978; Velichko *et al.* 1976).

An added problem which impeded and still continues to impede the acceptance of ^{14}C dating is the persistent inconsistency found in the dates derived from different materials and from different laboratories on the same sites. This problem is well illustrated by ^{14}C dates obtained for the site of Sungir, located 450 km to the east-northeast of the study area (Table 4.4). While large variances are more readily evident at Sungir, where a number of samples have been dated, similar difficulties exist in the dates obtained for the sites in the study area as well.

RADIOMETRIC DATES FOR THE STUDY AREA

Table 2.15 lists all ^{14}C dates available at present for the Upper Paleolithic sites in the area. Of the 33 dates presented in the table, 27 have been obtained by laboratories in the USSR over a period of some 20 years, and 5 have been obtained from the Radiocarbon Laboratory of Queens College, City University of New York, from 1978 to 1980. Three of the dates from the Queens College lab, those for Gontsy (QC 898) and Mezhirich (QC 897, 900), came from materials I collected from excavations in 1978 and 1979. The Eliseevichi sample (QC 889) came from materials collected by its most recent excavator L. V. Grekhova. The sample for Pushkari I (QC 899) came from materials excavated in the 1930s. These dates, like all those presented in Table 2.12, are "raw" and have not been corrected by the ^{12}C/^{13}C method.

The presented dates are of varying significance and reliability, and they require some discussion. There are four basic problems associated with them: (1) questionable provenience, (2) possible redeposition of the cultural remains, (3) non-equivalency of media tested, and (4) discrepancies between results from different laboratories. These problems affect a number of the dates, in some cases totally negating their significance and in others seriously questioning their accuracy.

Provenience.   Two dates, GIN 80 for Eliseevichi and GIN 4 for Mezin, are at issue here. Both appeared in the early 1960s in the literature and represent the first efforts by the Geology Institute of the Academy of Sciences of the USSR (AN USSR) at dating. In the case of Mezin, the date was reported for the first and only time by Ivanova *et al.* (1963). No provenience was given for the dated mammoth tooth, and the date has subsequently not appeared in any Soviet literature. The quick disappearance of the date from publications, its absence in the monograph on Mezin published after the date was obtained (Shovkoplyas 1965a), and the absence of any discussion in the literature on the merits of the date all lead me to conclude that, for reasons unknown, the date should not be accepted. A similar fate met the GIN 80 date of 33,000 ± 400 for Eliseevichi. The date was first reported by Ivanova *et al.* in 1963, who wrote that it was obtained from wood found in the cultural layer. Subsequently, other publications have stated that the dated material was bone, in other cases loess–loam (Kurenkova 1978; Shimkin 1978). Today the date is absent from the literature, the provenience of the dated material is held highly suspect, and the validity of the date is dismissed by Soviet investigators (Kalechitz 1978, personal communication; Kurenkova 1978; Lazukov *et al.* 1981).

Dates on Redeposited Materials.   Radiocarbon dates from two additional sites, Berdyzh and Yurovichi, pose problems of reliability as well. As was discussed in Chapter 2, cultural materials at both sites have been redeposited—partially at Berdyzh and totally at Yurovichi. Because of this the provenience of the dated materials (mammoth teeth in both cases) is highly questionable. Redeposition of organic materials in general exposes the materials to dangers of contamination by absorption of fresh carbon, thereby giving a younger date to the material. For bone, danger of contamination by older carbon exists as well (Butzer 1971). In the case of both Berdyzh and Yurovichi, the obtained dates appear much older than could be expected from the stratigraphy of the sites. I have noted in the earlier section of this chapter that while the geology of both the Sozh and Pripyat' valleys is less well known than that of the Desna, the two sites appear more or less coeval with those found on the Desna and Sudost'. At present, therefore, I suspect that some as yet unidentified factors are responsible for the relatively early dates obtained for both of the sites and that these factors are probably related to both the redeposition of the dated material and the nature of the dated medium itself. This, then, adds more uncertainty to the chronological assignment of these sites by radiometric criteria. This problem cannot be resolved by consulting either biostratigraphic or stylistic criteria, as those also fail to uniformly date the sites (see Tables 4.1 and 4.2). I am, therefore, forced to consider both possibilities that (1) the sites are two of the oldest found in the study area, and (2) they date to the same 18,000–12,000 B.P. period as the remainder of the sites (with the exception of Khotylevo II).

The Dated Medium.   It is generally agreed that wood charcoal is the optimal medium for radiocarbon dating. The absence of burned wood, however, is a notable feature of Upper Paleolithic sites in the study area, one that has been widely commented on in the literature (Klein 1973; Kurenkova 1978; Lazukov *et al.* 1981). This, by necessity, has led researchers to use a variety of less optimal media for dating; as Table 2.15 shows, dates have been obtained from burned bone, wood charcoal (one sample), unburned bone, and shell. Unburned bone, as both Butzer (1971) and Michels (1973) among others point out, is exposed to far greater dangers of contamination from both older and younger carbon. To combat this problem, Soviet researchers have focused on developing methods for dating the more impermeable type of bone, mammoth teeth, and a number of the Soviet ^{14}C dates in Table 2.12 come from this medium (see Kurenkova 1978, 1980; Velichko *et al.* 1976). Of the 33 dates listed in that table, 10 were obtained from mammoth teeth.

Radiocarbon dates obtained from Queens College, on the other hand, come from burned mammoth bone. These five dates, together with the LU 103 date for Yudinovo

B.P.	MAMMOTH TEETH		BURNED BONE	
10,000				
12,000				
	Timonovka I:	12,200 ± 300		
	Eliseevichi	12,970 ± 140 ⌉	Gontsy:	13,400 ± 185
			Yudinovo:	13,830 ± 850
14,000		14,470 ± 100 ⌐	Mezhirich:	14,300 ± 300; 14,320 ± 270; 14,530 ± 300
	Mezhirich:	14,700 ± 500		15,245 ± 1,350
	Timonovka II:	15,100 ± 530	Timonovka I:	15,300 ± 700
16,000	Yudinovo:	15,660 ± 180	Eliseevichi:	15,600 ± 1,350
		17,340 ± 170 ⌟	Pushkari I:	16,775 ± 605
				17,855 ± 950 ⌉
18,000	Mezhirich:	18,020 ± 600	Mezhirich ——	18,470 ± 550 ⌐
	Pogon:	18,690 ± 770		19,100 ± 500 ⌟
20,000				
22,000				
	Berdyzh:	23,430 ± 180		
		23,660 ± 270 ⌉		
24,000	Khotylevo I: —			
		24,960 ± 270 ⌟		
26,000				
	Yurovichi:	26,470 ± 420		
	Mezin:	27,500 ± 800		
28,000				

Figure 4.7   Comparison of ^{14}C dates from mammoth teeth and burned bone.

and GIN 2595 for Mezhirich also obtained from burned bone, appear to be consistently younger than the dates obtained from teeth. A comparison of dates from mammoth teeth to dates from burned mammoth bone (Figure 4.7) demonstrates the variability between media. In addition to showing chronological differences obtained from the two media, Figure 4.7 also shows a greater clustering of the dates obtained from burned bone. The significance of this observation cannot be evaluated at present, because only four of the sites have multiple dates obtained from different media. It is offered here as a suggestion for future work. Specifically, I suggest that burned bone as a dating medium may offer greater consistency and reliability than other media. The very wide range of dates obtained by the same lab on mammoth teeth at such sites as Eliseevichi, for example, appear to indicate that mammoth teeth are quite susceptible to contamination that is difficult to control.

Dates obtained from unburned mammoth bone as well as from mammoth teeth are unreliable for yet another reason. In Chapter 5 I offer a detailed discussion of fauna found at the sites and argue that some mammoth remains represent collection of bone rather than active hunting. If bone collection occurred during the Upper Paleolithic, some bone at the sites could have come from animals long dead whose remains may have fossilized and will probably yield much older dates than those obtained from bone burned.

Discrepancies between Laboratories.   Data in Table 2.12 indicate large differences in dates obtained on the same medium by different laboratories. This is particularly evident for Mezhirich, for which KI dates on burned bone are considerably older than those obtained by Queens College or the Geological Institute, AN USSR. A similar difference can be observed on materials from Mezin, although Mezin dates come from less reliable unburned bone and teeth. Because both Queens College and the Geological Institute radiocarbon laboratories have considerable experience dating archaeozoological remains, I consider their dates more reliable.

Summary and Conclusion

The discussion on radiometric dating has shown that this method of chronological ordering is as problematic as were the relative methods of chronological ordering discussed earlier. My observations on the tendency of mammoth teeth to produce older dates than those from other media puts into question the early dates obtained from Berdyzh, Khotylevo II, and Yurovichi. Younger dates, those ostensibly dating to the post–Valdai maximum such as Pogon and Timonovka II, may likewise be problematic and too old. In the case of Timonovka II, the date of $15,110 \pm 530$ is not consistent with the stratigraphic data from the site. The inconsistency may well be due to errors in radiometric dating of a particular medium.

Few concrete conclusions on chronological ordering of the sites can be drawn from this discussion. Those that appear justified are too general in nature to be of much use for archaeological questions. Available ^{14}C date generally indicate that Upper Paleolithic sites in the study area date to the late Valdai. Although there is some evidence of two periods of occupation, one preceding the glacial maximum and one following it, the older dates are too problematic to allow certainty to this possibility. On the other hand, the ambiguity of the data do not permit rejection of the hypothesis either. Clearly, much geological work remains to be done and many more chronometric dates are needed before a firm chronological ordering of the sites can be achieved.

PROPOSED CHRONOLOGICAL ORDERING OF THE SITES ─────────

Although no one method of dating the sites will yield unambiguous evidence, I suggest that a careful evaluation of both relative and chronometric data do allow for an assignment of occupation at the sites more specific than simply the general Upper Paleolithic period. Such subdivisions are shown in Figure 4.8. The late Valdai is divided into three stratigraphic units: the pre-maximum period between 26,000 and 20,000 B.P., when Bryansk soil formed and part of Loess II was deposited; the middle period of the glacial maximum itself (20,000–18,000 B.P.), when the remainder of Loess II was deposited; and the post-maximum period after 18,000 B.P., when Loess III, the gley layer, and the Timonovka soil layer were deposited. Conflicting conclusions from styl-

B. P.	Late Valdai Climate		Late Valdai Stratigraphy	Colder Periods	No Information on Climate	Warmer Periods
	Dryas III S		Contemporary Soil			
	Alleröd I					
— 12,000	Dryas II S					
	Bölling I	L o e s s	Gley Layer ? Timonovka Soil ?			
	Dryas I S					
— 14,000	Raunis I		Gley Layer ? Timonovka Soil ?	Chulatovo I, Eliseevichi, Klyusy(?), Mezhirich, Mezin, Pushkari I, II, Yudinovo(?)	Fastov, Kirillovskaya, Korshevo I, II, Kositsa, Novo-Bobovichi, Suponevo	Chulatovo II, Dobranichevka, Gontsy, Novgorod-Severskii, Timonovka I(?), Yudinovo(?), Zhuravka
— 16,000	Lascaux I	III	Gley Layer II?	Possibly: Berdyzh(?) and Khotylevo II (?)	Possibly: Radomyshl'(?), Yurovichi(?)	
	Laugerie I		Gley Layer I			
— 18,000				Valdai Maximum		
— 20,000		L o e s s				
— 22,000		II				
— 24,000	Tursac I			Berdyzh(?), Khotylevo II (?)	Radomyshl'(?)	
			Bryansk Soil			
26,000	Salpetriere I				Yurovichi(?)	

Figure 4.8 Suggested chronological ordering of sites: I, interstadial; S, stadial (climate data from Dol-ukhanov and Pashkevich 1977; stratigraphy adapted from Velichko 1961).

istic, stratigraphic, and chronometric data do not permit further subdivision. Biological information, however, suggests a delineation within each broad category of two distinct periods of occupation: sites occupied during colder climate and those occupied during warmer climate. Since paleoenvironmental information is lacking for some sites within each chronological period, I also delimit a third subcategory—one which belongs to a broad period but to no specific climatic episode within that period.

Sites Older than 20,000 B.P.

Combined dating methods suggest that four sites, Berdyzh, Khotylevo II, Radomyshl', and Yurovichi, were occupied during this period. Three of these sites, Berdyzh, Khotylevo II, and Yurovichi, have been dated chronometrically, but as discussed earlier, these dates are ambiguous. The fourth site, Radomyshl' is considered by Soviet researchers, on the basis of stylistic criteria, to be the oldest in the study area (e.g., Gladkih 1973; Lazukov et al. 1981; Shovkoplyas 1964).

The Valdai Maximum (20,000–18,000 B.P.)

No sites in the study area firmly date to this time, and it appears, as Velichko (1961) suggests, that the area may have been either totally uninhabited during this period or inhabited by a much smaller population. It is interesting to note that similar depopulation is also postulated for the other river valleys of the Russian Plain. Ivanova (1977) notes a cultural break in the Molodova sequence on the Dnestr that lasted from approximately 23,000 to 17,000 B.P. She writes that, while man did not totally leave the area, archaeological evidence suggests both a decrease in population and a change in subsistence practices and settlement systems. Zarrina and Krasnov (1979) note the same phenomenon in the Kostenki–Borschevo region during the 21,000–17,000 B.P. period. These observations are in agreement with my conclusion that the central Russian Plain was either totally uninhabited or had very sparce populations during this time.

The Post-Maximum Period (18,000–12,000 B.P.)

As Figure 4.8 shows, the vast majority of the sites (25 of 29) were probably occupied during this 6000-year period. Since conflicting data on the chronological assignment of each site preclude any intersite ordering, they are presented in alphabetical order only. While evidence suggests that chronological differences do exist between the sites, only paleoenvironmental differences can be monitored with any certainty at the present time. Roughly the same number of sites can be assigned to periods with warm climate (6–8) and to cold periods (6–10). The numerous climatic fluctuations between 18,000 and 12,000 B.P. preclude assignment of the sites in either group to a specific warm or cold oscillation.

It is significant to note that the most intensive occupation of the study area appears precisely during the period of climatic fluctuations. This co-occurrence of site occupation and climatic oscillations is clearly visible when paleoclimatic data is presented together with radiometric information (Figure 4.9). Mean dates were calculated for sites where more than one date was available; the range of dates reflects the extent of standard deviations of all of the dates per site combined.

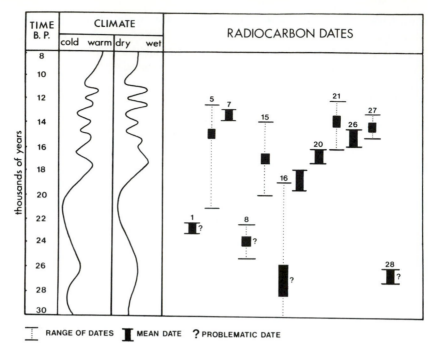

Figure 4.9   Late Pleistocene climate and ^{14}C dates from the sites: ^{14}C dates from Table 2.12 (climate curve after Chebotareva and Makaricheva 1982: Fig. 2; Dolukhanov 1978: Fig. 18).

UPPER PALEOLITHIC LAND USE: ———
THE LOCATION OF THE SITES

Upper Paleolithic sites in the study area are distributed not evenly across the landscape but in specific regions in association with river valleys. They are found between latitudes 49°30′ and 53°21 ′N and longitudes of 29°14′ and 34°20′ E in an area of some 180,000 km² (Figure 2.1). In this section I examine in detail various micro- and macrogeographic variables in the late Valdai landscape which conditioned patterns of land use. Since chronological controls are problematic and the sample size of sites possibly occupied before the glacial maximum very small (four), I discuss the location and distribution of all sites and limit myself to a series modifying statements about changes in land use through time.

MICROGEOGRAPHIC VARIABLES

Although very little work has been done by Soviet researchers on regional patterns of settlement location, all research to date assumes that the riverine location of the sites indicates that proximity to water and to subsistence resources in river valleys were important criteria in site location. River valleys, especially after the Valdai maximum, carried glacial runoff, drained numerous ice-dammed lakes, and were far broader and carried greater loads than their present-day equivalents. On the central Russian Plain these huge rivers held in their streams numerous chain lakes—creating a series of unique lacustrine and riverine environments along the river valleys. These locales, especially along the Desna, Sudost', and Pripyat', offered preferred locales for Upper Paleolithic settlements.

Table 2.3 lists the distances of sites to nearest rivers for 27 sites where distance could be estimated. The observed mean distance to the nearest river is 388 m with a range from 5–10 m to 3000 m. Only 3 sites (11%) are located farther than 1000 m from the river. These measurements reflect present-day distances. They were probably somewhat different in the late Valdai, but it is expected that they fluctuated within ranges observed today, and that present-day distances broadly reflect past conditions as well.

The location of sites in or near river valleys quite obviously does not reflect only site-selection criteria of late Valdai hunter–gatherers, but archaeological biases as well. No systematic surveys have ever been done in the study area. Past surveys accentuated the riverine bias by surveying only river valleys and their proximities (e.g., Polikarpovich 1968). The majority of the sites were discovered as a result of either river erosion or local earthworks such as road building and cellar digging. Local earthworks, while in theory randomly distributed across the landscape, are still more likely to occur in greater frequencies closer to river valleys. This is because population densities in agri-cultural communities have always tended to be greater closer to rivers. Therefore, we can expect that the distribution of modern populations in the study area contributes a specific bias in favor of discovering sites close to rivers.

I would argue however, that the *exclusive* presence of river valley sites in the study area is only partially due to these biases. The very exclusivity of this locale for site location suggests that legitimate factors, many the same as those *responsible* for mod-ern settlement distribution, are operative. Romanchuk (1974), for example, lists prox-imity to water, abundance of river valley, floral and faunal resources, and availability of lithic outcrops as the main site-selection criteria in Upper Paleolithic settlement sys-tems. Similar linearization of settlement systems has been observed elsewhere in the Old World as well during the Late Valdai (late Würm). White (1980), for example, notes this pattern in the location of the Magdalinean sites in southwestern France.

Proximity to Water.   Proximity to water was the first advantage offered by river valleys. Water, as has been pointed out by numerous researchers, exerts a strong pull on site location decisions of hunter–gatherers, as it is a necessary resource both for man and for the survival of faunal resources on which man preys (Binford 1982b; Jochim 1976; White 1980).

The specific features of river valleys in the study area produced characteric reg-ularities in Upper Paleolithic site selection. One is the presence of sites only on one side of the river valleys. This can be most clearly seen along the Desna and Sudost' where the 15 sites are all located on the left (northern or northwestern) banks. Velichko (1961) accounts for this regularity by pointing to the asymmetry of the rivers in the area. The left banks, therefore, offered some elevation and drainage in the past, while the right banks, as today, were low-lying, water-logged, and swampy. Some elevation was probably especially important in warm months between river break-up and freeze-up, when rivers presented the greatest problems to low-lying settlements.

A second regularity is the preferred placement of the sites on promontories bordered on one side by the river and on one or more of the other sides by ravines. Thus, of the 22 in situ or partially in situ sites listed in Table 2.3, 18 (82%) were located on such promontories at time of occupation. Velichko (1961) explains this locational preference as resulting from better drainage of such locales. Romanchuk (1974) adds such factors as improved visibility and natural protection from predators. He suggests that man settled in the late Valdai on either low-lying terraces, where these were present, or at the edges of adjacent plateaus. The presence of alluvial deposits both above and below cultural layers at such sites as Gontsy, Mezhirich, and Zhuravka indicates that the sites were indeed close to rivers and were periodically flooded. Table 2.3 estimates, where possible, altitudes of sites above the rivers at the time of occupation. Of the 19 sites, 9 (47%) were located either on the floodplain itself or 1–2 m above it. The others range from 5 to 40 m above the rivers.

Microclimate and Microenvironments.   In addition to providing water, river valleys today offer specific microclimatic conditions that are on the average milder than those of the surrounding plateau regions. It is expected that these advantages existed in the river valleys in the past as well (Romanchuk 1974; White 1980). These microclimates created a number of diverse microenvironments in the river valleys that were able to support both greater numbers and a greater variety of flora and fauna than was found in the interfluves (see Chapter 3 for a detailed discussion). This resource richness is expected to have exerted a very strong pull on the subsistence practices and settlement systems of late Valdai hunter–gatherers.

South-Facing Slopes and Promontories.   Table 2.3 lists the orientation of the sites in relation to cardinal points. Of the 24 site orientations that could be estimated, 15 (62.5%) face either true south or modified southerly directions. This indicates that after the first condition in site location was met, namely proximity to the river or lake, preferred site location was a south-facing slope or promontory. The climatic advantages of settlement on southern slopes is well known. As White (1980) reports, extensive ecological studies have shown that south-facing slopes receive considerably more solar radiation (2.5 times more in winter) than north-facing slopes. This implies that warmer and more favorable microclimate was to be found on south-facing slopes in the Late Valdai as well, and these advantages were likely taken into account by hunter–gatherers when selecting their site location.

White also shows how these microclimatic differences affected the distribution of biotic communities in late Pleistocene southwestern France: Lusher and more varied vegetation and greater overall numbers and variety of fauna existed on south-facing slopes. The lack of specific studies of north- versus south-facing slopes in the study area preclude further examination of additional subsistence-oriented advantages. It seem clear to me, however, that all other things being equal, late Valdai hunter–gatherers in the area did selectively locate their settlements on warmer and more hospitable south-facing river valleys.

Lithic Resources.   The presence of numerous flint outcrops in specific regions of river valleys exerted an additional locational pull on settlement systems. This is especially true for the Desna sites, which, as numerous authors have pointed out, are located near outcrops of high-quality flint (Boriskovskii 1953; Romanchuk 1974; Velichko 1961; Voevodskii 1952a,b). Unfortunately, no systematic work has been done to determine the exact locations of flint outcrops along the rivers in the study area. Observations on the proximity of Desna sites to good lithic sources are unquantified and anecdotal and preclude me from considering the pull that availability of lithic raw material may have played in settlement location.

Mammoth-Procurement Strategies.   Table 2.3 lists numbers of mammoth found at different sites in the study area. These estimates could be calculated for 21 of 28 sites. The same table indicates sites where mammoth-bone dwellings have been found. A comparison clearly shows that sites containing large numbers of mammoth are also those that have mammoth-bone dwellings. The difference of means test conducted on the MNI estimates of mammoth between the sites with dwellings and those without dwellings shows large differences significant at $p = .0001$ ($z = 5.30$; see Table 4.5).

Sites with mammoth-bone dwellings are also found in very specific geographic locales that differ from locales of sites without mammoth-bone dwellings. Table 2.3 lists geographic specifics of each site location (terrace or plateau, promontory or ravine) and estimates elevation of the sites above the river at the time of occupation. Of the 21 sites for which estimates could be listed, 15 were found in association with floodplains or ravines and 6 with neither floodplains nor ravines. Nine of the sites associated with ravines or floodplains had dwellings, whereas 2 of the 6 sites not located at floodplains or ravines had dwellings.

A comparison of location of sites with dwellings with the location of those without

Table 4.5   STATISTICAL TESTS: MAMMOTH-BONE DWELLINGS

Difference of means tests	N	$\overline{X}_1$	$\overline{X}_2$	z	p
1. Sites with mammoth-bone dwellings vs sites without—on number of mammoth	21	73.00	11.30	5.30	<.0001
2. Sites with mammoth-bone dwellings vs sites without—on nearest-neighbor distance	27	66.45	16.37	4.34	<.0001
3. Sites with mammoth-bone dwellings in the north vs those with them in the south—on nearest-neighbor distances to other like sites	10	65.16	80.00	0.56	.34
4. Sites without mammoth-bone dwellings in the north vs sites without them in the south—on nearest-neighbor distances to other like sites	16	22.33	145.00	11.40	<.0001

Chi square test of association	N	df	χ^2		p
Large accumulations of mammoth bones and dwellings in ravine or floodplain vs those in non-ravine and non-floodplain	21	1	41.05		<.001

dwellings ($\chi^2 = 41.05$, $df = 1$, $p = .001$; see Table 4.5) confirms that there is a significant association of sites with large numbers of mammoths and dwellings and floodplain–ravine location.

The preferential location of sites with large numbers of mammoths and mammoth-bone dwellings on the floodplains or near ravines is probably associated with mammoth-procurement strategies. Even though the exact strategies used in procuring mammoth are still unclear, any strategy, be it active hunting or collecting, would have taken place in or near floodplains and ravines (see Chapter 5). If active hunting strategies were responsible for the large accumulations found at the sites, and strategies these, as some researchers believe, included mass drives and kills, they could best be accomplished by driving herds off the precipices into the ravines (e.g., Kornietz 1962; Saunders 1980). On the other hand, if, as both Gromov (1948) and Vereschagin (1971, 1979) believe, some mammoths found at the sites were procured by scavenging mammoth cemeteries which had accumulated as a result of natural attrition, the location of these cemeteries would have also been on the floodplains or in ravines (for a discussion of the location of mammoth-bone cemeteries in the USSR, see Vereschagin 1979).

Role of Microgeographic Variables through Time.   Sites possibly occupied prior to the Valdai maximum are also located in river valleys, but at greater distances from the rivers. The mean distance is 1291 m; Berdyzh and Khotylevo II are located less than 100 m from the river, Radomyshl' and Yurovichi, 3000 m and 2000 m, respectively. The overall significance of this observed difference in mean distance may be moot because of both the difficulty of dating these sites firmly and the small sample size. If we assume, however, that these sites were indeed occupied early, then the observed differences point to a change in the paleogeography of the area and changes in cultural practices of site location. Specifically, as hypothesized previously, climatic factors and the enlargement of the rivers after the Valdai maximum effectively linearized the distribution of flora and fauna along the river valleys, and this linearization exerted a strong pull on the settlement systems and resulted in the riverine location of the Upper Paleolithic sites. The location of earlier sites farther from the rivers indirectly supports this interpretation and indicates either the absence of such linearization before the maximum or its much weaker "pull" on the settlement system.

Finally, an interesting difference emerges in the cardinal orientation of early versus late sites. As I noted previously, 15 (66.5%) sites face either true south or a modified southerly direction. Table 2.3 indicates that the pull of south-facing locations may have been less strong at early sites. Of the sites occupied after the Valdai maximum, 15 (75%) face either true south or a modified southerly direction, whereas only one site (Khotylevo II—25% of the sample) occupied early is oriented toward the south. The remaining three early sites, Berdyzh, Radomyshl', and Yurovichi, all face either true north or a modified northerly direction. The significance of this observation is open to discussion. If these sites are indeed early, then we can anticipate that they were occupied when climatic conditions were less severe than those postulated for the 18,000–12,000 B.P. period (see Chapter 3 for a discussion of the climate during the late Valdai). It is possible that milder climate reduced the attractiveness of south-facing locations for site selection and allowed for the predominance of other, as yet unknown, site-selection criteria.

MACROGEOGRAPHIC FEATURES

I have already noted one clear macrogeographic pattern in the distribution of sites: their association with river valleys. This pattern produced the linearized distribution of sites.

The regularity of site location on the left (north) banks of the river valleys appears to hold for the 4 early sites as well. These sites, like those occupied later, are found on the higher and better-drained sides of the valleys.

The height of the sites above the rivers also does not appear to exhibit significant change through time. Available data on 19 sites (Table 2.3) show that of the 17 later sites, 9 are found higher than 5 m above the river and 8 either on the floodplain or 1–2 m above it. For the early sites, information is only available on the elevation above the rivers for Khotylevo II and Radomyshl'. Both are located from 4 to 7 m above the river, and thus their location does not show a significant difference from those of later sites.

The noted association of sites with mammoth-bone dwellings and floodplain or ravine topography also appears to hold through time. Quantified data exist for 21 sites—18 dating after the glacial maximum and 3 to an earlier period of occupation. Of the early sites with a large number of mammoth, 2 (66%) have mammoth-bone dwellings (Berdyzh and Radomyshl'). Nine (50%) occupied during the later period have mammoth-bone dwellings as well. The observed difference in the percentage of sites with dwellings during the early and late periods of occupation is not statistically significant. Furthermore, the two early sites with mammoth-bone dwellings, like their counterparts in later periods, are also associated with floodplain or ravine topography. As Figure 2.1 shows, however, this linearization is not uniform across the area; sites are aggregated in specific parts of the region. I performed a series of dimensional analysis of variance tests to discern and identify these possible aggregations. This test, described by Whallon (1973), is designed to isolate and specify both the nature and location of point clusters across a given area. The relative sizes of quadrants used are offered in Figure 4.10.

The first test was performed on the distribution of all the sites in the area (Figure

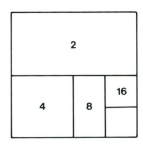

Figure 4.10   Size of quadrants for dimensional analysis of variance. Block sizes: block 2 = 90,000 km²; block 4 = 45,000 km²; block 8 = 22,500 km²; block 16 = 11,250 km².

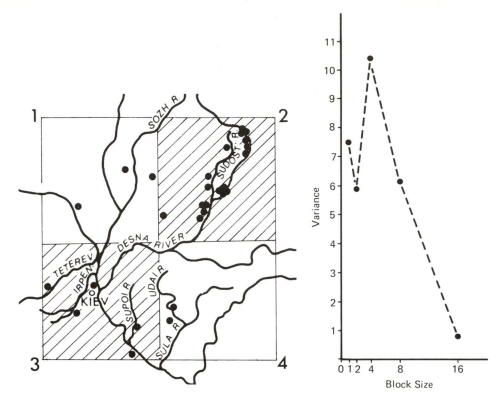

Figure 4.11 First-order clustering and dimensional analysis of variance—all sites: quadrants 2 and 3, block size 4.

4.11). As the resulting illustration shows, first-order clustering of the sites occurs in both the northeast (2) and southwest (3) quadrants. These quadrants are "block size 4," approximately 45,000 km² each. I interpret the results of this test to indicate that two clusters of sites are present in the area, one in the northeast, the other in the southwest.

Distribution of Sites without Dwellings.   Since distinct differences exist between the locations of sites with mammoth-bone dwellings (i.e., with large numbers of mammoths) and those without them, I also examined the distribution of these two groups of sites separately.

The dimensional analysis of variance on the distribution of sites with no mammoth-bone dwellings is depicted in Figure 4.12. As the graph suggests, first-order clustering of these sites occurs in the northeast quadrant. This quadrant, approximately 45,000 km², is situated along the upper half of the Desna and Sudost'.

Second-order clustering (Figure 4.13) occurs in quadrants 4 and 7 (block size 16). These quadrants cover 11,250 km² each. The strong second-order clustering shown in this figure occurs because of the linearization of clustering—a result of the location of the sites in river valleys. The second-order clustering is also found in the northeast part

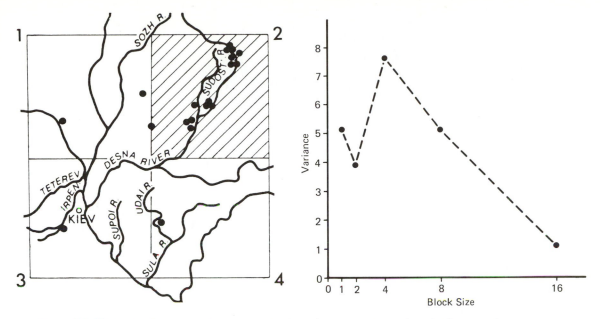

Figure 4.12   First-order clustering and dimensional analysis of variance—sites without dwellings: quadrant 2, block size 4.

of the study area and is associated with the Desna and Sudost. I therefore conclude that sites without mammoth-bone dwellings are not randomly or evenly distributed along all river valleys but are clustered in the northeastern section of the study area.

Distribution of Sites with Mammoth-Bone Dwellings.   Dimensional analysis of variance was also performed on the distribution of sites with mammoth-bone dwellings.

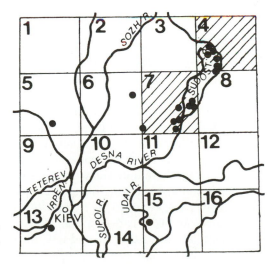

Figure 4.13   Second-order clustering—all sites (dimensional analysis of variance; quadrants 4 and 7, block size 16).

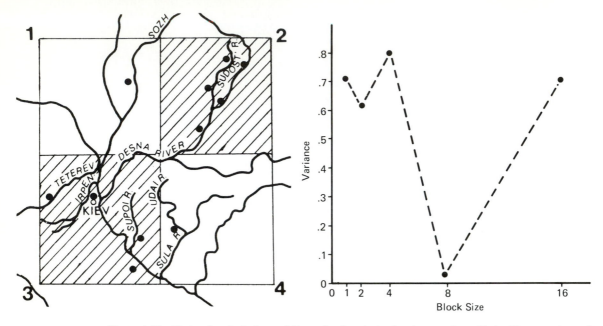

Figure 4.14   First-order clustering and dimensional analysis of variance—sites with dwellings: quadrants 2 and 3, block size 4.

The results (Figure 4.14) suggest that first-order clustering occurs in quadrants 2 and 3 (block size 4).

The presence of clustering in two quadrants related diagonally is like that observed for the distribution of all sites in the area (Figure 4.11) and is different from the pattern of clustering observed among the sites without dwellings (Figure 4.12).

Second-order clustering occurs in quadrants 4 and 14 (block size 16) (Figure 4.15). These occur in two noncontiguous blocks, again placed on a northeast–southwest diagonal. While the patterning of first-order clustering among the sites with mammoth-bone dwellings suggests a continuation of the linearized pattern of site distribution observed in the case of the distribution of sites without dwellings, the clear separation of second-order cluster quadrants with sites with dwellings suggests a different pattern. I interpret this pattern to reflect the existence of two separate regions of settlement for sites with dwellings. One of these is located in the northeastern part of the area and is associated with the Desna and Sudost'. The second group is located in the southwest and is associated with the Dnepr and Sula.

In summary, these tests show that sites without dwellings cluster in a very different manner from those with dwellings. The co-occurrence of two clusters with very similar types of sites suggests that the two clusters were not fully segregated from each other but possibly formed a part of a unified system with similar subsistence practices and settlement patterns. I develop and test this hypothesis in Chapters 5 and 6.

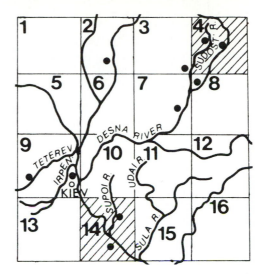

Figure 4.15   Second-order clustering, sites with dwellings: quadrants 4 and 14, block size 16.

Proximal Associations.   I have shown that specific clustering of sites is present on the central Russian Plain and that the sites with mammoth-bone dwellings and those without cluster in different sections of the study area. In this section I demonstrate that greater regularities exist in spacing of sites with dwellings across the study area than exists in the spacing of the non-dwelling sites.

Tables 4.6–4.8 list nearest-neighbor distances between all sites, sites with dwellings, and sites without dwellings. Difference of means tests performed on these distances are listed in Table 4.5. They show that the mean distance between sites with dwellings (66.45 km) is considerably greater than for sites without dwellings (16.37 km; $z = 4.34$, $p = .0001$). Additional tests revealed other significant regularities within each category of sites.

Since dimensional analysis of variance tests indicated a regional difference in the distribution of sites with dwellings, I divided the sites into those found in the north ($n = 6$, quadrants 1 and 2 [block size 4]) and in the south ($n = 5$, quadrants 3 and 4 [block size 4]) for new difference of means tests. The enlargement of quadrant size over those that showed maximal clustering in previous calculations was done to include all sites and offer the maximal number of sites for the calculation of this statistic. Test results (Table 4.5) indicate that there is no significant difference between mean nearest-neighbor distances of northern and southern sites with mammoth-bone dwellings ($z = 0.56$, $p = .34$). They indicate that sites with dwellings in both the north and south show a regularity of spacing across the landscape and are located approximately 70 km from each other. The one exception to this is Berdyzh, which is 160 km from its nearest neighbor. This large distance, well outside the expected range suggested by the standard deviation (51.74) for the northern sites, may indicate both archaeological bias and possible chronological differences between the sites. As noted previously, the Desna

Table 4.6 DISTANCE BETWEEN SITES (IN KILOMETERS)

	1	2	3	4	5	6	7	8	9	10	11	12	13	14	15	16	17	18	19	20	21	22	23	24	25	26	27	28	29
1. Berdyzh	0	195	195	260	180	240	260	230	230	100	200	200	200	125	258	175	175	55	170	170	170	170	250	218	220	220	160	140	240
2. Chulatovo I	195	0	0.5	233	135	300	160	180	260	90	175	175	175	52	241	18	7	127	27	27	27	27	280	160	162	162	100	270	160
3. Chulatovo II	195	0.5	0	233	135	300	160	180	260	90	175	175	175	52	241	18	7	127	27	27	27	27	280	160	162	162	100	270	160
4. Dobranichevka	260	233	233	0	325	140	70	387	132	200	390	390	390	282	70	220	235	275	250	250	250	250	186	360	362	362	322	220	90
5. Eliseevichi	180	135	135	325	0	420	280	45	355	160	30	30	30	85	362	150	130	140	108	108	108	108	390	28	30	30	50	320	265
6. Fastov	240	300	300	140	420	0	250	420	60	240	430	430	430	340	120	280	300	282	325	325	325	325	65	401	403	403	350	145	220
7. Gontsy	260	160	160	70	280	250	0	320	200	175	322	322	322	200	110	150	185	240	195	195	195	195	250	288	290	290	250	240	40
8. Khotylevo II	230	180	180	387	45	420	320	0	420	200	12	12	12	130	390	198	171	180	153	153	153	153	390	20	18	18	80	350	282
9. Kirillovskaya	230	260	260	132	355	60	200	420	0	240	430	430	430	290	100	220	265	282	285	285	285	285	70	413	415	415	325	140	145
10. Klyusy	100	90	90	200	160	240	175	200	170	0	190	190	190	100	217	85	85	55	55	55	55	55	242	198	200	200	120	175	145
11. Korshevo I	200	175	175	390	30	430	322	12	430	190	0	nd	nd	145	390	180	45	170	150	150	150	150	415	32	30	30	75	345	290
12. Korshevo II	200	175	175	390	30	430	322	12	430	190	nd	0	nd	145	390	180	45	170	150	150	150	150	415	32	30	30	75	345	290
13. Kositsa	200	175	175	390	30	430	322	12	430	190	nd	nd	0	145	390	180	45	170	150	150	150	150	415	32	30	30	75	345	290
14. Kurovo	125	52	52	282	85	340	200	130	290	100	145	145	145	0	282	60	45	100	25	25	25	25	325	113	115	115	40	280	185
15. Mezhirich	258	241	241	70	362	120	110	390	100	217	390	390	390	282	0	240	258	290	260	260	260	260	180	385	387	387	330	185	120
16. Mezin	175	18	18	220	150	280	150	198	220	85	180	180	180	60	240	0	25	120	45	45	45	45	260	178	180	180	105	260	145
17. Novgorod–Severskii	175	7	7	235	130	300	185	171	265	85	170	170	170	45	258	25	0	120	20	20	20	20	285	153	155	155	95	265	162
18. Novo-Bobovichi	55	127	127	275	140	282	240	180	245	55	170	170	170	100	290	120	120	0	120	120	120	120	290	178	180	180	100	180	215
19. Bugorok	170	27	27	250	108	325	195	153	285	55	150	150	150	25	260	45	20	120	0	0	0.2	0.4	325	133	135	135	63	260	180
20. Pogon	170	27	27	250	108	325	195	153	285	55	150	150	150	25	260	45	20	120	0	0	0.2	0.2	325	133	135	135	63	260	180
21. Pushkari I	170	27	27	250	108	325	195	153	285	55	150	150	150	25	260	45	20	120	0.2	0.2	0	0.2	325	133	135	135	63	260	180
22. Pushkari II	170	27	27	250	108	325	195	153	285	55	150	150	150	25	260	45	20	120	0.4	0.2	0.2	0	325	133	135	135	63	260	180
23. Radomyshl'	250	280	280	186	390	65	256	430	70	242	415	415	415	325	180	260	285	290	325	325	325	325	0	418	420	420	370	120	240
24. Suponevo	218	160	160	360	38	401	288	20	413	198	32	32	32	113	385	178	150	178	133	133	133	133	418	0	2	2	80	358	288
25. Timonovka I	220	162	162	362	40	403	290	18	415	200	30	30	30	115	387	180	150	180	135	135	135	135	420	2	0	0.2	90	360	290
26. Timonovka II	220	162	162	362	40	403	290	18	415	200	30	30	30	115	387	180	150	180	135	135	135	135	420	2	0.2	0	90	360	290
27. Yudinovo	160	100	100	322	55	350	250	80	325	120	75	75	75	40	330	105	95	100	63	63	63	63	370	88	90	90	0	280	180
28. Yurovichi	140	270	270	220	320	145	240	350	140	175	345	345	345	280	185	260	265	180	260	260	260	260	120	358	360	360	280	0	209
29. Zhuravka	240	160	160	90	265	220	40	382	145	145	290	290	290	185	120	145	162	215	180	180	180	180	240	288	290	290	230	209	0

Table 4.7   DISTANCE BETWEEN SITES WITH MAMMOTH-BONE DWELLINGS (IN KILOMETERS)

	1	4	5	7	9	15	16	21	23	24	27
1. Berdyzh	0	260	180	260	230	258	175	170	250	218	160
4. Dobranichevka	260	0	325	70	132	70	220	250	186	360	322
5. Eliseevichi	180	325	0	280	355	362	150	108	390	38	55
7. Gontsy	260	70	280	0	200	110	150	195	256	288	250
9. Kirillovskaya	230	132	355	200	0	100	220	285	70	413	325
15. Mezhirich	258	70	362	110	100	0	240	258	180	385	330
16. Mezin	175	220	150	150	220	240	0	45	260	178	105
21. Pushkari I	170	250	108	195	285	258	45	0	325	133	63
23. Radomyshl'	250	186	390	256	70	180	260	325	0	418	370
24. Suponevo	218	366	38	288	413	385	178	133	418	0	88
27. Yudinovo	166	322	55	250	325	330	105	63	370	88	0

region has undergone the most extensive archaeological investigation, and a large number of the known Upper Paleolithic sites are in that region. The Sozh, on the other hand, as well as the area between the Sozh and Pripyat', have been investigated far less extensively. Locational analyses presented here strongly suggest that one or more Upper Paleolithic sites with dwellings were located between the Berdyzh area and the Desna.

Difference of means tests conducted on nearest-neighbor distances of sites without dwellings in the northern and southern halves of the study area (same quadrants as used in the previous test) reveal additional differences. Sites without dwellings in the north have a mean distance of 22.33 km from each other; those in the south are far fewer in

Table 4.8   DISTANCE BETWEEN SITES WITHOUT MAMMOTH-BONE DWELLINGS (IN KILOMETERS)

	2	3	6	8	10	13[a]	14	17	18	19	20	22	25	26	28	29
2. Chulatovo I	0	0.25	300	180	90	175	52	7	127	27	27	27	162	162	270	160
3. Chulatovo II	0.25	0	300	180	90	175	52	7	127	27	27	27	162	162	270	160
6. Fastov	300	300	0	420	240	430	340	300	282	325	325	325	403	403	145	220
8. Khotylevo II	180	180	420	0	200	12	130	171	180	153	153	153	18	18	350	382
10. Klyusy	90	90	240	200	0	190	100	85	55	55	55	55	208	208	175	145
13. Kositsa[a]	175	175	430	12	190	0	145	170	170	150	150	150	30	30	345	290
14. Kurovo	57	57	340	130	100	145	0	45	100	25	25	25	115	115	280	185
17. Novgorod-Severskii	7	7	300	171	85	170	45	0	120	20	20	20	150	150	265	162
18. Novo-Bobovichi	127	127	282	180	55	170	100	120	0	120	120	120	180	180	180	215
19. Bugorok	27	27	325	153	55	150	25	20	120	0	0.20	0.20	135	135	260	180
20. Pogon	27	27	325	153	55	150	25	20	120	0.20	0	0.20	135	135	260	180
22. Pushkari II	27	27	325	153	55	150	25	20	120	0.20	0.20	0	135	135	260	180
25. Timonovka I	162	162	403	18	208	30	115	150	180	135	135	135	0	0.24	360	290
26. Timonovka II	162	162	403	18	208	30	115	150	180	135	135	135	0.24	0	360	290
28. Yurovichi	270	270	145	350	175	345	280	265	180	260	260	260	360	360	0	209
29. Zhuravka	160	160	220	382	145	290	185	162	215	180	180	180	290	290	209	0

[a]Estimates for Kositsa also include those for Korshevo I and II.

number ($n = 2$) and more distant from each other (mean distance = 145 km). The clustering of sites without dwellings in the northeastern quadrants of the study area has been discussed previously. It is reflected in these calculations as well as in the differences of both overall numbers and mean distances between the nearest-neighbor sites. I interpret the observed differences between the distribution of these sites in the north and south as primarily reflecting archaeological bias. The Desna and Sudost' regions are the best known, and it is therefore not surprising to find a large number of these "less visible" sites concentrated in the Desna area. I examine these differences in detail in Chapter 6.

Changes in Site Distribution through Time. Diachronic comparisons of macrogeographic variables indicate that some changes can be monitored in spatial arrangements. While sites possibly occupied early, like their later equivalents, are found in association with river valleys, they are at somewhat greater distances from the rivers themselves.

Differences can be observed in the location of site clusters as well. Early sites (Figure 4.16) are found primarily in the northern half of the study area. If we stretch the concept of clustering to include a discussion of just two sites, then the only observed clustering occurs in the northwestern quadrant (1), where both Berdyzh and Yurovichi are located. This pattern contrasts with that observed for all sites: Early sites are located in the north, whereas later sites are found in both the northern and southern parts of the study area.

Sites with mammoth-bone dwellings, Berdyzh and Radomyshl', are located in the west and show a straight vertical distribution, in contrast to later sites, which are diagonally spaced across the central Russian Plain. Nearest-neighbor distances (Table 4.9) indicate that early sites are found at much greater distances from each other. While the small sample precludes any firm conclusions, proximal associations and the distribution of these sites suggest tentatively both that a smaller population occupied the

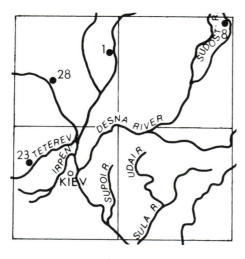

Figure 4.16   Early sites; quadrants block size 4. Sites: 1, Berdyzh; 8, Khotylevo II; 23, Radomyshl'; 28, Yurovichi.

Table 4.9   NEAREST-NEIGHBOR DISTANCE BETWEEN EARLY SITES (IN KILOMETERS)

	Berdyzh	Khotylevo II	Radomyshl'	Yurovichi
All				
Berdyzh	0	230	250	140
Khotylevo II	230	0	430	350
Radomyshl'	250	430	0	120
Yurovichichi	140	350	120	0
With dwellings				
Berdyzh			250	
Radomyshl'	250			
Without dwellings				
Khotylevo II				350
Yurovichi		350		

area prior to the glacial maximum and that this population was concentrated in the western part of the central Russian Plain.

CONCLUSIONS

This chapter discusses the dating and chronological ordering of the sites in the study area. It reiterates an important point: to date, no single dating technique, relative or chronometric, has yielded satisfactory chronologies. I advance a proposition that the central Russian Plain shows two periods of occupation during the Upper Paleolithic: an early phase dating between 26,000 and 20,000 years ago, and a late phase dating from 18,000 to 12,000 B.P. The area appears to have been either totally unoccupied or settled only very sparsely during the Valdai maximum itself, from 20,000 to 18,000 B.P.

The sites occupied during the early period are considerably fewer in number and appear to have been settled during a time of both milder and more gently oscillating climate. Only 4 sites are known from this early 6000-year period, giving a frequency of occupation of 1 site/1500 years. Sites occupied during the late period are far more numerous—25 are known from a period of 6000 years—giving a frequency of occupation of 1 site/240 years. These sites were occupied during a period replete with numerous climatic oscillations; sites occupied during the warm fluctuations appear to be as numerous as those occupied during the cold oscillations.

I also hypothesize that the distribution of the sites across the study area during the late period is different from that found during the early period. Late sites are linearily distributed across the central Russian Plain and cluster in the northeast and southwest parts of the region. The observed difference suggests that a change occurred in the pattern of utilization of the area—one that resulted in a change in the settlement systems themselves.

The patterning in distribution of Upper Paleolithic sites across the study area resulted from decisions conditioned by numerous logistic considerations: For all hunter–

gatherers, the foremost consideration is distribution of resources. Admittedly, settlement decisions are not exclusively conditioned by subsistence considerations. Social, ideological, and demographic factors play important roles as well (Heffley 1981; Jochim 1976; Yessner 1981). These factors, however, do not appear to be the prime ones conditioning settlement decisions. Rather, they act as modifiers which differentiate systems. The location of sites within a region is predominantly shaped by economic considerations—and these operate within a specific environment.

Climatic oscillations after the Valdai maximum effectively linearized the distribution of floral and faunal resources along river valleys. I suggest that such a linearization would have favored migratory behavior of mammoth and that these migrations occurred along the southwest–northeast trajectory. I conclude that the diagonal distribution of late sites and their clustering in the northeast and southwest correlates well with the proposed annual range of mammoth, and that the two phenomena may have been related. Such patterning is not discernable for the earlier period of occupation, where overall settlement preference was given to the northern half of the area. I consider the significance of these observations in Chapters 5 and 6.

Subsistence Practices and Duration of Occupation in the Late Valdai

Cultural systems articulate human actors with their environment, both natural and social, through their subsistence components. This chapter examines both the subsistence base and the organization of procurement during the Upper Paleolithic. By choosing to consider these man–land relationships first, I am in no sense affirming the primacy of techno-environmental variables in determining the nature of a cultural system. My approach mirror's Jochim's, who writes that "food procurement is simply one (albeit vital) aspect of human behavior. . . . If human behavior is to be viewed in systemic terms—then subsistence activities provide one point at which to enter the system for study" (1981:64).

I have selected the subsistence system as an entering point in spite of recent cogent criticism of the techno-environmental focus in archaeology (Bender 1978, 1981; Keene 1983; Moore 1983; Root 1983). This is because man–land relationships must first be outlined, however tentatively, before we can begin considering other pertinent variables. Simply put, while "what people do to make a living" and "how they do it" are affected by both natural and social phenomena, both are channeled by "what is available to make a living from."

The many approaches to reconstructing past subsistence practices found in the archaeological literature can be grouped into two categories: predictive and descriptive. The first, more sophisticated and rigorous, begins by modeling optimal subsistence behavior for a particular environmental setting and then tests these predictions against the data base (e.g., Jochim 1976; Keene 1981; Reidhead 1979, 1980; Winterhalder 1981a,b). Serious problems with these approaches, including the justification of certain behavioral assumptions, methodological difficulties in reconstructing past environments, and scalar problems, have all been discussed in the literature (Bettinger 1980; Jochim 1983a; Keene 1983; Yessner 1981). Such predictive modeling is first and foremost predicated on accurate environmental reconstruction, which, at present, is just not possible for the study area.

I have selected the second approach—descriptive modeling—and have investigated the subsistence economies using the excavated archaeological collections on hand. This approach is also beset with epistemological and methodological problems that have both been discussed in the literature and mentioned in previous chapters (for a discussion of the biases in faunal collections and their interpretations, see Behrensmeyer and Dechant-Boaz 1980; Binford 1981; Binford and Bertram 1977). I do so in spite of all the biases distorting the record because the record does, in this case at least, come closer to past behavioral realities than do modeling constructs erected on recent ethnographic analogies. Watanabe writes that

> man has his own view of environment: his activities react to and are limited by the nature of environment as seen by him. This implies that working of a given people in relation to their habitat should be understood not only in terms of ecology in the narrower sense but also in terms of the relationship between a people and their environment as perceived by the people themselves. (1978a:17)

Because of this, ethnographic analogies, no matter how close, cannot consider the "emic" component. Some will argue that neither can the archaeological record—or at least our present methods of working with the record. I suggest, however, that the record itself does contain this component, whether we recognize it as such or not, and should be our starting point. This is especially valid when dealing with past cultures for which no suitable ethnographic analogies exist.

In this chapter I offer a number of hypotheses to account for the observed synchronic and diachronic variability in the archaeological data. These hypotheses, where possible, are evaluated by a series of simple statistical procedures widely found in the literature, including measures of association (ϕ) (Thomas 1976), the Fisher exact test (Thomas 1976), the Pearson correlation coefficient and the comparison of correlation coefficients (Zar 1974), and the difference of means or student's t test (Blalock 1972). Since the sample sizes available for all calculations were small and came from finite populations, I apply Bessel's finite population corrections ($n/n - 1$) where appropriate (e.g., in the difference of means tests) (Moroney 1965:226). Unless otherwise indicated, probabilities are based on a two-tailed test and deemed significant at the .05 level. All probability estimates can be found in appropriate tables. In the discussion of the results of various tests, I list relevant test statistics in the text itself while the sample sizes (N), mean values ($\bar{X}$), and probability values are given in the appropriate tables. In cases where the test statistic is important but the probability estimate exceeds the .05 level, both the value and the probability associated with it are listed in the text. In cases where the statistical procedure employed is less common in the archaeological literature (e.g., the diversity index), I describe in detail the manipulations involved.

Finally, a cautionary note should be sounded about the use of statistical procedures, especially parametric statistics, on the data on hand. My sample sizes in all cases are exceedingly small, and in most cases a normal distribution cannot be assumed. Some may argue that the nature of my data does not warrant the use of any statistical evaluation other than the simplest nonparametric calculations on nominal scales. I have chosen more powerful procedures and argue that the repeated patterning observed is both relevant and important and does elucidate the patterning in the data themselves.

SUBSISTENCE AND FLORAL RESOURCES

Archaeological data relating to subsistence come in two forms: organic remains that testify to what was consumed or utilized, and tools used in the procurement and processing of these resources. Organic remains found at the Upper Paleolithic sites (Table 2.11) are composed exclusively of fauna, a fact that has led both Soviet and Western researchers to view late Valdai economies as based primarily on the procurement and consumption of meat. Ethnographic evidence on subsistence of hunter–gatherers, as well as the nature of recovery techniques used in excavating the sites in the study area, has led some researchers, especially Westerners, to wonder about the role of vegetal resources in subsistence (e.g., Klein 1973).

Ethnographically, as Lee (1968) and Watanabe (1968, 1969) have convincingly demonstrated, the role of vegetal resources in diet decreases latitudinally; all inhabitants of extreme northern latitudes meet their nutritional needs almost exclusively from animal products. Given the paleoenvironmental reconstruction of the late Pleistocene central Russian Plain offered in Chapter 3, I suggest that it is not the lack of appropriate recovery techniques that is responsible for the absence of floral remains in the archaeological record but rather the very minor role in subsistence played by floral resources. Both sifting and flotation were used in the excavation of some of the sites and have resulted in the recovery of microfauna and fish remains at Eliseevichi, Mezhirich, and Mezin. While it is true that use of such recovery techniques has been sporadic at best, I interpret the fact that when used, they did not recover floral remains, as support for my contention that vegetal resources were not a significant component in Upper Paleolithic diets. This is not to argue that mushrooms or berries or seeds were never eaten, but rather to state that, if eaten, these resources were opportunistically collected and played a role of "treats" rather than "basics" in diets.

Soviet researchers have long noted the presence of bone digging implements, variously interpreted as hoes and digging sticks, and have suggested that these were used to procure various roots and tubers (Pidoplichko 1976; Polikarpovich 1968; Shovkoplyas 1965a). But since these tools have been found at sites with storage pits (e.g., Eliseevichi, Mezhirich, Mezin), they could have just as easily been used to dig out pits as to procure roots and tubers.

Rogachev (1973) uses the presence of numerous grinding stones and slabs of sandstone, quartzite, and flint to argue for the procurement and processing of seeds and grains and for the importance of gathering and use of plant resources by Upper Paleolithic inhabitants of the Russian Plain. In his discussion, however, Rogachev does not consider the residue found on these grinding stones. Table 5.1 presents the data on grinding stones in the study area, as well as available evidence on what was ground by them. Semenov (1939), Shovkoplyas (1972), and Velichko, Grekhova, and Gubonina (1977) claim that slabs at Timonovka I and II and Dobranichevka held traces of ocher, and that Gontsy slabs seem to have been used for grinding bone. Since the residue found on some slabs indicated that these tools were associated with bone and ocher processing, I tested the association between slabs and worked bone and ocher. The

Table 5.1   CO-OCCURRENCE OF GRINDING STONES AND SLABS WITH OCHER, WORKED BONE, AND STORAGE PITS

	Grinding stones[a]			Presence at site	
Sites	N	Used on	Ocher	Worked bone	Storage pits
Berdyzh				+	+
Chulatovo I				+	
Chulatovo II	22	nd	+	+	
Dobranichevka	>1	ocher	+	+	+
Eliseevichi			+	+	+
Gontsy	some	bone	+	+	+
Khotylevo II			+	+	+
Kirillovskaya				+	
Kositsa	some	nd	+		
Mezhirich	~8	ocher	+	+	+
Mezin	~13	nd	+	+	+
Novgorod-Severskii				+	
Pogon			+		
Pushkari I	some	nd	+	+	+
Pushkari II	1	ocher	+		
Radomyshl'					+
Suponevo			+	+	+
Timonovka I	84	ocher	+	+	+
Timonovka II	some	ocher	+	+	+
Yudinovo			+	+	+
Yurovichi	some	nd	+	+	

[a]Grinding stones and slabs of sandstone, flint, and quartz.

resulting ϕ coefficients and probabilities (Table 5.2) show a positive association of worked bone and grinding stones ($\phi = .37$) and an even stronger association of ocher and grinding stones ($\phi = .66$). I interpret this to indicate that the stones were behaviorally associated with the production of bone implements and the processing of pigments. While they may also have been used for grain and seed processing, this still remains to be demonstrated.

The presence of grinding stones is also positively associated with the presence of storage pits ($\phi = .33, p = .06$). I argue at the conclusion of this chapter that sites with storage pits were occupied during cold-weather months. Accordingly, the stones would be used during cold-weather months—in seasons when plant resources would have been scarce, at best, or totally absent.

Finally, since I have argued for the existence of milder climatic conditions during the early period of occupation of the study area, and such conditions in turn imply the presence of a wider range of vegetal resources, we can anticipate that plant collecting played a greater role at sites occupied before the Valdai maximum. If, as Rogachev suggests, grinding stones were used in plant processing, we should observe a decrease

Table 5.2   MEASURES OF ASSOCIATION AND FISHER EXACT TESTS

	N	ϕ	p
1. Sites with storage pits and sites with dwellings	29	.60	.004
2. Grinding stones and worked bone	29	.37	.04
3. Grinding stones and ocher	29	.66	.0004
4. Grinding stones and storage pits	29	.33	.06
5. Sites with mammoth-bone dwellings and low diversity index	19	.41	.05
6. Sites with mammoth-bone dwellings and floodplain location	17	.65	.01
7. Sites with mammoth-bone dwellings and multiseasonal fauna	18	.64	.01
8. Sites with storage pits and multiseasonal fauna	21	.28	.17
9. All sites: number of cold- and warm-weather occupied sites in north vs. south	21	.18	.27
10. Late sites: number of cold- and warm-weather occupations in north vs. south	17	.20	.29
11. Early vs. late sites: number of cold- and warm-weather occupations	20	.13	.43
12. Northern sites occupied in warm- and cold-weather months: early vs. late	14	.17	.40

in their use through time. But data on hand on sites with grinding stones do not support Rogachev's hypothesis, indicating an increase rather than a decrease in the proportion of sites with grinding stones through time (Table 5.3).

I conclude then, that the data on hand, ethnographic and archaeological, do not permit us to consider vegetal resources as a major component of Upper Paleolithic diets in the study area.

Table 5.3   DISTRIBUTION OF GRINDING STONES

	Sites with grinding stones per total sites		
	Study area	North	South
All sites	15/29 (52%)	8/22 (36%)	3/7 (43%)
Early sites	1/4 (25%)	1/3 (33%)	0/1 (0%)
Late sites	9/25 (36%)	6/19 (32%)	3/6 (50%)

STORAGE STRATEGIES

Hunter–gatherers in the study area used storage throughout the Upper Paleolithic. Numerous storage pits have been discovered at sites occupied early (e.g., Berdyzh, Khotylevo II, Radomyshl') and late (Table 5.4). While pits found at 13 (45%) sites show a range in both size and volume, they can be broadly subdivided into two groups: (1) small pits, under 0.01 m³, and (2) large pits, over 0.5 m³. The difference in mean storage volume (Table 5.5) between these two groups of pits is significant ($z = 16.9$).

Table 5.4 STORAGE PITS AT THE SITES

| | Interior | | | | | | Exterior | | | | | | |
| | Large | | | Small | | | Large | | | Small | | | |
Sites	Number found	Mean volume (m³)	Σ Mean volume (m³)	Number found	Mean volume (m³)	Σ Mean volume (m³)	Number found	Mean volume (m³)	Σ Mean volume (m³)	Number found	Mean volume (m³)	Σ Mean volume (m³)	Σ Mean large pit volume (m³)
Berdyzh	1	0.2	0.2				3	0.9	2.7				2.9
Chulatovo II										few	0.005	0.01	
Dobranichevka	1?	nd	nd				12	2.5	30.0				30.0
Eliseevichi							>5	~2.0	~10.0				10.0
Gontsy				3	0.03	0.09	5.5[a]	1.5	~8.3				8.3
Khotylevo II							some	nd	nd				
Kirillovskaya	nd			nd									
Mezhirich							2	1.6	3.2				3.2
Mezin							7.5[a]	1.9	13.1	>4	nd	nd	13.1
Pushkari I				~50	0.007	0.04				3	~0.007	0.021	
Radomyshl'							1	3.14	3.14				3.14
Suponevo							1.5[a]	0.8	1.2				1.2
Timonovka I							2?	nd	nd				nd
Timonovka II							2	0.9	1.9	1	0.007	0.007	1.9
Yudinovo				~11	0.003	0.03	some?	nd	nd				

[a]Mean number found.

Table 5.5   DIFFERENCE OF MEANS TESTS ON STORAGE PIT VOLUMES

Difference of volume	N	$\overline{X}_1$	$\overline{X}_2$	z	p
Large pits vs. small pits	109	1.870	0.008	16.90	<.0001
Large pits: north vs. south	9	5.72	11.16	0.92	.36
Large pits: early vs. late	9	2.90	8.85	1.76	.08
Large pits, late: north vs. south	8	5.87	13.93	0.93	.06

Small pits have been recognized and reported at 4 (14%) sites and interpreted as roasting pits (Gontsy), possible postholes (Chulatovo II, Pushkari I, and Yudinovo), and small cache repositories for lithic and bone artifacts (possibly Eliseevichi and Mezin). Large pits, identified as storage pits, have been found at 10 sites in numbers ranging from 1 to 12 per site. Their presence is strongly associated with the presence of mammoth-bone dwellings: 9 (82%) of the sites with dwellings also have large storage pits (ϕ = .60).

Unfortunately, no systematic study has been done on the contents of the storage pits; the site reports just note the presence of large numbers of mammoth, horse, and reindeer bones and lesser amounts of carnivore remains in them. Soviet researchers have noted in passing some structural differences between the pits. Gladkih (1978, personal communication) states that two types of large pits exist at the sites: (1) the "hanging type," in which the individual bones are separated from each other and dispersed in loess and colluvium matrix, and (2) the "packed bone type," where no matrix or layers exist between the bones (see Figure 2.44 for an example). He interprets these differences to indicate that meat on the bone was stored in the first group and bone itself in the second. These observed differences may have resulted from different behavioral sequences in the use of the pits: sequential reuse of pits first for storing meat and then bone, for example. Gladkih's observations, however, do indicate that bone itself may have been the primary storable. Bone represented an important raw material used for both artifact production and fuel. Because of this, the storage of bone in pits dug into permafrost, where it would both retain its freshness and be inaccessible to predators, should not appear surprising. Ample documentation can be found in the literature, although not quantified, that some pits contained skeletal elements, such as antlers and tusks, that had no value as food but were important for tool manufacturing. The pits also held sizable amounts of flat bones such as pelvises and scapulae, which, while of low nutritional value, were useful as construction materials (Pidoplichko 1976; Shovkoplyas 1965a).

The discovery of filled storage pits at Upper Paleolithic sites on the central Russian Plain may seem unusual: Archaeologists working in northern latitudes today generally report finding empty storage pits (Arutyunov et al. 1982; McCartney 1979, 1980; R. White 1982, personal communication). This irregularity can, however, be explained by a number of scenarios from ethnographic and archaeological records. As Binford (1982, personal communication) reports, the exact location of cache pits is sometimes forgotten by present-day Nunamiut. This indeed may have been the case at Dobranichevka and

Mezin, where some of the "hanging-type" pits were covered by a layer of loess, and natural depressions created on the surface subsequently used as basins for small hearths. This hypothesis presupposes multiple reoccupation of some of the sites. In other cases, where no such diachronic evidence is present, a sequential use of pits mentioned earlier can also be suggested—first as meat caches and then as repositories for raw material. In these cases, sites may have been abandoned before all the bone supplies were used up. The evaluation of these two hypotheses must await further research.

The depth to which late Valdai storage pits were dug is interesting, as it never exceeds 1 m—a depth postulated (see Chapter 3) for the permafrost thaw layer in warm-weather months. The logistics of excavating pits in permafrost, as well as the documented depth of the pits, suggests that their dimensions were dictated by the thaw layer itself and implies that they were excavated in warm-weather months.

The use of storage facilities in the study area has a number of important implications for subsistence practices and settlement systems. The rationale behind storing behavior has been discussed in the literature and can be found in Colson (1979), Ingold (1983), Jochim (1976, 1981), O'Shea (1981), and Perlman (1980). In general, they focus on the techno-economic advantages that storage provides. Jochim terms storage a "short-term maintenance strategy" and states that

> if territoriality and conservation represent long-term maintenance strategies, resource storage, by contrast, is a relatively short-term anticipatory strategy. . . . Storage represents a security strategy aimed at providing sufficient resources for anticipated lean seasons. Storage may also represent a strategy efficiency, designed to take advantage of the short-term availability of particular resources. In either case, it implies significant environmental seasonality—strong seasonal contrasts in resource availability and sufficient seasonal regularity that lean seasons may be anticipated. As a result, northern- and temperate latitude groups of . . . farmers and hunter–gatherers should be more likely to practice food storage than tropical groups would be. (1981:176)

Perlman adds that

> populations are limited by the season of minimum yield, unless that season's yield can be counteracted. A group can utilize storage to achieve this objective by transferring the cost and benefits from one feeding period to another. (1982:532)

Elsewhere, Perlman notes that storage reduces return rate of the stored item and works to minimize subsistence activities during lean months by acquiring high-return resources when it is more productive, and he considers the practice of storage an independent variable.

For Testart,

> where some natural food resources are *bountiful* but *seasonal,* they can be gathered en masse while available and stored *on a large scale* once transformed through appropriate food preservation techniques, thus becoming the staple food year round. This possibility lies at the intersection of four conditions, two ecological (abundance and seasonality of resources) and two technical (efficient food-getting and food-storage techniques). The presence of these four conditions determines an economy in which storage provides the bulk of food during the season of scarcity. This economy has two main characteristics. . . . The first is a conspicuous seasonal variation in the intensity of food getting activities. . . . The second characteristic of the storing economy is its relative rigidity. . . . In storing economies planning plays a central role. (1982:524–525)

Underlying all of these conclusions is the assumption that storage is a beneficial subsistence strategy for hunter–gatherers in environments characterized by abundant but seasonally available resources. Two additional interesting qualifications have been offered to the above observations. Colson (1979), in discussing both short- and long-term fluctuations in resource availability in all environments, underscores the reality of recurrent periods of long-term scarcity and notes an *intensification* of such short-term coping mechanisms as storage during what she calls the "bad years." This suggests, then, that an increase in storage need not indicate increased abundance but may signal quite the reverse situation. Speth and Spielmann (1983), in reviewing nutritional requirements and regimens of northern-latitude groups, suggest that storage also may be designed to counteract seasonal imbalances and concomitant disturbances in human metabolism that come from ingestion of lean meat in late winter–early spring months. Storing is done in warm-weather months, when the animals in general are fatter.

We can summarize this discussion by saying that the techno-environmental rationale for storage favors the storage of seasonally abundant resources rich in calories, nutrients, and probably fats to offset the reduced availability of these resources during lean months. Such subsistence strategies are amply documented in both ethnographic and archaeological literature (Balikci 1970; McCartney 1979; Nelson 1971; Watanabe 1968, 1978b), confirming hypotheses about storing behavior discussed above. As I show in Chapter 3, natural conditions favoring storage economies were more than met by the late Pleistocene environment on the central Russian Plain—one that I characterize as having highly nucleated resources.

The emphasis on the individual as the unit of analysis of all ecologically based approaches to subsistence behavior is bound to lead to misinterpretation of the archaeological record. According to Keene,

> archaeologists have circumvented this problem to some extent by treating populations or societies as aggregates of individuals. . . . But clearly the problem is more complex than this, and we must consider whether a society isn't more than the sum of its parts. . . . The social demands on surplus production, reciprocity, and information sharing, for instance, are not entirely visible when the individual is the unit of analysis. Social reproduction necessitates more than the reproduction of the individuals. (1983:142)

The social component affecting subsistence practices and specifically storage behavior has received less attention in the literature. Work by Bender (1978, 1981), Ingold (1983), Moore (1983), and Weissner (1982) among others has increasingly drawn attention to this man–man component. Work by Bender, Weisner, Moore (1983), and Root (1983) indicates that it is the *social component* that crucially affects organizational strategies. For example, Bender, in discussing hunter–gatherer sedentism and related intensification of subsistence production, underlines the role played by establishment and maintenance of social alliances in making demands on production and promoting intensification of production. The form that these social alliances take is irrelevant for the moment (and is examined later). What is important is that we must consider this component when discussing any subsistence practices and especially changes in such practices.

Archaeological data (Tables 5.4 and 5.5) show a two-fold increase in mean storage volume at the sites through time ($z = 1.76$, $p = .08$). Such an increase indicates an intensification in subsistence practices, which, as I show later, is associated with an increase in subsistence risk due to climatic fluctuations and possibly with either an actual increase in human population or a linear realignment of groups inhabiting the central Russian Plain.

SUBSISTENCE AND FAUNAL RESOURCES

INTRODUCTION

In this chapter, as in preceding and subsequent discussions of faunal remains, I use MNB and MNI quantifications, which have been subjected to heavy and justified criticism in the literature (e.g., Casteel 1976; Grayson 1978, 1984). In Chapter 2 I discuss at length the reasons for reverting to these problem-laden values, and it is relevant to reiterate my main reasons for doing so. Most of the faunal data available for the majority of the sites in the study area exist only in archival form, where they are offered in traditional "laundry lists" which consist of MNI and MNB estimates per taxon. Since this is all there is and all there ever will be, two options are open to investigators interested in questions of late Pleistocene adaptations. One can either dismiss what is available as totally unreliable and thus change research concerns, or one can use what is available as a comparative heuristic devise. I have selected the latter.

As I note in Chapter 2, fauna present at the sites can be broadly divided into two categories: economically important taxa, and those of no economic significance that were deposited at the sites through the action of nonhuman agents. Soviet researchers have divided the economically important species into (1) those that constituted food resources, and (2) carnivores that played important nonfood roles in economies. The rationale behind this second division comes from the observed differential utilization of these taxa. As Pidoplichko (1969, 1976) and Vereschagin (1971, 1979, 1981) point out, while numerous remains of fur bearers are found at most of the sites, the bones belonging to these taxa *never* show any signs of food processing or food preparation. My own research on faunal materials, specifically focusing on the remains of fur bearing carnivores and lagomorphs, fully supports this division, and I evaluate the exploited taxa accordingly.

There are, however, a number of problems with such a subdivision based simply on a priori assumptions of the investigator and not on empirical evidence from the taxa themselves. These problems are less significant in separating species of economic importance from those of no importance. Likewise, there is little difficulty in designating those species that were not used as food. The residual group of food species, however, presents the crux of the problem. I have already mentioned the debate in Soviet literature on the exact role played by the mammoth in subsistence practices. Evidence exists that mammoth bone was used extensively for fuel, and the overwhelming majority of the hearths found at the sites contain burned bone and *burned bone only*. Similarly, dwellings found at the sites are made exclusively of mammoth bone. As noted before, bone was also an important raw material used in the manufacture of tools, jewelry, and *art mobiliere*.

The wide spectrum of use to which mammoth products were put—food, architecture, fuel, and raw material—did not all require utilization of freshly killed animals. If, for a moment, we omit the use of mammoth as food from consideration, we see that gathering of bone could have met the needs of the other activities. Specifically, the burning of bone for fuel only required relatively fresh or "green" bone with its collagen and fat content intact (see Buikstra and Swegle, 1982, on burning of bone in general). Given the climatic conditions reconstructed for the area at the time of occupation, we can anticipate that bone would have remained fresh for long periods of time, especially if gathered "green" and stored in pits in the permafrost. Bone also could have been collected from bone deposits accumulated in the permafrost as a result of natural agents. The freshness of bone from permafrost deposits was attested to by recent excavations at Berelekh as well as by numerous discoveries of frozen mammoth carcasses in Siberia, where not only the bone but the flesh was preserved fresh over thousands of years (Vereschagin 1979).

Bones for the construction of dwellings, likewise, could have been gathered. Although no taphonomic studies of differential weathering of bone used in construction have been undertaken, signs of differential weathering have been noted in the Soviet literature. These differences have generally been attributed to differential deposition rates (Pidoplichko 1976; Shovkoplyas 1965a; Vereschagin 1979, 1981). It is just as possible that differential weathering reflects the different times of death and different periods of exposure prior to use by man. Quite obviously, only future research can evaluate these conflicting hypotheses.

The collection of bone—whale bone in particular—for construction, from both discovered carcasses and extant structures, has been amply documented for the Thule culture in Alaska (McCartney 1980). This collecting behavior has led Alaskan researchers to question the extent to which active hunting contributed to the presence of whale bone in Thule assemblages and has forced a closer look at archaeological remains for corraborative evidence for active hunting (see discussion in McCartney 1979, 1980).

Finally, similar objections can be raised to the assumptions that bone used as raw material in manufacturing came from active hunting. Fresh bone, as has been shown in the literature, is more plastic and amenable to flaking (see Morlan 1980 with references). As I note above, however, bone under periglacial conditions would have remained fresh for longer periods and could have therefore been collected from carcasses. For some manufacturing tasks, for example those requiring the use of tusks, collection of ivory from carcasses was apparently required. As Semenov (1939) and Voevodskii (1952d) point out, removal of tusks from freshly killed mammoths could not have been accomplished without the breaking of the sustaining alveoli. Voevodskii (1952d) notes that the alveoli on mammoth crania at Pushkari I are intact, indicating that at least some of the 65 tusks there were collected after natural taphonomic processes had already disarticulated them. Filippov (1977) manufactured a number of bone and ivory implements experimentally and concludes that in many cases natural exfoliation patterns present in weathered tusks were utilized by Upper Paleolithic craftsmen who used the exfoliated layers as blanks. He concludes (Filippov 1979, personal communication) that some of the ivory objects were manufactured either from collected tusks or at least from tusks that had been left in the open to weather naturally.

Taphonomic research on post-depositional histories for different taxa conducted by Behrensmeyer and Dechant-Boaz (1980), Gifford (1980), and especially on elephant carcasses by Coe (1978) indicate that carcasses left on the surface and not subject to rapid burial will be disarticulated and scattered both horizontally and vertically in a short time. Evidence from Berelekh, on the other hand, points to the possibility of accumulation, more or less intact, of skeletal remains in particular microregions such as ravines and crevasses in river valleys under periglacial conditions (for a discussion on the natural processes leading to such accumulations, see Vereschagin 1979, 1981). Vereschagin's work strongly suggests that such bone accumulations, especially of mammoth bone, may have been present on the late Pleistocene landscape along river valleys, and that Upper Paleolithic hunter–gatherers found and utilized such accumulations. The procurement of mammoth tusks for ivory trade from just such deposits has been documented historically for Siberia (Vereschagin 1979, 1981). While, to date no late Pleistocene mammoth bone "cemeteries" have been found in the study area, this is not surprising, because the permafrost conditions favoring their preservation have not existed in the area since the onset of the Holocene, and possibly because they were regularly utilized during the Upper Paleolithic. Furthermore, such sites as Novo-Bobovichi, where the overwhelming number of faunal elements belong to mammoth (11 individuals) and cultural remains are represented by one burin, may indeed be remnants of just such past "cemeteries."

Similar difficulties arise if we interpret the presence of reindeer at the sites to indicate active hunting only. Pidoplichko (1969, 1976) notes that reindeer at many sites are represented by shed antlers which could have been collected. The collection of shed antlers is amply documented in the ethnographic and archaeological literature (Bouchud 1966, 1975; McCartney 1979; Spiess 1979 with references; White 1980; but also see Binford 1982a). Since, as pointed out in Chapter 2, we have no information on what skeletal elements were used in compiling the MNI estimates at the sites and we know that the antlers may have been collected, we must also question the role that active hunting played in the procurement of antlers.

Finally, animal teeth were extensively used as items of personal adornment during the Upper Paleolithic on the central Russian Plain. Teeth of various taxa, but especially of the wild boar, bear, steppe bison, horse, arctic fox, and wolf, were modified by circumferential grooving and piercing and used as pendants (see Pidoplichko 1976; Polikarpovich 1968; Shovkoplyas 1965a for illustrated examples). Since no indication exists in the literature on what skeletal elements of bear, steppe bison, and wild boar were used in tabulating the MNI values for them at the sites, and because of the high diagnostic value of teeth, it may well be that the presence of these species at the sites was established on identification of teeth alone. Such, indeed, is the case for wild boar at Dobranichevka, Gontsy, and Mezhirich (Kornietz 1979, personal communication). Here again, as with antlers and mammoth bone, collecting activities could have supplied the teeth without active hunting taking place.

The resolution of these problems necessarily lies in further archaeozoological and taphonomic research using the collections themselves. This avenue, however, is not possible for most of the materials excavated prior to the 1950s, as they are no longer in existence. Furthermore, as indicated in Chapter 3, remains of such large-size taxa as mammoth and woolly rhinoceros for logistical reasons are usually not curated. Lacking this avenue of research, I investigate procurement practices by considering the relationship between the MNB and MNI counts per taxon found at the sites. The assumptions I make are as follows: (1) Differential behavior used in obtaining different taxa are reflected in the MNB–MNI relationship; (2) Size-dependent differential preservation rates reported in the literature pattern equally through space and time; (3) Differential treatment accorded to high nutrition-yielding body parts is a size-dependent phenomenon (for a discussion of these assumptions see Binford 1981).

Since all faunal data present serious problems for interpretation of past behavior and since data from the central Russian Plain for many sites is "guesstimated" at best, I do not focus on the significance of any one particular test result, but instead argue that the overall consistent patterning observed in the behavior of the data is significant (see Guilday 1970 for a classic example). This point—*that it is the repeated patterning which is important*—should be especially kept in mind during the ensuing discussion of MNB–MNI correlation coefficients per taxon.

Because sites in the study area are known from excavations vastly differing in size, I first control for this difference by transforming raw MNB and MNI counts into density measures of MNB and MNI per square meter at each site (Tables 5.6 and 5.7). Eleven sites were eliminated from consideration because either they were totally redeposited (Chulatovo I, Kurovo, Novo-Bobovichi, Novgorod-Severskii, and Yurovichi) or no values existed for the MNB and MNI counts at the sites (Bugorok, Klyusy, Korshevo I and II, Kositsa, and Pogon).

Since possible chronological differences between the 16 sites used in these calculations are difficult to control (see Chapter 4 for discussion of chronology), I first consider all sites as if no significant chronological differences exist between them. After establishing a pattern for the study area, I control for chronology and monitor possible differences through time.

Finally, I treat the northern and southern halves of the study area separately and term them "regions" in all subsequent discussions. I separate the study area latitudinally because my locational analysis (see Chapter 4) suggests that some regional differences were present in settlement locations and thus implies a possible presence of more than one social group. Furthermore, Bibikova and Belan (1979) divide the area latitudinally into different faunal regions—mammoth complex in the north and mixed mammoth–reindeer–horse–bison in the south, suggesting that two distinct biotic communities existed on the central Russian Plain in the late Valdai. Tables 5.8 and 5.9 present summarized density-controlled MNI and MNB calculations per taxon for the two halves of the study area.

To investigate the procurement practices using faunal data, I performed two basic statistical calculations: (1) a calculation of the Pearson coefficient of correlation per taxon between the density-controlled MNB and MNI values both separately for the north

Table 5.6 DENSITY OF FAUNA PER m² AT UNDISTURBED SITES: FOOD TAXA

Sites	Birds MNB	Birds MNI	Fish MNB	Fish MNI	Mammoth MNB	Mammoth MNI	Horse MNB	Horse MNI	Rhinoceros MNB	Rhinoceros MNI	Boar MNB	Boar MNI	Summed cervids[a] MNB	Summed cervids[a] MNI	Reindeer MNB	Reindeer MNI
Berdyzh	—	—	—	—	nd	0.130	nd	0.003	nd	0.0028	—	—	—	—	—	0.0020
Chulatovo II	—	—	—	—	nd	0.010	nd	0.007	nd	0.0120	—	—	—	—	nd	0.0025
Dobranichevka	0.0005	0.0005	0.025	0.017	1.380	0.050	—	—	0.0010	0.0005	—	—	—	—	0.0150	0.0016
Eliseevichi	—	—	—	—	19.560	0.100	0.002	0.002	—	—	—	—	0.0016	0.0016	0.0030	0.0016
Fastov	—	—	—	—	1.160	0.050	0.290	0.020	—	—	—	—	—	—	—	—
Gontsy	0.240	0.058	—	—	4.880	0.010	—	—	—	—	0.005	0.012	—	—	1.2090	0.0171
Khotylevo II	—	—	—	—	1.230	nd	—	—	0.0040	0.0020	nd	nd	—	—	—	—
Kirillovskaya	—	—	—	—	0.060	0.010	—	—	0.0005	0.0003	—	—	—	—	—	—
Korshevo I	—	—	—	—	nd	nd	nd	nd	nd	nd	nd	nd	nd	nd	nd	nd
Korshevo II	—	—	—	—	nd	nd	nd	nd	nd	nd	nd	nd	nd	nd	nd	nd
Kositsa	—	—	—	—	nd	nd	nd	nd	nd	nd	nd	nd	nd	nd	nd	nd
Mezhirich	0.149	0.053	0.002	0.002	7.240	0.290	0.004	0.004	0.014	0.0025	0.004	0.002	—	—	0.0810	0.0197
Mezin	0.018	0.007	—	—	3.320	0.100	0.550	0.050	—	—	0.001	0.001	0.0008	0.0008	0.3700	0.0692
Bugorok	—	—	—	—	nd	nd	—	—	—	—	—	—	—	—	—	—
Pogon	—	—	—	—	nd	nd	—	—	—	—	—	—	—	—	—	—
Pushkari I	—	—	—	—	0.500	0.170	0.160	0.008	—	—	—	—	0.0025	0.0045	0.0020	0.0025
Pushkari II	—	—	—	—	20.170	0.290	0.020	0.020	0.2413	0.0344	—	—	—	—	0.1030	0.0172
Radomyshl'	—	—	—	—	1.900	0.080	0.010	0.002	—	—	—	—	—	—	0.0030	0.0017
Suponevo	—	—	0.010	0.005	1.440	0.040	0.270	0.005	0.0100	0.0050	—	—	—	—	0.0100	0.0050
Timonovka I	—	—	—	—	nd	0.080	—	—	—	—	—	—	—	—	nd	0.0025
Timonovka II	—	—	—	—	0.130	0.070	—	—	—	—	—	—	—	—	0.0610	0.0061
Yudinovo	—	—	—	—	0.490	0.110	—	—	0.0260	0.0140	—	—	0.0040	0.0040	0.0300	nd
Zhuravka	—	—	—	—	—	—	—	—	—	—	nd	0.003	nd	0.0030	—	—

Sites	All antlered taxa		Bison		Wild cattle		Musk-ox		Marmot		Beaver		Hare		All food taxa	
	MNB	MNI	MNB	MNI	MNB	MNI	MNB	MNI	MNB	MNI	MNB	MNI	MNB	MNI	MNB	MNI
Berdyzh	—	—	—	—	nd	0.0028	—	—	—	—	—	—	—	—	nd	0.0085
Chulatovo II	—	0.0200	nd	0.0040	—	—	—	—	nd	0.0250	—	—	nd	0.0010	nd	0.0570
Dobranichevka	0.0150	0.0025	0.001	0.0005	—	—	0.0010	0.0005	0.002	0.0002	—	—	0.0015	0.0010	0.0070	0.0035
Eliseevichi	0.0046	0.0032	—	—	—	—	—	—	—	—	—	—	0.0064	0.0032	0.0296	0.0200
Fastov	1.2090	—	—	—	—	—	—	—	—	—	—	—	—	—	0.2900	0.0020
Gontsy	—	0.0171	0.006	0.0024	—	—	—	—	0.045	0.0073	—	—	0.6268	0.0195	0.6828	0.0412
Khotylevo II	nd	nd	0.030	0.0020	—	—	—	—	—	—	—	—	0.0160	0.0020	0.2440	0.0600
Kirillovskaya	nd	nd	—	—	—	—	—	—	—	—	—	—	0.0001	0.0001	0.0006	0.0004
Korshevo I	nd	nd	nd	nd	nd	nd	nd	nd	nd	nd	nd	nd	nd	nd	nd	nd
Korshevo II	nd	nd	nd	nd	nd	nd	nd	nd	nd	nd	nd	nd	nd	nd	nd	nd
Kositsa	nd	nd	nd	nd	nd	nd	nd	nd	nd	nd	nd	nd	nd	nd	nd	nd
Mezhirich	0.0810	0.0197	0.033	0.0118	—	—	0.0980	0.0140	0.004	0.0033	—	—	5.1831	—	5.3757	0.2284
Mezin	0.3778	0.0700	0.016	0.0012	—	—	some	some	—	—	—	—	0.0308	0.0092	0.5016	0.0976
Bugorok	—	—	—	—	some	some	some	some	—	—	—	—	—	—	nd	nd
Pogon	—	—	—	—	—	—	—	—	—	—	—	—	—	—	nd	nd
Pushkari I	0.0045	0.0050	—	—	—	—	—	—	—	—	—	—	—	—	0.0045	0.0050
Pushkari II	0.1030	0.0172	—	—	—	—	—	—	—	—	—	—	0.0172	0.0172	0.3443	0.0510
Radomyshl'	0.0030	0.0017	0.002	0.0017	—	—	—	—	0.0020	0.0017	—	—	—	—	0.0140	0.0036
Suponevo	0.0100	0.0050	0.005	0.0050	—	—	—	—	—	—	—	—	0.0150	0.0050	0.0300	0.015
Timonovka I	nd	0.0025	—	—	—	—	—	—	—	—	—	—	nd	0.0008	nd	0.0025
Timonovka II	0.0610	0.0061	—	—	—	—	—	—	—	—	—	—	0.0307	0.0061	0.0610	0.0061
Yudinovo	0.0340	nd	0.052	0.0040	—	—	—	—	0.006	0.0020	0.006	0.002	0.0080	nd	0.0720	nd
Zhuravka	nd	0.0030	—	—	nd	0.0030	—	—	nd	0.054	—	—	—	—	nd	0.0600

[a]Summed Cervids include *Cervus elaphus*, *Cervus* sp., and *Megaloceros*.

Table 5.7 DENSITY OF FAUNA PER m² AT UNDISTURBED SITES: FUR BEARERS AND MICROFAUNA

Sites	Rare taxa[a]		Wolverine		Arctic fox		Wolf		Bear		All fur taxa		Fur taxa + hare		Microfauna	
	MNB	MNI	MNB	MNI	MNB	MNI	MNB	MNI	MNB	MNI	MNB	MNI	MNB	MNI	MNB	MNI
Berdyzh	—	—	—	—	nd	0.003	nd	0.0029	nd	0.0057	nd	0.0116	nd	0.0116	nd	0.010
Chulatovo II	nd	0.0230	—	—	nd	0.017	nd	—	nd	0.0010	nd	0.0230	nd	0.0430	nd	0.700
Dobranichevka	—	—	0.0035	0.0005	0.033	0.007	0.026	0.0015	0.0065	0.0005	0.069	0.0065	0.070	0.0075	0.019	0.004
Eliseevichi	0.0096	0.0032	0.0080	0.0016	24.760	0.456	1.677	0.0578	0.1540	0.0160	26.609	0.5346	26.615	0.5378	0.069	0.020
Fastov	—	—	—	—	—	—	—	—	—	—	—	—	—	—	—	—
Gontsy	0.0024	0.0024	0.0061	0.0024	0.080	0.015	0.054	0.0061	0.0061	0.0024	0.1490	0.0283	0.176	0.0478	0.037	0.015
Khotylevo II	—	—	0.3180	0.0120	0.380	0.004	0.552	0.012	0.0012	0.0020	1.2790	0.0300	1.295	0.0320	0.440	nd
Kirillovskaya	0.0004	0.0003	0.0001	0.0001	nd	—	0.001	0.0001	0.0005	0.0002	0.0020	0.0007	0.002	0.0008	—	—
Korshevo I	nd	nd	nd	nd	nd	nd	nd	nd	nd	nd	nd	nd	nd	nd	nd	nd
Korshevo II	nd	nd	nd	nd	nd	nd	nd	nd	nd	nd	nd	nd	nd	nd	nd	nd
Kositsa	nd	nd	nd	nd	nd	nd	nd	nd	nd	nd	nd	nd	nd	nd	nd	nd
Mezhirich	0.0059	0.0039	0.1200	0.0157	0.295	0.030	0.175	0.0236	0.0236	0.0059	0.6190	0.0791	5.802	0.2346	0.683	0.199
Mezin	—	—	0.0233	0.0042	1.540	0.094	0.837	0.0492	0.0292	0.0058	2.429	0.1532	2.460	0.1624	0.274	0.068
Bugorok	—	—	—	—	—	—	—	—	—	—	—	—	—	—	nd	nd
Pogon	—	—	—	—	—	—	—	—	—	—	—	—	—	—	nd	nd
Pushkari I	—	—	—	—	0.233	0.010	0.398	0.015	0.0025	0.0025	0.6330	0.0275	0.633	0.0279	0.030	0.008
Pushkari II	—	—	—	—	—	—	0.172	0.0689	0.0517	0.0172	0.2240	0.0861	0.241	0.1033	0.086	0.034
Radomyshl'	—	—	—	—	—	—	—	—	—	—	—	—	—	—	—	—
Suponevo	—	—	—	—	0.135	0.005	0.190	0.0100	0.0050	0.0050	0.3300	0.0200	0.345	0.0250	0.005	0.005
Timonovka I	—	—	—	—	nd	0.002	0.031	0.0008	nd	0.0017	nd	0.0046	nd	0.0054	nd	0.001
Timonovka II	—	—	0.0245	0.0061	0.479	0.037	0.064	0.0061	0.0061	0.0061	0.5410	0.0553	0.572	0.0614	0.006	0.006
Yudinovo	—	—	—	—	0.298	0.054	nd	0.0060	0.0260	0.0020	0.3880	0.0620	0.396	nd	0.088	nd
Zhuravka	—	—	—	—	nd	0.003	nd	0.0030	—	—	nd	0.0060	nd	0.006	—	—

[a]Rare taxa include cave lion, hyena, lynx, and mustelids.

Table 5.8   DENSITY OF ECONOMICALLY IMPORTANT TAXA: MNI PER m²

	Study area		Northern sites					Southern sites				
	No. sites	Σ MNI/m²	No. sites	% of sites	Σ MNI/m²	% of MNI	$\overline{X}$ of MNI	No. sites	% of sites	Σ MNI/m²	% of MNI	$\overline{X}$ of MNI
Birds	20	0.119	2	15.0	0.065	55.0	0.032	2	29.0	0.054	45.0	0.027
Fish	20	0.024	2	15.0	0.022	92.0	0.011	1	14.0	0.002	8.0	0.002
Other fur bearers[a]	21	0.012	2	14.0	0.005	42.0	0.003	3	43.0	0.007	58.0	0.002
Wolverine	20	0.043	4	31.0	0.024	56.0	0.006	4	57.0	0.019	44.0	0.005
Arctic fox	20	0.734	10	77.0	0.682	93.0	0.068	4	57.0	0.052	7.0	0.013
Wolf	20	0.266	11	85.0	0.232	87.0	0.021	5	71.0	0.034	13.0	0.007
Bear	20	0.074	10	77.0	0.060	81.0	0.006	4	57.0	0.014	19.0	0.003
Mammoth	17	1.590	10	100.0	1.100	69.0	0.110	6	86.0	0.491	31.0	0.080
Horse	21	0.121	7	50.0	0.095	78.0	0.010	3	43.0	0.026	22.0	0.009
Rhinoceros	20	0.071	7	54.0	0.070	99.0	0.010	2	29.0	0.0008	1.0	0.0004
Boar	20	0.018	1	8.0	0.001	6.0	0.001	3	43.0	0.017	94.0	0.006
Red deer	20	0.007	2	15.0	0.004	57.0	0.002	1	14.0	0.003	43.0	0.003
Deer sp.	20	0.002	1	8.0	0.002	100.0	0.002	—	—	—	—	—
Giant deer	20	0.003	2	15.0	0.003	100.0	0.001	—	—	—	—	—
Antlered taxa without reindeer	20	0.012	4	31.0	0.009	75.0	0.002	1	14.0	0.003	25.0	0.003
Reindeer	19	0.164	8	67.0	0.124	75.0	0.015	4	57.0	0.040	25.0	0.009
Antlered taxa with reindeer	19	0.173	8	67.0	0.129	75.0	0.023	5	71.0	0.044	25.0	0.009
Bison	20	0.031	5	38.0	0.015	48.0	0.004	4	57.0	0.016	52.0	0.004
Wild cattle	20	0.006	1	8.0	0.003	50.0	0.003	1	14.0	0.003	50.0	0.003
Musk-ox	21	0.015	1	8.0	0.014	97.0	0.014	1	14.0	0.005	3.0	0.005
Marmot	20	0.094	3	23.0	0.030	32.0	0.010	4	57.0	0.064	68.0	0.016
Beaver	20	0.002	1	8.0	0.002	100.0	0.002	—	—	—	—	—
Hare	19	0.240	8	67.0	0.064	27.0	0.008	4	57.0	0.176	73.0	0.044
All food taxa	19	0.680	10	83.0	0.323	47.5	0.032	7	100.0	0.357	52.5	0.051

[a]Includes cave lion, hyena, lynx, and mustelids.

and south and jointly for the study area, and (2) a comparison of the difference of means in both density-controlled MNI and MNB values per taxon in the two regions. The first procedure, a calculation of linear regression for the relationship of MNB to MNI, has received a good deal of attention in archaeozoological literature (e.g., Grayson 1984 with references). As both Grayson (1984) and Hesse (1982) have demonstrated, there is a positive linear or curvilinear (depending on sample size) relationship between the number of bones found and identified at a site and the number of individuals estimated. In this work I argue that, while we can anticipate a positive relationship between these two values, it is the deviation from this expected relationship observed for various taxa that is both interesting and a significant elucidator of past cultural practices. The resulting coefficients are listed in Table 5.10 and linear regressions per taxon are illustrated in figures throughout this chapter. Specific sites in these figures are number-coded as per Figure 2.1 and all tables in this work.

Table 5.9   DENSITY OF ECONOMICALLY IMPORTANT TAXA: MNB PER m²

	Study area		Northern sites					Southern sites				
	No. sites	Σ MNB/m²	No. sites	% of sites	Σ MNB/m²	% of MNB	$\bar{X}$ of MNB	No. sites	% of sites	Σ MNB/m²	% of MNB	$\bar{X}$ of MNB
Birds	20	0.401	2	15.0	0.251	63.0	0.126	2	29.0	0.150	37.0	0.075
Fish	20	0.037	2	15.0	0.035	95.0	0.018	1	14.0	0.002	5.0	0.002
Other fur bearers[a]	20	0.018	1	8.0	0.009	52.0	0.009	3	43.0	0.009	48.0	0.003
Wolverine	20	0.504	4	31.0	0.374	74.0	0.093	4	57.0	0.130	26.0	0.032
Arctic fox	16	28.238	7	70.0	27.830	99.0	3.970	3	50.0	0.408	1.0	0.136
Wolf	16	4.177	8	80.0	3.921	94.0	0.490	3	50.0	0.256	6.0	0.064
Bear	17	0.313	8	80.0	0.276	88.0	0.034	4	57.0	0.037	12.0	0.009
Mammoth	15	63.460	8	100.0	46.840	74.0	5.860	6	86.0	16.620	26.0	2.770
Horse	18	1.306	5	45.0	1.002	77.0	0.200	3	43.0	0.304	23.0	0.101
Rhinoceros	18	0.302	5	45.0	0.300	99.0	0.059	2	29.0	0.0015	1.0	0.0008
Boar	19	0.010	1	8.0	0.001	10.0	0.001	2	33.0	0.009	90.0	0.004
Red deer	19	nd	2	15.0	0.005	nd	0.003	1	17.0	nd	nd	nd
Deer sp.	20	0.002	1	8.0	0.002	100.0	0.002	—	—	—	—	—
Giant deer	19	0.003	2	16.0	0.003	100.0	0.001	—	—	—	—	—
Antlered taxa without reindeer	20	nd	4	31.0	0.009	nd	0.002	1	14.0	nd	nd	nd
Reindeer	21	1.786	7	50.0	0.479	27.0	0.068	4	57.0	1.308	73.0	0.327
Antlered taxa with reindeer	18	1.903	7	64.0	0.595	31.0	0.085	5	71.0	1.308	68.0	0.327
Bison	19	0.145	4	33.0	0.103	69.0	0.026	4	57.0	0.042	31.0	0.011
Wild cattle	19	nd	2	15.0	nd	nd	nd	1	17.0	nd	nd	nd
Musk-ox	21	0.099	2	14.0	0.098	99.0	0.098	1	14.0	0.001	1.0	0.001
Marmot	19	0.059	2	15.0	0.010	17.0	0.005	3	50.0	0.049	83.0	0.016
Beaver	19	0.006	1	8.0	0.006	100.0	0.006	—	—	—	—	—
Hare	18	5.935	7	64.0	0.124	2.0	0.018	3	50.0	5.811	98.0	1.937
All food taxa	16	7.654	8	80.0	1.283	17.0	0.160	6	100.0	6.371	83.0	1.062

[a]Includes cave lion, hyena, lynx, and mustelids.

As Table 5.10 and the figures illustrate, the coefficients for some taxa differ significantly when calculated separately for the north and the south. For example, mammoth shows values of $r = .75$ in the south and $r = .57$ ($p > .1$) in the north. Steppe bison show an even greater difference, $r = -.40$ in the north and $r = .99$ in the south. The significance of such differences is then evaluated by comparing the correlation coefficients and using a one-tailed test with critical values of $Z = 1.64$ and $p > .1$. The results are presented in Table 5.11. Results of the difference of means tests are listed in Tables 5.12 and 5.13.

Since the correlation coefficients are calculated on MNB and MNI values, and these values can reflect such cultural practices as the "schlepp effect" pointed out by Perkins and Daly (1968) and Binford (1981, 1983), I first investigate the overall relationship between the correlation coefficients and the size of the taxa. This relationship is illustrated in Figure 5.1, where live weights per taxon are plotted against the correlation

Table 5.10   PEARSON COEFFICIENTS OF CORRELATION BETWEEN DENSITY-CONTROLLED MNB AND MNI VALUES

	N	df	r	r²	p
Without Chronological Considerations					
Fish, all sites	3	1	.9877	.98	.10
Birds, all sites	4	2	.9655	.93	.05
Summed other fur bearers[a]					
all sites	4	2	.7804	.37	>.10
southern sites	3	1	.9684	.94	>.10
Wolverine					
all sites	8	6	.7497	.56	.05
northern sites	4	2	.9271	.86	.05 < p < .10
southern sites	4	2	.9951	.99	.01
Arctic fox					
all sites	10	8	.9870	.97	.001
all northern sites	7	5	.9874	.97	<.001
northern high-density sites (5,16,26,27)	4	2	.9967	.99	.010
northern low-density sites (8,21,24)	3	1	−.2680	.07	>.10
all southern sites	3	1	.9648	.93	>.10
Wolf					
all sites	12	10	.6307	.40	.05
all northern sites	8	6	.5465	.30	>.10
northern high-density sites (5,8,16,21)	4	2	.8805	.78	>.10
northern low-density sites (1,3,24,25,26,27)	4	2	.5404	.29	>.10
all southern sites	4	2	.9966	.99	.01
southern low-density sites (4,7,9)	3	1	.9648	.93	>.10
Bear					
all sites	12	10	.7888	.62	.01
all northern sites	8	6	.7709	.59	.05
northern high-density sites (5,16,22,27)	4	2	.6629	.44	>.10
northern low-density sites (8,21,24,26)	4	2	.9907	.99	.01
all southern sites	4	2	.9495	.90	~.05
southern low-density sites (4,7,9)	3	1	.5564	.31	>.10
All fur bearers excluding hares					
all sites	12	10	.9726	.95	<.0001
all northern sites	8	6	.9787	.96	<.0001
all southern sites	4	2	.9898	.98	.02
Mammoth					
all sites	13	11	.5400	.29	.10
all northern sites	7	5	.5700	.32	>.10
all southern sites	6	4	.7500	.56	.07
Horse					
all sites	8	6	.8079	.65	.02
all northern sites	5	3	.7660	.58	>.10
all southern sites	3	1	.9928	.99	.10
Woolly Rhinoceros					
all sites	7	5	.9558	.91	<.001
all northern sites	5	3	.9518	.91	.02
Boar, all sites	3	1	.7502	.56	>.10

(continued)

Table 5.10   (*Continued*)

	N	df	r	r²	p
Summed other cervids, all sites[b]	4	2	1.0000	1.00	<.001
Reindeer					
all sites	10	8	.3391	.11	>.10
all northern sites	6	4	.9933	.99	<.001
all southern sites	4	2	.5318	.28	>.10
All cervids including reindeer					
all sites	10	8	.3359	.11	>.10
all northern sites	6	4	.9915	.98	<.001
all southern sites	4	2	.5318	.28	>.10
Steppe bison					
all sites	8	6	.4310	.19	>.10
all northern sites	4	2	−.4020	.16	>.10
all southern sites	4	2	.9975	.99	.10
Steppe marmot					
all sites	5	3	.9385	.88	.02
all southern sites	3	1	.9862	.97	>.10
Hare					
all sites	10	8	.9946	.99	<.0001
all northern sites	6	4	.2545	.06	>.10
northern high-density sites (3,16,22,26)	4	2	−.9609	.92	>.10
northern low-density sites (5,8,24,25)	4	2	.0200	.0004	>.10
all southern sites	4	2	.9999	.99	<.0001
southern low-density sites (4,7,9)	3	1	.9992	.99	.05
All fur bearers including hare					
all sites	11	9	.9576	.92	<.0001
all northern sites	7	5	.9732	.95	<.0001
all southern sites	4	2	.9863	.97	.02
Arctic fox and marmot					
all sites on MNI/m²	6	4	−.4655	.22	>.10
all sites on MNB/m²	4	2	−.3691	.14	>.10
all northern sites on MNI/m²	3	1	−.8274	.68	>.10
all southern sites on MNI/m²	3	1	−.4633	.21	>.10
Summed large food taxa, northern and southern ones calculated separately, all sites	13	11	.9403	.88	<.0001
Summed large food taxa without consideration of regional differences, all sites	13	11	.6387	.41	.02
Summed all food taxa, northern and southern calculated separately					
all sites	13	11	.9317	.87	<.0001
all northern sites	7	5	.9600	.92	<.0001
all southern sites	6	4	.9988	.99	<.0001
Summed microfauna					
all sites	9	7	.9962	.99	<.001
all northern sites	6	4	.9834	.97	<.001
all southern sites	3	1	.9996	.99	.02
Size of taxon and coefficient of correlation	20	18	−.2779	.08	>.10

Table 5.10   (Continued)

	N	df	r	r²	p
Late Sites, After 18,000 B.P.					
Birds, all sites	3	1	.9991	.99	.05
Wolverine, northern sites	3	1	.9329	.87	>.10
Arctic fox					
all sites	9	7	.9885	.98	<.0001
northern sites	6	4	.9896	.98	<.0001
Wolf					
all sites	11	9	.6576	.43	.05
northern sites	7	5	.5769	.33	>.10
northern high-density sites (5,16,21)	3	1	.8720	.76	>.10
northern low-density sites (3,24,25,26,27)	5	3	.5404	.30	>.10
Bear					
northern sites	7	5	.8406	.71	.02
northern low density sites (21,24,26)	3	1	1.0000	1.00	<.0001
Summed all fur bearers					
northern sites	6	4	.9772	.95	<.0001
southern sites	4	2	.9898	.98	.02
Mammoth, southern sites	5	3	.7535	.57	>.10
Horse, all sites	7	5	.7886	.62	.05
Woolly rhinoceros, northern sites	4	2	.9569	.92	.05
Reindeer, southern sites	3	1	.4188	.18	>.10
Steppe bison					
all sites	6	4	.4669	.22	>.10
northern sites	3	1	−.8072	.65	>.10
southern sites	3	1	.9999	.99	.01
Steppe marmot, all sites	4	2	.9336	.87	~.06
Hare					
all sites	9	7	.9948	.99	<.0001
northern sites	5	3	.2017	.04	>.10
Summed all food taxa					
all sites	11	9	.9435	.99	<.0001
all northern sites	5	3	.9774	.95	.01
all southern sites	5	3	.9988	.99	.0001

[a]Summed other fur taxa include cave lion, hyena, and mustelids.
[b]Summed other cervids include red deer, deer sp., and giant deer.

coefficients for the taxa taken for the entire region. The live weights are taken from Tables 3.19 and 5.17. As Figure 5.1 clearly shows, the size of the taxon does not pattern with the correlation coefficient ($r = -.28$, $p = .10$).

To establish some parameters for evaluating coefficients, as well as to generate some expected values, I calculate coefficients for the summed and density-controlled remains of microfauna. These taxa, as noted, accumulated at the sites without human action. The figures and plots for microfauna (Table 5.11, Figure 5.2) show very high positive values (north, $r = .98$; south, $r = .99$; entire region, $r = .99$). Coefficients for reindeer (Figure 5.7), on the other hand, where gathering of antlers may have been responsible

Table 5.11 COMPARISON OF PEARSON COEFFICIENTS OF CORRELATION BETWEEN DENSITY-CONTROLLED MNB AND MNI VALUES

	N_1	N_2	z_1	z_2	Z	p
Without Chronological Considerations						
Summed other fur bearers,[a] all sites vs. southern						
sites	4	3	1.045	2.092	1.05	.23
Wolverine						
northern vs. southern sites	4	4	1.658	2.647	0.70	.31
northern sites excluding Khotylevo II vs. southern						
sites	3	4	1.658	2.647	0.99	.24
Arctic fox						
northern vs. southern sites	7	3	2.647	1.946	2.80	.008
northern high vs. low-density sites	4	3	2.647	−0.277	2.92	.005
high-density northern vs. southern sites	4	3	2.647	1.946	2.80	.008
low-density northern vs. southern sites	3	3	−0.277	1.946	1.58	.11
Wolf						
northern vs. southern sites	8	4	0.618	2.647	1.84	.07
northern high- vs. low-density sites	4	4	1.376	0.604	0.55	.34
low-density northern vs. southern sites	4	3	0.604	1.946	0.95	.21
Bear						
northern vs. southern sites	8	4	1.020	1.832	0.74	.30
northern low- vs. high-density sites	4	4	2.647	0.739	1.35	.16
northern low-density vs. southern sites	4	4	2.647	1.832	0.58	.34
northern high-density vs. southern sites	4	4	2.647	0.739	0.78	.29
low-density northern vs. southern sites	4	3	2.647	0.633	2.01	.05
northern high-density vs. southern low-density						
sites	4	3	0.793	0.633	0.16	.39
Mammoth, northern vs. southern sites	7	6	0.973	0.648	0.43	.36
Horse, northern vs. southern sites	5	3	1.02	2.647	2.29	.029
Reindeer, northern vs. southern sites	6	4	2.647	0.590	1.78	.08
All cervids, northern vs. southern sites	6	4	2.647	0.590	1.78	.08
Reindeer vs. other cervids at northern sites[b]	4	4	2.647	3.800	0.82	.29
Steppe bison, northern vs. southern sites	4	4	−0.424	2.647	2.18	.04
Steppe marmot, all vs. southern sites	5	3	1.738	2.647	1.28	.18
Hare, northern vs. southern sites	6	4	0.255	2.647	2.08	.05
Summed fur bearers						
including hare, northern vs. southern sites	7	4	2.092	2.647	0.48	.35
without vs. with hares, all sites	12	11	2.092	1.946	0.30	.38
without vs. with hares, northern sites	8	7	2.298	2.092	0.31	.38
without vs. with hares, southern sites	4	4	2.647	2.647	0.00	.00
Microfauna						
northern vs. southern sites	6	3	2.298	2.647	1.06	.23
vs. mammoth, all sites	9	13	2.647	0.604	3.93	<.0001
vs. mammoth, northern sites	6	7	2.298	0.648	2.17	.04
vs. mammoth, southern sites	3	6	2.647	0.973	2.89	.006
Summed food taxa, northern vs. southern sites	8	6	1.946	2.647	0.96	.25
Summed food taxa vs. mammoths						
all sites	13	13	1.658	0.604	2.34	.03
northern sites	8	7	1.946	0.648	1.94	.06
southern sites	6	6	2.647	0.973	2.07	.05

Table 5.11   (*Continued*)

	N_1	N_2	z_1	z_2	Z	p
Summed food taxa vs. microfauna						
northern sites	8	6	1.946	2.298	0.48	.35
southern sites	6	3	2.647	2.647	0.00	.00
With Chronological Considerations						
Bear, northern all vs. late sites	8	7	1.020	1.221	0.30	.38
Reindeer, southern all vs. late sites	4	3	0.590	0.448	0.14	.39
Steppe bison, northern all vs. late sites	4	3	−0.424	−1.127	0.70	.31
Hare, northern all vs. late sites	6	5	0.255	0.203	0.06	.39

[a]Other fur bearers include cave lion, hyena, and mustelids.
[b]Other cervids include red deer, deer sp., and giant deer.

for the presence of the bone at the sites, are considerably lower (entire area, $r = .33$). Similarily low coefficients ($r = .34$) are found for the summed values of all other antler-bearing taxa (giant elk, red deer, deer sp.; see Figure 5.8). In fact, the correlation coefficients for all taxa where collection may have played a role in procurement are appreciably lower than for those where such evidence of collection is lacking (mammoths, $r = .54$; steppe bison, $r = .46$; wild boar, $r = .75$). I interpret these differences to indicate that a selective presence of particular skeletal elements yields a lower correlation coefficient, whereas a nonselective presence of skeletal elements yields a higher r value. Such selectional introduction of particular elements can be anticipated from gathering.

As Table 5.10 and the linear regression figures show, regional differences in r values also emerge for some taxa, suggesting different procurement strategies in the north and south.

Before proceeding to my conclusions about the procurement practices employed, I must interject a few serious cautionary notes about the limits on inferences that can be drawn from any statistical manipulation of faunal data. First, both high and low positive correlation coefficients can reflect a number of different cultural practices. For example, let us consider possible behavioral variants associated with the exploitation of fur bearers. A spatial separation of the initial processing activities from the ultimate desposition of the processed products, that is, furs or hides, would produce very different coefficients for the two groups of sites. Sites where fur bearers were trapped and skinned would yield an abundance of skeletal elements such as long bones, the diagnostic value of which is lower than of the elements that may have been left on the furs (such as crania and phalanges). In this case we can anticipate higher MNB, lower MNI, and a lower correlation coefficient. At sites where the furs were deposited, on the other hand, assuming that the heads and feet were left attached to the furs, we would get a greater similarity in the MNB and MNI and a higher correlation coefficient. It is expected, however, that such possible intersite differences will be minimized when the study area is either considered as a whole or divided into two latitudinal components only.

Table 5.12 DIFFERENCE OF MEANS TESTS ON DENSITY-CONTROLLED MNI AND MNB VALUES, WITHOUT CHRONOLOGICAL CONSIDERATIONS

	N	$\overline{X}_1$	$\overline{X}_2$	z	p
1. Fish					
northern vs. southern sites, MNI	3	0.011	0.002	1.61	0.10
northern vs. southern sites, MNB	3	0.018	0.002	2.28	0.03
2. Birds					
northern vs. southern sites, MNI	4	0.032	0.027	0.55	0.34
northern vs. southern sites, MNB	4	0.126	0.075	0.36	0.37
3. Summed other fur bearers					
northern vs. southern sites, MNI[a]	5	0.003	0.002	0.36	.37
northern vs. southern sites, MNB	4	0.009	0.003	4.78	<.0001
4. Wolverine					
northern vs. southern sites, MNI	8	0.006	0.005	0.26	.39
northern vs. southern sites, MNB	8	0.093	0.032	0.81	.29
southern high- vs. low-density sites, MNI	4	0.016	0.001	24.50	<.0001
southern high- vs. low-density sites, MNB	4	0.120	0.003	83.57	<.0001
northern high- vs. low-density sites, MNI	4	0.012	0.004	8.00	<.0001
northern high- vs. low-density sites, MNB	4	0.318	0.019	56.36	<.0001
northern high- vs. low-density sites excluding Khotylevo II, MNI	3	0.005	0.002	3.77	<.0003
northern high- vs. low-density sites excluding Khotylevo II, MNB	3	0.024	0.008	31.80	<.0001
high-density northern vs. southern sites, MNI	4	0.005	0.016	10.70	<.0001
high-density northern vs. southern sites, MNB	4	0.239	0.120	238.00	<.0001
low-density northern vs. southern sites, MNI	4	0.002	0.001	1.00	.24
low-density northern vs. southern sites, MNB	4	0.009	0.003	3.57	.0006
northern high-density vs. southern low-density sites, MNI	5	0.005	0.001	3.63	<.0006
northern high-density vs. southern low density-sites, MNB	5	0.024	0.003	21.00	<.0001
5. Arctic fox					
northern vs. southern sites, MNI	14	0.068	0.013	0.17	.39
northern vs. southern sites, MNB	10	3.975	0.136	1.10	.22
northern high- vs. low-density sites, MNI	10	0.160	0.007	1.63	.10
northern high- vs. low-density sites, MNB	7	6.770	0.249	1.08	.22
southern high- vs. low-density sites, MNI	4	0.030	0.007	6.97	<.0001
southern high- vs. low-density sites, MNB	3	0.295	0.057	10.82	<.0001
high-density northern vs. southern sites, MNI	5	0.160	0.030	1.38	.15
high-density northern vs. southern sites, MNB	5	6.770	0.295	1.08	.22
low-density northern vs. southern sites, MNI	9	0.007	0.007	0.00	1.00
low-density northern vs. southern sites, MNB	4	0.184	0.057	2.39	.02
low-density northern vs. high-density southern sites, MNI	7	0.007	0.030	11.50	<.0001
low-density northern vs. high-density southern sites, MNB	3	0.184	0.295	2.36	.02
6. Wolf					
northern vs. southern sites, MNI	16	0.021	0.007	2.00	.05
northern vs. southern sites, MNB	11	0.490	0.001	2.14	.04
northern high- vs. low-density sites, MNI	11	0.040	0.009	7.04	<.0001

Table 5.12   (*Continued*)

	N	$\overline{X}_1$	$\overline{X}_2$	z	p
northern high- vs. low-density sites, MNB	8	0.727	0.095	2.38	.02
southern high- vs. low-density sites, MNI	5	0.024	0.003	19.00	<.0001
southern high- vs. low-density sites, MNB	4	0.175	0.027	10.46	<.0001
high-density northern vs. southern sites, MNI	6	0.040	0.024	4.68	<.0001
high-density northern vs. southern sites, MNB	6	0.727	0.175	2.12	.04
low-density northern vs. southern sites, MNI	10	0.009	0.003	1.91	.006
low-density northern vs. southern sites, MNB	6	0.095	0.027	1.36	.16
low-density northern vs. high-density southern sites, MNI	7	0.009	0.024	4.56	<.0001
low-density northern vs. high-density southern sites, MNB	4	0.095	0.027	1.45	.14
7. Bear					
northern vs. southern sites, MNI	14	0.060	0.003	1.50	.13
northern vs. southern sites, MNB	12	0.034	0.009	1.41	.15
northern high- vs. low-density sites, MNI	11	0.010	0.003	1.94	.06
northern high- vs. low-density sites, MNB	8	0.065	0.004	2.04	.05
southern high- vs. low-density sites, MNI	4	0.006	0.001	6.83	<.0001
southern high- vs. low-density sites, MNB	4	0.024	0.004	19.60	<.0001
high-density northern vs. southern sites, MNI	5	0.010	0.006	1.42	.14
high-density northern vs. southern sites, MNB	5	0.065	0.024	1.38	.15
low-density northern vs. southern sites, MNI	10	0.003	0.001	2.0	.05
low-density northern vs. southern sites, MNB	7	0.003	0.004	0.21	.39
8. Mammoth					
northern vs. southern sites, MNI	16	0.110	0.080	0.60	.33
northern vs. southern sites, MNB	14	5.860	2.770	0.95	.25
9. Horse					
northern vs. southern sites, MNI	10	0.010	0.009	0.12	.40
northern vs. southern sites, MNB	8	0.200	0.100	0.73	.31
10. Woolly rhinoceros					
northern vs. southern sites, MNI	9	0.010	0.0004	2.63	.01
northern vs. southern sites, MNB	7	0.060	0.001	1.28	.17
11. Boar					
northern vs. southern sites, MNI	4	0.001	0.006	1.55	.12
northern vs. southern sites, MNB	3	0.001	0.004	8.25	<.0001
12. Red deer					
northern vs. southern sites, MNI	3	0.002	0.003	2.36	.02
northern vs. southern sites, MNB	2	—	—	—	—
13. Summed all cervids without reindeer, northern vs. southern sites, MNI	5	0.002	0.003	1.37	.16
14. Reindeer					
northern vs. southern sites, MNI	12	0.015	0.010	0.56	.34
northern vs. southern sites, MNB	11	0.068	0.327	0.87	.27
15. Summed all cervids including reindeer					
northern vs. southern sites, MNI	13	0.016	0.009	0.78	.29
northern vs. southern sites, MNB	11	0.085	0.327	0.82	.29

(*continued*)

Table 5.12   DENSITY-CONTROLLED MNI AND MNB (*Continued*)

	N	$\overline{X}_1$	$\overline{X}_2$	z	p
16. Steppe bison					
northern vs. southern sites, MNI	9	0.004	0.0004	0.043	.40
northern vs. southern sites, MNB	8	0.026	0.011	1.20	.19
17. Wild cattle, northern vs. southern sites, MNI	2	0.003	0.003	—	—
18. Musk-ox					
northern vs. southern sites, MNI	2	0.014	0.0005	—	—
northern vs. southern sites, MNB	2	0.098	0.001	—	—
19. Steppe marmot					
northern vs. southern sites, MNI	7	0.010	0.016	0.40	.37
northern vs. southern sites, MNB	5	0.005	0.016	0.76	.30
20. Hare					
northern vs. southern sites, MNI	12	0.008	0.044	0.95	.25
northern vs. southern sites, MNB	10	0.018	1.937	0.72	.31
northern high- vs. low-density sites, MNI	8	0.013	0.003	3.07	.004
northern high- vs. low-density sites, MNB	6	0.026	0.012	2.61	.01
southern high- vs. low-density sites, MNI	4	0.087	0.0005	24.76	<.0001
southern high- vs. low-density sites, MNB	4	5.183	0.209	23.84	<.0001
high-density northern vs. southern sites, MNI	4	0.013	0.155	43.77	<.0001
high-density northern vs. southern sites, MNB	4	0.026	5.183	1146.00	<.0001
low-density northern vs. southern sites, MNI	6	0.003	0.007	0.80	.29
low-density northern vs. southern sites, MNB	6	0.012	0.209	0.95	.25
21. All fur bearers including hares					
northern vs. southern sites, MNI	15	0.101	0.059	0.62	.33
northern vs. southern sites, MNB	12	4.070	1.510	0.72	.31
northern high- vs. low-density sites, MNI	10	0.350	0.040	1.67	.09
northern high- vs. low-density sites, MNB	8	14.540	0.580	1.16	.20
southern high- vs. low-density sites, MNI	5	0.235	0.015	20.14	<.0001
southern high- vs. low-density sites, MNB	4	5.802	0.083	142.97	<.0001
high-density northern vs. southern sites, MNI	3	0.350	0.235	0.61	.33
high-density northern vs. southern sites, MNB	3	14.540	5.800	0.72	.31
low-density northern vs. southern sites, MNI	12	0.039	0.015	1.64	.10
low-density northern vs. southern sites, MNB	9	0.580	0.080	3.09	.003
22. Arctic fox and wolf at high-density northern vs. southern sites, MNI	3	0.329	0.054	1.48	.14
23. Summed food taxa excluding mammoth					
northern vs. southern sites, MNI	17	0.032	0.051	0.61	.33
northern vs. southern sites, MNB	14	1.062	0.160	1.03	.23
northern high- vs. low-density sites, MNI	9	0.070	0.010	4.25	<.0001
northern high- vs. low-density sites, MNB	8	0.363	0.039	4.30	<.0001
southern high- vs. low-density sites, MNI	7	0.228	0.021	23.00	<.0001
southern high- vs. low-density sites, MNB	6	5.376	0.199	39.82	<.0001
high-density northern vs. southern sites, MNI	4	0.070	0.228	11.56	<.0001
high-density northern vs. southern sites, MNB	4	0.363	5.376	67.73	<.0001
low-density northern vs. southern sites, MNI	11	0.010	0.021	1.14	.21
low-density northern vs. southern sites, MNB	10	0.039	0.199	1.22	.19
24. Summed microfauna					
northern vs. southern sites, MNI	12	0.091	0.030	0.18	.39
northern vs. southern sites, MNB	11	0.125	0.246	0.54	.35

[a]Summed other fur bearers include cave lion, lynx, hyena, and mustelids.

Table 5.13   DIFFERENCE OF MEANS TESTS ON DENSITY-CONTROLLED MNI AND MNB VALUES, WITH CHRONOLOGICAL CONTROLS

	N	$\overline{X}_1$	$\overline{X}_2$	z	p
1. Birds					
all early vs. late sites, MNI	4	0.058	0.020	2.53	.01
all early vs. late sites, MNB	4	0.240	0.054	6.00	<.0001
northern early vs. late sites, MNI	2	0.058	0.007	—	—
northern early vs. late sites, MNB	2	0.240	0.012	—	—
late northern vs. southern sites, MNI	3	0.007	0.027	0.77	.30
late northern vs. southern sites, MNB	3	0.012	0.075	0.85	.28
2. Wolverine					
northern early vs. late sites, MNI	4	0.012	0.004	8.00	<.0001
northern early vs. late sites, MNB	4	0.318	0.019	55.44	<.0001
northern high-density early vs. late sites, MNI	3	0.012	0.024	30.0	<.0001
northern high-density early vs. late sites, MNB	3	0.318	0.024	367.50	<.0001
late high-density northern vs. southern sites, MNB	3	0.024	0.120	137.14	<.0001
late high-density northern vs. southern sites, MNI	3	0.024	0.016	20.75	<.0001
3. Arctic fox					
northern low-density early vs. late sites, MNI	6	0.002	0.008	0.12	.39
northern low-density early vs. late sites, MNB	3	0.380	0.184	4.00	<.0003
late northern vs. southern sites, MNI	12	0.078	0.013	1.16	.20
late northern vs. southern sites, MNB	9	4.574	0.136	1.09	.22
late low-density northern vs. southern sites, MNI	7	0.085	0.007	0.36	.37
late low-density northern vs. southern sites, MNB	4	0.184	0.056	3.86	<.0004
4. Wolf					
northern high-density early vs. late sites, MNI	5	0.012	0.048	3.60	.0006
northern high-density early vs. late sites, MNB	5	0.552	0.771	0.66	.32
northern low-density early vs. late sites, MNI	5	0.003	0.006	1.63	.10
late high-density northern vs. southern sites, MNI	5	0.048	0.024	2.44	.02
late high-density northern vs. southern sites, MNB	5	0.771	0.175	1.80	.07
late low-density northern vs. southern sites, MNI	8	0.006	0.003	1.65	.10
late low-density northern vs. southern sites, MNB	6	0.095	0.027	1.36	.16
early northern high- vs. low-density sites, MNI	2	0.012	0.003	—	—
5. Bear					
northern low-density early vs. late sites, MNI	7	0.004	0.003	0.26	.39
northern low-density early vs. late sites, MNB	4	0.001	0.004	3.30	.001
late low-density northern vs. southern sites, MNI	8	0.003	0.001	2.30	.03
late low-density northern vs. southern sites, MNB	6	0.005	0.004	0.50	.35
6. Mammoth					
southern early vs. late sites, MNI	6	0.080	0.082	0.04	.40
southern early vs. late sites, MNB	6	1.900	2.940	0.78	.29
northern early vs. late sites, MNI	10	0.130	0.110	0.74	.30
northern early vs. late sites, MNB	8	6.510	1.640	1.23	.19
early northern vs. southern sites, MNI	2	0.130	0.080	—	—
early northern vs. southern sites, MNB	2	1.230	1.900	—	—
7. Horse					
northern early vs. late sites, MNI	7	0.003	0.015	1.71	.09
northern early vs. late sites, MNB		*nd*	*nd*	*nd*	*nd*
southern early vs. late sites, MNI	3	0.002	0.012	1.43	.14
southern early vs. late sites, MNB	3	0.001	0.150	1.07	.23

(continued)

Table 5.13 *(Continued)*

	N	$\overline{X}_1$	$\overline{X}_2$	z	p
8. Woolly rhinoceros					
northern early vs. late sites, MNI	7	0.002	0.014	2.49	.02
northern early vs. late sites, MNB	5	0.004	0.073	1.23	.19
9. Reindeer					
southern early vs. late sites, MNI	4	0.002	0.013	2.59	.01
southern early vs. late sites, MNB	4	0.003	0.435	1.11	.22
10. Steppe bison					
northern early vs. late sites, MNI	5	0.002	0.004	10.95	<.0001
northern early vs. late sites, MNB	4	0.030	0.024	0.42	.37
southern early vs. late sites, MNI	4	0.002	0.005	1.03	.23
southern early vs. late sites, MNB	4	0.002	0.013	1.20	.19
late northern vs. southern sites, MNI	7	0.004	0.005	0.19	.39
late northern vs. southern sites, MNB	6	0.024	0.013	0.85	.28
early northern vs. southern sites, MNI	2	0.002	0.002	—	—
early northern vs. southern sites, MNB	2	0.030	0.002	—	—
11. Steppe marmot					
southern early vs. late sites, MNI	4	0.017	0.020	1.35	.16
southern early vs. late sites, MNB	3	0.002	0.024	1.02	.24
late northern vs. southern sites, MNI	6	0.010	0.020	0.58	.34
late northern vs. southern sites, MNB	4	0.005	0.024	0.95	.25
12. Hare					
northern early vs. late sites, MNI	8	0.002	0.006	2.0	.05
northern early vs. late sites, MNB	7	0.016	0.018	0.42	.37
northern low-density early vs. late sites, MNI	4	0.002	0.003	0.83	.28
northern low-density early vs. late sites, MNB	4	0.016	0.010	3.0	.004
late low-density northern vs. southern sites, MNI	4	0.003	0.007	0.66	.32
late low-density northern vs. southern sites, MNB	4	0.010	0.209	0.91	.26
13. All fur bearers including hares					
northern early vs. late sites, MNI	10	0.022	0.120	1.55	.12
northern early vs. late sites, MNB	8	1.295	4.466	0.85	.29
northern low-density early vs. late sites, MNI	7	0.022	0.045	1.18	.20
northern low-density early vs. late sites, MNB	6	1.295	0.437	11.91	<.0001
late low-density northern vs. southern sites, MNI	9	0.045	0.016	1.45	.14
late low-density northern vs. southern sites, MNB	8	0.437	0.083	4.03	<.0002
14. Summed food taxa					
early northern vs. southern sites, MNI	3	0.034	0.004	1.21	.19
early northern vs. southern sites, MNB	2	0.244	0.014	—	—
late northern vs. southern sites, MNI	14	0.032	0.050	0.53	.35
late northern vs. southern sites, MNB	12	0.149	1.271	1.08	.22
northern early vs. late sites, MNI	10	0.034	0.032	0.06	.40
northern early vs. late sites, MNB	8	0.244	0.149	1.30	.17
southern early vs. late sites, MNI	7	0.036	0.006	1.58	.11
southern early vs. late sites, MNB	6	0.014	1.271	1.37	.16
late northern high- vs. low-density sites, MNI	8	0.075	0.018	2.47	.01
late northern high- vs. low-density sites, MNB	7	0.423	0.039	4.92	<.0001
northern high-density early vs. late sites, MNI	3	0.060	0.075	0.65	.32
northern high-density early vs. late sites, MNB	3	0.244	0.423	2.29	.02
northern low-density early vs. late sites, MNI	7	0.008	0.018	1.09	.22
southern low-density early vs. late sites, MNI	6	0.004	0.025	2.14	.04
southern low-density early vs. late sites, MNB	5	0.014	0.245	1.44	.14

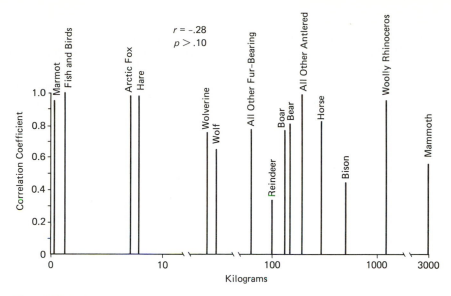

Figure 5.1 Relationship between size of taxa and coefficients of correlation.

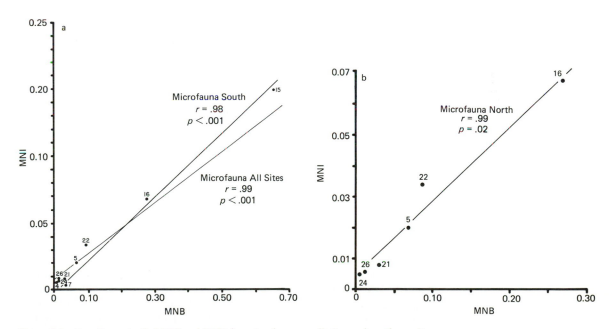

Figure 5.2 Density-controlled MNI and MNB for microfauna: a, all sites and southern sites; b, northern sites.

The selective use of long bones of some taxa as raw material for tool manufacture can also be expected to introduce ambiguity into the correlation coefficients. Such use of bone is amply documented for the study area during the Upper Paleolithic (Filippov 1977; Pidoplichko 1976; Polikarpovich 1968; Shovkoplyas 1965a). Worked bone, however, has been found at both the northern and southern sites, and I assume that no major interregional differences in bone-tool manufacture existed that would skew the correlation coefficients (for confirmation of rate of bone manufacture and densities of worked bone, see Chapter 6).

Another example of ambiguity in the correlation coefficients can come from considering the r values for mammoth. First, it is important to note that the r value for the region as a whole ($r = .54$) is fairly low and significantly different from the r value for microfauna ($r = .99$, $Z = 3.93$). Similar differences in r values are observed when comparing mammoth and microfauna in the north and the south separately (see Table 5.11). I interpret the low r values for mammoth to indicate that some bone was procured by activities other than active hunting and that the species was both hunted and gathered. Such an interpretation, however, raises a number of additional problems. First, if we consider the large size of the animals, we can anticipate that selective introduction of different skeletal elements to the sites took place. Such behavior would necessarily result in different r valus for this taxon than for smaller-size taxa. As I have demonstrated previously, size alone does not determine the magnitude of the correlation coefficient (see Figure 5.1). Second, data on the skeletal elements present at the sites indicate that such selective introduction did not play a determining role in the structuring of the mammoth remains at the sites. Kornietz (1962), Kornietz *et al.* (1981), and Shovkoplyas (1965a) all note the presence of fetal mammoth at Mezhirich and Mezin. The presence of whole articulated vertebral columns is known from Mezhirich (Soffer 1981). Data from other sites also indicate an abundance of crania, mandibles, scapulae, metatarsals and metacarpals, and phalanges—in a word, all the skeletal elements appear to be present. While no systematic study has quantified these observations for most of the sites, Pidoplichko does give these figures in his 1976 publication on Mezhirich (Table 5.14).

Another objection can be raised to my "gathering hypothesis" by pointing to the important role that mammoth bone played as fuel. It could be argued that such destructive use of bone could also produce lower r values. While it is more difficult to refute this argument since no studies identify what bones of which taxa were burned, I would suggest that (1) it is more reasonable to assume for now that selection of either taxa or skeletal elements did not play a significant role, and that (2) all bone, especially of large-size taxa, was probably used as fuel.

I examine and test the hypothesis that mammoth bone was gathered later in this chapter. I offer it here to account for the observed differences in the correlation coefficients in the north and south. If we assume that some bones were collected from "cemeteries," then the presence of such cemeteries either in greater numbers or in more undisturbed condition in the south could result in the observed differences in the r values between the north and south. Admittedly this is a fairly far-fetched explanation, and it is offered here as a suggestion for future research without which the role of mammoth in the economies cannot be evaluated.

Table 5.14   THE STRUCTURE OF MAMMOTH REMAINS
AT MEZHIRICH[a]

Skeletal elements	Total number found	
	MNB	MNI
Crania	97	97
Mandibles	109	109
Teeth	44	—
Tusks	92	—
Vertibrae	201	—
Ribs	266	—
Scapulae	102	53
Humeri	67	39
Radiae	27	18
Ulnae	14	13
Pelvises	129	71
Femora	105	57
Tibiae	36	21
Fibulae	5	—
Patellae	2	—
Carpals and tarsals	6	—
Metapodials	13	—
Phalanges	17	—
Sesamoid bones	2	—
Large bone fragments, longer than 15 cm	86	—
Other bone fragments, 10–15 cm	273	—
	1693	110

[a]After Pidoplichko (1976: 41). Remains excavated from 1966 to 1974.

In this "gathering hypothesis," I assume that the sites would have been selectively placed near such bone cemeteries out of logistical considerations; the cost of transporting mammoth would have been staggering. Weights of the different mammoth skeletal parts are listed in Table 5.15. Most of the listed values are a result of my weighing of mineralized bones in the collection of the Zoological Institute of the AN Uk. SSR in Kiev. Weights that could not be determined were kindly provided by N. K. Vereschagin. It is significant to note that, by and large, all mammoth skeletal elements are found at sites with mammoth-bone dwellings. My previous discussion, as well as Pidoplichko's values (Table 5.14), suggests that no selective transport of mammoth bone was employed and implies that the sites with dwellings were placed either directly on the kill sites or near mammoth "cemeteries." The low correlation coefficient for this taxon for the study region as a whole leads me to conclude that the second of the two practices was probably employed.

Such possible effects of cultural practices on the correlation coefficients prevent this index from being an absolute reflection of specific activities. As noted, the r value is ambiguous and should be considered only together with a comparison of the difference

Table 5.15   MEAN WEIGHT OF MINERALIZED MAMMOTH BONES[a]

Parts	N (weighed)	Weight (kg)
Skull (large)	1	100.0
Mandible with teeth	3	18.20
Teeth	3	5.0
Tusk	2	200.0
Scapula	2	4.90
Humerus	1	7.85
Radius and ulna	4	5.00
Pelvis half	1	16.50
Femur	1	15.00
Tibia	1	6.60
Long bone average	7	8.60
Vertibrae		
atlas	3	1.0
axis	3	0.54
thoractic	3	1.27
lumbar	5	2.0
coccyx	1	2.70
Rib	2	1.50
Tarsal and carpal	—	nd
Metatarsal	5	1.80
Metacarpal	5	1.85
Patella	1	0.20
Phalange	5	0.50
Calcaneus	5	0.95
Astrogalus	5	0.51

[a]For fresh weight, add ~10% (Kornietz 1979: personal communication).

of means calculated on density-controlled MNB and MNI values. I suggest, therefore, that all three together offer a viable entry into the reconstruction of hunting behavior and argue that it is the repeated patterning of the data that can be used to evaluate the hunting versus collecting hypotheses.

FOOD SPECIES

Analysis of Food Taxa

In this section I discuss the procurement of taxa used for food, and, using each taxon as a unit of analysis, I compare their harvesting in the north and south of the study area.

Mammoth.   Mammoths have been found at all northern sites and in 83% of the southern sites. As noted, there is a difference in correlation coefficients in the south ($r = .75$) and north ($r = .57$), but it is not significant ($Z = 0.43$) (Figure 5.3). Overall, correlation coefficients for this taxon are lower than those for other food species, and I interpret this to indicate that some mammoth bone was gathered. Similarly, a com-

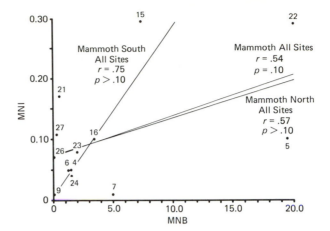

Figure 5.3   Density-controlled MNI and MNB for mammoth.

parison of both MNB and MNI values for mammoth found in the north and south shows no significant interregional difference (MNI, $z = 0.60$; MNB, $z = 0.95$). This lack of difference does not support my hypothesis offered in Chapter 3 on mammoth exploitation. There, after modeling mammoth behavior and placing the animals in the north for a short, 2 month warm season and in the south for the long, 8-month cold season, I predict that if this taxon was exploited in proportion to its availability, we should find approximately four times as many mammoth in the southern sites as in the northern ones. The lack of corroboration for this hypothesis further strengthens my interpretation that a good deal of mammoth bone was gathered.

At present, therefore, I conclude that mammoth did not play the major role in subsistence that has been widely attributed to them in both Soviet and Western literature. While some mammoth were undoubtedly hunted, how many remains a question for future research, as does determination of the frequency of mammoth kills, whether they were a seasonal or annual event, and if harvesting occurred at long intervals at frequencies similar to those postulated by Steward (1938) for Shoshone antelope drives (every 10 years) or by Frison (1978) for prehistoric bison kills (every 25 years or so). Since the contribution mammoth meat made to Upper Paleolithic diets is unclear, in this section I use two estimates—one if no mammoths found at the sites came from kills and the other if half the mammoths found were hunted. Also, because no differences have emerged in regional procurement behavior for this taxon (correlation coefficients, MNB and MNI comparisons), I assume that man–mammoth relationships were uniform throughout the area.

Woolly Rhinoceros.   Remains of woolly rhinoceros have been found at 65% of the sites in the study area. In contrast to mammoth, bones of this taxon were not used in construction of dwellings nor have they been found in storage pits. The correlation coefficient for this large-size taxon shows high positive values both in the north ($r = .96$) and in the study region as a whole ($r = .95$) (Figure 5.4). Since the species was only found at two southern sites, no correlation coefficients could be calculated for the

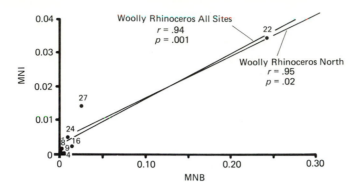

Figure 5.4 Density-controlled MNI and MNB for woolly rhinoceros.

south and no regional differences examined. The high positive correlation coefficient for density-controlled MNB and MNI values for rhinoceros at all sites suggests that this taxon was actively hunted over the entire study area. Remains are found in much higher densities in the north (MNI, $z = 2.63$). I conclude, therefore, that while this taxon was actively hunted all over the area, they were taken in greater numbers in the north. If the species was exploited in proportion to its availability, we can anticipate that it was far more numerous in the north.

Steppe Bison.   Remains of steppe bison have been found only at sites with large storage pits and, as I have noted, bison teeth were widely used as decoration. The taxon is represented at 37% of the northern and 57% of the southern sites. While a correlation coefficient for this taxon calculated for the entire study region shows a surprisingly low value ($r = .43$), a great difference ($Z = 2.18$) exists between the r values calculated for the north ($r = -.40$) and south ($r = .99$) (Figure 5.5). This evidence leads me to conclude that (1) the taxon was actively hunted in the south only, and (2) their presence

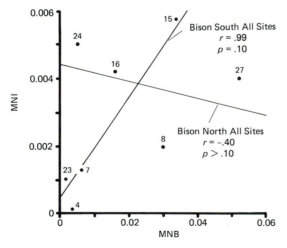

Figure 5.5 Density-controlled MNI and MNB for steppe bison.

in the north at densities indistinguishable from the south must have resulted from procurement practices other than active hunting. With the data on hand it is not possible to determine just what those practices may have been, as both gathering and interregional exchange are possibilities, especially if we assume that the northern sites mostly contain bison teeth. I present evidence for regional interactions in Chapter 7 and show that other items of personal adornment were parts of such networks.

At present, I take data on hand to indicate that a number of mechanisms existed for the procurement of this species. Biogeographic evidence indicates that steppe bison were found in larger numbers in the southern part of the study area during the late Pleistocene. Archaeological data from the Russian Plain as a whole also point to their extensive exploitation in the steppe zone south of the study area (Bibikova and Belan 1979; Boriskovskii 1953; Boriskovskii and Praslov 1964). These data support my conclusion that steppe bison were hunted only in the southern part of the study area.

Wild Cattle.   Cattle identified only to the genus *Bos* are reported at two sites: Berdyzh and Zhuravka. In both cases no MNB estimates exist. Therefore no coefficients could be calculated for this taxon and no interregional comparisons made. I arbitrarily treat this taxon together with the steppe bison in all future calculations but do not assume that they were actively hunted except in the south.

Musk-Ox.   This taxon was found only at three sites, two in the north and one in the south. Quantified data on MNB and MNI values exist only for Dobranichevka and Mezin. Table 5.8 shows that less than 10% of the sites contain remains of this taxon. Wilkinson (1974) argues that the logistics of hunting musk-oxen are such that the taxon very rarely plays a role in subsistence practices of hunter–gatherers and is only taken opportunistically when accidentally encountered. The low profile this taxon shows at sites indicates that similar man–musk ox relationships existed there as well. While a comparison of the number of musk-oxen found in northern sites (both MNI and MNB) is considerably larger than in the south, these differences, in all probability, are insignificant. All that can be concluded from this discussion is that musk-oxen did occasionally contribute to diet at both northern and southern sites, but that such contribution was irregular.

Horse.   Remains of horses were found at seven (50%) northern and three (43%) southern sites. While, as Figure 5.6 illustrates, correlation coefficients from the two parts of the study area show sizable differences (north, $r = .77$; south, $r = .99$; $Z = 2.29$), north–south comparisons of MNB and MNI values show no such disparities. Since horses are found at about the same proportion of sites and at similar densities in both the north and south, I interpret differences in r values to suggest that while horses at southern sites came exclusively from active hunting, those in the north may have been procured through other strategies as well. Horse teeth, like those of steppe bison and wild boar, were also used in decoration. It is possible that at some sites, northern especially, this taxon is mostly represented by teeth. While quantified information does not exist for the content of storage pits at the sites, Shovkoplyas (1965a) does report the presence of horse crania, mandibles, and long bones at Mezin. Pidoplichko (1976)

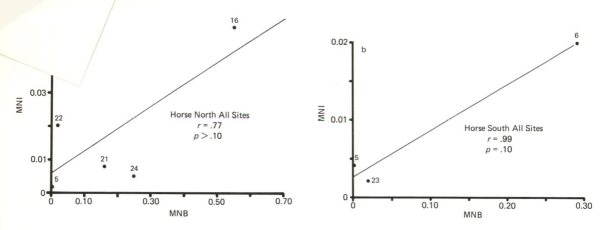

Figure 5.6   Density-controlled MNI and MNB for horse: a, northern sites; b, southern sites.

reports the same for Mezhirich. This indicates that parts other than teeth were found at the sites as well.

   Reindeer.   While density-controlled MNB and MNI values for reindeer show that approximately the same proportion of southern and northern sites have reindeer (about 50% for both MNI and MNB), correlation coefficients are significantly different between the north and south (north, $r = .99$; south, $r = .53$; $Z = 1.78$) (Figure 5.7). This difference supports my conjecture that reindeer were actively hunted only in the north, with the presence of antlers at southern sites an indication of collection. It is also possible that antlers, an important raw material used extensively for tool manufacturing, traveled along exchange networks and that at least some of the antlers reached southern sites through exchange. While this conclusion does not preclude occasional

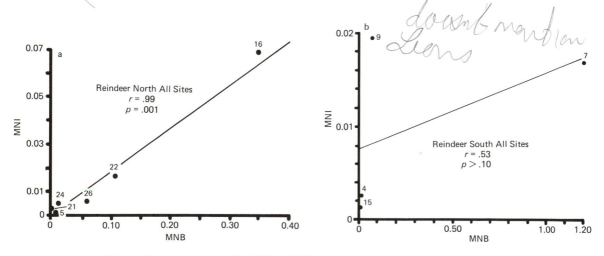

Figure 5.7   Density-controlled MNI and MNB for reindeer: a, northern sites; b, southern sites.

taking of a small number of reindeer in the south through hunting, the bulk of the evidence points to a prevalence of collecting. In further calculations I therefore assume that active hunting of this taxon occurred in the north only.

These observations on procurement practices also suggest that the taxon was a migratory form, at least in the southern part of the study area, whereas the northern region may have had a more sedentary reindeer population.

Other Antlered Taxa.   A small number of other deer groups (giant deer, red deer, deer sp.) have been found and quantified at four northern sites. The scarcity and disparity of these taxa has led me to group them together for the purposes of evaluating a relationship between their MNB and MNI counts. The correlation coefficient, as shown in Table 5.10 and Figure 5.8, is a perfect positive value of $r = 1.0$. This value, together with the locus of these taxa in the north, leads me to conclude that these species, like reindeer, were actively hunted only in the north. The presence of an unquantified amount of bone assigned to one red deer at Zhuravka may have come from collecting activities.

A comparison of mean MNI values for these taxa found in the north to those found in the south shows no significant difference and points to the minor role that these animals played in economies of the study area as a whole. They are found in approximately the same proportion of sites in both the north and south (31% in the north, 25% in the south). A comparison of the r values for reindeer to those for all antlered cervids in the north shows no significant difference between them ($Z = 0.80$), supporting my hypothesis about the role of these cervids in Upper Paleolithic economies.

Wild Boar.   Remains of wild boar, primarily if not exclusively represented by teeth, have been found and quantified at one northern and two southern sites. The hypothesis I offer for the role of this taxon in subsistence practices comes from a very small sample size and should be taken as a tentative estimation at best.

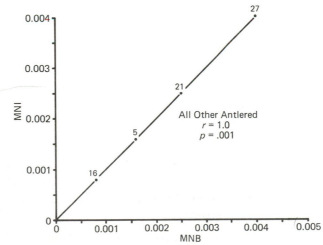

Figure 5.8   Density-controlled MNI and MNB for all other antlered taxa, northern sites.

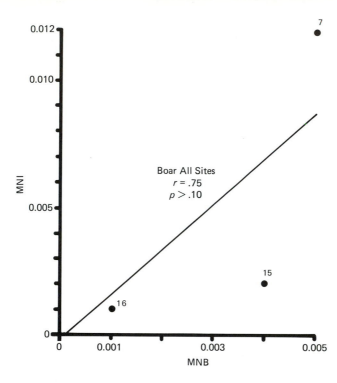

Figure 5.9 Density-controlled MNI and MNB for wild boar, all sites.

Comparisons of MNI and especially of MNB values between northern and southern sites show that this taxon was found in considerably larger numbers in the south. This observation conforms to the paleoenvironmental reconstruction for the area offered in Chapter 3, which projected a greater presence of deciduous forests in the south. The archaeological record shows not only that remains of wild boar were more abundant in southern sites, but also that a larger proportion of southern sites (43% on MNI, 33% on MNB) have this taxon present than northern sites (8% on MNI and MNB). A correlation coefficient calculated for the area as a whole yields a moderately high $r = .75$ ($p > .10$) (Figure 5.9).

As I have discussed earlier, this taxon is often represented by teeth, and presence of teeth does not necessarily signal active hunting. Since we know that boar teeth were used as decoration, it is interesting to look at the sites with boar teeth in greater detail. Teeth have only been found at sites used as winter base camps (see Chapter 6). These sites show numerous and diverse features and contain exotic materials. This co-occurrence is interesting and suggests that boar tooth decorations need not have resulted from active hunting alone. While I suspect that collecting and exchange played a role in movement of wild boar teeth across the landscape, I lack data to evaluate this proposition. I therefore assume that some hunting of this taxon did occur and that it occurred more often in the south.

Marmot.   The taxa discussed above have been considered primarily as contributing to Upper Paleolithic diets. Given ample ethnographic evidence on the use of hides, we

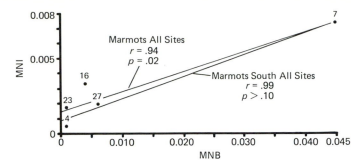

Figure 5.10   Density-controlled MNI and MNB for steppe marmots.

can anticipate that hides of these taxa were also utilized, as were their bones for bone-tool manufacture. In this work, however, I just consider their role as food resources. The following three species, however—marmot, beaver, and hare—clearly served a dual purpose, providing both energy and fur. Soviet researchers point to the systematic presence of both butchering and skinning marks on bones of these taxa and note that the bones are often charred and cracked (e.g., Pidoplichko 1969, 1976). My own analysis of lagomorph and marmot remains fully supports this interpretation.

Remains of steppe marmots have been found and quantified (both MNB and MNI values) at five sites. While no differences exist in mean densities of either MNI or MNB counts found in the north and south, a comparison of the ratio of sites with marmots shows that approximately twice as many southern sites as northern sites have this taxon (MNI, 23% of the northern and 57% of the southern sites; MNB, 15% of the northern and 50% of the southern sites). I interpret this to indicate a greater abundance of marmots in the south in general during the late Pleistocene.

Because of small sample size, correlation coefficients could not be calculated for northern sites. The r values for southern sites ($r = .99$) and for the study area as a whole ($r = .94$) are highly similar and lead me to conclude that marmots were hunted over the entire region (Figure 5.10). Since marmots were readily available only seasonally, they were, in all probability, taken in late summer–early fall (see discussion of marmot ecology in Chapter 3). The differences observed between the ratios of sites with marmots in the north and south suggest that the taxon was more abundant in the south and was hunted there more frequently.

Beaver.   This taxon is represented by remains of one individual at one site, Yudinovo. Its scarcity suggests that it did not play any significant role in late Pleistocene economies and its very rare procurement was probably highly opportunistic.

Hare.   Both MNI and MNB calculations indicate that hares were found at more than 50% of both northern and southern sites. Their frequency at sites, surpassed only by some gregarious herbivores, indicates that this taxon was systematically rather than opportunistically procured. While a comparison of overall differences in mean number of hares per square meter at the northern and southern sites does not show significant differences, the MNB–MNI relationship (Figure 5.11) shows the presence of two types of

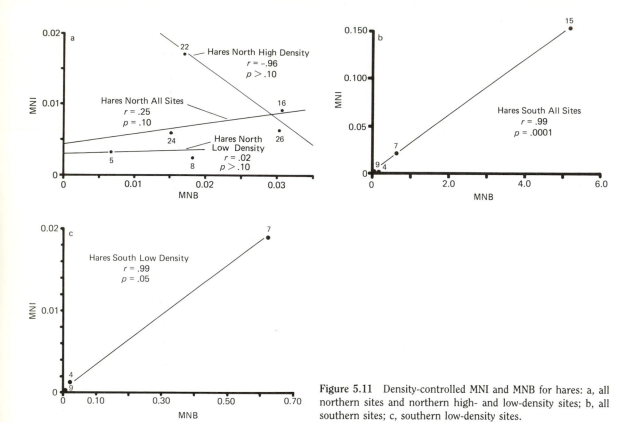

Figure 5.11 Density-controlled MNI and MNB for hares: a, all northern sites and northern high- and low-density sites; b, all southern sites; c, southern low-density sites.

sites with hares in both the north and south. As I show in a discussion of fur-bearing carnivores, this occurrence of two sample populations of sites (one with high and the other with low densities of fur bearers) is characteristic of the distribution of all fur bearers and is related to fur-procurement and -processing needs more directly than to nutritional requirements. Numerous difference of means tests calculated on density-controlled MNI and MNB values to distinguish sites with high mean numbers of hares from those with low mean numbers can be found in Tables 5.12 and 5.13. They show high-density sites in both the north and south (MNI, 170 times greater in the south and 25 times greater in the north; MNB, 25 times greater in the south and 2 times greater in the north). A comparison of high-density northern sites to one high-density southern site (Mezhirich) shows 11 times higher MNI and 199 times higher MNB in the south ($z = 43.8$ and $z = 1146.0$, respectively). No differences exist between densities of either MNB or MNI at low-density sites in the north and south. I interpret these statistics to indicate that (1) differential use of the taxon existed in both the north and south, with greater use at the high-density sites, and (2) hares played a greater role in the economy of the southern high-density site than they did in the northern ones.

   A calculation of the correlation coefficients for hares was first done for all of the northern and all of the southern sites. It shows a very high r value for the southern sites

$(r = .99)$ and a significantly lower one for the north $(r = .25; Z = 2.08)$. This indicates that active hunting played a significant role in the procurement of hares in the south only (Figure 5.11). Because of sample size, a separate calculation of correlation coefficients for the observed two groups of sites could only be done for high- and low-density northern sites and low-density southern sites. As Tables 5.12 and 5.13 show, they indicate no correlation at all at northern low-density sites $(r = .02)$ and a fairly high negative correlation at high-density sites $(r = -.96)$. The r value at the low-density southern sites is .99. These values further strengthen my argument that active hunting played a role in hare procurement in the south only.

The projection of active hunting for the southern sites only, however, still leaves open the question of procurement strategies employed at northern sites. As I discuss at the beginning of this chapter, a myriad of cultural practices affect the faunal record of archaeological sites. In the case of fur bearers, spatial separation of procurement and processing activities would profoundly affect the structure of remains. In the particular case of hares, the similarity of their behavior in faunal assemblages to that of fur-bearing carnivores strongly implies that this taxon was important for its fur.

As is shown in Chapter 6, the presence of fur bearers (including hares) at high densities at some sites is strongly associated with the presence of exotics. Both exotics and numerous fur bearers have been found at the more elaborate sites in the study area. The concentration of such activities as fur procurement or fur processing, importation of exotics, and construction of elaborate features all point to a behavioral complex at some sites that is not directly related to simple subsistence needs. These considerations lead me to conclude that the presence of hares at all northern sites can better be explained by invoking exchange rather than active hunting.

Birds. Bird remains of small MNI values but belonging to many taxa have been quantified at only four sites. I treat them categorically in this discussion. The proportion of sites with birds appears to be about equal in both the north and south when calculated on MNB values, whereas the MNI values show approximately twice as many

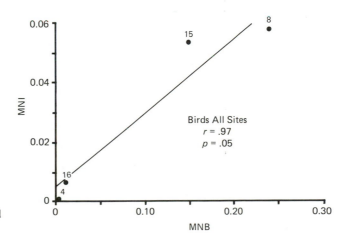

Figure 5.12 Density-controlled MNI and MNB for birds, all sites.

birds in the south. This difference, however, is not significant (MNI, $z = 0.55$; MNB, $z = 0.36$).

The small sample size of sites with birds precludes separate calculation of correlation coefficients for the north and south. Calculations for the study area as a whole (Figure 5.12) show a very high positive correlation ($r = .97$). I interpret the data to indicate that (1) birds were actively hunted over the entire study area, (2) they did not play an important role in the economies, and (3) they were most probably exploited opportunistically.

Fish.   Fish remains, like those of birds, have been documented for only a small proportion of the sites in the study area. As Tables 5.8 and 5.9 show, fish have been found at about 15% of the sites. The role of fish in diets of Upper Paleolithic hunter–gatherers, especially anadromous fish, has received a great deal of attention. Researchers have postulated that (1) fish contributed a far greater proportion of calories to prehistoric diets than has hitherto been considered, (2) the small number of fish remains found at prehistoric sites can be attributed to faulty recovery techniques, and (3) since fish remains are subject to greater destruction than mammalian remains, they should be present in lower numbers at prehistoric sites than mammal remains (Casteel 1976; Jochim 1979; Marschack 1979; White 1980).

While these observations are pertinent and interesting, the data from the central Russian Plain do not fully support the conjecture that fish were heavily exploited. The lack of sifting or flotation in the excavation repertoire of Soviet researchers has been noted previously. Neither is a standard procedure at excavations. Such recovery procedures, however, were employed at three sites: Eliseevich, Mezhirich, and Mezin. Polikarpovich (1968) describes the use of washing and flotation during the 1946 and 1948 field seasons at Eliseevichi, which led to the recovery of between 14 and 27 crystalline fish eye lenses which he identified as Cyprinids (carp). In Table 2.7 I list both the number of these lenses and the MNI they represent as ranging from 7 to 14, because my own subsequent research showed some of the lenses to be nonorganic. The presence of crystalline fish eye lenses at Eliseevichi intrigued me long before my first fieldwork in the USSR, because I had found no mention anywhere in the literature of the recovery of this element. While in the USSR in 1977 and 1978, I was able to locate and examine only 11 of the original 27. I submitted these to the Institute of Geology in Moscow for spectral analysis. This analysis showed that 6 items were nonorganic in nature (gley loess particles, quartz grains, etc.) while the remainder were possibly organic. The remaining 5 possibly organic pieces were examined by E. Sychevskaya, an ichthyologist at the Paleontology Institute in Moscow, who concluded that at least one of the specimens could belong to the Cyprinids, as identified by Polikarpovich (E. Sychevskaya 1978, personal communication). I therefore assume that only half of the lenses reported by Polikarpovich were such, treat both MNB and MNI values as a range, and use a means value in calculations.

Washing and sieving at Eliseevichi recovered both fish and rodent remains during the 1946 and 1948 excavations that were not found in 1935 and 1936 field seasons, when these recovery procedures were not employed. The small number of fish remains recovered out of a total 15,689 MNB reported by Vereschagin and Kuzmina (1977) (a number that does not include "many thousands of mammoth-bone fragments") suggests that fish did not constitute a significant or important component at the site.

Similarly, Pidoplichko (1976) employed sifting in his excavation at Mezhirich, and both he and Shovkoplyas (1965a) at Mezin. While this procedure, as at Eliseevichi, recovered a great deal of microfauna and some avian remains, it recovered no fish remains. My own application of dry sifting and flotation at Mezhirich resulted in the recovery, in two field seasons (1978, 1979), of one vertebra of an aged (8 years) pike. While it can be argued that most of the 1978 and 1979 excavations of Dwelling 4 and the surrounding area at Mezhirich (see floorplan in Figure 2.61) were done above the cultural layer, and that once the whole layer is excavated many more fish remains could be found, I suspect that this prognosis is just wishful thinking. Fish remains, by and large, either are not there or are there in such small numbers that they do not warrant a claim of an important role for fish in late Pleistocene economies of the central Russian Plain. One of the reasons for this, as is shown at the end of this chapter as well as in Chapter 6, where I present a typology for the sites, is that the majority of "high visibility" sites in the area (i.e., those having mammoth-bone features) are cold-weather occupations.

In summary, then, although I admit that fishing did play a role in the overall subsistence economies and that both direct and indirect evidence of fish remains exists (one possible bone fishing hook at Mezin reported by Shovkoplyas 1965a, as well as the predominance of water-related motifs in the ivory engravings from the study area reported by Marshack 1979), I do not see archaeological and faunal evidence to support a major role for fish procurement on the Upper Paleolithic central Russain Plain.

Density-controlled counts of fish remains are listed in Table 5.6. Difference of means tests in Tables 5.12 and 5.13 show that northern sites had larger MNI and MNB. The small sample size of sites used in these calculations, however ($N = 3$), precludes me from drawing any firm conclusions about the significance of these differences. A cal-

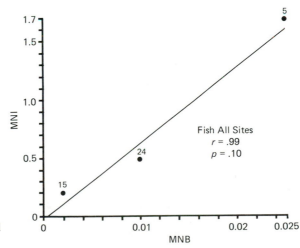

Figure 5.13 Density-controlled MNI and MNB for fish, all sites.

culation of the correlation coefficients for fish remains for the study area as a whole shows a very high positive value ($r = .99$). As the scatter plot of this linear regression (Figure 5.13) shows, the correlation is strong. I conclude that fishing was practiced all over the study region, but that fish was not a major food resource during the Upper Paleolithic.

Taxa Used as Food: Conclusions.   Table 5.16 summarizes the preceding discussion of species actively hunted for food in the different regions of the study area. The linear regression calculated for all food taxa, excluding taxa not actively hunted, is illustrated in Figure 5.14. The r values calculated separately for northern and southern sites that consider the role of active hunting do not show significant intraregional differences (north, $r = .93$; south, $r = .99$; Tables 5.10 and 5.11).

While a comparison of correlation coefficients calculated on microfaunal remains (done separately for the north and south) with those obtained for food species show no differences, differences can be observed in the r values between the food species and mammoth (see Table 5.11). The difference in the correlation coefficients for the summed food species in the north ($r = .96$) and mammoth in the north ($r = .57$) is significant ($Z = 1.94$). A similar difference is present in the southern sites between the r values for summed food species and for mammoth (food, $r = .99$; mammoth, $r = .75$; $Z = 2.07$). These observations conform to the general pattern observed in the behavior of mammoth when compared to food taxa separately and lead me to include this taxon in the food species list presented above as a food source of undetermined importance.

The similarity of r values for microfauna to those for the summed food species suggests, among other things, a high rate of transport for the food species. Specifically, since microfauna found at the sites can be expected to have died at the sites, the high

Table 5.16   FOOD TAXA ACTIVELY HUNTED[a]

Species	North	South
Mammoth	+(?)	+(?)
Woolly rhinoceros	+	+
Steppe bison	−	+
Wild cattle	+(?)	+
Musk-ox	+	+
Horse	+(?)	+
Reindeer	+	−
Other antlered taxa	+	−
Wild boar	+(?)	+
Marmot	+	+
Beaver	+	−
Hare	−	+
Bird	+	+
Fish	+	+

[a] +, active hunting or fishing; −, not procured by hunting; (?) role of active hunting problematic.

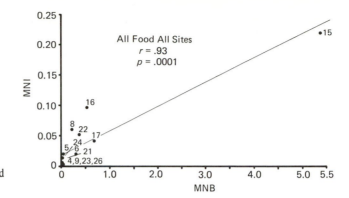

Figure 5.14 Remains of all food taxa actively hunted: all sites.

correlation coefficients for food species suggest that most of these taxa were also brought back to the sites without much processing done away from the sites. Such transport behavior can be expected in storage economies where food provisions are cached at or close to the sites. This expectation runs counter to much recent ethnoarchaeological information provided by Binford (1981) on curation and processing of food among the Nunamiut and the Navaho. I suggest, however, that this disparity between my data and Binford's is more apparent than real and is due to the coarse grain of my data.

Having outlined a general model for hunting behavior on the Upper Paleolithic central Russian Plain, it is interesting now to consider regional differences in the densities of food species. The comparison of density-controlled differences of means (MNB and MNI), excluding mammoth and including only those species actively hunted, shows no significant differences between the northern and southern sites (Tables 5.12 and 5.13). The only regional differences that can be observed are a greater number of both MNI and MNB for musk-oxen and fish at northern sites, and for wild boars at southern sites. These differences probably reflect biogeographic differences in the distribution of these taxa across the late Pleistocene landscape.

Kilocalories on the Central Russian Plain

The faunal record from the study area shows, in both number of sites and densities per site, that large gregarious herbivores were an important source of food. Groups in the south focused more on steppe bison and horses, while northern inhabitants exploited reindeer. Gregarious herbivores, however, were not the sole or even the most important source of food; a mix of both large- and small-size food species have been found at the sites. To evaluate the contribution made by different taxa to late Valdai diets, I transform faunal data on food species (Table 5.17) into density-controlled calculations of kilocalories per taxon per square meter per site (Table 5.18 and Figure 5.15). I have elected to evaluate prehistoric diets by looking only at energy values (kilocalories) even though recent research suggests that other nutrient values may be more relevant (Keene 1981; Reidhead 1979, 1980; Speth and Spielmann 1983). I do so because no nutritional values other than kilocalories appear in the literature for the

Table 5.17   BIOMASS ESTIMATES FOR LATE PLEISTOCENE FAUNA

Taxa	Live weight (kg)[a]	Usable meat (kg)[b]	kcal/kg[a]	kcal/individual	Daily requirement (kg)[c]
Mammoth	3,000 G	1,800.0	2,000 K	360,000,000	1.25
Woolly rhinoceros	1,200 P	720.0	1,750 K	1,260,000	1.43
Steppe bison	500 G	300.0	2,040 K	612,000	1.23
Cattle sp.	300 G	180.0	2,040 K	367,200	1.23
Horse sp.	290 G	174.0	1,150 K	200,100	2.20
Giant deer[d]	220	132.0	1,240 K	163,680	2.00
Red deer	220 G	132.0	1,240 K	163,680	2.00
Musk-ox	180 G	108.0	1,300 K	140,400	1.92
Deer sp.[e]	160	96.0	1,240 K	119,040	2.00
Boar	135 J	81.0	4,000 W	324,000	0.62
Reindeer	100 G	60.0	1,000 K	60,000	2.50
Beaver	20 J	12.0	4,000 J	48,000	0.63
Hare sp.	6 P	3.6	1,070 K	3,850	2.34
Steppe marmot	1 S	0.6	3,000 W	1,800	0.83
Fish	1.25 J	1.0	1,300 W	1,300	1.92
Birds	1.25 J	1.0	2,500 W	2,500	1.00

[a]References: G, Guthrie (1968); K, Klein (1969); J, Jochim (1976), P, Pidoplichko (1969); W, Wing and Brown (1979).
[b]Estimated as 60% of live weight for mammals and 80% of live weight for fish and birds, after Wing and Brown (1979).
[c]Average daily required caloric intake in Jochim (1976) given as 2000 kcal. Average daily required caloric intake in Wing and Brown (1978) given as 2400 kcal. I assume 2500 kcal for northern-latitude inhabitants.
[d]Estimated as red deer.
[e]Estimated as median between red deer and reindeer.

extinct taxa exploited on the central Russian Plain. These calculations, like others done on faunal remains in this volume, are not intended as definitive but rather are offered as heuristic devices that allow us to begin modeling some variables in late Valdai subsistence strategies.

Since at present it is impossible to determine what contribution mammoth made to the late Valdai diet, I offer kilocalorie estimates assuming that (1) all mammoth are used as a food source, (2) half are used, and (3) none are used.

I have postulated, using other data, that active hunting did not play a role in the procurement of some taxa. In Table 5.18 I evaluate the effect of the exclusion of species not hunted on the overall summary of kilocalories per square meter at the sites. Because no regional differences were observed for mammoth, I evaluate the effect of excluding species not hunted without using mammoth values. Row 18 summarizes kilocalories per square meter without taking active hunting into account; Row 19 lists values calculated only on taxa actively procured in the north and in the south. Row 20 lists the percentage of difference between the values in Rows 18 and 19. The maximal difference in values is 32%, and such high differences are found at two sites only. The other differences are all well below 20%. I conclude, therefore, that controlling for the

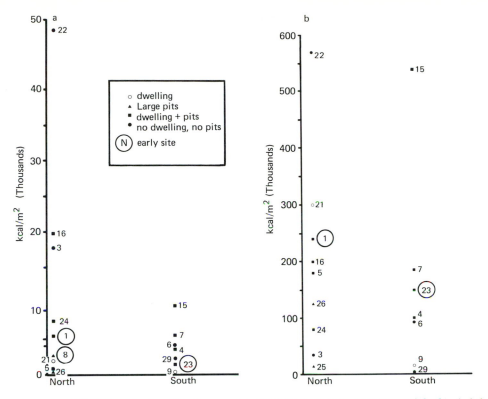

Figure 5.15   Density of kilocalories of food taxa: a, all mammoths excluded; b, half mammoth kcal included.

role of active hunting does not significantly depress kilocalorie calculations for those taxa that were actively hunted. Because of the sheer size of the animals, these differences become totally meaningless if mammoth kilocalories are added.

Table 5.19 presents the proportional contribution each taxon made to kilocalories at the sites: if no mammoths were actively hunted, if half of the mammoths found were hunted, and if all mammoths at each site were actively hunted. Regional north–south comparisons can be found in Table 5.20, again in three versions depending on the presence of mammoth. Difference of means tests (Table 5.21) are done at only two mammoth proportions: if no mammoth were eaten and if 50% were eaten. No calculations use all mammoth, because of their swamping effect on kilocalorie values.

It is important to note that although there are no significant differences in MNB, MNI, or kilocalorie estimates between northern and southern sites, there are differences in these values within each region: Both the north and the south have sites with high as well as low densities of food. I examine these differences at the conclusion of this chapter and in Chapter 6.

Table 5.18   KILOCALORIES PER SQUARE METER AT UNDISTURBED SITES

	Berdyzh	Chulatovo II	Dobranichevka	Eliseevichi	Fastov	Gontsy	Khotylevo II
1. Rhinoceros	3,528	15,120	630	—	—	—	2,530
2. Horse	600	1,400	—	400	4,002	—	—
3. Musk-ox	—	—	70	—	—	—	—
4. Wild cattle	1,028[a]	—	—	—	—	—	—
5. Steppe bison	—	2,448[a]	3,060	—	—	1,469	1,224[a]
6. Reindeer	—	1,200	150[a]	96	—	1,026[a]	—
7. Red deer	—	—	—	327	—	—	—
8. Deer sp.	—	—	—	—	—	—	—
9. Giant deer	—	—	—	—	—	—	—
10. Wild boar	—	—	—	—	—	3,888	—
11. Hare	—	77[a]	4	12[a]	—	75	8[a]
12. Steppe marmot	—	45	1	—	—	13	—
13. Beaver	—	—	—	—	—	—	—
14. Fish	—	—	—	22	—	—	—
15. Birds	—	—	12	—	—	—	145
16. All mammoth	468,000	36,000	180,000	360,000	180,000	360,000	nd
17. Half mammoth	234,000	18,000	90,000	180,000	90,000	180,000	nd
18. Summed calories, no mammoth, no north–south differences	5,156	20,290	3,927	857	4,002	6,471	3,897
19. Summed calories, no mammoth, north–south differences considered	4,128	17,765	3,777	845	4,002	5,445	2,665
20. Percentage difference between Rows 18 and 19	20	13	4	2	0	16	32
21. Summed calories, half mammoth	238,128	35,765	93,777	180,845	94,002	185,445	nd
22. Summed calories, all mammoth	472,128	53,765	183,777	360,845	184,002	365,445	nd

[a]Possibly not actively hunted.

The Subsistence Base

Herbivores.   I have already discussed the problematic role of mammoth in subsistence practices of Upper Paleolithic hunter–gatherers on the central Russian Plain (and see pp. 303–308). Similar difficulties also exist with the second largest herbivore, the woolly rhinoceros. While the correlation coefficients presented earlier suggest that this taxon was actively hunted, the distribution of MNI shows a strong regional difference and implies that woolly rhinoceros played a far more important role in the north. This point is clearly demonstrated in Table 5.20, which compares kilocalorie composition of sites in the north and south. Overall, this taxon is found in only 11 (46%) of the sites. Its

Kirillovskaya	Mezhirich	Mezin	Pushkari I	Pushkari II	Radomyshl'	Suponevo	Timonovka I	Timonovka II	Yudinovo	Zhuravka
379	—	3,150	—	43,344	—	6,300	—	—	17,640	—
—	800	10,005	1,601	4,002	400	1,000	—	—	—	—
—	—	2,022	—	—	—	—	—	—	—	—
—	—	—	—	—	—	—	—	—	—	1,102
—	7,222	2,570[a]	—	—	1,040	3,060[a]	—	—	2,448[a]	—
—	1,182[a]	4,152	150	1,032	102	300	150	366	nd	—
—	—	—	327	—	—	—	—	—	—	497[a]
—	—	—	—	—	—	—	—	—	238	—
—	—	327	—	—	—	—	—	—	327	—
—	648	324	—	—	—	—	—	—	—	972
<1	599	35[a]	—	66[a]	—	19[a]	3[a]	23[a]	—	—
—	—	6	—	—	3	—	—	—	4	97
—	—	—	—	—	—	—	—	—	8	—
—	3	—	—	—	—	6	—	—	—	—
—	133	17	—	—	—	—	—	—	—	—
36,000	1,044,000	360,000	612,000	1,044,000	288,000	144,000	28,800	252,000	396,000	—
18,000	522,000	180,000	306,000	522,000	144,000	72,000	14,400	126,000	198,000	—
380	10,581	22,608	2,078	48,444	1,545	10,685	153	389	nd	2,667
380	9,405	20,003	2,078	48,378	1,443	7,606	150	366	nd	2,171
0	11	12	0	1	7	29	2	6	nd	19
18,380	531,405	200,003	308,078	570,378	145,443	79,606	14,550	126,366	nd	2,171
36,380	1,053,405	380,003	614,078	1,092,378	289,443	151,606	28,950	252,366	nd	2,171

kilocalorie contribution, however, seems overwhelming at those sites and in the northern region as a whole. No information exists on skeletal elements of this taxon at the sites, and its bones did not contribute significantly to construction of bone dwellings or figure prominently in storage pits. Bone elements of woolly rhinoceros are quite distinct structurally, and therefore identification of them as to taxon can be expected to occur at fairly high rates. Although the species is thought to have been fairly solitary (Vereschagin 1979), its large size and defensive behavior suggest that it was pursued by a group of hunters rather than by single individuals.

Smaller gregarious herbivores (horse, steppe bison, reindeer, etc.) are found at the

Table 5.19 PERCENTAGE OF KILOCALORIES PER TAXON AT UNDISTURBED SITES[a]

Site	Mammoth	Rhinoceros	Horse	Musk-ox	Cattle	Bison	Reindeer	Red deer	Deer sp.	Giant deer	Boar	Hare	Marmot	Beaver	Fish	Birds	No. of taxa
No Mammoth																	
Berdyzh	—	68	12	—	20	—	—	—	—	—	—	—	—	—	—	—	3
Chulatovo II	—	84	8	—	—	—	7	—	—	—	—	ins	ins	—	—	—	4
Dobranichevka	—	17	—	2	—	81	—	—	—	—	—	ins	ins	—	—	ins	5
Eliseevichi	—	—	47	—	—	—	11	39	—	—	—	—	—	—	3	—	4
Fastov	—	—	100	—	—	—	—	—	—	—	—	—	—	—	—	—	1
Gontsy	—	—	—	—	—	27	—	—	—	—	72	1	ins	—	—	—	4
Khotylevo II	—	95	—	—	—	—	—	—	—	—	—	—	—	—	—	5	2
Kirillovskaya	—	99	—	—	—	—	—	—	—	—	—	ins	—	—	—	—	2
Mezhirich	—	—	9	—	—	77	—	—	—	—	7	6	—	—	ins	ins	6
Mezin	—	16	50	10	—	—	21	—	—	1	1	—	ins	—	—	—	7
Pushkari I	—	—	77	—	—	—	7	16	—	—	—	—	—	—	—	—	3
Pushkari II	—	90	8	—	—	—	2	—	—	—	—	—	—	—	—	—	3
Radomyshl'	—	—	28	—	—	71	—	—	—	—	—	—	ins	—	—	—	3
Suponevo	—	83	13	—	—	—	4	—	—	—	—	—	—	—	ins	—	4
Timonovka I	—	—	—	—	—	—	100	—	—	—	—	—	—	—	—	—	1
Timonovka II	—	—	—	—	—	—	100	—	—	—	—	—	—	—	—	—	1
Yudinovo	—	nd	—	—	—	—	nd	—	nd	nd	—	—	nd	nd	—	—	5
Zhuravka	—	—	—	—	51	—	—	—	—	—	45	—	4	—	—	—	3
Half Mammoth																	
Berdyzh	98	1	ins	—	ins	—	—	—	—	—	—	—	—	—	—	—	4
Chulatovo II	50	42	4	—	—	—	3	—	—	—	—	—	ins	—	—	—	5
Dobranichevka	96	ins	—	ins	—	3	—	—	—	—	—	ins	ins	—	ins	ins	7
Eliseevichi	99	—	ins	—	—	—	ins	ins	—	—	—	—	—	—	ins	—	5
Fastov	96	—	4	—	—	—	—	—	—	—	—	—	—	—	—	—	2
Gontsy	97	—	—	—	—	ins	—	—	—	—	2	ins	ins	—	—	—	5
Khotylevo II	nd	—	—	—	nd	—	—	—	—	—	—	—	—	—	—	nd	3

Site	%	n
Kirillovskaya	97	3
Mezhirich	98	7
Mezin	90	8
Pushkari I	99	4
Pushkari II	91	4
Radomyshl'	99	4
Suponevo	90	5
Timonovka I	99	2
Timonovka II	99	2
Yudinovo	nd	6
Zhuravka	—	3
All Mammoth		
Berdyzh	99	4
Chulatovo II	66	5
Dobranichevka	97	7
Eliseevichi	99	5
Fastov	98	2
Gontsy	98	5
Khotylevo II	nd	3
Kirillovskaya	99	3
Mezhirich	99	7
Mezin	95	8
Pushkari I	99	4
Pushkari II	95	4
Radomyshl'	99	4
Suponevo	95	5
Timonovka I	99	2
Timonovka II	99	2
Yudinovo	nd	6
Zhuravka	—	3

[a] ins < 0.9%.

Table 5.20   REGIONAL DISTRIBUTION OF KILOCALORIES

	North			South				
	No. of sites	Σ kcal/m^2	Percentage of calories	No. of sites	Σ kcal/m^2	Percentage of calories	Total	Percentage of total
No Mammoth								
Mammoth	—	—	—	—	—	—	—	—
Rhinoceros	7	91,602	73	2	1,009	4	92,611	61
Horse	7	21,409	17	3	5,202	20	26,611	18
Musk-ox	1	2,022	2	1	70	ins	2,092	1
Wild cattle	1	1,028	1	1	1,102	4	2,130	1
Bison	in southern sites only			4	12,791	48	12,791	9
Reindeer	8	7,446	6	in northern sites only			7,446	5
Red deer	2	654	ins	in northern sites only			654	ins
Deer sp.	1	238	ins	in northern sites only			238	ins
Giant deer	2	654	ins	in northern sites only			654	ins
Boar	1	324	ins	3	5,463	21	5,787	4
Hare	in southern sites only			4	679	2	679	ins
Marmot	3	55	ins	4	114	ins	169	ins
Beaver	1	8	ins	—	—	—	8	ins
Fish	2	28	ins	1	3	ins	31	ins
Birds	2	162	ins	2	145	ins	307	ins
Half Mammoth								
Mammoth	10	1,850,000	93	6	1,044,000	98	2,894,000	95
Rhinoceros	7	91,602	5	2	1,009	ins	92,611	3
Horse	7	21,409	1	3	5,202	ins	26,611	1
Musk-ox	1	2,022	ins	1	70	ins	2,092	ins
Wild cattle	1	1,028	ins	1	1,102	ins	2,130	ins
Bison	in southern sites only			4	12,791	1	12,791	ins
Reindeer	8	7,446	ins	in northern sites only			7,446	ins
Red deer	2	654	ins	in northern sites only			654	ins
Deer sp.	1	238	ins	in northern sites only			238	ins
Giant deer	2	654	ins	in northern sites only			654	ins
Boar	1	324	ins	3	5,463	ins	5,787	ins
Hare	in southern sites only			4	679	ins	679	ins
Marmot	3	55	ins	4	114	ins	169	ins
Beaver	1	8	ins	—	—	—	8	ins
Fish	2	28	ins	1	3	ins	31	ins
Birds	2	162	ins	2	145	ins	307	ins
All Mammoth								
Mammoth	10	3,700,800	97	6	2,088,000	98	5,788,800	97
Rhinoceros	7	91,602	2	2	1,009	ins	92,611	2
Horse	7	21,409	ins	3	5,202	ins	26,611	ins
Musk-ox	1	2,022	ins	1	70	ins	2,092	ins
Wild cattle	1	1,028	ins	1	1,102	ins	2,130	ins
Bison	in southern sites only			4	12,791	1	12,791	ins
Reindeer	8	7,446	ins	in northern sites only			7,446	ins
Red deer	2	654	ins	in northern sites only			654	ins
Deer sp.	1	238	ins	in northern sites only			238	ins
Giant deer	2	654	ins	in northern sites only			654	ins

Table 5.20 *(Continued)*

| | North | | | South | | | | |
	No. of sites	Σ kcal/m²	Percentage of calories	No. of sites	Σ kcal/m²	Percentage of calories	Total	Percentage of total
Boar	1	324	ins	3	5,463	ins	5,787	ins
Hare	in southern sites only			4	679	ins	679	ins
Marmot	3	55	ins	4	114	ins	169	ins
Beaver	1	8	ins	—	—	—	8	ins
Fish	2	28	ins	1	3	ins	31	ins
Birds	2	162	ins	2	145	ins	307	ins

[a] ins < 0.9%.

vast majority of sites (81% for the entire region; 79% of the northern and 86% of the southern sites). This fact together with the contribution they made to the late Pleistocene diet (38% of kilocalories if mammoth are excluded from consideration) suggests that they figured prominently in subsistence practices. As I discuss in Chapter 3, different taxa in this category probably had different aggregation schedules in the late Valdai and would have been optimally harvested at these times of peak abundance. The existence of storage economies in the study area indirectly confirms this prediction, and I conclude that these species were hunted by fairly large groups of hunters and that they figured prominently in scheduling decisions employed in the area. While regional differences exist between the northern and southern sites in types of gregarious herbivores exploited, no significant differences exist in either kilocalories available in the two regions or in overall numbers of animals found (Tables 5.8 and 5.20).

Small-Size Fauna. Faunal data from the central Russian Plain do not confirm the interpretation found too often in the literature that late Pleistocene groups there were *exclusively* large-game hunters. While the bulk of kilocalories did come from large herbivores, strong evidence exists for opportunistic exploitation of other taxa as well. Wild boar, for example, because of their high kilocalorie values, overcome the swamping effect of large herbivores—in the southern region especially (Table 5.20 shows 4% of kilocalories from southern sites come from this taxon).

Part of the difficulty in accurately evaluating the importance of smaller fauna in subsistence practices comes from the variable I selected to measure—kilocalories. Since this value is highly sensitive to the size of animal, such large disparities as observed in the fauna of the study area are bound to mask other pertinent variables. Speth and Spielmann (1983), as noted before, offer the fat content of taxa in northern latitudes as a variable to consider when evaluating subsistence practices. Their suggestion that fat plays a crucial role in diets of northern-latitude populations appears most germane for this study. It accounts nicely for the exploitation of such species as wild boar and marmot—both fat-intensive taxa.

Table 5.21   DIFFERENCES OF MEANS TESTS ON THE DISTRIBUTION OF KILOCALORIES

	N	$\bar{X}_1$	$\bar{X}_2$	z	p
Excluding All Mammoth					
1. All northern vs. southern sites	23	9,663	2,657	0.97	.25
2. All early vs. late sites	17	3,087	8,717	1.54	.12
3. Early sites with storage pits, north vs. south	3	3,910	1,443	1.98	.05
4. Late northern high-density sites with storage pits vs. without storage pits	3	19,676	33,071	1.00	.24
5. Late high-density sites with storage pits, north vs. south	2	19,676	9,405	—	—
6. Late northern low-density sites with storage pits vs. without storage pits	5	4,225	865	0.98	.25
7. Late southern low-density sites with storage pits vs. without storage pits	5	4,611	2,184	1.81	.07
8. Late low-density sites with storage pits, north vs. south	6	2,242	4,611	1.20	.19
9. Late low-density sites without storage pits, north vs. south	4	2,078	2,184	0.10	.40
10. Late northern high-density sites without storage pits vs. southern high-density sites with storage pits	3	33,071	9,405	1.55	.12
Including Half of Mammoth					
1. All northern vs. southern sites	25	141,116	97,325	0.27	.38
2. All early vs. late sites	16	192,299	174,317	0.27	.38
3. Early sites with storage pits and dwellings, north vs. south	2	239,156	145,443	—	—
4. Early vs. late sites with storage pits	10	192,299	176,459	0.13	.39
5. Early vs. late sites with storage pits and dwellings	8	192,299	184,666	0.05	.40
6. Late northern high-density sites with storage pits vs. without storage pits	4	190,260	439,228	1.89	.06
7. Late southern high-density sites with storage pits vs. without storage pits	1	531,405	—	—	—
8. Late northern low-density sites with storage pits vs. without storage pits	4	73,507	35,765	1.16	.20
9. Late southern low-density sites with storage pits vs. without storage pits	5	139,611	38,184	1.77	.08
10. Late high-density sites with storage pits, north vs. south	3	190,260	531,405	36.23	<.0001
11. Late low-density sites with storage pits, north vs. south	5	73,507	139,611	2.04	.05
12. Late low-density sites without storage pits, north vs. south	4	35,765	38,184	0.07	.40
13. Late northern high-density sites without storage pits vs. southern sites with storage pits	3	439,228	531,405	0.70	.31

HUNTING STRATEGIES AND TECHNIQUES

The nature of species exploited as food carries implications for both hunting technologies and hunting strategies.

A number of researchers, including Vereschagin (1971), suggest that different tool types were used in hunting different taxa during the Upper Paleolithic. Gvozdover (1974) reviewed this hypothesis and found absolutely no relationship between the lithic tool types present at the sites on the Russian Plain and the species exploited. The methods as well as the types of weapons used to harvest food species thus remain problematic. While the use of various spears and lances is widely accepted for the Upper Paleolithic, the use of bows and arrows is a point of debate. Praslov *et al.* (1981) advance a strong argument for the use of arrows at Kostenki–Borschevo sites. Gladkih (1973) has shown a fairly high rate of microlithization in tools at some southern sites. While he has not addressed the question of the function of these microliths, their presence can be taken to suggest a possibility that arrows were in use. Even though we cannot state just what sorts of weapons were used to kill various taxa, the broad variety of species exploited does point to a probable existence of a number of harvesting techniques.

The harvesting of small numbers of solitary species such as wild boar, musk-ox, and red deer indicates the use of single stalk and kill techniques. Pidoplichko (1976) suggests that snaring was widely used in the late Valdai for such small animals as willow ptarmigans and hares. Fish harvesting techniques are more difficult to reconstruct. The discovery of a part of a fishhook at Mezin suggests that this method was employed. The small number of fish remains found at the sites tends to imply that such mass harvesting techniques as netting or construction of fish dams were not in use.

Hunting the Mammoth

Nothing has generated as much debate in the literature as the possible methods employed in hunting species as large as the mammoth. Ethnographically, we do not know of any group that habitually hunted elephants in sizable quantities prior to the advent of the ivory trade (Carrington 1958; Sikes 1971; Vereschagin 1971, 1979). Much of the debate, as Saunders (1979) aptly puts it, is attributable to our inabilities to imagine how prehistoric hunters armed with stone implements could have taken down such large prey. Yet the archaeological evidence from both the Old and New Worlds amply documents that such successful hunts did indeed take place. This has led to a number of speculations on the hunting methods used (Saunders 1979; Vereschagin 1971). Kornietz, in her 1962 dissertation, first proposed the hypothesis that late Pleistocene hunters took mammoths by driving and slaughtering whole herds. She based her hypothesis on the analysis of the age composition of mammoths found at three Upper Paleolithic sites on the central Russian Plain: Dobranichevka, Mezin, and Radomyshl'. She concluded that the demographic distribution of the mammoth remains at these sites closely resembles the demographic composition of present-day Indian elephant herds and interpreted this to imply that Upper Paleolithic hunters took whole herds.

Saunders (1979, 1980), quite independently, has advanced the same argument for late Pleistocene hunters of the New World. Specifically, Saunders claims that the demographic composition of mammoth remains at such sites as Lehner Ranch, Dent, and Miami indicates that hunters killed whole herds of *Mammuthus columbi*. But at other sites, Saunders argues, (Murray Springs and Blackwater Draw) individual mammoths were hunted, and this resulted in a demographic profile quite different from those found among African elephant herds.

Both Kornietz and Saunders developed methods for aging mammoth teeth based on present-day elephant analogues. Kornietz also developed a method for sexing mammoth remains based on both sexual dimorphism of teeth and anatomical structure of the mandibles.

Saunders, unlike Kornietz, tested his conclusions by employing statistical techniques. Both Saunders and Kornietz relied on ethnographic analogues which report that indigenous populations, both in the Old and New Worlds, did indeed take large numbers of various species, such as bison and reindeer, in massive drives.

In the late 1960s a late Pleistocene "mammoth cemetery" was discovered in Siberia which contains sizable numbers of mammoth and other species. This site, Berelekh, carbon dated at 10,440 ± 100, 11,830 ± 110, 12,240 ± 160, and 13,700 ± 400, is located on the Berelekh River at the border of the tundra and boreal forest ecozones. Vereschagin (1977) investigated this locality and recorded all faunal remains. These are presented in Table 5.22. Table 5.23 presents Zherehova's (1977) demographic analysis of Berelekh mammoths. There is a discrepancy between the values for MNI of mammoth reported by Vereschagin and Zherehova: Vereschagin reports at least 140 individuals; Zherehova, using teeth, calculates a value of 166 individuals. In this work I use Ver-

Table 5.22   FAUNA FROM LATE PLEISTOCENE BERELEKH[a]

	MNI		kg per individual	Total kg	% of kg[b]
	Number	%			
Lagopus lagopus	1	0.6	3	3	ins
Panthera spelaea	1	0.6	240	240	ins
Gulo gulo	4	2.6	25	100	ins
Mammuthus primigenius[c]	140	89.8	3000	420,000	98.8
Equus caballus[d]	3	1.9	290	870	0.2
Coelodonta tichorhinus	1	0.6	2200	2,200	0.5
Bison priscus	2	1.3	500	1,000	0.2
Rangifer tarandus	4	2.6	100	400	<0.1
	156				

[a]After Vereschagin (1977: Tab. 2).
[b]ins < 0.9%.
[c]Vereschagin reports 140 mammoth at Berelekh; Zherehova (1977) estimates 166 on teeth (see Table 5.23).
[d]Vereschagin (1977) identified this species as *Equus lanensis*. Following Azzaroli (1982, personal communication), I list all late Pleistocene horses as *Equus caballus*.

Table 5.23   AGE AND SEX COMPOSITION OF BERELEKH MAMMOTH[a]

	Age group (yr)						
	0–2 MNI (%)	2–5 MNI (%)	5–10 MNI (%)	10–20 MNI (%)	>20 MNI (%)	>30 MNI (%)	N
Males	2 (3.0)	4 (6.1)	13 (19.7)	18 (27.3)	16 (24.2)	13 (19.7)	66
Females	2 (2.0)	6 (6.0)	24 (24.0)	18 (18.0)	28 (28.0)	22 (22.0)	100
All mammoth	4 (2.4)	10 (6.1)	37 (22.1)	36 (21.7)	44 (26.4)	35 (21.0)	166

[a]After Zherehova (1977: 56), on teeth.

eschagin's values when dealing with ecological reconstructions and Zherehova's when discussing demographic composition of mammoth populations.

While an Upper Paleolithic archaeological site has been found next to the bone deposits, Vereschagin (1977) argues that the Berelekh bone deposit represents a paleontological accumulation of animals who met their death through natural processes, and that their accumulation is in no way the result of human action (cf. Mochanov 1977). Thus Berelekh offers the first opportunity of testing the validity of conclusions about past hunting practices advocated by both Kornietz and Saunders. African data on elephant mortality indicates that death assemblages accumulate from accretional mortality of individual animals rather than from catastrophic deaths of whole herds. We can, therefore, assume that similar mortality patterns in the past would produce a demographic composition at Berelekh that should be significantly different both from those found at Old and New World mass-kill sites and from standing elephant herds.

I use Saunders (1980) as the source for data on both African elephant herds and the demographic composition of mammoths found at the New World archaeological sites. I use Kornietz (1962) and Pidoplichko (1976) for demographic composition of mammoths found on the central Russian Plain. Data on Berelekh is from Zherehova (1977). In my calculations I follow the categories used by Saunders in his tests and group the central Russian Plain and Berelekh mammoths accordingly. These are presented in Table 5.24.

My application of the Kolomogorov–Smirnov tests is presented in Table 5.25. I tested for the significance of differences between two data sets, using the .05 level of significance in a two-tailed test. My tests show the following: (1) no statistical difference between the demographic composition of Berelekh mammoths and African elephants ($\chi^2 = 2.23$, $df = 2$); (2) no statistical difference between the demographic composition of mammoths found at the New World sites taken cumulatively and those of Berelekh ($\chi^2 = 1.34$, $df = 2$); and (3) a significant statistical difference between the demographic composition of mammoth remains found at the Upper Paleolithic sites from the central Russian Plain taken cumulatively and those of Berelekh ($\chi^2 = 6.08$; $df = 2$).

Comparisons of the Berelekh mammoth remains with specific assemblages found in the New World sites show that remains at the Lehner Ranch ($\chi^2 = 6.33$; $df = 2$), Murray Springs ($\chi^2 = 9.70$; $df = 2$), and Blackwater Draw ($\chi^2 = 8.86$; $df = 2$) are significantly

Table 5.24   DEMOGRAPHIC COMPOSITION OF OLD AND NEW WORLD MAMMOTHS
AND AFRICAN ELEPHANTS

Sites	Juvenile (0–9) MNI (%)		Young (10–20) MNI (%)		Young adult (20–30) MNI (%)		Mature (>30) MNI (%)		N
Berelekh, Siberia[a]	51	(30.7)	36	(21.7)	44	(26.5)	35	(21.1)	166
Old World Upper Paleolithic Sites[b]									
Dobranichevka	2	(20.0)	6	(60.0)	2	(20.0)	—	—	10
Mezhirich	50	(45.9)	41	(37.6)	17	(15.6)	1	(0.9)	109
Mezin	9	(20.5)	12	(27.3)	14	(31.7)	9	(20.9)	44
Radomyshl'	11	(29.7)	6	(16.2)	14	(37.9)	6	(16.2)	37
All Old World sites	72	(36.0)	65	(32.5)	47	(23.5)	16	(8.0)	200
New World Paleoindian Sites[c]									
Blackwater Draw	—	—	—	—	1	(16.7)	5	(83.3)	6
Dent	4	(30.7)	4	(30.7)	4	(30.7)	1	(7.9)	13
Lehner Ranch	3	(21.5)	8	(57.1)	3	(21.4)	—	—	14
Miami	2	(40.0)	—	—	2	(40.0)	1	(20.0)	5
Murray Springs	—	—	—	—	—	—	4	(100.0)	4
Pooled Dent, Lehner, and Murray Springs	9	(28.1)	12	(37.5)	9	(28.1)	2	(6.3)	32
All New World sites	9	(21.4)	12	(28.6)	10	(23.8)	11	(26.2)	42
African Elephant Samples[c]									
34–47	5	(41.6)	2	(16.7)	4	(33.4)	1	(8.3)	12
52–61	3	(30.0)	3	(30.0)	2	(20.0)	2	(20.0)	10
108–114	2	(25.0)	3	(37.5)	1	(12.5)	2	(25.0)	8
25–33	3	(30.0)	3	(30.0)	4	(40.0)	—	—	10
130–135	1	(16.6)	3	(50.0)	2	(33.4)	—	—	6
88–92	2	(40.0)	2	(40.0)	—	—	—	—	5
71–82	6	(42.8)	2	(14.3)	4	(28.6)	2	(14.3)	14
207–217	2	(16.7)	4	(33.3)	4	(33.3)	2	(16.7)	12
218–226	2	(22.2)	4	(44.5)	1	(11.1)	2	(22.2)	9
227–235	4	(44.5)	1	(11.1)	3	(33.3)	1	(11.1)	9
236–245	1	(9.1)	4	(36.4)	5	(45.4)	1	(9.1)	11
298–310	3	(23.1)	4	(30.7)	5	(38.5)	1	(7.7)	13
311–322	5	(41.6)	4	(33.4)	3	(25.0)	—	—	12
333–336	—	—	2	(50.0)	1	(25.0)	1	(25.0)	4
Pooled African data	39	(28.9)	41	(30.4)	39	(28.9)	16	(11.8)	135

[a]From Zherehova (1977).
[b]From Kornietz (1962).
[c]From Saunders (1980).

Table 5.25   KOLOMOGOROV–SMIRNOV TWO-SAMPLE TESTS ON ELEPHANT AND MAMMOTH DATA ($df = 2$)

	N_1	N_2	D	χ^2	p
Berelekh vs. Pooled African Elephants	166	135	.09	2.23	.30
Berelekh vs. Paleoindian Sites					
Blackwater Draw	166	6	.62	8.86	.01
Dent	166	13	.13	0.84	.70
Lehner Ranch	166	14	.35	6.33	.05
Miami	166	5	.22	0.93	.70
Murray Springs	166	4	.79	9.70	.01
pooled Paleoindian data	166	42	.10	1.34	.70
Berelekh vs. Old World Sites					
Dobranichevka	166	10	.38	5.47	.10
Mezhirich	166	109	.20	10.53	.01
Mezin	166	44	.10	1.39	.50
Radomyshl'	166	37	.12	1.80	.50
pooled Old World data	166	200	.13	6.08	.05

different from those of Berelekh. Likewise, remains found at Mezhirich are also significantly different from those of Berelekh ($\chi^2 = 10.53$; $df = 2$). Remains from Old World Mezin, Dobranichevka, and Radomyshl' and New World Dent and Miami show no significant differences from Berelekh.

The statistical similarity of the majority of both Old and New World mammoth assemblages to both Berelekh and African elephant herd compositions leads me to conclude that no assumptions about taking of mammoth herds in the late Pleistocene are warranted. Vereschagin (1977, 1979, 1981), suggests that whole herds of mammoths could have perished at once—during crossings of thin ice on newly frozen rivers, for example. Under this hypothesis, late Pleistocene mammoth assemblages would reflect natural herds in their demographic profiles—and the Berelekh remains certainly support such an interpretation. This, in turn, implies that the phenomenon of equifinality may play a role in the composition of archaeological faunal assemblages: Both natural mortality and human hunting practices can leave behind the same demographic composition. Therefore, demographic profiles of mammoth remains alone cannot tell us the hunting methods employed by Upper Paleolithic hunters.

Quite obviously, my statistical tests do not exclude the possibility of hunters taking whole herds; rather these tests reduce what both Saunders and Kornietz have claimed as a *probability* to the ranks of *possibility*. That herd taking was a hunting strategy in mammoth exploitation must, at present, remain unproven.

Soviet researchers beginning with Gromov (1948) have suggested that Upper Paleolithic hunters not only hunted mammoth but also collected bone from already dead animals. Current data cannot refute this hypothesis either. If mammoths did indeed perish in herds from time to time during the late Pleistocene, as Vereschagin postulates, then the posthumous utilization of these carcasses could also have brought about the demographic compositions found at the Upper Paleolithic sites of both the Old and New Worlds.

Finally, the statistically different demographic profiles of mammoth at Blackwater Draw ($\chi^2 = 8.86$, $df = 2$) and Murray Springs ($\chi^2 = 9.70$, $df = 2$) compared to Berelekh are more difficult to evaluate. This is because of the classic multiple-sample problem in statistical calculations that at present cannot be controlled for (Blalock 1972). Thus these differences at Blackwater Draw and Murray Springs may, on the one hand, be just sampling aberrations; or, on the other hand, they may point, as Saunders (1980) has argued, to the taking of single individuals (solitary males?). Similar hunting practices may also be evident in mammoth assemblages at Mezhirich and Lehner Ranch as well.

The current state of research on the patterns of mortality of late Pleistocene mammoth does not permit us to discern the effects of particular human activities in the faunal assemblages using demographic profiles alone. This conclusion should also be extended to all speculations about elephant hunting in the Pleistocene (e.g., Freeman 1975 on Torralba–Ambrona). While I do intuitively agree with both Saunders and Kornietz that some mammoths were taken in herds, at present no analytic methods exist that can clearly demonstrate this, and our hypotheses must unfortunately remain "just-so stories"—unproven hypotheses. The abundance of the faunal assemblages in both the Old and New World sites together with documented evidence for taking of large numbers of other species in drives or jumps are documented both in the late Pleistocene and early Holocene (e.g., bison at the Upper Paleolithic site of Amvrosievka, Boriskovskii 1953; wild asses in Middle Paleolithic Staroselye, Lazukov et al. 1981; bison at Olson–Chubbock, Wheat 1972). This evidence argues for the sophistication of hunting skills of late Pleistocene–early Holocene populations. Also, as Saunders (1980) reports, present-day practice in Africa favors cropping of whole herds of elephants over the taking of individuals. This is because of the "mobbing" action of the herd around an injured individual, which prevents both present-day game wardens and, by analogy, past hunters from successfully retrieving their prey. This evidence favors the hypothesis that mammoths were most efficiently exploited in the past by taking whole herds. Our lack of suitable analytic methods for proving this hypothesis speaks for the need of future research on the subject and for the development of sensitive enough methods to distinguish the causes that produced particular demographic profiles in various mammoth assemblages.

Social Implications

The relationship between the type of resources hunted and the strategies employed has been widely explored in the literature. Woodburn, addressing strategies employed in hunting large animals, states that "where the number of hunters is greater, the interval between kills are not only smaller but more equal in length" (1972:199). Wilmsen (1970), in modeling late Pleistocene human ecology, uses patterns observed in predator–prey relationships of nonhuman species to suggest that hunting of concentrated large species is best achieved through group efforts that involve the participation of a number of hunters. Bishop (1973), based on a consideration of data accumulated by Rogers on the Ojibwa, concludes that the number of large game animals taken per capita increases with the number of men participating in the hunt, and that maximal efficiency is attained when 6–7 men are involved. He notes a decline in the number of kills per hunter when this optimal size is decreased or increased. Working with the relationship between group size and information-processing efficiency, Johnson (1982) offers a similar figure, 6 individuals, as a threshold for both comfortable and effective information exchange among egalitarian groups (see Chapter 7 for a fuller discussion of this phenomenon of "scalar stress"). The empirical evidence on the number of hunters involved in Ojibwa hunts conforms nicely to Johnson's observations: Both imply that cooperative hunts involving at least 6 hunters probably occurred during the late Valdai. Cooperative efforts by a number of hunters is implied by the presence of both large-size taxa and the sizable numbers of smaller gregarious herbivores at the sites.

This discussion of the optimal group size for harvesting of gregarious herbivores also carries implications for the size of the coresidential group. The cooperative hunting efforts of 6 to 7 men implies at least during hunting times, a total group size of the coresidential unit of 30 to 35 people (assuming a mean number of 5 individuals per family for each hunter). As numerous authors have pointed out, exploitation of season-ally available large clumps of resources such as gregarious herbivores is a labor-inten-sive activity, as is the processing of the animals killed in such hunts. In those economies in which forms of portable storage were practiced (e.g., the making and transportation of dried meat), such as among the Plains Indians in the New World, the requirement of manpower both for hunting and processing was combined in a short period of time. When the requirements for manpower for hunting is combined with the technology of nonportable storage (i.e., storage pits), we see a multiplication of labor requirements. In such cases, not only is planning and scheduling necessary for the hunt itself but also for construction of storage facilities before or after the hunt. Both Riches (1979) and Schalk (1977) argue that often it is the manpower to process the harvested resources that is the limiting factor among hunter–gatherers.

It could be argued that both Riches and Schalk have considered only manpower limitations in fish harvesting, and that these are unique because harvesting takes place in warm months when the catch must be quickly processed before it spoils. I argue that similar constraints apply to the exploitation of gregarious herbivores. As Wheat (1972) first noted, Paleoindian bison kills in the New World show that large numbers of killed bison were utilized only partially or not at all. Such underutilization has been in-terpreted as indicating a lack of resource management among hunter–gatherers. I suggest that such behavior can better be understood if we take into account manpower limitations.

Unfortunately, no unequivocable kill sites have been found in the study area. The only kill site known from the Upper Paleolithic Russian Plain, Amvrosievka, is located well to the south of the study area. Boriskovskii (1953) reports that over 950 steppe bison were found at the site but offers no information on the extent of butchering. Information on the skeletal elements present at the central Russian Plain sites is also lacking, and thus does not permit consideration of the processing sequences involved in procurement. I have previously suggested that storable resources were procured close to the sites with storage pits. Such synchronization of procurement, processing, and storage in nonmovable facilities would also select for large group size among hunter–gatherers. Specifically, I suggest that while the hunting of large herbivores favored the cooperation of a minimum of 6 to 7 hunters and their families, processing and storage required additional labor input.

This requirement for greater labor input, in turn, favored a decrease in the fluidity in group membership widely reported for some present-day hunter–gatherers. Group fluidity reported by Lee (1979) and Yellen (1977) for the !Kung San has been adopted all too readily as a model for all hunter–gatherers. Individual or family mobility can be anticipated in nonstoring economies where subsistence risk is primarily transferred into various social channels (see Weissner 1982b for a discussion of risk minimization). A reduction of both individual and family mobility can be expected among logistically organized groups who use nonmobile storage for risk minimization.

The origins of storage are a moot question and not germane to this work, since we find evidence for storage in both early (e.g., Berdyzh) and late sites in the study area. What is important, however, is a realization that once storage comes into existence—whether provoked by man–land or man–man factors (or both)—it favors both greater group sedentism and a decrease in fluidity of membership in the coresidential unit.

The relationship between storage and increased sedentism has received a great deal of attention in the literature. Researchers point to a connection between reduced residential mobility, both on an individual family level and on the level of the residential unit itself, and storage (Bender 1978, 1981; Hitchcock 1982; Ingold 1983). I address these points directly and extensively at the end of this chapter, as well as in Chapter 7. I raise the issue here both to classify Upper Paleolithic hunter–gatherers in the study area as logistically organized groups, and to indicate that, given the exploited resources and the use of storage, we can anticipate evidence of greater sedentism in the study area.

Fur Bearers

Fur bearers were exploited extensively in the study area and various parts of these taxa were used to satisfy clothing, raw material, and decorative needs. Carnivorous fur bearers, as well as hares, are differentially distributed in both regions of the central Russian Plain. Difference of means tests (Tables 5.12 and 5.13) on MNI and MNB values show that fur bearers are found at both high and low densities at northern and southern sites. For example, while summed MNI values for arctic fox densities show no overall difference between the northern and southern sites ($z = 0.17$), sites with a high density of fox remains in the north have twice as many individuals ($z = 1.63, p = .10$) as low-density northern sites; in the south, the one high-density site, Mezhirich, has more than four times the number of foxes as the other southern sites ($z = 6.97$).

A comparison of mean wolf densities between the two types of sites in the north and south similarly shows significant differences; four times as many wolves are found at high-density sites in the north ($z = 7.04$) and eight times as many in the southern high-density site ($z = 19.00$) as in the low density sites of each region. Finally, summed data for all fur bearers, including hares, show a similar large difference between the high-

and low-density sites (north MNI, $z = 1.67$; south MNI, $z = 20.14$). High- and low-density differences are summarized in Table 5.26.

Calculation of MNB–MNI correlation coefficients for fur bearers (Table 5.10) both per taxon and summarily shows high positive values for the study area as a whole as well as for northern and southern regions. The r values for arctic fox, for example, are high in both the north and south ($r = .99$ and $r = .96$) (Figure 5.16). Such broad treatment of the data, however, one that divides the area into just two segments, conceals some significant intraregional patterns. High-density northern sites show a correlation coefficient of .99, whereas low-density sites yield a significantly lower value of .27 ($Z = 2.65$).

Table 5.26   FUR BEARERS AT HIGH- AND LOW-DENSITY SITES

Species	Northern sites		Southern sites	
	High density	Low density	High density	Low density
Arctic Fox	Eliseevichi Mezin Timonovka II Yudinovo	Berdyzh Chulatovo II Khotylevo II Pushkari I Suponevo	Mezhirich	Dobranichevka Gontsy Zhuravka
Wolf	Eliseevichi Khotylevo II Mezin Pushkari I, II	Berdyzh Chulatovo II Suponevo Timonovka I, II	Mezhirich	Dobranichevka Gontsy Kirillovskaya
Bear	Chulatovo II Mezin Pushkari II Timonovka II	Berdyzh Chulatovo II Khotylevo II Pushkari I Suponevo Timonovka I	Mezhirich	Dobranichevka Gontsy Kirillovskaya
Wolverine	Khotylevo II Mezin Timonovka II	Eliseevichi	Mezhirich	Dobranichevka Gontsy Kirillovskaya
Hare	Chulatovo II Mezin Pushkari II Timonovka II	Eliseevichi Khotylevo II Suponevo Timonovka I Yudinovo	Mezhirich	Dobranichevka Gontsy Kirillovskaya
All fur bearers	Eliseevichi Mezin	Berdyzh Chulatovo II Khotylevo II Pushkari I, II Suponevo Timonovka I, II Yudinovo	Mezhirich	Dobranichevka Gontsy Kirillovskaya Zhuravka

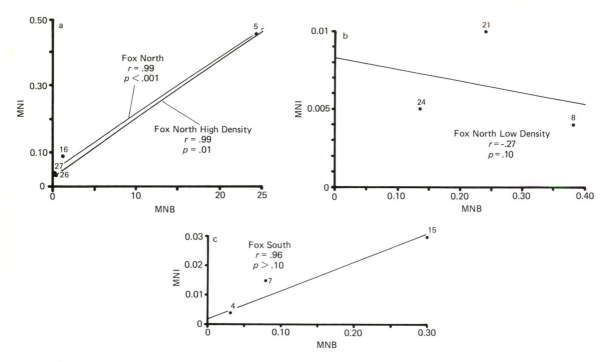

Figure 5.16 Density-controlled MNI and MNB for arctic fox: a, all northern sites and northern high-density sites; b, northern low-density sites; c, all southern sites.

Similar patterning can be observed for all fur bearers, but it is especially strong for two taxa: wolf and arctic fox. These two species are found at much greater densities (MNI and MNB) in both the northern and southern sites than are other fur bearers. Arctic fox, for example, is found at 77% of the northern and 57% of the southern sites at mean densities of $0.07/m^2$ and $0.01/m^2$, respectively. Wolverine, on the other hand, while found at the same percentage of sites in the south (57%), occurs in only 31% of the northern sites, and the mean respective densities are $0.005/m^2$ in the south and $0.006/m^2$ in the north. Similarly low mean densities can be observed for bear, as well as for summarized remains of other fur bearers such as lynx, cave lion, and hyena, which are found individually at a few of the sites.

It can be argued that small sample sizes as well as violation of some important statistical assumptions preclude us from assigning any significance to differences observed in r values and in MNB and MNI statistics. I suggest, however, that the repeated patterning of these values for each taxon evaluated separately, as well as for all fur bearers considered summarily, do reflect past human behavior. I document this patterning per taxon below, but first I offer some plausible hypotheses for such patterning. These, in turn, are evaluated with data from the sites.

A cautionary note should be sounded when dealing with remains of fur bearers. Hare, fox, marmot, and wolf bones were extensively used in the manufacture of bone tools and jewelry; long bones of these taxa were especially favored in tool making. Such use of long bones effectively removed these elements from inventories and left behind, at least at some sites, a disproportionately large number of highly diagnostic elements such as crania, mandibles, teeth, scapulae, pelvises, metapodials, and phalanges. Because of this, I believe that greater weight should be given to MNI values when evaluating the distribution of these taxa. I suspect, for example, that the discrepancies between densities of arctic fox MNI and MNB values at low-density southern and northern sites is due to "noise" generated by such selective removal of long bones (see Tables 5.12 and 5.13 for MNB and MNI values at low-density sites).

Four hypotheses can be proposed to account for the differential distribution of fur bearers in the study area:

1. biogeographic variability in the distribution of the taxa themselves;
2. differences in the season of procurement of the taxa and in the season of occupation of the sites;
3. demographic variability in demand for furs or pelts due to differences in group size and length of occupation at the sites;
4. differential social demands.

Each of these hypotheses carries a number of implications that can be evaluated with the data on hand. Thus, if the biogeographic distribution of the fur bearers was the independent variable and they were taken in direct proportion to their availability near the sites, we would expect both more fur bearers in the north in general and locational differences between high- and low-density sites. If the season of occupation played a decisive role in the accumulation of remains of these taxa in either high or low densities, then we can expect to find evidence for the occupation of the low-density sites in warm months and of the high-density sites during the cold seasons. Demographic variables as the independent variables responsible for the differential distribution of fur bearers imply that low-density sites should show evidence for shorter occupation or smaller group size and high-density sites the opposite.

To evaluate these hypotheses, I assume both similarity in clothing requirements for all groups in the study area and a uniform requirement for pelts or furs per individual. I primarily use data on the arctic fox, because it is found in greater densities at most of the sites than other fur bearers, and because age and sex data on the demographic composition of this taxon are available for some of the sites. The last hypothesis, that social variables are responsible for the observed distribution of some of the fur bearer remains (especially for arctic fox and possibly wolf and hare) is briefly examined in this chapter and evaluated in greater detail in Chapters 6 and 7.

Since we can expect that a number of these variables (i.e., biogeography, seasonality, demographic demands) could have affected the procurement of particular taxa differently, when possible I evaluate the importance of these variables per taxon as well.

Fur-Bearing Taxa

Arctic Fox.   Remains of this taxon have been found at a high proportion of sites in the study area. The correlation coefficients calculated on MNB and MNI values in both the north and south (Table 5.10 and Figure 5.16) show high positive values. Taken overall, the r values indicate that fox was actively hunted all over the study area.

Lack of uniform patterning in the data along the north–south axis excludes the biogeographic hypothesis as a viable explanation for the differential distribution of this taxon. First, as noted previously, no overall differences can be observed between the north and south either in MNB or MNI densities. The differences that do occur are intraregional. Thus, the one high-density southern site, Mezhirich, has a significantly greater number of foxes (MNI and MNB) than the low-density northern sites (MNB, $z = 2.36$; MNI, $z = 11.5$). At the same time, no significant differences exist in either MNB or MNI densities between Mezhirich and the high-density northern sites (MNB, $z = 1.08$, $p = .22$; MNI, $z = 1.38$, $p = .15$).

Age and sex profiles of the arctic fox at both high- and low-density sites appear to be very comparable. The similarity of age profiles of arctic fox at such northern sites as Eliseevichi and Mezin to those at the southern Dobranichevka, Gontsy, and Mezhirich indicates that we can eliminate the season of occupation as the independent variable responsible for its differential distribution.

The proposition that human population is the variable responsible for the observed differences is more difficult to evaluate. The question of population is addressed in detail in Chapter 6, where I argue that group size differences can be monitored at different sites. By and large, sites with high densities of fur bearers are those for which I project a larger population. At the same time, however, there appears to be no direct relationship between the projected population and the density of fox remains. No sizable population differences, for example, can be projected for Dobranichevka and Mezhirich, yet Dobranichevka has few foxes and Mezhirich many. Similarly, while a much smaller group is suggested for Eliseevichi than for Pushkari I, Eliseevichi fox density is significantly higher (MNI = $0.456/m^2$) than at Puskari I (MNI = $0.01/m^2$). These comparisons suggest that population of groups inhabiting the sites is also insufficient to fully account for the differential distribution observed.

I conclude, therefore, that the most viable explanation for the distribution of the arctic fox, and by extension of all fur bearers, is to be found in social relationships and the demands that such relationships generated. I return to this hypothesis and test some of its implications after a brief review of other fur bearers.

Wolf.   Correlation coefficients for wolf (Tables 5.10 and 5.11 and Figure 5.17) show high positive values in southern sites ($r = .99$) and a somewhat lower value in northern sites ($r = .55$). The correlation coefficient calculated for northern high-density sites shows a higher positive value ($r = .88$, p > .1) and a somewhat lower value for low-density sites ($r = .54$). The difference between these r values is not significant, however ($Z = 0.55$). While wolves are found in approximately the same proportion of sites in both regions of the study area (85% in the north and 71% in the south), wolf exploitation appears to have been more intensive at northern sites, as these show three times as many wolves present on MNI comparisons and over 300 times as many wolf bones on MNB values (Tables 5.12 and 5.13). These overall differences probably reflect a different biogeographic distribution of this taxon and are in marked contrast to those observed for arctic foxes.

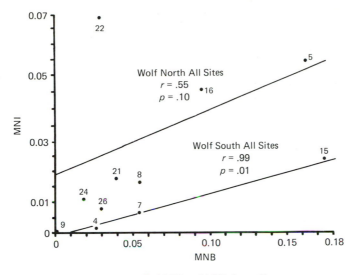

Figure 5.17   Density-controlled MNI and MNB for wolf.

Intraregional differences between the high- and low-density sites observed for arctic foxes are repeated in the distribution of wolves as well. Thus, both northern and southern high-density sites have significantly greater MNI and MNB than low-density sites. Intraregional comparisons show the one high-density southern site, Mezhirich, having fewer wolves (MNI and MNB) than northern high-density sites but more wolves (MNI) than low-density northern sites.

While no age profiles exist for wolves in the study area, both Pidoplichko (1969, 1976) and Vereschagin (1979, 1981) suggest that this taxon was hunted during cold-weather months. In a subsequent discussion, I show that no clear seasonal patterning exists that can account for the differential distribution of wolf remains at the sites.

I interpret the data to indicate that while wolves were opportunistically taken all over the study area, they were more intensively exploited in the north. The differential distribution of wolves within each region, like that of arctic foxes, cannot be adequately explained by biogeography, demographic demands, or seasonal variables alone.

Bear.   While bears have been found in 77% of northern and 57% of southern sites, they have been found at much lower mean densities than either wolves or foxes (Tables 5.8 and 5.9). The r values (Table 5.10 and Figure 5.18) show patterning very similar to that observed for arctic foxes and wolves and support my contention that this taxon was actively hunted throughout the study area. While higher r values come from low-density ($r = .99$) than from high-density sites ($r = .66$) in the north, these differences are not significant ($Z = 1.35$).

Difference of means tests in Tables 5.12 and 5.13 show that while no differences exist in bear densities (either MNB or MNI) between high-density northern and southern sites (MNB, $z = 1.41$; MNI, $z = 1.50$), both have considerably greater densities than do the low-density sites in each region (north MNI, $z = 1.94$, MNB, $z = 2.04$; south MNB,

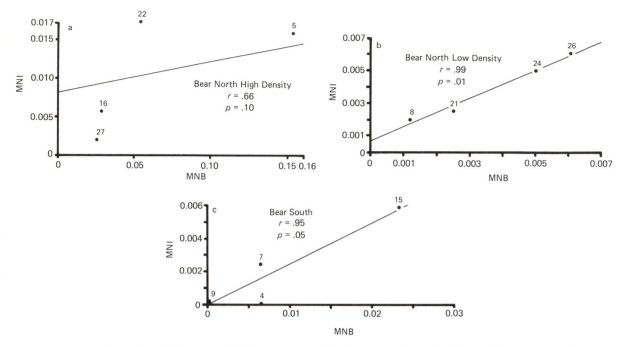

Figure 5.18 Density-controlled MNI and MNB for bear: a, northern high-density sites; b, northern low-density sites; c, all southern sites.

$z = 19.6$, MNI, $z = 6.83$). The fact that low-density northern sites have approximately three times as many bears on MNI counts ($z = 2.0$) as do southern low-density sites leads me to conclude that bears, like wolves, were possibly more abundant in general in the north.

No seasonal data can be inferred from bear remains because of the low density of bears at the sites. The types of bones found, predominantly cranial remains and phalanges, suggest the use of bear skins at sites and are in contrast to the structure of fox and wolf remains, where all skeletal elements are present (Pidoplichko 1976).

I conclude that while bears were actively hunted over the entire study area, their procurement can best be characterized as opportunistic with small numbers taken possibly in proportion to their general densities in the regions.

Wolverine.   The role of wolverines in late Pleistocene economies is difficult to evaluate for a number of reasons. First, as Table 5.7 shows, this taxon was found only at sites with storage pits. I argue in a later discussion that sites with storage pits were occupied during cold-weather months. The exclusive presence of wolverines at cold-weather sites suggests that this taxon was hunted from late fall through late winter. Correlation coefficients calculated on density-controlled MNB and MNI values (Table 5.10 and Figure 5.19) indicate that wolverines were hunted over the entire study area and that the distribution of wolverine remains shows no differences along the latitudinal axis.

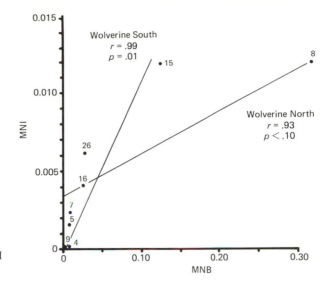

Figure 5.19 Density-controlled MNI and MNB for wolverine.

Intraregional comparisons of the distribution of this taxon shows the existence of both high- and low-density sites in the north and south. Data on density differences calculated from MNI values between high-density sites in the north and south conflict with those from MNB values; while Mezhirich has approximately three times more wolverines than the northern high-density sites of Khotylevo II, Mezin, and Timonovka II (MNI, $z = 10.70$), the northern sites have twice the number of wolverine bone remains (MNB, $z = 238.00$). Similarly, while low-density northern sites do not differ from their equivalents in the south on MNI, significantly greater mean numbers of wolverine bones come from northern low-density sites ($z = 3.57$). At the same time, a smaller proportion of the northern sites (31%) than of the southern sites (57%) has this taxon.

The small sample size of sites precludes me from attaching a behavioral significance to these statistical differences and leads me to conclude that the overall distribution of wolverines broadly conforms to that observed for other carnivores exploited opportunistically in the study area. Differences in the distribution of wolverine remains suggest that this taxon was exploited in proportion to its biogeographic distribution, being taken in greater numbers in cold months and near the sources of its principal prey—mammoth carcasses (see Vereschagin 1979 on wolverine–mammoth predator–prey relationship).

Other Fur-Bearing Carnivores. A small number of cave lions, lynx, weasels, and hyenas have been found at five of the sites. I summarize their densities under the heading "Other fur bearers" in all tables in this chapter. As Tables 5.10–5.13 and Figure 5.20 show, the pattern in their correlation coefficients and mean distribution of both MNI and MNB values are similar to those observed for other fur bearers. In contrast to the fur bearers already discussed, this group does not occur in different densities

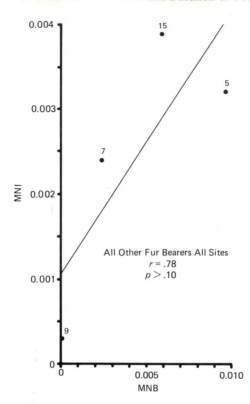

Figure 5.20   Density-controlled MNI and MNB for all other fur bearers, all sites.

intraregionally, and, like wolverines, these taxa are found only at sites with storage pits. They are found at a slightly greater number of sites in the south (43%) than in the north (14%). Since, however, a larger proportion of southern sites have storage pits, higher rates of occurrence of these taxa in the south can best be explained as a function of the season of occupation. In general, I conclude that these fur bearers, while being actively hunted over the entire study area, were opportunistically taken as encountered and were not objects of specific exploitation.

Conclusions on the Exploitation of Fur Bearers

As noted in a previous discussion, one food species, hare, shows interregional differences in distribution which conform to the pattern outlined for fur bearers, suggesting that hares were probably utilized for both food and pelts. Exploitation of hares was especially prevalent in the southern part of the study area, and I concluded that this taxon was actively hunted only in the south. Having presented data on carnivorous fur bearers, I now evaluate the proposition that hare exploitation in the south was conditioned by the desire for pelts.

In Chapter 3 I project optimal hunting for hares in two distinct seasons—late summer (August) if food patch size was being selected for, and late fall or early winter (December) if pelt conditions were of prime value. I have already noted that arctic foxes were probably taken in cold-weather months. Because of this, we can predict that if hares were taken at prime pelt condition—December—their densities should be highly correlated with densities of arctic foxes, whereas if hares were taken in late summer, no positive relationship should be observed between the two. This prediction assumes seasonal occupation of sites, an assumption that is evaluated and confirmed in the concluding section of this chapter.

To test the prediction I calculated the Pearson coefficient of correlation on density-controlled MNI values of arctic fox and hare at southern sites where both taxa were actively hunted. The resulting high positive correlation ($r = .94$, Figure 5.21) supports my hypothesis that hares were taken in cold months. This observation permits us to better understand density differences in the distribution of this taxon at southern sites; simply put, they are southern equivalents of the general pattern observed for all other fur bearers in the north. Of all fur-bearing taxa studied—arctic fox, wolf, bear, wolverine, hare, and grouped infrequent others—all were actively hunted in the south, and all but hare were actively hunted in the north.

I conclude this review by suggesting that we can discern two types of hunting behavior in exploitation of fur bearers: (1) opportunistic or utilitarian, and (2) specialized. The first, which I call "opportunistic exploitation," satisfied clothing, decorative, and industrial needs. Different taxa were exploited to these ends in proportion to their availability in the area; thus, we have more emphasis on hares in the south and greater numbers of wolves and bears in the north. It is this sort of opportunistic

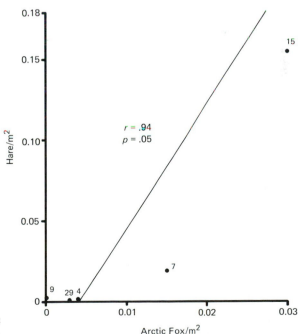

Figure 5.21   Relationship between arctic fox and hare calculated on MNI densities.

exploitation, controlled as it was by both local biogeography and population of local hunter–gatherer groups, that leads to the lack of visible differences in densities of different taxa when overall north and south summed values are compared. It is quite probable that all fur bearers were exploited to meet utilitarian needs, and we can expect that some of the procurement of arctic foxes and wolves also satisfied these needs. To some as yet undetermined extent, some differences observed in the density distribution of fur bearers intraregionally (i.e., between the high- and low-density sites) can be attributed to such factors as population differences and differences in the season of occupation. As I have shown in the discussion of the arctic fox, however, these variables fail to fully account for the observed differences, and social needs have to be considered.

Specifically, I suggest that specialized hunting was also carried on in the study area, focused on procurement of arctic foxes and possibly wolves in the north, possibly hares in the south, and that these taxa were taken in quantities beyond those needed to meet utilitarian needs. The results of this specialized hunting, as noted, can best be seen in the faunal inventories at high-density sites. Thus, as Table 5.12 shows, arctic foxes and wolves are six times as numerous at the high-density northern sites of Eliseevichi and Mezin as at Mezhirich. The density of hares is the exact opposite, with 11 times more hares at Mezhirich than at high-density northern sites (MNI, $z = 43.77$). My conclusions on specialization in hare procurement are more tenuous than for foxes and wolves.

As noted previously, greater densities of fur bearers at some sites cannot be adequately explained by biogeographic or demographic variability. Social relationships have been proposed as an explanation, but before I can evaluate this hypothesis I must examine the relation between high- and low-density sites. To this end, it is interesting to consider whether (1) more intensive hunting and processing went on at the high-density sites in toto, or if (2) high concentrations of fur bearers at these sites resulted from initial hunting and processing at the low-density sites and the transportation of furs or pelts themselves to the high-density sites.

If more hunting per se went on at Eliseevichi, Mezhirich, and Mezin, then we can anticipate finding far greater MNB and MNI per taxon at these sites, as well as most of the skeletal elements of the hunted taxa in their faunal assemblages. The following MNB and MNI have been reported:

Site	Taxon	MNB	MNI	MNB:MNI
Eliseevichi	Arctic fox	15,374	278	55:1
	Wolf	1,045	36	29:1
Mezhirich	Hare	2,633	79	34:1
	Arctic fox	146	11	13:1
	Wolf	89	12	7:1
Mezin	Arctic fox	1,842	112	16:1
	Wolf	1,004	59	17:1

These data, especially for arctic fox at Eliseevichi, tend to confirm the hypothesis that more intensive hunting took place at these sites. The wide range in the MNB:MNI ratios, however, also suggests that factors other than intensive active hunting played a role. To test the second hypothesis—that some of the fur bearers entered high-density sites as prepared furs—I computed the correlation coefficient between fur bearers and fur-processing tools at both high- and low-density fur sites.

In order to work with the largest sample size possible, I compare the relationship between arctic fox MNI and the combined end scraper and burin densities at northern sites. Soviet researchers associate both end scrapers and burins with hide processing as well as with manufacture of bone tools (Filippov 1977; Gvozdover 1974; Leonova 1977; Semenov 1939, 1968). While end scrapers are more directly associated with skin and hide work, and burins with bone work, I combine them for this analysis, assuming that processing of fur and tool manufacture from bones of fur bearers would tend to occur at the same locales. Furthermore, more reliable results can be obtained if larger counts of tool types are used as units of analysis.

Good-quality flint outcrops existed all along the Desna Valley. Upper Paleolithic hunter–gatherers in the region used these outcrops extensively, while those occupying the southern part of the central Russian Plain used lower quality cobble flint. This difference in availability of raw material is widely noted in the Soviet literature and can be expected to have had an effect on the rate of lithic utilization. In general, as Gladkih (1973) and Shovkoplyas (1965a) note, there is a much greater density of lithics as well as a lower overall percentage of tools at northern than at southern sites. They interpret this to indicate that far greater conservation was practiced by southern flint knappers than by their northern equivalents. I test this observation in discussions of interregional differences in Chapter 6. For the purposes of the present discussion, these observations are offered to suggest that we can anticipate finding different lithic–tool density relationships between the southern and northern sites.

Table 5.27 divides the area regionally and lists densities of both lithics and combined end scrapers and burins at the sites. Since I anticipated that there would be a relationship between the numbers of end scrapers and burins and overall lithic densities at the sites, I first tested for the presence of such a relationship in each region. Table 5.27 shows a significant high correlation between these two lithic categories (north $r = .45$; south $r = .90$). In order to control for that proportion of end scrapers and burins due to tool manufacture itself and therefore not related to fur processing and bone manufacture, I calculate the residuals of end scrapers and burins from lithic densities and thus obtained density values for this category of tools that were not related to overall lithic densities or lithic manufacture at the sites.

The relationship between end scraper and burin residuals and density-controlled values of arctic fox (MNI) at northern sites is shown in Table 5.28. While there is a strong negative correlation ($r = -.99$) at high-density fox sites, there is a much weaker and positive correlation at low-density sites ($r = .43$). The difference between these r values (Table 5.30) is significant ($Z = 3.10$) and supports my hypothesis that some pelts reached the high-density fur sites as finished products. A similar positive correlation was also obtained for the end scraper and burin residuals and fox densities at the low-density southern sites ($r = .70, p = .1$).

It could be argued that this observed patterning reflects either seasonal differences in occupation of the sites or improper identification of hide- and pelt-processing tools. The

Table 5.27   END SCRAPER PLUS BURIN (ESB) AND LITHIC DENSITIES

	ESB/m²	Lithics/m²	ESB expected	ESB residuals
North				
Chulatovo II	0.46	13.4	−4.17	4.63
Eliseevichi	0.74	128.4	3.76	−3.02
Kositsa	0.80	20.0	−3.71	4.51
Mezin	2.80	94.4	1.42	1.38
Bugorok	13.90	308.60	16.18	−8.58
Pogon	0.40	400.00	22.48	−22.08
Pushkari I	~1.03	10.60	−4.36	5.39
Pushkari II	0.02	1.50	−4.99	5.01
Timonovka I	4.90	85.00	0.77	4.13
Timonovka II	3.12	85.50	0.80	2.32
South				
Dobranichevka	0.006	0.17	−0.170	0.176
Fastov	0.040	8.60	0.270	−0.230
Gontsy	0.310	3.70	0.015	0.295
Kirillovskaya	0.0004	0.50	−0.150	0.154
Mezhirich	1.300	29.30	1.350	−0.050
Zhuravka	0.060	11.20	0.410	−0.350

Pearson Coefficients of Correlation

	N	df	r	r²	p
North	10	8	.4500	.20	>.10
South	6	4	.8960	.80	.02

first explanation is at odds with data I present in a later discussion on seasonality, where I show that no seasonal differences exist between such high-density sites as Mezhirich and low-density sites as Dobranichevka and Gontsy in the south or high-density northern sites Eliseevichi and Mezin and low-density Pushkari I and Timonovka I. The second explanation is equally untenable. While it is certainly true that much more research is needed on use wear of different lithic tools, sufficient data exist from microwear studies to justify considering end scrapers and burins as pelt- and hide-working tools (Filippov 1977; Moss 1983; Semenov 1939, 1968).

The very small sample sizes I use in all these calculations clearly do not permit me to consider the hypothesis that some fur bearers entered high-density sites as prepared furs as confirmed. Rather, these statistical exercises point out some interesting patterning that can be fully evaluated only by further research. Specifically, if the observed relationships are valid and if we can assume uniform skinning practices that removed heads and feet with hides, we can then anticipate a disproportionately larger number of crania and foot bones at the high-density sites than at the low-density sites, and conversely, a far greater ratio of long bones and other nonextremity parts at the low-density sites.

In general, this discussion has shown that both utilitarian or opportunistic and

Table 5.28 END SCRAPER AND BURIN (ESB) RESIDUALS AND DENSITY-CONTROLLED ARCTIC FOX MNI

	North			South		
	ESB	Fox MNI			ESB	Fox MNI
High Density			*High Density*			
Eliseevichi	−3.02	0.456	Mezhirich		−0.05	0.03
Mezin	1.38	0.094				
Timonovka II	2.32	0.037				
Low Density			*Low Density*			
Chulatovo II	4.63	0.017	Dobranichevka		0.176	0.004
Pushkari I	5.39	0.010	Gontsy		0.295	0.015
Timonovka I	4.13	0.002	Zhuravka		−0.350	0.003

Pearson Correlation Coefficients	N	df	r	r^2	p	slope	intercept
North high-density	3	1	−.9993	.99	.05	−0.080	0.213
North low-density	3	1	.4291	.18	>.1	0.005	−0.014
South low-density	3	1	.6983	.49	>.1	0.014	0.007

Comparison of Correlation Coefficients	N_1	N_2	z_1	z_2	Z	D
North low-density vs. high-density	3	3	−2.467	0.460	3.107	.003
North low-density vs. south low-density	3	3	0.460	0.867	0.407	.37

specialized exploitation of fur bearers existed in the study area in late Pleistocene. I suggest that specialized exploitation of fur bearers was propelled by regional social interactions and that exchange networks existed in the area. Since, as is shown below, these networks greatly intensified through time and are more clearly visible during the second period of occupation, between 18,000 and 12,000 B.P., I return to this hypothesis after reviewing changes in subsistence practices through time.

CHANGES IN SUBSISTENCE STRATEGIES THROUGH TIME

Data from early sites is problematic, and the number of sites possibly dating to this period of occupation woefully small—factors that make the ensuing discussion highly tentative at best. The observed patterning in the data, however, is suggestive and can be used to sketch "just so stories" for future evaluation.

Procurement of Food Taxa

Sample sizes involved do not permit interregional comparison of early sites or an examination of possible differences in hunting practices between early and late sites. Overall, I suggest that the patterning of *r* values per taxon (coefficients of correlation on density-controlled MNB and MNI values) indicates that no significant changes can be monitored in active procurement of different taxa through time. Thus, for example, the correlation coefficient for woolly rhinoceros for the late period in the north ($r = .96$) is not significantly different from that reported for all northern sites ($r = .95$). Correlation coefficients for steppe bison in the south in the late period ($r = .99$) are the same as those for which chronology is not controlled ($r = .99$, $p > .1$).

A comparison of correlation coefficients per taxon (Tables 5.10 and 5.11) between all sites and sites occupied during the late period shows, in general, no significant changes for the following taxa: mammoth, woolly rhinoceros, horse, reindeer, marmot, and the summed food species. I interpret this to indicate that these taxa were actively procured in the area throughout the entire period of occupation.

At the same time that we observed a continuation of the basic subsistence pattern in the area, we can also see a diversification in the food base through time. The following taxa are found only in late sites: red deer, giant deer, deer species, musk-ox, wild boar, beaver, and fish. Hare and birds occur only at one early site, Khotylevo II, whereas they are found at numerous late sites.

We can also see an intensification in gathering behavior through time: Reindeer antlers become more prevalent in the late southern sites and steppe bison tooth remains in the north. This increase in the collection of antlers and teeth depresses the correlation coefficient for each taxon in each region. For example, the MNI–MNB r value for steppe bison from late northern sites is $-.81$ ($p > .1$), whereas it is .59 for all of the southern sites.

Difference of means comparisons between densities of different taxa through time (Table 5.13) also indicate an increase in the exploitation of food species through time. Much greater MNI and MNB of the following species are found in the study area later in time: woolly rhinoceros, horse, steppe bison, and probably birds. This increase is especially evident for woolly rhinoceros values at northern sites, where a five-fold increase in MNI can be observed ($z = 2.49$). And a comparison of densities of horse found at the early and late northern sites shows a six-fold increase (MNI, $z = 1.71$, $p = .09$).

At the same time that we observe changes in the rate of exploitation and monitor the appearance of new food species, other taxa do not show any change in density. Data on mammoth (Table 5.13) indicate no change either regionally or for the study area as a whole in mean densities of either MNB or MNI. Summed data on all food species likewise show no chronological changes either in the northern or southern regions (MNI north, $z = 0.06$; south, $z = 1.58$). For both the early and late periods we can observe the presence of high- and low-food-density sites in the north. In the south, on the other hand, no high-food-density sites exist in the early period—they appear only later. These differences, however, can better be examined for significance and implications if we take energy value (kilocalories) rather than individual animals as our unit of analysis.

Comparisons of the difference in mean kilocalories found at the early and late sites are presented in Table 5.21 and offer values both if no mammoth were taken for food and if half of the mammoths were consumed. Here again, as in previous calculations, the unclear role that mammoths played in subsistence does not permit a formulation of firm conclusions. In general, at both mammoth values, a comparison of energy values available in the north and south during the early period suggests that more kilocalories were available at northern sites (no mammoths, $z = 1.98$). At the same time, no significant differences can be discerned between all early and all late sites (no mammoths, $z = 1.54$; half mammoths, $z = 0.27$). While calculations without mammoth show greater values at northern late sites, calculations with half of the mammoths show more kilocalories available at late southern sites with storage pits. In brief, the evidence is ambiguous and no clear patterning is discerned through time other than more food at early northern sites than at their southern equivalents.

Data from comparisons of MNB, MNI, and energy values indicate the presence of both high- and low-food-density sites in both parts of the study area. All three early sites, Berdyzh, Khotylevo II, and Radomyshl', fall into a group of low-food-density sites if mammoths are omitted from the calculations, whereas with half of the mammoths included, Berdyzh falls into the high-density group. Table 5.29 summarizes the data for sites occupied late, between 18,000 and 12,000 B.P.

While we can anticipate a general increase in both numbers of individuals and taxa through time due solely to taphonomic factors, data from the central Russian Plain do not pattern in such a manner only. Although no changes in overall calories available are indicated, several other deviations in pattern can be monitored—deviations that reflect changes in human behavior through time:

1. Intensification in the exploitation of some taxa, especially gregarious herbivores, and diversification of species harvested for food indicates increased solitary hunting or hunting by smaller groups as well as diversification of harvesting techniques.
2. Increased storage capacity (Table 5.5 shows a three-fold increase in storage volume at late sites: $z = 1.76$, $p = .08$) indicates increases in food preservation by storage.

Table 5.29   HIGH- AND LOW-DENSITY LATE SITES

	North		South	
Site category[a]	Without pits	With pits	Without pits	With pits
Without Mammoth				
High kcal	Chulatovo II Pushkari II	Mezin	—	Mezhirich
Low kcal	Pushkari I	Eliseevichi Suponevo Timonovka I Timonovka II	Fastov Kirillovskaya Zhuravka	Dobranichevka Gontsy
With Half of Mammoth				
High kcal	Pushkari I Pushkari II	Mezin Eliseevichi	—	Mezhirich
Low kcal	Chulatovo II	Suponevo Timonovka I Timonovka II	Fastov Kirillovskaya Zhuravka	Dobranichevka Gontsy

[a]Kilocalories calculated (1) without mammoths and (2) with one half of mammoths.

I offer a number of hypotheses to account for these differences in the context of site typology and settlement system analysis in Chapter 6.

Procurement of Fur Bearers

Because of the small sample size of early sites, no correlation coefficients could be calculated for fur bearers. A comparison of r values per taxon calculated for all northern and southern sites without chronological controls to those calculated per region on late sites (Table 5.10) shows no significant differences. For example, the r value for arctic fox is .99 at all northern sites and .99 at late northern sites. The correlation coefficient for wolverine is .93 in all northern sites and .93 ($p = .1$) for the late northern sites. While no fur bearers have been found at the only early southern site, Radomyshl', this site's singularity and the poor preservation of its fauna make this observation statistically insignificant. The majority of evidence indicates that fur bearers were actively hunted over the entire study area throughout the entire Upper Paleolithic period.

Table 5.30 summarizes frequency data on the exploitation of all fur bearers in the northern region in both early and late periods, and Table 5.31 further analyzes the late-period data into southern and northern areas. All calculations are based on MNI and MNB mean values in Table 5.13. In general, these tables show both an increase through time in the exploitation of fur bearers in the study area as a whole and an increase in the numbers of these taxa at northern sites. With the exception of wolverines, there is an overall increase in the proportion of sites exploiting fur bearers. And while the densities of some species show no change through time, other taxa are present in greater numbers in the late sites. For example, mean MNI values for bear and arctic fox at the low-density northern sites do not show an increase through time (bear, $z = 0.26$; arctic fox, $z = 0.12$). Wolves, on the other hand, show a two-fold increase in MNI densities at the late low-density northern sites (MNI, $z = 1.63$, $p = .10$). Such increases at low-density sites can best be interpreted as intensification of opportunistic exploitation of fur bearers.

Table 5.30   EXPLOITATION OF FUR BEARERS: NORTHERN SITES

| | Early | | | | | | Late | | | | | |
| | | % of MNI | | % of MNB | | | | % of MNI | | % of MNB | |
	Number of sites	% of sites	high density	low density	high density	low density	Number of sites	% of sites	high density	low density	high density	low density
Arctic fox	2	67	0	50	0	67	8	73	100	50	100	33
Wolf	2	67	20	33	50	nd	9	82	80	67	50	nd
Wolverine	1	33	33	0	92	0	3	27	67	100	8	100
Bear	2	67	0	50	0	20	9	82	100	50	100	80
Hare	1	33	0	50	0	60	8	73	100	50	100	40
Summed all fur bearers	2	67	0	50	0	67	9	82	100	50	100	33

Table 5.31   EXPLOITATION OF FUR BEARERS: LATE SITES

| | North | | | | | | South | | | | | |
| | | | % of MNI | | % of MNB | | | | % of MNI | | % of MNB | |
	Number of sites	% of sites	high density	low density	high density	low density	Number of sites	% of sites	high density	low density	high density	low density
Arctic fox	8	73	50	50	50	75	3	43	50	50	50	25
Wolf	9	82	67	50	80	50	4	57	33	50	20	50
Wolverine	3	27	75	50	67	67	4	57	25	50	33	33
Bear	9	82	67	50	80	50	4	57	33	50	20	50
Hare	8	73	8	50	0.5	50	4	57	92	50	99.5	50
Summed all fur bearers	9	82	50	50	50	83	4	57	50	50	50	17

With the exception of Khotylevo II, all early sites have fur bearers present in low densities. Khotylevo II does not fit this pattern—both wolverine and wolf are there in high densities. While Khotylevo II is poorly known in the literature and is still undergoing excavation, its uniqueness in both features and assemblages has drawn much attention from Soviet researchers. Zavernyaev (1978) writes that, stylistically, Khotylevo II lithics best resemble those found at the Kostenki–Borschevo early sites. Gvozdover (1982, personal communication) states that Khotylevo II *art mobiliere* and engravings place the site in the Kostenki–Avdeevo culture. As I show in Chapter 6, the features found at this site as well as the nature of its living floor are also more similar to those of Kostenki–Borschevo sites than to any found in the study area. While it is too early to assign this site either to a different culture or a different settlement system than the other Dnepr–Desna sites, there is enough data to warrant its consideration as unique to the study region and not representative of the overall Dnepr–Desna pattern.

Omitting Khotylevo II from the discussion, we see that the sites with high densities of fur bearers, especially those where particular attention was paid to the procurement of arctic fox, wolf, and hare, date to the late period of occupation in both the north and south. Khotylevo II notwithstanding, sites with a high fox density date only to the late period of occupation, and wolf density increases from the early to the late period. A comparison of mean wolf densities on MNI counts shows a four-fold increase in the north high-density late sites ($z = 3.60$).

I conclude, therefore, that the following changes in the exploitation of fur bearers can be observed through time:

1. a moderate increase in opportunistic exploitation of all fur bearers;
2. a rise of specialized exploitation of fur bearers with particular emphasis on the procurement of arctic fox and possibly wolf and hare;
3. a differentiation of the distribution of fur bearers which resulted in the existence of both high- and low-density fur sites in both the northern and southern regions of the central Russian Plain.

SEASONALITY OF OCCUPATION

The nature of occupation at different Upper Paleolithic sites in the study area—whether year-round or seasonal—has not received serious attention. Soviet researchers, relying heavily on sheer volume of presumed food remains and assuming that what was found at the sites represented just a portion of food taken, have generally concurred that many of the sites (especially those with dwellings and storage pits) were occupied by fully sedentary groups who remained at the settlements for decades (Bibikov 1969; Pidoplichko 1969, 1976; Shovkoplyas 1965a). Pidoplichko (1969:148), using meat weight estimates, postulates the following lengths of uninterrupted occupation for the sites: Dobranichevka, 8 years; Gontsy, 9 years; Kivillovskaya, 7 years; Mezhirich, 20 years; Mezin, 8 years. Other Soviet researchers, citing the presence of particular taxa at the sites that were presumably harvested in different seasons, have also argued also for year-round occupation of the sites. Kornietz *et al.* (1981) for example, cite the presence of reindeer to indicate fall, birds for spring to fall, and fur bearers for winter occupation of Mezhirich. English-language literature on the area has either repeated Soviet conclusions or avoided the issue altogether (see Klein 1973; Shimkin 1978; but also see Sklenar 1975, 1976). Researchers working at more ephemeral Upper Paleolithic sites in the area (those lacking storage pits and dwellings) have, on the other hand, presumed that such sites as Chulatovo II, Fastov, Pushkari II, and Zhuravka were seasonal occupations (Boriskovskii 1953; Boriskovskii and Praslov 1964; Leonova 1977; Voevodskii 1952a).

All of these uni- and multiseasonal estimates have been based either on intuitive guesses or very problematic assumptions. Estimates of duration of occupation based solely on available kilograms of meat have met strong criticism on both sides of the Atlantic (Guilday 1970; Vereschagin 1971, 1981). Determination of the season or seasons of occupation based on the recognition of a few elements of a few small taxa are equally untenable.

Faunal remains have been extensively used in archaeology as indicators of the season of occupation. The rationale for such uase of faunal data is too well known to warrant a discussion (Chaplin 1971; Gilbert 1973; Monks 1981). Faunal data in and of themselves, however, do not offer clear and unequivocal solutions to the problem of seasonality. This is because a number of behavioral stances can profoundly distort information on seasonality. This problem is especially acute when dealing with hunter–gatherers who also practice food storage. Binford (1980, 1981, 1982) describes the distortions that such practices can introduce into the faunal record of sites. The most obvious example of distortion we can expect in the study area is that remains of taxa found in storage pits may reflect hunting that took place during different seasons than when the sites were occupied. To control for possible distortions, I have compiled evidence on the season of occupation from a number of different sources, including faunal remains, density of indoor and outdoor hearths at the sites, abundance of fur bearers, as well as altitude of the sites above the floodplain. Finally, because of the nature of data on hand, I distinguish only two seasons in the study area: warm-weather (May–September) and cold-weather (October–April) months. Final conclusions on seasonality are compiled in Table 5.43.

DIVERSITY INDEX

Ecologists have long used a diversity index or information statistic in comparing populations inhabiting different environments in terms of both the numbers of categories (species) present and the distribution of the population within each category (MacArthur and MacArthur 1961; Odum 1971; Pielou 1969). Of a number of indices available, two in particular have achieved great popularity—Simpson's diversity index, which tends to favor the more abundant species, and the Shannon (or Shannon–Weiner) diversity index, which favors the rarer species.

Archaeologists have primarily used these indices, especially the Shannon index, to examine similarities and differences in lithic, ceramic, or portable art inventories (Conkey 1980; De Boer and Moore 1982; Kintigh 1984; Yellen 1977). Yessner (1977) has used the Shannon index on faunal data from Aleutian sites as a way of comparing richness or diversity in the subsistence bases.

I calculate the diversity index on the proportions of taxa found in assemblages at the sites. The mechanics of the application of this index are discussed at length in Zar (1974:35–38, 115–117), who also presents a way of testing the difference between the diversity indices. Shannon's basic formula for the calculation of the index is

$$H = -\sum_{i=1}^{k} p_i \log p_i$$

where k is the number of categories and p_i the proportion of the observations found in category i. Inasmuch as H is affected by number of categories as well as distribution, *relative* diversity, J, is used to express observed diversity as a proportion of maximum possible diversity: $J = H/H_{max}$.

Hutcheson (see Zar 1974:115–116) has developed the following t test for comparing two H values:

$$t = \frac{H_1 - H_2}{s_{H_1 - H_2}}$$

The degrees of freedom associated with this t test are approximated by

$$v = \frac{(s_{H_1}^2 + s_{H_2}^2)^2}{\dfrac{(s_{H_1}^2)^2}{n_1} + \dfrac{(s_{H_2}^2)^2}{n_2}}$$

The range for both the H and J statistic are from 0 to 1.0 with the higher values reflecting greater diversity. In the ensuing discussion, I use the J values. The H statistics are used only for comparison when t tests are calculated between different indices.

Ethnographic literature on hunter–gatherers in northern latitudes amply documents a great diversity in food resources available during the warm months and a reduction in this diversity during cold weather (Binford 1981; Boas 1964; Helm 1968; Jochim 1976; Keene 1981; Nelson 1971). Because of this, I assume that, all other things being equal, fauna caught during warm months should produce a higher diversity index than that caught during the cold season in northern latitudes and, by extention, in the study area as well. To test the validity of this assumption, I calculated the H and J values on ethnographic data first.

Binford and Chasko (1976:102) offer data on game taken by a Nunamiut hunter from June 1950 through May 1951. I retabulated their data into categories suitable for the calculation of the index by dividing their month by month record into groupings of taxa taken during the cold October–March months and those taken in the warm April–September season. These retabulations are presented in Table 5.32, as are the H and J values calculated on both MNI values and kilocalories per taxon. As this table shows, the choice of energy value rather than MNI as the unit of analysis does not significantly alter the indices (cold MNI, $H = .27$; cold kcal, $H = .32$; warm MNI, $H = .68$; warm kcal, $H = .52$). A comparison of H values between the warm and cold seasons gives $t = 3.80$ at $v \cong 200$ and $p < .001$. As Table 5.32 shows, the two indices discriminate the season of harvest well.

A second test for the diversity index as a seasonal indicator is presented in Table 5.33. Data on the Ojibwa come from Jochim (1976) and have again been recalculated into energy values per taxon as the unit of analysis. While the Ojibwa H indices for both cold and warm months were considerably lower than those for the Nunamuit data (cold, $H = .005$; warm, $H = .12$), the t test shows a significant difference between them ($t = -2.08$, $v \cong 115$, $p = .05$).

Table 5.32   NUNAMIUT HUNTING RECORD, 1950–1951[a]

Species	kcals per individual	Cold weather (October–March)		Warm weather (April–September)	
		N (%)	Total kcals (%)	N (%)	Total kcals (%)
Caribou	80,500	279 (89.4)	22,459,500 (87.7)	173 (72.7)	13,926,500 (67.2)
Sheep	86,487	30 (9.7)	2,594,610 (10.1)	42 (17.6)	3,632,454 (17.4)
Bear	272,400	2 (0.6)	544,800 (2.1)	10 (4.2)	2,724,000 (13.1)
Moose	407,000	0 —	— —	1 (0.4)	407,000 (1.9)
Squirrel	1,000	0 —	— —	4 (1.7)	4,000 (0.1)
Marmot	1,800	1 (0.3)	1,800 (0.1)	8 (3.4)	14,400 (0.3)
		312 (100)	25,600,710 (100)	238 (100)	20,708,354 (100)

Comparison of Diversity Indices

	Cold			Warm					
	J	H_1	N_1	J	H_2	N_2	v	t	p (two-tailed)
MNI	.16	.27		.53	.68				
kcal	.19	.32	4	.41	.52	6	~200	3.8023	<.001

[a]After Binford and Chasko (1976: Tab. 22). Live weights, edible weights, and kilocalories per kilogram of taxa taken from Klein (1969), except for squirrel (assume 1 kg and 1000 kcal/kg) and marmot (see Table 5.17).

Table 5.33   OJIBWA FOOD HARVEST RECORD[a]

		Cold weather (October–March)			Warm weather (April–September)		
Species	kcals per individual	Food taken (kg)	Total kcals (%)		Food taken (kg)	Total kcals (%)	
Moose	320,000	132,448.97	4.2384×10^{10} (99.93)		3447.30	1.103×10^9 (96.85)	
Beaver	4,000	4,277.38	17,109,480 (0.04)		3669.56	14,678,240 (1.28)	
Fish	1,300	3,964.40	5,153,720 (0.01)		10332.83	13,432,679 (1.19)	
Small game	1,800	5,320.64	9,577,152 (0.02)		4322.76	7,780,968 (0.68)	
			4.2416×10^{10} (100)			1.1390×10^9 (100)	

Comparison of Diversity Indices

	Cold			Warm					
J	H_1	N_1		J	H_2	N_2	v	t	p (two-tailed)
.003	.005	4		.07	.12	4	~115	−2.08	.05

[a]After Jochim (1976: Tab. 10). In calculating values in this table, I omit some unquantifiable entries in Jochim (1976). I eliminate approximately the same amount of kilograms from both the cold and warm seasons: cold—1918.70 kg; warm—2059.31 kg. Caloric values per taxon from Jochim (1976: 42–43).

Having tested the assumption that the diversity index can be a powerful tool in discerning seasonality at sites, I proceeded to calculate the H and J statistics for all undisturbed sites in the study area using density-controlled energy values per taxon as the unit of analysis (Table 5.34). In these calculations I include only those taxa that were procured by active hunting. Also, since mammoth remains an ambiguous food source, I calculate the indices for each site at three levels of mammoth inclusion: none, half, and all.

A number of qualifying factors should be mentioned before examining the indices. While the index is sensitive to the season of procurement, other independent variables can also affect it. For example, a low density index at sites without storage pits can reflect either the hunting season or exploitation of just one resource. Thus, both weather and specialization in procurement can result in a low index. At sites with storage pits, on the other hand, a low diversity index does not necessarily reflect a cold season of occupation; the practice of storing one or a few abundant resources caught during the warm season will also result in a low index. In general then, the index should be seen as a heuristic or exploratory device—one that will give first approximations within a particular region. These seasonal estimates should then be checked against other independent data.

In calculating the H and J values, I deal cumulatively with taxa present in very small quantities (those listed in Table 5.19 as insignificant). I assign each taxon so listed an arbitrary proportion of 0.01. For example, in the calculation of the index for Mezin (omitting mammoth), the following proportions were obtained:

Species	p_i (Proportion)
Horse	50.00
Woolly rhinoceros	16.00
Reindeer	21.00
Musk-ox	10.00
Giant deer	1.00
Wild boar	1.00
Marmot	0.01
Bird	0.01

Since the diversity index is sensitive only to the number of categories or species and to the distribution of individuals per taxon, and as both statistics are also available for the severely disturbed and redeposited sites, I also calculate the H and J values for those sites. As with the undisturbed sites, I first convert the MNI per taxon values (without controlling for density) into kilocalories per taxon and then estimate for each taxon a proportional contribution. These calculations, as well as values for summarized kilocalories available per site at the three mammoth densities, are given in Tables 5.35 and 5.36. The H and J values for the disturbed sites are listed in Table 5.37.

As noted before, some Soviet researchers have hypothesized migratory behavior for

Table 5.34   DIVERSITY INDEX AT UNDISTURBED SITES[a]

Site	Without mammoths		With half mammoths		With all mammoths	
	H	J	H	J	H	J
Berdyzh	.36	.75	.03	.05	.01	.02
Chulatovo II	.23	.33	.41	.59	.36	.51
Dobranichevka	.24	.31	.08	.09	.06	.07
Eliseevichi	.46	.77	.01	.02	.01	.02
Fastov	0	0	.07	.02	.04	.13
Gontsy	.25	.42	.05	.08	.03	.05
Khotylevo II	.09	.29	nd	nd	nd	nd
Kirillovskaya	.0004	.001	.046	.09	.007	.01
Mezhirich	.34	.48	.04	.05	.02	.02
Mezin	.56	.62	.23	.24	.10	.10
Pushkari I	.30	.62	.01	.02	.01	.02
Pushkari II	.16	.34	.13	.21	.08	.13
Radomyshl'	.26	.54	.01	.02	.01	.02
Suponevo	.24	.40	.15	.22	.08	.11
Timonovka I	0	0	.02	.08	.02	.08
Timonovka II	0	0	.03	.01	.03	.01
Zhuravka	.36	.75	.36	.75	.36	.75

[a]Calculated on percentages of calories per taxon per square meter.

Table 5.35   KILOCALORIES PER TAXON AT DISTURBED SITES

	Chulatovo I	Kurovo	Novgorod-Severskii	Novo-Bobovichi	Yurovichi
Mammoth—all	39,600,000	3,600,000	54,000,000	39,600,000	63,000,000
Mammoth—half	19,800,000	720,000	27,000,000	19,800,000	31,500,000
Rhinoceros	2,520,000	2,520,000	16,380,000	—	—
Horse	400,200	200,100	1,600,800	—	200,100
Wild Cattle	—	—	—	—	367,000
Reindeer	360,000	—	1,500,000	—	—
Marmot	3,600	—	55,800	—	—
Fish	2,600	—	57,200	—	—
Birds	—	—	140,000	—	—
Totals with					
all mammoth	42,886,400	6,320,100	73,733,800	39,600,000	63,567,100
half mammoth	23,086,400	3,440,100	46,733,800	19,800,000	32,067,100
no mammoth	3,286,400	2,720,100	19,733,800	0	567,100

Table 5.36   PERCENTAGE OF KILOCALORIES AT DISTURBED SITES

	Chulatovo I	Kurovo	Novgorod-Severskii	Novo-Bobovichi	Yurovichi
Excluding Mammoth					
Rhinoceros	76	93	83	—	—
Horse	12	7	8	—	35
Wild Cattle	—	—	—	—	65
Reindeer	11	—	8	—	—
Marmot	ins[a]	—	ins	—	—
Fish	ins	—	ins	—	—
Birds	—	—	ins	—	—
Including Half Mammoth					
Mammoth	85	21	58	100	98
Rhinoceros	11	73	35	—	—
Horse	2	6	3	—	ins
Wild Cattle	—	—	—	—	1
Reindeer	1	—	3	—	—
Marmot	ins	—	ins	—	—
Fish	ins	—	ins	—	—
Birds	—	—	ins	—	—
Including All Mammoth					
Mammoth	92	57	73	100	99
Rhinoceros	6	40	22	—	—
Horse	1	3	2	—	ins
Wild Cattle	—	—	—	—	ins
Reindeer	ins	—	2	—	—
Marmot	ins	—	ins	—	—
Fish	ins	—	ins	—	—
Birds	—	—	ins	—	—

[a]ins < 0.9%.

Table 5.37   DIVERSITY INDEX AT DISTURBED SITES[a]

Sites	All mammoth		Half mammoth		No mammoth	
	H	J	H	J	H	J
Chulatovo I	.13	.16	.22	.29	.31	.44
Kurovo	.34	.71	.31	.64	.11	.37
Novgorod-Severskii	.32	.38	.40	.48	.25	.30
Novo-Bobovichi	—	—	—	—	—	—
Yurovichi	.007	.01	.03	.06	.28	.93

[a]Calculated on MNI percentages of calories per taxon per site.

gregarious herbivores of the late Pleistocene central Russian Plain that would have placed the taxa only seasonally in the northern or southern regions of the study area (Pidoplichko 1969, 1976; Vereschagin 1979). Kornietz (1962) postulates a latitudinal migration pattern for some herbivores that would have made these taxa available only seasonally in the river valleys. Finally, in my own reconstruction of the behavior of some taxa in the study area (Chapter 3), I also hypothesize that seasonal migrations would place some taxa in the north of the study region during the warm months and in the south in the cold season. There are a number of interesting archaeological implications from these projections that can be tested with the diversity index. Specifically, we can hypothesize that if some herbivores were available in the north only during warm months and in the south during the cold seasons, then the hunter–gatherers exploiting them may also have been seasonally mobile—living in the north during the warm months and in the south in the fall and winter. If this was the settlement pattern during the Upper Paleolithic, then the diversity index for the northern sites should be higher than for the southern sites.

Cumulative indices for the northern and southern sites at the three levels of mammoth inclusion are presented in Table 5.38. All undisturbed sites are included in these calculations without consideration of possible chronological differences. No significant differences are found in the H values between the north (H_1) and the south (H_2) with all the mammoths included ($H_1 = .08, H_2 = .05, t = 0.57$), or with half of the mammoths included ($H_1 = .12, H_2 = .05, t = 1.32$). The only significant difference in the H values

Table 5.38   HUTCHESON t TEST ON DIFFERENCES IN DIVERSITY INDICES

	N_1	N_2	J_1	J_2	H_1	H_2	v	t	p (two-tailed)
Northern (1) vs. Southern (2) Sites									
No mammoth	13	10	.36	.59	.40	.59	~200	2.92	.005
Half mammoth	14	11	.11	.05	.12	.05	200	1.32	.20
All mammoth	14	11	.07	.05	.08	.05	~200	0.57	.50

emerged in calculations when no mammoths were included, showing that the H values for the north ($H_1 = .40$) were significantly *lower* than for the south ($H_2 = .59$, $t = 2.92$).

The conclusions from these regional comparisons are ambiguous at best since, once again, the uncertain role that mammoths played in the economies prevents me from selecting a specific index as the more significant one. Overall, however, the tests do strongly suggest that we can exclude seasonal migration as an explanation for the settlement system and exploitation strategies. I have arbitrarily selected to use the values obtained if half of the mammoths are included in the calculations in all future evaluations in this chapter.

Figure 5.22 graphically presents the distribution of the J values of all sites, dividing the study area into northern and southern regions. As this figure shows, sites with high indices (warm-weather occupations) are found in both the north and south. Figure 5.22 also shows that the sites with mammoth-bone dwellings all have relatively low diversity indices, suggesting that these sites were occupied during the cold season.

I tested the association of sites with low indices ($J < .20$) and sites with dwellings using the measures of association (ϕ) and the Fisher exact test. The results show a strong positive association between sites with dwellings and low diversity indices ($\phi = .47, p = .05$, see Table 5.2). I conclude, therefore, that sites with dwellings appear to have been occupied during the cold months.

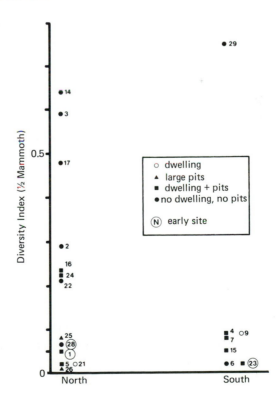

Figure 5.22   Diversity indices: regional distribution.

Diversity indices could be calculated for only three of the early sites with 50% of mammoths included. All three, Berdyzh, Radomyshl', and Yurovichi, have a low index, suggesting occupation during cold months. Berdyzh and Radomyshl' also have remains of mammoth-bone dwellings. Since mammoths found at Khotylevo II have not been quantified, no index could be calculated for the site including this taxon. The site yields a relatively low index when calculated without mammoths. We can anticipate that its index would be equally low with half of the mammoths included as well. Khotylevo II's J value is considerably lower than the values for Berdyzh, Radomyshl', and Yurovichi (without mammoths) and would remain equally low with half the mammoths counted. This suggests that Khotylevo II was also occupied during cold months.

Figure 5.22 shows that most of both northern and southern sites with storage pits and dwellings occupied during the late period have low J values; the two exceptions are Mezin and Suponevo in the north. Sites without dwellings or storage pits in both the north south, on the other hand, have either very low or very high indices. I have previously discussed different behavioral variables that would affect the index and suggested that while high indices in general would reflect warm-weather occupation, low values could also be generated by specialized exploitation of one resource. I suspect that this indeed is the reason for low values at Fastov and possibly Pushkari II. I interpret the high indices at the other sites without storage pits and without dwellings as indicating warm-weather occupation.

In general, Figure 5.22 shows a greater diversity in the north, where we can monitor the presence of numerous cold- and warm-weather occupations. Only one site in the south, Zhuravka, has produced a high index indicating warm-weather occupation. At first glance, the differential distribution of warm-weather sites in the north and south appears interesting. However, as I have argued previously, the diversity index itself is ambiguous, and low values can also be generated by specialized exploitation of one resource.

When dealing with the diversity indices from the Upper Paleolithic central Russian Plain sites, we also have to consider the effect of climatic fluctuations. The J values were calculated without considering such fluctuations. As I show in Chapter 4, the sites cannot be unequivocally assigned to a specific cold or warm fluctuation. It could, therefore, be argued that the presence of cold- and warm-weather occupations in the north date to a warm interstade and the cold-weather occupations in the south to a cold interstade. This suggestion implies a latitudinal shift in settlements through time as a response to climatic fluctuations. As I show in Chapter 3, biological data on the climate at the time of occupation are sparce and often contradictory. What data are available have been plotted against the diversity indices of the sites in Figure 5.23 for the north and south separately. Climatic ratings from "warm" (1) to "cold" (4) have been presented and discussed in Chapter 3.

As this figure shows, the data do not support the hypothesis of a shift of settlement systems along the latitudinal gradient during the warm and cold interstades as an adequate explanation for the distribution of cold-weather sites in the study area. Sites with dwellings in the south, such as Dobranichevka and Gontsy, were occupied during a warm climate phase. In the north, Mezin, with its relatively high diversity index, was

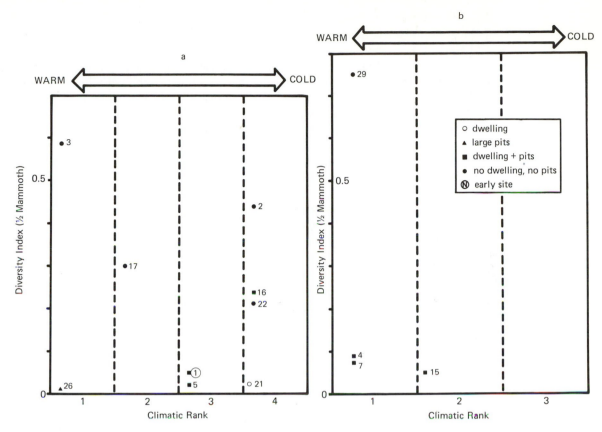

Figure 5.23 Diversity index and climatic ranking of the sites: a, northern sites; b, southern sites.

occupied during a cold climate phase. Both Eliseevichi and Pushkari I, with mammoth-bone dwellings and low diversity indices, also seem to date to a cold climatic episode.

Quite clearly we cannot, at present, fully reject the hypothesis that the north and south were occupied only seasonally. Much work remains to be done on chronologies as well as on climatic reconstruction before it can be fully demonstrated that year-round occupation occurred in both the north and south of the study area. The data I have presented, however, indicate just such a conclusion, with sites with dwellings in both parts of the study area being occupied during the cold season and those without dwellings or storage pits being occupied during warm weather.

SEASON OF OCCUPATION BASED ON TAXA EXPLOITED

Food Taxa

In Chapter 3 I discuss the ecology of some of the more abundant taxa found at the sites and project an optimal time for their harvesting. These projections are listed in

Table 3.18. For the purpose of this discussion, I assume that species taken were hunted at the season of their greatest abundance.

In some cases, especially when dealing with small taxa such as hare and marmot, finer estimations of the season of actual hunting can be obtained. Evidence earlier in this chapter (see pp. 318–320) suggests that hares were taken in early winter (possibly December), when their pelts were in optimal condition. Similarly, since arctic fox was hunted in late winter (p. 190), I can test the hypothesis that marmots were taken in late summer and early fall. If the sites in the study area were seasonally occupied and if marmots were taken in late summer, then we could expect to find a negative correlation between the MNI of marmot and fox. Their scatter plot and regression line (Figure 5.24) show such a negative correlation ($r = -.46, p > .1$), although the sample size ($N = 6$) is too small for this correlation to be statistically significant. I interpret this correlation as a confirmation of my hypothesis that marmots were taken in warm-weather months while they were out of their burrows.

In order to estimate the season of occupation of the sites based on the food taxa exploited, I first eliminate both mammoth and woolly rhinoceros from consideration, as these taxa offer no information on the season of exploitation. Second, I also exclude fish and birds, since they are subjects of separate analyses. I group the taxa per season of exploitation (warm or cold weather) where such estimates can be made, and I also create a third category of species that cannot be assigned to a particular season of exploitation. The units of analysis for this exercise are density-controlled kilocalories per taxon at the undisturbed sites and MNI counts converted to kilocalories per taxon for the severely disturbed and redeposited sites. New values for kilocalories per site (without mammoth and woolly rhinoceros) are then calculated and proportional weights assigned to the different taxa (Table 5.39). The final column in this table lists, in

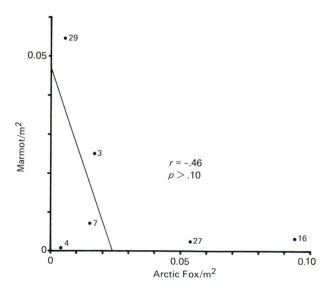

Figure 5.24 Co-occurrence of marmot and arctic fox calculated on MNI densities.

Table 5.39   PROPORTIONAL CONTRIBUTION OF FOOD TAXA TYPED PER OPTIMAL SEASON FOR HARVESTING[a]

| | Optimal season for harvesting | | | | | | | | | | | | |
| | Cold season (%) | | | | | Warm season (%) | | | | No data on optimal season (%) | | | |
Sites	Red deer	Deer sp.	Giant deer	Reindeer	Hare	Horse	Bison	Marmot	Boar	Wild cattle	Musk-ox	Beaver	Season of occupation
Berdyzh	—	—	—	—	—	37	—	—	—	63	—	—	nd + W
Chulatovo I	—	—	—	70	—	—	—	30	—	—	—	—	C + W
Chulatovo II	—	—	—	46	—	52	—	2	—	—	—	—	W + C
Dobranichevka	—	—	—	—	—	—	97	ins	—	—	2	—	W + nd
Eliseevichi	39	—	—	11	—	46	—	—	—	—	—	—	C + W
Fastov	—	—	—	—	—	100	—	—	—	—	—	—	W
Gontsy	—	—	—	—	1	—	27	ins	71	—	—	—	nd + W
Kirillovskaya	—	—	—	—	100	—	—	—	—	—	—	—	C
Mezhirich	—	—	—	—	6	9	76	—	7	—	—	—	W + nd + C
Mezin	—	—	ins	25	—	60	—	ins	—	—	12	—	W + C + nd
Novgorod-Severskii	—	—	—	39	—	13	—	48	—	—	—	—	W + C
Pushkari I	16	—	—	7	—	77	—	—	—	—	—	—	W + C
Pushkari II	—	—	—	21	—	79	—	—	—	—	—	—	W + C
Radomyshl'	—	—	—	—	—	28	—	ins	—	71	—	—	nd + W
Suponevo	—	—	—	23	—	76	—	—	—	—	—	—	W + C
Timonovka I	—	—	—	100	—	—	—	—	—	—	—	—	C
Timonovka II	—	—	—	100	—	—	—	—	—	—	—	—	C
Yudinovo	—	some	some	some	—	—	—	some	—	—	—	some	C + W
Yurovichi	—	—	—	—	—	50	—	—	—	50	—	—	W + nd
Zhuravka	—	—	—	—	—	—	—	4	45	51	—	—	nd + W

[a] Calculated without mammoth and woolly rhinoceros; ins < 0.9%; nd = no data on optimal season for harvesting; W = warm-weather months; C = cold-weather months. In some cases where fish or birds contributed more than 1.0% of calories, summed percentages for the site are below 100.

order of magnitude, the season or seasons of occupation based on the data in the table. For example, the entry for Chulatovo II, where 46% of kilocalories come from reindeer harvested during the cold months and 54% come from taxa hunted during the warm months, is listed in the last column as W + C. Berdyzh, on the other hand, where 37% of kilocalories come from warm-weather hunting and 63% from hunting during an undeterminable season, is listed as W + nd (no data).

The resulting seasonal indications are ambiguous at best. As I have discussed previously, in storage economies one can anticipate a lack of clear seasonality at sites where storage is practiced. What the seasonal indications do reveal, however, is a prevalence of multiseasonal fauna at sites with dwellings and storage pits and uniseasonal fauna at sites without such features. I tested the association of sites with dwellings with the presence of multiseasonal faunas, as well as the association of sites with storage pits with multiseasonal faunas. The results of the Fisher exact test and the φ values are listed in Table 5.2. As that table indicates, there is a significant positive association

(ϕ = .64) between sites and dwellings and the presence of multiseasonal faunas (p = .01), while no significant association is found between sites with multiseasonal faunas and those with storage pits (ϕ = .28, p = .17). These results suggest two conclusions:

1. Two types of storage behavior may be present in the study area: one for sites with storage pits and dwellings, where diverse resources were cached for later use in winter base camps, and a second, at such sites without dwellings as Timonovka I and II, where one specific abundant resource was stored at the time of harvest.

2. Sites without dwellings show subsistence practices best characterized as opportunistic exploitation of available resources during the occupation of the sites.

These conclusions imply that sites with storage pits but without dwellings should exhibit a faunal composition low in diversity, while those with storage pits and dwellings should show greater diversity. Data on hand on the diversity indices confirm these predictions—sites with storage pits and dwellings show somewhat higher indices than Timonovka I and especially Timonovka II. At the present time, however, the sample sizes are too small (e.g., two sites with storage pits and without dwellings, Timonovka I and II) to fully evaluate this prediction.

Fur Bearers

I have previously shown that fur bearers, especially arctic fox, wolf and hare, were exploited in the study area during the cold months. Also, as noted, all body parts of these taxa are represented at the sites. In this discussion I use densities of fur bearers found at the sites as seasonal indicators. I assume that the density of fur bearers only reflects their availability in the area at the time of occupation and assign sites with low densities of fur bearers to warm months and those with high densities to cold months. The assignments are listed in Table 5.43.

Fish

Fish have long been recognized in archaeology as highly sensitive indicators of season of occupation. Ethnographic evidence amply documents concentrated efforts at securing fish by northern-latitude groups during fish spawning periods when they are most abundant (Boas 1964; Casteel 1976; Jochim 1976, 1981; Keene 1981; Nelson 1971). While the small numbers of fish found at the sites suggest that fishing was an opportunistic strategy not keyed to maximal exploitation, for the purposes of this discussion I assume that the fish found were taken at the period of their greatest abundance as well.

Data in both the archaeological and ichthyological literature indicate that northern-latitude fish have widely varying spawning seasons, with some species such as pike spawning in late winter to early spring while others such as catfish exhibit far greater sensitivity to water temperatures and spawn in summer months only (Berg 1964; Carlander 1969; Cleland 1982; Wheeler 1969). Table 2.7 lists economically important fish exploited in the study area and shows that both these species, pike and catfish, were present in the faunal assemblages. Table 5.40 groups fish remains on the basis of spawning season. Spawning season could be determined only for those taxa identified to species. In cases where fish remains are identified to the genus only (e.g., salmon, carp,

Table 5.40 FISH USED AS FOOD: MNI[a]

Site	Cold late winter–early spring		Spring		Late spring–early summer		Summer		Warm		Unidentified	Typed per spawn season	% cold spawners	% Warm spawners	Fishing season
	Pike	Burbot	Roach	Dace	Pike-perch	Perch	Catfish	Salmon-ids	Carps	Bream					
Chulatovo I	—	—	—	—	—	—	—	—	—	—	1	0	0	0	nd
Eliseevichi	—	—	—	—	—	—	—	—	10.5	—	—	10.5	0	100	W?
Mezhirich	1	—	—	—	—	—	—	—	—	—	—	1	100	0	C
Novgorod-Severskii	2	1	1	1	1	1	1	1	1	1	25	11	27	73	W
Suponevo	—	—	—	—	—	—	—	—	—	—	1	0	0	0	nd

[a]Spawning data from Berg (1964), Carlander (1969), and Wheeler (1969).

Table 5.41 AVIAN FOOD TAXA: MNI

Site	Terrestrial		Waterfowl						Unidentified	Total identified	% O	% M	Season
	Willow ptarmigan (O)[a]	Black grouse (M)	Silver gull (M)	Black-headed gull (M)	Field geese (M)	Duck (M)	Golden eye (M)	Swan (M)					
Dobranichevka	1	—	—	—	—	—	—	—	1	1	100	0	C
Eliseevichi	1	—	—	—	—	—	—	—	—	1	100	0	C
Khotylevo II	10	—	2	14	—	2	—	—	—	28	36	64	W
Mezhirich	21	1	—	—	3	1	1	1	11	28	75	25	C
Mezin	3	—	—	—	1	—	—	—	2	4	75	25	C
Novgorod-Severskii	5	1	—	—	2	13	—	—	24	21	24	76	W
Yudinovo	+	—	—	—	—	—	—	—	+	nd	nd	nd	nd

[a]O, overwintering; M, migratory. Season of return for all migratory taxa except black grouse (no data) from Voitenko (1965).

and bream families), I can only project spawning during warm months, based on their descriptions in the literature as temperature-sensitive spawners (see Carlander 1969; Wheeler 1969).

Two taxa in Table 5.40 are cold-weather spawners, while the remaining eight are warm-weather spawners. Combined MNI of all fish assigned to a spawning season, proportions of cold- and warm-spawners, and implied season of fish harvesting are listed in the final columns.

Fish remains at Eliseevichi, contrary to other indicators (see Table 5.43), suggest that fishing may have been done during the warm months. But since fish remains from Eliseevichi are problematic (see pp. 290–291) and identified to the genus only, this inconsistency may not be too serious. As Berg (1964), Carlander (1969), and Wheeler (1969) indicate, the carp family includes a number of species with widely ranging sensitivities to water temperatures; some Cyprinids spawn in early spring while others do so in the fall. This suggests that Eliseevichi carp could have also been harvested during the early spring, when the bulk of the fur bearers found at the site were procured.

Birds

Umanskaya (1978) has investigated avian remains at the central Russian Plain Upper Paleolithic sites and divides them into two categories: (1) those of economic importance to man, which became a part of the faunal inventories as a result of direct procurement, and (2) those not exploited or utilized by man. Birds that she identifies as economically important belong to two broad categories: terrestrial and waterfowl. Terrestrial birds include two taxa: the willow ptarmigan and the black grouse. The willow ptarmigan today is an overwintering species in northern latitudes and can be presumed to have been such in the late Pleistocene as well. The black grouse, as well as all the waterfowl, are migratory today. In a discussion of the present-day biogeography of the Ukraine, Voitenko (1965:101–102) notes that migratory taxa return to the environs of Kiev no earlier than mid-March. These data can be used to approximate the return dates for the migratory taxa to the study area during the late Pleistocene as well.

Exploited avian taxa are listed in Table 5.41 in groupings that designate their terrestrial or aquatic habitat as well as their sedentary or migratory behavior. As this table indicates, only one species, the willow ptarmigan, would have been available year-round. The remaining taxa were available for exploitation during warm-weather months only. Ethnographic literature on northern-latitude hunter–gatherers repeatedly indicates that the willow ptarmigan is usually harvested in winter months and constitutes what Watanabe (1969) calls "starvation food" (see also Boas 1964; McGovern et al. 1983; Nelson 1971). To test the proposition that the willow ptarmigan also constituted a winter "starvation food" for the inhabitants of the Upper Paleolithic central Russian Plain, I calculate a correlation coefficient between the MNI values of hare and willow ptarmigan. Ideally such a correlation should be calculated for only the southern sites, since I have suggested that active procurement of hare occurred only in the south. Hare and willow ptarmigan, however, are only found at two southern sites—Dobranichevka and Mezhirich. If, on the other hand, we include the northern sites where these taxa co-

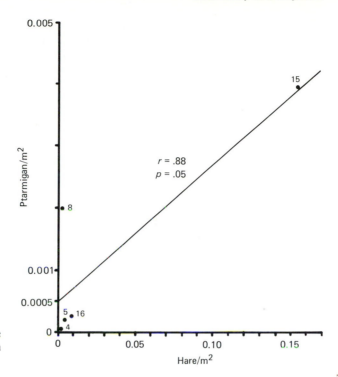

Figure 5.25 Co-occurrence of hare and willow ptarmigan calculated on MNI densities.

occur in the sample, the sample size is sufficient for *r* values to be calculated. The inclusion of northern sites where hares were not actively hunted in this sample is justified because we can assume that the hares found at northern sites came from kills outside the region. As I have shown previously, hares were hunted in the south at the onset of winter. Therefore, if we assume that willow ptarmigans were winter food as well, we can predict a high positive correlation between the MNI counts of these taxa at the sites. As Figure 5.25 illustrates, a high positive correlation does exist between the density controlled-MNI values of hare and willow ptarmigan (*r* = .88), confirming my hypothesis that willow ptarmigans were taken during cold-weather months.

Table 5.41 presents the numbers and proportions of overwintering birds (i.e., willow ptarmigan) and migratory birds found at the sites and estimates the season of occupation based on these proportions. While the data for both Dobranichevka and Eliseevichi suggest cold-weather occupation (100% of the birds at both sites are overwintering willow ptarmigans), those from Khotylevo II, Mezhirich, Mezin, and Novgorod-Severskii are more ambiguous. The low ratios of overwintering to migratory taxa at both Khotylevo II (36%:64%) and Novgorod-Severskii (24%:76%) suggest that most birds were taken in warm months; those from Mezhirich and Mezin (75%:25% at both sites) suggest procurement during the cold months. To test the validity of such seasonal assignment of the sites, I performed a difference of means test on the avifaunal proportions. Since the variables are proportions rather than absolute values, they had to be first submitted to the arcsine transformation. (The statistical justification as well as the mechanics of arcsine transformations are discussed in Zar, 1974:185–186). The following arcsine-transformed values were obtained for the sites:

	Arcsine-transformed proportions	
Sites	Overwintering	Migratory
Khotylevo II	35.67	54.33
Mezhirich	60.00	30.00
Mezin	60.00	30.00
Novgorod-Severskii	27.27	62.73

The difference of means test shows a significant difference between mean proportion values from Mezhirich and Mezin, on one hand, and Khotylevo II and Novgorod-Severskii, on the other ($X_1 = 60.00$, $X_2 = 31.47$, $N = 4$; $z = 6.79$, $p < .0001$). I interpret these results as support for my hypothesis for winter occupation of Mezhirich and Mezin and warm-weather occupation for Khotylevo II and Novgorod-Severskii.

ALTITUDE OF SITES ABOVE THE FLOODPLAIN

Ethnographic literature on settlements in northern latitudes, especially in tundra regions with permafrost, repeatedly indicate that while cold-weather settlements are located on or near floodplains, warm-weather ones are either further inland or higher up and away from the floodplain (e.g., Nelson 1971). The reasons for such movement of villages or camps relate to the marshy, swampy terrains of river valleys and the consequent enumerable mosquitoes and gnats during warm months. Given the paleoenvironmental reconstruction of the late Pleistocene central Russian Plain, it is reasonable to suppose that similar terrain and insect problems existed on the floodplains.

With this assumption in mind, we can consider the altitudinal location of the sites as a possible source of information on the season of occupation. My working assumption here is that warm-weather sites should be located higher above the floodplains than cold-weather settlements. I have already hypothesized that sites with mammoth-bone dwellings appear to be cold-weather settlements and have shown the association of sites with dwellings with floodplain and ravine topography (Chapter 4). If sites with dwellings are indeed cold-weather occupations, they should be located either on the floodplains themselves or close to them. Sites without dwellings, which I have previously indicated may have been warm-weather occupations, should be found higher above the floodplains. The results of a Fisher exact test and ϕ calculation on the association of sites with dwellings with floodplains (Table 5.2) indicates a strong positive association ($\phi = .65$, $p = .01$). I interpret these results to confirm my hypothesis that there is a difference in the altitudinal location of warm- and cold-weather sites. Table 5.43 repeats data on site altitude and presence of dwellings from Table 2.3 and summarizes estimates of season of occupation made on this basis.

This seasonal indicator, as can be seen in the case of Zhuravka, is not unambiguous. Zhuravka's location on the floodplain argues for winter occupation, while all the other seasonal indicators considered heretofore suggest that it was occupied during warm weather. This discrepancy does not invalidate the conclusions reached on the season of occupation using altitude as a variable; it does remind us that no one indicator is sufficient and should be considered along with information from other independent data bases.

Data from Hearths

The indoor or outdoor location of hearths as well as volume differences between them represents another source of information on the season of occupation of the sites with dwellings. As Table 2.4 indicates, hearths have been found both inside and outside the dwellings at some sites, and data are available on both volume of ash in the hearths and density of hearths per sites. This information is tabulated for the undisturbed sites in Table 5.42. We can use these data to test for the season of occupation after making the following assumptions: (1) all other things being equal, more time will be spent indoors and more activities performed inside dwellings during cold months; (2) more time will be spent outdoors and more activities performed outside dwellings during warm months; and (3) the volume and density of hearths are sensitive to both duration of occupation and number of occupants at the sites. Given these assumptions, we can predict that both the number of indoor hearths and their volumes should be consider-

Table 5.42   COMPARISON OF HEARTH VOLUME AND DENSITY

	Interior hearths				Exterior hearths				All hearths	
	No. hearths	Mean vol. (m^3)	Total vol. (m^3)	Density/ m^2	No. hearths	Mean vol. (m^3)	Total vol. (m^3)	Density/ m^2	Total vol. (m^3)	Total density/ m^2
Dobranichevka	2	0.1	0.2	0.2	7	0.1	0.7	0.2	0.9	0.2
Mezhirich	3	0.05	0.15	0.2	6	0.05	0.3	0.03	0.45	0.11
Mezin	6	0.004	0.024	0.01	9	0.2	1.8	0.1	1.82	0.05
Pushkari I	3	0.2	0.6	0.1	2	0.2	0.3	0.1	0.9	0.10

Difference of means tests	N	$\overline{X_1}$[a]	$\overline{X_2}$[b]	z	p
total hearth volume (m^3)	4	0.75	1.824	7.16	<.0001
interior hearth volume (m^3)	4	0.32	0.024	2.06	.04
exterior hearth volume (m^3)	4	0.43	1.80	10.27	<.0001
interior hearth density (m^2)	4	0.17	0.01	4.76	<.0001
exterior hearth density (m^2)	4	0.11	0.10	0.21	.39
total hearth density (m^2)	4	0.14	0.05	2.81	.007

[a] Summed Dobranichevka, Mezhirich, and Pushkari.
[b] Mezin.

ably greater at sites occupied during the cold season than at sites occupied during the warm weather.

To control for the differences in the sizes of excavated portions of the sites, I transformed the raw density or volume data into measures of both density and volume per square meter of site. The necessary data to test the stated hypothesis are available for only four sites: Dobranichevka, Mezhirich, Mezin, and Pushkari I (Table 5.42). The values for the mean hearth volume for each site were obtained by multiplying the mean depth of the hearths by the mean number of hearths found at the sites.

A comparison of total hearth volumes found in interior hearths to those of exterior hearths at these four sites shows large differences. For example, interior hearths at Dobranichevka hold 3.5 times the volume of ash as do the exterior hearths. Similarly high ratios of interior to exterior volume can be observed at Mezhirich, and a somewhat smaller one at Pushkari I. At Mezin, on the other hand, exterior hearths hold about 75 times more volume than the interior hearths. These differences suggest that the four sites were occupied during different seasons—the first three in cold months and Mezin during the warm season. I evaluate these differences through a difference of means test on both the volume and hearth densities. The test results show that both the interior hearth volume (about 13 times greater, $z = 2.06$) and the interior density of hearths per square meter (about 16 times denser, $z = 4.76$) are significantly higher at Dobranichevka, Mezhirich, and Pushkari I. The volume of exterior hearths at Mezin is about four times greater than at Dobranichevka, Mezhirich, and Pushkari I ($z = 10.27$). The density of exterior hearths per square meter, however, shows no difference between sites.

From these comparisons I conclude that more people spent more time indoors at Dobranichevka, Mezhirich, and Pushkari I and more time outdoors at Mezin. I therefore estimate cold-weather occupation for the first three sites and warm-weather occupation for Mezin.

In these tests I assume that all other things were equal, including both population and length of stay. These two variables, however, cannot be considered equal, as both affect hearth density and hearths volume and can be expected to range at the sites. If we assume, for example, that hearth volume roughly reflects the duration of occupation and that the number of hearths is sensitive to population, then the results of the difference of means tests reported here carry additional implications for the sites. I examine these in greater detail in Chapter 6.

CONCLUSIONS

Seasonality estimates from the diverse sources discussed in this chapter are listed in Table 5.43. A comparison of seasonality estimates between sources shows a great deal of ambiguity and contradiction. I suggest that conclusions on seasonality based on mammalian food species are the weakest indicators. This, as discussed previously, is because we are dealing with logistically organized hunter–gatherers who extensively utilized storage in their procurement practices and subsisted on stored provisions during at least a part of the year. In a discussion of food taxa as seasonal indicators, I have

Table 5.43   ESTIMATES OF SEASON OF OCCUPATION

Site	Diversity index[a]	Food sp.	Fur taxa	Pits	Dwellings	Fish	Birds	Height above floodplain (m)	Season on height	Season on hearths	Summed estimated season
Berdyzh	Lo	W + nd	W	+	+	−	−	nd	nd	nd	C
Chulatovo I	Hi	C + W	W	−	−	nd	−	0–5	W?	nd	W
Chulatovo II	Hi	C + W	W	−	−	−	−	15–20	W	nd	W
Dobranichevka	Lo	W + nd	W	+	+	−	C	nd	nd	C	C
Eliseevichi	Lo	C + W	C	+	+	W?	C	0	C	nd	C
Fastov	Lo	C + W	W	−	−	−	−	nd	nd	nd	W
Gontsy	Lo	W + nd	W	+	+	−	−	0	C	nd	C
Khotylevo II	Lo	nd	C	+	−	−	W	5–7	W	nd	C–W
Kirillovskaya	Lo	C	W	−?	+	−	−	0	C	nd	C
Klyusy	nd	nd	nd	−	−	−	−	nd	nd	nd	nd
Korshevo I	nd	nd	nd	−	−	−	−	nd	nd	nd	nd
Korshevo II	nd	nd	nd	−	−	−	−	nd	nd	nd	nd
Kositsa	nd	nd	nd	−	−	−	−	nd	nd	nd	nd
Kurovo	Hi	W	W	−	−	−	−	nd	nd	nd	W?
Mezhirich	Lo	W + C + nd	C	+	+	C	C	1–2	C	C	C
Mezin	Hi	W + C + nd	C	+	+	−	C	0?	C	W	C–W
Novgorod-Severskii	Hi	W + C	W?	−	−	W	W	10–15	nd	nd	W
Novo-Bobovichi	Lo	−	W	−	−	−	−	10?	W	nd	W?
Bugorok	nd	nd	W	−	−	−	−	35–40	W	nd	W
Pogon	nd	nd	W	−	−	−	−	15–20	W	nd	W
Pushkari I	Lo	W + C	?	+?	+	−	−	15–20	W	C	C?
Pushkari II	Hi	W + C	?	−	−	−	−	15–20	W	nd	W
Radomyshl'	Lo	W + nd	W	+	+	−	−	4–5	W?	nd	C–W?
Suponevo	Hi	W + C	W	+	+	nd	−	0	C	nd	C–W?
Timonovka I	Lo	C	W	+	−	−	−	18–23	W	nd	C?
Timonovka II	Lo	C	?	+	−	−	−	15–20	W	nd	C?
Yudinovo	Lo?	C + W + nd	?	+	+	−	−	0	C	nd	C
Yurovichi	Lo	W + nd	W	−	−	−	−	nd	nd	nd	C?
Zhuravka	Hi	W + nd	W	−	−	−	−	0	C	nd	W

[a]Diversity index: Hi > .20; Lo < .20; + = present; − = absent.

demonstrated that all sites with dwellings and storage pits show the presence of multi-seasonal faunas and that only sites without such facilities show uniseasonal occupation. I conclude, therefore, that the practice of storage effectively obliterates the utility of most faunal seasonal indicators.

The density of fur bearers is equally unreliable as an indicator of the season of occupation. While the assignment of high-density fur sites to a cold-weather occupation conforms to the estimates from other sources, the assignment of all sites with low densities of fur bearers to the warm season is clearly in conflict with other evidence. This is because low densities of fur bearers reflect a number of both technological and social variables. I therefore conclude that data on fur bearers in its present form is unsuitable for use as an unambiguous source of information.

Seasonality estimates based on both fish and bird remains appear to be more reliable and consistent. Unfortunately, these data are available for only a very small number of sites and in numbers too small to be significant. Similarly, data on hearth volumes and densities appear interesting but again suffer from the problems of sample size.

I offer seasonality estimates based on the diversity indices and on the height of the sites above the floodplains as the most reliable. As discussed, both are problematic and rely on a number of assumptions that need to be tested in future research. Overall, however, I suggest that it is these two indicators that are in closest accord with each other and come closest to accurately estimating the season of occupation of the sites. Consequently, I have heavily favored conclusions on the season of occupation listed in these two columns in reaching my final estimates.

Some will question the value of estimates obtained without adequate climatic or chronological controls. I concur that both paleoenvironmental and chronological controls are problems that cannot be surmounted with the data on hand, but I also argue that as problematic as my seasonal estimates are, they do further our understanding of the Upper Paleolithic settlement practices in the study area and they or some comparable estimates must be made if we are to get beyond looking at individual sites as Upper Paleolithic universes.

I conclude from this discussion that *all sites in the study area were seasonally occupied and do not represent permanent settlements inhabited for years or decades.* I examine the duration of occupation of the sites in Chapter 6 and offer possible ranges for the extent of sedentism on the central Russian Plain.

I also conclude that *the northern and southern regions of the study area do not represent territories exploited seasonally by one group.* The presence of both warm- and cold-weather occupations is documented for both parts of the study area and indicates local or regional territorial fidelity. Regional comparisons between the numbers of cold- and warm-weather sites listed in Table 5.44 show very similar proportions of cold- to warm-weather sites both interregionally as well as through time. For example, 47% of all northern sites and 67% of all southern sites were occupied during the cold season. The proportions for warm-weather sites during the late period of occupation are similarly close: 55% for the north and 33% for the south. As the results of the Fisher exact test and associations presented in Table 5.2 show, these differences in proportions are not significant given the nature of the data on hand and the history of archaeological research in the study area.

Because of sample size it is more difficult to evaluate the possible changes through time. It is obvious that time factors themselves would favor the preservation of sites with more permanent features such as storage pits or bone dwellings and would remove a disproportionately large number of the more ephemeral sites from the archaeological record. Given these assumptions, it is not surprising to find, as Table 5.44 shows, that the three early northern sites all appear to have been occupied during cold seasons. In light of my discussion on the association of cold-weather sites with more permanent features, both the lack of bone dwellings at Khotylevo II and its location above the

Table 5.44   REGIONAL PATTERNS IN SEASONAL OCCUPATION OF SITES

	Number of sites with determined season	Sites occupied in cold season		Sites occupied in warm season		Number of sites with ambiguous season
		N	%	N	%	
All sites: no chronological controls						
North	15	7	47	8	53	2
South	6	4	67	2	33	0
Total	21	11	52	10	48	2
Early sites						
North	2	2	100	0	0	1
South	0	0	0	0	0	1
Total	2	2	100	0	0	2
Late sites						
North	11	5	45	6	55	2
South	6	4	67	2	33	0
Total	17	9	53	8	47	2

floodplain are surprising. As I note earlier, however, Khotylevo II is a unique site, differing from the other Dnepr–Desna Upper Paleolithic sites stylistically in its lithic and bone assemblages and its portable art. As a subsequent discussion in Chapter 6 demonstrates, Khotylevo II is enigmatic and does not easily fit into the site typology I offer for the study area.

Finally, I offer the following generalizations on the season of occupation of the sites in the study area: (1) sites with mammoth-bone dwellings, with or without storage pits, were occupied during cold-weather months, (2) sites with neither dwellings nor storage pits were occupied during the warm-weather months, and (3) sites without dwellings but with storage pits were occupied during cold-weather months. Three of the sites with storage pits and dwellings, Mezin, Radomyshl', and Suponevo, do not fit this pattern perfectly. For Radomyshl' I offer an explanation based on its early period of occupation and its location in the southern part of the study region. Since it was occupied during a relatively warm period of the Bryansk Interstadial, prior to the general post-Bryansk cooling, we can anticipate a more temperate environment with greater faunal diversity. Given milder climatic conditions and greater faunal diversity in the region, we should expect that the diversity indices of the cold-weather sites from this period would show higher values than the indices from cold-weather sites occupied during the subsequent, much harsher post-Valdai maximum. Data from Mezin and Suponevo are more difficult to account for. First, the mixed cold–warm seasons of occupation cannot be taken to indicate year-round sedentism at these sites. As I show in Chapter 6, neither the cultural layer, available energy values, number of features, nor densities of lithics and bone assemblages at these sites differ significantly from other sites with mammoth-bone dwellings and storage pits. I suggest that Mezin and Suponevo show multiple seasons of occupation because the sequences of reoccupation are more visible at these sites. I have already suggested that transport costs and logistics imply that procurement of the stored foods went on in the vicinity of the storage pits. If we suppose that this provisioning and stocking of the storage pits was done during the warm months, we find the hunter–gatherers present near the storage pits during both the cold, and at least partially, the warm seasons. The locus of warm-weather activities in some cases would be concentric with the locus of the subsequent cold-weather activities and, depending on the rates of sedimentation in the area, would be indistinguishable from one another. In other cases, because of some highly local topographic or geomorphological factors, there could be a greater separation in the seasonal loci of activities. This would result in a spatial separation of season-specific behavior. The first may indeed be the case at Mezin, where both warm- and cold-weather occupations are indicated. The second case may exist in the Pushkari group sites. Pushkari I, which I have classified as a cold-weather occupation, is located just some 300 m from Pushkari II, occupied during the warm season. The relationship between these two sites remains unclear in the Soviet literature (see Boriskovskii 1953; Voevodskii 1952c, 1952d). Both are known from relatively small excavations, and the area between them has not been investigated. Finally, Suponevo data are insufficient to offer either one of these two explanations to account for the multiseasonality indicated for the site. In conclusion, I suggest that in spite of these three discrepancies, the overall seasonal patterning observed is significant and warrants our acceptance of the sites as seasonally occupied settlements.

MODELING CHANGES IN SUBSISTENCE PRACTICES

This chapter has examined the nature of man–land interactions on the late Pleistocene central Russian Plain. I close with a brief review of what changes have been noted through time, both in the landscape itself and in the man–land interactions, and offer a model to account for the observed changes.

In Chapter 3 I present evidence for two major changes in the late Pleistocene landscape through time as seen in the gross numbers of sites for each period of occupation. In Chapter 4, comparing the distribution of settlements through time, I conclude that we see not only an increase in the number of sites but also a change in the location of sites. In time they become linearized along the river valleys. I relate this change in settlement pattern directly to the observed linearization of the resources.

In a discussion of subsistence practices in this chapter, I show a general intensification of exploitation of economically important taxa as well as a diversification of the species used as food. Similar intensification is also noted in storage behavior.

At the same time, this chapter also shows a lack of change in a number of important components of the subsistence practices—most notably in the organization of subsistence activities and in the fundamental composition of the subsistence base. As I have demonstrated, gregarious herbivores formed the subsistence base during the entire period of Upper Paleolithic occupation of the study area, and the strategies employed in harvesting them did not undergo major changes.

Allowing for gaps in the data, I monitor a continued presence of both warm- and cold-weather sites, for which there are no differences in either MNB or MNI densities of economically important taxa. Summarized energy values on food available at the sites also do not exhibit significant change.

These observations represent the major components of my model; their relationships are illustrated in Figure 5.26. This model is offered only for the observed changes in man–land relationships and does not consider social relationships. It is a heuristic device designed to account for just a part of the variables; as such, it explains the function of one of the subsystems of the total Upper Paleolithic adaptation complex.

Stress brought on by climatic fluctuations is seen here as the independent variable responsible for the observed changes through time. Environmental stress was felt and reacted to by man on the level of resource availability and predictability. The linearization of the resources after the Valdai maximum brought about a rearrangement of the settlement system and created both demographic and resource circumscription.

It is a moot point whether the observed moderate increase in population was real or just a product of a different (in this case linear) arrangement of the same number of people in the study area. I argue here that even if no actual increase in number of people occurred, the linearization of the population created linear circumscription, which can be considered an equivalent of demographic increase. This demographic circumscription or linearization in turn amplified the resource stress and brought about intensification and diversification of the subsistence base as well as intensification in storage behavior.

It is important here to reiterate that the organization of procurement did not change; the basic subsistence practices remained the same but were intensified. This intensification was a behavioral response to stress. At present, little additional evidence can be brought to support my argument, because archaeologists working on Upper Paleolithic adaptations have implicitly assumed that these populations lived in rich, stable environments (e.g., Dolukhanov 1982; Mellars 1985). I argue that stress was felt and reacted to

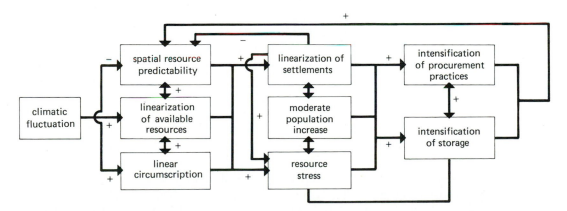

Figure 5.26 Model for man–land relationships after the Valdai maximum. + indicates positive feedback; − indicates negative feedback.

much earlier than the terminal Pleistocene—from around 18,000 B.P. and onward. Jacobs (in press) has shown that early Upper Paleolithic populations were morphologically both more robust and more sexually dimorphic than those who inhabited Europe after 20,000 B.P., and that late Upper Paleolithic hominids cannot be morphologically distinguished from their Mesolithic antecedents. He argues that both decreased robusticity and diminished sexual dimorphism after the glacial maximum indicate populations under greater stress than existed before 20,000 B.P. These observations support my conclusions about environmental stress in the study area in the late Valdai after 18,000 B.P.

The model offered here is similar in a number of aspects to those put forth by Hayden (1981) for late Pleistocene and Price (1981) for Mesolithic Europe. Hayden (1981) proposes resource stress as the most important motive for patterned directional change in cultural systems. Price (1981) argues for the importance of demographic stress in rich but environmentally circumscribed regions in promoting increasing complexity in hunter–gatherer settlement and subsistence systems. Both authors see these stresses, environmental in the first case and environmental cum demographic in the second, as bringing about directional change that can be termed "evolutionary." I also emphasize the importance of both environmental and environmental–demographic stress in bringing about the observed changes. In contrast to both Hayden and Price, however, I suggest that the observed change can be better understood as fluctuational than as unidirectional.

Recently, both systems theorists and ecologists, as well as an increasing number of anthropologists, have come to recognize that dynamic systems, especially living ones, display fluctuations in even their most stable states (Glansdorff and Prigogine 1971; Nicolis and Prigogine 1977). In ecology, Haber (1980) and May (1973a, 1977) have shown that nondirectional fluctuations (i.e., those that do not lead to directional or permanent change) are present in most living systems. This indicates that we should expect to find diachronic variability in systems that has no unidirectional evolutionary significance. Friedman (1979) has applied some of these observations to culture and history in general and criticized the acceptance of the cybernetics model in anthropology. Approaching past human cultural systems from this perspective, one that allows for fluctuations, I would argue that we must expect to find a great deal of variability in all adaptation practices, be they related to subsistence or settlement. Given this, when we note change in one or more of the components of a cultural system, we cannot assume that such change, ipso facto, is evidence for directional change or evolution. Translating this into archaeological implications, I suggest that we can argue for directional or evolutionary significance in observed change only after we have eliminated the possibility that what we are witnessing does not fall within the normal range of expected variability.

Archaeologists, following Steward's (1955) lead, have long accepted the idea that a given environment does not determine or prescribe a particular cultural behavior but just imposes certain rather broad limits on such behavior. It follows that in any given environment there are a number of organizational strategies that can satisfy subsistence needs—a conclusion empirically demonstrated by Bettinger (1978) with Great Basin data. I argue here that we can project the existence of these alternate solutions in time as well. Their coexistence in space is a synchronic analogue of temporal fluctuations. From this perspective, most changes in cultural systems through time first and foremost represent behavioral adjustments (or alternate strategies) that need not, in most cases do not, have evolutionary significance.

The data from the central Russian Plain presented in Chapters 3–5 show both the presence of change, especially in some aspects of the subsistence behavior, and evidence for the continuity of basic adaptive strategies through time. I interpret the type of changes observed as "variations on a theme," quantitative rather than qualitative.

6

Site Types
and the Settlement System

SETTLEMENT SYSTEMS: PRESENT AND PAST ─────────

In Chapter 4 I briefly examine the location of sites in the study area and point out some regularities in the distribution of particular kinds of sites (e.g., sites with and without mammoth bone dwellings). In Chapter 5 I show that all sites were seasonally occupied. Both of these characteristics, duration of occupation and site location, are aspects of the second major component of Upper Paleolithic cultural systems in the central Russian Plain. They are variables of the settlement system. I have elected to work with the settlement system as an analytic tool for studying past human adaptations because, at present, it is the most powerful method available for understanding the temporal and spatial operation of hunter–gatherer groups in their environment. This approach has been used extensively by both ethnographers and archaeologists (e.g., Balikci 1970; Binford 1982b; Damas 1972; Jochim 1976; Lee 1979; Winters 1969; and Yellen 1977).

Since all ethnographically know hunter–gatherers exhibit locational mobility in their subsistence pursuits, numerous settlements or camps for a given group in time and space result (for a detailed discussion of hunter–gatherer settlement variability, see Binford 1980, 1982b; Watanabe 1968).

Lee offers a second universal strategy for hunter–gatherer settlements: aggregation and dispersal. He writes:

> What are central to all these cases . . . are a pattern of concentration and dispersal, usually seasonal. . . . The worldwide occurrence of this pattern of spatial organization in vastly different kinds of environments indicates the degree to which it is basic to the hunting and gathering adaptation. (Lee 1979:360–361)

This second mechanism, if equally universal in the past, implies that we can anticipate finding very different sizes of sites for a given group of hunter–gatherers.

The settlements themselves, as numerous authors have pointed out, can and do vary along a number of parameters including season, duration of occupation, location, and composition. These parameters, in turn, are affected by such factors as subsistence and social needs (see Jochim 1981 for a thorough discussion). While the settlements or sites themselves are features of a specific adaptation strategy of a given group, their variety across all groups is not limitless. In general, two broad classes of sites have been distinguished for hunter–gatherers on the basis of the range of activities occurring in them and the size of the group performing these activities and occupying the sites: base camps and special-purpose or extractive camps (Binford 1980; Binford and Binford 1966; Binford 1980; Price 1978). Base-camp activities include construction of shelter, tool and clothing manufacture, food preparation, and other routines generally involving the whole coresidential group. Extractive camps, which may be occupied by only a specifically functioning element of the coresidential group, show the varying evidence of different irregular activities: hunting, gathering, quarrying. Finally, special-purpose camps can also include locations for ritual or ceremonial activities.

Binford (1980) has focused on the different settlement types generated by more mobile foragers and by logistically organized food collectors. He writes:

> Collectors, like foragers, actually procure and/or process raw materials at locations. However, since logistically organized producer parties are generally seeking products for social groups far greater than themselves, the debris generated at different locations may frequently vary considerably. (Binford 1980:10)

This implies, then, that we can anticipate a wide range both in site size and assemblage density at extractive camps or locations of logistically organized groups.

These general observations on the two basic classes of hunter–gatherer sites carry archaeological implications for site composition. If we assume either single episodes of occupation or repeated occupation for the same range of activities per site, the nature of both features and assemblages at the sites should reflect past activities and allow us to classify the sites into either maintenance or extractive types. The following site classes can be expected in the study area.

Extractive or Special-Purpose Camps or Locations.   These include, (1) *lithic workshops,* which should lack any features and have assemblages related to initial lithic processing. There should be little or no food remains and no evidence for exploitation of nonfood taxa. The sites themselves should be small and show short-term occupation by small task forces; (2) *hunting and collecting camps* should be smaller in size and show shorter duration of occupation than base camps (see following). They should show occupation by smaller groups and lack such features as dwellings, storage pits, and sizable hearths. Since we are dealing with logistically organized hunter–gatherers who harvested food in large quantities and may have also collected bone in volume, we can predict the presence of two types of faunal-procurement camps—one used in active hunting and the other in collecting practices. The assemblages at both should contain a smaller number and more limited variety of tools than at base camps, and these should be related to procurement and possibly to initial processing of food at hunting camps and to procurement of bone in collecting camps. Since active hunting would have required a greater use of tools than collecting, more tools should be found at hunting camps. Faunal remains should be sparcer at these sites than at base camps and should reflect the presence of just one or two taxa. Evidence for exploitation of nonfood species should not be present.

Base Camps.   These large sites should contain the widest array of features such as dwellings, hearths, and storage pits. The archaeological assemblages should contain a variety of tools associated with diverse maintenance activities as well as exotics, jewelry, and art. The size of the occupying group should be larger than those of extractive or special-purpose camps. Food remains should show greater abundance (MNB, MNI, kcals) as well as a greater variety of taxa exploited. Evidence for exploitation of nonfood species should be present as well. In addition, we should find base camps occuied during various seasons.

In generating these archaeological expectations, I assume single episodes of occupation or reoccupation for the same range of activities per site. Both archaeological data and ethnographic evidence, however, show that in the real world these assumptions are untenable. Binford (1982b) has documented regular reoccupation of sites by different groups for different purposes. Thus, what is once a Nunamiut food-extraction location can subsequently become a base camp, and then can be either abandoned or occupied again as a special-purpose camp, and so on. Nunamiut are not alone in such behavior. McCartney (1979) documents temporal changes in Thule settlement function for sites with whale-bone dwellings—first as base camps and then, after abandonment, as quarry or extraction camps for the procurement of whale bone itself.

The data on the Upper Paleolithic central Russian Plain sites also strongly suggest that at least some of the sites were occupied more than once. First, as I note in Chapter 5 in a discussion of ambiguous data on the season of occupation of such sites as Mezin and Suponevo, evidence exists that these sites were occupied during different seasons. Hearths separated by thin loess or colluvium layers from underlying storage pits have been found at Dobranichevka (Shovkoplyas 1972) and Mezin (Shovkoplyas 1965a). Pidoplichko (1976) reports bone charcoal over one Mezhirich storage pit as well. As noted in Chapter 2, the possibility of more than one cultural layer in at least a part of the site has been suggested for Gontsy, Kirillovkaya, Mezhirich, and Mezin. Shovkoplyas (1951) proposes that two types of settlements, one long- and one short-term, may have existed at Suponevo, and Pidoplichko (1976) suggests a similar dual occupation for Mezhirich.

It is also unclear if all parts of the Upper Paleolithic sites were occupied at the same time. This question has received little attention in Soviet literature, and a working assumption of most researchers has been that the entire area of the sites was occupied simultaneously (e.g., Boriskovskii 1953; Velichko, Grekhova *et al.* 1981). Sergin (1974b) uses evidence of regular site layout at such sites as Dobranichevka, Mezin, and Radomyshl' to argue for a synchronic occupation. Shovkoplyas (1965a), on the other hand, while arguing for long-term occupation of Mezin, suggests that different parts of the site were occupied in sequence. Similarily, Pidoplichko (1976) speculates that the occupants of Mezhirich lived at the site for a while before constructing mammoth-bone dwellings. Voevodskii (1952a), in noting the presence of separate clusters of debris at Chulatovo II (see Figures 2.22 and 2.23), allows for the possibility of diachronic occupation at this site too.

Leonova (1977) indirectly addressed this question. She examined both the nature of archaeological remains (features and lithics) and the spatial distribution of different lithic categories at a number of sites, including Chulatovo II and Dobranichevka. Leonova's plot of conjoinables, different lithic pieces from a single nucleus, at Chulatovo II shows that out of the 156 objects that could be matched, 153 were found in adjoining squares less than a meter apart (see Figure 2.24). The longest distance at which conjoinables were separated was approximately 12 m. Leonova outlines three concentrations of archaeological remains at Chulatovo II that showed strong spatial segregation and concludes that the question of synchronic occupation of all three areas still remain open.

Leonova was less successful at conjoining Dobranichevka lithics because of the excavation methodology (see Chapter 2). She could conjoin only two burins with their spalls—found during the 1967 excavation of Complex 1. These were found more than 10 m apart but well within the area of the complex itself, and their relatively short separation did not conclusively show synchronic occupation of the different complexes. Overall, Leonova's spatial analysis of the distribution of cultural remains at Dobranichevka indicates the presence of four non-overlapping complexes. She concludes that the question of synchronic occupation of the four remains open.

Gladkih (1973, 1977a) also indirectly considered the issue of occupational sequence at Dobranichevka. Working with traditional tool classes as well as stylistic criteria, he examined the different proportions of tool classes found at the four complexes and concluded that a great similarity exists in the assemblages of all four. He interprets this to suggest a more or less synchronic occupation for the entire site.

As these examples indicate, then, we cannot expect to find evidence for single or even uniform occupations, but rather superimpositions of mixed occupations that yield a great deal of contradictory data on the nature of behavior at the sites.

A second and perhaps more serious caveat should be kept in mind when generating ethnographically derived implications for archaeological sites. The problem is twofold. First, since we generate expectations from ethnographic observations, we tend to recognize only those patterns that conform to the record. Such cultural uniformitarianism puts us in danger of either omitting or totally misunderstanding those past behaviors for which we have no present-day analogues. Second, we are in danger of forgetting that no ethnographic data comes from "pristine" groups, as Leacock (1954) and Schrire (1980; 1984) among others have repeatedly pointed out. The ethnographic data we have on hand is of groups and cultures that have been affected to varying degrees by contact with complex state societies and the market system and are a part of what Wallerstein (1974) terms "the world-system." We must be flexible in applying our ethnographically derived models to date from the past; we must allow for a great deal of deviation in the fit between the two. Likewise, when warranted, we must allow for the existence of settlement types in the past without recognizable present-day analogues. Failing this, we just illustrate what is known historically, creating Paleolithic clones of Netsilik, or Nunamiut, or Ojibwa, or of some other ethnographic group currently in vogue in the literature.

DATA FROM THE CENTRAL RUSSIAN PLAIN

Data on features and assemblages found at the sites are presented in Tables 2.7, 2.8, and 2.11. Most values in these tables represent estimates derived from the literature and from my examination of collections and such archival data as field notes. In a few cases, such as Mezhirich and Mezin, for which full lists of excavated lithics have been published, the values are more exact.

Some arbitrary decisions had to be made on quantification of features because neither large storage pits nor mammoth-bone dwellings were recognized as such prior to the late 1920s. As a result, subsequent researchers do not agree on just how many dwellings and storage pits were found at such sites as Gontsy, Kirillovskaya, and Suponevo. I therefore treat the estimated numbers as ranges and use mean values in all calculations. Similarly, since stratigraphic controls are in many cases the deciding element in distinguishing between very large storage pits and small bone dwellings, the identification of pits or dwellings at sites excavated prior to the 1930s remains problematic (e.g., Kirillovskaya or Timonovka I).

As noted earlier, human groups who occupied the sites were logistically organized hunter–gatherers, and the sites they left behind vary greatly in both features and assemblages. These range from such sites as Bugorok, with no features and an abundance of lithics, to elaborate sites such as Mezhirich and Mezin, with multiple features and diverse assemblages. I compare the 29 sites in the study area in terms of general attributes outlined below and base my typology on data from the undisturbed sites. My basic assumptions in using these attributes for site classification are that (1) there is a behavioral correlation, however muted, between material remains and past human behavior, and (2) a greater variety of material remains indicates a greater variety in behavioral repertoire (but see Binford 1982b).

The attributes selected for consideration can be broadly divided into three categories: assemblages, site characteristics, and features. The first group includes anything portable, and some items in this category were found at each site; this category includes objects and faunal remains. The second group refers to geographic and stratigraphic attributes such as location, site size, and the thickness of the cultural layer. The third category includes such immovable attributes as mammoth-bone dwellings, hearths, and storage pits. In some cases, attributes are given as raw counts. In others, reported quantities are subjected to simple statistical manipulations such as residualization (via the calculation of Pearson correlation coefficients and subtraction of the dependent proportions), arcsine transformations, calculation of ϕ values of association, and comparison through difference of means tests. These procedures have been previously presented and used in Chapter 5.

ASSEMBLAGES: OBJECTS

Density of Lithics.   This value is defined as a mean number of all lithics found per square meter of each site. These values (Table 6.1) range widely and show higher values, in general, in northern sites. Difference of means tests in Table 6.2 indicate that northern sites have approximately eight times more lithics per square meter than do the southern sites ($z = 2.33$).

Overall density of lithics at sites can be affected by a number of variables, including length of occupation and group size as well as general availability of raw materials. In order to see if these observed interregional differences were due to group size or

Table 6.1   DENSITY OF ARTIFACTS[a]

Site	Lithics/m²	Tools/m²	End scrapers + burins/m²	Nuclei/m²	MNB/m²[b]	Worked Bone/m²
Berdyzh	4.3	nd	nd	nd	nd	nd
Chulatovo II	13.4	0.5	0.46	0.16	nd	0.0006
Dobranichevka	6.8	0.6	0.17	0.15	1.50	0.005
Eliseevichi	128.4	6.4	0.74	0.52	46.10	0.50
Fastov	8.6	0.8	0.04	0.42	1.45	—
Gontsy	3.7	0.4	0.31	0.02	6.90	0.02
Khotylevo II	41.4	10.0	nd	nd	2.80	0.60
Kirillovskaya	0.5	0.01	0.004	<0.0009	0.06	0.0009
Kositsa	20.0	2.0	0.80	0.24	0.02	—
Mezhirich	29.3	2.5	1.30	0.66	13.30	0.50
Mezin	94.4	3.7	2.80	0.48	6.9	0.20
Bugorok	308.6	19.7	13.90	9.56	nd	—
Pogon	10.6	1.1	0.40	0.38	nd	—
Pushkari I	400.0	8.0	1.00	8.0	1.30	0.01
Pushkari II	1.5	0.03	0.02	0.29	3.50	—
Radomyshl'	16.7	1.9	nd	nd	1.90	—
Suponevo	150.0	1.0	nd	nd	2.08	1.00
Timonovka I	85.0	0.1	4.90	2.55	nd	0.10
Timonovka II	85.5	0.01	3.12	1.32	0.80	0.01
Yudinovo	>25.0	nd	nd	nd	1.01	nd
Zhuravka	11.2	0.2	0.06	0.01	nd	—

[a]Number per square meter of site.
[b]MNB/m² calculated only for economically important taxa.

duration of occupation, I examine the relation between thickness of cultural layer (see Table 2.3) and lithic density. I assume that the thickness of the cultural layer roughly reflects both duration of occupation and group size. The resulting r values for the area as a whole as well as for the northern and southern sites separately (Table 6.3) show that no significant relation exists between these two variables. I conclude that the differences in density of lithics, especially at northern sites, can best be explained by the differential distribution of lithic resources in the study area.

In general, keeping interregional differences in mind, I assume that greater lithic densities at some sites reflect a prevalence of lithic production there, and I anticipate finding higher densities at lithic workshops than at base camps or hunting and collecting camps.

Density of Lithic Tools.   This value (Table 6.1) is defined as the mean number of tools per square meter of site. I assume that, as with the density of all lithics, greater densities of tools reflect more lithic workmanship at sites.

The density of stone tools at sites, however, can be influenced by general lithic density. Table 6.3 shows a strong positive correlation between general lithic densities and densities of tools at both northern and southern sites (northern sites, $r = .68$; southern sites, $r = .92$). To control for that proportion of lithic tools directly related to

Table 6.2   DIFFERENCE OF MEANS TESTS ON THE DISTRIBUTION OF ASSEMBLAGES[a]

	N	$\overline{X}_1$	$\overline{X}_2$	z	p
1. Density of lithics per m² of site					
northern vs. southern sites	21	87.10	10.82	2.33	.02
northern sites with vs. without storage pits	10	112.67	70.82	0.59	.32
southern sites with vs. without storage pits	7	10.08	9.90	0.16	.39
sites with storage pits, north vs. south	13	112.67	10.08	2.58	.01
sites without storage pits, north vs. south	7	70.82	9.90	1.02	.24
2. Density of tools residualized against lithic densities; northern and southern sites residualized separately					
late northern vs. southern sites	16	0.006	0	0.05	.40
late northern sites with vs. without storage pits	10	−0.66	0.67	0.52	.35
late southern sites with vs. without storage pits	6	0.12	−0.24	0.88	.27
late sites with storage pits, north vs. south	9	−0.66	0.12	0.44	.36
late sites without storage pits, north vs. south	7	0.67	−0.24	0.49	.35
all northern sites with vs. without storage pits	11	0.06	−0.07	0.04	.40
all southern sites with vs. without storage pits	7	0.13	−0.32	1.07	.23
sites with storage pits, north vs. south	11	0.06	0.13	0.04	.40
sites without storage pits, north vs. south	7	−0.07	−0.32	0.12	.40
3. Densities of end scrapers plus burins, residualized against lithic densities					
northern vs. southern sites	16	−0.02	−0.002	0.02	.40
sites with vs. without storage pits	16	0.38	−0.23	0.40	.37
high-density vs. low-density sites	16	1.52	−1.55	2.52	.01
high-density sites, north vs. south	8	2.92	0.13	1.53	.13
low-density sites, north vs. south	8	−1.97	−0.26	1.86	.07
4. Densities of nuclei, residualized lithic densities					
all (= late) northern vs. southern sites	15	−0.005	−0.002	0.008	.40
northern sites with vs. without storage pits	10	−0.83	0.82	2.89	.006
southern sites with vs. without storage pits	5	0.06	0.005	0.24	.39
sites with storage pits, north vs. south	8	−0.83	0.06	1.71	.09
sites without storage pits, north vs. south	7	0.82	0.005	1.71	.09
northern sites, high density vs. low density	10	−1.26	0.83	4.02	<.0001
southern sites, low density vs. high density	5	−0.14	0.09	2.11	.04
low-density sites, north vs. south	5	−1.26	−0.14	2.97	.004
high-density sites, north vs. south	9	0.83	0.09	2.00	.05
high-density vs. low-density sites	15	0.58	−0.89	3.44	<.0009
5. Densities of residualized values of end scrapers plus burins and of residualized values of nuclei					
northern vs. southern sites	15	−0.001	−0.002	0.00	0
sites with storage pits, north vs. south	8	4.45	−0.37	1.74	.08
sites without storage pits, north vs. south	8	−3.31	−0.56	0.22	.39
high-density vs. low-density sites	15	5.21	−4.36	4.45	<.0001
high-density sites with vs. without storage pits	6	5.48	11.84	5.05	<.0001
low-density sites with vs. without storage pits	9	−1.32	−5.71	1.66	.10
high-density sites with storage pits, north vs. south	5	6.13	2.89	1.51	.13
high-density sites without storage pits, north vs. south	1	11.84			

Table 6.8 DENSITIES OF END SCRAPERS PLUS BURINS, RESIDUALIZED AGAINST MNI DENSITIES OF ALL FUR BEARERS

	All fur bearers/m²	ESB residuals[a]	New ESB residuals[b]
Sites with high densities of fur bearers			
Eliseevichi	0.5378	−3.02	0.24
Mezhirich	0.2346	−0.05	−0.32
Mezin	0.1624	1.38	0.26
Sites with low densities of fur bearers			
Chulatovo II	0.0430	4.63	1.90
Dobranichevka	0.0075	0.17	−1.36
Fastov	0.0000	−0.23	−1.51
Gontsy	0.0478	0.29	−2.61
Kirillovskaya	0.00008	0.15	−1.14
Kositsa	0.0000	4.51	3.23
Bugorok	0.0000	−8.58	−9.86
Pogon	0.0000	−22.08	−23.36
Pushkari I	0.0279	5.39	3.16
Pushkari II	0.1033	5.01	0.24
Timonovka I	0.0054	4.13	2.66
Timonovka II	0.0614	2.32	−1.23
Zhuravka	0.0060	−0.35	−1.84

[a]Densities of end scrapers plus burins residualized against lithic densities.
[b]End-scraper and burin densities residualized from lithic density and density of all fur bearers.

data on tool types made from nonlocal lithics and therefore not able to correlate particular behavior with them, I assume that the rate of use of these items is roughly proportional to (1) the range of activities performed with them, (2) the size of the group using them, and (3) the duration of occupation. I also assume the existence of a direct relation between the value of an object and the distance to its source. This implies that, all other things being equal, we should find greater numbers of nonlocal lithics at base camps than at extractive camps and should not find them at lithic workshops.

While the range of activities for which ocher was used in the study area is still to be determined, mammoth bones painted with ocher have been found at Mezhirich and Mezin (see Pidoplichko 1969, 1976), and ocher has been found in the few burials reported for the Upper Paleolithic Russian Plain at Sungir and the Kostenki sites (see Bader 1978; Praslov and Rogachev 1982). Taking into account all the other possible uses that ocher may have been put to, such as tanning of hides, body decoration, and healing practices, it is reasonable to presume that this item would be used far more often at base camps and that very little, if any, ocher will be found at extractive locales of any kind.

Decorative Objects.   The second group of rare items at the sites—decorative objects—includes amber, art objects, fossil marine shells, and jewelry. As with exotic lithics, I treat these four groups of items both as individual attributes in some calculations and as a single group attribute.

Table 6.9   PROVENIENCE OF LITHICS

| | Types present[a] | | | | | Summed data on lithics | | |
Site	Ocher	Flint	Sandstone	Mountain crystal	Slate	(1) Presence-absence of exotics	(2) Coded values[b]	(3) Dimension-scaled codes[c]
Berdyzh	L	nd	—	—	—	—	0	nd
Chulatovo I	L	L	—	—	—	—	0	0
Chulatovo II	E	L	—	—	—	+	0	1
Dobranichevka	E	L	L	E	—	+	1	2
Eliseevichi	E	E	E	—	—	+	1	3
Fastov	L	L	—	—	—	—	0	0
Gontsy	E	L	—	E	—	+	1	2
Khotylevo II	E	nd	nd	—	—	+	0	nd
Kirillovskaya	L	L	—	—	—	—	0	0
Klyusy	L	nd	—	—	—	—	0	nd
Korshevo I	L	nd	nd	—	—	—	0	nd
Korshevo II	L	nd	nd	—	—	—	0	nd
Kositsa	E	nd	nd	—	—	+	0	nd
Mezhirich	E	L	L	E	L	+	1	2
Mezin	E	L	—	—	—	+	0	1
Novgorod-Severskii	E	L	—	—	—	+	0	1
Novo-Bobovichi	L	L	—	—	—	—	0	0
Bugorok	L	L	—	—	—	—	0	0
Pogon	E	E	—	—	—	+	1	2
Pushkari I	E	L	—	—	L	+	0	1
Pushkari II	E	L	—	—	—	+	0	1
Radomyshl'	L	E	—	—	—	+	0	1
Suponevo	E	L	—	—	—	+	1	1
Timonovka I	E	L	nd	—	E	+	1	nd
Timonovka II	E	L	—	—	—	+	0	1
Yudinovo	E	E	—	—	—	+	1	2
Yurevichi	E	L	L?	—	—	+	0	1?
Zhuravka	L	E	—	—	—	+	0	1

[a]— = absent; + = present; E = present, nonlocal origin; L = present, local origin; nd = present, no data on source of origin.
[b]0 = exotic material present in less than 2 categories, 1 = exotic materials present in more than 2 categories.
[c]1 = exotics present in 1 category, 2 = exotics present in 2 categories, 3 = exotics present in 3 categories.

Varying amounts of disintegrating amber have been reported at Chulatovo II, Dobranichevka, Gontsy, Mezhirich, and Mezin. Pidoplichko (1976) convincingly demonstrates that much of this amber was originally in the form of beads, but he has also suggested that some may have been burned in hearths for the pleasant scent it releases. While no definite studies have been done to pinpoint its source, Kornietz *et al.* (1981), Pidoplichko (1976), and Shovkoplyas *et al.* (1981) all state that (1) amber-bearing deposits are found along the right bank of the Dnepr in the vicinity of Kiev, and (2) this area most probably served as the source for the material found at the Upper Paleolithic sites. In Chapter 2 I translate their observations into distance measures from base maps,

Table 6.10   DISTRIBUTION OF AMBER

Site	No. found	Distance to source (km)	Distance-scaled values[a]	Code[b]
Chulatovo II	1	260	2.6	1
Dobranichevka	12	130	15.6	2
Gontsy	some[c]	200	10.0	1.5?
Mezhirich	>348	100	348.0	3
Mezin	>1	220	2.2?	1

[a]Distance-scaled values = $N \times$ *distance to source*/100.
[b]Code on distance-scaled values: 1, <10; 2, 10–100; 3, >100.
[c]Assume 5 items.

rounded off to the nearest 10 km, and I list them along with amber counts in Table 6.10. Since I assume a positive relation between distance and value, I also transform raw amber counts to account for the distances at which amber was found from it suggested source. These distance-scaled values are then coded 1 through 3 (low to high). Given the aforementioned possible uses of amber, I presume that it should be behaviorally associated with maintenance activities and found at base camps rather than extractive camps.

Total counts of art objects, excluding anything obviously wearable, which I have classified as jewelry, are listed in Table 6.11. In addition, coded values are assigned 1 through 3 (low to high). As with other decorative items, I assume that art objects will be found at base camps rather than at extractive locales.

Table 6.11   ART AND JEWELRY

Site	Art		Jewelry	
	No. found	Coded values	No. found	Coded values[b]
Dobranichevka	2	1	—	—
Eliseevichi	1	1	>32	3
Gontsy	—	—	2	1
Khotylevo II	~16	2	—	—
Kirillovskaya	3	1	—	—
Mezhirich	15	2	28	3
Mezin	~40	3	44	3
Pushkari I	—	—	1	1
Suponevo	2	1	16	2
Timonovka I	27	3	0	—
Timonovka II	1	1	0	—
Yudinovo	some[c]	2	some[c]	2
Yurovichi	1	1	—	—

[a]Coding for art: 1, 0–10; 2, 11–25; 3, >26.
[b]Coding for jewelry: 1, <10; 2, 11–20; 3, >20.
[c]Assume more than 10 items.

Table 6.12   DISTRIBUTION OF FOSSIL MARINE SHELLS

Site	No. found	Distance to source (km)	Distance-scaled values[a]	Code[b]
Chulatovo II	4	550	22.0	1
Eliseevichi	105	600	630.0	2
Mezhirich	3	300	9.0	1
Mezin	~800	500	4000.0	3
Timonovka I	>9	650	58.5	1.5?
Yudinovo	>150	650	975.0	2?

[a]Distance-scaled values = $N \times$ *distance to source*/100.
[b]Codes on distance-scaled values: 1, 1–50; 2, 51–1000; 3, >1000.

Table 6.13   TESTS OF ASSOCIATION: ARTIFACTS, FEATURES, AND DECORATIVE OBJECTS

	N[a]	φ	p[b]
Sites with storage pits or dwellings and sites with thick cultural layers	19	.11	.34
Interior and exterior hearths	22	.40	.05
Sites with hearths and sites with dwellings	22	.56	.01
Hearths and large storage pits at the sites	22	.75	.0007
End scrapers plus burins and nuclei	16	.63	.02
High and low percentages of end scrapers plus burins and of nuclei (of all lithics)	10	.20	.40
High and low blade–nuclei ratios and sites with storage pits	18	−.55	.02
Density of nuclei and percentage of nuclei of total number of tools	15	.04	.90
Presence of art and jewelry	29	.44	.03
Presence of art and jewelry and dwellings, all sites	28	.63	.01
Presence of art and jewelry and dwellings, late sites	24	.91	.000008
Presence of art and jewelry and storage pits, all sites	28	.86	.000005
Presence of art and jewelry and storage pits, late sites	25	1.00	.000002
Presence of art and storage pits, all sites	28	.75	.00007
Presence of art and storage pits, late sites	25	.85	.00002
Presence of marine shells and storage pits, all sites	25	.39	.003
Presence of marine shells and art	11	.13	.51
Presence of marine shells and amber	25	.42	.06
Presence of amber and storage pits	25	.36	.08
Presence of amber and art	29	.21	.21
Presence of amber and jewelry	25	.37	.10
Presence of ocher and storage pits	22	.43	.05
Presence of decorative items and exotic lithics and ocher, on dimensionally scaled codes	29	.67	.001
Presence of decorative items and exotic lithics and ocher, on presence or absence	29	.56	.003
Presence of grinding stones and worked bone	29	.37	.04
Presence of grinding stones and ocher	29	.66	.0004
Presence of grinding stones and storage pits, all sites	29	.33	.06
Presence of grinding stones and exotic lithics (without ocher)	24	.22	.19

[a]N refers to number of sites in the sample.
[b]Probability estimated by Fisher exact test.

Fossil marine shells representing a number of taxa have been found at Chulatovo II, Eliseevichi, Mezhirich, Timonovka I, and Yudinovo (see Table 2.11). Most were perforated and found close to each other, suggesting to Soviet researchers that they were used as beads in necklaces and bracelets (see Shovkoplyas 1965a). Some shells, however, both at Eliseevichi and Mezin, were either not perforated or partially perforated, indicating that they were also processed into beads at the sites (Polikarpovich 1968; Shovkoplyas 1965a). Motuz (1969), Rudenko (1957, 1959), and Shovkoplyas (1965a) indicate that the shells were mined from both the Karangat and Sarmatian marine deposits, and that the closest area where both deposits had surface exposure was in the far south of European Russia, near the shores of the Black Sea and the Sea of Azov. I translate these observations into rough distance measures to the closest possible region in the south where shells could have been obtained, calculated from base maps in Chapter 2 and figured "as the crow flies" (Table 6.12). Assuming, as for other nonlocal materials, a direct relation between the distance from which an object was procured and its value, I incorporate information on distances and multiply the raw numbers of shells found per site by the distance measures (then dividing the resultant figures by 100). Finally, I code the resulting distance-controlled measures, using 1 through 3 (low to high). As noted above, unspecified large numbers of fossil shells were perforated and presumably utilized as beads. A high positive correlation coefficient ($r = .72$, Table 6.3) is found between shells and other items of personal adornment (termed "jewelry" in this work), supporting the interpretation that shells were used as jewelry. Therefore I anticipate that shells, as jewelry, should be found in significantly greater numbers at base camps rather than extractive camps.

I define jewelry to include a range of items such as perforated animal teeth, beads from long bones, bracelets, and pendants. Raw values for this category are listed in Table 6.11, as are their codes. I assume that the making and wearing of jewelry is behaviorally associated with base camps.

Since I assume that all decorative artifact classes should be found in greater numbers at base camps, I evaluate correlations between different categories of these objects. The individual test statistics for these relations, listed in Tables 6.3 and 6.13, can be summarized as follows:

	Amber	Art	Shells	Jewelry
Amber		$-C$	$+C$	$-C$
Art	$-C$		$-C_1$	$+C$
Shells	$+C$	$-C_1$		$-C_2$
Jewelry	$-C$	$+C$	$+C_2$	

While the negative association between amber and jewelry indicates some problems in classifying amber exclusively as a jewelry item, the overall positive correlations do roughly indicate a behavioral connection between these classes of artifacts. At the same time, however, they also indicate the existence of two distinct behavioral complexes—one, involving exchange, associated with nonlocal materials such as amber and shells,

Table 6.14   DECORATIVE OBJECTS

Site	Coded values				(1) Presence/absence	(2) Scaled codes[a]	(3) Dimension-scaled codes[b]
	Amber	Art	Fossil shells	Jewelry			
Berdyzh	—	—	—	—	—	0	0
Chulatovo I	—	—	—	—	—	0	0
Chulatovo II	1	—	1	—	+	1	2
Dobranichevka	2	1	—	—	+	1	2
Eliseevichi	—	1	2	3	+	1	3
Fastov	—	—	—	—	—	0	0
Gontsy	1.5?	—	—	1	+	1	3
Khotylevo II	—	2	—	—	+	0	1
Kirillovskaya	—	1	—	—	+	0	1
Klyusy	—	—	—	—	—	0	0
Korshevo I	—	—	—	—	—	0	0
Korshevo II	—	—	—	—	—	0	0
Kositsa	—	—	—	—	—	0	0
Kurovo	—	—	—	—	—	0	0
Mezhirich	3	2	1	3	+	1	4
Mezin	1	3	3	3	+	1	4
Nogvorod-Severskii	—	—	—	—	—	0	0
Novo-Bobovichi	—	—	—	—	—	0	0
Bugorok	—	—	—	—	—	0	0
Pogon	—	—	—	—	—	0	0
Pushkari I	—	—	—	1	+	0	1
Pushkari II	—	—	—	—	—	0	0
Radomyshl'	—	—	—	—	—	0	0
Suponevo	—	1	—	2	+	1	2
Timonovka I	—	3	1.5?	—	+	1	2
Timonovka II	—	1	—	—	+	0	1
Yudinovo	—	2	2?	2	+	1	3
Yurovichi	—	1	—	—	+	0	1
Zhuravka	—	—	—	—	—	0	0

[a]Scaled coding: 0, no or one category present; 1, present in two or more catetgories.
[b]Coding by number of categories present.

and the other, purely local display of art and jewelry made of locally available materials. I return to these observations when I consider Upper Paleolithic social interactions in Chapter 7.

As indicated earlier, for some evaluations I combine data on all decorative items into a single attribute. Table 6.14 lists coded values for individual decorative types and (1) presence or absence of any decorative objects, (2) scaled values of 0 for the presence of no or only one category of item and 1 for the presence of two or more categories, and (3) a dimensional coding system based on the number of categories (1–4) present.

Since I assume that both exotic lithics and decorative items are associated with a range of base-camp behaviors, I also test the association of these two summed attributes at the sites. This is done on both presence–absence data and coded values (Table 6.13). Both tests show the two summed attributes to be associated at the sites (presence–absence, $\phi = .56$; scaled codes, $\phi = .67$), corroborating my assumptions.

Assemblages: Faunal Remains

Information on the economically important taxa found at the sites is used as attributes in the following manner.

Number of Taxa Exploited.   This attribute is defined as the total number of hunted or collected species utilized per site (see Table 2.7).

Number of Taxa Exploited as Food.   Also derived from Table 2.7, this attribute is modified to include only those species actively hunted in the north and south (see Chapter 5 for a discussion of hunting and collecting). In this discussion, I consider individual species of fish and birds independently, not combining them into a summed taxa as done in Chapter 5.

Summed MNI and MNB Values for Food Species.   These values are defined in Chapter 5 as measures of density per square meter of either MNI or MNB. Individual values per site can be found in Tables 5.6 and 5.7. As I show in Chapter 5, food taxa, quantified in both MNI and MNB, were found at high and low densities at the sites. In this chapter I simply use these "high" and "low" density categories.

Given the assumptions about the division of activities between base camps and extractive camps, I anticipate (1) a greater number of economically important taxa, (2) a greater number of food species, and (3) higher MNI and MNB values for summed food taxa at base camps than at extractive camps.

Density of Fur Bearers.   This attribute is based on data presented in Chapter 5 (see Table 5.7) and is used in two ways: (1) evaluated simply by presence or absence of summed fur bearers, and (2) as density-controlled values for MNI/m² of all fur bearers found at sites. In the second case I define the attribute as either "high" or "low" density value per site.

Presence of fur bearers at sites resulted from at least two behavioral complexes: fulfilment of need for clothing and specialized exploitation for furs in quantities above simple consumer needs. Some sites may have served as initial procurement and processing stations for fur bearers. We can, therefore, anticipate fur bearers at high densities both at extractive camps used for procuring this resource and at base camps occupied by larger groups.

Kilocalorie Density.   Available energy is defined, as in Chapter 5, as total caloric value per square meter of site obtained from the taxa exploited as food. This attribute is used in this chapter at two ranges—one omitting all mammoths from consideration and the second including half of the mammoths present at each site. As I have shown in Chapter 5, the sites in the study area can be divided into high- and low-kcal groups.

We can anticipate high kilocalorie values at base campes as well as at some extractive locations, especially at those where provisioning for storage took place. I argue in

Chapter 5, however, that procurement behavior in the study area did not include much initial processing of food resources before they were taken to the sites. This in turn implies that we should not find evidence for extensive use of mass-procurement hunting camps in the area, and consequently that high kilocalorie values should be found at base camps and low values at extractive locales.

SITE PROFILES

Attributes that can be subsumed under the term "site profiles" offer another set of measures for classifying the sites in the study area. These include such characteristics as the thickness of the cultural layer, location and size of site, and season at which the site was occupied. This set of attributes, however, is the most problematic of all examined here. The thickness of a cultural layer can be affected by a number of diverse behaviors including the duration of occupation, frequency of reoccupation, and group size, as well as by a number of depositional or taphonomic variables. Since most of the sites have not been fully excavated, the size of a site is also a problematic measure. Site location, as I show in Chapter 5, is probably most directly related to the season of occupation, and, as such, is useful in secondary refinement of a classificatory scheme. Finally, the season of occupation is also suitable only as an attribute to refine a typology rather than to create one. In general, then, I use this set of attributes not for initial classification but only for secondary elaboration or corroboration. These attributes are characterized as follows:

Season of Occupation.   This has been estimated for the sites in Table 5.43. These estimates, cold- or warm-weather months, are used as such in this chapter as well.

Site Location.   Data on the location of sites vis-à-vis the floodplain are presented in Chapter 4, where I show that sites with mammoth-bone dwellings or storage pits tend to be found close to the rivers, whereas those without them are located at higher elevations.

Thickness of the Cultural Layer.   Thickness of cultural layer is defined for sites found in situ as either "high" or "low." These values are obtained by comparing northern to southern sites as well as comparing sites with features to those without them through difference of means tests (Table 6.15). These comparisons show considerably thicker cultural layers at some sites than at others but do not show either regional or feature-associated differences between sites (Figure 6.1). In general, the observed differences can be summarized as follows:

1.   "high" cultural layer thickness at Berdyzh, Bugorok, Fastov, Khotylevo II, Kositsa, Radomyshl', Suponevo, and Yudinovo;
2.   "low" cultural layer thickness at Chulatovo II, Dobranichevka, Gontsy, Eliseevichi, Pushkari I, Pushkari II, Mezhirich, Mezin, Timonovka I and II, and Zhuravka.

Since a number of independent factors can be suggested to account for differential thickness of the cultural layers, I use this attribute not for initial classification but only

Table 6.15   DIFFERENCE OF MEANS TESTS ON CULTURAL LAYER THICKNESS

	N	$\overline{X}_1$	$\overline{X}_2$	z	p
All Sites					
with vs. without storage pits	20	0.11	0.17	1.50	.13
northern vs. southern sites	18	0.18	0.11	1.75	.08
northern sites with vs. without storage pits	13	0.20	0.13	1.40	.16
southern sites with vs. without storage pits	6	0.13	0.08	1.67	.10
with storage pits, high vs. low density	10	0.29	0.11	6.00	<.0001
without storage pits, high vs. low density (all = late)	6	0.15	0.05	2.78	.008
with storage pits, north vs. south	13	0.20	0.13	1.60	.11
without storage pits, north vs. south	6	0.13	0.08	1.00	0.32
with storage pits, high density, north vs. south	5	0.31	0.20	5.50	<.0001
with storage pits, low density, north vs. south	8	0.104	0.10	0.18	.39
without storage pits, high densisty, north vs. south	4	0.16	0.10	1.50	.12
without storage pits, low density, north vs. south	2	0.04	0.06	—	—
northern high-density sites with vs. without storage pits	7	0.31	0.16	3.75	<.0001
northern low-density sites with vs. without storage pits	6	0.104	0.04	30.00	<.0001
southern high-density sites with vs. without storage pits	2	0.20	<0.10	—	—
southern low-density sites with vs. without storage pits	4	0.10	0.006	4.48	<.0001
Late Sites					
with vs. without storage pits	16	0.14	0.11	0.75	.45
northern vs. southern sites	15	0.15	0.09	2.00	.05
with storage pits, high vs. low density	10	0.25	0.10	1.07	.23
with storage pits, high vs. low density					
if Suponevo eliminated	9	0.30	0.10	40.00	<.0001
without storage pits, north vs. south	6	0.13	0.08	1.25	.18
without storage pits, high vs. low density	6	0.15	0.05	2.78	.008
with storage pits, high density, north vs. south	2	—	—	—	—
with storage pits, low density, north vs. south	8	0.104	0.10	0.18	.39
without storage pits, high density, north vs. south	4	0.16	0.10	1.50	.13
without storage pits, low density, north vs. south	2	0.04	0.06	—	—
with storage pits, north vs. south	10	0.16	0.10	2.00	.05

to examine regional differences and changes of settlement types and settlement patterns through time.

FEATURES

This last category of attributes includes mammoth-bone dwellings, bone charcoal, hearths, small pits, large storage pits, and mammoth-bone heaps or accumulations not identified as dwellings.

Mammoth-Bone Dwellings.   Since dwellings as such were only recognized by archaeologists in the study area in the late 1920s, the numbers of dwellings found at sites excavated before that decade have been subsequently estimated through various reconstructive efforts. Table 6.16 lists the number of dwellings reported for each site and estimates the roofed space for each reported dwelling. In this chapter I use these data as

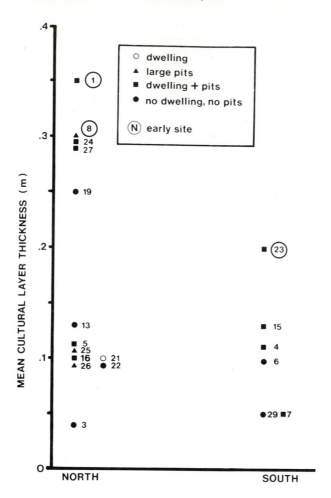

Figure 6.1 Thickness of cultural layers at the sites.

nominal at times and also work with both presence–absence of dwellings and interval quantifications.

Table 6.16 shows that two categories of dwellings have been found at the sites—those averaging less than 13 m² and those of over 20 m². As Table 6.17 shows, the difference between these sizes is significant ($z = 11.84$), and we can divide the sites on dwelling size as follows:

1. only small dwellings: Dobranichevka and Radomyshl';
2. only large dwellings: Gontsy(?), Eliseevichi, Kirillovskaya, Suponevo, and Yudinovo;
3. both small and large dwellings: Mezhirich and Mezin.

In addition to size of dwellings and mean number per site, I use an estimation of labor invested in the construction of the dwellings to classify sites with dwellings into two types. To arrive at labor investment values I performed the following calculations:

Table 6.16   LABOR EXPENDITURE IN THE CONSTRUCTION OF DWELLINGS

Sites	No. of dwellings	Dwelling area (m²)					Small dwellings	Large dwellings	Dwellings per site (mean)	Estimated bone (kg)[a]	Days of Labor per site	
		1	2	3	4	5					10 workers	20 workers
Berdyzh	2	12.5	45?				←—omit (questionable reconstructions)—→					
Dobranichevka	4	12.5	12.5	12.5	12.5		4	—	4	19,260	5.4	2.7
Eliseevichi	2?	←——— ~20. for each ———→					—	2	2	31,442	8.8	4.4
Gontsy	2	←——— ~20 for each? ———→					—	2	2	31,442	8.8	4.4
Kirillovskaya	3–4	←——— ~20 for each ———→					—	4?	—	←—omit (reconstructed)—→		
Mezhirich	4	24	20	12?	20		1	3	4	51,978	14.5	7.3
Mezin	2–5	20	8	28	8	23	2	3	3.5	56,793	15.9	8.0
Pushkari I[b]	1–3	(48)	(12.5)	(12.5)			3	—	2	14,445	4.0	2.0
Radomyshl'	5–6	12.5	12.5	10	12.5	10	5–6	—	5.5	28,890	8.1	4.0
Suponevo	1–3	23.76	27.5	nd					2	47,163	13.2	6.6
Yudinovo	3–4	20–44	24	20–28	20–30		—	4	3.5	62,884	17.6	8.8

[a]Small dwelling = 4815 kg bone; large dwelling = 15,721 kg bone.
[b]If one dwelling, then area = 48 m²; if 3 dwellings, then each area = 12.5 m²; calculated as 3 small dwellings for maximal bone estimates.

1. First, I obtained from the literature (where possible) a total list of mammoth skeletal elements used in each dwelling. These are only available in tabulated form for Dwellings 1, 2, and 3 at Mezhirich (Pidoplichko 1976). Those for Dwelling 4 are taken from my 1978 and 1979 field notes. Mezhirich data is presented in Table 6.18.

2. Table 5.15 presents weights of different mammoth skeletal elements. These values are multiplied by the number of each element per dwelling, and the total weights of bone per dwelling are listed in Table 6.19. Data on the skeletal elements per dwelling at Dobranichevka, Gontsy, and Mezin were extracted from the literature and at best represent minimal estimates. Although the bone weights offered in this table are rough estimates, they do pattern consistently to show a positive correlation between size of dwelling (interior area) and kilograms of bone used in its construction ($r = .79$, $.05 < p < .1$).

3. Using data on worker-hours of labor for transporting and erecting of earthworks and stone monuments from Coles (1973, 1979), Table 6.20 offers worker-day estimates for the assemblage of bone and the construction of dwellings for each site. The values assume (1) total transport of 500 kg (over a distance of 750 m) per worker per day, and (2) 250 kg per worker per hour for a 5-hour work day (i.e., 1250 kg of bone per worker per day) as a rate for the construction of the dwellings (after Coles 1973:73, 1979:138–139). These values are then translated into labor estimates per dwelling for groups of 10 and 20 workers.

4. Since firm data on skeletal elements per dwelling are available only for a few dwellings at a few sites, I calculate mean labor investment values for the assemblage and construction of small and large dwellings. These are based on a mean weight of 4815 kg for small dwellings and 15,721 kg for the large ones. These mean values are multiplied by the number of small and large dwellings reported for the sites and totaled per site (Table 6.16). Note that these mean estimates are different from the actual values

Table 6.17 DIFFERENCE OF MEANS TESTS ON FEATURES

	N	$\overline{X}_1$	$\overline{X}_2$	z	p
Hearths					
Density at the sites, m² per hearth, all sites					
northern vs. southern sites	12	95.42	226.95	2.91	.005
sites with vs. without dwellings	12	186.30	111.10	1.73	.08
northern sites with vs. without dwellings	6	87.03	112.20	0.78	.29
southern sites with vs. without dwellings	6	285.50	110.00	4.74	<.0004
northern vs. southern sites with dwellings	8	87.09	285.30	5.15	<.0001
northern vs. southern sites without dwellings	4	112.20	110.00	0.07	.40
northern sites with vs. without storage pits	8	124.51	142.90	0.41	.37
Density at the sites, m² per hearth, late sites					
sites with vs. without storage pits	12	167.21	120.97	1.10	.22
northern vs. southern sites	12	84.30	227.00	3.12	.003
northern sites with vs. without storage pits	6	72.78	142.90	11.73	<.0001
southern sites with vs. without storage pits	6	285.50	110.00	4.74	<.0001
northern vs. southern sites with storage pits	9	72.78	285.30	5.67	<.0001
northern vs. southern sites without storage pits	6	70.73	110.00	6.22	<.0001
Volume of hearths, all sites					
northern vs. southern sites	7	2.10	0.68	1.54	.12
northern vs. southern sites with dwellings	6	2.52	0.68	1.77	.08
sites with vs. without dwellings	7	1.91	0.40	2.04	.03
northern vs. southern sites with storage pits	6	2.53	0.68	2.09	.05
northern sites with vs. without storage pits	5	2.53	0.40	2.13	.04
Volume of hearths, late sites					
sites with vs. without storage pits	6	1.21	0.40	2.70	.01
northern vs. southern sites	6	1.28	0.68	1.36	.16
northern sites with vs. without storage pits	4	1.57	0.40	3.44	<.0009
northern vs. southern sites with storage pits	5	1.57	0.89	2.70	.008
Dwellings					
number of dwellings at northern vs. southern sites	11	2.50	3.80	2.06	.05
number of dwellings at late northern vs. late southern sites	9	2.60	3.38	1.30	.17
large vs. small dwellings (on area per dwelling)	32	23.13	11.29	11.84	<.0001
Facilities					
Numbers of storage pits, dwellings, and surface bone accumulations per square meter at simple vs. complex sites with storage pits and dwellings (base camps)	10	114.42	67.85	1.76	.08
Square meters per facilities and hearths at simple vs. complex sites with storage pits and dwellings (base camps)	10	67.90	59.52	0.73	.31
Labor investment of 10 workers at sites with dwellings at simple vs. complex base camps	9	6.58	13.98	3.92	<.0004

observed at Mezhirich and that the actual weight there (63,567 kg) is greater than the value derived by this calculation (51,978 kg). This transformation of Mezhirich data from real into mean values enables the use of comparable values for the largest possible number of sites.

Table 6.18 DISTRIBUTION OF MAMMOTH SKELETAL ELEMENTS AND THEIR WEIGHTS PER DWELLING AT MEZHIRICH[a]

	Dwelling 1		Dwelling 2		Dwelling 3		Dwelling 4[b]	
	N	kg	N	kg	N	kg	N	kg
Cranea	46	9200.0	34	6800.0	17	3400.0	40	8000.0
Mandibles	95	1729.0	2	36.4	12	218.4	11	200.2
Teeth	10	50.0	13	65.0	21	110.0	—	
Tusks	40	8000.0	41	8400.0	11	2200.0	35	7000.0
Vertibrae	47	61.1	70	91.0	84	109.2	9	4.7
Ribs	9	13.5	192	288.0	65	97.5	1	1.5
Scapulae	31	341.0	42	642.0	29	319.0	13	143.0
Humeri	20	157.0	32	351.2	15	117.8	6	47.1
Radii	8	8.0	15	60.0	10	40.0	—	
Ulnae	2	2.0	5	5.0	7	7.0	4	4.0
Pelvises	46	506.0	61	671.0	22	242.0	28	308.0
Femora	26	390.0	59	885.0	20	300.0	7	105.0
Tibiae	6	39.6	12	79.2	18	118.8	1	6.6
Fibulae	1	1.0	2	2.0	2	2.0	—	
Patellae	—		1	0.2	1	0.2	—	
Tarsals	2	3.6	3	5.4	1	1.8	—	
Metapodials	3	3.6	5	9.0	6	10.8	—	
Phalanges	3	1.5	9	4.5	5	2.5	—	
Sesamoids	—		2	ins	—		—	
Long bone fragments	18	77.4	58	249.4	283	1216.9		
	406	20,584.3	658	18,643.3	629	8518.9	155	15,827.1

[a]Data on skeletal elements in Dwellings 1, 2, and 3 from Pidoplichko (1976); on Dwelling 4 from my field notes on excavations during the 1978–1979 field seasons. Weights of skeletal elements from Table 5.15.
[b]Counts incomplete; Dwelling 4 under excavation.

5. Lacking data on skeletal elements and their total weights for most sites, I also arrive at mean labor estimates to use on mean kilogram estimates per site. The mean value of kilograms of bone moved (through either assemblage or construction) per person per site is based on the values of the firmly quantified sites. For example, the 8209-kg Dwelling 1 at Dobranichevka represent 2.3 days of labor of 10 workers giving an estimated 357 kg of bone per worker per day (3570 kg for 10 workers, 7140 kg for 20 workers per day).

6. Using this mean estimate of 357 kg per day as the amount of labor per person per site, I calculate the time it would take both 10 and 20 workers to construct the dwellings at the sites (Table 6.16).

Given my assumptions about the differences in activities performed at base camps and extractive camps, I anticipate finding mammoth-bone dwellings only at base camps.

Large Storage Pits.   Data on the number of large storage pits and their volume per site are reported in Table 5.4. In this discussion I use both presence–absence of storage pits and their numbers at sites, and I assume that this attribute will be found exclusively at base camps.

Table 6.19 MAMMOTH-BONE DWELLINGS

	Dwelling	Interior area (m²)	Mammoth-bone (kg)
Dobranichevka[a]	1	12.5	8,209
	2	12.5	1,045
	3	12.5	1,490
	4	12.5	nd
Gontsy[b]	1	$\overline{X}$ =20.0	>11,789
	2	$\overline{X}$ =20.0	nd
Mezhirich[c]	1	24.0	20,583
	2	20	18,643
	3	12.0	8,514
	4	27.0	15,827
Mezin[d]	1	20	8,202
	2	8	nd
	3	28	>2,944
	4	8	>362
	5	28	1,669

*Area for Mezhirich dwelling/3 given in Pidoplichko 1976. This estimate is questionable as he gives a diameter of ~2 m.
[a]From Shovkoplyas et al. (1981); Shovkoplyas (1972).
[b]From Pidoplichko (1969).
[c]From Kornietz et al. (1981); Pidoplichko (1969). Questionable estimate for Dwelling 3 from Pidoplichko (1976), based on ~2 m diameter.
[d]From Shovkoplyas 1965a.

Small Pits.   As discussed in Chapter 5, a number of both exterior and interior small pits, variously identified as possible postholes, roasting pits, and caches, have been found at three sites: Gontsy, Pushkari I, and Yudinovo. Small exterior pits have been reported at Chulatovo II, Mezin, Pushkari I, and Timonovka II. While it is impossible to associate these small pits with specific behaviors, the interpretations offered for these pits all suggest that we can anticipate finding them more readily at base camps. For the purposes of this discussion, small pits will be evaluated either as present or absent at the sites.

Bone Charcoal.   Because a number of sites in the study area have been either severely disturbed or redeposited, and because of the disparate sizes of excavations at the sites, I include the presence or absence of severely burned bone or bone charcoal at the sites as an independent attribute in this chapter. This attribute however, is noted only when present at the sites where no definite hearths have been reported. I assume that charcoal is behaviorally associated with some form of food processing and therefore anticipate finding it at both food procurement camps and base camps.

Hearths.   Data on hearth volume per site and density of hearths per site is presented in Table 6.21. Both are used in this chapter and illustrated in Figure 6.2. As this figure shows, the presence of hearths at the sites is associated with the presence of storage

Table 6.20 ESTIMATES OF LABOR INVESTED IN THE ASSEMBLAGE AND CONSTRUCTION OF MAMMOTH-BONE DWELLINGS

	Assembly (days)[a]		Construction (days)[b]		Total (days)	
	10 workers	20 workers	10 workers	20 workers	10 workers	20 workers
Dobranichevka						
Dwelling 1	1.6	0.8	0.7	0.3	2.3	1.1
Dwelling 2	0.2	0.1	0.08	0.04	0.3	0.1
Dwelling 3	0.3	0.1	0.1	0.05	0.4	0.15
Dwelling 4	ins	ins	ins	ins	ins	ins
Gontsy						
Dwelling 1	2.4	1.2	0.9	0.5	3.3	1.7
Dwelling 2	2.4	1.2	0.9	0.5	3.3	1.7
Mezhirich						
Dwelling 1	4.0	2.0	1.6	0.8	5.6	2.8
Dwelling 2	3.7	1.8	1.5	0.7	5.2	2.5
Dwelling 3	1.7	0.8	0.7	0.3	2.4	1.1
Dwelling 4	3.1	1.5	1.2	0.6	4.3	2.1
Mezin						
Dwelling 1	1.6	0.8	0.7	0.3	2.3	1.1
Dwelling 2	nd	nd	nd	nd	nd	nd
Dwelling 3	0.6	0.3	0.2	0.2	0.8	0.4
Dwelling 4	ins	ins	0.1	0.05	ins	ins
Dwelling 5	0.3	0.2	ins	ins	ins	ins

[a]Assume 500 kg/person/day over 750 m, after Coles (1970:138–139); insignificant (ins) less than 0.01 days.
[b]Assume 250 kg/person/hour and a 5-hour work day, after Coles (1973).

pits. The tests of this association show $\phi = .75$ and a value of $\phi = .56$ is obtained for the association of hearths and mammoth-bone dwellings (Table 6.13).

A comparison of mean differences in hearth volume at northern and southern sites does not show a significant difference ($z = 1.54$), but large differences are observed in the mean hearth volume between sites with storage pits ($\overline{X}_1 = 1.91$) and without them ($\overline{X}_2 = 0.40$, $z = 2.04$). Similarly, large differences are observed in mean hearth volume between the northern and southern sites with storage pits ($z = 2.09$). A comparison of hearth volume between these categories of sites indicates the presence of the following two groups of sites:

1. high-volume sites: Berdyzh, Mezin, and Suponevo;
2. low-volume sites: Chulatovo II, Dobranichevka, Pushkari I, and Mezhirich.

For the purposes of this chapter, I assume that, all other things being equal, hearth volume roughly reflects the length of stay at sites; I use the "high" and "low" volume estimates to define this characteristic.

Figure 6.2 shows that a difference can also be observed in the density of hearths at the sites. I have quantified this value as square meters of site per hearth. Using difference of means tests, significantly greater densities of hearths are found at northern sites

Table 6.21   VOLUME AND DENSITY OF HEARTHS

Site	Interior			Exterior			All hearths	
	No. found	Mean volume (m³)	Total volume (m³)	No. found	Mean volume (m³)	Total volume (m³)	Total hearth volume (m³)	m² of site per hearth
Berdyzh	3	1.8	5.4	—	—	—	5.4	116.7
Chulatovo I	—	—	—	7	0.06	0.4	0.4	142.9
Dobranichevka	2	0.1	0.2	7	0.1	0.7	0.9	222.2
Fastov	—	—	—	2	nd	nd	nd	110.0
Gontsy	1	nd	nd	2	nd	nd	nd	273.3
Khotylevo II	—	—	—	some	nd	nd	nd	nd
Kirillovskaya	—	—	—	>20	nd	nd	nd	~392.0
Mezhirich	3	0.05	0.15	6	0.05	0.3	0.45	254.5
Mezin	6	0.004	0.024	9	0.2	1.8	1.824	80.0
Pushkari I	3	0.2	0.6	2	0.15	0.3	0.9	80.0
Radomyshl'	some	nd	nd	some	nd	nd	nd	nd
Suponevo	1–2	0.2	~0.4	1–2?	0.8	1.6?	~2.0	50.0
Timonovka I	nd	nd	nd	1	0.6	0.6	nd	nd
Timonovka II	—	—	—	2	nd	nd	nd	81.5
Yudinovo	2	0.04	0.08	5	nd	nd	nd	71.4
Zhuravka	—	—	—	3	nd	nd	nd	110.0

(z = 2.91, Table 6.17) as well as between sites with mammoth-bone dwellings and sites without them (z = 1.73, p = .08). Northern sites with dwellings have considerably more hearths than their southern equivalents (z = 5.15). At the same time, no differences in hearth densities are found between northern sites with storage pits and without them (z = .41). If we assume that the number of hearths at sites is positively related to the number of occupants, the regional differences noted above appear to indicate that greater numbers of people occupied northern sites. I have argued previously, however (see a discussion on indoor vs. outdoor hearths in Chapter 5), that data at some northern sites, especially those with dwellings, suggest that (1) those sites do not represent single occupations, and (2) those sites may have had some disparate occupational episodes during warm and cold seasons. I therefore suggest that, lacking controls on the reoccupational sequences at sites, we should not interpret the differences in hearth densities as unequivocal indications of larger group sizes at northern sites. All that can be concluded is that some sites show larger numbers of hearths than others, and that the following two groups are present in the area:

1. high density of hearths at Berdyzh, Mezin, Pushkari I, Suponevo, Timonovka II, and Yudinovo in the north; Fastov and Zhuravka in the south;
2. low density of hearths at Chulatovo II in the north; Dobranichevka, Gontsy, and Mezhirich in the south.

In general, assuming single occupational episodes at the sites, I anticipate greater hearth volume at base camps, while either the density of hearths should be very much

tures, and site characteristics found at these sites is offered in Table 6.24. The following attributes are found predominantly in this category of sites: (1) worked bone ($z = 2.85$); (2) art and jewelry ($\phi = .86$); (3) shells ($\phi = .39$); (4) amber ($\phi = .36$, $p = .08$); (5) ocher ($\phi = .43$); and (6) grinding stone ($\phi = .33$, $p = .06$) (Tables 6.2 and 6.13). In addition to the co-occurrence of storage pits, hearths, and mammoth-bone dwellings, this category of sites also has greater hearth volume ($z = 2.04$), and in both north and south, sites with storage pits or dwellings have more hearths ($z = 11.73$ and $z = 4.74$, respectively, Table 6.17).

Data on hand for Mezin and Suponevo, and possibly for Dobranichevka, Gontsy, and Mezhirich, suggest that these sites were occupied more than once. It is unclear if various reoccupations were functionally alike. As Binford (1982b) points out, base camps can and do become extractive locales, and vice versa. Given this ambiguity, we should anticipate some unclear patterning in the distribution of attributes at these sites.

Considering only the two most visible diagnostic attributes, storage pits and mammoth-bone dwellings, we see three categories of in situ sites:

1. sites with both dwellings and storage pits: Berdyzh, Dobranichevka, Eliseevichi, Gontsy, Radomyshl', Mezhirich, Mezin, Suponevo, and Yudinovo;
2. sites with dwellings but without storage pits: Kirillovskaya and Pushkari I;
3. sites with storage pits but without dwellings: Khotylevo II and Timonovka I and II.

I suspect that the second group, with dwellings but no storage pits, really belongs to the first group, and I categorize them as such in the following. I would argue that Kirillovskaya and Pushkari I lack storage pits only because of archaeological biases. In the case of Kirillovskaya, lack of stratigraphic controls and the failure of nineteenth-century excavators to recognize these features is probably to blame. Pushkari I, located on the heavily utilized Pushkari promontory, requires additional excavation, which, I suspect would yield storage pits.

In addition, large MNI counts of mammoth (17–22) at the totally redeposited Yurovichi suggest that dwellings or storage pits were present at this site as well.

Using the data from Table 6.24, we can recognize at least two types of base camps among these sites. In considering the distribution of assemblages among the sites, however, regional differences should be kept in mind in the patterning of lithic remains, as they crosscut and overshadow all other differences. Specifically, the superior lithic outcrops in the north and cobble flint in the south should be reflected in lithic distribution. While I attempt to control for much of this effect through residualization in attribute definition, in this discussion I argue that the distribution of any lithic attribute should be evaluated separately at the northern and southern sites. For example, low overall densities of lithic tools are observed for all but Khotylevo II and Timonovka I in the north, while they are found at low densities only in Mezhirich in the south. Likewise, since we have no lithic workshops in the south, the consistently high blade–nuclei ratios at southern sites contrast with the low ratios at such northern sites as Pushkari I and Timonovka I (Table 6.24).

Keeping these regional differences in mind, we can clearly distinguish two types of

Table 6.24   PROFILE OF SITES WITH DWELLINGS OR STORAGE PITS[a]

	Simple base camps						
	Berdyzh	Dobranichevka	Gontsy	Kirillovskaya[b]	Pushkari I	Radomyshl'	Yurovichi[b]
Objects							
lithic tool density	nd	Hi	Hi	Hi	Lo	Hi	nd
nuclei density	nd	Hi	Lo	nd	Lo	nd	nd
nuclei proportion	nd	Lo	Lo	nd	Hi	nd	nd
blade-nuclei ratio	nd	Lo	Hi	Hi	Lo	nd	nd
ESB ratio[c]							
measure 1	nd	Hi	Hi	Hi	Hi	nd	nd
measure 2	nd	Lo	Lo	Lo	Hi	Lo	nd
grinding stones	—	+	+	—	+	—	+
worked bone	—	Lo	Hi	Lo	Hi	—	+
exotic lithics	nd	+	+	—	—	+	—
ocher	—	+	+	—	+	—	+
amber	—	+	+	—	—	—	—
art	—	+	—	+	—	—	+?
marine shells	—	—	—	—	—	—	—
jewelry	—	—	+	—	+	—	—
Faunal remains							
No. of exploited taxa	7	13	13	8	7	4	3
No. of food taxa	4	7	5	3	4	4	3
MNI + MNB, food taxa	Lo	Lo	Lo	Lo	Lo	Lo	nd
fur-bearer density	Lo	Lo	Lo	Lo	Lo	—	nd
kcal density							
no mammoth	Lo	Lo	Lo	Lo	Lo	Lo	nd
half mammoth	Lo	Lo	Lo	Lo	Hi	Lo	nd
Site profiles							
season of occupation	C	C	C	C	C?	C	C?
cultural layer thickness	Hi	Lo	Lo	nd	Lo	Hi	R
Features							
small pits	—	—	+	—	+	—	nd
bone charcoal	+	+	+	+	+	+	+
hearth volume	Hi	Lo	nd	nd	Lo	nd	nd
hearth density	Lo	Lo	Lo	Lo	Hi	nd	nd
bone heaps	—	—	?	nd	—	—	nd
dwellings	+	+	+	+	+	+	+?
storage pits	+	+	+	—	—	+	nd

[a]Hi = high density; Lo = low density; W = warm season; C = cold season; R = redeposited.
[b]Classification problematic.
[c]ESB = end scrapers plus burins; Measure 1 is density residualized against lithic density (bone and hide work); Measure 2 is density residualized against lithic density and density of fur bearers.
[d]Unquantified; from personal inspection at the Institute of History, AN BSSR and The Historical Museum in Minsk.

base camps—*simple* and *complex*—but also a third residual category of problematic base camps. I begin by examining sites where both dwellings and storage pits have been found. The simple base camps have fewer storage pits and dwellings, as well as surface bone accumulations and hearths, than their more complex equivalents (see Table 6.22). I have eliminated Berdyzh and Kirillovskaya from consideration; in the first case, data are unclear on the nature, number, and size of the features; in the second, the features assigned by Pidoplichko (1969) come from his reconstruction of the site from nineteenth-century archival sources and can be expected to include numerous omissions

Complex base camps					Problematic base camps		
Eliseevichi	Mezhirich	Mezin	Suponevo[b]	Yudinovo[b]	Khotylevo II	Timonovka I	Timonovka II
Lo	Lo	Lo	nd	nd	Hi	Hi	Lo
Lo	Hi	Lo	nd	nd	nd	Hi	Lo
Lo	Lo	Lo	nd	nd	nd	Hi	Hi
Hi	Hi	Hi	nd	nd	nd	Lo	nd
Lo	Lo	Hi	nd	nd	nd	Hi	Hi
Hi	Hi	Hi	nd	nd	nd	Hi	Lo
—	+	+	—	—	—	+	+
Hi	Hi	Hi	Hi	Hi[d]	Hi	Hi	Hi
+	+	—	—	+	nd	+	—
+	+	+	+	+	+	+	+
—	+	+	—	—	—	—	—
+	+	+	+	+	+	+	+
+	+	+	—	+	—	+	—
+	+	+	+	+	—	—	—
14	19	16	10	14	13	6	7
6	11	8	5	7	7	2	2
Lo	Hi	Hi	Lo	Lo	Hi	Lo	Lo
Hi	Hi	Hi	Lo	Lo	Lo	Lo	Lo
Lo	Hi	Hi	Lo	nd	Lo	Lo	Lo
Hi	Hi	Hi	Lo	nd	Lo	Lo	Lo
C	C	C-W	C-W	C	C-W	C?	C?
Lo	Lo	Lo	Hi	Lo	Hi	Lo	Lo
—	—	+	—	+	—	—	+
+	+	+	+	+	+	+	+
nd	Lo	Hi	Hi	nd	nd	nd	Hi
nd	Lo	Hi	Hi	Hi	nd	nd	Hi
+	+	+	+	+	—	?	+
+	+	+	+	+	—	—	—
+	+	+	+	+	+	+	+

and errors. A comparison of the differences in mean densities of facilities only (i.e., storage pits, dwellings, and bone heaps) among sites with dwellings shows significantly higher density at Eliseevichi, Mezhirich, Mezin, Suponevo, and Yudinovo than at Dobranichevka, Gontsy, Pushkari I, and Radomyshl' ($z = 1.76$, $p = .08$). A similar division of sites into two groups can be observed if we use labor investment as a measure; twice as much effort was invested in construction at Eliseevichi, Mezhirich, Mezin, Suponevo, and Yudinovo than at Dobranichevka, Gontsy, Pushkari I, and Radomyshl' ($z = 3.92$, Table 6.17 and Figures 6.4–6.6).

While impossible to quantify, labor investment beyond that used in this discussion can also be postulated at some of the complex sites. Both Rogachev (1970) and, indirectly, Polikarpovich (1968) note that some kind of patterning or bone sorting can be

Figure 6.4   Reconstructed Dwelling 3 from Dobranichevka, on display at the Periyaslov–Khmelnitsky open air museum.

observed in the construction of at least one dwelling at Yudinovo. As Kornietz *et al.* (1981) report, bone sorting is also evident at Mezhirich. Dwelling 1 features outside facing or "retaining walls" made of mammoth skulls and 95 mandibles stacked one on top of the other in a herringbone "chin down" pattern (Figure 6.5 and 6.6). In Dwelling 2, these facings or outside walls are of long bones. In Dwelling 4, different sections of the outside walls are made up of different skeletal elements and sectionally reflect the other dwellings at the site. Gladkih notes an additional fascinating detail in the construction of Mezhirich Dwelling 4—the use of mirror imagery and repetition in the construction of the outside wall (Soffer 1981); for example, the mandible section features two rows with "chin down," then a row with "chin up," then another row with "chin down" (Figure 6.7). In an adjacent section, a skull is bracketed on the left and right sides with identical sequences of scapula–scapula–pelvis (Figure 6.8). The same rhythmic repetition is also seen in the placement of the vertebrae and the skeletal elements next to them. As noted, I have not translated these observations into quantified estimates of labor; they do, however, strongly suggest that the estimation I do use represents just minimal ranges of labor employed in constructing the dwellings.

Likewise, significantly greater numbers of decorative items have been found at the sites with more labor and facilities. A comparison of mean art and jewelry counts shows

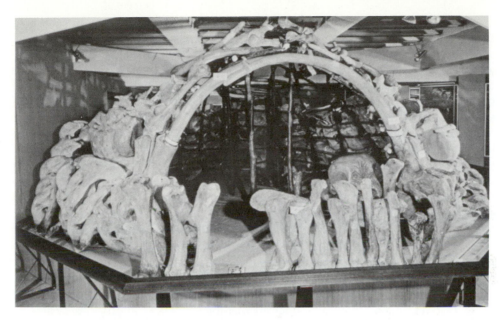

Figure 6.5 Reconstructed Dwelling 1 from Mezhirich (front), on display at the Museum of Paleontology, Kiev. Note painted mammoth skull inside (detail, Figure 2.73).

Figure 6.6 Reconstructed Dwelling 1 from Mezhirich (back).

86 times as many of these items at complex base camps ($z = 3.72$). In fact, as Table 6.11 shows, high values for art and jewelry can only be observed at these sites.

At the same time that this group of artifacts, requiring a good deal of labor but locally available raw materials, are found at complex base camps, nonlocal exotic materials—amber and fossil marine shells in particular—show a more ambiguous distribution. I have demonstrated previously that the distribution of all of these artifacts is associated at the sites, but it could be argued that this association is a result of different and unrelated behaviors. In order to test such a hypothesis—that the two sets of decorative items, one of local and one of exotic materials, are behaviorally related—I calculate a Kendall's tau correlation coefficient between them using data only from the in situ sites showing the presence of any of these items. To do so, coded values for these objects are transformed and recoded as follows: (1) the coded values for amber (Table 6.10) and shells (Table 6.12) and for art and jewelry (Table 6.11) are added and listed in Table 6.25; (2) these summed coded values are halved since objects could be found in either one or two categories; (3) to control for the differences in the sizes of excavations, these values are further divided by square meters excavated for each site (Table 6.25). These values are ranked, and the resulting tau value of .24 transformed into a $z = 1.09$ score (Table 6.26). The correlation between these two groups of decorative objects is not significant at the .05 level, which I interpret to indicate that the two sets of objects—those of local

Figure 6.7   Details of Mezhirich Dwelling 4, mandible section.

Figure 6.8 Details of Mezhirich Dwelling 4, scapula section.

Table 6.25 ASSOCIATION OF DECORATIVE OBJECTS AND FUR BEARERS

Site	Amber and shells		Art and jewelry		Fur bearers	
	Combined code values	Density-controlled coded values	Combined code values	Density-controlled coded values	Fox and hare density (m²)	All fur bearers density (m²)
Chulatovo II	2	0.0010	0	0.00000	0.037	0.0400
Dobranichevka	2	0.0005	1	0.00025	0.005	0.0080
Eliseevichi	2	0.0016	4	0.0032	0.459	0.540
Gontsy	1.5	0.0009	1	0.0006	0.034	0.050
Kirillovskaya	0	0.0000	1	0.00006	0.0001	0.0008
Mezhirich	4	0.0039	5	0.00492	0.185	0.2300
Mezin	4	0.0017	6	0.0025	0.103	0.1600
Pushkari I	0	0.0000	1	0.00125	0.010	0.0300
Pushkari II	0	0.0000	0	0.0000	0.017	0.1000
Suponevo	0	0.0000	3	0.0075	0.01	0.0300
Timonovka I	1.5	0.0006	3	0.00127	0.003	0.0050
Timonovka II	0	0.0000	1	0.0033	0.043	0.0600
Yudinovo	2	0.0020	4	0.0040	nd	nd
Zhuravka	0	0.0000	0	0.000	0.003	0.0060

Table 6.26   CORRELATION COEFFICIENTS: KENDALL'S TAU

	N	τ	z	p
Amber and shells vs. fox and hare	13	.40	9.09	<.0001
Amber and shells vs. art and jewelry	12	.24	1.09	.22
Amber and shells vs. all fur bearers	13	.40	9.09	<.0001
Art and jewelry vs. all fur bearers	13	.26	1.24	.18
Art and jewelry vs. fox and hares	13	.34	1.62	.11

material that require a good deal of labor and those of exotic material—are associated with two distinct behavioral complexes. I argue that decorative objects of local material are related more to intragroup signaling of status, while those of exotic materials, while possibly also used as status markers, were more closely associated with intergroup or regional exchange networks (O'Shea 1981; Root 1983; Wobst 1977). Table 6.24 also shows that the distribution of densities of fur bearers, MNI and MNB counts of food taxa, and kilocalorie values show similar patterning and are found at high densities at complex base camps and low densities at simple base camps. Due, however, to the early date of excavation of Suponevo, periglacial disturbances at Eliseevichi, and the incomplete reporting of faunal data from Yudinovo (as well as the fact that it is still under excavation), this patterning is less clear than for the distribution of facilities, labor investment, and decorative items. Thus, high densities of fur bearers are found only at Eliseevichi, Mezhirich, and Mezin. High kilocalorie values (including half of the mammoths in calculations) occur at Eliseevichi, Mezhirich, and Mezin and high MNI and MNB values for all food taxa at Mezhirich and Mezin.

Faunal remains likewise show clear-cut patterning. A comparison of mean numbers of economically important taxa shows approximately two times the variety at complex base camps ($N = 12$, $\overline{X}_1 = 14.60$, $\overline{X}_2 = 7.86$, $z = 3.22$, $p = .002$). Similar disparity can be observed in species exploited as food ($N = 12$, $\overline{X}_1 = 7.40$, $\overline{X}_2 = 4.29$, $z = 2.70$, $p = .01$).

As I demonstrate in Chapter 5, fur bearers were objects of specialized exploitation and are found at some sites in quantities well above those that can be projected for purely utilitarian consumer needs. It will be recalled that the three sites with significantly higher densities of fur bearers are Eliseevichi, Mezhirich, and Mezin. These sites, as noted above, are also the locales where high densities of both local and exotic decorative items were found. To test for a behavioral relationship between fur bearers and decorative items, I calculate Kendall's correlation coefficients. Data on summarized density-controlled MNI per square meter for arctic fox and hare, as well as on all fur bearers, are presented in Table 6.25. I calculate tau and z scores for the following pairs of attributes: (1) summed amber and shell values and summed arctic fox and hare values; (2) summed amber and shell values and summed values for all fur bearers; (3) summed art and jewelry and summed arctic fox and hare values; (4) summed art and jewelry values and summed values for all fur bearers (Table 6.26). Ranking for all tests is done only for those sites where at least one of the two attributes tested for the correlation is present. As these analyses indicate, decorative objects of exotic material (i.e., amber and shell) are highly correlated with both fox and hare and with all fur bearers (both $\tau = .40$, both $z = 9.09$). Much weaker positive correlations are found between decorative objects of local materials (art and jewelry) and either summed fox and hare densities ($\tau = .34$, $z = 1.62$) or densities of all fur bearers ($\tau = .26$, $z = 1.24$), and these are not significant at the .05 level. I interpret these tests to indicate that while amber and shells were a part of the same exchange network as furs or pelts, art and jewelry of local material did not figure prominently in such networks. I conclude that (1) both status demarcation and exchange figured far more prominently in the behavioral repertoire at complex base camps than at simple base camps, (2) emphasis on status demarcation is seen primarily at complex base camps, and (3) long-distance exchange involving exotic materials and furs is behaviorally associated with complex base camps.

While I have demonstrated clear patterning in the distribution of attributes that can be roughly equated with social and possibly ideological behavior and have found much greater evidence for such behavior at complex base camps, this clear patterning cannot be observed in the distribution of attributes related to everyday subsistence or maintenance needs. Thus, while lithic tools tend to be found at low densities at the complex base camps, they are also low at the northern site of Pushkari I and consistently high at the simple southern base camps. While high blade–nuclei ratios are found at all southern sites, they are high only at northern complex sites and low at other northern sites. Data on end-scraper and burin densities are equally ambiguous. As suggested above, I interpret the lack of clear patterning among these attributes to be a result of both the distribution of high-quality raw materials interregionally and historic or prehistoric factors of limited significance to this discussion.

Finally, a lack of clear patterning can be observed in the densities of worked bone as well. First, a comparison of mean densities of worked bone between the sites with and without storage pits shows that bone working primarily occurred at sites with storage pits ($z = 2.85$). Bone working appears to have been more important, in general, in the north. A comparison of mean densities of worked bone between northern and southern sites with storage pits yields a z value of 1.30 ($p = .17$). Similarily, values for end-scraper and burin densities residualized from lithic density in general, as well as from fur bearer densities (Table 6.8), which I associate with bone working, show more intensive bone working in the north, with high densities found in the south only at Mezhirich.

I conclude this discussion by suggesting that we can identify the following simple and complex camps among the sites with storage pits and dwellings:

1. simple base camps: Berdyzh, Dobranichevka, Gontsy, Kirillovkaya, Pushkari I, Radomyshl', and in all probability Yurovichi;
2. complex base camps: Eliseevichi, Mezhirich, Mezin, and probably Suponevo and Yudinovo.

I suggest that the differences between the two types of cold-weather camps does not lie in basic maintenance—subsistence–related activities, but rather in the sphere of behavior associated with social and possibly ideological factors. It could be argued, however, that what I have identified as complex base camps were not in fact base camps at all but possibly special locales for ritual or ceremonial activities. I delay evaluating this hypothesis until all sites have been typed and questions of population and duration of occupation examined.

SITES WITH STORAGE PITS BUT WITHOUT DWELLINGS

Three sites, Khotylevo II, Timonovka I, and Timonovka II, have storage pits but lack mammoth-bone dwellings. This pattern differs from that observed at other base camps and merits a closer examination. As indicated in Chapter 2, data on features at these three sites are problematic. Khotylevo II is still under excavation and only preliminary information on the features and assemblages found at the site have appeared in the literature. Soviet researchers assign this early Desna site to the spatially distant Kostenki–Avdeevo culture; my analysis of faunal remains also shows Khotylevo II to be anomalous (see discussion in Chapter 5). The distribution of features and assemblages at this site appears to conform broadly to that identified at base camps, but while these distributions are similar to those found at other sites with storage pits or dwellings, lithic and bone assemblages as well as art objects show great differences (see Zavernyaev 1978). For example, Khotylevo II has yielded a number of female Venus figurines like those found only at the eastern Kostenki–Avdeevo sites. Likewise, the distribution of features on the Khotylevo II living floor is far more similar to those at Kostenki I-1 and I-2 and Avdeevo than to the Desna sites (see, for example, floor plans in Velichko, Zavernyaev et al. 1981 for a comparison). At present, all that can be said about Khotylevo II is that it represents some sort of base camp with an unclear season of occupation and unclear cultural affinities. Thus, I do not include this site in the discussion of the Upper Paleolithic settlement system in the study area.

Timonovka I and II may represent a sequential occupation rather than distinct sites (see Chapter 2). While they have been traditionally treated as two sites in the literature (a practice that I also adopt for this work), Grekhova (Velichko, Grekhova, and Gubonina 1977) hypothesizes that a part of the promontory, including sections of both Timonovka I and II, was occupied first and that a second occupation sequence (or a continuation of occupation at a slightly later period) took place at other sections of Timonovka I. Such an interpretation, while intriguing, has not been empirically substantiated.

Treating the two as separate sites, we see that a good deal of lithic manufacture went on at both. Data in Table 6.24 indicate a somewhat higher rate of original tool making at Timonovka II, with low lithic tool densities, than at Timonovka I, with high densities of this attribute. Data on nuclei densities, with high values at Timonovka I and low ones at Timonovka II, contradict this conclusion. The low blade–nuclei ratio at Timonovka I likewise indicates tool manufacture. High densities of end scrapers and burins associated with hide and bone processing at both sites indicate bone working at both. This is also confirmed by high densities of worked bone found at both sites. Both sites also show the presence of grinding stones, ocher, and art, and the absence of jewelry and amber. A small number of marine shells (~9) have been found at Timonovka II.

The distribution of features at the two sites is similar—both have large storage pits, hearths, and surface bone heaps. On these attributes, both Timonovka I and II, other than lacking mammoth-bone dwellings, are indistinguishable from simple base camps. And as other simple base camps with storage pits, they show occupation during the cold season and have low densities of fur bearers, kilocalories, and MNB and MNI counts of food taxa. What distinguishes these two sites from others I have classified as simple base camps is the number of species exploited as food: Only two food taxa have been found at Timonovka I and II. A comparison of mean numbers of taxa exploited as food at simple cold-weather base camps to those at Timonovka I and II shows significant differences ($N = 9$, $\overline{X}_1 = 4.29$, $\overline{X}_2 = 2.0$, $z = 8.25$, $z < .0001$). A similar difference can also be observed between the mean numbers of food taxa at warm-weather base camps and Timonovka I and II ($N = 8$, $\overline{X}_1 = 6.67$, $\overline{X}_2 = 2.0$, $z = 1.60$, p $= .11$). At the same time, no differences in mean densities of economically important taxa can be found between simple cold-weather base camps and Timonovka I and II ($N = 9$, $\overline{X}_1 = 7.86$, $\overline{X}_2 = 6.50$, $z = 0.87$, $p = .27$) or between warm-weather base camps and Timonovka I and II ($N = 8$, $\overline{X}_1 = 11.33$, $\overline{X}_2 = 6.50$, $z = 1.15$, p $= .21$). The low variety of food taxa at Timonovka I and II is indistinguishable from that at sites I classify as hunting or collecting locales (i.e., Fastov, Kurovo, and Novo-Bobovichi). A difference of means test between mean numbers of food taxa at these two groups of sites shows a z value of 0.00 ($N = 5$, $\overline{X}_1 = 2.0$, $\overline{X}_2 = 2.0$).

I interpret the distribution of attributes at Timonovka I and II to indicate that these two sites were base camps associated with much hunting and food provisioning. This, together with information that both were occupied during cold-weather months, further indicates that they represent yet another type of base camp, one where processing and caching of one or two abundant food resources took place. While there is no data on the exact content of the storage pits at these sites, and the role of mammoth in Upper Paleolithic diets unclear, it is tempting to speculate that both sites were base camps associated with intensive exploitation of reindeer. This species is the only one other than mammoth that was actively procured here (Table 5.6). Since reindeer in the study area would have been optimally hunted from fall to spring (see Chapter 3), and since storage pits were likely excavated during warm months, fall seems the probable time for hunting and storing of this taxon.

Data on the densities of fur bearers at Timonovka I and II, however, indicate that fall was not the only time the Timonovka promontory was occupied. High densities of arctic fox and wolverine are also present at Timonovka II. Data on arctic fox from other sites indicate that they were taken in late winter–early spring. Assuming this taxon was taken during this same season at Timonovka, we can conclude that the site was occupied in late winter–early spring. Thus, faunal evidence broadly supports Grekhova's hypothesis about the occupation sequence at Timonovka I and II, indicating that Timonovka I was probably a fall provisioning base camp and Timonovka II a late winter–early spring base camp, possibly subsisting on provisions cached in the fall.

It could also be argued that Timonovka I and II were exactly what other simple cold-weather base camps looked like before mammoth-bone dwellings were erected on them, and that the lack of dwellings at these two sites is due to some unknown prehistoric factor. In other words, the following Upper Paleolithic occupation sequence could be suggested: (1) at the end of warm weather, establishment of provisioning base camps for active hunting and storage, as well as intensive gathering of mammoth bone for construction (hence the surface bone heaps), and (2) in the fall, construction of dwellings. In this scenario, Timonovka I represents the locus of an early fall settlement at which dwellings were either never constructed or were constructed but subsequently destroyed after the site was abandoned. In the first instance, the inhabitants would have left the site, wintered in mammoth-bone dwellings elsewhere, and returned with the onset of warm weather to use the stored resources. In the second instance, they would have wintered over in the later destroyed dwellings, remaining in the area until spring. Unfortunately, data on hand do not permit a full evaluation of these alternatives. The faunal record on the food species appears to favor the second reconstruction, and I therefore classify the Timonovka sites as a second type of simple cold-weather base camp: the hunting base camp.

SUMMARY OF SITES AND SITE TYPES

The types of sites found in the study area and my assignment of the study sites according to these types is as follows:

1. lithic workshops—warm weather: Bugorok, Klyusy, Korshevo I and II, Pogon, and Pushkari II;
2. hunting camps—warm weather: Fastov and Kurovo;
3. collecting camps—warm weather: Novo-Bobovichi;
4. simple base camps—(a) warm weather: Chulatovo II, Zhuravka, Chulatovo I, Kositsa, Novgorod-Severskii, and Pushkari II; (b) cold weather: Berdyzh, Dobranichevka, Gontsy, Kirillovskaya, Pushkari I, Radomyshl', and Yurovichi;
5. hunting base camps: Timonovka I and II;
6. complex base camps—cold weather: Eliseevichi, Mezhirich, Mezin, Suponevo, and Yudinovo;
7. anomalous: Khotylevo II base camp.

POPULATION AND DURATION OF OCCUPATION

Questions about the size and duration of site occupations often found in the literature, present perhaps the thorniest of archaeological questions. Numerous approaches have been offered by researchers, ranging from the now classic caloric values of White (1953) to the equally popular values based on dwelling space per individual of Naroll (1962). A persistent problem in the application of these formulas has always been the separation of data dependent on population from data dependent on length of occupation. Yellen (1977) attempts to control these variables by dividing sites into central and peripheral portions, showing that areal values in the center reflect group size and those in the periphery the duration of occupation. And while this refinement certainly represents an improvement on ready-made recipes of the past, it assumes a single episode of occupation—an assumption that cannot be made for the sites on the late Pleistocene central Russian Plain. But in spite of a lack of suitable analytic tools for estimating population and duration of occupation for sites like those in study area, the establishment of even tenuous parameters is of heuristic value, and such parameters should be considered before an outline of settlement patterns is attempted. Because of my reservations about each single method for estimating either population or length of stay, I examine these variables with an array of approaches and look for evidence of patterning.

With the exception of White's (1953) caloric approach, estimations of population and length of occupation are either for very mobile hunter–gatherers (e.g., Weissner 1974; Yellen 1977) or for any group residing in dwellings, regardless of subsistence practices (e.g., Cook and Heizer 1968; Naroll 1962). Since the sites in the study area fall into both categories, I basically follow such a division in my discussion. First I apply methods based simply on site size, then I examine data from cold-weather base camps with dwellings, with or without storage pits, warm-weather base camps without any of these features, and finally Timonovka I and II, without dwellings but with storage pits.

POPULATION ESTIMATES FROM SITE SIZE

The most reliable estimates of site size for those few sites that have been fully excavated, as well as maximal sizes for sites only partially excavated (from Table 2.3), are listed in Table 6.27. I eliminate from consideration all cases, such as Eliseevichi and Yudinovo, where huge discrepancies exist between what has been excavated and what is postulated as maximal site size, as well as data on redeposited sites. Table 6.27 offers three estimates of populations per site, using formulas from Yellen (1977) and Weissner (1974) and a ratio of square meters per individual derived from Leroi-Gourhan and Brezillon's (1972) Pincevent study. These estimates are derived as follows:

Yellen's Formula.   Based on his work with the !Kung San, Yellen (1977) estimates population at sites by $y = 6.43 + 1.15x$, where y is the area of the core of the site and x the total number of inhabitants. While his delineation of the core is based on a comparison of artifact densities at the center and the periphery, lack of appropriate provenience data for the sites in the study area necessitates a relaxation of Yellen's requirements. Table 6.28 offers approximate areas for complexes delimited at Dobranichevka, Mezhirich, Mezin, Timonovka I, and Timonovka II and population estimates for each complex. These estimates are compared with those based on Weissner's method and the Pincevent data in Table 6.27.

Weissner's Formula.   While Weissner (1974), again using !Kung San data, has demonstrated a logarithmic relation between group size and living area at sites, her formula is applicable only to sites between 50 and 250 m² and for groups not numbering above

Table 6.27   POPULATION ESTIMATES FOR FULLY EXCAVATED SITES

Site	Site size	Population		
		Per Yellen[a]	Per Weissner[b]	On Pincevent data[c]
Chulatovo II	2000	342	185	50
Dobranichevka	5500[d]	487	509	138
Kirillovskaya	7840	nd	724	196
Mezin	1200	>408	111	30
Timonovka I	2800	655	259	70
Timonovka II	500	136	46	13

[a]Estimated after Yellen (1977); see Table 6.28.
[b]Estimated after Weissner (1974), assuming 10.8 m²/person.
[c]Estimated at 40 m²/person, derived from Leroi-Gourhan and Brezillon (1972).
[d]See p. 51 on site size.

25 individuals. Relaxing many of Weissner's requirements, and roughly assuming maximal floor space of 10.8 m² per individual for groups of 25 and above (Weissner's ratio for a group of 25), I estimate populations for the sites (Table 6.27).

Data from Pincevent.   Leroi-Gourhan and Brezillon (1972) have identified the remains of three temporary dwellings at Pincevant Section 36 and postulated that each was occupied by a family of about 5 individuals. Knowing that the total site encompasses approximately 600 m², and assuming (with Leroi-Gourhan and Brezillon) that the three dwellings were occupied simultaneously, we can determine a ratio of 40 m² per person at Pincevent. The results of applying this ratio to the data from the central Russian Plain sites are also listed in Table 6.27.

The results of these three approaches vary widely, casting doubt on the utility of site size for population estimations. Furthermore, there is no obvious rationale for preferring one approach from among the three. The resulting range in group sizes probably results from a lack of control for the number of reoccupations, as well as from a basis in spatial relationships (man/area) for groups no larger than those of the !Kung San.

ESTIMATES FOR SITES WITH DWELLINGS

Population

Another approach to estimating group size utilizes the roofed-over dwelling space per individual. Two ratios figure prominently in the English-language literature: Naroll's (1962) 10 m² per person, derived from a survey of agricultural groups, and Cook and Heizer's (1968) 6.1 m² per person, based on a survey of aboriginal California populations (the metric value here is my conversion and simplification of their more complex version expressed in inches). Soviet archaeologists, without discussing the empirical basis for their assumptions, have used 1–3 m² per person in their estimates (e.g., Bibikov 1969; Pidoplichko 1969, 1976; Shovkoplyas 1965a). This ratio is in fairly close accord with that reported by Watanabe (1972) for the sedentary Ainu. He reports that

Table 6.28 POPULATION BASED ON APPROXIMATIONS OF CORE AREA[a]

	Approximate core (m²)[b]	Population
Chulatovo II	400?	342
Dobranichevka		
complex 1	130	107
complex 2	200	168
complex 3	130	107
complex 4	128	106
		487
Mezhirich		
complex 1	120	99
complex 2	130	107
complex 3	112	92
		298
Mezin		
complex 1	232	196
complex 5	250	212
		408
Timonovka I		
complex 1	247	209
complex 2	194	163
complex 3	40	29
complex 4	298	254
		655
Timonovka II	163	136

[a]Based on Yellen (1977).
[b]Dobranichevka estimates from Leonova (1977); Timonovka I and II estimates from Velichko, Grekhova, and Gubonina (1977); Mezin and Mezhirich estimates by Soffer.

dwellings averaging about 5 m² in area were occupied by a single nuclear family of about 5 people. Similar ratios can also be obtained from Nelson (1971) for the Bering Strait Eskimo. For them, I calculate an average of 2.5 m² per person for winter houses and 2.8 m² per person for summer houses. Ives and Sinopoli (1979–1980) report a mean house size of 38 m² for a group of 20 among the Kaska—yielding a ratio of 1.9 m² of house floor space per individual. Balikci's (1970) data indicate approximately 4 m² per person in Netsilik winter houses, and the ratio for Siberian Nganasan can be estimated at about 1.6 m² per person from Chard (1963).

Table 6.29 gives population estimates per site using Naroll's, Cook and Heizer's, and Soviet ratios. Where ranges are given for number or size of dwellings, mean values are used. In order to select among these estimates, it is useful to briefly examine some ethnographic data on northern-latitude groups. Table 6.30 lists village sizes reported for

Table 6.29   POPULATION BASED ON HOUSE FLOOR SPACE

Site	Area excavated (m²)	Dwelling space (m²)	Population			Mean population
			Per Naroll[a]	Per Cook and Heiser[b]	1–3 m² per person	
Berdyzh	350	57	~6	~7	19–57	38
Dobranichevka	2000[c]	71	~7	~7	24–71	48
Eliseevichi	623	40	~4	~6	13–40	27
Gontsy	820	40	~4	~6	13–40	27
Kirillovskaya	7840	70	7	~7	23–70	47
Mezhirich	508	75	~7	~7	25–75	50
Mezin[d]	1200	70	~7	~7	23–70	47
Pushkari I	400	48	~5	~6	16–48	32
Radomyshl'	600	66.5	~6	~7	22–66	44
Suponevo	200	62	~6	~7	21–62	42
Yudinovo[d]	500	91.4	~9	~8	30–91	61

[a]10 m²/person from Naroll (1962).
[b]6.1 m²/person from Cook and Heizer (1968).
[c]See discussion on site size p. 51.
[d]Calculated on mean number and size of dwellings.

Holarctic populations of hunter–gatherers. As these show, population estimates for the central Russian Plain sites derived either from Naroll's or Cook and Heizer's ratios are too low to be viable. The size ranges derived from the use of 1–3 m² of floor space per individual come closer to ethnographically reported coresidential units. I therefore use estimates derived from this ratio in all future calculations.

Duration of Occupation

Even though all sites in the study area, with or without storage pits or dwellings, were temporary occupations (see Chapter 5), it is of some interest to see if the duration of this seasonal occupation can be roughly estimated, and to determine whether warm-weather sites were occupied for shorter periods than cold-weather sites. I offer three approaches to the problem of duration of occupation—through kilocalorie values, through the volume of lithics discovered, and through Yellen's formula for the size of the outer or peripheral area of the site. All three approaches share numerous problematic assumptions that I have mentioned earlier. For example, kilocalorie values reflect, in all probability, just a portion of what was consumed, and the effects of group size versus duration of occupation cannot be distinguished. The use of lithic density as an indicator assumes a uniform rate of lithic deposition per man as well as a direct relation between the rate of lithic deposition and duration of occupation. Yellen's (1977) formula is based both on a careful delineation of the periphery at sites using distribution of artifacts from single-occupation sites. I use these approaches, not to accurately estimate lengths of stay, but rather to derive some parameters for this variable which will be useful both for intersite comparisons and for our understanding of the settlement system in the study area.

Table 6.30   HOLARCTIC VILLAGE SIZES

Group[a]	Village size	Reference
Alaska		
Bering Strait Eskimo (w,s)	20–125	Nelson 1971
Central Eskimo (w,s)	mean 33	Boas 1964
Kaska (w,s)	~20	Ives and Sinopoli 1979–1980
Netsilik (w)	50–100	Balikci 1970
Point Barrow Eskimo (w)	mean 30	de Montmollin 1979–1980
Siberia		
Bering Strait–East Cape (nd)	250	Nelson 1971
Giliyak (w,s)	50–100	Black 1973
Nganasan (w)	38–45	Chard 1963

[a]w, winter camp; s, summer camp.

Kilocalorie Data.   Table 6.31 estimates duration of occupation using kilocalorie values per square meter of site. The basic assumptions are (1) group size within the parameters obtained through the use of 1–3 m² of dwelling space per individual and (2) a daily caloric requirement of 2400 kcals per individual. Two categories of estimate are offered in this table—one assuming minimal group size per site (i.e., 3 m² of dwelling space per individual) and the other assuming maximal group size per site (i.e., 1 m² of dwelling space per individual). Within each category, two values are considered, one excluding all mammoths and the other including half of the mammoths per site. Estimates of site area and of population from the 1–3-m² ratio are given in Table 6.2. Kilocalories available from actively hunted taxa per site are given in Table 5.18.

As the range of results indicates, estimates of duration of occupation based on kilocalorie values are severely limited by the problematic role mammoths played in Upper Paleolithic diets. Thus, for example, a group of 19 individuals could have remained from 1.4 months to 5.5 years at Berdyzh, or a group of 75 from 0.9 months to 4.1 years at Mezhirich, depending on whether mammoths are included in the calculations. Clearly the magnitude of such ranges shows this method of estimation to be of little use, even heuristically. I suggest, therefore, that this approach, like the estimation of population from the site area, is of little value for understanding demographic and temporal variability of the study sites.

Rate of Lithic Deposition.   Another approach to the problem of duration of occupation is the use of lithic density as a rough indicator. Taking the reliable Pincevent data reported by Leroi-Gourhan and Brezillon (1972) as a starting point, I calculate a rate for lithic deposition per man per month per square meter of site. A total of 16,040 pieces of lithics were found at the 600 m² excavated at Pincevent, giving a density of 26.7 lithics/m². The excavators suggest that Section 36 at Pincevent was occupied for about 5 months, giving a value of 5.34 lithics deposited per month. Finally, since Pincevent may have been occupied by three nuclear families (15 individuals), and assuming one flint maker per family, we can estimate a deposition rate of 1.78 lithics per man per month as a rough measure.

Table 6.31   DURATION OF OCCUPATION AT SITES WITH DWELLINGS BASED ON AVAILABLE KILOCALORIES

Site	Minimal group size[a]				Maximal group size[b]			
	Person/ m^{2c}	kcal/ person/ m^{2d}	No mammoth (mo)	Half mammoth (mo)	Person/ m^{2c}	kcal/ person/ m^{2d}	No mammoth (mo)	Half mammoth (mo)
Berdyzh	0.05	120	1.4	66	0.16	384	0.4	21
Dobranichevka	0.01	24	5.2	130	0.04	96	1.3	33
Eliseevichi	0.02	48	0.6	126	0.06	144	0.2	50
Gontsy	0.02	48	3.8	129	0.05	120	1.5	52
Kirillovskaya	0.004	10	1.3	61	0.01	24	0.5	26
Mezhirich	0.05	120	2.6	148	0.15	360	0.9	49
Mezin	0.02	48	14.0	139	0.06	144	4.5	46
Pushkari I	0.04	96	<1.0	107	0.12	288	0.2	36
Radomyshl'	0.04	96	0.7	51	0.11	264	~0.2	18
Suponevo	0.10	240	~1.0	11	0.31	744	0.3	4
Yudinovo	0.06	144	nd	nd	0.18	nd	nd	nd

[a]Maximal density, 0.33 person/m^2 of dwelling.
[b]Minimal density, 1.0 persons/m^2 of dwelling.
[c]Population estimates from Table 6.29.
[d]Presumes 2400 kcal/person/day requirement.

Some will argue that this permutation is an exercise in futility serving no useful archaeological purpose, since it is based on information from just one site. I offer it here as an interesting exercise that can be used on the central Russian Plain data and compared to other independently derived data to see if any patterning can be discerned. Such an approach has not been used widely because of the number of assumptions that must be made. Spiess (1979) uses a much higher value of 0.7 lithics per man per day (21 per man per months) for Abri Pataud, basing this on his observation of the rate of lithic production (10.2 per man per month) for the Dorset Eskimo. I use the much lower value derived from the Pincevent data to favor longer estimates in the duration of occupation.

Table 6.32 lists lithic densities found at the study sites. I have previously argued that, in general, lithic densities are about eight times greater at northern than at the southern sites, probably due to the ready availability of superior flint outcrops in the north. In order to control for this phenomenon, I divide lithic densities at northern sites by a factor of eight. Then, using a rate of 1.78 lithics per man per month, I calculate the duration of occupation for both minimal and maximal group-size estimates. I offer two estimates for the duration of occupation for each group size: one from uncontrolled and one from controlled lithic densities. For example, at Eliseevichi I estimate 13–40 inhabitants (Table 6.29). If we consider the minimal size (i.e., 13 people—3 families), we can suppose that 3 knappers were at work depositing a total of 5.3 lithics/m²/month. Using the lithic density of 128.4/m² reported for Eliseevichi, we obtain a duration of occupation of approximately 24 months. Or if we use the controlled value of 16.05 lithics/m² we obtain a duration of 3.1 months.

Table 6.32   DURATION OF OCCUPATION BASED ON RATE OF LITHIC DEPOSITION[a]

			Minimal Group Size				Maximal Group Size			
Site	Lithic density	Corrected lithic density[b]	Group size	Number of toolmakers[c]	Stay on lithic density (mo)	Stay on corrected lithic density (mo)	Group size	Number of toolmakers[c]	Stay on lithic density (mo)	Stay on corrected lithic density (mo)
Berdyzh	4.3	0.54	19	4	0.5	0.08	57	11	0.2	0.03
Dobranichevka	6.8	6.8	24	5	0.8	0.8	71	14	0.3	0.3
Eliseevichi	128.4	16.05	13	3	24.0	3.1	40	8	9.0	1.1
Gontsy	3.7	3.7	13	3	0.7	0.7	40	8	0.3	0.3
Kirillovskaya	0.5	0.5	23	5	0.06	0.06	70	14	0.02	0.02
Mezhirich	29.3	29.3	25	5	3.3	3.3	75	15	1.1	1.1
Mezin	94.9	11.8	23	5	10.6	1.3	70	14	3.8	0.5
Pushkari I	400.0	50.0	16	3	75.5	9.4	48	10	22.5	2.8
Radomyshl'	16.7	16.7	22	4	2.3	2.3	66	13	0.7	0.7
Suponevo	150.0	18.8	21	4	21.1	2.6	62	12	7.0	0.9
Yudinovo	>25.0	>3.1	30	6	2.3	0.3	91	18	0.8	0.1

[a]Rate of lithic deposition assumed to be 1.78 lithics/man/month/m², after Leroi-Gourhan and Brezillon (1972).
[b]Densities at northern sites divided by 8, see discussion in text.
[c]Assume a family of 5 people and 1 toolmaker per family.

As this table indicates, if we control for the greater availability of raw materials in the north, the length of stay at all sites is less than a year. In fact, the longest stay for a minimal group, observed at Pushkari I, is a little over 9 months. While I agree that the range in estimated duration of occupation per site is wide (from 24 to 1.1 months at Eliseevichi), and that the required assumptions are problematic, I argue that the data indicate temporary sedentism (1–4 months if controlling for raw material availability in the north; 4–13 months if not taking this factor into account) and conform to my conclusions about the seasonal occupation of the sites reached in Chapter 5.

Size of Peripheral Areas.   Yellen (1977) gives the following formula for duration estimations: *number of days of occupation = 0.1 (peripheral area) + 1.87.* Estimated durations of occupation obtained by this method are given in Table 6.33. Size of the

Table 6.33   DURATION OF OCCUPATION BASED ON PERIPHERAL AREA[a]

Site	Peripheral area (m²)	Length of stay (days)
Chulatovo II	600	62
Dobranichevka	1412	143
Fastov	188	20
Timonovka I	2021	214
Timonovka II	337	36

[a]Based on Yellen (1977).

Table 6.34   GROUP SIZE AND DURATION OF OCCUPATION AT WARM-WEATHER SITES

	Area (m²)	Flint/ m²	kcal per complex[a]		Group size per		Stay per Yellen (days)[a]		Stay per Weissner (days)[a]		No. of knappers[b]		Stay on flint/ m² (mos)[b]		Stay on corrected flints/m² (mos)[b,c]	
			1	2	Yellen	Weissner	1	2	1	2	3	4	3	4	3	4
Chulatovo II																
Complex 1	41[d]	59.4[e]	728,365	1,466,365	30	~9	10	20	34	68	6	2	5.6	16.7	0.7	2.1
Complex 2	20[d]	62.9[e]	355,300	715,300	12	—	12	25	—	—	2	—	18.0	—	2.2	—
Complex 3	72[d]	99.0[e]	1,279,080	2,575,081	57	11	9	19	48	97	11	—	5.0	28.0	6.6	3.5
total					99	>20	31	59	82	165	19	2	28.6	73.3	9.5	5.6
mean					60								51		8	
Fastov																
2 work areas	15	8.6	60,030	1,410,030	7	—	3.5	84	—	—	1	—	4.3	—	4.3	—
	17	8.6	68,034	1,588,034	9	—	3	74	—	—	2	—	2.4	—	2.4	—
total					16	—	6.5	158	—	—	3	—	6.7	—	6.7	—
mean					16								7.0		7.0	
Zhuravka																
3 work areas	~110	11.2	79,603	79,603	80	14	1	1	4	4	16	3	0.4	2.1	0.4	2.1
	~110	11.2	79,603	79,603	80	14	1	1	4	4	16	3	0.4	2.1	0.4	2.1
	~110	11.2	79,603	79,603	80	14	1	1	4	4	16	3	0.4	2.1	0.4	2.1
total					240	42										
mean					141								1.3		1.3	

[a]1, kcal excluding mammoth; 2, kcal including half of mammoth.
[b]3, population estimate based on Yellen (1977) formula; 4, population estimate based on Weissner (1974) formula.
[c]Northern site lithic densities divided by eight.
[d]Part of complex only.
[e]From Leonova (1977).

peripheral areas at Chulatovo II, Dobranichevka, Timonovka I, and Timonovka II are calculated from core areas (Table 6.28) and total excavated areas (Table 6.29) at each site. The estimates for Fatov use 32 m² on which Shovkoplyas (1956) reported the densest concentration of remains as the core area.

Lengths of stay obtained through this method are in overall accord with those derived from the rate of lithic deposition, showing ranges of 1–5 months at cold-weather base camps, 2 months at Chulatovo II, occupied in warm weather, and less than 20 days at Fastov, a hunting station.

ESTIMATES FOR SITES WITHOUT DWELLINGS OR STORAGE PITS

Three in situ sites, the warm-weather base camps Chulatovo II and Zhuravka and the hunting station Fastov, are considered in this section. Table 6.34 summarizes estimates for both the duration of occupation and group size at these sites. Since there is no conclusive proof that the three concentrations of remains at Chulatovo II and Zhuravka and the two at Fastov reflect synchronic occupation, I calculate both estimates for each concentration per site. The area of each concentration at Chulatovo II is calculated from Leonova's map (Figure 2.24) and includes all squares where the observed lithic density was above 1/m². Areas listed for Fastov and Zhuravka, where no maps of lithic distribu-

Table 6.35   GROUP SIZE AND DURATION OF OCCUPATION FOR TIMONOVKA I AND II

	Timonovka I	Timonovka II
Total area (m²)	2,800	500
Kcals, no mammoths	420,000	183,000
Kcals, half mammoths	40,740,000	63,183,000
Duration of occupation, per Yellen 1977 (days)	214	36
Kcals per day, no mammoths	1,962.6	50,833.3
Kcals per day, half mammoths	190,373.8	1,755,083.3
Number of people, no mammoths	1	21
Number of people half mammoths	79	731
Lithic density (per m²)	85.0	85.5
Corrected lithic density[a] (per m²)	10.6	10.7
Length of stay, on lithic density (months)	9.5	9.6
Length of stay, on corrected lithic density (months)	1.1	1.0
Mean length of stay (months)	5.3	5.3

[a]Corrected lithic density = density at northern sites divided by 8.

tion are available, are estimated by dividing the total area of the site by 2 and 3, respectively.

Population estimates based on site size (as in Table 6.26) follow Yellen (1977) and Weissner (1974). In computing the latter, I use the total size of each cluster at Chulatovo but only 90% of the area for Fastov and Zhuravka (see Price 1978 for a discussion of area size and the Weissner formula). These two sets of population figures are then each applied in estimations of duration of occupation based on available kilocalories (as in Table 6.31) and lithic distribution (as in Table 6.32).

The values for both group size and length of stay show wide ranges—at Zhuravka, for example, from 42 to 240 individuals who stayed from 0.4 to 2.1 months on lithic densities and from 1 to 4 days on kilocalories. While these ranges do not permit me to establish firm parameters for either one of these variables, they can be used for a comparison with the values obtained for sites with mammoth-bone dwellings.

In general, I suggest that the data indicates considerably shorter duration of occupation at warm-weather base camps (1–3 months?) than at their cold-weather equivalents. Estimates for Fastov broadly conform to the expectations for hunting stations, showing both smaller group size and shorter length of stay than base camps.

ESTIMATES FOR SITES WITHOUT DWELLINGS BUT WITH STORAGE PITS

Table 6.35 presents temporal and demographic estimates for Timonovka I and II. Duration of occupation based on Yellen's pheripheral area formula is taken from Table 6.33. Population size based on kilocalories with no mammoths and half of the mammoths included is calculated as in Tables 6.31 and 6.34. Since these population esti-

Table 6.36   MEAN VALUES FOR GROUP SIZE AND DURATION OF OCCUPATION

			Duration of occupation (months)			Lithics + kcal	
Sites	(1) Group size	(2) Lithics	(3) kcal no mammoth	(4) kcal half mammoth	(5) Mean kcal	(6) No mammoth	(7) Mean kcal
With dwellings							
Berdyzh	38	0.05	0.9	44	22	0.5	11
Dobranichevka	48	0.55	3.3	82	43	2.0	22
Eliseevichi	27	2.10	0.4	88	44	1.0	23
Gontsy	27	0.50	2.7	91	47	1.6	24
Kirillovskaya	47	0.04	0.9	44	22	0.5	11
Mezhirich	50	2.20	1.8	99	50	2.0	26
Mezin	47	2.55	9.3	93	51	6.0	27
Pushkari I	32	6.10	0.6	72	36	3.0	21
Radomyshl'	44	1.50	0.5	35	18	1.0	10
Suponevo	42	1.75	0.6	7.3	4	1.0	3
Yudinovo	61	0.20	nd	nd	nd	nd	nd
Without dwellings							
Chulatovo II	60	8	2.00	4.00	3.00	5.0	6.0
Fastov	16	7	0.08	0.08	0.08	4.0	4.0
Timonovka I[a]	nd	← 1.1–5.3 →				6.0	6.0
Timonovka II[a]	nd	← 1.0–5.3 →				3.0	3.0
Zhuravka	42	1	0.20	5.00	2.60	0.6	1.8

[a]Estimates for duration of occupation at Timonovka I and II from Table 6.35.

mates show improbable ranges of 1–79 individuals at Timonovka I and 21–731 at Timonovka II, I forego their use in calculating lengths of stay. Instead, I arbitrarily assume five flint knappers at each site and calculate lengths of stay as Tables 6.32 and 6.34, for uncontrolled lithic densities and for lithic densities controlled for northern high-quality flint. These estimates broadly conform to the pattern observed at other cold-weather base camps, indicating that the two sites were also occupied temporarily.

SUMMARY AND CONCLUSIONS

It should be reiterated that no estimates in this section, whether for population or duration of occupation, are offered as absolute measures. There are a myriad of problems associated with such calculations. But however unrealistic these values are, they may be equally unrealistic for all types of sites and therefore useful for comparison of different site types. To this end, Table 6.36 summarizes all estimates of population and duration of occupation for all sites from Tables 6.29–6.35. All values in Table 6.36 are means of the alternate values and ranges given in each category. Populations are either the means of the 1–3-m² per person ratio or the means of the Yellen- and Weissner-based estimates (Column 1); Zhuravka, an exception, simply takes the less unlikely Weissner-based value. Durations of occupation based on lithic deposition are means of

Table 6.37 DIFFERENCE OF MEANS TESTS ON POPULATION AND DURATION OF OCCUPATION

	N	$\overline{X}_1$	$\overline{X}_2$	z	p
Population at cold- vs. warm-weather base camps	13	42.09	51.00	0.93	.26
Duration at cold- vs. warm-weather base camps (no mammoths)	14	1.86	3.65	1.38	.15
Duration at cold- vs. warm-weather base camps (mean kcal)	14	15.58	3.90	3.47	<.0009
Population at simple vs. complex cold-weather base camps	11	39.33	45.40	0.93	.26
Duration at simple vs. complex cold-weather base camps (no mammoths)	12	2.20	2.50	0.22	.39
Duration at simple vs. complex cold-weather base camps (mean kcal)	12	13.50	19.97	0.98	.25
Population at cold- vs. warm-weather simple base camps	8	39.33	51.00	1.21	.19
Duration at cold- vs. warm-weather simple base camps (no mammoths)	10	2.20	2.80	0.26	.39
Duration at cold- vs. warm-weather simple base camps (mean kcal)	10	13.63	3.90	2.84	.007

the minimal and maximal estimates based on corrected density values (Column 2). Durations of occupation based on available kilocalories are given with mammoths excluded (Column 3), half of mammoths included (Column 4), and for the mean of these two (Column 5). In addition, mean lengths of stay based on lithics plus kilocalories excluding mammoths (Column 6) and on lithics plus mean kilocalories (Column 7) are calculated. Duration of occupation for Timonovka I and II are taken from the values given in Table 6.35. No population estimations are offered for these two sites because those calculated (Table 6.35) appear totally unrealistic.

Table 6.37 shows the results of statistical analyses on the population and duration variables and site types. Comparison of mean populations at all cold- and warm-weather base camps ($z = 0.93$), as well as at simple and complex cold-weather base camps ($z = 0.93$), shows no significant differences. Similarily, no differences are found in population of simple cold- and warm-weather base camps ($z = 1.21$). I conclude, therefore, that no seasonal aggregations can be projected for the Upper Paleolithic central Russian Plain, and that similar-size coresidential units remained together during both cold and warm weather.

Comparing the duration of occupation at these three types of base camps, no differences are observed if the values used exclude mammoths (Table 6.36, Column 6), either between all cold- and warm-weather base camps ($z = 1.38$), simple cold- and warm-weather base camps ($z = 0.26$), or simple and complex cold-weather base camps ($z = 0.22$). When duration of occupation estimates include mammoths, however, cold-weather base camps show a considerably longer occupation ($z = 3.47$) than warm weather base camps, as do simple cold-weather base camps when compared to warm-

Table 6.38 BERING STRAIT ESKIMO
SETTLEMENT PATTERN[a]

Village[a]	Population	Number of houses
Ignituk (w)	120	nd
Kushungil (w)	100	20
Razbinsky (w)	~125	25
Starikwikhpak (w)	40	nd
Ukagamiut (?)	20	nd
Karaligamiut (w,s)	100	nd
Cape Espenberg (s)	30	5
Point Hope (s)	300–400	2–10
Hotham Inlet (s)	600–800[c]	18
East Cape, Siberia (nd)	250	54

[a]From Nelson (1971).
[b]w, winter camp; s, summer camp.
[c]special trading camp.

weather base camps ($z = 2.84$). No differences are observed in the duration of occupation between simple and complex cold-weather base camps ($z = 0.98$) using these values. These conflicting results once again underscore the difficulty of establishing any demographic or temporal parameters for site occupation until the role of mammoths in the diet is clearly established.

In spite of this conflict, I argue that consistent patterning in test results indicates that cold-weather base camps, both simple and complex, were occupied for about the same length of time, and consequently that this variable is not responsible for the complexity observed at some cold-weather base camps. Estimated lengths of stay at warm-weather base camps consistently indicate shorter duration of occupation than at either of the two types of cold-weather base camps. Just how much longer cold-weather camps were occupied cannot be determined with the data on hand, because mean differences vary depending on the values used. Thus, while a comparison between simple cold- and warm-weather base camps on kilocalories (including mammoths) indicates three times longer stays at cold-weather camps, a comparison of all cold-weather to warm-weather camps shows seven times longer occupation at cold-weather camps. Intuitively, I suggest that a realistic estimate lies somewhere between these two, with stays of about 6 months at cold-weather camps and about 1 to 1.5 months at their warm-weather equivalents.

Although I have argued against too strict an adherence to ethnographic models when evaluating late Pleistocene cultures, it is interesting to compare the emerging Upper Paleolithic settlement pattern to ethnographic data. I suggest that of Holarctic hunter–gatherer cultures, the Bering Strait Eskimo as described by Nelson (1971) show the greatest similarity to the central Russian Plain pattern (see Table 6.38).

As Nelson describes them, Bering Strait groups lived in large, distinct aggregations during winter and summer. The two types of settlement were quite near each other (within a kilometer or two), and at times were even adjacent—summer dwellings being located on one side of the village and winter dwellings on another. This pattern appears rather similar to that of the central Russian Plain when size differences between the coresiding units are considered. While groups around the Bering Strait lived in considerably larger groups in the villages, there was no dispersal into smaller sizes in summer months. Although Nelson offers no information on the duration of occupation of summer villages, climatic factors would suggest that in northern latitudes, where the warm season is much shorter than the cold season, summer villages would be occupied for shorter periods. Black (1973) reports this pattern for Siberian Gilyak, and Chang (1962) traces similar seasonal settlement stability among a number of circumpolar societies in Siberia and Alaska. The central Russian Plain data appear to conform to this general pattern of year-round, large coresidential units which remain at winter settlements longer than at summer ones, and which do not show dispersal in warm-weather months.

SETTLEMENT SYSTEM ANALYSIS

Two further topics should be considered before my model for the settlement system is presented: the relationship between simple and complex cold-weather base camps, and possible north–south regional differences in seasonal site type, duration of occupation, and group size.

SIMPLE VERSUS COMPLEX BASE CAMPS

While I demonstrated previously that real differences exist between simple and complex cold-weather base camps, I only alluded to possible explanations for these differences, including the possibility that what I identify as complex base camps are not such at all but rather some sort of special gathering places for trade, ritual activities, and so forth.

Ethnographic data on Bering Strait groups can be used to generate yet another explanation for the observed differences—that what I identify as complex base camps are sites that included some sort of ritual or men's club houses, where a great deal of nonsubsistence behavior occurred which, in site-level analysis, would make these sites appear different and more complex. Nelson (1971) describes special ritual dance houses in some winter villages. These dance houses were considerably larger than residential houses and locales of nonsubsistence behavior; yet no food was cooked there, no one lived there, no maintenance activities were performed there. Using Nelson's data, I estimate the mean size of these dance houses to be 54 m², with the reported winter houses averaging 12.5 m², and summer houses ranging from 3 to 28 m². While no systematic estimates can be obtained Nelson's data on the relation between number of houses per village and number of dance houses per village, he does suggest that larger villages had more special houses (*kashin*) than did the small villages. Since both small and large mammoth-bone dwellings are found at winter base camps in the study area, it could be argued that the large ones were not residential structures but some sort of ritual constructions. Assuming such a function for the large houses, one could then simply argue that complex base camps had such dwellings and the simple ones did not.

While data on hand are not firm or adequate enough to properly evaluate these two hypotheses—that complex base camps were either aggregation sites or base camps with ritual houses—some evidence can be brought to bear on the two. First, if we argue that the complex base camps were not base camps at all but some sort of special aggregation sites, we can derive the following archaeological implications: (1) that there will be a noticeable difference in the densities of such subsistence-related attributes as total lithics and lithic tools, percentage of specific tool types, density of worked bone, and so forth at these sites; (2) that there will be a difference in the duration of occupation of these sites, with base camps being occupied longer than special gathering locales; and (3) that special gathering locales will have larger populations than base camps. The data on hand (e.g., Tables 2.4–2.11) do not meet the expectations necessary to identify Eliseevichi, Mezhirich, Mezin, Suponevo, or Yudinovo as special locales; no significant differences are found in either population or duration of occupation between these and other base camps. Taking regional differences in lithic use into account, complex base camps have been shown to have comparable densities for both tools in general and specific tool types. Overall, Table 6.24 shows no difference in the range of activities performed at simple and complex sites. In fact, densities of worked bone are higher at complex base camps, as are densities of kilocalories, indicating both more manufacturing of bone implements and more intensive procurement of food resources. Observed higher densities of fur bearers at complex sites also argue for more intensive exploitation of these taxa. In summary then, data on hand do not support the hypothesis that complex base camps were not base camps but special-purpose gathering locales.

The second hypothesis, that some of the dwellings were not residential but ritual constructions, and that they may have been found at only some sites, is more difficult to evaluate because the type of data necessary for a dwelling–dwelling comparison is generally not available for the study sites. As I have noted, both small and large constructions have been found, but their distribution does not pattern according to the predictions of this second hypothesis. Thus, for example, while both large and small dwellings have been found at Mezhirich and Mezin (both identified as complex base camps), and only small dwellings unearthed at Dobranichevka and Radomyshl' (identified as simple base camps), data from Eliseevichi, Gontsy, Kirillovskaya, Suponevo, and Yudinovo do not conform to the pattern. These sites have yielded only large constructions. Since it could be argued that the last group represents either sites excavated very early, before dwellings were recognized (Gontsy, Kirillovskaya, Suponevo), or severely disturbed sites (Eliseevichi), or sites still undergoing excavation (Yudinovo), and that, therefore, the reported sizes and numbers of dwellings there are at best "guesstimates," I compare the distributin of some attributes between the different dwelling complexes at the two sites most recently excavated for which such data could be obtained: Mezhirich and Dobranichevka. These comparisons are presented in Table 6.39. Each complex listed represents a combination of dwelling and outside work area. I use the complex as a unit of analysis because the excavators, Pidoplichko (1976) and Shovkoplyas (1972),

Table 6.39   DISTRIBUTION OF INVENTORIES AT DOBRANICHEVKA AND MEZHIRICH[a]

Inventory[b]	Dobranichevka				Mezhirich		
	Complex 1	Complex 2	Complex 3	Complex 4	Complex 1	Complex 2	Complex 3
Area of complex (m²)	130	200	120	128	68	64	~68
Area of dwelling (m²)	12.5	12.5	12.5	12.5	24	20	12
Mammoth bone per m² of dwelling (kg)	656.7	83.6	119.2	nd	857.6	932.1	709.5
Type of dwelling	small	small	small	small	large	large	small
Mammoth bone in dwelling (kg)	8209	1045	1490	nd	20,583	18,643	8514
Lithics density	25.0	7.0	12.0	25.0	66.5	116.8	32.8
Lithic tool density	4.2	0.5	1.1	2.1	8.2	10.3	3.8
End scraper + burin density	5.8	1.9	nd	nd	4.9	6.2	2.0
Nuclei density	0.7	0.2	0.4	0.9	1.1	1.8	0.6
Worked bone density	some	some	some	nd	0.8	1.5	0.7
Amber density	some	some	—	—	1.0	3.6	0.6
Art density	some	some	some	—?	0.06	0.03	0.04
Red and yellow ocher density	some	some	—?	—?	0.9	1.1	0.3

[a]Dobranichevka data from Leonova (1977) and Shovkoplyas (1965a); Mezhirich data from Kornietz et al. (1981) and Pidoplichko (1976).
[b]Densities of inventories calculated per square meter of complex.

use such subdivisions in their reports. While the data in this table are far from adequate in some cases—for example, the distribution of art, amber, ocher, and bone could not be estimated per complex for Dobranichevka—they still indicate no radical differences in the densities of attributes at the different complexes. At Mezhirich, in fact, maintenance-related attributes such as flint density, density of end scrapers and burins, and tool density, are higher in Complexes 1 and 2 with large dwellings than at Complex 3 with a small dwelling. At the same time, Complexes 1 and 2 feature higher densities of art, amber, and ocher. Nor are the differences in densities of subsistence-related attributes at the three Mezhirich complexes significantly greater than between the four Dobranichevka complexes with small dwellings. Finally, while similar qualification could not be presented for Mezin, Shovkoplyas (1965a) reports that art objects were found in Dwellings 1, 2, 3, and 5 at the site. This distribution again shows no association of decorative objects with larger dwellings (at Mezin, Dwellings 1, 3, and 5 are large).

I conclude, therefore, that data on hand do not support the hypothesis that large dwellings were some sort of special-activity locales where behavior unrelated to subsistence took place, and that these types of dwellings were located at just some of the winter base camps. It is not the dwellings themselves that were different, but rather the sites. Eliseevichi, Mezhirich, Mezin, Suponevo, and Yudinovo were locales where a set of activities above and beyond subsistence needs took place, and these activities occurred there more intensively than at the other base camps. I have already discussed evidence for special planning and sorting in the construction of dwellings at Mezhirich and possibly Yudinovo. This, along with the use of rhythmic repetition and symmetry in the construction of both individual dwellings and in the relationship of the structural elements of the different dwellings argues for site-centered rather than dwelling-centered behavior.

The complex sites were locales where status demarcation was important (art and jewelry distribution), as well as repositories of goods involved in exchange networks (amber, shell, furs). This behavioral complex reflects both intra- and intergroup social relationships. At the same time, and at the same sites, there is also evidence of behavior associated with ideology. The elaborate site planning at Mezhirich and possibly Yudinovo suggests this. And while it could be argued that painted mammoth skulls, scapulae, and pelvises found at Mezhirich (see Figure 2.72 and illustrations in Pidoplichko 1976) and Mezin (see Figure 2.82 and illustrations in Shovkoplyas 1965a) were also used in personal status signaling, I suspect they were more closely allied with ideological behavior. Bibikov (1981) suggests that remains of a number of percussion instruments were found at both sites, although his postulation of Upper Paleolithic rhythm bands has not been widely accepted (Semenov 1978, personal communication). I can neither firmly prove the association of these attributes with ideology nor state whether such behavior was related to corporate or cosmic ideologies (most probably to a combination of the two). I argue, however, that it is precisely this sort of behavior that distinguishes complex from simple base camps. In brief, I identify two spheres of behavior at complex sites above those related to subsistence needs: social and ritual.

I am also unable, at present, to clearly delimit the sorts of activities carried on at these complex sites nor to exhaustively delimit the behavioral differences between simple and complex base camps. I find no similar pattern in the hunter–gatherer ethnographic literature to draw on for analogy and would argue that in these five sites we have evidence for Upper Paleolithic behavior for which we may have no clear present-day equivalents.

On the other hand, it may well be that both simple and complex base camps represent two ends of a continuum—just as some Bering Strait villages are larger, have more numerous dance houses, and are residential locales of rich and esteemed men. Recognition of some of the attributes used to make the distinction between simple and complex base camps clearly varies with the work of particular excavators. Thus, for example, Pidoplichko, a paleontologist, was the first researcher to identify amber in the study area. This attribute, in fact, has only been reported at those sites at which he worked. As noted in Chapter 2, a similar fate befell the quantification of mammoth. Those sites where paleontologists were involved have quantified counts of this taxon; those without their participation do not. It may well be that archaeological bias itself is responsible for some of the differences I note between simple and complex base camps.

Second, before we can full understand the differences between these two types of camps, we must have much finer chronological controls than are available now. In looking at the location of these complex sites, for example, it is tempting to speculate that they may have been some sort of hunter–gatherer "central places" (Figure 6.9). If the four northern sites spanned a long period of time and only one existed during any one period, we would see a rather neat pattern of one complex site in the south and one in the north at any given time. Certainly, if Eliseevichi and Yudinovo on the Sudost' and Mezin and Suponevo on Desna were not contemporary, then they are most interestingly

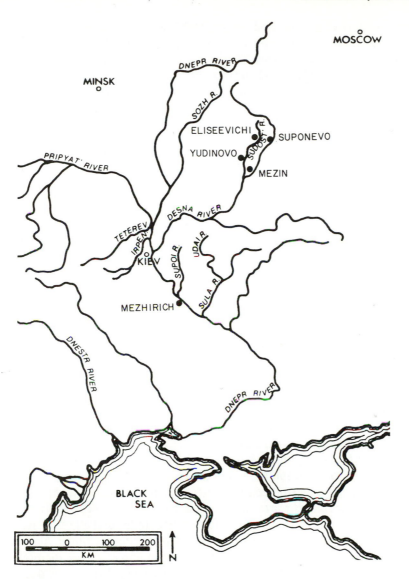

Figure 6.9 Location of complex base camps.

and regularily situated along the Desna and Sudost' water courses. If Mezin, for example, was earliest, as some have speculated (see Shovkoplyas 1965a), it would have been located in the center of the study area. If Mezhirich, then, was a contemporary of any one of the other three other northern complex sites, they would have each been located at the edges of the study area, and so on.

Such positioning of complex sites may related to linearization itself. Although linear settlement patterns have received far less attention than hexagonal lattices, Flannery (1976a) and Reynolds (1976) address the subject, pointing out some regularities governing site location in linear systems. They hypothesize that initial sites will be located in the center of linear regions and subsequent sites at regular intervals upstream and downstream from the first one. Their work is based on early agricultural settlements in Mesoamerica, where extensive river trade was an important factor. A fairly regular distribution of complex sites along water courses on the late Pleistocene central Russian Plain seems to pattern similarily and may also have been conditioned by transport requirements.

All of these speculations, however, as tantalizing as they are, represent less than "just so stories" and await further research before they can be evaluated in detail. I examine the special behavior at some of these sites as well as the social implications of settlement linearization in Chapter 7.

REGIONAL DIFFERENCES IN THE DISTRIBUTION OF SITE TYPES

The history of Paleolithic research in the study area has been such that the northern region, especially along the Desna and Sudost' valleys, saw a longer period of intensive research than did the southern region (see Chapter 1). This factor undoubtedly greatly affects the archaeological record and must be considered when evaluating possible regional differences in either the nature of sites found or the proportions of different types.

At the completion of locational analysis in Chapter 4, I suggest that clustering of sites with mammoth-bone dwellings in northeastern and southwestern quadrants may indicate the presence of two different social groups with different settlement systems. I now return to this suggestion, evaluating it with data on site types, distribution, demographic parameters, and the temporal variability in duration of occupation. Table 6.40 gives the distribution of site types per region. At first glance, this breakdown tends to suggest that a larger proportion of southern sites are cold-weather base camps. I would argue that this regional difference reflects archaeological bias. Thus, as can be expected given the history of research in the area, we find both a greater number of different site types in the north (seven types, as opposed to four in the south) and a greater ratio of high-visibility sites in the south (those with mammoth-bone constructions). A comparison of the distribution of mammoth-bone dwellings, for example, shows them to be more numerous in the south ($z = 2.06$, Table 6.17). This, again, I suspect is due to archaeological bias.

Comparisons of the distribution of various attributes does reveal some regional differences. Thus, as noted, far higher densities of lithics, lithic tools, and tool classes are found at northern sites. These differences are in all probability caused by the greater availability of superior block flint in the north (see Chapter 5). While Table 6.2 shows lower blade-nuclei ratios in the northern sites than in their southern equivalents ($z = 2.15$), no differences in these ratios are found when the same types of sites are compared (north vs. south, sites with storage pits, $z = 0.92$; north vs. south high-ratio sites, $z = 0.01$; north vs. south low-ratio sites, $z = 0.96$).

Table 6.40   REGIONAL DISTRIBUTION OF SITE TYPES

Site type	Northern sites $N = 23^a$ (%)	Southern sites $N = 7$ (%)
Lithic workshop	26	0
Hunting and Collecting Station	9	14
Warm-weather base camp	22	14
Cold-weather hunting base camp	9	0
Cold-weather simple base camp	13	58
(including Timonovka I and II)	(22)	(58)
Cold-weather complex base camp	17	14
Anomalous—Khotylevo II	4	0

[a]Pushkari II counted twice, both as a lithic workshop and as a warm-weather base camp.

Similarily, no overall interregional differences are found in density of worked bone ($z = 0.85$), but more sites with high densities of worked bone are found in the north. However, since bone working occurred at base camps (in Table 6.2 identified as sites with storage pits, $z = 2.85$), and since a lower proportion of sites in the north belong to this category than in the south, I suspect that more bone processing actually occurred in the north.

No interregional differences are observed in available kilocalories, duration of occupation, or population. Table 6.2 also shows no differences in the densities of art, jewelry, and amber when the latter are coded and the distance to the source is controlled (Table 6.10). Overall, as difference of median tests indicate (Table 6.41), no north–south differences are found in the distribution of (1) all decorative items that have been dimensionally scaled and coded or (2) coded values of exotic lithics and ocher (Table 6.14). Marine shells (Table 6.12), however, show a considerably higher density in the north ($z = 1.53, p = .12$) when coded and distance-controlled. Comparison of high-density to low-density sites yields $z = 1.72, p = .09$; comparison of north and south low-density sites shows $z = 2.05, p = .06$ (Table 6.2). I argue in the following chapter that the distribution of shells, at least in part, was controlled by various exchange networks that spanned the entire study area. Thus I interpret the higher density of shells in the north as a reflection of different social factors rather than different settlement patterns.

Soviet researchers have not been able to define systematically any stylistic differences in lithics, worked bone, or art and decorative objects found in the north and south (see Chapter 4). While Gladkih (1973) argues for a greater stylistic similarity between lithic assemblages at Mezhirich and Dobranichevka than between these two southern sites and Mezin, he does not interpret this to signify two synchronic style zones. He suggests that chronological factors were responsible for these differences. Problematic as stylistic criteria are for the definition of cultural regions and, by extension, social groups, the inability of Soviet researchers over a 100-year period to distinguish such differences between northern and southern sites indicates that in all probability no differences of this sort exist (see the disagreement between Hodder, 1981 and Wobst, 1977, in particu-

Table 6.41   DIFFERENCE OF MEDIAN TESTS: REGIONAL AND CHRONOLOGICAL

	N	Median	p^a
Dimensionally scaled and coded values for exotics and decorative objects, including art			
all northern vs. southern sites	14	.69	.44
early vs. late sites	14	.69	.23
late northern vs. southern sites	11	.75	.36
northern early vs. late sites	10	.63	.22
Dimensionally scaled and coded values for exotics and decorative objects, excluding art: all (= late) northern vs. southern sites	10	.56	.41
Exotic lithics and ocher			
all northern vs. southern sites	16	1.00	.29
all early vs. late sites	10	1.00	.29
Exotic lithics without ocher: late northern vs. southern sites	9	1.00	.48

^{a}Probability estimated by Fisher exact test.

lar, on the significance of stylistic differences in general). I suggest that we are dealing with very similar, socially connected groups, and I extend this to support my conclusion that no large-scale differences existed in the settlement systems in the north and south.

Three attributes related to the nebulous variables of duration of occupation and group size show consistent interregional differences: thickness of the cultural layer, density of hearths per square meter of site, and hearth volume per site. All three are end products of factors related to both human activity and local geological processes. If we roughly correlate thickness of cultural layer and hearth volume with duration of occupation, the consistently higher values found for these attributes in northern sites appear to show that these sites were occupied either longer or more often than their southern equivalents. Thus, for example, a comparison of cultural layer thickness at northern sites with thick cultural layers of southern sites shows northern sites with 1.5 times thicker layers ($z = 5.5$, Table 6.15). Similarly, northern sites without storage pits with thick cultural layers have significantly thicker deposits than their southern equivalents ($z = 1.50, p = .12$). Table 6.17 shows that northern sites with storage pits have about four times as much hearth volume as southern sites ($z = 2.09$). This consistent patterning of data appears to indicate some interregional differences in the settlement system.

If, for the sake of argument, we assume that the density of hearths roughly reflects population (assuming that a given hearth will accommodate only a limited number of people, and that if such a number is exceeded, a second hearth will be used), we can speculate that higher densities of hearths at northern sites may indicate higher populations. For example, while southern sites yield mean densities of one hearth every 227 m^2, hearths at northern sites are found every 95 m^2 ($z = 2.91$, Table 6.17). Northern sites with dwellings have about three times as many hearths as southern sites ($z = 5.15$), while not interregional differences are found in the densities of hearths at sites without dwellings ($z = 0.07$).

Since other data (e.g., kcal) indicate no differences in either duration of occupation or size of the occupying group between the north and south, the seeming contradiction offered by hearth and cultural layer data merits closer examination. I have previously noted that some northern sites classified as cold-weather base camps may have been occupied more than once (e.g., Mezin and Suponevo). While logically we should expect that all the sites, especially those with numerous features, resulted from more than one occupation, I would argue that such reoccupation sequences have been observed at northern sites precisely because they were more frequent there. It could be argued that, since much of our knowledge of Mezin and Suponevo come from archival reconstructions, recognition of reoccupation at these sites is posthumous and speculative at best. I suspect, however, that somewhat greater mobility existed in the north: (1) the greater number of site types recognized in the north, (2) the unique hunting base camps occupied during cold-weather months only in the north (e.g., Timonovka I and II), (3) the existence of lithic workshops only in the north, and (4) the speculation of multiple occupation for some northern sites, all support this interpretation. Such greater mobility, however, does not significantly differentiate the settlement system of the north from that of the south. I suggest that data presented in this chapter demonstrate a single settlement pattern in the study area. The observed interregional differences represent local variatons of this pattern—variations that could have resulted, in the north, from factors including (1) greater population density (if we assume that number of sites very roughly reflects population density), (2) shorter period of availability of most food resources, (3) closer proximity to the Scandinavian Ice Sheet, or even (4) greater linear circumscription, which in combination with the first two factors could result in more frequent returns to particular locales.

THE BASIC SETTLEMENT SYSTEM

Cold Season

Upper Paleolithic hunter–gatherers of the central Russian Plain spent cold-weather months on or near river floodplains in base camps with numerous features and mammoth-bone dwellings. Coresident groups at such camps numbered from about 30 to 60 individuals (6 to 12 families). Data on floor space in winter mammoth-bone dwellings suggest occupation by both single and multiple families (2 to 3 families at most). Some coresident units occupied simple base camps, while others lived in camps at which much nonsubsistence-related behavior occurred. While no unambiguous data exist on the duration of occupation of these cold-weather base camps, I argue that sedentism extended over a number of months (6?) but was not year-round.

Although the archaeological record has yielded no examples of cold-weather extractive camps, such locations probably existed as satellites to the base camps. Since cold-weather subsistence was based on stored foods, I would expect these satellite camps to be very ephemeral, related to opportunistic exploitation (e.g., of willow ptarmigan or hare). Because of the small size and portability of such food resources, little archaeological debris would have been left at these sites, diminishing archaeological visibility. Some procurement of lithics may have occurred in the north during the cold season, and lithic workshops used during cold weather may be discovered. However, since the type of data which indicates seasonality (i.e., flora and fauna) is generally lacking at lithic workshops, our chances of discovering such workshops and identifying them to cold-weather occupation appear very slim.

Warm Season

With the onset of the short warm season, coresident groups moved into summer base camps. This relocation, however, did not involve abandonment of the region but was highly localized. With the onset of river breakup and marshing up of river valleys, residential settlements relocated higher above the floodplain close to the winter base camps. Using data reported by Nelson (1971) for the Bering Strait, and considering possible multiseasonal occupations at Mezin and Suponevo, I suggest that in some cases summer base camps may have been located adjacent to winter ones.

Warm- and cold-weather base camps appear to have been inhabited by groups of similar size. No seasonal aggregation and dispersal can be observed for the study area during the Upper Paleolithic. Since there are only two clear warm-weather base camps in our sample, I cannot generalize about this site type's duration of occupation. Data from Zhuravka, with low kilocalorie values and low lithic densities, suggest only brief occupation; data from Chulatovo II suggest full warm-season occupation (2 to 3 months). It may well be that northern camps were occupied longer than the southern camps. Since we can expect that migratory as well as social behavior (see Chapter 3) of food taxa affected the duration of occupation in summer months, and since the north saw an influx of food taxa (particularly mammoth) only during the warm season (see Chapter 3), data from Zhuravka and Chulatovo II may reflect more food and greater sedentism in the north and more mobility in the south during the summer.

Mobility, as has been amply noted in the literature, is not only a group-specific phenomenon but also varies by age grade as well as by gender (see Watanabe 1968, 1978a). The presence of summer lithic workshops, hunting stations, and collection locales indicates that such variability existed during the Upper Paleolithic. While a group of 40 to 60 (8 to 12 families) was settled in summer base camps, special-task groups occupied satellite extraction camps for the procurement of raw materials, food resources, and so forth.

Earlier in this chapter I argue that, while cold-weather months were spent living off stored provisions, greater opportunistic exploitation and immediate consumption of food resources occurred during warm-weather months. If we accept Binford's (1980) distinction between foragers and logistically organized hunter–gatherers, we can interpret the data from the study area as showing seasonal switches in subsistence strategies, with logistical organization prevailing during cold weather and opportunistic foraging during the warm seasons.

At some point during summer months, perhaps with the onset of colder weather, or more likely with the appearance of abundant gregarious herbivores, a third type of base camp was occupied, at which group efforts were directed toward the procurement and storage of food resources for overwintering camps. It is unclear if these hunting base camps were spatially distinct occupations or just temporal sequences that, in most cases, turned into overwintering camps. As noted, I favor the latter interpretation for Timonovka I and II; that is, that they are prehistoric "accidents" where for some reason the normal occupational sequence was interrupted.

DIACHRONIC CHANGES IN THE SETTLEMENT SYSTEM

Sample-size problems come to the fore in comparisms of the nature of sites occupied early to those occupied after the Valdai maximum (after 18,000 B.P.). Of the four sites possibly occupied early, only three are in situ. Of these three, Khotylevo II does not fit the general pattern for the area. Only one of the early sites, Radomyshl', is located in the south. Clearly, it is dangerous to draw conclusions from such a sample size.

In Chapters 4 and 5 it was observed that (1) a smaller population of hunter–gatherers may have occupied the study area before 20,000 B.P.; (2) this population was located predominantly in the north; (3) the early sites were located farther from the river valleys than the late sites, indicating a lack of linear circumscription during the early period; (4) subsistence practices during the early period were focused on the exploitation of a smaller number of taxa and directed to the gregarious herbivores; (5) procurement practices during the early period did not show the intensity observed at the late sites.

The early sites, with the exception of the anomalous Kohtylevo II, all represent simple cold-weather base camps. I therefore restrict diachronic comparisons to those appropriate to this type. It should be noted that the presence of only one site type in the record of early sites in no way signals a difference in settlement system prior to the Valdai maximum; rather, it is a result of archaeological bias. Cold-weather base camps, because of their features, have such inordinately high archaeological visibility that we should expect these sites to be most frequent in the record. Lithic workshops are notoriously hard to date, and it may well be that some of those known in the study area were used during the early period. Food extraction camps, as noted, would leave such ephemeral marks on the landscape that, as a norm, they can be expected to escape archaeological detection. Thus, taking archaeological and taphonomic biases into account, it is not surprising that the three early sites, Berdyzh, Radomyshl', and Yurovichi, are winter base camps.

What is significant, however, when comparing early to late cold-weather base camps, is the complete absence of complex base camps among the early sites. It could be suggested that complex early sites were substantially different from the late ones, and that perhaps the anomalous Khotylevo II is such a site. I have argued, however, that Khotylevo II, with its abundant art and worked bone as well as its unique living floor, is from another cultural system and is intrusive in the study area. I assume here that Khotylevo II is not part of the early settlement system in the area and should not be seen as an early complex base camp. To mitigate sample-size problems, however, I include data from this site in the comparisons discussed below.

Comparison of early and late sites can be made using only some of the attributes outlined in this chapter; data are missing on the counts of different tool types found at the early sites. I therefore restrict my comparison primarily to features and site profiles and use whatever comparable data are available on artifacts (Table 6.42).

Features

Although early sites have both large and small dwellings and the number of dwellings per site does not show a change through time ($z = 0.75$), a diachronic comparison of storage pits and hearths does show chronological differences. About three times as many storage pits are found at the late sites ($z = 1.76$, Table 5.5). A comparison of mean densities of hearths per site area does not show change through time ($z = 0.05$ comparing all early and late sites; $z = 1.30$ for early sites with storage pits vs. late sites with storage pits). Noticeably greater volume of burned material, however, is present in the hearths of early sites. All early sites have about four times more hearth volume than all late sites ($z = 15.43$), as do early sites with storage pits when compared to their late equivalents ($z = 13.79$, Table 6.42). Similar patterning is observed in thickness of cultural layer. Early sites have layers twice as thick as their late counterparts ($z = 3.00$). Early sites with pits have much thicker cultural layers ($z = 3.00$). Northern early sites with storage pits have thicker layers than northern late sites with pits ($z = 3.40$). The one southern early site with storage pits, Radomyshl', has about twice as thick a cultural layer as late southern sites with these features ($z = 5.00$). If we presume that thickness of cultural layer roughly reflects duration of occupation or frequency of reoccupation, this repeated patterning indicates that early sites were occupied longer or more frequently than the late sites. I return to this hypothesis after comparing the diachronic distribution of other attributes.

Assemblages

No chronological differences can be observed in kilocalories available at the sites if half of the mammoths are included in the calculations. If mammoths are totally excluded, early sites appear to have a fewer kilocalories available, but this difference is not significant (see Tables 5.19 and 5.20). Faunal data also indicate that no specialized exploitation of fur bearers was practiced during the early period of occupation. Fur bearers, when found at the early sites, are all present in low densities (see Chapter 5).

Comparison of general lithic densities (taking into account the noted difference in the availability of raw material between the regions) indicates that a considerably greater number of lithics in general were found at the late sites. For example, all late sites have about five times as many lithics as early sites ($z = 1.96$), and late northern sites with storage pits have about six times as many as their early equivalents ($z = 2.33$). If we assume a steady rate of lithic deposition per knapper, these figures suggest that more lithic workers occupied the late sites. Densities of stone tools, on the other hand, produce the opposite patterning, showing about six times as many stone tools at early sites, both in the north ($z = 5.49$) and south ($z = 4.46$) (using values that have been residualized against general lithic density separately for the north and south). If we again assume that the rate of tool production is roughly sensitive to temporal factors

Table 6.42   CHRONOLOGICAL COMPARISONS: DIFFERENCE OF MEANS TESTS

	N	$\overline{X}_1$	$\overline{X}_2$	z	p
Assemblages					
Lithic density					
all early vs. late sites	20	16.35	76.15	1.96	.05
early vs. late sites with storage pits	14	20.80	91.69	1.96	.05
early vs. late northern sites with storage pits	9	22.85	138.33	2.33	.03
early vs. late southern sites with storage pits	5	16.70	10.08	1.01	.24
early sites with storage pits, north vs. south	3	22.85	16.70	0.33	.38
late northern vs. southern sites	16	106.40	9.64	2.43	.02
late sites with vs. without storage pits	18	91.69	53.41	0.70	.31
late sites with storage pits, north vs. south	11	138.33	10.08	2.98	.003
late sites without storage pits, north vs. south	7	70.82	9.90	1.02	.24
Lithic tool density residualized against lithic density					
early vs. late northern sites	11	6.14	−0.61	5.49	<.0001
early vs. late southern sites	7	0.50	−0.08	4.46	<.0001
early vs. late northern sites with storage pits	6	6.14	−1.15	4.42	<.0001
early vs. late southern sites with storage pits	5	0.50	0.04	11.50	<.0001
Worked bone density at sites with storage pits: early vs.					
late sites	11	0.60	0.33	2.25	.03
Art density					
northern early vs. late sites	4	8.50	14.20	0.51	.35
early vs. late high-density sites	4	16.00	27.33	1.57	.12
early vs. late low density sites	6	1.00	18.00	2.16	.04
Site Profiles					
Thickness of cultural layer					
all early vs. late sites	19	0.28	0.13	3.00	.004
early vs. late sites with storage pits	13	0.28	0.14	3.00	.004
early vs. late northern sites with storage pits	9	0.33	0.16	3.40	.0012
early vs. late southern sites with storage pits	4	0.20	0.10	5.00	<.0001
early vs. late sites with thick cultural layers and storage pits	4	0.33	0.25	1.60	.11
early vs. late sites with thin cultural layers and storage pits	9	0.20	0.10	5.88	<.0001
early vs. late northern sites with thick cultural layers and storage pits	4	0.33	0.25	1.60	.11
early vs. late southern sites with thin cultural layers and storage pits	4	0.20	0.09	5.50	<.0001
early sites with storage pits, north vs. south	3	0.33	0.20	4.33	<.0001
early sites with storage pits with thick vs. thin cultural layers	3	0.33	0.20	6.50	<.0001
Features					
Hearths					
density of hearths at early vs. late sites	13	116.70	143.86	0.05	.39
volume of early vs. late hearths	7	5.40	1.08	15.43	<.0001
density of hearths at early vs. late sites with storage pits	12	116.70	159.75	1.30	.17
volume of early vs. late hearths	6	5.40	1.21	13.97	<.0001
Dwellings, numbers at the sites: early vs. late sites	11	3.75	2.94	0.75	.30
Group Size and Duration of Occupation					
Mean group size at early vs. late sites with storage pits	11	41.00	42.33	0.27	.38
Duration of occupation on kcals (without mammoths) plus lithics at early vs. late sites	12	0.75	2.61	2.30	.03
Duration of occupation on kcals (with half mammoths) plus lithics at early vs. late sites	12	10.50	16.60	1.96	.05

(i.e., the longer people stay at a site, the more tools they will use up), this patterning is in accord with that observed for the thickness of the cultural layer and for hearth volume.

Data on the densities of worked bone found at the early sites is available only for the anomalous Khotylevo II. This attribute is associated with storage pits, and more worked bone is found at complex than at simple base camps. Worked bone is found at a very high density at Khotylevo II; this one early site has twice as many worked bone pieces as late sites with storage pits ($z = 2.25$). As noted, however, the uniqueness of this site weakens its significance as a chronological marker. Since no quantified data on worked bone is available for either Berdyzh or Yurovichi (no worked bone has been found at Radomyshl'), I am unable to evaluate the changes in worked-bone density through time. Some bone working apparently did go on at the early sites, but whether this activity intensified must await further research.

The most apparent differences to be noted between the early and late sites are in the distributions of exotic lithics and decorative objects. These have been found primarily at late sites. Only art and ocher occur at early sites. Art objects have been reported at both Khotylevo II and Yurovichi. While no differences can be observed in the mean numbers found at the northern early and late sites ($z = 0.51$), art objects have only been found at the late sites in the south. Since art shows a bimodal distribution at the study sites, it is interesting to compare art densities at both the high- and low-density sites through time. These comparisons show that considerably more art is found in both late high-density ($z = 1.57, p = .12$) and low-density sites ($z = 2.16$). In general then, data on hand indicate an intensification in the production and use of art objects from the early to the late period. Other attributes belonging to the category of decorative objects—amber, marine shells, and jewelry—have only been found at late sites. The same is true for exotic lithics. Ocher, on the other hand, is present in the same proportion of early (50%) and late (60%) sites.

In summary, then, both art and ocher were associated with behavior that existed in the study area during the entire period of occupation, whereas procurement, production, and use of jewelry, shells, amber, and nonlocal lithics seem evident only during the late period. It is not surprising, therefore, given the strong relationship between these objects and complex base camps discussed earlier, that the lack of these objects at early sites co-occurs with the absence of complex sites.

Since no early warm-weather base camps have been found in the study area, I cannot address the issue of different settlement patterns prior to the Valdai maximum. I would argue that, given the general similarities observed between all sites, we should assume for now that such warm-weather occupations were not significantly different during the early period. I would anticipate smaller coresidential units occupying such early sites, but with durations of occupation similar to the corresponding later sites. In general, since I have postulated a milder climate prior to the Valdai maximum, I anticipate more warm-weather occupations for the early period simply because the warm season itself was longer.

Finally, turning to the most nebulous "guesstimates" presented in this chapter—population and duration of occupation—a comparison of mean population between the early and late sites shows no differences ($z = 0.27$) but appears to indicate, using values that both exclude mammoths and include some mammoths, that late sites were occupied longer. These conclusions run counter to those reached on cultural layer thickness, hearth volume, and lithic density data. Since they are based on the most speculative values presented in this chapter, I dismiss them from this analysis.

Conclusions

Sample sizes used as comparative units are small, and within this small sample, comparison of different attributes generate several contradictory conclusions. The main factor responsible for these contradictions has not been controlled. I identify this factor as my inability to distinguish demographic variability from temporal variability and to distinguish variables related specifically to group size from those related to duration of occupation. In addition, the very nature of the archaeological data limits chronological comparisons to just one site type. Nonetheless, I suggest that duration of occupation is most responsible for the observed differences. Three attributes—hearth volume, cultural layer thickness, and density of lithic tools, all indicate longer stays at early sites. Assuming that early sites were occupied longer, we can interpret the lack of differences in kilocalories through time to indicate that larger numbers of people occupied the later sites. In brief, I see smaller groups staying longer at early cold-weather base camps and larger groups staying a shorter time at late cold-weather base camps.

In this argument I assume the same frequency of reoccupation through time—an assumption that may clearly be unjustified. My interpretation is also just one of the explanations that can be generated using evidence on hand. I offer it only tentatively, a sort of working hypothesis that requires a great deal of additional work for either substantiation or refutation. I argue, however, that increases in both storage and density of lithics at later sites support such an interpretation.

Using these conclusions of demographic and temporal changes in site occupation, we can postulate increased mobility through time in general. I have already suggested that northern sites were reoccupied more frequently and that more site types existed in the north than in the south; both of these observations testify to greater mobility in the north. This is especially evident if we control for time and look at only the late sites. A similar pattern, though less clear because of sample size, can be observed in the south, where there are more site types later in time as well. This increase in mobility coincides with the linear circumscription postulated for the area after the Valdai maximum. If I am correct, and later groups in the study area were more mobile in a linearized environment, we should expect to find a considerably greater number of late sites that look alike, are in a similar locale, and are located closer to each other than during the early period. In other words, it is possible that the population density increase I postulate for the area may have simply resulted from a change in the demographic arrangement rather than from a real increase in population. The resolution of this question, as of so many others this discussion has raised, must await future research.

If we assume both greater mobility and an increase in the size of coresident groups, we can next generate a series of social problems related to information flow (Moore 1979), the maintenance of mating networks (Wobst 1974, 1976), and the maintenance of egalitarian social relationships (Johnson 1982) that would have faced Upper Paleolithic hunter–gatherers on the central Russian Plain after the Valdai maximum. I address these issues in the next chapter of this work and argue that it is precisely the solutions to these problems that are responsible for the proliferation of nonsubsistence-related artifacts, the specialized exploitation of fur bearers, and the rise of complex base camps seen in late settlements on the central Russian Plain.

I conclude this discussion by emphasizing that the single most visible and diagnostic difference in the study area through time is the absence of complex cold-weather base camps during the early period. This absence, together with the absence of attributes associated with these camps, including exotic materials, intensive labor investment in the construction of dwellings, and probably communal ritual behavior, clearly indicates a change in settlement system. It might be argued that archaeological bias alone is responsible for this. However, since the type of attributes missing at early sites have the highest archaeological visibility, and are also perennial archaeological favorites, their absence is not likely explained by excavator bias alone.

In short, as with subsistence practices discussed in Chapter 5, what we see for settlement systems during the 15,000 years of occupation is a continuation of the basic pattern—one that sees modification and elaboration but does not show any radical breaks through time.

7

Sociopolitical Integration

Human adaptation involves not only man–land relationships (considered so far), but man–man relationships as well. These sociopolitical relationships affect subsistence practices and settlement locations, as well as sociopolitical integration and ideological behavior. Noting, after Flannery (1972), that all systems must exchange not only energy and matter but also information, Root states:

> The direction, frequency, and intensity of information flow structures both man–man and man–land interactions. Information, thus, may be seen as a common denominator of human interaction, and social processes, such as subsistence–settlement arrangements, are mediated by information exchange on a regional basis. (1983:200)

Bender, in criticizing the ecological approach inherent in a man–land focus as an explanation for subsistence–settlement patterns, writes that "for gatherer–hunter studies . . . the failure to consider the social impetus behind much human strategy has made it difficult to understand why human, in contrast to other animal, societies have developed along so many different historical trajectories" (Bender 1982:1). Her theoretical orientation in looking at hunter–gatherer economies is "that at both intra- and inter-regional levels it is the analysis of social relations—seen as to some extent, the determinants of technological process, but also acting within the constraints imposed by techno-environmental factors—that permits an explanation of origins and change" (Bender 1982:24).

The sociopolitical component in hunter–gatherer adaptation has received, however, a good deal less attention in both the archaeological and ethnographic literature than the ecologico-economic one (e.g., Binford 1982b; Jochim 1976; Lee and DeVore 1968; Winterhalder 1981a,b). As a result, our theoretical constructs and inferential machinery for examining sociopolitical organization through the archaeological record are under-explored. While this is not the place for an examination of root causes, it is relevant to lay a part of the blame on the simplistic application of general evolutionary paradigms popular in archaeology in the last 20 years. In general evolutionary schemes of Fried (1967), Sahlins (1972), and Service (1962), the accent was placed on modal behavior for each level of economic, social, or political integration. Additional problems have been generated by coupling the evolutionary schemes based on subsistence behavior to those

433

based on sociopolitical organization. As Price (1981) points out, hunter–gatherer adaptation thus became equated with a "simple, small, and mobile" paradigm. This coupling and the resulting paradigm are now being questioned. Sheehan (1983), for example, argues for the existence of hierarchical and perhaps even ranked organization among some Alaskan coastal groups. The sophisticated and complex Pacific Northwest Coast societies have always belied the appropriateness of the "simple, small, and mobile" characterization for all hunter–gatherers (e.g., Ames 1985, with references).

Influenced in some cases by the work of Flannery (1972), Wilmsen (1970, 1972, 1973), and Wobst (1974), and in others by Marxist or neo-Marxist theory, a number of researchers including Bender (1978, 1981, 1982, 1985), Conkey (1980), Moore (1979, 1983), O'Shea (1981), Root (1981, 1983), and Weissner (1982a, b, 1983, 1984), systematically examine the social component in hunter–gatherer adaptations. The results of their approach have been both thought-provoking and promising, but not without serious problems. Of these, perhaps the most pressing for archaeology is the relationship of theoretical constructs to the material correlates of these constructs. As both Hodder's (1978, 1979) and Weissner's (1983, 1984) work clearly indicates, the phenomenon of equifinality is ever-present in all attempts to firmly connect social messages to their material expressions. Both researchers conclude that although social information is contained in material culture, the correspondence is far from straightforward.

In brief then, while the focus of this chapter is on the social and political relationships of Upper Paleolithic groups in the study area viewed both as one component of their adaptation strategies and also as a set of variables responsible for some changes, the lack of inferential machinery does not permit me to either perform an exhaustive examination of these variables, or come to any unequivocal conclusions. This chapter, then, considers some aspects of sociopolitical relationships and offers a modification to the subsistence and settlement model presented in Chapters 5 and 6. The refinements are tentative—a series of plausible "just so stories" that can be tested and used to generate new directions for research.

ASSUMPTIONS AND METHODOLOGY

Data presented in the first six chapters of this work clearly indicate that we are dealing neither with small nor simple foraging groups but rather an example of complex Upper Paleolithic hunter–gatherer adaptation. Since I have shown that the economic behavior of these groups was fairly complex (e.g., storage economy, specialized exploitation of fur bearers, the presence of long-distance exchange networks, etc.), we can also anticipate evidence for sociopolitical complexity. In this discussion I assume, after Flannery (1972:409), that complex adaptation strategies have both greater *segmentation* (the amount of internal differentiation and specialization) and *hierarchization* of their subsystems than do simple strategies. Thus, in this work, the term *complexity* describes an entity, economic or sociopolitical, that consists of many interrelated parts, some of which are in a hierarchical relationship. I also assume that a complex hunter–

gatherer adaptation can be seen archaeologically in sizable coresidential units, technological innovations, multiple facilities, decorative and exotic objects, intensive resource procurement and preservation, and ritual activity. Various connections between sociopolitical factors and economic and demographic complexity have received strong theoretical and empirical backing in the literature: between intensification in procurement and storage practices and social relationships (Bender 1978, 1981, 1985); between size of coresidential unit, increase in information flow, and increasing complexity of social organization (Johnson 1982, 1983); between stylistic variability and man–man relationships (Conkey 1980; Weissner 1983, 1984; Wobst 1977); between the demographic component and more complex hunter–gatherer adaptation (Binford 1968; Cohen 1977); between the demographic component and more complex social relationships (Bender 1978; Testart 1982). The aspects of sociopolitical organization I examine in this chapter can be categorized as (1) social networks, (2) sociopolitical relationships, and (3) ritual or ideological behavior.

SOCIAL NETWORKS

Exchange of information is a vital component of all human adaptation. Ample ethnographic evidence indicates that information exchange fulfills both economic and demographic needs; it keeps hunter–gatherer groups informed on the availability and location of resources and helps distribute them advantageously across the landscape. Information is transmitted along social networks, and these networks extend well beyond the coresiding groups themselves (Moore 1983; Root 1983). Such networks, by pooling subsistence risk over a large area, also function to reduce risk (Colson 1979; Weissner 1982a, b). Social networks also fulfill mating requirements and serve as channels along which mates are exchanged (Wobst 1974, 1976). Finally, these social or alliance networks underwrite social reproduction (Bender 1981).

Exchange Networks

Flanner (1972) notes that exchange conveys information and that regular exchange networks can therefore be seen as establishing permanent information channels. Because material flows accompany the flow of information, we can view material remains relating to exchange as archaeological correlates of past social and information networks.

The existence of such networks has been amply documented for ethnographically known hunter–gatherers (e.g., Boas 1964; Butinov 1960; Nelson 1971; Weissner 1982a, b; Yegoyan 1972). Archaeologically, such networks can be inferred from the presence of nonlocal goods and materials at sites. Such evidence, however, may be ambiguous. Ethnographic evidence shows that nonlocal materials can also be either procured in the course of a group's annual rounds or obtained by specially organized expeditions for exotics; the mere presence of exotic materials does not demonstrate exchange.

Similar ambiguities exist on the route and mode by which exotic materials move through exchange networks. Both occasional trade-partner exchange (e.g., San *hxaro*) and trading centers are reported for hunter–gatherers (Boas 1964; Butinov 1960; Nelson 1971; Weissner 1982a, b). Plog (1977) outlines a number of characteristics that should be noted when studying or modeling exchange networks; these include diversity and size of the network, directionality and symmetry, as well as whether or not centralization is evident. Archaeological attention to exchange networks, most notably by Renfrew (1977) and Ericson (1977), has produced various fall-off curves symptomatic of different sorts of exchange mechanisms. While both Hodder (1980) and Renfrew (1977) warn that similar curves may, in fact, mask very different behavioral patterns, the two distribution patterns potentially most relevant to this discussion are what Renfrew (1977) terms "down-the-line" and "directional" models. For the first case, Renfrew writes:

> When a commodity is available only at a highly localized source or sources for the material, its distribution in space frequently conforms to a very general pattern. Finds are abundant near the source, and there is a fall-off in frequency or abundance with distance from the source. (1977:22)

In the second case, directional exchange, various sociopolitical factors operate to obliterate the decrease-with-distance effect and produce evidence for preferential supplies in large quantities of exotic materials at locations other than those that can be predicted by distance considerations. In brief then, both the presence of exotics and their distribution must be taken into account when reconstructing past exchange behavior. Data on nonlocal materials found at the study sites indicate two categories of material: nonlocal lithics and decorative objects, including amber and fossil marine shells. Each is now considered.

Lithics

Nonlocal lithics including flint, sandstone, slate, and mountain crystal have been found at a number of study sites (see Table 6.9). No research has been done on the exact source of these materials, and no data exist on the exact nature of artifacts made of nonlocal lithics. Anecdotal evidence suggests that exotic lithics were not used differently than locally available lithics. Shovkoplyas (1955, 1965c, 1972)does not find any difference between tools fashioned of mountain crystal at Dobranichevka and tools made of local flint. Gladkih (1973), likewise, sees no difference between the tools fashioned from mountain crystal either at Dobranichevka or at Mezhirich and those made from local materials.

The closest source of mountain crystal found at the southern sites of Dobranichevka, Gontsy, and Mezhirich lies in the vicinity of Smela, about 150 km south of Dobranichevka and Gontsy and 100 km southeast of Mezhirich (Shovkoplyas 1965a). Shovkoplyas (1978, personal communication) also lists two more distant regions for this material: Volyn' to the northwest of the sites and the Donetsk Basin to the southeast (Figure 7.1). Pidoplichko (1969) notes the occurrence of mountain crystal near the city of Zhitomir, 300 km to the east of the sites. While the exact source of the mountain crystal found at the sites remains to be determined, both Pidoplichko and Shovkoplyas consider the

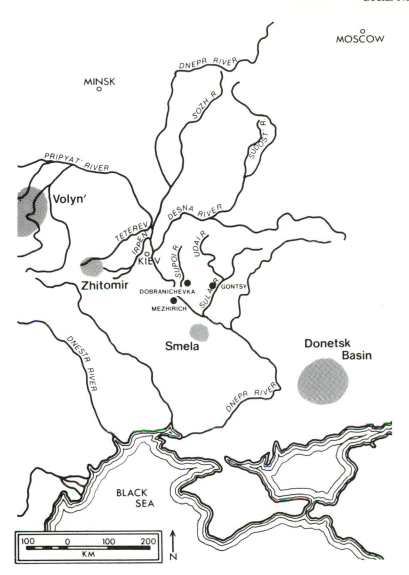

Figure 7.1   Sources of mountain crystal (shaded areas).

Smela region to be the most likely. Finally, finished tools, unworked fragments, and waste flakes of mountain crystal have been found at Dobranichevka—suggesting that the material arrived at the site as blanks or nuclei and was fashioned into various blades and scrapers at the site.

Polikarpovich (1968) reports that all Yudinovo lithics were of nonlocal origin. Abramova (1983, personal communication) sees a great similarity between Yudinovo flint and the highly diagnostic superior Desna flint and suggests that Yudinovo flint may have been obtained from Desna outcrops. If she and Polikarpovich are correct, flint used at Yudinovo would have come from at least 60 km south-southeast of the site.

While information on the sources of nonlocal lithics at the sites is far from satisfactory, it does support my interpretation that nonlocal lithics, in all probability, were procured directly by the inhabitants of the sites; the relative proximity of the sources suggests that the distances involved were well within the range of annual rounds. Nonlocal lithics have been found at both simple and complex base camps, as well as at sites I classify as lithic workshops (Table 6.9). Such a distribution strongly argues for the utilitarian role of exotic lithics in Upper Paleolithic economies, as does the use to which exotic lithics were put. In summary, I argue that the procurement and use of nonlocal lithics in no way differed from the behavior associated with local materials; I suggest that, like locally available materials, exotic lithics were obtained by direct procurement. Pending evidence to the contrary, I suggest that such direct procurement most probably occurred during the group's annual rounds.

Amber

Varying amounts of amber, probably originating from the vicinity of Kiev, have been found at Chulatovo II, Dobranichevka, Gontsy, Mezhirich, and Mezin. Coded and distance-scaled values for this material are listed in Table 6.10 (see the discussion of scaling and coding in Chapter 6). We know that some amber was fashioned into beads, but the poor condition of the amber at the sites makes it unclear whether bead manufacturing occurred on these sites or elsewhere (see illustrations of amber in Pidoplichko 1969, 1976). Amber was also probably used for nondecorative purposes.

Assuming after Shovkoplyas et al. (1981), Kornietz et al. (1981), and Pidoplichko (1976) that amber-bearing deposits in the vicinity of Kiev were the source for this material, we can note an interesting pattern of amber distribution in the study area (Figure 7.2). Distance-coded values in Table 6.10 and Figure 7.2 generally conform to Renfrew's (1977) "down-the-line" model of nondirectional exchange. Sites closest to the source have larger quantities of amber than do those farther away. Thus, Mezhirich, located 100 km south of Kiev, has over 348 pieces of amber (coded value of 3), while the more distant Chulatovo II, about 260 km from Kiev, has only one piece (coded value of 1).

While the distribution of amber conforms to Renfrew's model, such a conformity does not preclude the possibility that amber was procured directly. Since I project only seasonal sedentism at the study sites, it is also feasible that amber could have been obtained in the course of annual rounds. While, to my knowledge, no definitive theoretical or empirical studies exist on the relationship of distance to quantity of material obtained by direct procurement, one can theorize a similar pattern of fall-off as observed in the "down-the-line" model of exchange. As is shown below, however, this directional interpretation is less likely, and amber probably reached the more distant sites via nondirectional exchange.

Finally, it is significant to note that amber has been found only at base camps. As Table 6.10 shows, the nature of the base camp (simple or complex, warm- or cold weather) does not influence the amount of amber. For example, the simple warm-

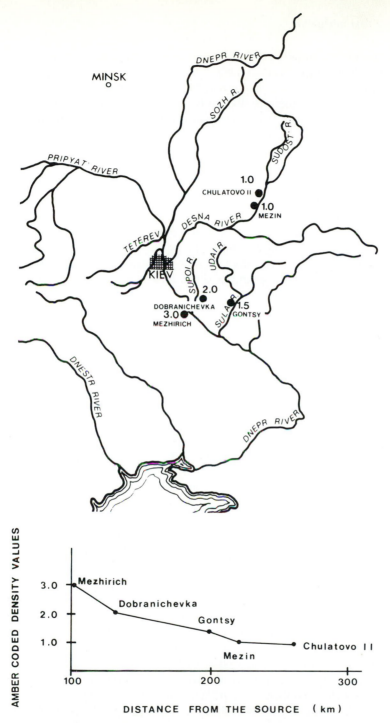

Figure 7.2 Source (shaded area) of amber and fall-off curve for volume of amber; see Table 6.10 (Soffer 1985).

weather base camp Chulatovo II had approximately the same amount as the complex cold-weather base camp Mezin. Likewise, simple base camps located close to amber sources (i.e., Gontsy and Dobranichevka) have more amber than the distant, complex Mezin. This patterning suggests that amber was associated with behavior at all base camps, a marked difference from the other exotic decorative material—fossil marine shells.

Fossil Marine Shells

Marine shells belonging to a number of taxa have been found at six sites in the study area (Table 6.12). Soviet researchers indicate that these shells were in all probability obtained from the Karangat and Sarmat marine deposits, located considerably south of the study area near the shores of the Black Sea and the Sea of Azov (Motuz 1969; Polikarpovich 1968; Shovkoplyas 1965a). As noted in Chapter 6, shells were used as beads or pendants, and both perforated and unperforated shells have been found at the sites, indicating that the processing of shells into items of personal adornment took place at the sites themselves.

While the greater abundance of amber at the southern sites indicates the importance of amber procurement and exchange there, the distribution of fossil marine shells indicates that their procurement and use was more important in the north. As Table 6.12 shows, the greatest number of shells are found at the more distant northern sites. And whereas shells in the north appear at both simple and complex base camps (e.g., Chulatovo II and Eliseevichi), in the south they are only found at the complex base camp Mezhirich. Complex northern base camps (Elizeevichi, Mezin, and Yudinovo) have high numbers of fossil marine shells, whereas complex southern and simple northern sites have considerably fewer shells. I conclude, therefore, that the procurement and distribution of shells exhibits behavior unlike that for amber—behavior that conforms more closely to Renfrew's model of "directional" exchange (see Figure 7.3).

The presence of shells at Eliseevichi, Mezin, and Yudinovo might be explained by two different mechanisms: (1) "down-the-line" exchange and accumulation or hoarding at complex base camps, or (2) specially organized procurement expeditions. The distribution of shells argues against the first hypothesis; if unworked shells were exchanged to and processed at complex base camps, we would find much greater quantities of them at Mezhirich. I suspect, therefore, that the second mechanism operated the study area; that procurement expeditions to the Sarmat and Karangat deposits were organized from northern complex base camps, and that shells were subsequently processed into jewelry at these camps. The distribution of shells depicted in Figure 7.3 supports such an interpretation. It also suggests that the distribution of shells across the study area was controlled by the northern complex base camps; shells from these sites found their way to simple northern base camps as well as to complex southern sites.

Such a hypothesis carries implications about social relationships, relationships of production, as well as control of labor. While long-distance procurement expeditions are known for Australia as well as northern-latitude groups (Boas 1964; Butinov 1960; Thompson 1949) I argue that the behavior during the Upper Paleolithic—taken together with other examples of complex sociopolitical relationships I discuss below—indicates greater complexity than found among most ethnographically known hunter-

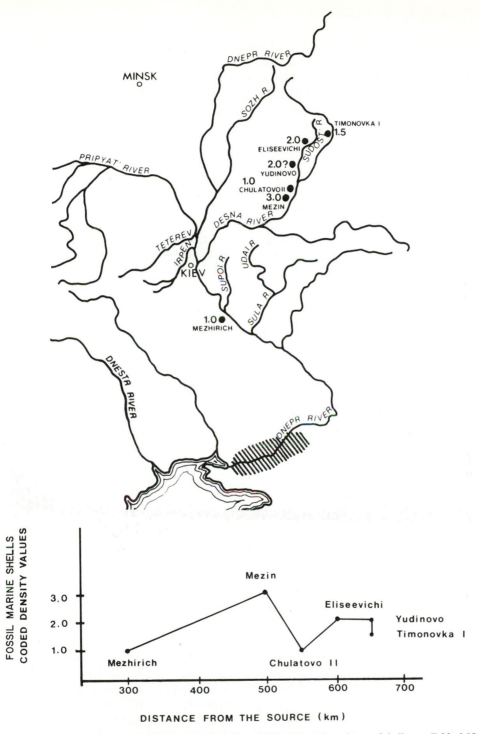

Figure 7.3 Source (shaded area) of fossil marine shells and fall-off curve for volume of shells; see Table 6.12 (Soffer 1985).

gatherers. My arguments for greater sociopolitical complexity during the late Valdai are based not on a single line of evidence, but rather on directional patterning of multiple sources of information. While, admittedly, each source of information, such as marine shells, is problematic, taken together they warrant consideration of more complex sociopolitical relationships than we have assumed for the Upper Paleolithic.

Conclusion and Implications

Soviet researchers have long noted the presence of nonlocal materials at the Upper Paleolithic sites in the study area but have generally explained this presence as stemming from residential mobility (Pidoplichko 1969, 1976; Shovkoplays 1965a; cf. Masson 1976). This explanation is especially curious, since the same investigators claim fairly long residential sedentism at the sites (see Chapter 5).

The presence of nonlocal materials including lithics and shells has been documented for a number of European Upper Paleolithic sites, but the explanation for their presence either has been ignored, is anecdotal in nature, or is the subject of heated debate (e.g., Hemingway 1979; Hemingway and Bahn 1982; Taborin 1972). Kozłowski (1972–1973) invokes residential mobility to explain nonlocal lithics at Czech, Hungarian, and Polish Paleolithic sites. More recently, he argues for unspecified "contacts" (Kozłowski 1986).

Data on the exotics from the study area presented in this work clearly demonstrate that not only did exchange networks exist during the Upper Paleolithic, but also that various mechanisms were in operation. Given the projected settlement system for the study area, one with only limited local residential and logistical mobility, the sources postulated for different exotic materials argues against direct procurement. Simply put, the exotics come from too many directions and from too great a distance. For example, while amber sources may have been within the annual range of Mezin or Chulatovo II residents, shell procurement would have taken them all beyond areas covered by annual residential moves. Likewise, multidirectionality of source areas for Dobranichevka exotics (i.e., amber from the north and mountain crystal from either the south or west) argues against mobility as the sole explanation for the presence of exotics there. Some of the exotic materials, particularly lithics, in all probability were obtained via residential mobility. Neither distances from which they came nor the utilitarian use to which they were put permit more complex explanations.

The existence of clear, distinct, and disparate patterning in the distribution of amber and shells suggests that exchange rather than direct procurement is a better explanation for the distribution of these items. While it could be argued that the fall-off curve for amber presented in Figure 7.2 could also be generated by direct procurement, a hypothesis of direct procurement requires a greater presence of amber at all sites close to the source. This, however, is clearly not the case: Kirillovskaya, located right at the source, and Fastov, 60 km away, have no amber. Quite clearly, social mechanisms and not proximity alone regulated the flow of amber, and nondirectional exchange explains the distribution of this material better than does direct procurement.

Directional exchange appears the best explanation for the distribution of marine shells. The occurrence of amber and shells is strongly associated (see Table 6.13) and suggests that these two nonlocal items were behaviorally connected and distinct from behavior associated with art and jewelry made of local materials (see Chapter 6). Also, specialized procurement is correlated with the procurement of amber and shells (see Table 6.26). I interpret the various test results obtained and discussed in Chapter 6 as indicating that furs or pelts were a part of the same exchange network as amber and shells. The occurrence of this third item—obtained through specialized procurement and moved across the area through exchange—strengthens my argument for the existence of multiple and complex exchange networks.

The types of items that moved along these exchange networks can be best described as nonutilitarian or luxury goods. It could be argued that furs and pelts were utilitarian items. I suggest however, that since fur bearers were available and exploited over the entire study region, their inclusion in the exchange networks satisfied social rather than utilitarian needs.

The movement of exotic goods through exchange networks carries a number of social implications. Pires-Ferreira and Flannery (1976) term long-distance trade in exotics a form of "foreign relations." As such, they regularize and direct social and economic relations with more distant groups. There are also intragroup implications. Since locally available materials are equally available to all, they are ineffectual as status markers (Rowlands 1982). Exotics, by their scarcity and costliness, are better suited for status demarcation. Bender (1981, 1982, 1985) indicates that alliances sustained by exchange networks also have a potential for manipulating the relations of production in egalitarian societies. Her observations imply that once we notice the presence of exotic goods in hunter–gatherer economies, we should search for other evidence of emerging inequality. Some of this evidence would include disparity in the volume and distribution of storage facilities at the sites as well as specialization in production. As I show in a later section of this chapter (see pp. 453–463), such evidence is present at the study sites—albeit often in ambivalent form.

It is interesting to note that the nodes of long-distance exchange, as delineated by the distribution of amber, shells, and fur bearers, co-occur at locales with some evidence of organized ritual activity (see the discussion of complex base camps in Chapter 6). This co-occurrence, rather than being fortuitous, is clearly to be expected. Dalton (1977), Flanner (1976b), Jochim (1981), and Wilmsen (1972) note that exchange activity and ritual activity are intimately connected in premarket systems. Exchange activity sustains ritual activity, and ritual activity in turn provides the ideological rationale by which social groups justify themselves. Because these types of behavior co-occur at the Upper Paleolithic complex base camps, and in light of ethnographic data that characterize hunter–gatherer exchange behavior as ceremonial or ritualistic (Dalton 1977; Jochim 1981), I suggest that the long-distance exchange in the study area was probably also ceremonial or ritualistic in nature.

Halstead and O'Shea (1982) argue that exchange networks may be confronted with problems of inflation. Two solutions maintain the value of goods: (1) removal of goods from circulation, and (2) creation of hierarchies of valuables. The second solution would favor the incorporation of exotic goods into exchange networks. The first would find expression in burial and possibly destruction of goods. Exotic goods were indeed an integral part of Upper Paleolithic exchange networks on the central Russian Plain.

While no caches of exotics or burials with exotics have been found in the study area, the famed burials at Sungir, located some 650 km to the northeast, have produced evidence for just such "dumping" behavior. I return to this data below in examining social relationships.

It is most significant that evidence for long-distance exchange networks comes only from the later occupied sites. Evidence for specialized procurement of fur bearers, marine shells, and amber appears only at sites occupied after the Valdai maximum. If this is an accurate reflection of the period, the origin of long-distance exchange must be examined. As is shown below, its rise can best be understood as a response to geographic factors (the linearization of the settlement system) and changing social relationships.

STYLISTIC VARIATION

Stylistic variation in Upper Paleolithic lithic assemblages from the study sites has been noted and widely discussed in the literature (see discussion in Chapter 4). Stylistic variation in lithics has long been used by Old World archaeologists to classify sites into archaeological cultures. This approach has been singularly unsuccessful in delineating cultures in the study area (see Chapters 1 and 4). This "stylistico-cultural" impasse— namely, the inability of researchers to agree on the significance of observed intersite variability—can be attributed to the narrowness of the assumptions traditionally used in stylistic classification and systematics. I argue, after Wobst (1977), that more fruitful and interesting results can be gained if style and stylistic demarcation are viewed as functional parts of adaptive complexes.

In this work, after Weissner (1983:256), I define *style* as "formal variation in material culture that transmits information about personal and social identity." Since it can be expected that the imprinting of stylistic information on items of material culture requires additional labor input, and given that for much of the Pleistocene such stylistic imprinting is absent from the archaeological record, it is logical to ask when and why such imprinting arises. Proceeding from theoretical considerations, Wobst (1977) predicts that signaling of group identity or group membership via stylistic demarcation will arise with closure of mating or alliance networks, that is, when corporate identity comes into being. For Wobst (1977) and Conkey (1980) after him, social closure could only develop in the late Pleistocene after certain population-density thresholds were crossed and such signaling of social identity was advantageous for groups exploiting high-return resources, where cooperation of large work groups was required. Hodder (1978, 1979) demonstrates that such signaling is favored under conditions of intergroup competition. Weissner (1983), on the other hand, argues that ecological stress can also initiate such signaling. More important, Weissner demonstrates that two very distinct types of identity signaling can be imprinted on material cultures: *emblemic* and *assertive*. She, after Wobst (1977), defines emblemic style as "formal variation in material culture that has a distinct referent and transmits a clear message to a defined target population about conscious affiliation or identity. . . . Most frequently its referent will be a social group" (1983:257). Assertive style is "formal variation in material culture which is personally based and which carries informative supporting individual identity, by separating persons from similar others as well as by giving personal translation of membership in various groups. . . . It has no distinct referent as its support" (Weissner 1983:258). Weissner's separation of emblemic and assertive styles is based on her work with simple egalitarian hunter–gatherers—the Kalahari San. If we consider possible permutations of stylistic messages among more complex hunter–gatherers, we can envision additional causes for stylistic demarcation. For example, in groups where clear positions of status exist (religious specialist or hunt leader), such positions might also be signaled through stylistic variation. In such groups, we can anticipate emblemic styles proclaiming both corporate (we are the XXX) and individual (I am the ritual specialist of the XXX) identities. While consideration of yet another source of stylistic message may be theoretically important when dealing with complex hunter–gatherers, our poor empirical understanding of the material correlates of different style messages make such concerns fairly academic. Hodder (1979, 1981) and Weissner (1983, 1984) show clearly that ambivalence is the norm in the relationship of message and its manifestation in material culture, and that much more work needs to be done on identifying which attributes carry which stylistic message. Among the San, for example, different attributes on a given item can simultaneously carry different social messages, and, what is even more unfortunate for archaeologists, the same attribute can signal different messages from one time to another.

If we consider style and stylistic demarcation as a functional part of an adaptation complex, we can anticipate that once a need arises for conveying corporate identity through style, such information will be stylistically imprinted across a number of media. Such redundancy, as Moore (1983) points out, would be favored to insure both reception and validation of the message. Recent work on style imprinting suggests that lithics, art and engravings, jewelry, and structural features of sites may carry such information (e.g., Conkey 1980; Hodder 1979, 1981; Weissner 1983, 1984; Wobst 1977).

Two media, lithics and art and engravings, have longe been the focus of Soviet archaeological interest and research. As noted earlier, they, along with most of their Old World colleagues, assume that stylistic similarity in lithics reflects archaeological cultures. While the relationship of such cultures to any ethnographic groupings remains a moot point, work on lithic assemblages from Dnestr and Don Upper Paleolithic sites generally led to the recognition of different cultures, each with distinct lithic assemblages (e.g., Davis 1983; Efimenko 1938; Grigor'ev 1970; Klein 1969). But the sites from the study area presented a thornier problem for Soviet researchers. Some sort of consensus of opinion does exist on the cultural identity of lithic assemblages from the sites I place in the early period of occupation; most Soviet researchers assign both Berdyzh and Khotylevo II lithics to the Kostenki–Avdeevo culture, see Radomyshl' as having no cultural analogues, and note similarities of Yurovichi lithics to those from Eliseevichi (Budko 1967b; Lazukov et al. 1981; Shovkoplyas 1965a; Zavernyaev 1978, 1981). But assemblages from sites occupied between 18,000 and 12,000 B.P., are interpreted with far less agreement. In fact, with the exception of Grekhova (1970; 1983, personal communication) and Grigor'ev (1983), Soviet researchers describe each site as having unique stylistic and therefore cultural features. They either claim archaeological cultural status for each site or lump all of them into a rather amorphous Desna–Dnepr

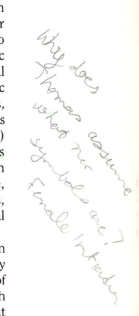
why does Thomas assume whether her symbols are? female intruders

cultural co-tradition (Dolukhanov 1982; Gladkih 1973; Shovkoplyas 1965). Grekhova (1970), working with materials from Desna and Sudost' sites, has been the only specialist to claim local style similarities on the level of distinct archaeological cultures. Grigor'ev, on the other hand, has departed from his previously held position that the lithic assemblages from the Dnepr–Desna sites represent a regional co-tradition and now argues that with the exception of Berdyzh, Khotylevo II, and possibly Klyusy, no archaeological cultures proper can be delineated in the study area (see Grigor'ev 1970 and compare with Grigor'ev 1983). Grigor'ev places Berdyzh and Khotylevo II in the Kostenki–Avdeevo culture.

A study of art and engravings has similarly failed to produce clear distinctions in the area. Zavernyaev (1978, 1981) shows that portable art from Khotylevo II can be classified into a recognized cultural style: the Kostenki–Avdeevo tradition. While both whole and fragmented classic "Venus" figurines and engravings are found at Khotylevo II (Figure 2.51), other Dnepr–Desna sites contain unique, site-specific portable art (Figures 2.31, 2.71, and 2.81). A study of engraving motifs on bone at the Dnepr–Desna sites has led both Abramova (1962, 1966) and Marshack (1979) to identify complex geometric motifs, linear marks, and fishlike or "diamond" designs as characteristic for the central Russian Plain. It should be noted, however, that with the exception of Marshack's (1979) work on decorative systematics on the Upper Paleolithic Russian Plain, no analytic research has been done on the subject of styles in art and engraving. Abramova's (1962) monograph on Upper Paleolithic art from the USSR is largely descriptive and only distinguishes the European from the Asiatic zone.

Finally, Soviet researchers, while noting a similarity in dwelling construction at the Dnepr–Desna sites, see this attribute as reflecting not archaeological culture, but rather similar economic modes of life (Dolukhanov 1982; Gladkih 1977b; Shovkoplyas 1965a).

A careful examination of stylistic data, however, reveals some interesting patterning which can best be understood in context of social networks. This patterning is especially visible if the sites are divided according to period of occupation, and when each medium (i.e., lithics, art, engravings, jewelry, site layout, and architectural detail in dwelling construction) is considered separately (Table 7.1). The chronological division of sites into just two categories—those occupied early and late—presents some problems. The sample of early sites is very small and the dating problematic. A more serious problem for this discussion, however, is presented by Khotylevo II. Its lithics, art, and worked bone bear strong similarity to the assemblages from the Kostenki–Avdeevo Upper Paleolithic sites lying to the southwest. It is the only early site that has yielded art, and, with the exception of one clear piece from Yurovichi, all examples of engraved bone from the early sites also come from Khotylevo II. The site's living floor, with a plethora of hearths and various-size pits and an absence of mammoth-bone constructions, likewise comes closer to Kostenki–Avdeevo sites than to either cold- or warm-weather Dnepr–Desna base camps (compare Figures 2.48 and 8.1). In brief, Khotylevo II appears to belong to another archaeological culture and probably a different settlement system. I control for such a possibility by both including and excluding this site from consideration in Table 7.1. I include it in my sample because (1) my hypothesis that it was a part of a more eastern settlement system remains to be investigated, (2) its relationship to

Table 7.1   LOCAL STYLISTIC DIFFERENCES ON THE CENTRAL RUSSIAN PLAIN[a,b]

| | Early sites | | |
Medium	Excluding Khotylevo II	Including Khotylevo II	Late sites
Lithics	+	+	−
Art			
figurative	−	+	−
engraved and painted	−	+	−
Jewelry	none found	none found	−
Site structure	−	+	−
Architectural details	−	−	+

[a]Adapted from Soffer (1985).
[b]+ = significant local differences present; − = significant local differences absent.

another early site, Berdyzh, remains unclear—Berdyzh lithics have also been identified with the Kostenki–Avdeevo culture, and (3) its inclusion gives a broader perspective on stylistic variation on the whole Upper Paleolithic Russian Plain.

Comparing stylistic variation from the early sites to those occupied late, I note both a change in the media used to signal corporate identity and a reduction in the number of distinct corporate groups occupying the area. Specifically, these changes are as follows:

Lithic Assemblages.   At the early sites, both including and excluding Khotylevo II, lithic assemblages show a great deal of stylistic variability. Both Shovkoplyas (1965a) and Grigor'ev (1970) clearly distinguish Radomyshl's lithics into a separate early archaeological culture. Yurovichi lithics are said to be stylistically similar to those of Eliseevichi (Budko 1967). Berdyzh stone tools resemble those of Kostenki–Avdeevo sites, as do the lithics from Khotylevo II. Stone tools from the late sites, on the other hand, have not been classified into agreed-upon local cultures. While the criteria used by Soviet researchers in either assigning assemblages to different archaeological cultures or pointing to similarities between assemblages from any two sites remain problematic (see Klein 1973), they are not the main issue here. I suggest that the fact that Soviet researchers note such similarities for the assemblages from early sites and generally fail to note them for the late sites is itself significant. I argue, therefore, that some stylistic signaling, however ambiguous, is present in the lithics from early sites and absent from those sites occupied after the Valdai maximum.

Figurative Art.   Portable art depicting human forms has been identified as such at Eliseevichi, Khotylevo II, and Mezhirich (see Figures 2.39, 2.51, and 2.72). In addition, 17 "phallic" figurines, more than 6 "birds," and 5 pieces transitional between the two found at Mezin are classified as stylized female figurines (Figure 2.81; see Shovkoplyas 1965a; Marshack 1981, personal communication). Likewise, Shovkoplyas (1972) identifies the badly weathered amber and sandstone artifacts from Dobranichevka as fragments of female figurines (Figure 2.31).

As Table 7.1 shows, this traditional carrier of stylistic information is absent from the early sites other than Khotylevo II. Those whole and fragmented classic "Venus" figurines from Khotylevo II are stylistically similar to those from the Kostenki–Avdeevo sites. Figurative art depicting either female or generic human forms found at the late sites, on the other hand, is all notably site-specific in style. Thus, while the Mezin collection of "birds" and "phallic" forms is said to be an abstracted representation of the female, the same gender identification cannot be made for the three anthropomorphic forms from Mezhirich, nor, despite Shovkoplyas' views to the contrary, for the two pieces from Dobranichevka (see Figure 2.31). In brief, figurative art from the late sites does not seem to reflect coherent style zones or demarcate bounded corporate identity.

Engraved and Painted Objects. While engraved and painted motifs found on bone at the study sites have not been subject to systematic regional analysis until recently, Marshack's 1979 study does confirm general observations by Abramova (1962, 1966) and Klein (1973) that complex geometric linear and "diamond" motifs prevail at the study sites. An exception to this pattern is again found at Khotylevo II, where the engraved motifs bear a much stronger resemblance to those from the Kostenki–Avdeevo sites (Figure 2.51; Zavernyaev 1981; Gvozdover 1983, personal communication). Comparing engraved motifs from early sites to those from the late ones, we again see the presence of distinct local differences at the early sites if Khotylevo II is included in the sample. A piece from Yurovichi (in Budko 1967b) bears the fishlike or "diamond" motif characteristic of the Dnepr–Desna design repertoire, while objects from Khotylevo II mirror Kostenki–Avdeevo design elements. At the late sites, while different sites show some individual preference for particular geometric or linear motifs, these differences are less significant than the general prevalence of complex geometric motifs. This is especially evident if we compare two engraved plaques of ivory from Eliseevichi and Mezhirich (Figures 2.37, 2.38, 2.74, and 2.75). Kornietz (1978, personal communication) identifies the Mezhirich piece as possibly representing the first "map." Marshack (1979), on the other hand, focusing on the sequential placement of different motifs on each plaque, claims that neither represents a conscious composition. He suggests that both pieces contain a series of ritual markings which were made over an indefinite period of time. In his argument for sequential ritual marking of these plaques, Marshack fails to note what for me is the most important feature of both plaques—their conceptual similarity. I offer both plaques here as an illustration of the unity in the Dnepr–Desna and Sudost' design repertoire. Both contain very similar elements, show great conceptual likeness to each other, and can be seen as material expressions of very similar concepts.

Finally, mammoth crania, mandibles, scapulae, and pelvises decorated with red ocher linear designs have been found at both Mezhirich in the south and Mezin in the north. Again, while showing some specific differences, both exhibit great overall similarity in design motifs (see Figures 2.73 and 2.82).

In brief, this discussion shows the existence of repetitive, local style differences in portable decorative pieces at the early sites and an atomization of this disinct local differentiation at the late sites. The late sites, while showing some overall conceptual similarity, exhibit site-specific style in portable decorated objects. We see regional or local style zones collapse with time, and decorated objects appear to signal messages other than those of bounded corporate identity.

At the same time that significant local stylistic differences (in both figurative and decorated objects) decrease with time, the number of these objects greatly increases. Considerably more art has been found in late high-density sites (nearly double the amount, $z = 1.57, p = .12$) and late low-density sites (18 times more, $z = 2.16$) than at early sites (see Table 6.42).

Jewelry.   Items of personal adornment have been found only at the late sites—heavily concentrated at complex base camps. Jewelry pieces include a usual assortment of shell and amber beads, elongated beads made of wolf long bones, tie-on bracelets from mammoth ivory, ivory pendants, perforated carnivore canines presumably worn as pendants or beads, as well as decorated bone pins. While no regional study has been made of these objects to date, and no analysis exists on the similarities and differences between jewelry from the study area and that from the Kostenki–Avdeevo sites, visually little or no difference can be seen between the two. Also, it appears that items of personal adornment from the entire study region are very similar stylistically. Thus, pending future information to the contrary, I argue that this mode does not carry significant stylistic information.

Site Structure.   As I demonstrate in Chapter 6, late sites in the study area show no north–south differences in site structure, and I interpret this to indicate that these two were a part of the same settlement system. If Khotylevo II is included in the sample, this is not the case for the sites occupied during the early period. While Berdyzh, Radomyshl, and probably the redeposited Yurovichi conform to the Dnepr-Desna pattern, Khotylevo II is startlingly different. Root (1983) argues that site structure should more directly reflect a subsistence–settlement system rather than more abstract social phenomena. If this is so, then the difference in the site structure of Khotylevo II, once again very similar to Kostenki–Avdeevo sites, may indicate a different and more eastern pattern. Thus, as with style motifs in art and lithics, significant local differences present at the early sites disappear in the site structuring of the late ones.

Architectural Details.   In Chapter 6 I describe architectural details discovered at Mezhirich. These include the use of such principles as mirror imagery and symmetry in Dwelling 4 (see Figures 6.7 and 6.8). Similar selective patterning may have been present in some of the dwellings at Yudinovo excavated by Polikarpovich and Bukdo. Abramova (1983, personal communication) reports evidence of symmetrical patterning in the use of mammoth bones in a Yudinovo dwelling. While the significance of this patterning remains unclear, I suggest that it can be seen as stylistic encoding of information. After Fritz (1978), I argue that at Mezhirich and Yudinovo we have information encoding in space and in building medium that transmits a secular and, probably, a sacred message. The style is clearly emblemic and the message corporate at both sites. I further argue that, at least at Mezhirich, similar encoding of stylistic information can be seen at the level of the site itself. Dwellings 1 and 2 (Figures 2.64 and 6.6) feature purposefully sorted mammoth skeletal elements (Dwelling 1—mandibles; Dwelling 2—long bones), and Dwelling 4 reflects Dwellings 1 and 2 sectionally. I suggest that similar site-wide transmission of emblemic information should be expected to occur at other complex base camps in the study area. Such stylistic information in architectural mode is absent at the sites occupied during the early period.

A cursory look at chronological differences in stylistic behavior (Table 7.1) appears to indicate an overall decrease in stylistic signaling through time. While distinct local style differences have been noted for both lithics and site structuring at the early sites, these become muted or disappear at the late sites. The same can be observed for figurative and decorated art. Price (1981) suggests that a change in the amount of stylistic signaling should reflect change or variation in social complexity. Wobst (1977) argues that a greater amount of style signaling reflects greater complexity. Taking these arguments into account, one could conclude that we are witnessing a decrease in social complexity in the study area through time. Such a conclusion, however, is greatly at odds with the changes noted in the subsistence and settlement patterns discussed in previous chapters.

I suggest, however, that this seeming contradiction is only a by-product of the scale of analysis used: One can argue for a decrease in social complexity through time only if one assumes an equal value for any and all stylistic signaling. This presupposes that it is the sheer redundancy, as expressed in the number of modes through which style messages are transmitted, that reflects social complexity or simplicity. But, as Root (1983) cogently argues, not all modes of stylistic signaling are of equal social significance. In her analysis of the social costs of information processing among egalitarian groups, she distinguishes two types of information encoding—the curated (i.e., artifacts) and noncurated (i.e. features) modes. She predicts that the noncurated mode, found in such features as dwellings and storage pits, should contain little or no stylistic information and show little or no concentration of surplus labor in egalitarian societies. A similar argument has been advanced by McGuire and Schiffer (1983), who note that structural investment in symbolic functions increases in response to greater social differentiation. Root (1983) predicts that curated items with style messages in egalitarian societies, those messages that transmit information of a corporate nature, should be homogeneously distributed over a region and found in concentrations at aggregation sites only.

Root's distinction between the curated and noncurated modes of style imprinting, as well as her association of each of these modes with social relationships, is of interest for this discussion. Media carrying stylistic information at the study sites, as noted, is of both curated and noncurated categories. A comparison in the use of these categories as carriers of stylistic information through time indicates (1) great redundancy in stylistic encoding on curated objects during the early period, and (2) a reduction in both redundancy (i.e., the number of media used) and stylistic signaling in curated objects at the late sites. The redundancy in style messages signals the presence of at least two archaeological cultures in the area during the early period of occupation. Berdyzh and Khotylevo II on lithics and Khotylevo II on art can be seen as local analogues of the Kostenki–Avdeevo culture. The stylistically different lithics from Radomyshl' and Yurovichi as well as the engraved piece from Yurovichi appear to indicate the presence of another cultural pattern in the area. Such redundancy in stylistic signaling of group identity is absent in the curated items from the late sites. In brief, we see an erasure of some social or corporate message that had been transmitted through curated items before 20,000 B.P.

At the same time that curated items show a decrease in style imprinting, late sites exhibit an increase in style imprinting on noncurated items, most clearly seen in architectural detailing at Mezhirich and Yudinovo. This is accompanied by a significant increase in the amount of art as well as the appearance of jewelry and exotics. These curated decorative items do not appear to carry any corporate message or emblemic style, and I suspect that information is *not imprinted on them but signaled by their very existence*.

I argue that the observed changes in stylistic signaling indicates the following pattern: During the early period of occupation, emblemic style on curated objects signaled corporate identity of different social groups. Some of these groups, those inhabiting Khotylevo II and possibly Berdyzh, for example, may not have been independent social entities but parts of larger social configurations settled to the east and southeast of the study area. During the late period, curated items lost their signaling power as emblemic markers of local corporate identity. I argue in Chapters 5 and 6, that the study area during the late period of occupation appears to have been inhabited by two groups, and that these groups were not socially independent but a part of the same social network. The lack of any localized concentration of style imprinting on curated items from late sites appears to support such an argument. During this period, corporate identity may have been signaled through noncurated features. The proliferation of stylistically indistinct art and decorative items, as well as of exotics and jewelry at complex base camps, argues for their use as status markers—carriers of corporate but also assertive information.

If, for the purposes of this discussion, we assume that the data from early sites (including Khotylevo II) is generally characteristic of these sites, then the observed differences in style behavior through time indicate either a change in social organization or the existence of at least two distinct social groups with different subsistence practices and settlement systems during the early period of occupation. In light of my analysis of changes in subsistence practices and settlement systems, I suspect the second of these to be more accurate. I tentatively suggest that the anomalous Khotylevo II was part of an adaptation complex of hunter–gatherers settled east of the study area—those whose sites have been traditionally classified as belonging to Kostenki–Streletskaya and Kostenki–Avdeevo cultures. I further suggest that this eastern adaptation strategy may have featured greater residential mobility and an aggregation–dispersal pattern of social integration. It is this system which utilized curated objects as carriers of emblemic style. It well may be that the art-rich anomalous Khotylevo II base camp represents an aggregation site of this eastern strategy.

The second subsistence–settlement pattern present during the early period was located in the study area proper and is represented by Berdyzh, Radomyshl', and Yurovichi. This system featured a logistically organized subsistence strategy and a storage economy. In time, this system intensified and, under conditions of reduced mobility selected for by both logistical organization and storage economy, underwent social intensification as well. Portable items no longer signaled generalized corporate identity, and some increasingly began signaling intragroup status differences. It is the stationary features that took on the role of carrying corporate identity information, and this identity was region-wide, not localized. While this hypothesis is speculative, it does appear to have some support in data on the social organization to be presented below.

SOCIOPOLITICAL RELATIONSHIPS AND ORGANIZATION ─────────

Suitable evidence on sociopolitical relationships and organization is notoriously hard to come by in prehistoric archaeology of hunter–gatherers, and ambiguous to boot. First, as Root (1981, 1983), Moore (1979, 1983), and Wobst (1974, 1976, 1977) point out, the site-specific focus of much of prehistoric archaeology does not recover the type of information necessary for the reconstruction of this subsystem. These authors advocate a regional approach, one that, while undoubtedly far more promising, also ignores part of data base. We need both a fine-scale site-specific focus and a more general regional focus when considering questions of sociopolitical relationships.

In this work I use a regional approach in which each site is a unit of analysis. Although this approach is best suited to the nature of the archaeological record, the use of the site as a unit of analysis precludes from consideration finer intrasite differences in frequency and distribution of archaeological remains. Because of this, I have effectively eliminated much potential information on sociopolitical relationships from this work. Since I see sociopolitical organization as a functional component of an adaptation strategy, I also view the structuring of such organization as a solution to existing environmental, demographic, economic, and social problems. So far I have outlined the following variables that have a bearing on sociopolitical organization:

1. A subsistence economy based on storage. In such an economy, individual or family mobility does not offer a solution to potential social problems, as it does in non-logistically organized foraging economies. In addition, the procurement and storage of seasonally abundant subsistence resources creates certain labor demands that both reduce the mobility option for individual families and facilitates potential manipulations and control of labor.

2. In Chapter 6 I document some evidence, albeit ambiguous, for smaller group size and possibly longer lengths of stay at the early sites and larger group size and shorter stay at the late sites. However, as Tables 6.36 and 6.42 show, the mean sizes of coresidential units during both the early and late periods were fairly sizable.

3. I have documented an increase in the environmental stress during the late period of occupation. In Chapter 5 I argue that this increased stress partially selected for intensification in procurement practices and storage. Riches (1979), using data from the Northwest Coast, argues that environments with increasing productive uncertainty bring increasing need for the control of manpower. His argument can be extended to include a comparison between more stable and more fluctuating environments—and to argue that, given a particular logistically organized subsistence strategy, periods with

greater environmental stress select for more control of labor than those under less stress.

GROUP DYNAMICS

Johnson (1983) has brought forth convincing ethnographic and historical evidence to show that group size and complexity of sociopolitical organization are directly related. Discussing the increase in social strain between individuals with an increase in group size, he writes: "Scalar stress in non-hierarchical groups is an exponential function of organization size, and small increments in size may result in large increments in scalar stress" (Johnson 1983:8). Johnson identifies information-processing overload as the mechanism that may constrain the size of cofunctioning or coresiding groups and suggests an organizational threshold at around six individuals.

Making a distinction between different-size organizational units in social systems (i.e. individual, nuclear family, extended family, etc.), Johnson notes that for hunter–gatherers organized into nuclear families, this scalar-stress threshold empirically surfaces when the number of nuclear families exceeds about 11 (over 35 individuals). He identifies three types of potential social response to scalar stress: (1) group fission, (2) expansion of basal or organizational unit size (i.e., the change from nuclear to extended family), and (3) hierarchization and the development of specialized positions of leadership. Johnson concludes his analysis by admitting that we cannot predict which responses to scalar stress are most likely to occur (Johnson 1983:45).

Given the size of coresidential units I project for the study area, we can anticipate that problems of scalar stress were operating on the Upper Paleolithic central Russian Plain. One of the solutions to this stress, mobility, was not viable. Data on hand suggest that the other two solutions, increase in basal unit size and hierarchization, were adopted at various times. My argument against the viability of the mobility solution is based on subsistence practices and storage behavior. Given this organization, mobility, at best, would be an ad hoc solution. The settlement pattern outlined for both the early and late periods indicates that the solution to scalar stress did not involve residential mobility on the level of individual families and did not result in the aggregation–dispersal pattern suggested for other Old World late Pleistocene–Early Holocene groups (Conkey 1980; Jochim 1976; Spiess 1979; White 1980). While undoubtedly a family did occasionally move out of an unpleasant base camp, it was hierarchization and increase in household size that were institutionalized as societal responses to scalar stress.

While I have documented the absence of mobility or fission as a solution, it is more difficult to convincingly document the two solutions I argue for. The data on hand are nebulous and can be used to argue for very different interpretations if each source is taken individually. I suggest, however, that the sum of the evidence, taken in toto, does warrant such hypotheses.

Hierarchization: Status Demarcation

I define *hierarchization* here as vertical differentiation in sociopolitical roles and see it as an introduction of specialized leadership or decision-making positions (see Johnson 1977, 1983; Lightfoot and Feinman 1982). Such leadership roles in societies are expected to be clearly marked both directly, by items of material culture, and indirectly. Indirect evidence for the existence of hierarchical status positions includes evidence for specialization in production and for activity differentiation, for control of labor, and for control of resources (see Braun and Plog 1982; Lightfoot and Feinman 1982; Peebles and Kus 1977; Price 1981).

Fried (1967) distinguishes two ways that positions of status are obtained in society—through achievement and through ascription. He associates the first recruitment process with simpler egalitarian societies and the second with more complex tribal and chiefdom formations. Following his lead, many archaeologists have attempted to distinguish and monitor these two types of status as a way of gauging the simplicity or complexity of a group under study.

Archaeological evidence for status demarcation, however, is notoriously ambivalent and inconclusive, and the mere fact that status is marked in the archaeological record does not imply hierarchization. Since it can be expected that all social systems will have some status positions, what is of interest in questions of social differentiation is the presence or absence of hierarchization of status positions. Direct archaeological correlates of status mentioned in the literature include exotic materials, items of personal decoration that bear evidence of costly labor investment, and ritual paraphernalia. These materials, in and of themselves, however, do not indicate status hierarchization. For example, the differential distribution of elaborate burials with voluminous grave goods has been interpreted as signaling hierarchization of status. As Bender (1982) points out, however, messages from the grave can be most equivocal, and grave goods can signal status reached only in death as well as that earned in life. In the ensuing discussion I limit myself to examining evidence for hierarchical behavior in general and omit from consideration questions of how individuals were recruited to fill particular status positions (i.e., if through individual achievement, through inheritance, through some ritual process, etc.).

Data from the study area do indicate that such artifacts as art, jewelry, and especially exotic amber and shells probably functioned as status markers. While these items are found in far greater numbers at complex base camps, no evidence can be brought to argue for their unequal distribution within these sites. No burials of any kind and no caches of valuables have been found in the study area itself. The few Upper Paleolithic burials known for the Russian Plain all come from Sungir and Kostenki sites lying to the northeast and southeast of the study area. Although I argue in Chapter 6 that sites belonging to the Kostenki–Streletskaya and Kostenki–Avdeevo cultures all probably belong to a different settlement system than that of the Dnepr–Desna basin, I turn here to burial evidence from this eastern part of the Russian Plain because it does have a bearing on the issue at hand. I argue here that these data are relevant because Khotylevo II was probably a part of this eastern adaptation strategy, and because mortuary behavior in evidence there does reveal some interesting, although speculative, patterning of relevance to the study area proper. I include data on the three Sungir burials in my sample because Sungir has been classified by Bader as belonging to the Kostenki–Streletskaya or Kostenki–Sungir culture (Bader 1978; Sukachev et al. 1966).

Table 7.2   BURIAL DATA FROM THE UPPER PALEOLITHIC RUSSIAN PLAIN[a]

Site	N	Age	Sex	Grave construction	Grave goods Tools	Ornaments	¹⁴C date
Kostenki II[b,c] (Zamyatninskaya)	1	Old	M	Bone-lined	—	—	11,000 ± 200
Kostenki XIV[b,d] (Markina Gora) Layer III	1	25	M	Pit	—	—	14,300 ± 460
Kostenki XV[b,e] (Gorodtsovskaya)	1	6–7	nd	Pit	70 flakes, knife, needles, burnisher	~150 beads or fox pendants	21,720 ± 570
Kostenki XVIII[b,f] (Hvoikovkaya)	1	9–10	nd	Bone cover	—	—	Not dated[h]
Sungir[g]	3–9?	55–65	M	Pit	flint knife	>3000 bone beads, pendants, fox pendants	25,500 ± 200 24,430 ± 400
		7–9	F	Pit	bone spears	>3000 bone beads, pins, bracelets, stone pendants, 100 fox pendants, figurine	22,500 ± 600 21,800 ± 1000 20,540 ± 120 16,200 ± 400 14,600 ± 600
		9–13 plus possibly two more F	M	Pit	4 shaft straighteners	>3000 bone beads, pins, bracelets, stone pendants, fox pendants, shells	

[a]Adapted from Soffer (1985).
[b]Gerasimova (1982).
[c]Boriskovskii and Dmitrieva (1982).
[d]Rogachev and Sinitsyn (1982a).
[e]Rogachev and Sinitsyn (1982b).
[f]Rogachev and Belyaeva (1982).
[g]Bader (1978, 1984).
[h]Assignment to early period of occupation uncertain.

The five sites with human interments from the Upper Paleolithic Russian Plain are presented in Table 7.2, including demographic breakdown of the buried individuals and the accompanying burial inventories. In spite of the very small sample of burials for a period that appears to have spanned some 25,000 years, I suggest that two factors related to status demarcation are significant in these data. First, if we divide the burials into early and late chronological subdivisions, as done for the study area, we note that burials accompanied by grave goods date only to the early period—before 20,000 B.P. The two burials dating to the late period, Kostenki II and Kostenki XIV, contain no grave goods.

The nature of the grave goods found in early burials is the second relevant issue. Note that while varying amounts of labor investment are suggested by the goods, from moderate at Kostenki XV to very costly in the burials of the adult male and two adolescents at Sungir, the vast majority of burial goods were made of locally available materials. Bader (1978; and in Sukachev *et al.* 1966) reports that while over 10,000 beads were found in the three Sungir interments, distributed approximately equally between the deceased, fewer than 10 of them are perforated shells and the rest are made of mammoth ivory. The shells used as decoration are from freshwater species of *Unio* and *Ostrea* and could have been obtained locally (Chepalyga 1983, personal communication; Sukachev *et al.* 1966). Bader (1978) also reports an unspecified number of both finished beads and bead blanks, presumably in the process of being fashioned into beads, on the living floor at Sungir. This suggests that bead manufacturing went on at the site itself. The beads were not ground but produced by cutting mammoth-ivory blanks and then perforating bead preforms by incision and drilling. Bader (1978) and Abramova (1962) divide Sungir beads into four very standardized and uniform categories.

Using data from Coles (1979) on the rate of bone-bead manufacturing, and assuming that each Sungir bead would have taken approximately 15 minutes to manufacture (including preparing ivory blanks, cutting preforms, cutting and then drilling holes, etc.), I estimate that over 2500 man-hours of labor are reflected in beads alone in the three Sungir burials. Bader (1978) argues that Sungir represents a single episode of summer to fall occupation. If we assume this interpretation to be correct, translate it into days of occupation, and assume a 5-month stay at the site, the labor investment in beadmaking carries a number of implications for both specialization in production and at least a partial control of labor. I define specialization in production as differentiation in activities beyond the level of simple task segregation by age and gender. Assuming a 6-hour workday per individual, Sungir beads represent 417 days of work for one person, 42 days for 10 people, and full-time bead manufacturing during the entire length of stay if 3 people were involved in bead manufacturing. The standardization of bead size and shape noted by Bader, although not confirmed by any empirical studies, suggests that beads were not manufactured by a large number of individuals but rather produced by a few specialists. If beads were produced by a small group of individuals, then the relatively short duration of occupation at Sungir argues for either full-time or nearly full-time specialization in beadmaking.

On the other hand, it is possible, and more likely, that Sungir does not represent a single occupational episode and that the beads found in the three burials were not all made over a 5-month period. The noted standardization in bead shapes and sizes still argues for their manufacture by a limited number of beadmakers. The amount of labor put in by them, whether done over a 5-month period or over a longer span of time, was still invested in just three burials. This labor investment and standardization, in turn, implies that bead manufacturers were (1) supported while beadmaking, (2) persuaded to devote some portion of their working time to this task, and (3) persuaded to contribute their products to the grave inventories of just three individuals.

In addition to all the beads, the three Sungir burials also contain rich inventories of bone and ivory objects, including the famed long spears (one over 2 m in length), an animal figurine, four carved shaft straighteners, as well as pendants, bracelets, and pins. Thus the 2500 man-hours of labor I project for beadmaking represents just a fragment of the labor involved in the manufacturing of Sungir grave goods.

I interpret the Sungir data as implying that status hierarchization was in existence on the Russian Plain some 24,000 years ago and that some individuals, regardless of their age, occupied higher positions of status than others. At Sungir, both the 7–9-year-old girl and the 9–13-year-old boy received as many grave goods as the adult male buried with them. Bender (1982, 1985) argues that the seeds of social inequality may lie in the control of access to social and ritual knowledge. In light of her observations, I suspect that the association of labor investment with the ritual act of burial at Sungir indicates that social differences marked in the burials were associated with some sort of ritual control. While much work remains to be done to ascertain the exact nature of these high-status positions, the age of the two adolescents buried elaborately at Sungir argues for such an interpretation.

Sites dating since 18,000 B.P., on the Russian Plain as a whole and in the study area itself, have not yielded any examples of burials accompanied by burial goods. At the same time, the study sites, and especially complex base camps, contain a variety of exotic and special items that I indirectly associate with status demarcation. I argue here that if we accept the role of exotics and decorative objects as status markers, then both their restricted distribution at complex base camps and their association with long-distance exchange networks suggests that, in time, positions of status were associated not only with ritual mortuary behavior but also with the behavior of the living. Such an emerging "secularization" is most clearly seen in the long-distance exchange networks that spanned the area during the late period. While these exchanges were in all probability heavily cloaked in sacred justification and ritual, they were clearly also affairs of the living, manipulated and controlled by just some of the living.

Hierarchization: Relationships of Production

Specialization.   My examination of burials indicates that some specialization in production may have been present during the early period of occupation. Data from the late sites in the study area proper indicate an increase in this specialization. While it can be argued that specialized bead production, if it existed, existed well east of the study area, data on the specialized exploitation of fur bearers and on the procurement of exotic materials come from the study area itself. In addition to exotics and fur bearers, I suggest that specialized production of blades can also be projected (see Table 6.7 for blade and nuclei data). Two types of site can be found during the late period of occupation—those with high blade–nuclei ratios, where four times as many blades as nuclei are found, and those with low ratios ($N = 18, z = 4.71, p < .0001$, see Table 6.2). Sites with low blade–nuclei ratios are those where blade manufacturing predominated, and those with the high ratios are sites where blade use predominated. Ten sites shown in Table 6.7 have low ratios: Chulatovo I, Chulatovo II, Fastov, Kurovo, Novgorod-Severskii, Bugorok, Pogon, Pushkari I, Pushkari II, and Timonovka I. The north–south breakdown on the distribution of high- and low-ratio sites shows that of the 19 sites in the north, 10 (53%) have low ratios and 9 (47%) high ratios. In the south, 1 (17%) site has a low ratio and 5 (83%) high ratios. The sizable presence of blade-manufacturing sites in the north is to be expected, given the availability of superior flint. It will be recalled from Chapter 6 that all recognized lithic workshops are in the north.

Sites with low ratios have generally been identified in Chapter 6 as warm-weather occupations. The only exceptions are Dobranichevka, Pushkari I, and Timonovka I—all of which have been classified as simple base camps occupied during the cold season. Table 7.3 presents the results of various comparisons in the distribution of blade–nuclei ratios between the different types of sites. While no regional north–south differences are observed between the high- ($z = 0.96$) or low-ratio sites ($z = 0.01$), there is a significant difference between northern and southern sites in general ($z = 2.50$) that shows lower ratios at northern sites. A comparison of ratios at the different types of sites indicates seasonal differences both in the north and south at base camps. Northern cold-weather base camps have much higher ratios than their warm-weather equivalents ($z = 2.16$). Southern cold-weather base camps, on the other hand, have significantly lower ratios than their warm-weather analogues ($z = 6.14$). Likewise, a significant difference is also present in the ratios of northern and southern warm-weather base camps ($z = 18.63$), while no differences can be observed between northern and southern cold-weather occupations ($z = 1.11$).

Since I have previously argued in Chapter 6 that (1) no significant differences existed in the sizes of coresidential units between the warm- and cold-weather base camps, (2) a full range of procurement and manufacturing activities went on at both cold- and warm-weather base camps, and (3) northern warm-weather base camps may have been occupied longer than their southern equivalents (or subject to more reoccupation), the magnitude in the differences of blade–nuclei ratios between northern and southern warm-weather base camps appears interesting. In this discussion I assume a steady year-round demand for blades that would be about equal at both northern and southern warm- and cold-weather base camps and would vary only as a result of either population or duration of occupation. Given this assumption, I interpret the prevalence of low blade–nuclei ratios at northern warm-weather base camps as suggesting specialized procurement and production but not use of blades at these locales. These regional differences become even more pronounced if we add northern lithic workshops occupied in warm-weather months to our northern sample ($z = 13.40$).

The possible existence of at least seasonal specialization in blade production at warm-weather northern sites leaves open the question of the final destination of these blades. I suggest that some may have found their way through exchange networks to southern sites. Such possible seasonal specialization suggests additional labor demands for the curation and transport of blades. In this discussion I leave open the question of whether this specialization was seasonal for the whole coresidential unit (for a particular age and gender category within this unit), or if it was individual specialization by just a few members of the unit. Quite clearly, all of these questions will have to be considered before I can unequivocally demonstrate specialization in blade production on the Upper Paleolithic central Russian Plain. In addition, and more important, the origin of both

Table 7.3   DIFFERENCE OF MEANS TESTS ON THE DISTRIBUTION OF BLADE–NUCLEI RATIOS[a]

	N	$\overline{X}_1$	$\overline{X}_2$	z	p
Northern vs. southern sites, all	18	16.87	35.71	2.50	.04
Northern vs. southern high-ratio sites	7	36.00	46.47	0.96	.25
Northern vs. southern low-ratio sites	11	12.89	12.83	0.01	.40
Northern lithic workshops vs. Fastov	4	10.21	8.91	0.48	.36
Northern vs. southern cold-weather base camps	8	30.33	32.08	1.11	.22
Northern vs. southern warm-weather base camps (Pushkari II omitted)	4	15.44	74.32	18.63	<.0001
Northern cold- vs. warm-weather base camps (Pushkari II omitted)	7	30.33	15.44	2.16	.04
Southern cold- vs. warm-weather base camps	5	32.08	74.32	6.14	<.0001
Northern warm-weather lithic workshops and base camps vs. southern warm-weather sites (Kurovo and Fastov omitted)	8	16.71	74.32	13.40	<.0001

[a]Arcsine transformed values; see Table 6.7.

northern and southern lithics will have to be firmly established. I argue here that the evidence I have presented, while both ambiguous and inconclusive, does indicate a possibility of specialization in blade manufacturing, and that more significant, it only comes from the late sites.

Finally, in all three examples of possible specialization in production during the late period, I have only been able to demonstrate this specialization per site rather than per individual or per household. Such site-specific accumulation could admittedly also result from cultural and social practices unrelated to specialization in production. I also realize that the sample sizes I work with are quite inadequate and that my chronological controls are problematic. In spite of all these problems, there is a reasonably strong case for at least some specialization in production and an increase in such specialization through time.

Control of Labor and Resources.   While part-time specialists are known from the ethnographic literature on hunter–gatherers, the ability to control labor has traditionally been seen as a feature of hierarchically organized sedentary groups (e.g., Lightfoot and Feinman 1982; Peebles and Kus 1977). We do have ethnographic evidence for control of labor from complex and nonegalitarian hunter–gatherers (e.g., the Northwest Coast), and Bender's (1978, 1982, 1985) work clearly indicates that nascent forms of labor control should be anticipated when working with any but the simplest hunter–gatherer groups.

Archaeological data from the study area on storage pits and construction of mammoth-bone dwellings indirectly argue for the existence of some sort of control of labor. Specifically, if we assume that unequal distribution of resources accompanies hierarchization, then the distribution of storage pits at some of the sites bears on the discussion. Unfortunately, information on the contents of storage pits is most incomplete and does not permit comparisons of storage volume per dwelling or per site. Data are available, however, on the location of the pits at some of the sites in relation to the dwellings at these sites; these are illustrated for Radomyshl' in Figure 2.99 and for Dobranichevka in Figure 2.28.

The identification and distribution of storage pits at Mezin is a more difficult problem. Shovkoplyas excavated only one of the five possible dwellings at the site, and his plan for the site presented in Figure 2.77 illustrates his archival reconstruction of Dwelling Complexes 2–5. On his plan (Shovkoplyas 1965a), Shovkoplyas does not depict the location of the 7 or 8 pits he excavated, because 5 of them lay directly below the hearths that surrounded Dwelling 1 and the others were found up to 60 cm below what he considered to have been the living surface of the site. The location of these pits is illustrated in Figure 7.4.

Compounding the problem at Mezin is the fact that Shovkoplyas did not reconstruct any pits surrounding Dwellings 2–5. On his floor plan, he does note the presence of bone accumulations or bone heaps around some of these dwellings. Since he was working with archival fieldnotes and excavator diaries that in some cases dated to the beginning of the twentieth century—with data on the vertical provenience of the finds was lacking, it is understandable that Shovkoplyas demured from considering bone accumulations as storage pits. As Table 2.4 indicates, both surface bone heaps and storage pits are present at other sites in the study area—a fact that also forbids an assumption that any past excavation of bone accumulations had necessarily unearthed storage pits.

If, for the purposes of this discussion, we assume that only 7 or 8 pits were present at Mezin, then 6 out of these were located in a semicircle 1 to 2 m from Dwelling 1. If, on the other hand, we include surface bone accumulations surrounding Dwellings 2–5, then the 19 surface or subterranean bone accumulations depicted in Figure 7.4 are associated with dwellings as follows:

Dwelling	Number of associated bone accumulations
1	9
2	2
3	4 (?)
4	2 (?)
5	none

I place question marks after estimates for Dwellings 3 and 4 because their proximity to each other does not permit a clear distinction in the association of at least two bone accumulations. One or two storage pits and one bone accumulation depicted in Figure 7.4 were found on the periphery of the site and not associated with any one of the dwellings.

For Gontsy, Sergin (1983) demonstrates conclusively that the 5 or 6 storage pits excavated at the site all bracketed just one of the two possible dwellings at the site

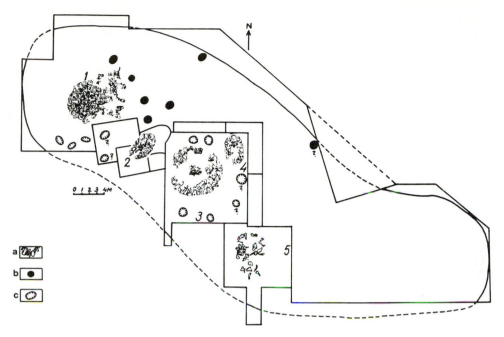

Figure 7.4 Distribution of bone heaps and storage pits at Mezin: a, mammoth-bone dwellings; b, storage pits; c, bone heaps; 1–5, dwelling numbers; ?, association unclear (Soffer 1985).

(Figure 2.45 shows three of these pits; Sergin's 1976–1981 work on two other pits around this dwelling is unpublished and not included in this figure). Finally, Grekhova (1983, personal communication) states that the more than five storage pits documented at Eliseevichi also surround only one of the dwellings there.

Past excavations at Mezhirich unfortunately focused on unearthing the dwellings themselves and not on investigating the living floors adjacent to the dwellings. Because of this bias, we simply do not know how many storage pits were located at the site nor how they were distributed. Current work at the site is uncovering large areas of the living floor adjacent to Dwelling 4 and should in time supply information pertinent to this discussion.

A comparison of the distribution of storage pits to dwellings at these sites shows three patterns: (1) central location of the pit between the dwellings at Radomyshl', (2) fairly equitable distribution of pits around the dwellings at Dobranichevka, and (3) clustered distribution of pits predominantly surrounding one dwelling at Mezin, Gontsy, and Eliseevichi.

As I note in a discussion of storage pits in Chapter 5, the chronological change in pit use throughout the life of a site or dwelling resulted in some pits containing solid-packed bone while others held remains of just a few bones suspended in a loess matrix. Sergin (1983) likewise suggests that, at least during the last stages of occupation at some sites, some pits may have been refuse pits while others served as storage facilities.

If we assume that all of the pits initially served as storage facilities and some turned into refuse pits only later, the distribution of pits at the late sites suggests that an unequal distribution of resources existed at some sites. This become especially apparent if we compare pit location at Radomyshl', occupied early, to that at the late sites. The central location of Radomyshl's pit argues for open, visible, and equal access to stored resources for all inhabitants of the site. Resources at Dobranichevka, on the other hand, were distributed around each dwelling, and this distribution implies a restriction of access to the pits limited to the residents of the dwelling only. The fairly similar numbers and sizes of pits surrounding each Dobranichevka dwelling imply that, while access to resources was controlled by each household, the amount per household was fairly equal. The concentration of 6 of the 7 or 8 Mezin pits (or of 9 of the 17 heaps and pits) around one dwelling suggests that one household at Mezin controlled more than its even share of the resources at the site. Similar interpretations can be suggested for Gontsy and Eliseevichi.

A chronological comparison in pit distribution through time appears to suggest that control of resources changed from open and accessible to all to fairly equal but restricted to each household at simple base camps (i.e., Radomyshl' and Dobranichevka). In other cases, most clearly seen at complex base camps such as Mezin and Eliseevichi, resources may have come not only under the control of each household or dwelling, but also unequally distributed among the households.

I am aware that the problematic and ambiguous nature of my data base, as well as the unit of analysis I use in this exercise, are all fairly controversial, and that pit location alone is a poor indicator of unequal resource distribution. A number of different behavioral sequences totally unrelated to the control of resources could also have produced a similar pattern. A multiple reoccupation of some dwellings and singular occupations of others, for example, could have resulted in more pits around those dwellings that were reoccupied more frequently. It could be also argued that in assuming a mean value of 2 m^2 of dwelling space per person in my population estimates per site (see Chapter 6), I imply that larger dwellings were occupied by larger numbers of people. If more people lived in the larger dwellings, it can be anticipated that larger dwellings would have more storage pits associated with them. However, the magnitude of the differences in pit- and bone-heap distribution between the dwellings at Mezin argues against population as the only determinant of pit distribution. Mezin Dwelling 1 measures 20 m^2 and has 6 storage pits and 9 pits and heaps around it, while Dwelling 3, measuring 28 m^2, has no pits and only 4 bone heaps around it. This information, of course, comes from only one site, and while being suggestive, it does not eliminate alternate hypotheses. As before, I argue that while the distribution of storage pits around dwellings alone is not sufficient enough a proof of unequal distribution of resources, this evidence together with data from other sources does warrant such a proposal. I see this possible unequal distribution as yet another indirect indication that social and economic hierarchization was taking place on the Upper Paleolithic central Russian Plain.

Additional indirect evidence for hierarchization can be also observed in the architectural construction at complex base camps. I suggest that site planning evident at Mezhirich (i.e., the conceptual unity in the selection and use of the different mammoth skeletal elements per dwelling), as well as the use of symmetry, mirror imagery, and rhythmic repetition at Mezhirich and Yudinovo, implies both public works and monumental architecture. While the contemporaneity of the dwellings at these sites is still to be clearly demonstrated, Pidoplichko (1976) notes that bones belonging to the same mammoth were used in different dwellings at Mezhirich. This and the site-wide planning evident at Mezhirich suggest interpreting this site as one of unified conception and construction. Similar patterning is present at Yudinovo as well, and I suspect that it was also present at the other complex base camps excavated earlier. If we take human labor as a gauge, we can see that three times as much labor went into the construction of these complex base camps as into the construction of simple base camps (see Tables 6.16 and 6.17). While the 14.5 days of labor for 10 workers, I postulate for Mezhirich and 16 days for Mezin do not approach the kinds of massive labor investment estimated for monumental architecture of more complex societies (e.g., Coles 1979), they are indeed impressive investments for hunter–gatherers and qualify as examples of late Pleistocene monumental architecture. Although we do not know of ethnographic equivalents for Mezhirich and Yudinovo, it does not mean that such architectural feats were not part of hunter–gatherer adaptation in the past. Elaborate bone constructions discovered on Yttigran Island off the Bering Strait, called Whalebone Alley by Arutyunov *et al.* (1982), suggest that such monumental constructions may have been more frequent for hunter–gatherers in the past than we have suspected.

Labor investment seen at such sites as Mezhirich and Yudinovo, as well as the stylistic encoding of social information in these constructions, indicate behavior more compatible with hierarchically organized societies than with egalitarian ones. As Peebles and Kus (1977) and McGuire and Schiffer (1983) point out, this sort of directed mass labor investment is an archaeological equivalent of social complexity beyond that modeled for egalitarian groups. The planning and labor coordination necessary for such projects as Mezhirich implies some form of leadership and suggests a hierarchical sociopolitical organization. Thus, I offer data on Mezhirich and Yudinovo constructions as yet another line of evidence for hierarchization in the study area during the Upper Paleolithic—particularly during the late period of occupation.

Increase in Size of Basal Units

Johnson (1983) notes that an increase in the size of the basal organizational unit is another solution to problems of scalar stress. He notes that in simple human social systems this can be a change from the nuclear family to the extended family as the basic coresidential and cooperating unit. Archaeological data from the study area indicate that this second solution may have also been instituted during the late period of occupation. In Chapter 6, I estimate a mean value of 2 m^2 of dwelling space per individual and show that two sizes of dwellings were present at the sites: large ones, measuring over 20 m^2, and small ones, under 13 m^2. Table 6.42 shows significant difference in the numbers of dwellings through time ($z = 0.75$). A comparison of mean dwelling size between simple and complex base camps shows that the 21.52 m^2 observed at complex base camps is significantly greater than the 15.63 m^2 per dwelling at simple base camps ($N = 36$, $z = 1.98$, $p = .05$). I have noted previously that complex

Table 7.4   DWELLINGS AND INTERIOR HEARTHS

Dwelling	Area (m^2)	Number of hearths
Berdyzh		
1	12.5	2
2	45.0 (?)	1
Dobranichevka		
1	12.5	0
2	12.5	1
3	12.5	1
4	12.5	0
Gontsy		
1	20.0	1
Mezhirich		
1	24.0	1
2	20.0	1
3	12.0 (?)	1
Mezin		
1	20.0	3
2	8.0	0
3	28.0	2
4	8.0	0
5	28.0	1
Pushkari I[a]		
1	12.5	1
2	12.5	1
3	12.5	1
Suponevo		
1	23.76	1
2	27.5	1[c]
Yudinovo[b]		
1	32.0	2
2	24.0	1

[a]Pushkari I considered as 3 small dwellings (see Table 2.4).
[b]Yudinovo areas per dwelling taken as mean values (see Table 2.4).
[c]Suponevo hearths in Dwelling 2 taken as a mean value.

base camps were an inherent feature of the late period of occupation and that these types of cold-weather occupations were not found among the early sites.

Although both early and late cold-weather base camps contain large and small dwellings (see Table 6.16), large dwellings are strongly associated with the late period ($\phi = .41$, $p = .02$, calculated by Fisher exact test). In fact, if we eliminate the problematic Berdyzh second dwelling from consideration (the area given for this dwelling in Table 6.16 is a questionable 45 m^2), we see that all the large dwellings date only to the late period. I interpret this increase in dwelling size to indicate a change in size of

Table 7.5   PEARSON CORRELATION COEFFICIENTS ON DWELLING SIZES AND NUMBER OF INTERIOR HEARTHS

	N	df	r	r^2	p
All sites: dwelling size and number of hearths	22	20	.40	.16	.05<p<.1
Late sites: dwelling size and number of hearths	20	18	.61	.38	.01
All sites excluding Berdyzh Dwelling 2: dwelling size and number of hearths	21	19	.53	.28	.02

coresidential units. I further suggest that this change can be best understood as a change from the nuclear family to the extended or multiple family as a minimal unit of socioeconomic organization. It is interesting to note that these extended families, presumably occupying the larger dwellings, are especially associated with complex base camps. As Table 6.16 shows, all complex base camps have large dwellings. However, large dwellings are also found at what I identify as simple base camps (e.g., Gontsy, Kirillovskaya). At other simple base camps, such as Dobranichevka and Pushkari I, only small dwellings have been reported. This unclear patterning in the distribution of large dwellings appears to indicate that extended or multiple families were not a feature of just complex base camps, but an integral organizational unit after 18,000 B.P.

It can be argued that an increase in dwelling size need not reflect an increase in family size—that it could just reflect hierarchization itself. Specifically, given hierarchization of status positions in the study area, we could anticipate that families of high-status individuals would reside in larger dwellings than families with lower status. Data on dwelling size and distribution of storage pits and bone heaps at Mezin, for example, could be used for just such an argument—one that fills Mezin Dwelling 1 with the nuclear family of a high-status individual who controlls much of the resources stored at the site. In order to evaluate these two hypothetical explanations—(1) that large dwellings housed families of high-status individuals, or (2) that large dwellings housed larger extended families—I examine the relationship between house area and number of interior hearths. If we assume a rough relationship between number of occupants and number of interior hearths per dwelling, we should find no relationship between house size and hearth number if the first hypothesis is correct. A positive relationship between these two variables favors the second hypothesis.

Table 7.4 lists dwelling sizes and number of hearths per dwelling. Pearson correlation coefficients between areas of dwellings and hearth numbers can be found in Table 7.5, which indicates a strong positive correlation between these two variables at sites occupied late ($N = 20$, $r = .61$, $p = .01$). A positive correlation also exists if we include both early and late sites in the calculation, although data from the one early site, Berdyzh, lower both the correlation ($N = 22$, $r = .40$) and the level of significance (.05 $> p > .1$). Information on Berdyzh, however, is quite problematic (see Chapter 2), and Budko's (1969a; Budko et al. 1971) reconstructions of dwelling areas may be quite erroneous. Overall, I interpret these test results as confirmation of the second hypothesis—that larger dwellings were occupied by larger numbers of people than small dwellings. The association of large dwellings with more numerous hearths in the late period of occupation indicates that an increase probably occurred in the size of the basal unit of socioeconomic organization. Thus, although Johnson (1983) offers both hierarchization and an increase in basal unit size as equally viable and separate solutions to problems of scalar stress, data from the study area suggest that an interesting sequential relationship may exist between them.

SETTLEMENT HIERARCHIES

In this section I examine the significance of different site types and their ranges of activities as they relate to sociopolitical integration. Johnson (1977) suggests that a range in activities can be used as a measure of the relationship of sites or settlements to each other and has termed this measure "settlement function size." A comparison within site types of function size can reveal whether sites are in a hierarchical relationship or are exact equivalents. For Johnson, as well as Peebles and Kus (1977) and Renfrew (1983), clear-cut settlement hierarchies are characteristic of hierarchical societies, whereas egalitarian societies are expected to show a lack of such structuring in regional settlements.

Data on settlement types in the study area clearly indicate a seasonal difference in function size; cold-weather base camps show a wider range of activities than do warm-weather sites. Storage behavior, for example, is only evident at cold-weather base camps, as is the specialized procurement of fur bearers and site-wide architectural planning. While such seasonal differences in activities find analogues in the ethnographic record of egalitarian groups (e.g., Mauss 1966), the differences observed between the activities at simple and complex cold-weather base camps suggest the existence of settlement hierarchies and dictate a closer look at the functional relationship of these two types of sites to each other.

I have so far observed (1) a much greater density of status goods, (2) specialized procurement of fur bearers, (3) evidence for planned architectural constructions, and (4) the presence of larger basic socioeconomic units at complex base camps. No differences are found in subsistence-related behavior between simple and complex cold-weather base camps (Chapter 6). Complex base camps differ in their additional social and ritual behavior. In brief, I identify complex base camps as (1) nodes of long-distance exchange networks, (2) residential locales of high-status individuals, (3) residential locales of extended or multiple families, and (4) locales of elaborate architectural activities requiring the coordination of sizable labor forces. With these differences, it could be argued that the coexistence of simple and complex cold-weather base camps indicates a hierarchical relationship between these sites and, indirectly, suggests ranked sociopolitical organization in the area.

Working primarily with "small and simple" paradigms, archaeologists dealing with hunter–gatherers have implicitly assumed the absence of any hierarchization among settlements (Binford 1982b; Jochim 1976; Price 1981). In fact, however, a brief look at the ethnographic literature on logistically organized northern-latitude groups reveals significant differences in settlement types. For example, both Spencer (1959) and

Nelson (1971) describe the coexistence of small and large winter villages. The latter has greater numbers of wealthy individuals and more dance houses and hosts more large festivals such as the Messenger Feast or the Great Feast of the Dead. We can anticipate that such settlements would leave behind a richer and more diverse archaeological record than the small villages, and that these differences would reflect ritual behavior as well as economic differentiation at the larger villages.

Arguing theoretically, Wobst (1974, 1976) shows that, in egalitarian societies distributed hexagonally over the landscape, centrally positioned groups would have locational advantages in both mate- and information exchange. Flannery (1976a) and Reynolds (1976) show that in linearized settlement systems, travel distance alone would favor centrally located settlements and would result in their being larger. All these observations indicate an innate advantage to central location, one that would be expressed in material correlates and function size. On both ethnographic and theoretical evidence, then, I conclude that functionally differentiated settlements can and do exist among egalitarian groups; the mere presence of settlement differentiation is an insufficient measure of nonegalitarian sociopolitical organization in prehistoric groups.

Data from the study area indicate that complex cold-weather base camps are only known from the late period of occupation, after strong linearization of the settlement system had taken place (see Figure 6.9). Depending on different chronological assumptions, various explanations can be offered from the distribution of these sites (see Chapter 5). Lacking firm chronological controls, however, I can offer little beyond speculation about the synchronic relationship of these sites to the simple cold-weather base camps. Quite clearly, given the linearization of the settlement system, one can argue that linearization itself selected for this differentiation; in other words, that complex base camps represent just fortuitously located sites. This explanation, however, does not take into account data on social differentiation found only at complex base camps. High-status individuals residing at these camps appear to have been able to partially control labor, exchange, and ritual behavior. Since such controls and the residence of high-status individuals was localized at complex base camps, this can be used as evidence of settlement hierarchization—if one assumes a contemporaneity of occupation of simple and complex sites. It is possible, on the other hand, that complex base camps reflect very temporary and rare prehistoric events that were not permanently associated with particular types of sites; this would also produce the sort of archaeological patterning found in the study area. Quite clearly, the issue cannot be resolved until a synchronic existence of hierarchically related or nested settlements can be demonstrated.

While the existence of social hierarchization, differential distribution of resources, public works or monumental architecture, and long-distance trade suggests that we are indeed dealing with hierarchically organized groups, this evidence is suggestive rather than conclusive. Simply stated, I suggest that we are monitoring something akin to a middle ground between egalitarian and ranked sociopolitical organization in the archaeological record of the study area after 18,000 B.P. At times, this hierarchical organization may have been coupled with economic inequality as well. At present, however, given standard evolutionary models for subsistence behavior and sociopolitical organization, I cannot claim with any certainty either egalitarian or ranked organization on the Upper Paleolithic central Russian Plain. Rather, what this chapter repeatedly illustrates is a set of Upper Paleolithic economic, social, and political behaviors too complex for egalitarian groups, as we modeled them, and too simple for ranked societies. I return to these issues of theory versus archaeological record in the concluding chapter of this work.

RITUAL BEHAVIOR

Past ideologies and ritual behavior are possibly the most difficult of all to document unequivocally. The material correlates of this behavior, ones Binford (1962) terms "idiotechnic artifacts," are very elusive and have been the subject of great abuse in archaeology. All too often we have tended to categorize all unidentified objects as ritual or cult artifacts.

In this discussion I assume, after Rappaport (1971), that ideological beliefs are manifest in ritual activity. I therefore focus on material correlates of ritual activity as these appear in the archaeological record of the study area. Ethnographic literature on ritual behavior of hunter–gatherers documents a range in behavior from simple one-person curing ceremonies to more complex and more organized communal ritual feasts (e.g., Boas 1964; Nelson 1971; Spencer 1959). Archaeological data reveal a myriad of other ritual activities in the past that are poorly understood today—such as those associated with the construction and function of Eskimo Whalebone Alley in the Bering Strait reported by Arutyunov *et al.* (1982), or bison kills in the High Plains investigated by Frison (1978).

Ritual behavior functions on multiple fronts; it reinforces group solidarity, regulates man–land relationships, transmits social and ecological information, helps redistribute resources, and so forth. Rappaport (1971) notes that rituals, aside from serving integrative functions, also "invest social conventions with sanctity . . . to hide their arbitrariness in a cloak of seeming necessity" (1971:36). Root (1981) suggests that ritual acts both hide and legitimize inequality. The ability to manipulate ritual knowledge carries with it a potential to control production and social reproduction (Bender 1982). Thus, it is clear that ritual behavior functions along two trajectories: the sacred and the secular. The roles it plays in the secular realm are those we can expect to recognize in the archaeological record (but see Hodder 1982, for differing views). I focus on the effects of ritual behavior on the secular realm and consider some of the recognizable material correlates of ritual practices in the study area.

Archaeological evidence for ritual behavior is difficult to delimit. Implements associated with ritual behavior, while often fairly distinct in the ethnographic present, become muted in the archaeological record. While archaeologists have in the past claimed ritual status for a given category of items, time and additional research tend to reveal the uncertainty of such identification (e.g., the history of the *bâton des commandement* or debates over the function of cave art). Some Soviet researchers have claimed ritual status for particular artifacts found at the study sites. Bibikov (1981), for one, insists that the ivory bracelets and painted mammoth bones at Mezin are ritual musical instruments. The anecdotal foundation for such claims, and, more important, our inability to adequately evaluate such hypotheses at present, lead me to eliminate from this discussion all possible portable ritual artifacts. Instead, I focus on two features traditionally identified with the ritual and ideological spheres: burials and monumental architecture (see Binford 1971; Fritz 1978).

In the previous discussions of burials and monumental architecture, I treat them as conveyors of corporate information. Here I also consider them material expressions of invested labor. After Root (1981, 1983), I see burials as "dumps" of controlled labor. While both burials and monumental architecture certainly reflect the ability to control or marshall labor, I argue that they differ in the manifestation of such control. I suggest that, in the case of burials, labor control is visibly exercised during the interment ritual itself but is then taken out of public view. The burial of this labor investment effectively decreases the conscious realization of social asymmetry. In short, elaborate or rich burials spotlight hierarchical social relationships prior to and during the interment itself. This public manifestation is then concealed from everyday view under the ground. Such practices, when not accompanied by visible and permanent aboveground re-minders (e.g., menhirs, stelae, or earthworks), are associated with early stages of hierarchization in sociopolitical relationships. I argue that, given societal strains that accompany social asymmetry noted by Keene (1983), hierarchical social differentiation will initially be less overt than after such differentiation becomes fully entrenched in the social matrix. Such differentiation will be revealed and sanctified during occasional events or ceremonies but will not be present and apparent in everyday life. I therefore suggest that burials present ideal ceremonial events for marking this incipient social differentiation. Monumental architecture or public works, on the other hand, are per-manent visual reminders of social differentiation. They are expected to occur after social differentiation has been fully established and possibly after it is accompanied by some degree of economic differentiation as well. Following Flannery's (1976a) and Drennan's (1976) distinction between ad hoc or situational and regular or time-dependent rituals, I would argue that burials are situational rituals while monumental architectural pro-jects reflect time-dependent ones.

Burial data from the Russian Plain (see Table 7.2) suffer from small sample size and distance from the study area proper. Interments dated to the early period of occupation show a much greater labor investment than do the late burials. I interpret this as showing an association of ritual behavior and fairly incipient social differentiation. These early burials reflect the ability of some individuals to manipulate and control ritual and social knowledge. This ability was visibly demonstrated in a ritual context, but the end product—the interment—removed its manifestation from daily life. The miniscule size of the burial population, one totally inadequate to have equitably met the needs of the entire population, indicates that the interment ritual was bestowed selec-tively. This, in turn, argues for the association of status positions with the ability to control both ritual knowledge and ritual behavior.

Although early sites show no visible aboveground evidence for the cooperative labor, late sites, particularly complex base camps, do indicate such practices. Gladkih and

Kornietz (1983) argue convincingly that the highly patterned architectural details of individual dwellings and the relationship between dwellings at Mezhirich reflect aesthetic and ritual behavior. If we accept Mezhirich (and possibly Yudinovo) constructions as the results of ritual behavior, we see that ritual behavior and coordinated labor efforts at these late sites became far more permanently visible than in burials. I argue that the building of these sites represents public ritual actions that required an impressive amount of planning and coordination. They differ from earlier burials, which also required sizable labor investment, because they are aboveground and more visible, and as such they functioned as daily reminders of social asymmetry for the group occupying the sites. I further suggest that this transition in the manifestation of social asymmetry from underground and covert to aboveground and overt could only come about after status differentiation had passed the incipient stage to become firmly rooted in the social matrix. While it could be argued that the man-hours of labor invested in early burials (I estimate 2500 man-hours for one aspect at Sungir, for exmple) is greater than that needed for the later public constructions (a maximum of 1080 hours at Yudinovo; see Table 6.16), I contend that *visibility itself* is the crucial variable here.

Much of this discussion, admittedly, is highly speculative and should be taken as an indication for future direction in research. Nonetheless, given the data on hand, I would argue that groups occupying the central Russian Plain after the Valdai maximum were coordinated through corporate rituals and corporate ideologies. I further suggest that the emergence of ritual focus from under the ground was systemically related to greater social complexity. While, clearly, it is impossible to say exactly what form rituals at such sites as Mezhirich took, whether they validated status positions or marked the rites of passage of some category of individuals, they appear to have routinely involved larger numbers of people, required more coordination and planning, and marked more visibly and permanently the late Pleistocene landscape than did their earlier equivalents.

In conclusion, this discussion indicates a possible trajectory that ritual behavior followed through time in the study area. The speculated changes, while open to much debate, in general correlate with the changes noted in subsistence behavior and more notably in sociopolitical organization. While differing from each other, both early burials and late constructions indicate a marking of particular place. Bender (1982) argues for the "importance of place" in prehistory, suggesting that this permanent association of a group with a particular location may have been an important feature of complex hunter–gatherers. Such permanent marking of the landscape bespeaks certain territorial fidelity and permanence of association between group and territory. I argue here that an increase in the marking of this association can be observed through time.

SUMMARY AND CONCLUSIONS

This chapter examines some aspects of sociopolitical integration on the Upper Paleolithic central Russian Plain. The discussed components by no means constitute an all-inclusive list of important features; rather, they should be seen as an entrée into the complex and changing social matrix of Upper Paleolithic adaptations. I have shown that significant changes in man–man relationships can be monitored in the area through time.

Early Period

In Chapters 5 and 6 I demonstrate that subsistence practices in the study area involved large coresidential units, were logistically organized, and were based on storage. I argue here that the use of storage pits allowed for and favored larger coresidential units. At the same time, this economy generated specific labor requirements; sufficient numbers of people had to be available to dig the storage pits, procure storable resources, process the resources, and lay away supplies for the cold season. This intrinsic and permanent need for manpower maintained large coresidential units and also resulted in scalar stress. Given the nature of subsistence practices and storage, fissioning or dispersal was not a viable solution to this stress. I suggest that this scalar stress was aleviated by hierarchization, which, in turn, established high-status individuals who served as labor coordinators and information processors.

Hunter–gatherers occupying the study area prior to 20,000 B.P., in addition to requiring energy from the environment, also had certain information and mating requirements. These requirements were met by regional mating and information networks. During the early period of occupation, these networks were fairly closed social systems and probably signaled their corporate identity through curated objects such as stone tools, art, and engravings. It is a moot point whether this emblemic signaling arose as a byproduct of population density (suggested by Wobst 1977), or as a reaction to social or ecological stress (proposed by Hodder 1979, 1981, and Weissner 1983). What is germane to the discussion is that at least two such corporate groups may have been present in the study area between 26,000 and 20,000 B.P.

Hierarchization also would have selected for emblemic signaling, because high-status individuals were socially differentiated within a particular group and it would have been to their advantage to maintain and signal the corporate cohesion of the group. These high-status individuals generated a need for particular goods that marked their social differences. As shown in this chapter, they probably supported some specialization in the manufacturing of such status items as beads. Since the type of control over production these individuals held was at best partial, and since status goods were made of local materials, we can anticipate that there may have also existed problems in restricting access to these goods. Being made of locally available materials, the goods could have been manufactured and amassed by anyone. In addition, and perhaps more important, high-status individuals also had to deal with problems of inflation or bead saturation. I would argue that problems of this sort were resolved by burying large numbers of beads with the deceased.

It can also be anticipated that hierarchization, in addition to solving problems of scalar stress, generated new problems of social asymmetry and conflict (Keene 1983). These social conflicts, in turn, selected for ritual validation of status positions. In this context, rituals both validated status and helped cope with problems of inflation and potential usurpation of status goods (Pollock 1983). The mode, evident in the archaeological record of the Russian Plain prior to 20,000 B.P., was ritual burial. Both Root (1983) and Brose (1978) argue for precisely this kind of a solution to similar social problems—theoretically in the first instance, and for prehistoric Eastern Woodland in North America in the second. Root (1983) also suggests that caches are another solution for problems of inflation in valuables. While these have not been found in the study area, their existence can be anticipated. I would suspect, however, that if caches are found, they will also have a heavy ritual connotation to them and contain such status goods as jewelry, portable art, and fine and exotic flint pieces.

In this model I argue that positions of high status during the early period of occupation were closely allied with the control and manipulation of ritual knowledge, and that this is exhibited in the burial data.

Finally, since much of the data for sociopolitical relationships comes from east of the study area, it may well be that the model offered here is more applicable to an eastern social system that occupied areas around the Don and Sejm rivers.

In brief, the ethnographic reconstruction I offer for this early period is one that has local autonomous and hierarchically organized social groups. High-status positions in this system were occupied by ritual specialists who marked their status through an abundance of personal adornments. These individuals may have been like the "elders" or leaders of corporate groups known from the ethnographic record—people who possess a great deal of authority, can commandeer labor for ritual purposes, but who have no significant economic advantages over the remainder of the population.

LATE PERIOD

It is important to reiterate that this second period of occupation, after 18,000 B.P., followed an approximately 2000-year hiatus during which the study region may have been totally unoccupied. Given the model for sociopolitical integration prior to the Valdai maximum, I argue that hierarchization had already been established by the onset of this second period of occupation. The economy during this period was basically like that during the early period, and the use of nonportable storage was an inherent feature of these subsistence practices. The new variable, one not present during the early period, was the linearization of the settlement system. In Chapter 5 I argue that this linearization was a response to the linearization of resources during the period of climatic fluctuations between 18,000 and 12,000 B.P. A linear settlement system carries with it a number of features related purely to geometric and geographic factors. As numerous authors argue, centrally located settlements have locational advantages in linear systems. Wobst (1976) and Moore (1979) show that a linearization of the settlement system increases the cost of maintaining mating networks and information networks. Since the linearization of settlements in the study area was related to an increase in environmental variability and unpredictability, I argue that it was also accompanied by an increased need for information, a need to monitor greater linear expanses in both northern and southern extentions of the study area. For example, I argue for the north–south migration of the main food resources during the post-Valdai period. Such linear resource mobility would require tracking or monitoring over longer distances. The model offered here posits that all three of these factors, locational advantages of some groups, increased cost of maintaining social networks, and increased need for information, would possibly have jointly selected for decreasing autonomy and resulted in a decrease of local emblemic encoding of corporate information in portable objects.

Increased need for information, in this perspective, would select for a slight increase in mobility noted at the late sites and reenforce hierarchization. The presence of high-status individuals, with their requirements for restricted status goods, as well as the increased need for information, would favor the development of long-distance exchange networks. These ties would provide the needed information, cement alliances, and supply exotics for status demarcation.

Hierarchization, in and of itself, as Bender (1981, 1982) argues, would favor an increase in the size of the coresiding unit, and allow for the manipulation and control of labor. Control of labor (even a partial one) together with larger group sizes, in turn, would further select for an expansion of specialization of production; some of this specialized production would have been directed toward fueling the long-distance exchange networks. Larger group size, noted at the late sites, together with social conflict stemming from hierarchization, would create additional scalar stress. I argue here that both this added scalar stress and labor demands exerted by hierarchization would, in turn, favor the expansion of basal unit sizes and result in a change from the nuclear to the extended or multiple families (cf. Ember and Ember 1971).

Whether this increase was universal or occurred primarily among the families of high-status individuals remains to be investigated. Bender (1981, 1982) hypothesizes that high-status individuals would exert greater demands on household production and thus stimulate growth in the sizes of all households. Sahlins (1972), on the other hand, notes that families of "big men" and petty chiefs are more productive and larger. Data from the study area are ambiguous on this question; they suggest, however, an association of larger households and status. Thus, for example, at simple cold-weather base camps such as Dobranichevka we have only small households, while at Mezin or Mezhirich, the locus of high-status individuals, we have both small and large households. The resolution of this issue, like that of many others raised in this chapter, must await further work on temporal and spatial relationships between simple and complex cold-weather base camps.

Since status differentiation during the late period appears to have been associated with an unequal distribution of resources as well, we can anticipate that this social and economic asymmetry would have generated added social conflict. It would have selected for some ritual or cultural means of validating the favorable positions enjoyed by some individuals. I argue here that the means employed were ritual. In this model, I see high-status individuals overtly as ritual specialists who controlled and manipulated the long-distance exchange networks.

Whereas status during the early period was marked by personal adornments made of local materials, it was the exotics that most clearly signaled status after 18,000 B.P. I argue here that the partial control over labor exercised by high-status individuals during the early period selected for visual display of this control—thus an abundance of beads, lances, bone jewelry, and ornaments of ivory at early burials. During the late period, on the other hand, both a greater control over labor (seen in the increase of specialization of production) and an increased need for information (and thus for an expansion of exchange networks) selected for the use of exotics as status markers.

In the model for sociopolitical integration after 18,000 B.P., I also suggest that the need to control labor, maintain supraregional long-distance ties, and validate status differences jointly selected for the development of public works and resulted in Pleistocene monumental architecture. I argue here that ritual validation of status differences occurred in the context of communal architectural undertakings. The resulting constructions, in turn, carried encoded emblemic messages of corporate identity and at the same time bore highly visible and permanent witness to the control over labor and information enjoyed by high-status individuals. The occurrence of such architecture in both the northern and southern parts of the study area is interesting and suggests a cultural unity for the central Russian Plain. The exact nature of this unity is unclear at present, and although I suggest that both north and south were parts of one corporate social matrix after 18,000 B.P., this suggestion is tentative and requires a great deal of future work for validation.

The locational advantages enjoyed by some settlements are expressed in the archaeological record by the concentration of exchange goods and monumental architecture at these locations. Since both exchange and construction were innately connected to ritual, evidence for all three is found localized at the same sites—complex cold-weather base camps.

It is both tempting and at the same time impossible to offer an ethnographic analogue for the late period of occupation of the central Russian Plain. The model I present is reminiscent of social relationships and settlement patterns of northern-latitude hunter–gatherers exploiting sea mammals or fish. This similarity is not surprising—I did turn to these more complex groups in an attempt to understand the data from the study area. These data indicated that the subsistence practices and settlement systems were far from the "simple, small, and mobile" paradigms currently employed for late Pleistocene hunter–gatherers. While these ethnographic analogues serve a purpose, they come basically from groups with subsistence based on marine resources. Data from the study area, on the other hand, clearly indicate that whatever social complexity was achieved, it was embedded in subsistence strategies based on the exploitation of terrestrial resources. Many authors have stated that a coupling of social complexity with a reliance on terrestrial resources should be expected for prehistoric hunter–gatherers who occupy nonmarginal environments (e.g., Jochim 1981; Mellars 1985; Price 1981). Others, like Schalk (1977) and Sheehan (1985), argue cogently that the high degree of reliability assigned to marine resources may be illusory. Schalk's (1977) discussion of the exploitation of anadromous fish along the Northwest Coast indicates that the accepted connection between rich and reliable fish resources and social complexity among hunter–gatherers is unwarranted, and that the supposed causal relationship between the two has to be reexamined. The stability and reliability of terrestrial resources was certainly augmented by storage practices in the study area. Binford (1982b), Testart (1982), and Jochim (1981), among others, argue that storage is a technical means for regulating resource reliability and predictability. Thus, both the location of the study area and the technology of Upper Paleolithic groups added to the operational richness of the Upper Paleolithic resource base. Given this techno-environmental context, the noted complexity of sociopolitical organization should come as no surprise.

The social, political, and ritual complexity seen at the late sites, especially at complex base camps, is reminiscent of Eskimo winter villages where various large festivals were held (Boas 1964; Mauss 1966; Nelson 1971; Spencer 1959). I suspect that ethnoarchaeological research among such groups as the Bering Strait Eskimo would present an archaeological picture not too dissimilar to the one observed in the study area during the late period of occupation. At the same time, however, much more work must be done on the relationship of complex to simple cold-weather base camps before we can offer a clear ethnographic model for the Upper Paleolithic. At present, we have no archaeological analogues for monumental architecture among late Pleistocene hunter–gatherers. While such behavior has been associated with sedentary ranked or tribal societies (Peebles and Kus 1977; Renfrew 1982), I would argue that sedentism is not a necessary and sufficient cause for such behavior. Data from the study area indicate that the central Russian Plain lacked full-time sedentism, yet it does have such examples of public works. Examples of such behavior among hunter–gatherers of the historic past are rare, but Whalebone Alley off the Bering Strait and the Hopewell sites in the New World offer us just such examples.

In brief, I suggest that the Upper Paleolithic central Russian Plain after 18,000 B.P. was peopled by hierarchically organized groups who had some degree of status hierarchization associated with ritual roles. The groups were not fully sedentary, exhibiting both residential and logistical seasonal mobility. Even though they meet a number of the criteria for ranked societies suggested by Peebles and Kus (1977) and Renfrew (1982), these groups should not be seen as such; rather, they reflect a level of sociopolitical integration between egalitarian and ranked society. I address this issue—data versus model—in greater detail in the concluding chapter of this work.

Finally, the most important conclusion I reach from this analysis is that the trajectory of culture change as seen through social complexity varies with the time scales used for monitoring it. The two patterns of complexity I describe in this chapter, one for the early and the other for the late period, represent ecological and social solutions to problems of adaptation. In both periods we did not see a further evolution in complexity, but rather a collapse. The early period was followed by an approximately 2000-year period when the area was either totally or predominantly uninhabited. The second period of occupation also did not lead to a steady increase in complexity—it just led to the early Mesolithic, a time of much greater residential and logistical mobility as well as smaller group size (see Dolukhanov 1982 on the Mesolithic on the Russian Plain).

Given these patterns, I would argue, after Bender (1982) and Friedman (1979), that the observed changes in sociopolitical integration should be seen as fluctuational. Fluctuations have been documented for sedentary groups and we accept such oscillations as the norm in history as well as in later prehistory (e.g., the numerous rises and falls of the early state in the Near East). I close this discussion by suggesting that fluctuations in sociopolitical complexity were also an intrinsic feature of hunter–gatherer adaptations in the past—a claim that I expand in the following chapter.

8

Conclusions and Implications

INTRODUCTION

Two major objectives guide this work. Original data on the sites have been unavailable to an English-speaking audience, and when published in Russian, either in the Soviet Union or in the West, have been hard to obtain. My first objective, then, is to present as complete a compilation of original information as possible. My second major objective is to examine and model human adaptation strategies in the study area that operated from 26,000 to 12,000 B.P. These two objectives, one descriptive and synthetic and the other analytic, shape the form of this work.

The preceding chapters amply demonstrate that the central Russian Plain during late Pleistocene was an important part of the European Upper Paleolithic world—one inhabited by groups of hunter–gatherers with a complex behavioral repertoire. In this concluding chapter, I first summarize my environmental, subsistence, and settlement system models, and the data on which they are based, and then begin to evaluate these models with important qualifications and suggestions for further research. I then examine the Central Russian Plain in the wider context of Upper Paleolithic Europe. Last, I comment on traditional hunter–gatherer theory, and particularly on the significance of the disparity between this theory and data from the central Russian Plain.

DATA AND MODELS

THE ENVIRONMENTAL GIVEN

The data available on late Pleistocene environments show that traditional models and reconstructions are on a scale too gross to address questions of human adaptations. The archaeological record spans four major climatic periods: the Bryansk Interstadial, the cooling period between 24,000 and 20,000 B.P., the Valdai maximum itself (20,000–18,000 B.P.), and the period after the glacial maximum from 18,000 to approximately 12,000 B.P.

While broad climatic and environmental trends indicate a cold periglacial landscape during the entire Upper Paleolithic period of occupation, it is the climatic and environmental differences between the habitats before and after the Valdai maximum which were crucial to human adaptation. During the early period of occupation, the climatic trend was one of gradual long-term deterioration, going from warmer and moister interstadial conditions at 26,000 B.P. to colder and more arid conditions at the onset of the glacial maximum. This gradual change in climate is in sharp and significant contrast to the rapid climatic oscillations that occurred in the area between 18,000 and 12,000 B.P. This late period saw fluctuations from warmer and wetter to colder and drier conditions approximately every 1000 years. Each oscillation was "saw-toothed," featuring rapid climatic deterioration and a slow period of recovery, and confronting living organisms with climatic stress for periods of 100 to 200 years.

While throughout the Upper Paleolithic the central Russian Plain supported abundant food resources, these resources were very patchily distributed across the study area and found in large concentrations only during some times of the year—specifically in or near the floodplains during cold-weather months. The majority of resources used both for food and clothing probably undertook seasonal north–south migrations along the river valleys. This variability in distribution and abundance of resources was especially significant during the late period of occupation, which saw linearization along river valleys and greater seasonal and long-term fluctuations and greater resource stress.

Late Pleistocene populations on the central Russian Plain have in general been characterized as mammoth-hunters. The demographics and paleoecology of this taxon indicate that the mammoth would have been under extreme demographic stress during the period of climatic oscillations—one that would have brought population numbers down to catastrophically low numbers without any human interference. Modeled population estimates, information on mammoth skeletal elements found at the study sites, and independent data on the age and sex composition of mammoth from the Berelekh mammoth-bone cemetery demonstrate that our assumptions that mammoth were the major food resource during the late Pleistocene and that all mammoth were procured by active hunting are unwarranted.

While my reconstruction of late Pleistocene landscapes and models of resource behavior allow for a subsequent examination of human adaptation strategies, they also highlight a number of important and unresolved problems. Two major areas in need of attention are (1) a refinement of chronological controls, and (2) taphonomic research on faunal assemblages to evaluate the role that active hunting played in the procurement of some resources.

HUMAN BEHAVIOR

The Upper Paleolithic in the study area consisted of three distinct episodes: (1) an early period of occupation (26,000–20,000 B.P.), (2) an occupational hiatus during the Valdai maximum (20,000–18,000 B.P.), and (3) a late period of human occupation (18,000–12,000 B.P.).

Subsistence Practices

Faunal remains from the 29 sites considered in this work show that the central Russian Plain was occupied during the entire Upper Paleolithic by logistically organized hunter–gatherers who exploited seasonally abundant and aggregated resources and relied heavily on nonportable storage strategies. Their subsistence practices centered on the exploitation of large gregarious herbivores, including some mammoth, steppe bison, horse, and reindeer. As noted, serious problems must be resolved before we can characterize the subsistence base with certainty; foremost among these is the role of mammoth as a food resource. Paleontological and archaeological faunal evidence show that both mammoth and reindeer were not only hunted but also "collected"; that is, skeletal elements of these taxa were gathered. Such gathering could have occurred without active hunting being involved at all.

While we can monitor a general continuation of similar subsistence strategies during the entire period of occupation, a comparison of data between the early and late periods shows an intensification in procurement of both food and nonfood resources: Greater numbers of some gregarious herbivores, a greater number of taxa, including solitary and small species, and more evidence of storage appears at the late sites. This intensification and diversification was most probably a response to the linearization of resources after 18,000 B.P. A comparison of exploitation of fur bearers between the early and late periods indicates that specialized procurement of these taxa arose during the late period and that it was associated with the rise of exchange networks in the area.

Settlement Systems

Geographic and faunal data as well as information on the nature and contents of features at the sites indicate that all sites were seasonal occupations, not year-round residential locales. Twenty-eight variables, including geographic information as well as data on site inventories and features, were used to classify the sites into the following site types:

Cold-Weather Occupations	*Warm-Weather Occupations*
complex base camps	simple base camps
simple base camps	lithic workshops
hunting base camps	hunting stations
	bone collecting stations

A consideration of groups size and length of stay at the sites, while admittedly beset by serious epistemological and methodological problems, in general indicate that (1) sizable groups, probably numbering well over 30 individuals, coresided at both warm- and cold-weather base camps during the entire period of occupation, (2) smaller numbers of people may have occupied earlier sites but remained there longer, and (3) larger numbers of people who stayed for shorter periods inhabited base camps during the late period of occupation. The settlement patterns during both periods of occupation were ones with long occupational episodes during cold months at base camps located on or near floodplains. During this season, coresidential units lived off stored resources. With the onset of warm weather, these units moved, as a group, short distances but off the floodplains, to warm-weather base camps. Thus, the settlement system of Upper Paleolithic hunter–gatherers on the central Russian Plain does not feature seasonal aggregation–dispersal pulsations.

Chronological and regional comparisons indicate that (1) the northern section of the study area was more extensively (possibly exclusively) occupied during the early period, but that these settlements were not linearized along the river valleys; (2) both the north and south were occupied during the late period and settlements were linearized along the floodplains; (3) while some north–south differences were noted, these indicate not different settlement patterns but rather variations on a theme; and (4) the major chronological difference in settlement type and system is the absence of complex cold-weather base camps during the early period of occupation.

Finally, a comparison of complex cold-weather base camps to their simple cold- and warm-weather analogues indicates that the differences between these settlements were not related to utilitarian behavior but rather lay in the sphere of social and political relationships and ideological behavior.

Sociopolitical Integration and Ideology

A model for the sociopolitical integration of the early period suggests some activity differentiation and some form of nascent social hierarchization. Prior to 20,000 B.P., both leadership and activity differentiation were heavily associated with ritual behavior. High-status ritual specialists could probably commandeer labor for ritual activity but did not have major economic advantage. Stylistic signaling in different media suggest that the area was occupied by more than one social group during the early period. This early period was followed by a 2000-year hiatus, when the central Russian Plain, like river valleys to the east (Don) and west (Dnestr), was either totally devoid of human inhabitants or occupied very sporadically and sparsely.

After 18,000 B.P., we can monitor the emergence of a different, and perhaps more complex, pattern of sociopolitical integration. Individuals occupying high-status positions had economic as well as social advantage over the rest of the population. While nuclear families formed the basic socioeconomic unit prior to 20,000 B.P., AFTER 18,000 B.P. extended or multiple families increasingly became the basal organizational unit. As well as unequal distribution of resources and increased activity differentiation, the late period also saw the development of long-distance exchange networks and the construction of public work and monumental architecture. The central Russian Plain during this period was settled by at least two social groups who were probably parts of a larger social matrix which not only spanned the entire study area but also had ties to populations in adjacent river valleys.

The reconstruction of sociopolitical relationships offered in this work are meant to be suggestive, not definitive; admittedly, the data used to model these relationships are sparce. Problematic as my hypotheses may be, they do carry a number of testable implications. For example, future work on the origin of exotic materials found at the sites can be used to evaluate my hypothesized exchange networks. The existence of an unequal distribution of resources can be evaluated with data on the distribution of exotics and other items among different dwellings at sites. Further analysis of intersite distribution of blades and beads can be used to evaluate the activity segregation suggested in this work. Rigorous, extensive, and quantified analyses of portable art, engravings, and decorative objects, something not done heretofore, will go a long way toward evaluating my conclusions about the number of social groups present in the area.

PROBLEMS OF TEMPORAL AND SPATIAL SCALE

In the course of this work a set of temporal and spatial problems emerged that can best be characterized as scalar. These problems are relevant not only to this study, but to all our attempts to reconstruct past human behavior. Marquardt notes that "observations of sociocultural lifeworlds come to us not as "totalities," but as apparently patterned facts at *particular spatial and temporal scales*" (1985:69). For example, one spatial scale may be appropriate for questions about regional interactions and quite another for questions about status differentiation. Problems of appropriate scales come to the fore in any archaeological reconstruction. It is germane to examine some of these problems with reference to the area and period under study.

Temporal Scales

All hypotheses of man–land relationships in prehistory are clearly heavily dependent on the temporal scale selected for analysis. Thus Mellars (1985), Dolukhanov (1982), and Velichko, Zavernyaev *et al.* (1981), who take the entire Upper Paleolithic period of occupation (in the Périgord in the first case and on the Russian Plain in the second and third) as a single climatic and paleoenvironmental unit, argue for stable and highly productive habitats which allowed for stable and complex adaptations in both regions of the Old World. David (1973), on the other hand, taking smaller time units as his base, argues for demographic and cultural fluctuations in southwestern France during the Upper Paleolithic. In this work, I also break down the long span of late Pleistocene occupation into a series of fluctuations in climate and habitat.

We are just beginning to establish some chronological controls in the study area. The ^{14}C dates available for the sites are quite clearly inadequate for many questions explored in this work. By using the region rather than the site as my analytic universe, I assume a rough contemporaneity for at least some of the sites, as well as for all portions of a given site. This sort of contemporaneity is, however, inappropriately gross. For example, I implicitly assumed that some of the different types of sites (e.g., simple and complex cold-weather base camps) were contemporaneous and parts of the same settlement system. Binford (1983), using Nunamiut data, argues that logistically organized hunter–gatherers are quite mobile when their location is viewed in longer time scales. He reports that the length of stay of a Nunamiut group in any one residential core area lasts approximately 10 years, after which they move to a completely new territory. He indicates that at any one time such a group has available to them approximately four times the territory that it is currently using and that, therefore, there is a cyclical pattern of land use. He offers a figure of 22,000 km^2 as the area that a group of 36 Nunamiut would utilize during their lifetime (Binford 1983:205). Binford's observations raise the possibility that the settlement patterns I project for the Upper Paleolithic central Russian Plain could have been generated by behavior different from that which I assume. Lacking fine chronological controls, I cannot argue with certainty that any two sites in the study area were contemporary rather than sequential occupations. The kind of fineness of chronological controls called for by Binford's (1983) work, however, will probably never be available to researchers working with Pleistocene groups. But while we may never know with certainty that any two sites were occupied at the same time, a refinement of chronological controls will get us a bit closer to reconstructing past behavior—although these reconstructions will always remain what Leach (1973:768) has called "well-informed guesses."

SPATIAL SCALES

In previous discussions, I note that various spatial scales are necessary when one investigates past human adaptations. In this work, I select the site itself as the unit of analysis and a particular drainage system as the analytic universe. In selecting the site rather than a structural component of the site as a basal unit, I immediately eliminate information pertinent to some questions raised in this work. Such information as the contemporaneity of occupation of the different parts of a site, as well as data on possible differential distribution of assemblages and features at the sites, are effectively excluded. Yet a discussion of sociopolitical relationships clearly required these kinds of information. My decision to use the site itself as a basal unit is predicated on the nature of information available. For the vast majority of past excavations in the study area, information on intrasite variability is irretrievable. Thus, some of the hypotheses on sociopolitical integration offered in this work can be tested only with data on storage pit contents and on the distribution of features and artifacts obtained from ongoing excavations at such sites as Mezhirich and Yudinovo.

In classifying the sites in the study region, I encountered an anomaly: Khotylevo II. This site does not fit the Dnepr–Desna pattern and is deemed more similar to sites found along the Don which Soviet researchers assign to the Kostenki–Borschevo culture (Figure 8.1). Sites along the Don, however, also contain at least two anomalies: Anasovka II (Kostenki XI) and Kostenki II (for their description see Klein 1969; Praslov and Rogachev 1982). Both have round or oval mammoth-bone dwellings and storage pits characteristic of the sites in the Dnepr–Desna basin (Figure 8.2). While neither Soviet nor Western scholars have treated these two Kostenki–Borschevo sites as regional anomalies, I suspect that the presence of Khotylevo II on the Desna and of Anasovka II and Kostenki II on the Don indicate that neither river valley was a closed, self-contained social universe during the Upper Paleolithic. The location of these sties outside of their own "cultural" regions argues for the use of an additional spatial scale to the one employed in this work. Specifically, the location of these anamolous sites argues for the need to look at the entire Russian Plain when examining sociopolitical relationships.

It is even more important to use this larger spatial scale when considering change in sociopolitical integration through time. I argue that at least two settlement patterns were present in the study area during the early period of occupation. I go on to suggest that one of these was characteristic of a more eastern region: the Don basin. I hypothesize that Khotylevo II was a part of this more eastern system, and that groups inhabiting the Don region may have had an aggregation–dispersal pattern of social integration. This hypothesis, in turn, suggests that groups along the Don had greater residential mobility and "mapped on" to resources more than the groups in the study area (see Binford 1982b for a distinction between "mapping-on" and logistical organization). While it is tempting to suggest that one adaptation pattern existed along the Don and another, with greater year-round residential and social stability, along the Dnepr and Desna, the presence of the anomalous sites in each region indicates that adaptations in both regions may have been more complex and not independent of each other. To understand the relationship of Don and Dnepr–Desna groups to each other—whether genealogical or contemporary, we must firmly control chronology and take the whole Russian Plain as our analytic universe.

Different chronological assumptions can clearly give us different scenarios. For example, if the anomalous sites are located where they are due to time alone, then, given the greater number of early sites along the Don, we should suspect that human settlements on the central Russian Plain at the onset of the Upper Paleolithic some 35,000 years ago saw denser populations along the Don. Khotylevo II, in this case, would be a

Figure 8.1   Excavations at Kostenki I-2, 1979.

Figure 8.2   Excavations at Anosovka II (Kostenki XI), 1979.

most western outpost of this population (see Praslov and Rogachev, 1982, for the chronology of the Don sites). Khotylevo II dates well after the earliest Upper Paleolithic sites on the Don; is it, therefore, evidence of expanding or moving Kostenki–Borschevo groups? If so, did these groups change from "mapping-on" strategies to logistical organization in their subsistence pursuits after reaching the Desna? Long-distance migrations have been proposed for Upper Paleolithic groups on the Russian Plain by Grigor'ev (1968). He argues that groups coming from Austria and Czechoslovakia (from the Willendorf and Pavlov cultures) went eastward across the Russian Plain, settled along the Don, and developed the Kostenki–Avdeevo culture. His scenario can be expanded to suggest that descendents of these groups, after settling along the Don, expanded westward and settled along the Desna and subsequently along the Dnepr as well. This prehistoric scenario, while accounting for Khotylvo II and the noted Kostenki–Borschevo influences in Berdyzh lithics, leaves the origin or affiliation of Kostenki II and Anosovka II unexplained. Both appear to date to the late period of occupation, after 18,000 B.P. (see Boriskovski and Dmitrieva 1982a; Rogachev and Sinitsyn 1982b). Are they a result of yet another and later eastern move of Dnepr–Desna groups?

On the other hand, if chronology cannot be evoked, and I suspect that it will prove an unsatisfactory causal variable, how do we explain the anomalous sites in both regions without considering them as parts of the same large social and analytic universe?

Clearly none of these issues or speculations can either be considered or resolved without taking the entire Russian Plain as a unit of analysis. They also cannot be considered given the chronological controls available today. I raise these issues here both to qualify models presented in this work and to indicate some directions for research.

THE CENTRAL RUSSIAN PLAIN MICROCOSM AND THE EUROPEAN UPPER PALEOLITHIC WORLD

This work offers a reconstruction of both culture history and human adaptation strategies over a particular period in a particular part of the European Upper Paleolithic world. How does this dynamic microcosm fit into what we know about the whole of Upper Paleolithic Europe? Numerous authors claim unique status for groups who inhabited the Périgord region of southwestern France during the Upper Paleolithic and consider that region the center of Upper Paleolithic development (e.g., Jochim 1983b; Mellars 1985). In general, these claims rest on observations and assumptions that include (1) the density of sites found, (2) the high archaeological visibility of these sites, and especially (3) the high volume of artifacts and features recovered (e.g., cave art, portable art, beautiful Solutrean blades). Important historical factors in large part responsible for a Périgord bias are that (1) Paleolithic research began very early in France, (2) excavations were conducted most intensively and systematically in the Périgord, and (3) systematized classification schemes for Upper Paleolithic lithic inventories were proposed by French researchers (see Wobst and Keene 1983 for a somewhat ascerbic but important discussion of these points). Yet in examining what we know of human adaptations in the Périgord, one is struck by the dearth of human focus. As White (1980) and Audouze and Leroi-Gourhan (1981) point out, much of French research employed and still employs the geochronological type-fossil approach and focuses on questions of technology in tool manufacturing, stylistic variability in lithics, and the significance of observed lithic variability. In this approach, where lithics in a particular stratigraphic context are the analytic universe, other sites, regardless of their locations, are of interest only if their lithics are similar. If they are, then the two sites are considered members of the same archaeological culture (e.g., Smith 1966).

Another direction of research in Paleolithic archaeology, one I see as an offshoot of the lithic focus, is a concern with features. Thus numerous studies exist, some quite detailed and exhaustive, of the nature and change of such features as dwellings or Upper Paleolithic art (e.g., Leroi-Gourhan 1965b; Sklenar 1975, 1976). These studies, like their lithic counterparts, focus on object behavior rather than human behavior.

Human behavior began to be of interest to archaeologists working in France in the late 1960s. This resulted in a number of valuable monographs, such as those by Leroi-Gourhan and Brezillon (1972) and Movius (1977). These, however, deal with human behavior at a particular site rather than within a particular region. By accounting for what a particular small group of hunter–gatherers did in a cave or rockshelter for two or three months some 15,000 years ago, they explain only moments in prehistory. When researchers expanded their focus beyond a specific site, a compilation of site descriptions resulted in which the only connection between the sites considered was their proximity to each other in the published volume (e.g., Bhattacharya 1977). At the same time that these object- and site-specific foci were the norm of the day, other discussions tended to leap across questions of human behavior to grandiose scales of analysis that used huge time spans and broad, in some cases continent-wide, expanses of space as arenas of social interaction (e.g., Gamble 1982, 1983).

In this discussion I am focusing primarily on the state of Upper Paleolithic research in France, because France has been the "law-giver" and role model for archaeological research in the rest of Europe. Our understanding of Upper Paleolithic human adaptations in the rest of Europe, with a few site-specific exceptions, is not much better (see Rust 1937, 1958, on Magdalenian occupations of Germany). As in France, research elsewhere has focused on technological and stylistic classificatory schemes of lithics as the criteria of archaeological cultures—that is, on analytic universes strangely devoid of human actors. As a result of such research focus in the past, we have today, on the one hand, details of objects through time and space and, on the other, little if any understanding of how the creators and users of these objects lived. In brief, there is a huge gap in our knowledge about human adaptations during the Upper Paleolithic in Europe—in France and elsewhere.

The filling of this crucial gap has become the primary aim of researchers working in Europe. Their work is bringing forth models in which late Pleistocene man and not flint is the focus. For example, Clark and Straus (1983) examine man–land relationships in Cantabria and White (1980) considers ecological variables and the perception and use of these variables by Upper Paleolithic groups in the Périgord region. Larick (1983) has used information on lithic resources to examine the issue of residential mobility in Solutrean adaptations in Southwestern France, and Weniger (1982) examined settlement systems in Germany during the Magdalenian period. Interest in paleoenvironmental reconstruction is strongly felt in Europe today. But, as White notes "Environment and culture in French archaeology have most often been studied and presented as separate entities with little concern for the relationship between the two" (1980:30). This observation can be extended to the treatment of man–land relationships in the rest of Europe as well. Researchers are now increasingly focusing on this relationship, but perhaps to the exclusion of the second, equally important component of human adaptation: the social matrix, or man–man relationships.

Pertinent data on sociopolitical relationships is clearly available, and some, like Conkey (1980), have begun examining Upper Paleolithic art as an entry point into this social component of human adaptation. Others, like Bahn (1977, 1982) and Taborin (1972), have once again focused on exotics at the sites, which with systematized consideration should disclose factors responsible for the long distances that some of these artifacts apparently moved. Social and ideological concerns have surfaced in the work of Freeman and Gonzalez-Echegaray (1981), whose excavations at El Juyo may have uncovered an Upper Paleolithic ritual site. The relatively rich burial data from Europe has consistently been the focus of archaeological interest: Unfortunately, this interest has centered only on the variability in burial behavior and not on the functional relationship of particular behavioral units with specific groups (see Harrold 1980, with references).

While the various analytic universes in each of these research directions is promising, we still have very little middle-range research about subsistence and settlement patterns. Many of my European colleagues, no doubt, would counter that the data on hand do not permit anything beyond a descriptive treatment of sites and inventories, and that such "anthropologizing" of archaeological concerns is a purely New World and "New Archaeology" fashion. I, in turn, would argue that even though data are far from satisfactory in any part of the Old World, they are sufficient for initial model building, and, more important, we will only obtain better data if we ask new questions and become aware of the sort of data needed to answer them. I would also argue that even if one rejects "anthropologizing" of archaeological research, one still must accept the need for making man and his specific adaptation the center of our analysis if we expect to produce any semblance of culture history that is broader than the history of objects.

Many important questions remain about particular culture histories by region, as well as about processes of change during the Upper Paleolithic in Europe. These questions, however, cannot be meaningfully raised until we have some comprehension of how different groups made a living in different parts of Europe during the different periods of the late Pleistocene.

In this work, using 180,000 km² of European space, I argue that we can monitor changes in social organization—changes that should be interpreted as fluctuational, not directional. Such an interpretation can be viewed from a wider, European perspective to see if such fluctuations were local phenomena or if they reflect universal patterns. If we expand our Upper Paleolithic analytic universe to include data from Central Europe, we can also see evidence for differences in sociopolitical complexity west of the Dnestr. The archaeological record of Upper Paleolithic Czechoslovakia includes complex sites with elaborate features and inventories (e.g., Barca, Dolni Vestonice, Pavlov, Tibava). These sties, dating to about 25,000 B.P., in some aspects (inventories, and some features) resemble sites along the Don (see Grigor'ev 1970, 1979; Klima 1976; Sklenar 1977). Other features, as well perhaps as the subsistence practices employed, resemble more those of the central Russian Plain after 18,000 B.P. After the glacial maximum, however, Czechoslovakia seems to have been occupied by less complex hunter–gatherers, ones who left behind far more ephemeral marks on the landscape than their Pavlov predecessors (see Sklenar 1977). Thus, by taking Central and Eastern Europe as a whole, we can detect what appear to be two distinct periods of complex hunter–gatherer adaptation—one at about 25,000 B.P. and the other at about 15,000 B.P.

If we expand our analytic universe to include all of Europe and use the abundance of art as a rough gauge of more complex social behavior, we again see distinct periods of such complexity. In France, as Leroi-Gourhan (1965b) and Jochim (1983b) point out, the abundance of portable art peaks at two periods: the Aurignacian–Perigordian (30,000–22,000 B.P.) and after 18,000 B.P. during the Magdalenian. Bosinksi (1976) notes three periods with abundant art in Germany: one perhaps earlier than 30,000 B.P., the second before 20,000 B.P. (at about 24,000 B.P.?), and the last at about 13,000 B.P. If we assume that intensification in production and use of art broadly reflect intensification in some aspect of social behavior, these peaks suggests fluctuations in social behavior, not unidirectional progress.

Researchers, selecting different variables as the determinant ones, interpret these patterns differently. Jochim (1983b) and Grigor'ev (1968, 1970) argue that demographic shifts and population movements are partially responsible for the uneven abundance of art during the different segments of the Upper Paleolithic. Gamble (1982), on the other hand, uses the spatial distribution of abundant portable art to argue for chronological shifts in corporate awareness among late Pleistocene populations. Thus, both in situ developments and migration have been proposed as likely causes. Clearly, given our present minimal understanding of stylistic signaling, we cannot demonstrate responsibility of any variable for the distribution of art across Upper Paleolithic time and space. It is probable that different processes produced similar patterns of distribution; that is, once again, we may have the phenomenon of equifinality operating on the archaeological record.

At the same time, if these two or three peaks in the abundance of art do signal peaks in some form of social behavior, we must ask why these peak periods occurred. While intuitively I favor local developments as the most likely progenitors of change, we should not dismiss hypotheses of population shifts. Given ethnographic and ethnoarchaeological data on both short- and long-distance movement of hunter–gatherers, we cannot dismiss population movement as a possibly important variable during the 25,000 years of Upper Paleolithic occupation in Europe. In light of the stormy history that population migration has had as an explanation for change in the archaeological record, it is not surprising that today we favor in situ developments over migration. This bias, however, should not be allowed to dominate our paradigms. Population movements, as the ethnographic record implies, undoubtedly did occur in the past.

The archaeological record calls for a study of long-distance population and resource movements. Adaptation strategies in Upper Paleolithic Central and Eastern Europe in comparison to the distribution of large gregarious, herbivores, for example, is interesting. In Czechoslovakia we see subsistence based on the exploitation of these taxa coupled with cultural complexity at about 25,000 B.P. After 18,000 B.P., groups in Czechoslovakia switched to primary dependence on reindeer and left behind evidence for simpler cultural patterns (see Sklenar 1977). On the Russian Plain, particularly along the Dnepr and Desna valleys, we see subsistence based on large gregarious herbivores together with analogous complex cultural patterns after 18,000 B.P. In light of these co-occurences, I wonder how the movement of complexity from west to east through time is related to the extinction front or movement of large gregarious herbivores. Vereschagin (1979) calls the grouping of late Pleistocene, large gregarious herbivores that includes mammoth, rhinoceros, bison, and horse the "mammoth faunal complex." Martin (1982) offers a west to east trajectory for the extinction of this faunal complex. On the surface, the two trajectories—one for the location of the mammoth faunal complex and the other for evidence of complexity in hunter–gatherer adaptations—seem to overlap rather nicely in time. Is their co-occurence purely fortuitous? How are the two related?

The record from the Kostenki–Borschevo sites is admittedly less clear. There, we probably see a steady occupation from perhaps as early as 38,000 B.P. to the onset of the

Holocene, albeit with a hiatus between 20,000 and 18,000 B.P. (see Praslov and Roga-chev 1982). Judging by burial data, we should suspect that some sort of social complex-ity existed along the Don before 20,000 B.P. After 18,000 B.P., such sites as Anosovka II and Kostenki II, with mammoth-bone dwellings and storage pits, indicate possible complexity in adaptation as well. What we do not know is how these sites are related to other very different-looking sites along the Don, as well as to their look-alikes along the Dnepr and Desna. It is interesting to note that Don sites dating after the Valdai max-imum have much greater numbers of mammoth than those that were probably oc-cupied before the maximum: Borschevo II (Boriskovskii and Dmitrieva 1982a), Anosovka II (Rogachev and Popov 1982), and Kostenki II (Boriskovskii and Dmitrieva 1982) contain over 20, 39, and over 28 mammoth, respectively (for MNI estimates per taxon at the Kostenki–Borschevo sites see Vereschagin and Kuzmina, 1977); sites probably occupied before the Valdai maximum, on the other hand, have at most 7 mammoth. At present we do not know the role mammoth played in subsistence prac-tices at the Don sites, or if the increased utilization of mammoth was primarily spurred by social requirements (e.g., increased use of mammoth bone for construction). Given this record, however, I would argue that their greater use during the late period of occupation, whether a result of hunting or of gathering, probably indicates that more mammoth were available (whether in live or skeletal form) along the Don after the Valdai maximum. If this is so, we may have yet a third example of co-occurence of the mammoth faunal complex with a particular type of complex hunter–gatherer adaptation.

In summary, this discussion shows much similarity between Upper Paleolithic data from the study area and information from other parts of Europe. I have indicated that information on the abundance of artifacts, art, and exotics, on rich and elaborate burials, and so forth, can stimulate questions about social relationships. Likewise, different patterning of these data during different periods of the Upper Paleolithic should generate questions about culture change. I have also argued, however, that before we can begin asking social questions, we must work with smaller scales of time and space and understand human adaptations at a given moment in a given area of Upper Paleolithic Europe. As McGuire (1983) notes, before explaining change, we must have a functional or systemic model of the phenomenon that does or does not change. After more than 150 years of research, we still have very few such models for Europe.

THE DATA AND OUR THEORETICAL CONSTRUCTS

In closing, I consider how various issues discussed throughout this work relate to broad theoretical concerns in anthropology and anthropological archaeology. The rela-tionships between archaeological research and theoretical issues in any work, including this one, are multiple and complex. Taking this work as an example, it is clear that the issues raised are all derived from a specific body of theory. The relationship between theory and particular research is not unidirectional, however. Various relationships between different systemic variables all carry implications for our theoretical constructs about hunter–gatherer adaptation. I have directly and indirectly referred to a number of theoretical issues. Three that stand out are (1) uniformitarian assumptions, (2) causal primacy or problems of the "prime mover," and (3) our theoretical constructs about hunter–gatherers and about culture change. Each of these has a significant and problematic bearing on this work and on all our attempts to reconstruct past lifeways.

UNIFORMITARIAN ASSUMPTIONS AND THE ANALYTIC UNIVERSE

I consider this work an exercise in anthropological archaeology. As such, it shares a number of basic problematic assumptions with other similar efforts in diachronic anthropology. One of these is that understanding obtained from the ethnographic record is a suitable key for deciphering the past. When we assume this, we argue implicitly or explicitly that we can know the distant past because it was not all that dissimilar from the present and the recent past (both Wobst, 1978, and Bailey, 1983, warn of the dangers of such cultural uniformitarianism).

Throughout the body of this work, especially in Chapters 6 and 7 where I deal with settlement types, settlement systems, and sociopolitical integration, I repeatedly argue that some features of the adaptation systems in the study area during the Upper Paleolithic have no present-day analogues. My interpretation of complex cold-weather base camps with their examples of monumental architecture is an apt case in point. Another example is the complex sociopolitical and economic behavior I model for the area, behavior based on the exploitation of terrestrial resources. While we can find ample suggestions in the literature that complex hunter–gatherer adaptations based on the exploitations of such resources could have existed in the distant past, we have no ethnographic record of such patterns. Thus, part of the data from the study area cannot be understood through ethnographic analogy. Groups who inhabited the central Russian Plain were clearly not like the Netsilik, the Nunamiut, or the Ojibwa, nor were they like the Eskimo around the Bering Strait, to whom I have turned for rough analogues. They had a different adaptation—one that undoubtedly had much in common with adaptations of known northern latitude hunter–gatherers, but also one with its own important unique features. My brief consideration of data from adjacent regions of Upper Paleolithic Europe, most notably Czechoslovakia, suggests that adaptations on the central Russian Plain may have had closer analogues in the distant past.

In brief, I am not arguing against the use of any uniformitarian assumptions whatsoever, but rather suggesting that our present-day assumptions about hunter–gatherers are based on a narrow range of behavioral variation available to us in the ethnographic record. It is not that the principle of uniformitarianism itself is at fault, but rather that the universe we draw on for analogy is too narrow. By reconstructing different adaptation patterns in the past, ones for which we have no known analogues, we expand this universe. Thus archaeological research adds to our knowledge of the range of hunter–gatherer behaviors. These additions need not, and will not, only mirror what is already known; they will offer us examples of the unknown. In short, uniformitarian assumptions, based as they are on incomplete analytic universes, should be used with great care in prehistoric archaeology.

PRIME MOVERS—OVERT AND COVERT

Gould (1985) describes the "stage of the art"in studies of culture change as one where two paradigms, the evolutionary and the transformational, are battling for supremacy. Under the first, he means paradigms based on evolutionary ecology; under the second, paradigms based on considerations of societal dialectic. Examples of ecological evolutionism referred to in this work include, for the Old World, the work of Hayden (1981) and Jochim (1976, 1981). The transformationalist viewpoint is expressed by Bailey (1983), Bender (1982), Friedman (1979), and Root (1983). While each of these researchers would vociferously argue that they are indeed not advocating the primacy of their variable—ecological or social—as the "prime mover," I contend that, in effect, that is precisely what they are doing, albeit in muted terms. Thus, when Bender writes that "The theoretical orientation of my paper is that at both intra- and inter-regional levels it is the analysis of social relations—seen as, to some extent, the determinants of technological progress, but also acting within the constraints imposed by techno-environmental factors—that permit an explanation of origins and change" (1982:4), she is arguing for the acceptance of the social variable as a prime mover. Likewise, Hayden, in writing that "cultural ecology provides the most productive framework for explaining these terminal Pleistocene transformations . . . . this periodic resource stress was the most important motive for patterned, directional change (1981:520), is in fact arguing for the ecological component, or man–land relationships, as the prime mover. That we do have these two disparate directions or paradigms to explain culture change indicates that we still tend to oversimplify problems of human adaptation and favor looking for *the* component, or prime mover, in change.

While such approaches may be suitable for dealing with theoretical issues and model building in general, I suspect that their utility diminishes for empirical work that focuses on specific adaptations. Clearly, both ecological and social concerns are indispensable for a reconstruction of past adaptations. Yet few voices have been raised to argue for a synthesis of these direction of empirical research. One that has, Marquardt (1985), calls for archaeology to become synthetic processual anthropology, one that includes both ecological–evolutionary rationalism and historical materialism.

In this work, I consider both the ecological and sociopolitical components of Upper Paleolithic adaptation strategies. Neither component is given preference; their intricate interrelationship is underscored. Thus, this work is an exercise in neither prehistoric cultural ecology nor prehistoric materialism. It is an amalgam of both. The fact that the ecological variable receives greater attention should not be taken as a tacit indication of the primacy of this component. Such an allocation of attention just reflects our greater facility for reconstructing this component—it is a reflection of the history of research, and no more. The equally important sociopolitical variable received less attention because our methods for reconstructing these relationships lag behind and because data on multiple scales of time and space necessary for a consideration of this component are far more sparce and problem laden.

CENTRAL RUSSIAN PLAIN DATA AND OUR THEORIES

Two disparate theoretical issues have been repeatedly mentioned in this work: our modal constructs of hunter–gatherer adaptation and trajectories along which culture change occurs. Throughout this volume, I note an apparent ill fit between our theoretical constructs and the data from the study area. It is important, here, to see if this is due to faulty theorizing or a result of erroneous use of theories.

Our anthropological theories about the organization of culture and about culture change, be they based on subsistence behavior as in Sahlins (1972), on social organization as in Service (1962), or on political organization as in Fried (1967), are both directional and evolutionary. In addition, and perhaps more important, all of them deal with huge blocks of time as well as with averaged behavior.

Taking model behavior as the first issue, we can, after Price (1981), state that the equation of a hunting and gathering way of life with a "small, simple, and mobile" adaptation is no longer valid. It is certainly true that following the Man The Hunter symposium in 1966, many archaeologists did tend to adopt the San as models of typical hunter–gatherers. More recently, however, a number of researchers have focused on distinguishing two subtypes of hunter–gatherer economic behavior. Thus we have Bettinger and Baumhoff's (1982) travellers and processors, Binford's (1982b) foragers and logistically organized groups, Testart's (1982) groups without and with storage, and Woodburn's (1980) groups with immediate or with delayed returns on invested labor. These differences are held to carry numerous implications for sociopolitical integration (both real and potential), as well as for the archaeological record (see especially Binford 1982b). Given the archaeological record of late Pleistocene–early Holocene Europe, it is not surprising that we are now arguing that it is the second, more complex type of hunter–gatherers, those with logistical organization, who inhabited the Old World in prehistory. If this is so, and the data presented in this work certainly support such a conclusion, then what do we do with our past theoretical constructs? How valid or useful are they today?

I would argue that a problem in our appreciation of theoretical insights comes with faulty use of both scales and models. I suggest, first, that we have been at fault in adhering too strictly to modal behavior outlined in our evolutionary models. Modal behavior presented in Fried (1967), Sahlins (1972), or Service (1962) is a heuristic device and not an empirical yardstick. In stressing the mean or modal points within their analytic universes, we in no way deny the existence of behavioral continua. Data on these ranges have always existed. We have no ethnographic information on such complex hunter–gatherers as the Ainu, the Bering Strait Eskimo, and the Northwest Coast groups for many years. Yet even with these data, we still favored seeing the San as our prototypical hunter–gatherers.

Second, we fail to consider that faulty coupling of disparate variables diminishes the value of our models. As I noted earlier in Chapter 7, each of the three researchers, Fried,

Sahlins, and Service, who offered evolutionary schemes modeled different components of culture—the political, the economic, and the social. They did not claim that developments within their selected components were synchronized to those in all other subsystems of culture. Problems arose with our theoretical constructs after we tried to firmly conjoin and synchronize these developments. In the real world each of these components shows, not a discrete distribution of attributes, but rather a continuous one. Schrire (1980) shows that even our paradigmatic foraging San at times kept impressive amounts of cattle and thus switched to pastoral pursuits. Groups in Australia exhibit social configurations quite unlike simple sodality-free constructs expected in model bands. In the political sphere, few would characterize slave-owning Northwest Coast groups as egalitarian. Feinman and Nietzel (1984) document an overwhelming lack of modality in political behavior in pre-state societies in general and find no clear-cut criterial that can be used by archaeologists to separate prehistoric groups into distinct theoretical categories. The same point is made by Schrire (1980) for subsistence behavior of hunter–gatherers. In brief, by equating foraging behavior with egalitarian sociopolitical relationships, by merging the means of the two, we eliminate the range of variability present in each construct.

A second major theoretical issue drawing criticism today is the notion of directional progress inherent in all our evolutionary models, whether based on cultural ecology or on the tenets of historical materialism (Dunnell 1980; Marquardt 1985). In this work, I do not presume that all evidence of change signals directional progress; I argue that some changes are just fluctuations. Such fluctuation in sociopolitical integration is advocated by Bender (1982) and Friedman (1979). I argue that while on one scale we can monitor some progressive and directional change in socioeconomic complexity in the study area, a broader spatial and temporal scale reveals fluctuations in complexity (see Bailey 1981). Whatever social complexity has been monitored on the Upper Paleolithic central Russian Plain, it did not directly lead to greater complexity. Ultimately it led to the early Mesolithic—a time of simpler adaptation strategies. (see Dolukhanov 1982 on the Mesolithic record of the area). It could be argued, albeit with numerous and glaring problems, that drastic climatic changes at the end of the Pleistocene may have aborted such an evolution in complexity. These arguments, however, cannot be offered for the archaeological record of Czechoslovakia. What we have there is a case of complexity in adaptation at about 25,000 B.P. and a simplification of this complexity after 20,000 B.P. In the study area proper, the 2000-year hiatus in occupation during the glacial maximum likewise undermines a notion of a steady and directional increase in complexity through time. My argument about this observed patterning points to the importance of fluctuations in complexity as the norm. I argue that when we look at human adaptation on time scale smaller than those of archaeological or geological periods, we can see nondirectional fluctuations in complexity.

As the data from the study area suggest, directional increases in cultural complexity can be claimed only on some time scales. I would, therefore, argue that both the phenomenon of cultural complexity or simplicity and their interpretations change, depending on the scale used for their analysis. In discussing some broad issues (e.g., the general trajectory of culture change over the entire period of hominid history), where broad scales on the order of geological periods are appropriate, we can see directional, evolutionary change to greater complexity. For concrete questions of culture history and human adaptation, where finer chronological scales are appropriate, this work indicates a lack of such directional patterning to change. Instead, I argue for oscillatory change. The trajectory of culture change at one time scale appears directional, but on others it consists of an amalgamation of multiple fluctuations, some progressive and others not. This argument is similar to that presented for late Pleistocene climatic profiles. In the case of climatic fluctuations, I show that profiles could be seen either as linear and direct, if large periods were taken as units of analysis, or oscillatory, if finer scales were considered. I argue, then, that some of our present discourse about the general applicability and validity of evolutionary models comes from a confusion of time scales.

It should be noted that our debates about the patterning and trajectories of cultural evolution to some degree echo the debates among biologists and paleontologists about the nature of evolutionary change in general—whether this process occurs gradually or through a pattern of long periods of fluctuating stasis followed by bursts of rapid change (Dunnell 1980). The first model, one advocated by Darwin (1859) and his followers, sees a steady process of minor and cumulative change through time. The second, advocated by Eldredge and Gould (1972), sees the evolutionary process as one of punctuated equilibria. In many ways our models of culture change, especially those grounded in cultural ecology, mirror the Darwinian model of biological evolution. Models offered by such transformationalists as Friedman (1979), on the other hand, appear to come closer to the punctuated equilibria model. Having taken from nineteenth-century natural sciences the concept of evolution, we find ourselves today directly reflecting their theoretical disagreements as well. I have not considered the equally serious problems that we inherited from another nineteenth-century donor of evolutionary thought—the social philosophers. This issue has been admirably dealt with by Dunnell (1980).

Stebbins and Ayala (1981) argue that whether biologists see evolution as slow and steady or abrupt and discontinuous in part depends on the units they use to measure change and have called for the recognition of differences between micro and macro patterns in evolution. My interpretations of the archaeological record from the study area show that similar scalar differences have to be considered in cultural evolution as well.

Given all these problems associated with our theoretical models, one may well ask if our constructs serve any purpose at all. I suggest that the debate about the validity of our models does not reflect the inherent faulty nature of our models, but rather their misuse as empirical yardsticks. I see our theoretical constructs, be they on general cultural evolution or on specific evolutionary sequences, as heuristic devices that roughly outline patterns but in no way impose them on the data base. Archaeological research, especially studies dealing with the deep recesses of prehistory, cannot be expected to illustrate our theoretical models. It should, however, both evaluate them and augment or expand them. This work, rather than seriously questioning our models, simply draws attention to often ignored aspects in our theoretical constructs.

References

Abramova, Z. A.
  1962   Paleoliticheskoye iskustvo na territorii SSR. In *Svod Arkheologischeskih Istochnikov* Vyp.A 4-3 Moscow–Leningrad: AN SSSR
  1966   *Izobrazheniye cheloveka v paleoliticheskom iskustve.* Moscow–Leningrad: Nauka.
  1983   Tri goda roskopok pozdnepaleoliticheskoi stoyanki Yudinovo. *Tezisy Dakladov,* Arkheologicheskii Plenum: Moscow.

Abramova, Z. A., and L. V. Grekhova
  1981   Raskopki stoyanki Yudinovo I. *Arkheologischeskiye otkritiya 1980 goda,* p. 40. Moscow: Nauka.

Adlerberg, G. P., B. S. Vinogradov, N. A. Smirnov, and K. K. Flerov
  1935   *Zverki Arktiki.* Leningrad: Glavsovmorputi.

Ager, T. A.
  1982   Vegetational history of western Alaska during the Wisconsin glacial interval and the Holocene. In *Paleoecology of Beringia,* edited by D. M. Hopkins, J. V. Matthews, Jr., C. S. Schweger, and S. B. Young, pp. 75–94. New York: Academic.

Akhmanova, O. S.
  1962   *Russko-Angliskii Slovar'.* Moscow: Gosudarstvenoye Izdatel'stvo Inostrannih i Natsional'nih Slovarei.

Allan, G. M.
  1920   Dogs of the American aboriginees. *Bulletin of the Museum of Comparative Zoology* 63:9.

Allen, P. M.
  1982   The genesis of structure in social systems: the paradigm of self-organization. In *Theory and explanation in archaeology,* edited by C. Renfrew, M. J. Rowlands, and B. Abbott Seagraves, pp. 347–374. New York: Academic.

Ames. K. M.
  1985   Hierarchies, stress, and logistical strategies among hunter–gatherers in Northwestern North America. In *Prehistoric hunter–gatherers,* edited by T. D. Price and J. A. Brown, pp. 155–180. Orlando: Academic.

Amsden. C. W.
  1979   Hard times: a case study fron northern Alaska and implications for Arctic prehistory. In *The Thule culture and anthropological retrospection,* edited by A. McCartney, pp. 395–410. *Mercury Publications 88.* Museum of Man. Ottawa.

Andreev, V. N., and V. D. Aleksandrova
  1981   Geobotanical division of the Soviet Arctic. In *Tundra ecosystems: a comparative analysis,* edited by L. C. Bliss, O. W. Heal, and J. J. Moore, pp. 25–34. Cambridge: Cambridge University Press.

Andrews, J. T., and R. G. Barry
  1978   Glacial inception and disintegration during the last glaciation. *Annual Reviews of Earth Planetary Science* 6: 205–228.

Arutyunov, S. A., I. I. Krupnik, and M. A. Chlenov
  1982   *Kitovaya alleya.* Moscow: Nauka.

Aseev, A. A., V. V. Brongulev, and A. N. Makaveev
  1973   Rekonstruktsiya poslednego Evropeiskovo lednikovogo pokrova. In *Paleogeografiya Evropi v*

pozdnem Pleistotsene: rekonstruktsii i modeli, pp. 26–30. Moscow: Institute of Geography, AN SSSR.

Audouze, F., and A. Leroi-Gourhan
1981   France: a continental insularity. *World Archaeology* 13(2): 170–189.

Averkieva, J.
1971   The Tlingit Indians. In *North American Indians,* edited by E. B. Leacock and N. O. Lurie, pp. 317–343. New York: Random House.

Bader, O. N.
1978   *Sungir. Verhnepaleoliticheskaya stoyanka.* Moscow: Nauka.
1984   Paleoliticheskiye pogrebeniya i paleoanthropologicheskiye nakhodki na Sungire. In *Sungir,* edited by A. A. Zubov and V. M. Kharitonov, pp. 6–13. Moscow: Nauka.

Bahn, P. G.
1977   Seasonal migration in southwest France during the late glacial period. *Journal of Archaeological Science* 4: 245–257.
1982   Inter-site and inter-regional links during the Upper Paleolithic: the Pyrenean evidence. *Oxford Journal of Archaeology* 1(3) 247–268.

Bailey, G. N.
1981   Concepts, time-scales, and explanations in economic prehistory. In *Economic archaeology,* edited by A. Sheridan and G. Bailey, pp. 97–118. *British Archaeological Reports, International Series* 96.
1983   Hunter-gatherer behavior in prehistory: problems and perspectives. In *Hunter-gatherer economy in prehistory,* edited by G. N. Bailey, pp. 1–6. Cambridge: Cambridge University Press.

Balikci, A.
1970   *The Netsilik Eskimo.* Garden City, N.J.: The Natural History Press.

Batzli, G. O.
1981   Population and energetics of small mammals in the tundra ecosystem. In *Tundra ecosystems: a comparative analysis,* edited by L. C. Bliss, O. W. Heal, and J. J. Moore, pp. 376–377. Cambridge: Cambridge University Press.

Batzli, G. O., R. G. White, and F. L. Bunnell
1981   Herbivory: a strategy of tundra consumers. In *Tundra ecosystems: a comparative analysis,* edited by L. C. Bliss, O. W. Heal, and J. J. Moore, pp. 359–376. Cambridge: Cambridge University Press.

Behrensmeyer, A. C., and D. E. Dechant-Boas
1980   The recent bones of Amboseli Park, Kenya, in relation to East African paleoecology. In *Fossils in the making: vertibrate taphonomy and paleoecology,* edited by A. K. Behrensmeyer and A. P. Hill, pp. 72–92. Chicago: University of Chicago Press.

Bender, B.
1978   Gatherer–hunter to farmer: a social perspective. *World Archaeology* 10: 204–222.
1981   Gatherer–hunter intensification. In *Economic archaeology: towards and integration of ecological and social approaches,* edited by A. Sheridan and G. N. Bailey, pp. 149–157. *British Archaeological Reports, International Series* 96.
1982   *Emergent tribal formations in eastern North America: a study in gatherer–hunter intensification.* Paper presented at the Meeting of the Society for American Archaeology, Minneapolis, Minn.
1985   Emergent tribal formations in the American midcontinent. *American Antiquity* 50: 52–62.

Benesz, J.
1975   The Würmian foxes of Bohemian and Moravian karsts. *Sborník Národního Muzea v Praze* vol. XXXB no. 3–5.

Berg, L. S.
1964   *Freshwater fishes of the USSR and adjacent countries* (fourth ed.). Translation from Russian. Published for the Smithsonian Institution and the NSF, Washington, D.C.: Israel Program for Scientific Translations.

Bettinger, R. L.
1978   Alternative adaptive strategies in the prehistoric Great Basin. *Journal of Anthropological Research* 34: 27–36.

Bettinger, R. L., and M. A. Baumhoff
    1982   The Numic spread: Great Basin cultures in competition. *American Antiquity* 47: 485–503.
Bhattacharya, D. K.
    1977   *Paleolithic Europe.* New Jersey: Humanities Press.
Bibikov, S. N.
    1969   Nekotoriye aspekti paleoekonomicheskogo modelirovaniya paleolita. *Sovetskaya Arheologiya* 4: 5–23.
    1981   *Drevneishii muzikal'nii kompleks iz kostei mamonta.* Kiev: Naukova Dumka.
Bibikova, V. I., and N. G. Belan
    1979   Lokal'niye varianti i grupirovki pozdnepaleoliticheskogo teriokompleksa yugo-vostochnoi Evropi. *Byulleten' Moskovskogo Obschestva Ispitaniya Prirodi, Otdel Biologii* T. 84. Vyp. 3: 3–14.
Binford, L. R.
    1962   Archaeology as anthropology. *American Antiquity* 28: 217–225.
    1968   Post-Pleistocene adaptations. In *New perspectives in archeology,* edited by S. R. Binford and L. R. Binford, pp. 313–341. Chicago: Aldine.
    1971   Mortuary practices: their study and their potential. In *Approaches to the social dimensions of mortuary practices,* edited by J. A. Brown, pp. 6–29. *Society for American Archaeology Memoirs* 25.
    1980   Willow smoke and dog's tails: hunter–gatherer settlement systems and archaeological site formation. *American Antiquity* 45: 4–20.
    1981   *Bones: ancient men and modern myths.* New York: Academic.
    1982a   Comments on Middle–Upper Paleolithic transition by R. White. *Current Anthropology* 23:177–181.
    1982b   The archaeology of place. *Journal of Anthropological Archaeology* 1: 5–31.
    1983   *In pursuit of the past.* London: Thames and Hudson.
Binford, L. R., and J. B. Bertram
    1977   Bone frequencies and attribitional processes. In *For theory building in archaeology,* edited by L. R. Binford, pp. 77–153. New York: Academic.
Binford, L. R., and S. R. Binford
    1966   A preliminary analysis of functional variability in the Mousterian of Lavallois facies. *American Anthropologist* 68: 238–259.
Binford, L. R., and W. J. Chasko, Jr.
    1976   Nunamiut demographic history: a provocative case. In *Demographic anthropology,* edited by E. B. W. Zubrow, pp. 63–143. Albuquerque, New Mexico: University of New Mexico Press.
Birks, H. J. B.
    1981   Late Wisconsin vegetational–climatic history at Kylen Lake, Northeastern Minnesota. *Quaternary Research* 16: 322–355.
Bishop, C.
    1973   Cultural and biological adaptations to deprivation: the northern Ojibwa case. In *Extinction and survival in human populations,* edited by C. Laughlin, Jr., and I. Brady, pp. 209–230. New York: Columbia University Press.
Black, L.
    1973   The Nivkh (Gilyak) of Sakhalin and the lower Amur. *Arctic Anthropology* X: 1–106.
Blalock, H. M., Jr.
    1972   *Social statistics* (second ed.). New York: McGraw-Hill.
Bliss, L. C., G. M. Courtin, D. L. Pattie, R. R. Riewe, D. W. A. Whitfield, and P. Widden
    1973   Arctic tundra ecosystems. *Annual Review of Ecology and Systematics* 4: 359–399.
Bliss, L. C., and J. H. Richards
    1982   Present-day arctic vegetation and ecosystems as a predictive tool for the arctic-steppe mammoth biome. In *Paleoecology of Beringia,* edited by D. M. Hopkins, J. V. Matthews, Jr., C. S. Schweger, and S. B. Young, pp. 241–258. New York: Academic.
Boas, F.
    1964   *The Central Eskimo.* Lincoln, Nebraska: University of Nebraska Press.

Bonch-Osmolovskii, G. A.
 1931   O narezkah na paleoliticheskih kostyah. *Soobscheniya Gosudarstvennoi Akademii Istorii Mater-yalnoi Kulturi* no. 8: 27.
Bordes, F.
 1961   *Typologie du Paléolithique Ancien et Moyen.* Memoire 1. Bordeaux: Delmas.
 1968   *The Old Stone Age.* New York: McGraw-Hill.
Boriskovskii, P. I.
 1953   Paleolit Ukraini. *Materiali i Issledovaniaya po Arheologii SSR 40.* Moscow–Leningrad: Izdatel'st-vo An SSSR.
Boriskovskii, P. I., and T. N. Dmitrieva
 1982   Kostenki 2 (stoyanka Zamyatnina). In *Paleolit Kostenkovsko-Borschevskogo raiona na Donu 1879–1979,* edited by N. D. Praslov and A. N. Rogachev, pp. 67–71. Leningrad: Nauka.
 1982b   Borschevo 2. In *Paleolit Kostenkovsko–Borschevskogo raiona na Donu 1879–1979,* edited by N. D. Praslov and A. N. Rogachev, pp. 217–221. Leningrad: Nauka.
Boriskovskii, P. I., and A. P. Okladnikov
 1953   O preodolenii vul'garizatorskih psevdo-Marksistkih kontseptsij N. Y. Marra v izuchenii rannih etapov razvitiya pervobytno-obschinnogo stroya. In *Protiv vul'garizatsii Marksizma v arheologii,* edited by A. D. Udaltsev, pp. 70–93. Moscow: AN SSSR.
Boriskovskii, P. I., and N. D. Praslov
 1964   Paleolit Dnepra i Priazovya. *Arheologiya SSSR–Svod Arheologicheskih Istochnikov* vyp. 1, t. 5. Moscow–Leningrad: AN SSSR.
Boriskovskii, P. I., A. A. Velichko, T. D. Morozova, and T. A. Halcheva
 1981   Pushkari I. In *Arheologiya i paleogeografiya Pozdnego Paleolita Russkoi ravnini,* edited by A. A. Velichko, pp. 93–97. Moscow: Nauka.
Bosinski, G.
 1976   L'art mobilier paléolithique dans l'ouest de l'Europe Centrale et ses rapports possibles avec le monde franco-cantabrique et Méditerranéen. In *Les courants stilistiques dans l'art mobilier au Paléolithique Supérieur,* edited by Z. A. Abramova and P. Graziosi, pp. 97–117. *Actes du IXᵉ Congrés de l'Union Internationale des Sciences Préhistoriques et Protohistoriques, Colloque XIV.* Prétirage. Nice.
Bouchud, J.
 1966   *Essai sur le renne et la climatologie du Paléolithique Moyen et Supérieur.* Perigeux: Magne.
 1975   Etude de la faune de l'Abri Pataud. In *Excavation of the Abri Pataud, Les Eyzies (Dordogne),* edited by H. L. Movius. *American School of Prehistoric Research Bulletin* 30: 69–153.
Bourliere, F.
 1963   Observations on the ecology of some large mammals. In *Human ecology and evolution,* edited by F. C. Howell and F. Bourliere, pp. 43–55. Chicago: Aldine.
Bourliere, F., and M. Hadley
 1970   The ecology of tropical savannas. *Annual Review of Ecology and Systematics* 1: 125–152.
Braestrup, F. W.
 1941   A study on the Arctic fox in Greenland. *Meddeleser om Grønland* 131(4): 1–110.
Braun, D. P.
 1977   *Middle Woodland–early Late Woodland social change in the prehistoric central midwestern U.S.* Ph.D. dissertation, University of Michigan. Ann Arbor: University Microfilms.
Braun, D. P., and S. Plog
 1982   Evolution of "tribal" social networks: theory and prehistoric North American evidence. *American Antiquity* 47: 504–525.
Brose, D. S.
 1978   A speculative model of the role of exchange in the prehistory of the eastern woodlands. In *Hopewell archaeology,* edited by D. S. Brose and N. Graber, pp. 3–12. Kent, Ohio: Kent State University Press.
Budko, V. D.
 1962   *Paleolit Byelorussii.* Aftoreferat dissertatsii na soiskaniye uchenoi stepeni kandidata istoricheskih nauk. Leningradskoye Otdeleniye Instituta Arheologii AN SSSR.

1964   O zhilischah Berdyzhskoi paleoliticheskoi stoyanki. *Kratkiye Soobscheniya Instituta Arheologii* 101: 31–34.

1966   Verhnii paleolit severo-zapada Russkoi ravnini. In *Drevnosti Byelorussii,* edited by V. F. Isaenko, A. G. Mitrofanov, and G. V. Shitihov, pp. 6–21. Minsk: An BSSR.

1967a   Novoye sooruzheniye is kostei mamonta v punkte Yudinovo I. *Doklady Akademii Nauk BSSR* (7): 651–653.

1967b   Yurevicheskaya paleoliticheskaya stoyanka. In *Byelorusskiye drevnosti,* pp. 6–47. Minsk: AN BSSR.

1969a   Paleolit Byelorussii i smezhnih teritorii. In *Drevnosti Byelorussii,* edited by V. D. Budko, P. I. Lysenko, L. D. Pobol, and M. M. Chernyavskii, pp. 4–27. Minsk: AN BSSR.

1969b   Yudinovskoye verhnepaleolitischeskoye poselenye. In *Tezisi dokladov k Konferentsii po arheologii Byelorussii,* pp. 16–19. Minsk: Institut Istorii AN BSSR.

Budko, V. D., and A. G. Mitrofanov
1967   Arheologiya Byelorussii za Sovetskii period. *Kratkiye Soobscheniya Instituta Arheologii* Vyp. 101: 31–34.

Budko, V. D., and V. V. Obodenko
1974   Ostatki sooruzhenii iz kostei mamonta v Berdyzhe. *Doklady AN BSSR* XVII (12): 1135–1137.

Budko, V. D., and L. M. Voznyachuk
1969   Nekotoriye rezul'tati raskopok Berdyzhskoi stoyanki v 1969 godu. In *Tezisi dokladov k konferentsii po arheologii Byelorussii,* pp. 5–7. Minsk: Institut Istorii AN BSSR.

Budko, V. D., L. M. Voznyachuk, and E. G. Kalechitz
1971   Paleoliticheskaya stoyanka Berdyzh. In *Arheologicheskiye Otkritiya 1970 Goda,* pp. 303–304. Moscow: Nauka.

Budyko, M. I.
1967   On the cause of extinction of some animals at the end of the Pleistocene. *Soviet Geography—Review and Translations* 8(10) 783–797.

1977   *Climate change.* Translated by R. Zolina. Washington, D.C.: American Geophysical Union.

1980   *Global ecology.* Moscow: Progress.

Buikstra, J. B., and M. Swegle
1982   Cremated bone: experimental evidence. Ms. on file, Department of Anthropology, Northwestern University.

Bulkin, V. A., L. S. Klejn, and G. S. Lebedev
1982   Attainments and problems of Soviet archaeology. *World Archaeology* 13: 272–295.

Bunnell, F. L.
1980   Ecosystem synthesis—a "fairytale." In *Tundra ecosystems: a comparative analysis,* edited by L. C. Bliss, O. W. Heal, and J. J. Moore, pp. 637–646. Cambridge: Cambridge University Press.

Burch, E. S., Jr.
1972   The caribou/wild reindeer as a human resource. *American Antiquity* 37: 339–368.

Butinov, N. A.
1960   Razdeleniye truda v pervobytnom obschestve. *Trudy Instituta Etnografii* IV. New Series V. LIV.

Butler, L.
1953   Population cycles in Canadian mammals. *Canadian Journal of Zoology* 31: 242–262.

Butzer, K.
1971   *Environment and archaeology.* Chicago: Aldine.

1976   Pleistocene climate. In *Ecology of the Pleistocene,* edited by R. C. West and W. G. Haag, pp. 27–44. *Geoscience and Man* vol. XIII.

Carlander, K. D.
1969   *Handbook of freshwater fishery biology* (Vol. I, third ed.). Ames, Iowa: Iowa State University Press.

Carneiro, R.
1970   A theory of the origin of the state. *Science* 169: 733–738.

Carrington, R.
1958   *Elephants.* London: Chafto-Windus.

Casteel, R. W.
1976   *Fish remains in archaeology.* New York: Academic.

Chang, K. C.
1962   A typology of settlement and community patterns in some circumpolar societies. *Arctic Anthropology* 1 (1): 42–51.

Chaplin, R. E.
1971   *The study of animal bones from archaeological sites.* New York: Seminar.

Chard, C. S.
1963   The Nganasan wild reindeer hunters of the Taimyr peninsula. *Arctic Anthropology* 1(2): 105–122.

Chebotareva, N. S.
1969a   Recession of the last glaciation in Northesatern European USSR. In *Quanternary geology and climate,* edited by H. E. Wright, Jr., pp. 79–83. Washington, D.C.: National Academy of Science.
1969b   Obschiye zakonomernosti degradatsii Valdaiskogo oledeneniya. In *Poslednii lednikovii pokrov na severo-zapadnoi evropeiskoi chasti SSSR,* edited by I. P. Gerasimov, pp. 276–300. Moscow: Nauka.

Chebotareva, N. S., and I. A. Makaricheva
1974   *Posledneye oledineniye Evropy i ego geokhronologiya.* Moscow: Nauka.
1982   Geokhronologiya prirodnih izmenenii lednikovoi oblasti Vostochnoi Evropy v Valdaiskuyu epohu. In *Paleogeografiya Evropy za posledniye sto tysyach let,* edited by I. P. Gerasimov and A. A. Velichko, pp. 16–26. Moscow: Nauka.

Chernysh, A. P.
1959   Pozdnii Paleolit srednego Pridnestrov'ya. In *Paleolit Srednego Pridnestrov'ya,* edited by V. I. Gromov and A. P. Okladnikov. *Trudy Komissii po Izucheniyu Chetvertichnogo Perioda* XV: 5–214.
1973   *Paleolit i Mezolit Pridnestrov'ya.* Moscow: Nauka.

Chesemore, D. L.
1975   Ecology of the Arctic fox (*Alopex lagopus*) in North America—a review. In *The wild canids,* edited by M. W. Fox, pp. 143–161. New York: Van Nostrand Reinhold.

Churcher, C. S.
1980   Did the North American mammoths migrate? *Canadian Journal of Anthropology* 1(1): 103–105.

Clark, G. A., and L. G. Straus
1983   Late Pleistocene hunter–gatherer adaptations in Cantabrian Spain. In *Hunter–gatherer economy in prehistory,* edited by G. N. Bailey, pp. 131–148. Cambridge: Cambridge University Press.

Clark, J. G. D.
1954   *Excavations at Starr Carr: an early Mesolithic site at Seamer near Scarborough, Yorkshire.* Cambridge: Cambridge University Press.

Clason, A. T. (editor)
1975   *Archaeozoological studies.* New York: American Elsevier.

Cleland, C. E.
1982   The Inland Shore fishery of the northern Great Lakes: its development and importance in prehistory. *American Antiquity* 47: 761–784.

CLIMAP Project Members
1976   The surface of the Ice-Age earth. *Science* 191(4232): 1131–1137.

Coe, M.
1978   The decomposition of elephant carcasses in the Tsavo (East) National Park, Kenya. *Journal of Arid Environment* 1: 71–86.

Cohen, M. N.
1977   *The food crisis in prehistory.* New Haven: Yale University Press.

Coles, J.
1973   *Archaeology by experiment.* New York: Scribner.
1979   *Experimental archaeology.* London: Academic.

Colinvaux, P. A.
1967   Quaternary vegetational history of Arctic Alaska. In *The Bering Land Bridge,* edited by D. M. Hopkins, pp. 207–231. Stanford, California: Stanford University Press.

1980   Vegetation of the Bering Land Bridge revisited. *The Quarterly Review of Archaeology* 1(1): 2–15.

1981   Grand Pile the Great. *The Quarterly Review of Archaeology* 2(3): 12.

Colson, E.

1979   In good years and in bad: food strategies of self-reliant societies. *Journal of Anthropological Research* 35(1): 18–29.

Conkey, M. W.

1980   The identification of prehistoric hunter–gatherer aggregation sites: the case of Altimira. *Current Anthropology* 21: 609–630.

Cook, S. F., and R. F. Heizer

1968   Relationship among houses, settlement area and population in aboriginal California. In *Settlement archaeology,* edited by K. C. Chang. Palo Alto: National Press.

Cornwall, I. W.

1968   *Prehistoric animals and their hunters.* London: Faber & Faber.

Cowgill, G.

1975   Population pressure as a non-explanation. *Society for American Archaeology Memoire* 30: 127–131.

Cwynar, L. C., and J. C. Ritchie

1980   Arctic steppe–tundra: a Yukon perspective. *Science* 208(4450): 1375–1377.

Dalton, G.

1977   Aboriginal economies in stateless societies. In *Exchange systems in prehistory,* edited by T. K. Earle and J. E. Ericson, pp. 191–212. New York: Academic.

Daly, P.

1969   Approaches to faunal analysis in archaeology. *American Antiquity* 34: 146–153.

Damas, D.

1972   The Copper Eskimo. In *Hunters and gatherers today,* edited by M. G. Bicchieri, pp. 3–50. New York: Holt, Rinehart and Winston.

Dansgaard, W., S. J. Johnsen, and H. Clausen

1973   Climatic fluctuations during the late Pleistocene. In *The Wisconsin stage,* edited by R. F. Black, R. P. Goldthwait, and H. B. Willman, pp. 317–321. *The Geological Society of America Memoire* 136.

Darwin, C.

1859   *Origin of species.* London: John Murray.

David, N. C.

1973   On Upper Paleolithic society, ecology, and technological change: the Noaillian case. In *The explanation of culture change,* edited by C. Renfrew, pp. 277–304. London: Duckworth.

Davis, M. B.

1976   Pleistocene biogeography of emperate deciduous forests. In *Ecology of the Pleistocene,* edited by R. C. West and W. G. Haag. *Geoscience and Man* XIII: 13–26.

Davis, R. S.

1983   Theoretical issues in contemporary Soviet Paleolithic archaeology. *Annual Review of Anthropology* 12: 403–428.

De Boer, W. R., and J. A. Moore

1982   The measurement and meaning of stylistic diversity. In *Essays in honor of John H. Rowe and Dorothy Menzel.* A special issue of *Nawpa Pacha,* Berkley, California: Institute of Andean Studies.

de Montmollin, O.

1979–   The archaeological record of an Alaskan whale-hunting community. In *The archaeological corre-*

1980   *lates of hunter–gatherer societies: studies from the ethnographic record,* edited by F. E. Smiley, C. M. Sinopoli, H. E. Jackson, W. H. Wells, and S. A. Gregg, pp. 1–21. *Michigan Discussions in Anthropology* 5(1,2).

Dolgov, V. A., and O. L. Rossolimo

1966   Vozrastniye izmenneniya nekotorih osobenostei stroyeniya cherepa i bakunum hishnih mlyekopi tayuschih i metodika opredeleniya vozrasta na primere pestsa. *Zoologicheskii Zhurnal* 45(7): 1074–1080.

Dolukhanov, P. M.
1979   *Geografiya kamennogo veka.* Moscow: Nauka
1982   Upper Pleistocene and Holocene cultures of the Russian Plain and Caucasus: ecology, economy, and settlement patterns. In *Advances in world archaeology* (Vol. I), edited by F. Wendorf, pp. 323–358. New York: Academic Press.

Dolukhanov, P. M., J. K. Kozłowski, and S. K. Kozłowski
1980   Multivariate analysis of Upper Paleolithic and Mesolithic stone assemblages. *Prace Archeologiczne.* Zeszyt 30. Uniwersytet Jagiellonski.

Dolukhanov, P. M., and G. A. Paskevich
1976   Ekologiya verhnego Paleolita, Mezolita, i Neolita. Unpublished Ms. Kiev.
1977   Paleogeograficheskiye rubezhi verhnego Pleistotsena–Golotsena i razvit'ye khozyaistvennih tipov na yugo-vostoke Evropy. In *Paleogeografiya drevnego cheloveka,* edited by I. K. Ivanova and N. D. Praslov, pp. 134–146. Moscow: Nauka.

Dreimanis, A., and Goldthwail, R. P.
1973   Wisconsin glaciation in the Huron, Erie, and Ontario lobes. In *The Wisconsin stage,* edited by R. F. Black, R. P. Goldthwail, and H. B. Willman. *The Geological Society of America Memoire 136* (7): 1–106.

Drennan, R. D.
1976   Religion and social evolution in Formative Mesoamerica. In *The early Mesoamerican village,* edited by K. V. Flannery. pp. 345–368. New York: Academic.

Douglas-Hamilton, I.
1972   *The ecology and behavior of the African elephant.* Unpublished Ph.D. dissertation, University of Oxford.

Dunbar, M. J.
1973   Stability and fragility in Arctic ecosystems. *Arctic* 26: 179–185.

Dunnell, R. C.
1980   Evolutionary theory and archaeology. *Advances in archaeological methods and theory* (Vol. III) edited by M. B. Schiffer, pp. 35–99. New York: Academic.

Efimenko, P. P.
1928   Nekotoriye itogi izucheniya Paleolita SSSR. *Chelovek* 1: 45–59.
1938   *Pervobytnoye obschestvo* (second ed.). Gosudarstvenoye Sotsial'no-Ekonomicheskoye Izdatel'stvo.
1953   *Pervobytnoye obschestvo,* (third ed.).

Eidt, R. C.
1966   Economic features of land opening in Peruvian montaña. *The Professional Geographer* XVIII (3); 146–150.
1967   Modern colonization as a facet of land development in Columbia, South America. *Yearbook of the Association of Pacific Coast Geographers* 29: 21–42.
1971   *Pioneer settlement in Northeast Argentina.* Madison: The University of Wisconsin Press.
1975   Agrarian reform and the growth of new rural settlements in Venezuela. *Erdkunde, Archiv Für Wissenschaftuche Geographie* 29(2): 118–133.

Eldredge, N., and S. J. Gould
1972   Speciation and punctuated equilibria: an alternative to phyletic graduation. In *Models in paleobiology,* edited by T. Schopf, pp. 82–115. San Francisco: W. A. Freeman.

Ellen, R.
1982   *Environment, subsistance, and system.* Cambridge: Cambridge University Press.

Elton, C.
1924   Periodic fluctuations in the numbers of animals: their causes and effects. *British Journal of Experimental Biology* 2: 119–163.
1942   *Voles, mice, and lemmings: problems in population dynamics.* Oxford: Oxford University Press.

Ember, M., and C. R. Ember
1971   The conditions favoring matrilocal vs patrilocal residence. *American Anthropologist* 73: 571–594.

Engels, F.
1948   *The Origin of the family, private property, and the state.* Translation of 1891 edition. Moscow. (originally published 1884).

Ericson, J. E.
1977   Egalitarian exchange systems in California: a preliminary view. In *Exchange systems in prehistory,* edited by T. K. Earle and J. E. Ericson, pp. 109–126. New York: Academic.

Ermolova, N. M.
1963   O faune mlyekopitayuschih epohi Paleolita i Neolita Pribaikalya. *Materialy po Etnografii* (vyp. 4), pp. 27–64. Leningrad: Geograficheskoye Obschestvo SSSR.

Fainberg, L. A.
1975   Vozniknoveniye i razvitiye rodovogo stroya. In *Pervobytnoye Obschestvo,* edited by A. I. Pershitz, pp. 49–87. Moscow: Nauka.

Feinman, G., and J. Neitzel
1984   Too many types: an overview of sedentary prestate societies in the Americas. In *Advances in archaeological method and theory* (Vol. VII), edited by M. B. Schiffer, pp. 39–102. New York: Academic.

Filippov, A. K.
1977   *Svyaz' formi i funktsii izdelii cheloveka v Paleolite.* Avtoreferat dissertatsii na soiskaniye uchenoi stepeni kandidata istoricheskih nauk. Leningradskoye Otdeleniye Instituta Arheologii AN SSSR.
1983   Antropomorfniye statuetki iz Mezina. In *Plastika i risunki drevnih kul'tur,* edited by R. S. Vasil'evskii, pp. 34–38. Novosibirsk: Nauka.

Finerty, J. P.
1981   *The population ecology of cycles in small mammals.* New Haven: Yale University Press.

Fink, J.
1969   Zametki o nauchnih rezul'tatah polevykh ekskursii provedennih po probleme Lyoss–Periglyatsial–Paleolit. In *Lyoss–periglyatsial–Paleolit na Territorii Srednei i Vostochnoi Evropy,* edited by I. P. Gerasimov, pp. 13–32. Moscow: AN SSSR.

Flannery, K. V.
1972   The cultural evolution of civilization. *Annual Review of Ecology and Systematics* 3: 339–428.
1976a   Linear stream patterns and riverside settlement rules. In *The early Mesoamerican village,* edited by K. V. Flannery, pp. 173–180. New York: Academic.
1976b   Interregional religious networks. In *The early Mesoamerican village,* edited by K. V. Flannery, pp. 329–345. New York: Academic.

Flohn, H.
1979   On time scales and causes of abrupt paleoclimatic events. *Quaternary Research* 12: 135–149.

Formozov, A. N.
1946   *Snow cover as an integral factor of the environment and its importance in the ecology of mammals and birds.* English translation. University of Alberta, Edmonton. *Boreal Institute Occasional Paper* 1.
1970   Ecologie des plus importantes especes de la fauna subarctique. *Ecology of the Subarctic regions. Proceedings of the Helsinki Symposium,* pp. 257–276. Paris: UNESCO.

Freeman, L. G.
1973   The significance of mammalian faunas from Paleolithic occupations in Cantabrian Spain. *American Antiquity* 38: 3–44.
1975   Acheulean sites and stratigraphy in Iberia and the Meghreb. In *After the Australopithecines,* edited by K. W. Butzer and G. L. Isaac, pp. 661–744. The Hague: Mouton.

Freeman, L. G., and J. Gonzalez-Echegaray
1981   El Juyo: a 14,000 year old sanctuary from northern Spain. *History of Religion* 21(1): 1–19.

Frenzel, B.
1973   *Climatic fluctuations of the Ice Age.* Cleveland: The Press of Case Western Reserve University.

Fried, M.
1967   *The evolution of political society.* New York: Random House.

Friedman, J.
1979   Hegelian ecology: between Rousseau and the World Spirit. In *Social and ecological systems,* edited by P. C. Burnham and R. F. Ellen, pp. 253–271. London: Academic.

Frison, G. C.
1978   *Prehistoric hunters of the High Plains.* New York: Academic.

Fritz, J. M.
1978   Paleopsychology today: ideational systems and human adaptation in prehistory. In *Social archaeology,* edited by C. L. Redman, M. J. Berman, E. V. Curtin, W. T. Longhorne, Jr., N. M. Varsagg, and J. C. Wanser, pp. 37–59. New York: Academic.

Gaiduk, V. E.
1970   Ekologo-morfologicheskiye osobennosti zaitsa belyaka Byelorussii. In *Popul'yatsionnaya struktura vida mlyekopitayuschih,* edited by V. E. Flint. Moscow: Nauka.

Gamble, C.
1982   Interaction and alliance in Paleolithic society. *Man* 17: 92–107.
1983   Culture and society in the Upper Paleolithic of Europe. In *Hunter–gatherer economy in prehistory,* edited by G. N. Bailey, pp. 201–211. Cambridge: Cambridge University Press.

Gellner, E.
1975   The Soviet and the savage. *Current Anthropology* 16: 595–618.

Geografiya Byelorussii
1977   Edited by V. A. Dement'yeva, N. I. Romanovsky, and I. I. Truhan. Minsk: Vyshaya Shkola.

Gerasimov, I. P.
1969   Degradation of the last European ice sheet. In *Quaternary geology and climate,* edited by H. E. Wright, Jr., pp. 70–78. *Proceedings of the VII Congress of the International Association for Quaternary Research* (Vol. 16). Washington, D.C.: The National Academy of Science.
1973   Pervobytnii chelovek, ego zavisimost' ot prirodnoi sredy v Pleistotsene, i razvitiye ego material'noi kulturi. In *Chelovek, obschestvo, i okruzhayuschaya sreda,* edited by I. P. Gerasimov and A. A. Velichko, pp. 35–47. Moscow: Mysl'.

Gerasimov, I. P., and K. K. Markov
1939   Lednikovii period na territorii SSSR. *Trudy Instituta Geografii* (Vyp. 33). Moscow–Leningrad.

Gerasimov, I. P., and A. A. Velichko (editors)
1982   *Paleogeografiya Evropy za posledniye sto tysyach let.* Moscow: Nauka.

Gerasimov, M. M.
1931   *Malta—paleolitischeskaya stoyanka.* Irkutsk.

Gerasimova, M. M.
1982   Paleoantropologicheskiye nahodki. In *Paleolit Kostenkovsko–Borschevskogo raiona na Donu 1879–1979,* edited by N. D. Praslov and A. N. Rogachev, pp. 245–256. Leningrad: Nauka.

Gifford, D. P.
1980   Ethnoarchaeological contributions to the taphonomy of human sites. In *Vertibrate taphonomy and paleoecology,* edited by A. K. Behrensmeyer and A. P. Hill, pp. 93–106. Chicago: University of Chicago Press.

Gilbert, A. S.
1980   *Quantification experiments on simulated faunal collections.* Paper presented at the 79th Annual Meeting of the American Anthropological Association. Washington, D.C.

Gilbert, M. B.
1973   *Mammalian osteo-archaeology: North America.* Special Publications of the Missouri Archaeological Society. Columbia, Missouri.

Gladkih, M. I.
1973   *Pozdnii Paleolit Lesostepnogo Pridneproviya.* Avtoreferat kandidatskoi dissertatsii na soiskaniye uchenoi stepeni kandidata istoricheskih nauk. Leningradskoye Otdeleniye Instituta Arheologii AN SSSR.
1977a   Nekotoriye kriterii opredeleniya kultornoi prinadlezhnosti Pozdnepaleolitischeskih pamyatnikov. In *Problemy Paleolita Tsentral'noi i Vostochnoi Evropy,* edited by N. D. Praslov, pp. 127–136. Leningrad: Nauka.
1977b   K voprosu o razgranichenii khozyaistvenno-kul'turnih tipov i istoriko-etnograficheskih

obschnostei pozdnego Paleolita. In *Paleoekologiya drevnego cheloveka,* edited by I. K. Ivanova and N. D. Praslov, pp. 127–136. Moscow: Nauka.

Gladkih, M. I., and N. L. Kornietz
    1983   Aesthetic aspects of construction-oriented utilization of hunting prey by Paleolithic man. *Abstracts, XI INQUA Congress.* (Vol. III), p. 88. Moscow.

Glansdorff, P., and I. Prigogine
    1971   *Structure, stability, and fluctuations.* New York: Wiley.

Golomshtok, E.
    1938   The Old Stone Age in European Russia. *Transactions of the American Philosophical Society* 29 (Pt. 2): 191–468.

Gorodtsov, V. A.
    1923   Kamenii period. *Arheologiya* 1.
    1935a   Timonovskaya Paleoliticheskaya stoyanka. *Trudy Instituta Antropologii, Etnografii, i Arheologii* (Vyp. 3), pp. 1–50. Moscow-Leningrad: AN SSSR.
    1935b   Sotsialno-ekonomicheskii stroi drevnih obitatelei Timonovskoi Paleoliticheskoi stoyanki. *Sovetskaya Etnografiya.* 3.

Gould, R. A.
    1985   "Now let's invent agriculture": a critical review of concepts of complexity among hunter–gatherers. In *Prehistoric hunter–gatherers,* edited by T. D. Price and J. A. Brown, pp. 427–435. Orlando: Academic.

Grayson, D. K.
    1973   On the methodology of a faunal analysis. *American Antiquity* 38: 432–439.
    1974   The Riverhaven No. 2 vertibrate faunas: comments on methods in faunal analysis and on aspects of the subsistence potential of prehistoric New York. *Man in the Northeast* 8: 23–40.
    1978   Minimal numbers and sample size in vertibrate faunal analysis. *American Antiquity* 43: 53–64.
    1981   The effects of sample size on some derived measures in vertibrate faunal analyses. *Journal of Archaeological Science* 8: 77–88.
    1984   *Quantitative vertibrate faunal analysis in archaeology.* Orlando: Academic.

Grekhova, L. V.
    1970   *Timonovskiye stoyanki i ih mesto v Pozdnem Paleolite Russkoi ravnini.* Avtoreferat kandidatskoi dissertatsii na soiskaniye uchenoi stepeni kandidata istoricheskih nauk. Kafedra Arheologii, Istoricheskii Fakultet, Moskovskii Gosudarstvenii Universitet.
    1971   Rabota Desninskoi ekspeditsii Gosudarstvennogo Istoricheskogo Muzeya. In *Arheologicheskiye otkritiya 1970 goda,* pp. 46–47. Moscow: Nauka.
    1977   Raskopki v Eliseevichah. In *Arheologicheskiye otkritiya 1976 goda,* pp. 48–49. Moscow: Nauka.
    1981   Raskopki Eliseevicheskoi stoyanki. In *Arheologicheskiye otkritiya 1980 goda,* p. 49. Moscow: Nauka.

Grichuk, V. P.
    1969a   Rastitel'nii pokrov v pozdnem Pleistotsene. In *Lyoss–periglyatsial–Paleolit na territorii Srednei i Vostochnoi Evropy,* edited by I. P. Gerasimov, pp. 465–481. Moscow: AN SSSR.
    1969b   Znacheniye paleobotanicheskih mater'yalov dlya stratifikatsii Valdaiskih otlozhenii. In *Poslednii lednikovii pokrov na severo-zapade Evropeiskoi chasti SSSR,* edited by I. P. Gerasimov, pp. 57–71. Moscow: Nauka.
    1969c   Rastitel'nii pokrov periglyatsial'nih oblastei. In *Lyoss–periglyatsial–Paleolit na territorii Srednei i Vostochnoi Evropy,* edited by I. P. Gerasimov, pp. 571–577. Moscow: AN SSSR.
    1972   Osnovniye etapy istorii rastitel'nosti yugozapada Russkoi ravnini v pozdnem Pleistotsene. In *Palinologiya Pleistotsena,* edited by V. P. Grichuk, pp. 9–53. Moscow: Nauka.
    1982a   Rastitel'nost' Evropy v pozdnem Pleistotsene. In *Paleogeografiya Evropy za posledniye sto tysyach let,* edited by I. P. Gerasimov and A. A. Velichko, pp. 92–109. Moscow: Nauka.
    1982b   Rastitel'nost' Evropy v pozdnem Pleistotsene. In *Paleogeografiya Evropy za posledniye sto tysyach let,* edited by I. P. Gerasimov and A. A. Velichko, Map 10. Moscow: Nauka.

Grichuk, V. P., N. S. Chebotareva, M. A. Faustova, and V. G. Lodakov
    1975   Rekonstruktsiya lednikovogo pokrova i rastitel'-notsti Evropy v pozdnem Pleistotsene (20–10,000 let nazad), pp. 1–15 *Materialy VI Syezda Geograficheskogo Obschestva SSSR.* Leningrad.

Grigor'ev, G. P.

1968   *Nachalo verhnego Paleolita i proishozhdeniye Homo Sapiens.* Leningrad: Nauka.

1970   Verhnii Paleolit. In *Kamennii vek na territorii SSSR,* edited by A. A. Formozov. *Materyali i Issledovaniya po Arheologii SSSR* 166: 43–63.

1972   Vostanovleniye obschestvennogo stroya Paleoliticheskih okhotnikov i sobiratelei. In *Okhotniki-sobirateli–rybolovi,* edited by A. M. Reshetov, pp. 11–26. Leningrad: Nauka.

1979   Kostenkovskaya kul'tura: metodicheskiye problemy eyo vydeleniya. In *Verhnii Pleistotsen i razvitiye Paleolitichekoi kul'turi v tsentre Russkoi ravnini,* pp. 28–30. *Tezisi dokladov k vsesoyuznomu soveschaniyu posvyaschennomu 100-letiyu otkritiya Paleolita v Kostenkah.* Voronezh.

1983   Razvitiye kul'tury v epohu verhnego Paleolita v Evropeiskoi chasti SSSR. *Tezisy Dokladov,* Moscow: Arkheologischeskii Plenum.

Gromov, V. I.

1925   Ostatki drevnego cheloveka Sibiri i sovremennoi emu fauni. *Zhizn' Sibiri* 5–6: 166.

1933a O geologii i faune Paleolita SSSR. *Problemy Istorii Mater'yalnoi Kul'tury* 1–2.

1933b Problemy mnozhestvennosti oledenenii v svyazi s izucheniyem Chetvertichnykh mlekopitayuschih. *Problemy Sovetskoi Geologii* 7.

1936   Itogi izucheniya Chetvertichnykh mlekopitayuschikh i cheloveko na territorii SSSR. *Materialy po Chetvertichnomu Periodu SSSR.* Moscow–Leningrad.

1948   Paleontologicheskiye i arheologicheskiye obosnovaniya stratigrafii kontinental'nih otlozhenii Chetvertichnogo perioda na territorii SSSR. *Trudy Instituta Geologicheskih Nauk* (Vyp. 64). Geologicheskaya Seriya no. 17. Moscow-Leningrad: AN SSSR.

Grosswald, M. G.

1980   Late Weichselian Ice Sheet of Northern Eurasia. *Quaternary Research* 13: 1–32.

Gubonina, Z. P.

1975   Palinologicheskiye issledovaniya osnovnih gorizontov lyossov i iskopaemykh pochv yuzhnoi chasti Russkoi ravnini. In *Problemy regional'noi i obschei paleogeografii lyesoovikh i periglyatsial'nih oblastei,* edited by A. A. Velichko, pp. 43–58. Moscow: Institut Geografii AN SSSR.

Guilday, J. E.

1970   Animal remains from archaeological excavations at Fort Ligioner. *Annals of the Carnegie Museum* 43: 177–186.

Gureev, A. A.

1964   Zaitseobrazniye. *Fauna SSSR.* Novaya Seriya 87. Mlekopitayuschiye T. 3. V. 10. Moscow: Nauka.

Gurskii, I. G.

1978   Uchastok obitaniya volka i kharakter ego izpol'zovaniya v severo-zapadnom Prichernomor'ye. *Tezisy dokladov II s'ezda vsesoyuznogo teriologicheskogo obschestva.* Moscow: Nauka.

Guthrie, R. D.

1968   Paleoecology of large mammal communities in Alaska. *American Midland Naturalist* 79: 346–363.

1980   Bison and man in North America. *Canadian Journal of Anthropology* 1: 55–75.

1982   Mammals of the mammoth steppe as paleoenvironmental indicators. In *Paleoecology of Beringia,* edited by D. M. Hopkins, J. V. Matthews, Jr., C. S. Schweger, and S. B. Young, pp. 307–328. New York: Academic.

Gvozdover, M. D.

1947   Paleoliticheskaya stoyanka "Bugorok." *K soobscheniyam o dokladah, polevikh issledovaniyah Instituta Istorii Mater'yalnoi Kultury* (Vyp. XV). Moscow–Leningrad: AN SSSR.

1974   Spetsializatsiya ohoty i kharakter kremnevogo inventarya verhnego Paleolita. In *Pervobytnii chelovek, ego materyalnaya kul'tura, i prirodnaya sreda v Pleistotsene i Golotsene,* edited by A. A. Velichko, pp. 45–56. Moscow: Institute Geografii AN SSSR.

Gvozodover, M. D., and A. M. Rogachev

1969   Razvitiye Verhnepaleoliticheskoi kul'tury. In *Lyoss–periglyatsial–Paleolit na teritorii srednei i Vostochnoi Evropy,* edited by I. P. Gerasimov, pp. 487–531. Moscow: AN SSSR.

Haber, G.

1980   The balancing act of moose and wolves. *Natural History* 89: 38–50.

Haber, R. D.
1971   Criteria of sex and age. In *Wildlife management techniques* (third ed.), edited by R. H. Giles, Jr., pp. 325–402. Washington, D.C.: The Wildlife Society.

Halcheva, T. A.
1975   Spetsifika izucheniya minerologicheskogo sostava lyessovoi tolschi Pleistotsena basseina Dnepra. In *Problemy paleogeografii lyessovih i perigl'nih oblastei,* edited by A. A. Velichko, pp. 69–79. Moscow: Institut Geografii AN SSSR.

Halstead, P., and J. O'Shea
1982   A friend in need is a friend indeed: social storage and the origins of social ranking. In *Ranking, resource, and exchange,* edited by C. Renfrew and S. Shennan, pp. 92–99. Cambridge: Cambridge University Press.

Harrold, F. B.
1980   A comparative analysis of Eurasian Paleolithic burials. *World Archaeology* 12: 196–211.

Hassan, F. A.
1981   *Demographic archaeology.* New York: Academic.

Hayden, B.
1981   Research and development in the Stone Age: technological transitions among hunter–gatherers. *Current Anthropology* 22: 519–548.

Heffley, S.
1981   The relationship between Northern Athaspaskan settlement patterns and resource distribution: an application of Horn's model. In *Hunter–gatherer foraging strategies,* edited by B. Winterhalder and E. A. Smith, pp. 126–147. Chicago: University of Chicago Press.

Helm, J.
1968   The nature of Dogrib socioterritorial groups. In *Man the hunter,* edited by R. B. Lee and I. DeVore, pp. 118–125. Chicago: Aldine.

Hemingway, M. F.
1979   Possible long-distance contact in Magdalenian: a comment. *Antiquity* LIII(208): 136–138.
1980   The initial Magdalenian in France. *British Archaeological Reports. International Series* S-90.

Hemingway, M. F., and P. Bahn
1982   The Laugerie Basse shell case. *Antiquity* LVI (218): 212–215.

Hesse, B.
1982   Bias in the zooarchaeological record: suggestions for interpretation of bone counts in faunal samples from the Plains. In *Plains Indian studies: a collection of essays in honor of John C. Ewers and Waldo R. Wedel,* edited by D. H. Ubelakes and H. J. Viola, pp. 157–172. *Smithsonian Contributions to Anthropology* 30.

Higgs, E. S. (editor)
1975   *Paleoeconomy.* Cambridge: Cambridge University Press.

Hitchcock, R.
1982   Patterns of sedentism among Bosarwa of eastern Botswana. . - In *Politics and history in band societies,* edited by E. B. Leacock and R. B. Lee, pp. 223–267. Cambridge: Cambridge University Press.

Hodder, I.
1978   The maintenance of group identities in the Baringo District, Western Kenya. In *Social organization and settlement,* edited by D. Green, C. Haseglove, and M. Spriggs, pp. 47–74. *British Archaeological Reports, International Series 47.*
1979   Economic and social stress and material culture patterning. *American Antiquity* 44: 446–454.
1980   Trade and exchange: definitions, identification, and function. In *Models and methods in regional exchange,* edited by R. E. Frey, pp. 151–156. *Society for American Archaeology Paper* 1.
1981   Society, economy, and culture: an ethnographic case study amongst the Lozi. In *Patterns of the past: studies in honor of David Clarke,* edited by I. Hodder, G. Isaac, and N. Hammond, pp. 67–86. Cambridge: Cambridge University Press.

Hodder, I. (editor)
1982   *The archaeology of mind.* Cambridge: Cambridge University Press.

Howe, J. E.
1976   Pre-agricultural society in Soviet theory and method. *Arctic Anthropology* XIII: 84–115.
1980   *The Soviet theories of primitive history: 40 years of speculation on the origins and evolution of people and society.* Unpublished Ph.D. dissertation, University of Washington, Seattle.

Hvoiko, V. A.
1901   Kievo-Kirillovskaya stoyanka i kul'tura epohi Madlen. *Trudy XI Arheologicheskogo S'yezda v Kieve v 1899 Godu.* Moscow.

Ingold, T.
1983   The significance of storage in storage societies. *Man* 18(3): 553–571.

Isaenko, V. F.
1968   *Arheologicheskaya karta Beylorussii.* Minks: Polymya.
1978   Osnovniye tipy kremnevih orudii yuzhnoi Byelorussii. In *Orudiya Kamennogo Veka,* edited by D. Ya. Telegin, pp. 70–88. Kiev: Naukova Dumka.

Ivanova, I. K.
1969   Rasprostraneniye i vozrast Paleoliticheskih stoyanok Russkoi ravnini. In *Lyoss–periglyatsial– Paleolit na territorii Srednei i Vostochnoi Evropy,* edited by I. P. Gerasimov, pp. 465–481. Moscow: AN SSSR.
1977   Prirodniye uslov'ya obitaniya l'yudei kamennogo veka v basseine reki Dnestr. In *Paleoekologiya drevnego cheloveka,* edited by I. K. Ivanova, and N. D. Praslov, pp. 7–18. Moscow: Nauka.

Ivanova, I. K., N. V. Kind, and V. V. Cherdyntsev (editors)
1963   *Absol'yutnaya geochronologiya Chetvertichnogo perioda.* Moscow: Nauka.

Ives, J. W., and C. M. Sinopoli
1979–   The archaeological correlates of Athapaskan Kaska. In *The archaeological correlates of hunter–*
1980   *gatherer societies: studies from the ethnographic record,* edited by F. E. Smiley, C. M. Sinopoli, H. E. Jackson, W. H. Wells, and S. A. Gregg, pp. 23–39. *Michigan Discussions in Anthropology* 5(1,2).

Jacobs, K. H.
1985   Evolution in the postcranial skeleton of late glacial and early postglacial European hominids. *Zeitschrift fur Morphologie und Anthropologie* (in press).

Jochim, M. A.
1976   *Hunter–gatherer subsistance and settlement: a predictive model.* New York: Academic.
1979   Catches and caches: ethnographic alternatives for prehistory. In *Ethnoarchaeology,* edited by C. Kramer, pp. 219–246. New York: Columbia University Press.
1981   *Strategies for survival: cultural behavior in an ecological context.* New York: Academic.
1983a   Optimization models in context. In *Archaeological hammers and theories,* edited by J. A. Moore and A. S. Keene, pp. 157–172. New York: Academic.
1983b   Paleolithic cave art in ecological perspective. In *Hunter–gatherer economy in prehistory,* edited by G. N. Bailey, pp. 212–219. Cambridge: Cambridge University Press.

Johnson, G. A.
1977   Aspects of regional analysis in archaeology. *Annual Reviews of Anthropology* 6: 479–508.
1982   Organizational structure and scalar stress. In *Theory and explanation in archaeology,* edited by C. Renfrew, M. J. Rowlands, and B. A. Segraves, pp. 389–421. New York: Academic.
1983   *System scale and decision making organization: implications for ethnology and archaeology.* Paper prepared for AN SSSR–IREX Archaeological Exchange Meeting. Samarkand. September.

Kabo, V. R.
1979   Teoreticheskiye problemy rekonstruktsii pervobytnosti. In *Etnografiya kak istochnik rekonstruktsii istorii pervobytnogo obschestva,* edited by A. I. Pershitz, pp. 60–107. Moscow: Nauka.

Kaiser, K.
1969   The climate of Europe during the Quarternary ice age. In *Quarternary geology and climate,* edited by H. E. Wright, pp. 10–37. Washington, D.C.: National Academy of Science.

Kalechitz, E. G.
1972   *Paleogeografiya epohi verhnego Paleolita na territorii Byelorussii i Bryanskoi oblasti.* Av-

toreferat dissertatsii na soiskaniye uchenoi stepeni kandidata geograficheskih nauk. Minsk: Byelorusskii Gosudarstvennii Universitet.

1973   Znacheniye arheologicheskih issledovanii dlya paleogeografii verhnego Antropogena Byelorussii. In *Prablemy paleogeografii Antrapagene Belarussi,* edited by E. A. Levkoe, pp. 204–209. Minsk: Nauka i Tehnika.

1984   *Pervonachal'noye zaseleniye territorii Byelorussii.* Minsk: Nauka i Tekhnika.

Kaminiskii, F. I.

ca. 1873   Sledy dervneishei epohi kamennogo veka po r. Sule i eyo pritokam. *Trudy III Arheologicheskogo S'yezda v Kieve* 1: 147.

Keene, A. S.

1981   *Prehistoric foraging in a temperate forest: a linear programming model.* New York: Academic.

1983   Biology, behavior, and borrowing: a critical examination of optimal foraging theory in archaeology. In *Archaeological hammers and theories,* edited by J. A. Moore and A. S. Keene, pp. 137–155. New York: Academic.

Khodakov, V. G.

1982   Aktualisticheskaya model' Evropeiskogo pokrovnogo lednika. In *Paleogeografiya Evropy za posledniye sto tysyach let,* edited by I. P. Gerasimov and A. A. Velichko, pp. 48–63. Moscow: Nauka.

Khotysnki, N. A.

1977   *Golotsen severnoi Evrazii.* Moscow: Nauka.

Kintigh, K. W.

1984   Measuring archaeological diversity by comparison with simulated assemblages. *American Antiquity* 49: 44–54.

Kirikov, S. V.

1979   *Chelovek i priroda Vostochnoevropeiskoi lesostepi v X–nachale XIX V.* Moscow: Nauka.

Klein, R. G.

1969   *Man and culture in the late Pleistocene: a case study.* San Francisco: Chandler.

1973   *Ice-Age hunters of the Ukraine.* Chicago: University of Chicago Press.

Klejn, L.

1977   A panorama of theoretical archaeology. *Current Anthropology* 18: 1–42.

Klima, B.

1962   The first ground-plan of an Upper Paleolithic loess settlement in Middle Europe and its meaning. In *Courses towards urban life,* edited by R. J. Braidwood and G. R. Willey, pp. 193–210. Chicago: Aldine.

1963   *Dolni Vestonice.* Praha: Nakladatelstvi Ceskoslovenske Akademie Vĕd.

1976   Le Pavlovien. In *Périgordien et Gravettien en Europe,* edited by B. Klima, pp. 128–141. *Actes du IXe Congrés de l'Union Internationale des Sciences Préhistoriques et Protohistoriques, Collogue XV.* Prétirage. Nice.

Kornietz, N. L.

1962   Pro prichini vimirannya mamonta na teritorii Ukraini. In *Vikopni fauni Ukraini i sumizhnih teritorii,* edited by I. G. Pidoplichko, pp. 93–169. Kiev: AN USSR.

Kornietz, N.L., M. I. Gladkih, A. A. Velichko, G. V. Antonova, Y. N. Gribchenko, E. M. Zelikson, E. I. Kurenkova, T. A. Halcheva, and A. L. Chepalyga

1981   Mezhirich. In *Arheologiya i paleogeografiya pozdnego Paleolita Russkoi ravnini,* edited by A. A. Velichko, pp. 106–119. Moscow: Nauka.

Kozłowski, J. K.

1972–   The origin of lithic raw materials used in the Paleolithic in the Carpathian countries. *Acta*
1973   *Archaeologica Carpathica* XIII: 5–19.

1986   Gravettian in Central and Eastern Europe. In *Advances in world archaeology* (Vol. 5), edited by F. Wendorf and A. Close. Orlando: Academic (in press).

Kozłowski, J. K., and S. K. Kozłowski

1979   Upper Paleolithic and Mesolithic in Europe. *Prace Komisji Archeologicznej* 18. Warsaw: Polska Akademia Nauk.

Krainov, D. A.
    1956   Zhilischa Timonovskoi Paleoliticheskoi stoyanki. *Sovetskaya Arheologiya* 25: 13–34.
Ksenzov, V. P., L. N. Voznyachuk, and V. E. Kudryashev
    1977   Raskopki Yurovicheskoi Verhnepaleoliticheskoi stoyanki. In *Arheologicheskiye otkritiya 1976 goda*, pp. 408–409. Moscow: Nauka.
Kukla, G. J.
    1972   Insolation and glacials. *Boreas* 1(1) 63–96.
    1975   Loess stratigraphy of Central Europe. In *After the Australopothecines*, edited by K. W. Butzer and G. L. Isaac, pp. 99–189. The Hague: Mouton.
Kurenkova, E. I.
    1978   Radiouglerodniye datirovki i paleogeografiya nekotorih stoyanok pozdnego Paleolita v basseine srednego techeniya Desni. *Izvestiya Akademii Nauk SSSR, Seriya Geograficheskaya* 1: 192–110.
    1980   *Radiouglerodnaya khronologiya i paleogeografiya Pozdnepaleoliticheskih stoyanok verhnego Pridneprov'ya*. Avtoreferat dissertatsii na soiskaniye uchenoi stepeni kandidata geograficheskih nauk. Moscow: Institut Geografii AN SSSR.
    1985   Radiouglerodniye datirovki i paleogeografiya Mezhirich. *Byulleten' Komissii po Izucheniye Chetvertichnogo Perioda* 54.
Kurten, B.
    1968   Pleistocene mammals of Europe. Chicago: Aldine–Atherton.
Kuzmina, I. E.
    1977   O proishozdenii i istorii teriofauni Sibirskoi Arktiki. In *Flora i fauna Antropogena severo-vostoka Sibiri*, edited by O. A. Strelkov, pp. 18–55. Trudy Zoologicheskogo Instituta AN SSSR. Leningrad: Nauka.
    1978   Pozdnepleistotsenovaya shirokolapaya loshad' verhnego Dona. *Tezisy dokladov II s'yezda vsesoyuznogo teriologicheskogo obschestva*. Moscow: Nauka.
Lamb, H. H.
    1966   *The changing climate*. London: Methuen.
    1977   *Climate* (Vol. 2). London: Methuen.
Landsborough-Thompson, A.
    1964   *A new dictionary of birds*. New York: McGraw-Hill.
Larick, R. R.
    1983   *The circulation of Solutrean foliate point cherts: residential mobility in the Prigord*. Ph.D. Dissertation, Department of Anthropology, State University of New York, Binghamton. Ann Arbor: University Microfilms.
Laville, H. L., J. P. Rigaud, and J. Sackett
    1980   *Rock Shelters of the Périgord*. New York: Academic.
Lawrence, B.
    1966   Early domestic dogs. *Zeitschrift für Säugetier-Kunde* 32: 44–59.
Lawrence, B., and W. H. Bossert
    1967   Multiple character analysis of *Canis lupus, latrans,* and *familiaris,* with a discussion of the relationship to *Canis niger. American Zoologist* 7: 223–232.
    1975   Relationships of North American Canis shown by a multiple character analysis of selected populations. In *Wild canids,* edited by M. W. Fox, pp. 74–86. New York: Van Nostrand Reinhold.
Laws, R. M., I. S. C. Parker, and R. C. B. Johnstone
    1975   *Elephants and their habitats*. Oxford: Clarendon.
Lazukov, G. I., M. D. Gvozdover, Y. Y. Roginskii, M. I. Urynson, V. M. Haritonov, and V. P. Yakomov
    1981   *Priroda i drenvii chelovek*. Moscow: Mysl'.
Leach, E.
    1973   Concluding address. In *The expectation of culture change,* edited by C. Renfrew, pp. 761–771. London: Duckworth.
Leacock, E. B.
    1954   The Montagnais "hunting territory" and the fur trade. *American Anthropological Association Memoire* 78. Washington, D.C.

Lebedev, V. D.
1944   K voprosu ob izmerenii ikhtiofauny reki Desny v period ot poslednei mezhledovoi do sovremennoi epohi. *Zoologicheskii Zhurnal* 23(5): 240–249.
1952   Materyaly po promyslovoi ikhniofaune gorodisch rek Desny i Seima. *Ucheniye Zapiski Moskovskogo Gosudarstvennogo Universiteta* 158: 253–273.

Lee, R. B.
1968   What hunters do for a living, or how to make out on scarce resources. In *Man the hunter,* edited by R. B. Lee and I. DeVore, pp. 30–48. Chicago: Aldine–Atherton.
1979   *The !Kung San.* Cambridge: Cambridge University Press.

Lee, R. B., and I. DeVore (editors)
1968   *Man the hunter.* Chicago: Aldine–Atherton.

Leonova, N. B.
1977   *Zakonomernosti raspredeleniya kremnevogo inventarya na Verhnepaleoliticheskih stoyankah i otrazheniye v nih spetsifiki Paleoliticheskih poselenii.* Avtoreferat dissertatsii na soiskaniye uchenoi stepeni kandidata istoricheskih nauk. Leningradskoye Otdeleniye Instituta Arheologii AN SSSR.

Leroi-Gourhan, A., and M. Brezillon
1965a   The Würm climate during the Upper Paleolithic from 36,000–8,000 b.c. *Abstracts, VII INQUA Congress* p. 290. Boulder, Colorado.
1965b   *Treasures of prehistoric art.* New York: Abrams.

Leroi-Gourhan, A., and M. Grezillon
1972   *Fouilles de Pincevent.* Essai d'Analyse ethnographiqu d'un habitat Magdalénien. *Gallia Prehistoire, VIIe Supplément.* Paris: CNRS.

Levitskii, I. F.
1947   Gontsivs'ka Paleolitichna stoyanka. In *Paleolit i Neolit Ukraini* (Vol. 1, No. 3), pp. 197–247. Kiev: AN USSR.

Levkovskaya, G. M.
1974   Paleogeografiya i khronologiya kul'tur kamennogo veka na territorii Evropeiskoi chasti SSSR, Sibiri, i sopridel'nih territorii. In *Pervobytnii chelovek, ego materyal'naya kul'tura, i prirodnaya sreda v Pleistotsene i Golotsene,* edited by A. A. Velichko, pp. 204–210. Moscow: Institut Geografii AN SSSR.
1977   Palinologicheskaya kharakteristika razrezov Kostenkovsko–Borschevskogo raiona. In *Paleoekologiya drevnego cheloveka,* edited by I. K. Ivanova and N. D. Praslov, pp. 74–83. Moscow: Nauka.

Lightfoot, K. G., and G. M. Feinman
1982   Social differentiation and leadership development in early pithouse villages in the Mogollon region of the American Southwest. *American Antiquity* 47: 64–86.

Likhachev, I. M., and E. S. Rammel'meier
1962   *Terrestrial mollusks of the fauna of the USSR.* Translated from Russian for N. S. F. Jerusalem: Israel Program for Scientific Translations.

Lundelius, E. L., Jr.
1976   Vertibrate paleontology of the Pleistocene: an overview. In *Ecology of the Pleistocene,* edited by R. C. West and W. G. Haag, pp. 45–59. *Geoscience and Man* 13.

Lyell, C.
1889   *Principles of geology.* New York: D. Appleton. (originally published 1830–1833)

Lyman, R. L.
1982   Archaeofaunas and subsistence studies. In *Advances in archaelogical method and theory,* (Vol. V) edited by M. B. Schiffer, pp. 332–394. New York: Academic.

MacArthur, R., and J. MacArthur
1961   On bird species diversity. *Ecology:* 42: 594–598.

McBurney, C. B. M.
1975   *Early man in the Soviet Union: implications of some recent discoveries.* London: British Academy.

McCartney, A. P.

1979   A processual consideration of Thule whale bone houses. In *Thule Eskimo culture: an anthropological retrospective,* pp. 301–323. *Archaeological Survey of Canada Paper 88, Mercury Series.* National Museum of Man, Ottawa.

1980   The nature of Thule Eskimo whale use. *Arctic* 33: 517–541.

McGovern, T., P. C. Buckland, G. Sveindjarnardottir, D. Savory, C. Andeasen, and P. Skidmore

1983   A study of floral and faunal remains from two Norse farms in the western settlement in Greenland. *Arctic Anthropology* 20: 2.

McGuire, R. H.

1983   Breaking down cultural complexity: inequality and heterogeniety. In *Advances in archaeological method and theory* (Vol. VI), edited by M. J. Schiffer, pp. 91–142. New York: Academic.

McGuire, R. H., and M. B. Schiffer

1983   A theory of architectural design. *Journal of Anthropological Archaeology* 2: 277–303.

Mania, D.

1969   Klimaticheskiye tsikly pozdnego Antropogena i v predgoryakh Gartsa, byvshee Asherslabenskoye ozero i Geizel'tail'. In *Lyoss-periglyatsial-Paleolit na teritorii Srednei i Vostochnoi Evropy,* edited by I. P. Gerasimov, pp. 487–531. Moscow: AN SSSR.

Marakov, S. V.

1970   Nekotoriye cherty morfologii i struktury populyatsii golubogo pestsa ostrova Mednogo (Komandorskiye Ostrova). In *Populyatsionnaya struktura vida mlekopitayuschih,* edited by V. E. Flint, pp. 130–131. Moscow: Nauka.

Markova, A. K.

1975   Palegeografiya verhnego Pleistotsena po dannim analiza izkopaemykh melkih mylekopitayuschih verhnego i srednego Pridneprovya. In *Problemy regional'noi i obschei paleogeografii lyossovih i peiglyatsial'nih oblasted,* edited by A. A. Velichko, pp. 59–68. Moscow: Institut Geografii AN SSSR.

1982   *Pleistotsenoviye gryzuny Russkoi ravnini.* Moscow: Nauka.

Marquardt, W. H.

1985   Complexity and scale in the study of fisher–gatherer–hunters: an example from the Eastern United States. In *Prehistoric hunter–gatherers,* edited by T. D. Price and J. A. Brown, p. 59–98. Orlando: Academic.

Marshack, A.

1979   Upper Paleolithic symbol systems of the Russian Plain: cognitive and comparative analysis. *Current Anthropology* 20: 271–311.

Martin. P. S.

1973   The discovery of America. *Science* 179: 969–974.

1982   The pattern and meaning of Holarctic mammoth extinction. In *Paleoecology of Beringia,* edited by D. M. Hopkins, J. V. Matthews, Jr., C. E. Schweger, and S. B. Young, pp. 399–408. New York: Academic.

Marx, K., and F. Engels

1939   *Sochineniya* (Fol 46). Moscow: Gospolitizdat. (*Grundrisse* originally published 1857–1858)

Masson, V. M.

1976   *Ekonomika i sotsialnii stroi drevnih obschestv.* Leningrad: Nauka.

Matthews, J. V., Jr.

1982   East Beringia during Late Wisconsin time: a review of the biotic evidence. In *Paleoecology of Beringia,* edited by D. M. Hopkins, J. V. Matthews, Jr., C. S. Schweger, and S. B. Young, pp. 75–94. New York: Academic.

Mauss, M.

1966   Sur les variation saisonnieres des societes Eskimos. *Sociologie et Anthropologie Pt. 8.* Paris: Presse Universitaires de France. (originally published 1904)

May, R. M.

1983a   Stability in randomly fluctuating versus deterministic environments. *The American Naturalist* 107: 621–651.

1973b   *Stability and complexity in model ecosystems.* Princeton: Princeton University Press.

1977   Thresholds and break points in ecosystems with multiplicity of stable states. *Nature* 269: 471–477.

1980   Cree-Ojibwa hunting and the hare–lynx cycle. *Nature* 286: 108–109.

Mech, D. L.

1970   *The wolf.* New York: Natural History Press.

Mellars, P. A.

1985   The ecological basis of social complexity in the Upper Paleolithic of Southwestern France. In *Prehistoric hunter–gatherers,* edited by T. D. Price and J. A. Brown, pp. 271–297. Orlando: Academic.

Mel'nikovskaya, O. N.

1950   Pamyatniki Paleolita Novgorod—Severskogo Raiona. *Kratkiye Soobscheniya Instituta Istorii Materyal'noi Kultury* XXXI: 185–192.

Michels, J. W.

1973   *Dating methods in archaeology.* New York: Seminar.

Miller, M. O.

1956   *Archaeology in the USSR.* New York: Praeger.

Mirchink, G. F.

1934   Geologicheskiye usloviya nahozhdeniya Paleoliticheskih stoyanok v SSSR i ih znacheniye dyla vostanovleniya Chetvertichnoi istorii. *Trudy Vtoroi Mezhdunarodnoi Assotsiatsii po Izucheniyu Chetvertichnogo Perioda Evropy.* (Vyp. 5). Leningrad.

1937   Dostizheniya v oblasti izucheniya Chetvertichnyh otlozhenii. *Byulleten' Moskovskogo Obschestva Ispytaniya Prirody. Otdel Geologicheskii.* (Tom 15. Vyp. 5).

Mochanov, Yu. A.

1977   *Drevneishiye etapi zaseleniya chelovekom severo-vostochnoi Azii.* Novosibirsk: Nauka.

Mongait, A. L.

1961   *Archaeology in the USSR.* Baltimore: Penguin.

Monks, G. G.

1981   Seasonality studies. In *Advances in archaeological method and theory* (Vol. IV), edited by M. B. Schiffer, pp. 177–240. New York: Academic.

Moore, J. A.

1979   The effects of information networks in hunter–gatherer societies. In *Hunter–gatherer foraging strategies,* edited by B. Winterhalder and E. A. Smith, pp. 194–217. Chicago: University of Chicago Press.

1983   The trouble with know-it-alls: information as a social and ecological resourse. In *Archaeological hammers and theories,* edited by J. A. Moore and A. S. Keene, pp. 173–191. New York: Academic.

Morlan, R.

1980   Taphonomy and archaeology in the upper pleistocene of northern Yukon Territory: a glimpse of the peopling of the New World. *Archaeological Survey of Canada Paper* 94. Mercury Series. National Museum of Man. Ottawa.

Mörner, N. A.

1969   The late Quaternary history of the Kattegatt Sea and the Swedish west coast: deglaciation, shore level displacement, chronology, isostacy, and eustasy. *Sveriges Geologiska Undersöknings Årsbok* C 640.

1972   World climate during the last 130,000 years. *24th International Geological Congress, Section 12,* pp. 72–79. Montreal.

1974   Ocean paleotemperature and continental glaciation. *Colloques Internationaux du CNRS* 219: 43–49.

Mörner, N. A., and A. Dreimanis

1973   The Erie interstade. In *The Wisconsin stage,* edited by R. F. Black, R. P. Goldthwait, and H. B. Willman, pp. 107–134. *The Geological Society of America Inc. Memoire* 136.

Moroney, M. J.

1965   *Facts from figures.* Baltimore, MD.: Penguin.

Morozova, T. D.
1969   Verhnepleistotsenoviye iskopaemiye pochvy. In *Lyoss–periglyatsial–Paleolit na territorii Srednei i Vostochnoi Evropy,* edited by I. P. Gerasimov, pp. 438–444. Moscow: AN SSSR.

Morton, J. E.
1979   *Molluscs.* (fifth ed.). London: Hutchinson.

Moss, E. H.
1983   The functional analysis of flint implements. *British Archaeological Reports. International Series* S177.

Motuz, M. V.
1969   O faune morskih mollyuskov iz Verhnepaleoliticheskoi stoyanki Yudinovo, Bryanskoi oblasti, pp. 16–20. *Tezisi dokladov k konferentsii po arheologii Byelorussii.* Minsk: Institut Istorii AN BSSR.

Movius, H. L. (editor)
1977   *Excavation of the Abri Pataud, Les Eyzies (Dordogne). American School of Prehistoric Research Bulletin* 30. Cambridge, Mass.

Naroll, R. S.
1962   Floor area and settlement population. *American Antiquity* 27: 587–588.

Naumov, N. P.
1948   *Otcherki po sravnitel'noi ekologii gryzunov.* Moscow: AN SSSR.
1972   *The ecology of animals.* Translated by F. K. Plous, Jr. Edited by N. D. Levine. Urbana: University of Illinois Press.

Naumov, N. P., and V. G. Gentner (editors)
1967   *Mlekopitayuschiye Sovetskogo Soyuza.* Part 2. Moscow: Vyshaya Shkola.

Nelson, E. W.
1971   *The Eskimo about Bering Straits.* New York: Johnson Reprint Corporation. (originally published 1899)

Nicolis, G., and I. Prigogine
1977   *Self-organization in nonequilibrium systems.* New York: Wiley.

Odum, E. P.
1971   *Fundamentals of ecology* (third ed.). Philadelphia: Saunders.

Official Standard Names Gazeteer No. 42
1970   (second ed.). U.S. Army Topographical Comission, Geographic Names Division. Washington, D.C.

Oliver, R. C. D.
1982   Ecology and behavior of living elephants: bases for assumptions concerning the extinct wooly mammoths. In *Paleoecology of Beringia,* edited by D. M. Hopkins, J. V. Matthews, Jr., C. S. Schweger, and S. B. Young. pp. 291–306. New York: Academic.

Olsen, S. J., and J. W. Olsen
1977   The Chinese wolf, ancestor of New World dogs. *Science* 197: 533–535.

O'Shea, J.
1981   Coping with scarcity: exchange and social storage. In *Economic Archaeology,* edited by A. Sheridan and G. Bailey, pp. 167–186. *British Archaeological Reports. International Series* 96.

Pashkevich, G. A., and V. A. Dubnyak
1978   Paleogeograficheskaya kharakteristika razreza s. Dobranichevka. In *Ispol'zovanie metodov estestvennih nauk v arheologii,* edited by V. F. Gening, pp. 69–85. Kiev: Naukova Dumka.

Pécsi, M., M. A. Pevzner, and E. Szébenyi
1979   Upper Pleistocene litho- and chronostratigraphical type profile from the loess exposure at Mende. In *Guide-book for conference and field—workshop on the stratigraphy of loess and alluvial deposits,* edited by M. Pécsi, pp. 11–37. INQUA Comission on Loess, IGCP International Geological Correlation Programme Magnetostratigraphy. Budapest-Szeged, Hungary.

Peebles, C. S., and S. M. Kus
1977   Some archaeological correlates of ranked societies. *American Antiquity* 42: 421–448.

Perkins, D. J., and P. Daly
1968   A hunters village in Neolithic Turkey. *Scientific American* 219: 96–106.

Perlman, S. M.
1980   An optimum diet model, coastal variability, and hunter–gatherer behavior. In *Advances in ar-*

chaeological method and theory (Vol. III), edited by M. B. Schiffer, pp. 257–310. New York: Academic.

1982   Comments to Testart's "The significance of food storage among hunter–gatherers: residence patterns, population densities, and social inequalities." *Current Anthropology* 23: 532.

Peterson, G. M., I. T. Webb, III, J. E. Katzback, T. van der Hammer, T. A. Wijmstrata, and F. A. Street
1979   The continental record of environmental conditions at 18,000 years B.P.: an initial evaluation. *Quaternary Research* 12: 47–67.

Peterson, R. O., R. E. Page, and K. M. Dodge
1984   Wolves, moose, and the allometry of population cycles. *Science* 4655: 1350–1352.

Pianka, E. R.
1974   *Evolutionary ecology.* New York: Harper & Row.

Pidoplichko, I. G.
1933   Chetvertichii period na Ukraine. In *Chetvertichnii period* (Vyp 5) pp. 113–119.
1939   K istorii fauni SSSR. *Doklady AN SSSR, Novaya Seriya* 23(6) 609–612.
1947a   Paleolitichna stoyanka Chulativ I. In *Paleolit i Neolit Ukraini* (Vol. 1, Vyp. II), pp. 123–153.
1947b   Piznyopaleolitichna stoyanka Novgorod-Sivers'k. In *Paleolit i Neolit Ukraini* (Vol. 1, Vyp. II), pp. 65–106. Kiev: AN USSR.
1969   *Pozdnepaleoliticheskiye zhilischa is kostei mamonta na Ukraine.* Kiev: Naukova Dumka.
1976   *Mezhirichskiye zhilischa iz kostei mamonta.* Kiev: Naukova Dumka.

Pidoplichko, I. G., and P. S. Makaeev
1955   *O klimate i landshafte proshlogo* (second ed.). Kiev: AN USSR.

Pidoplichko, I. G., and I. G. Shovkoplyas
1961   Paleolit Ukrainskogo polessya. In *Voprosy Stratigrafii i Periodizatsii Paleolita* XVIII: 75–88.

Pielou, E. C.
1969   *An introduction to mathematical ecology.* New York: Wiley.

Pimlott, D. M.
1975   The ecology of the wolves in North America. In *Wild canids,* edited by M. W. Fox, pp. 280–285. New York: Van Nostrand Reinhold.

Pires-Ferreira, J., and K. V. Flannery
1976   Ethnographic models for Formative exchange. In *The early Mesoamerican village,* edited by K. V. Flannery, pp. 286–291. New York: Academic.

Plog, F.
1977   Modeling economic exchanges. In *Exchange systems in prehistory,* edited by T. K. Earle and J. E. Ericson, pp. 127–140. New York: Academic.
1979   Alternative models of prehistoric change. In *Transformations,* edited by C. Renfrew and K. L. Cooke, pp. 221–235. New York: Academic.

Polevoi, N. I. (editor)
1974   *Geokhronologiya SSSR.* Leningrad: Nedra.

Polikarpovich, K. M.
1968   *Paleolit verhnego Podneprov'ya.* Minsk: Nauka i Tehnika.

Pollock, S. M.
1983   *The symbolism of prestige: an archaeological example from the royal cemetery of Ur.* Ph.D. dissertation, University of Michigan. Ann Arbor: University Microfilms.

Praslov, N. D.
1982   Rasseleniye cheloveka v Evrope v pozdnem Pleistotsene (map 14). In *Paleogeografiya Evropy za posledniye sto tysyach let,* edited by I. P. Gerasimov and A. A. Velichko, p. 113. Moscow: Nauka.

Praslov, N. D., M. A. Ivanova, L. A. Gugalinskaya, I. E. Kuz'mina, V. M. Motuz, E. S. Malyasova, E. Y.
Mednikova, E. Y. Prosvirina, S. A. Piserevskii, and G. V. Holmovoi
1981   Kostenki XXI. In *Arheologiya i paleogeografiya pozdnego Paleolita Russkoi ravnini,* edited by A. A. Velichko, pp. 6–17. Moscow: Nauka.

Praslov, N. D., and A. N. Rogachev (editors)
1982   *Paleolit Kostenkovsko-Borschevskogo raiona na Donu 1879–1979.* Nauka: Leningrad.

Price, T. D.
1978   Mesolithic settlement systems in the Netherlands. In *The early postglacial settlement of Northern Europe,* edited by P. A. Mellars, pp. 81–113. London: Duckworth.
1981   Complexity in "non-complex" societies. In *Archaeological approaches to the study of complexity,* edited by S. E. van der Leeuw, pp. 53–97. Amsterdam: Institut voor Pre- en Protohistorie.

Pruitt. W. O.
1970   Some ecological aspects of snow. In *Ecology of the subarctic regions: Proceedings of the Helsinki Symposium,* pp. 83–101. Paris: UNESCO.

Pulliainen, E.
1975   Wolf ecology in Northern Eruope. In *Wild canids,* edited by M. W. Fox. New York: Von Nostrand Reinhold Company.

Rappaport, R. A.
1971   The sacred in human evolution. *Annual Review of Ecology and Systematics* 2: 23–44.

Ravdonikas, V. I.
1939   *Istoriya pervobytnogo obschestva.* Part 1. Leningrad: Izdatel'stvo Leningradskogo Universiteta.

Redman. C. L.
1978   *The rise of civilization.* San Francisco: Freeman.

Reidhead, V. A.
1979   Linear programming models in archaeology. *Annual Review of Anthropology* 8: 543–578.
1980   The economics of subsistence change: a test of an optimization model. In *Modeling change in prehistoric subsistence economies,* edited by T. Earle and A. Christenson, pp. 141–179. New York: Academic.

Renfrew, C.
1977   Alternative models for exchange and spatial distribution. In *Exchange systems in prehistory,* edited by T. K. Earle and J. E. Ericson, pp. 71–90. New York: Academic.
1982   Socio-economic change in ranked societies. In *Ranking, resources, and exchange: aspects of the archaeology in early European societies,* edited by C. Renfrew and S. Shennan, pp. 1–8. Cambridge: University of Cambridge Press.

Reynolds, R. G. D.
1976   Linear settlement systems on the upper Grijalva River: the application of Markovian model. In *The early Mesoamerican village,* edited by K. V. Flannery, pp. 180–194. New York: Academic.

Riches, D.
1979   Ecological variation on the Northwest Coast: models for generation of cognatic and matrilineal discent. In *Social and ecological systems,* edited by P. C. Burnham and R. F. Ellen, pp. 145–160. London: Academic.

Ritchie, J. C., and L. C. Cwynar
1982   The Late Quaternary vegetation of the North Yukon. In *Paleoecology of Beringia,* edited by D. M. Hopkins, J. V. Matthews, Jr., C.S Schweger, and S. B. Young, pp. 113–126. New York: Academic.

Rogachev, A. N.
1957   Mnogosloiniye stoyanki Kostenkovsko-Borschevskogo raiona na Donu i problema razvit'ya kul'tury v epohy verhnego Paleolita na Russkoi ravnine. *Materialy i Issledovaniaya po Arheologii SSSR* 57: 9–134.
1961   Nekotoriye voprosy stratigrafii i periodizatsii verhnego Paleolita Vostochnoi Evropy. *Trudy Komissii po Izucheniyu Chetvertichnogo Perioda* XVIII: 40–45.
1970   Paleoliticheskiye zhilischa i poseleniya v Vostochnoi Evrope. *Doklady, VII Mezhdunarodnii Kongress Antropologicheskih i Etnograficheskih Nauk* (Vol. 5), pp. 432–438.Moscow: AN SSSR.
1973   Ob uslozhnennom sobiratel'stve kak forme khozyaistva v epohu Paleolita na Russkoi ravnine. In *Antropologicheskaya rekonstruktsiya i problemy paleoetnografii,* edited by G. V. Lebedinskaya and M. G. Rabónovich, pp. 127–142. Moscow: Nauka.

Rogachev, A. N., and V. I. Belyaeva
1982   Kostenki 18 (Hvoikovskaya stoyanka). In *Palelit Kostenkovsko-Borschevskogo raiona na Donu 1879–1979,* edited by N. D. Praslov and A. N. Rogachev, pp. 190–196. Leningrad: Nauka.

Rogachev, A. N., and V. V. Popov
1982   Kostenki 11 (Anosovka 2). In *Paleolit Kostenkovsko–Borschevskogo raiona na Donu 1879–1979*, edited by N. D. Praslov and A. N. Rogachev, pp. 116–131. Leningrad: Nauka.

Rogachev, A. N., and A. A. Sinitsyn
1982a   Kostenki 14 (Markina Gora). In *Paleolit Kostenkovsko–Borschevskogo raiona na Donu 1879–1979*, edited by N. D. Praslov and A. N. Rogachev, pp. 145–161. Leningrad: Nauka.
1982b   Kostenki 15 (Gorodtsovskaya stoyanka). In *Paleolit Kostenkovsko–Borschevskogo raiona na Donu 1879–1979*, edited by N. D. Praslov and A. N. Rogachev, pp. 162–170. Leningrad: Nauka.

Romanchuk, S. P.
1974   Rasprostrananiye stoyanok Paleolita i Mezolita sredi drevnih landshaftov basseina srednego Dnepra. In *Pervobytnii chelovek, ego material'naya kultura i prirodnaya sreda v Pleistotsene i Golotsene*, edited by A. A. Velichko, pp. 131–133. Moscow: Institut Geografii AN SSSR.

Root, D.
1981   *Ritual and the arrangement of information flow in egalitarian systems.* Paper presented at the American Association for Anthropology Annual Meetings, Los Angeles.
1983   Information exchange and the spatial configurations of egalitarian systems. In *Archaeological hammers and theories*, edited by J. A. Moore and A. S. Keene, pp. 193–219. New York: Academic.

Rossolimo, O. L., and V. A. Dolgov
1965   Zakonomernosti izmenchivosti cherepa volka (*Canis lupus Linnaeus*, 1758) na territorii SSSR. *Acta Theriologica* X(12): 195–207.

Rowlands, M. J.
1982   Processual archaeology as historical social science. In *Theory and explanation in archaeology*, edited by C. Renfrew, M. J. Rowlands, and B. A. Segraves, pp. 157–174. New York: Academic.

Rudenko, A. S.
1957   *Lyoss i makroskopicheskiye ostatki v lyossah.* Avtoreferat dissertatsii na soiskaniye uchenoi stepeni kandidata zoologicheskih nauk. Kiev: Institut Zoologii AN USSR.
1959   Morskiye molyuski iz Mezinskoi stoyanki. *Kratkiye Soobscheniya Instituta Arheologii AN USSR* 8: 110–112.

Rudinskii, M.
1928   Doslidi v Zhuravtsi. *Antropologiya* II: 140–152.
1929   Zhuravka. *Antropologiya* III: 97–123.
1930   Deyki pidsumki ta blizhchi zavdannya Paleontolichnih vivchenj v mensah USSR. *Antropologiya* IV: 145–185.

Rust, A.
1937   *Das eiszeitliche Rentierlager Meiendorf.* Neumünster: Karl Wachholtz.
1958   *Die jungpälaolithischen Zentanlagen von Ahrensburg.* Neumünster: Karl Wachholtz.

Sahlins, M. D.
1972   *Stone-Age economics.* Chicago: Aldine.

Sahlins, M. D., and E. R. Service (editors)
1960   *Evolution and culture.* Ann Arbor: University of Michigan Press.

Saunders, J.
1979   Reply, idea exchange. *AMQUA Newsletter* 9(1): 2.
1980   A model for man–mammoth relationship. *Canadian Journal of Anthropology* 1: 87–98.

Schalk, R. F.
1977   The structure of an anadromous fish resource. In *For theory building in archaeology*, edited by L. R. Binford, pp. 207–249. New York: Academic.

Schrire, C.
1980   An inquiry into the evolutionary status and apparent identity of San hunter–gatherers. *Human Ecology* 8: 9–32.

Schrire, C. (editor)
1984   *Past and present in hunter–gatherer studies.* Orlando: Academic Press.

Schweger, C. E.

1982   Late Pleistocene vegetation of Eastern Beringia: pollen analysis of dated alluvium. In *Paleoecology of Beringia,* edited by D. M. Hopkins, J. V. Matthews, Jr., C. S. Schweger, and S. B. Young, pp. 95–112. New York: Academic.

Semenov, S. A.

1939   Izucheniye funktsii Verhnepaleoliticheskih orudii truda po sledam ot upotrebleniya na materialah Kostenok I, Timonovki, i Pescheri Virhova. *Kandidatskaya Dissertatsiya. Archiv 1157.* Leningradskoye Otdeleniye Instituta Arheologii AN SSSR.

1968   *Razvitiye tekhniki v kamenom veke.* Moscow: Nauka.

Semenov, Y. I.

1979   O metodike rekonstruktsii razvitiya pervobytnogo obschestva po dannim etnografii. In *Etnografiya kak istochnik rekonstruktsii istorii pervobytnogo obschestva,* edited by A. I. Pershitz, pp. 108–124. Moscow: Nauka.

1980   The theory of socio-economic formations and world history. In *Soviet and Western anthropology,* edited by E. Gellner, pp. 29–58. New York: Columbia University Press.

Serebryannaya, T. A.

1972   Paleophitologicheskaya kharakteristika lyessov iz razreza u poselka Karachizh v raione g. Bryanska. In *Palinologiya Pleistotsena,* edited by V. P. Grichuk, pp. 55–72. Moscow: Institut Geografii AN SSSR.

Sergin, V. Y.

1974a   O razmere pervogo Paleoliticheskogo zhilischa v Yudinove. *Sovetskaya Arheologiya* 3: 236–240.

1974b   O khronologicheskom sootnoshenii zhilisch i prodolzhitel'nosti obitaniya na pozdnepaleoliticheskih poseliniyah. *Sovetskaya Arheologiya* 1: 3–11.

1977   Raskopki v sele Yudinovo. *Arheologicheskiye otkritiya 1976 goda,* p. 70. Moscow: Nauka.

1978   Raskopki Paleoliticheskogo zhilischa v Gontsah. *Arheologicheskiye otkritiya 1977 goda,* p. 83. Moscow: Nauka.

1979a   Raskopki Gontsovskogo Paleoliticheskogo poseleniya. *Arheologicheskiye otkritiya 1978 goda,* p. 402. Moscow: Nauka.

1979b   Paleoliticheskiye poseleniya srednedneprovskogo tipa i ih istoriko-kul'turnoye znacheniye. *Kratkiye Soobscheniya Instituta Arheologii* 157: 15–20.

1981a   Raskopki v Gontsah. *Arheologicheskiye otkritiya 1980 goda,* p. 310. Moscow: Nauka.

1981b   Zhilischa na Gontsovskom Paleoliticheskom poselenii. *Kratkiye Soobscheniya Instituta Arheologii* 165: 43–50.

1981c   Raskopki Paleoliticheskogo poseleniya Yudinovo 3 i punkta Yudinovo 2. *Arheologicheskiye otkritiya 1980 goda,* p. 80. Moscow: Nauka.

1983   O naznachenii bol'shih yam na Paleoliticheskih poselen'yah. *Kratkiye Soobscheniya Instituta Arheologii* 173: 23–31.

Service, E. R.

1962   *Primitive social organization.* New York: Random House.

Sheehan, G. W.

1985   Whaling as an organizing focus in Northwestern Alaskan Eskimo society. In *Prehistoric hunter–gatherers,* edited by T. D. Price and J. A. Brown, pp. 123–154.Orlando: Academic

Shilo, N. A., A. V. Loshkin, E. E. Titov, and Y. V. Shumilov

1983   *Kirgilyachskii mamont.* Moscow: Nauka.

Shilyaeva, L. M.

1970   Prostranstvennaya i ekologicheskaya struktura Severnoevropeiskoi popul'yatsii pestsa. In *Popul'yatsionnaya struktura vida mlekopitayuschih,* edited by V. E. Flint, pp. 58–59. Moscow: Nauka.

Shimkin, E. M.

1978   The Upper Paleolithic in north-central Eurasia: evidence and problems. In *Views of the past, essays in Old World prehistory and paleoanthropology,* edited by L. G. Freeman, pp. 193–315. The Hague: Mouton.

Shovkoplyas, I. G.
1950   Suponevskaya Paleolitichna stoyanka. *Arheologiya* IV: 177–183.
1951   Zhitla Suponevs'koi Paleolitichnoi stoyanki. *Arheologiya* V: 127–142.
1952   Kistyani virobi Suponevskoi Paleolitichnoi stoyanki. *Arheologiya* VI: 81–94.
1955   *Starodavnii kamyanii vik na Ukraini.* Kiev: AN USSR.
1956   Fastovskaya Pozdnepaleoliticheskaya stoyanka. *Kratkiye Soobschenia Instituta Istorii Mater'ialnoi Kul'tury* 65: 68–74.
1964   Paleolitichna stoyanka Radomyshl'. *Arheologiya* XVI: 88–102.
1965a   *Mezinskaya stoyanka.* Kiev: Naukova Dumka.
1965b   Radomyshl'skaya stoyanka—pamyatnik nachal'noi pory pozdnego Paleolita. In *Stratigrafiya i periodizatsiya Paleolita Vostochnoi i Tsentral'noi Evropy,* edited by O. N. Bader, I. K. Ivanova, and A. A. Velichko, pp. 104–116. Moscow: AN SSSR.
1965c   O kharaktere svyazei naseleniya v pozdnem Paleolite. In *Mater'yaly po Chetvertichnomu periodu Ukraini,* pp. 312–321. Kiev: AN USSR.
1967   Novaya pozdnepaleoliticheskaya stoyanka na Chernigovschine. *Arheologicheskiye otkritiya 1966 goda,* pp. 187–189. Moscow: Nauka.
1971   Issledocanıya Dobranichevskoı stoyanki. *Arheologicheskiye Otkritiya 1970 Goda,* Moscow: Nauka. pp.229-230.
1972   Dobranichevskaya stoyanka na Kievschine—nekotoriye itogi issledovaniaya. In *Paleolit i Neolit SSSR* (Vol. 7). *Materialy i Issledovaniya po Arheologii SSSR* 185: 177–189.
1974   Raskopki v Dobranichevka. *Arheologicheskiye otkritiya 1973 goda,* pp. 363–364. Moscow: Nauka.
1976   Issledovaniya v Dobranichevka na Kievschine. *Arheologicheskiye otkritiya 1975 goda,* pp. 407–408. Moscow: Nauka.
Shovkoplyas, I. G., N. L. Kornietz, and G. A. Pashkevich
1981   Dobranichevskaya stoyanka. In *Arheologiya i paleogeografiya Pozdnego Paleolita Russkoi ravnini,* edited by A. A. Velichko, pp. 97–106. Moscow: Nauka.
Sikes, S. K.
1971   *The natural history of African elephants.* London: Weindenfield & Nicholson.
Silver, I. A.
1969   The ageing of domestic animals. In *Science in archaeology,* edited by D. Brothwell and E. Higgs, pp. 283–302. London: Thames & Hudson.
Sklenar, K.
1975   Paleolithic and Mesolithic dwellings: problems of interpretation. *Pamatky Archeologicke* LXVI: 266–304. Praha.
1976   Paleolithic and Mesolithic dwellings: an essey in classification. *Pamatky Archeologicke* LXVII: 249–340. Praha.
1977   *Najstarši lidská obydli v Českoslovsnsku.* Praha: Narodni Museum.
Slobodkin, L. B., and A. Rappaport
1974   An optimal strategy of evolution. *Quarterly Review of Biology* 49: 181–200.
Smirnov, S. V.
1973   *Paleolit Dniprovs'kogo Nadporizzya.* Kiev: Naukova Dumka.
Smith, E. A.
1981   Optimal foraging theory and analysis of hunter and gatherer group size. In *Hunter–gatherer foraging strategies,* edited by B. Winterhalder and E. A. Smith, pp. 36–65. Chicago: University of Chicago Press.
Smith, P. E. L.
1966   *Le Solutréen en France.* Bordeaux: Delmas.
Soffer, O. (Soffer-Bobyshev)
1981   *Social intensification among hunters–gatherers: the case of the Upper Paleolithic on the Russian Plain.* Paper presented at the Annual Meeting of the Society for American Archaeology, San Diego, California.
1983   The politics of the Paleolithic in the USSR: a case of paradigms lost. In *The socio-politics of*

archaeology, edited by J. M. Gero, D. L. Lacy, and M. L. Blakey, pp. 91–106. *Research Report 23,* Department of Anthropology, University of Massachusetts, Amherst.

1984   *Upper Paleolithic of the central Russian Plain: a study of fluctuational trajectories of culture change.* Ph.D. dissertation, Graduate Center, C.U.N.Y. Ann Arbor: University Microfilms.

1985   Patterns of intensification as seen from the Upper Paleolithic Central Russian Plain. In *Prehistoric hunters and gatherers.* edited by T. C. Price and J. A. Brown, pp. 235–270. Orlando: Academic.

Sonneville-Bordes, D. de

1960   *Le Paléolithique Supérieur en Périgord.* Bordeaux: Delmas.

Soviet Ukraine

1965   Editor in chief, M. P. Bazhan. Kiev: AN USSR.

Spencer, R. F.

1959   *The North Alaskan Eskimo.* A study in ecology and society. *Bureau of American Ethnology Bulletin* 171. Washington, D.C.: Smithsonian Institute.

Speth, J. D., and K. A. Speilmann

1983   Energy source, protein metabolism, and hunter–gatherer subsistence strategies. *Journal of Anthropological Archaeology* 2: 1–31.

Spiess, A. E.

1979   *Reindeer and caribou hunters: an archaeological study.* New York: Academic.

Spjeldnaes, N.

1964   Climatically induced faunal migrations: examples from the littoral faunas of the late Pleistocene of Norway. In *Problems in paleoclimatology,* edited by E. A. M. Nairn, pp. 353–356. London: Interscience.

Stebbins, G. L. and F. J. Ayala

1981   Is a new evolutionary synthesis necessary? *Science* 218, 967–971.

Steward, J.

1938   *Basin–Plateau aboriginal sociopolitical groups. Bureau of American Ethnology Bulletin* 120. Smithsonian Institution.

1955   *Theory of culture change.* Urbana, Ill.: University of Illinois Press.

Stroganov, S. V.

1969   *Carnivorous mammals of Siberia.* Translated from Russian. Published for the Smithsonian Institution and NSF by Israel Program for Scientific Translations. Jerusalem.

Sukachev, V. N., V. I. Gromov, and O. N. Bader

1966   Verhnepaleoliticheskaya stoyanka Sungir. *Trudy Geologicheskogo Obschestva* 162. Moscow.

Taber, R. D.

1971   Criteria of sex and age. In *Wildlife management techniques* (third edition), edited by R. H. Giles, Jr., pp. 325–402. Washington, D.C.: The Wildlife Society.

Taborin, Y.

1972   Les Cardium triforés du Placard. *Bulletin de la Societe Prehistorique Française* 69: 269–273.

Tarasov, L. M.

1976   Issledovaniye Paleolita na Desne v raione Betovo. *Arheologicheskiye otkritiya 1975 goda,* pp. 91–92. Moscow: Nauka.

1977   Raskopki Paleoliticheskih stoyanok na verhnei Desne. *Arheologicheskiye Otkritiya 1976 goda,* pp. 74–75. Moscow: Nauka.

1981   Pozdnepaleoliticheskaya stoyanka Kositsa. *Kratniye Soobscheniya Instituta Arheologii* 165: 50–55.

Ter-Akopian, N. B.

1979   Pokhod K. Marksa i F. Engels k issledovaniyu problemy pervobytnoi istorii i mesto v nem etnograficheskih metodov. In *Etnografiya kak istochnik rekonstruktsii istorii pervobytnogo obschestva,* edited by A. I. Pershitz, pp. 5–25. Moscow: Nauka.

Testart, A.

1982   The significance of food storage among hunter–gatherers: residence patterns, population densities, and social inequalities. *Current Anthropology* 23: 523–537.

Thomas, D. H.
  1976   *Figuring anthropology.* New York: Holt, Rinehart, and Winston.
Thompson, D.
  1949   *Economic structure and the ceremonial exchange cycle in Arnhem Land.* Oxford: Oxford University Press.
Tieszen, L. L., M. C. Lewis, P. C. Miller, J. Mayo, F. S. Chapin, III, and W. Oechel
  1980   An analysis of processes of primary production in tundra growth forms. In *Tundra ecosystems: a comparative analysis,* edited by L. C. Bliss, O. W. Heal, and J. J. Moore, pp. 285–356. Cambridge: Cambridge University Press.
Ukraina—Obschii Obzor.
  1969   Edited by V. P. Zamkovskii, L. M. Koretskii, I. A. Kuchekalo, G. K. Makarenko, A. M. Marinich, and V. I. Naulko. Moscow: Mysl'.
Ukraintseva, V. V.
  1979   Rastitel'nost' tyoplykh epokh pozdnego Pleistotsena i vymiraniye nekotorikh krupnikh rastitel'noyadnikh mlekopitayuschikh. *Botanicheskii Zhurnal* 64: 318–328.
Umanskaya, A. S. (Bryuzgina)
  1975   *Pozdneantropogenoviye ptitsy Ukraini i smezhnih territorii (preimuschestvenno po materyalam iz arheologicheskih pamyatnikov).* Avtoreferat dissertatsii na soiskaniye uchenoi stepeni kandidata biologicheskih nauk. Kiev: Institut Zoologii AN USSR.
  1978   Ptitsy pozdnego Paleolita Ukraini. *Doklady AN USSR Seriya B* 7: 659–662.
Valoch, K.
  1968   Evolution of the Paleolithic in Central and Eastern Europe. *Current Anthropology* 9: 351–390.
Van Den Brink, F. H.
  1968   *A field guide to the mammals of Britain and Europe.* Boston: Houghton Mifflin.
Veklich, M. F.
  1974   *Stratigrafiya lyossovih otlozhenii Ukrainii.* Kiev: AN USSR.
Velichko, A. A.
  1961   *Geologicheskii vozrast verhnego Paleolita tsentral'nih raionov Russkoi Ravnini.* Moscow: AN SSSR.
  1969a   Paleogeografiya stoyanok pozdnego Paleolita baseina srednei Desni. In *Priroda i razvitiye pervobytnogo obschestva na territorii Evropeiskoi chasti SSR,* edited by I. P. Gerasimov, pp. 97–103. Moscow: Nauka.
  1969b   Razvitiye merzlotnyh protsessov v verhnem Pleistotsene. In *Lyoss–periglyatsial–Paleolit na teritorii Srednei i Vostochnoi Evropy,* edited by I. P. Gerasimov, pp. 429–438. Moscow: AN SSSR.
  1973   *Prirodnii process v Pleistotsene.* Moscow: Nauka.
  1979   Problemy korrelyatsii Pleistotsenovih sobitii v lednikovoi, periglyatsial'no-lyessovoi, i primorskih oblastyah Vostochno-Evropeiskoi ravnini. In *Problemy regional'noi i obschei paleogeografii lyossovyh i perglyatsial'nyh oblastei,* edited by A. A. Velichko. Moscow: Nauka.
  1982a   Osnovniye osobennosti poslednego klimaticheskogo makrotsykla i sovremennoye sostoyaniye prirodnoi sredy. In *Paleogeografiya Evropy za posledniye sto tysyach let,* edited by I. P. Gerasimov and A. A. Velichko, pp. 131–143. Moscow: Nauka.
  1982b   Paleogeografiya Pozdnepleistotsenovoi periglyatsial'noi oblasti. In *Paleogeografiya Evropy za posledniye sto tysyach let,* edited by I. P. Gerasimov and A. A. Velichko, pp. 67–70. Moscow: Nauka.
Velichko, A. A. (editor)
  1974   *Pervobytnii chelovek, ego materyal'naya kul'tura, i prirodnaya sreda v Pleistotsene i Golotsene.* Moscow: Institut Geografii AN SSSR.
  1977   *Atlas Pleistotsena.* Moscow: Nauka.
Velichko, A. A. (editor) (with V. P. Liubin, N. D. Praslov, and E. I. Kurenkova)
  1981   *Arheologiya i paleogeografiya pozdnego Paleolita Russkoi ravnini.* Moscow: Nauka.
Velichko, A. A., H. A. Arslanov, and E. I. Kurenkova
  1976   Radiouglerodniye opredeleniya vozrasta Verhnepaleoliticheskih stoyanok tsentra Russkoi ravnini (po kostnomu mater'ialu). *Doklady AN SSSR* 228(3): 713–716.

Velichko, A. A., L. V. Grekhova, and Z. P. Gubonina
1977   *Sreda obitaniya pervobytnogo cheloveka Timonovskih stoyanok.* Moscow: Nauka.
Velichko, A. A., L. V. Grekhova, and V. P. Udartsev
1977   Noviye danniye po arheologii, geologii, i paleogeografii stoyanki Eliseevichi. In *Paleokologiya drevnego cheloveka,* edited by I. K. Ivanova and N. D. Praslov, pp. 96–105. Moscow: Nauka.
Velichko, A. A., L. V. Grekhova, S. P. Gubonina, E. I. Kurenkova, V. P. Udartsev, and T. A. Halcheva
1981   Timonovskiye stoyanki. In *Arheologiaya i paleogeografiya pozdnego Paleolita Russkoi ravnini,* edited by A. A. Velichko, pp. 69–77. Moscow: Nauka.
Velichko, A. A., Y. N. Gribchenko, A. D. Markova, and V. P. Udartsev
1977   O vozraste i uslovyah obitaniya stoyanki Khotylevo II na Desne. In *Paleoekologiya drevnego cheloveka,* edited by I. K. Ivanova and N. D. Praslov, pp. 40–49. Moscow: Nauka.
Velichko, A. A., and T. D. Morozova
1969   Osnovniye cherty paleogeografii. In *Lyoss–periglyatsial–Paleolit na teritorii Srednei i Vostochnoi Evropy,* edited by I. P. Gerasimov, pp. 577–589. Moscow: AN SSSR.
1982   Izmeniye prirodnoi sredy v pozdnem Pleistotsene po dannim izucheniya lyossov, kriogennih yavlenii, iskopaemykh pochv, i fauni. In *Paleogeografiya Evropy za posledniye sto tysyach let,* edited by I. P. Gerasimov and A. A. Velichko, pp. 115–120. Moscow: Nauka.
Velichko, A. A., T. D. Morozova, I. L. Sokolovskii, and T. A. Halcheva
1969   Lyoss Russkoi Ravnini. In *Lyoss–periglyatsial–Paleolit na teritorii Srednei i Vostochnoi,* edited by I. P. Gerasimov, pp. 405–429. Moscow: AN SSSR.
Velichko, A. A., F. M. Zavernyaev, Y. N. Gribchenko, E. M. Zelikson, A. K. Markova, and V. P. Udartsev
1981   Khotylevskiye stoyanki. In *Arheologiya i Paleogeografiya pozdnego Paleolita Russkoi ravnini,* edited by A. A. Velichko, pp. 57–69. Moscow: Nauka.
Vereschagin, N. K.
1971   Okhota pervobytnogo cheloveka i vymiraniye Pleistotsennovih mlyekopitayuschih v SSSR. In *Materialy po faunam Antropogena SSSR,* edited by N. K. Vereschagin. *Trudy Zoologicheskogo Instituta* XLIX: 123–193. Leningrad: Nauka.
1977   Berelyohskoye "kladbische" mamontov. In *Mamontovaya fauna Russkoi ravnini,* edited by A. O. Skarlato. *Trudy Zoologicheskogo Instituta* LXXII: 5–50. Leningrad: Nauka.
1979   *Pochemu vymerli mamonty.* Leningrad: Nauka.
1981   *Zapiski paleontologa.* Leningrad: Nauka.
Vereschagin, N. K., and G. F. Baryshnikov
1982   Paleoecology of the mammoth fauna in the Eurasian Arctic. In *Paleoecology of Beringia,* edited by D. M. Hopkins, J. V. Matthews, Jr., C. S. Schweger, and S. B. Young, pp. 267–280. New York: Academic.
Vereschagin, N. K., and I. E. Kuzmina
1977   Ostatki mlyekopitayuschih iz Paleoliticheskih stoyanok na Donu i verhnei Desne. In *Mamontovaya fauna russkoi ravnini,* edited by A. O. Skarlato. *Trudy Zoologicheskogo Insituta* LXXII: 77–110.
1979   Ekologiya mlyekopitayuschih verhnego Dona v epohu pozdnego Paleolita. In *Verhnii Pleistotsen i razvitiye Paleoliticheskih kul'tur v tsentre russkoi ravnini. Tezisy dokladov k vsesoyuznomu soveschaniyu posvyaschenomu 100-letiyu otkritiya Paleolita v Kostenkah.* Voronezh.
Vibe, C.
1967   Arctic animals in relation to climatic fluctuations. *Meddetelser om Grønland* 170. Pt. 5: 101–210.
1970   The Arctic ecosystem influenced by fluctuations in sun-spots and drift-ice movement. In *Productivity and conservation in northern circumpolar lands,* edited by W. A. Fuller and P. G. Kwan, pp. 115–120. *International Union for Conservation of Nature and Natural Resources Publication* 16.
Vigdorchik, M. E., E. P. Zarrina, I. I. Krasnov, and V. G. Auslender
1974   Pozdnii Pleistotsen. In *Geokhronologiya SSSR* (Vol. 3), edited by V. A. Zubakov. Leningrad: Nedra.
Voevodskii, M. V.
1940   Rezul'taty rabot Desninskoi ekspeditsii po izucheniyu Paleolita (1936–1937). *Byulleten' Komissii po Izucheniyu Chetvertichnogo Perioda* 6–7: 54–57.

1947a   Rezul'taty raboty Desninskoi ekspeditsii 1936–1938 roku. *Paleolit i Neolit Ukraini* Vol. 1, pp. 41–57. Kiev.

1947b   Kremyani i kistyani vyroby Paleolitichnoi stoyanki Chulativ I. *Paleolit i Neolit Ukraini.* Vol. 1, pp. 107–117. Kiev.

1949   Paleoliticheskaya stoyanka Pogon. *Kratkyie Soobscheninya Instituta Istorii Material'noi Kul'tury* XXXI: 40–54.

1952a   Paleoliticheskaya stoyanka Rabochii Rov (Chulatovo II). *Ucheniye Zapiski Moskovskogo Gosudarstvennogo Universiteta* 158: 101–132.

1952b   Stoyanka Burorok. *Ucheniye Zapiski Moskovskogo Gosudarstvennogo Universiteta* 158: 87–100.

1952c   Stoyanka Anikeev Rov I (Pushkari II). *Ucheniye Zapiski Moskovskogo Gosudarstvennogo Universiteta* 158: 75–86.

1952d   K voprosu o Pushkarevskom zhilische. *Ucheniye Zapiski Moskovskogo Gosudarstvennogo Universiteta* 158: 71–74.

Voitenko, A. M.
1965   Do fenologii vesnyanogo pril'otu ptahiv v okolytsi g. Kieva. In *Nazemni hrebetni Ukraini,* edited by I. G. Pidoplichko, pp. 90–103. Kiev: Naukova Dumka.

Voznyachuk, L. M.
1973   K stratigrafii i paleogeografii Neopleistotsena Byelorussii i smezhnih territorii. In *Problemy paleogeografii Antrapagena Belarussi,* edited by E. A. Levkoe, pp. 45–75. Minsk: Navuka i Tekhnika.

Voznyachuk, L. M., and V. D. Budko
1969   O znachenii Berdyzhskoi Paleoliticheskoi stoyanki dlya opredeleniya vozrasta rechnih terras basseina Dnepra. In *Tezisy dokladov k konferentsii po arheologii Byelorussii,* pp. 7–16. Minsk: AN BSSR.

Voznyachuk, L. M., V. D. Budko, and E. N. Kalechitz
1969   Stratigrafo-paleogeograficheskaya shema Neopleistotsena Byelorussii i smeznih oblastei. In *Drevnosti Byelorussii,* edited by V. D. Budko, P. F. Lysenko, L. D. Pobol, and M. M. Chernyavskii, pp. 179–212. Minsk: AN BSSR.

Walker, E. P.
1975   *Mammals of the world* (third ed.). Baltimore: John Hopkins University Press.

Wallerstein, E.
1974   *The modern world-system.* New York: Academic.

Watanabe, H.
1968   Subsistence and ecology of northern food gatherers with special reference to the Ainu. In *Man the hunter,* edited by R. B. Lee and I. DeVore, pp. 69–77. Chicago: Aldine-Atherton.

1969   Famine as a population check. Comparative ecology of Northern peoples. *Journal of the Faculty of Science* Vol. III, Pt. 4, Section V, pp. 237–252. University of Tokyo.

1972   *The Ainu ecosystem.* Seattle: University of Washington Press.

1978a   *Natural resources and human activity system: a spatiotemporal view.* UNU–NR Task Force Meeting on "Resource-Systems Theory and Methodology." Manila, Philippines.

1978b   Systematic classification of hunter–gatherers' food habits: an ecological–evolutionary perspective. *Journal of the Ethnological Society of Japan* 43: 111–137.

Watts, W. A.
1980   Regional variation in the response of vegetation to Late Glacial climatic events in Europe. In *Studies in the Late Glacial of North-West Europe,* edited by J. J. Lowe, J. M. Grey, and J. E. Robinson, pp. 1–21. Oxford: Pergamon Press.

Weissner, P.
1974   A functional estimator of population from floor area. *American Antiquity* 39: 343–350.

1982a   Beyond willow smoke and dog's tails: a comment on Binford's analysis of hunter–gatherer settlement systems. *American Antiquity* 47: 171–178.

1982b   Risk, reciprocity, and social influence on !Kung San economies. In *Politics and history in band societies,* edited by E. B. Leacock and R. B. Lee, pp. 61–84. Cambridge: Cambridge University Press.

1983   Style and social information in Kalahari San projectile points. *American Antiquity* 48: 253–276.

1984   Reconsidering the behavioral basis for style: a case study among the Kalahari San. *Journal of Anthropological Archaeology* 3:190–234.

Weniger, G. -C.

1982   *Wildbeuter und ihre Umwelt.* Tubingen, W. Germany: Archaeologica Ventoria.

Whallon, R., Jr.

1973   Spatial analysis of occupation floors I: application of the dimensional analysis of variance. *American Antiquity* 38: 266–277.

Wheat, J. B.

1972   The Olsen–Chobbuck site. *Memoirs of the Society for American Archaeology* 26.

Wheeler, A.

1969   *The fishes of the British Isles and North-West Europe.* East Lansing: Michigan State University Press.

White, L. A.

1949   *The science of culture.* New York: Ferrar, Straus, and Giroux.

White, R. G., F. L. Bunnell, E. Gaare, T. Skogland, and B. Hubert

1981   Ungulates on Arctic ranges. In *Tundra esosystems: a comparative analysis,* edited by L. C. Bliss, O. W. Heal, and J. J. Moore, pp. 397–485. Cambridge: Cambridge University Press.

White, R. K.

1980   *The Upper Paleolithic occupation of the Perigord: a topographic approach to subsistence and settlement.* Unpublished Ph.D. dissertation, Department of Anthropology, University of Toronto.

1982   Rethinking the Middle–Upper Paleolithic transition. *Current Anthropology* 23: 169–192.

White, T.

1953   A method of calculating the dietary percentage of various food animals utilized by aboriginal peoples. *American Antiquity* 18: 396–398.

Wiens, J. A.

1976   Population response to patchy environments. *Annual Review of Ecology and Systematics* 7: 81–120.

Wilkinson, P. F.

1974   The relevance of musk ox exploitation to the study of prehistoric animal economies. In *Paleoeconomy,* edited by E. S. Higgs. Cambridge: Cambridge University Press.

Wilmsen, E. N.

1970   Late Pleistocene human ecology. *AMQUA Abstracts.* p. 153.

1973   Interactions, spacing behavior, and the organization of hunting bands. *Journal of Anthropological Research* 29: 1–31.

Wilmsen, E. N. (editor)

1972   *Social exchange and interaction. Anthropological Papers, University of Michigan Museum of Anthropology* 46.

Wilson, E. O.

1975   *Sociobiology.* Cambridge: Harvard University Press.

Wing, E. S., and A. B. Brown

1979   *Paleonutrition.* New York: Academic.

Wing, L. D., and I. O. Buss

1970   *Elephants and forests. Wildlife Monograph* 19. Louisville, Kentucky: Publication of the Wildlife Society.

Winterhalder, B.

1981a   Optimal foraging strategies for hunter–gatherer research in anthropology: theory and models. In *Hunter–gatherer foraging strategies,* edited by B. Winterhalder and E. A. Smith, pp. 13–35. Chicago: University of Chicago Press.

1981b   Foraging strategies in the boreal forest: an analysis of Cree hunting and gathering. In *Hunter–gatherer foraging strategies,* edited by B. Winterhalder and E. A. Smith, pp. 66–98. Chicago: University of Chicago Press.

Winters, H. D.

1969   The Riverton culture. *Illinois State Museum Reports of Investigations* 73.

Wobst, H. M.
    1974   Boundary conditions for Paleolithic social systems: a simulation approach. *American Antiquity* 39: 147–178.
    1976   Locational relationships in Paleolithic society. *Journal of Human Evolution* 5: 49–58.
    1977   Stylistic behavior and information exchange. In *For the director: Essays in honor of James B. Griffin,* edited by C. Cleland, pp. 74–81. *Anthropological Papers, University of Michigan Museum of Anthropology* 61.
    1978   The "archaeo-ethnology of hunter–gatherers" or the tyranny of the ethnographic record in archaeology. *American Antiquity* 43: 303–309.

Wobst, H. M., and A. S. Keene
    1983   Archaeological explanations as political economy. In *The sociopolitics of Archaeology,* edited by J. M. Gero, D. M. Lacy, and M. L. Blakey, pp. 79–90. *Research Report 23,* Department of Anthropology, University of Massachusetts, Amherst.

Woillard, G. M.
    1978   Grand Pile Peat Bog: a continuous pollen record for the last 140,000 years. *Quaternary Research* 9: 1–21.
    1979   Abrupt end of the last interglacial s.s in north-east France. *Nature* 281: 558–562.

Woillard, G. M., and W. G. Mook
    1982   Carbon 14 dates at Grande Pile: correlation of land and sea chronologies. *Science* 215: 159–161.

Woodburn, J.
    1972   Ecology, nomadic movement, and the composition of local groups among hutners and gatherers: an East African example and implications. In *Man, settlement, and urbanism,* edited by P. J. Ucko, R. Tringham, and G. W. Dimbleby. London: Duckworth.
    1980   Hunters and gatherers today and reconstruction of the past. In *Soviet and Western anthropology,* edited by E. Gellner, pp. 95–118. New York: Columbia University Press.

Wright, H. E., Jr.
    1976   Pleistocene ecology: some current problems. In *Ecology of the Pleistocene,* edited by R. C. West and W. G. Haag. *Geoscience and Man* XIII: 1–13.

Yegoyan, A. A.
    1972   Ritual and exchange in aboriginal Australia: an adaptive interpretation of male initiation rites. In *Social exchange and interaction,* edited by E. N. Wilmsen, pp. 5–10. *Anthropological Papers, University of Michigan Museum of Anthropology* 46.

Yellen, J. E.
    1977   *Archaeological approaches to the present: models for reconstructing the past.* New York: Academic.

Yessner, D. R.
    1977   Resource diversity and population stability among hunter–gatherers. *The Western Canadian Journal of Anthropology* VII(2): 18–77.
    1981   Archaeological applications of optimal foraging theory: harvest strategies of Aleut hunter–gatherers. In *Hunter–gatherer foraging strategies,* edited by B. Winterhalder and E. A. Smith, pp. 148–170. Chicago: University of Chicago Press.

Yoshino, M. M.
    1975   *Climate in a small area.* Tokyo: University of Tokyo Press.

Yurtsev, B. A.
    1982   Relics of the xerophyte vegetation of Beringia in northeastern Asia. In *Paleoecology of Beringia,* edited by D. M. Hopkins, J. V. Matthews, Jr., C. S. Schweger, and S. B. Young, pp. 157–178. New York: Academic.

Zaharuk, Y. N.
    1978   Paradoks arheologicheskoi kul'tury. In *Problemy Sovetskoi arheologii,* edited by V. V. Kropotkin, G. N. Matyushin, and B. G. Peters, pp. 49–54. Moscow: Nauka.

Zamyatnin, S. N.
    1930   Raskopki Berdyzhskai Paleolitichnai stoyanki u 1927 g. *Pracy Arheologichai Komisii Belarusskai Akademii Navuk* II. Mensk.

1951   O vozniknovenii lokal'nyh razlichii v kul'ture Paleoliticheskogo perioda. *Trudy Instituta Et-nografii AN SSSR* 16: 89–152.

Zar, J. H.
1974   *Biostatistical analysis.* Englewood Cliffs, N.J.: Prentice-Hall.

Zarrina, E. P., and I. I. Krasnov
1979   Stratigrafiya i paleogeografiya tsentral'nih oblastei Russkoi ravnini v epohu Pozdnego Paleolita. In *Verhnii Pleistotsen i razvitiye Paleoliticheskoi kul'tury v tsentre Russkoi Ravnini,* pp. 31–37. *Tezisy dokladov k vsesoyuznomu soveschaniyu posvyaschennomu 100-letiyu otkritiya Paleolita v Kostenkah.* Voronezh.

Zarrina, E. P., I. I. Krasnov, and I. A. Spiridonova
1980   Klimatostratigraficheskaya korrelyatsiya i khronologiya pozdnego Pleistotsena severozapada i tsentra Russkoi ravnini. In *Chetvertichnaya geologiya i geomorfologiya,* edited by I. I. Krasnov, pp. 46–50. Moscow: Nauka.

Zavernyaev, F. M.
1978   Antropomorfnaya skulptura Khotylevskoi verhnepaleoliticheskoi stoyanki. *Sovetskaya Arheologiya* 4: 145–161.
1981   Gravirovka na kosti i kamne Khotylevskoi verhnepaleoliticheskoi stoyanki. *Sovetskaya Arheologiya* 4: 141–158.

Zeeman, E. C.
1977   *Catastrophy theory.* Reading, Mass.: Addison-Wesley.
1982   Decision making and evolution. In *Theory and explanation in archaeology,* edited by C. Renfrew, M. J. Rowlands, and B. Abott Seagraves, pp. 315–346. New York: Academic.

Zelikson, E. M., and M. H. Monoszon
1974   Usloviya obitaniya cheloveka na stoyanke Khotylevo II po palinologicheskim dannim. In *Pervobytnii chelovek, ego materyal'naya kul'tura, i prirodnaya sreda v Pleistotsene i Golotsene,* edited by A. A. Velichko, pp. 137–142. Moscow: Institut Geografii AN SSSR.

Zhadin, V. I.
1965   *Mollusks of fresh and brackish waters of the USSR.* Translated from Russian for the Smithsonian Institution and NSF by the Israel Program for Scientific Translations. Jerusalem.

Zherehova, I. E.
1977   Opisaniye i izmereniya zubov mamonta Berelyohi. In *Mamontovaya fauna Russkoi ravnini i vostochnoi Sibiri,* edited by A. O. Skarlato. *Trudy Zoologicheskogo Instituta* LXXII: 50–57.

Zimina, R. P.
1953   Ocherk ekologii stepnogo i serogo surkov. *Trudy Instituta Geografii AN SSSR* 54: 351–382.

Zimina, R. P., and I. P. Gerasimov
1970   Surki (Marmota) kak tipichniye obitateli periglyatsial'noi zony lednikovogo perioda. *Izvestya AN SSSR, Seriya Geograficheskaya,* No. 4 pp. 24–35.
1971   Periglyatsial'naya ekspansiya surkov v Srednei Evrope v techenii Verhnego Pleistotsena. *Byulleten'Moskovskogo Obschestva Ispytaniya Prirody, Otdeleniye Biologii* LXXVI: 37–50.

Zubrow, E. (editor)
1976   *Demographic anthropology: quantitative approaches.* Albuquerque: University of New Mexico Press.

Index